W9-BUY-196

TABLE SAW TECHNIQUES

REVISED EDITION

ROGER W. CLIFFE

Sterling Publishing Co., Inc.
New York

About the Author

Roger Cliffe has been a woodworker for the past 30 years. Currently, he is a Distinguished Teaching Professor at Northern Illinois University. Cliffe has acted as a consultant in woodworking safety and training to many organizations. He currently has several books in print with Sterling, including *Table Saw Basics, Woodworker's Handbook, Radial Arm Saw Techniques, Radial Arm Saw Basics, Shaper Handbook,* and *Table Saw Techniques.*

Cliffe has worked at many woodworking shows, providing lectures and demonstrations for those attending. He has also conducted summer classes in his studio and as a guest of studios throughout the Midwest.

Cliffe has recently developed a series of videos for the home cabinetmaker entitled "Faceplate Cabinetmaking." There are currently twelve titles in the series.

Library of Congress Cataloging-in-Publication Data

Cliffe, Roger W.
Table saw techniques / Roger W. Cliffe. — Rev. Ed.
p. cm.
Includes index.
ISBN 0-8069-4268-1
1. Circular saws. 2. Woodwork. I. Title.
TT186.C554 1997
684'.083—dc21 97-19321
CIP

1 3 5 7 9 10 8 6 4 2

Published by Sterling Publishing Company, Inc.
387 Park Avenue South, New York, N.Y. 10016
© 1997 by Roger Cliffe
Distributed in Canada by Sterling Publishing
% Canadian Manda Group, One Atlantic Avenue, Suite 105
Toronto, Ontario, Canada M6K 3E7
Distributed in Great Britain and Europe by Cassell PLC
Wellington House, 125 Strand, London WC2R 0BB, England
Distributed in Australia by Capricorn Link (Australia) Pty Ltd.
P.O. Box 6651, Baulkham Hills, Business Centre, NSW 2153, Australia
Manufactured in the United States of America
All rights reserved

Sterling ISBN 0-8069-4268-1

Acknowledgments

Table Saw Techniques represents the work and cooperation of many people. No project of this magnitude could be done by the author alone.

The photos for this book were shot by Jim Schmitz and Bill Peters. The custom darkroom work was done by Bill Peters. Special thanks to the photo models, Dave Miles and Chris Sullens.

The drawings for projects and jigs were done by Don Simon and Steve Piatak. Their work has made project construction much easier for the reader.

The manuscript critique by Dr. John Beck has also been very helpful. His work and advice have made the written portion of the book easier to read and understand.

Manuscript typing by Bea Paulus and Ruth Odynocki transformed the writer's longhand into a workable product. Many thanks to these patient women.

Commercial photographs were generously furnished by the following people and organizations.

John Baenisch
James Bates
Marilyn Brock
Garretson W. Chinn
Jay Dykstra
Dale Fahlbeck
Jim Forrest and Wally Kunkel (Mr. Sawdust)
John Greguric
Mike Mangan
Fred Slavic
Clayt Williams

Biesemeyer Manufacturing Corporation
Boice Crane Industries
Brett Guard™
Delta International Corporation
Fisher Hill Products (Ripstrate™)
Foley-Belsaw Company
The Foredom Electric Co.
Forrest Manufacturing
Garrett Wade
Marvco Tool and Manufacturing
Oliver Machinery
Power Tool Institute
Sears, Roebuck and Company

Roger Cliffe
Cliffe Cabinets

—Contents—

Metric Equivalents

INCHES TO MILLIMETRES AND CENTIMETRES

MM—millimetres   CM—centimetres

Inches	MM	CM	Inches	CM	Inches	CM
1/8	3	0.3	9	22.9	30	76.2
1/4	6	0.6	10	25.4	31	78.7
3/8	10	1.0	11	27.9	32	81.3
1/2	13	1.3	12	30.5	33	83.8
5/8	16	1.6	13	33.0	34	86.4
3/4	19	1.9	14	35.6	35	88.9
7/8	22	2.2	15	38.1	36	91.4
1	25	2.5	16	40.6	37	94.0
1 1/4	32	3.2	17	43.2	38	96.5
1 1/2	38	3.8	18	45.7	39	99.1
1 3/4	44	4.4	19	48.3	40	101.6
2	51	5.1	20	50.8	41	104.1
2 1/2	64	6.4	21	53.3	42	106.7
2	76	7.6	22	55.9	43	109.2
3 1/2	89	8.9	23	58.4	44	111.8
4	102	10.2	24	61.0	45	114.3
4 1/2	114	11.4	25	63.5	46	116.8
5	127	12.7	26	66.0	47	119.4
6	152	15.2	27	68.6	48	121.9
7	178	17.8	28	71.1	49	124.5
8	203	20.3	29	73.7	50	127.0

Part I:
Table Saw Fundamentals

—1—
Introduction to the Table Saw

Types of Table Saw

There are many different types of table saw sold today. Each type has its own unique features, but all table saws can be classified according to the following categories or groups.

Motorized or Motor Driven A table saw is classified as motorized or motor driven. A motor-driven table saw uses a motor and one or more belts to drive the blade (Illus. 1-1–1-3). The blade is mounted on one end of an arbor, and the driven pulley is mounted on the other end. The motor is usually mounted under the table.

The blade on a motorized table saw attaches directly to the motor (Illus. 1-4). The motor is mounted to the underside of the table. Some motorized table saws operate at a higher noise level than motor-driven saws. This is due to increased vibration and motor echo. Some motorized table saws are classified as universal table saws. These saws have two arbors and two blades (Illus. 1-5). The blade in the upper position is the only one that moves when the saw is turned on.

Universal saws are large industrial saws. Raising the blade causes them to move on a large arc. As one blade disappears beneath the table, the other blade appears. This minimizes the amount of blade changing, as one blade may be a rip blade and the other a crosscut blade.

Tilting Table or Tilting Arbor Cutting stock at an angle is done by tilting the blade or tilting the table. Most newer saws use a tilting blade (Illus. 1-6). This allows the stock to remain horizontal while it is being cut. The blade is attached to an arbor. The

Illus. 1-2. The belt transfers power from the motor to the blade through a pair of pulleys. Note the perfect alignment of the pulleys. This reduces saw vibration.

Illus. 1-3. This series of belts transfers power from the motor to the arbor which drives the blade. The blade is attached to the arbor behind the nut and between the two arbor washers. (Photo courtesy of Delta International Machinery Corporation.)

Illus. 1-4. This is a motorized table saw. The blade attaches directly to the motor arbor. No belts or pulleys are used.

Illus. 1-5. This motorized table saw is called a universal saw. It has two arbors. Only the arbor in the up position turns when the saw is turned on.

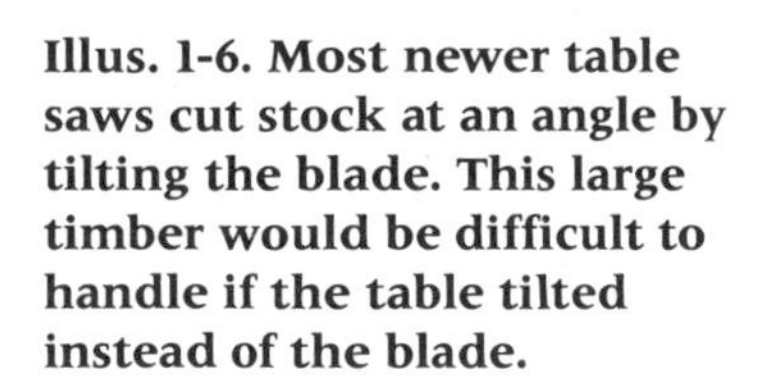

Illus. 1-6. Most newer table saws cut stock at an angle by tilting the blade. This large timber would be difficult to handle if the table tilted instead of the blade.

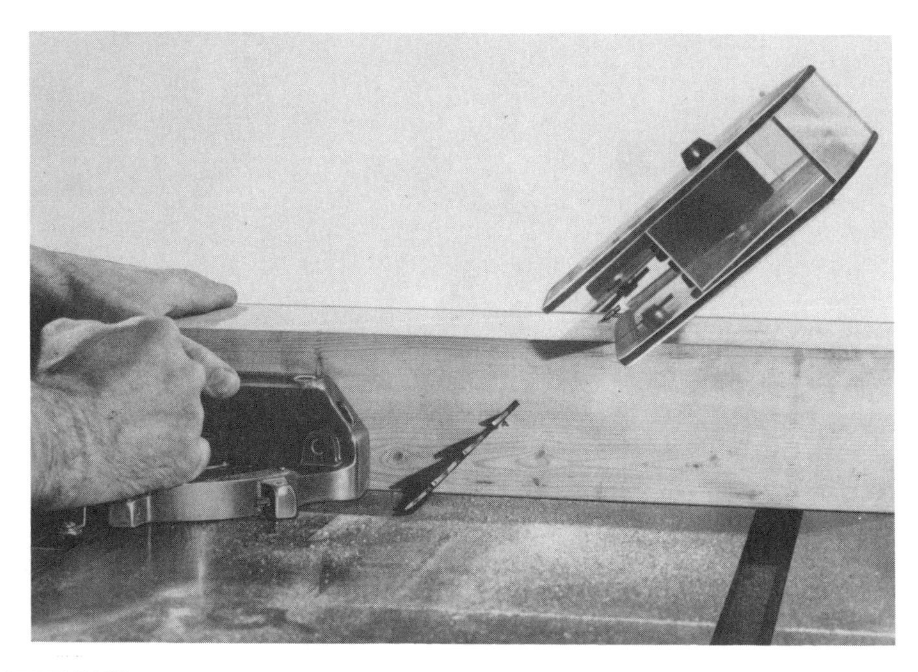

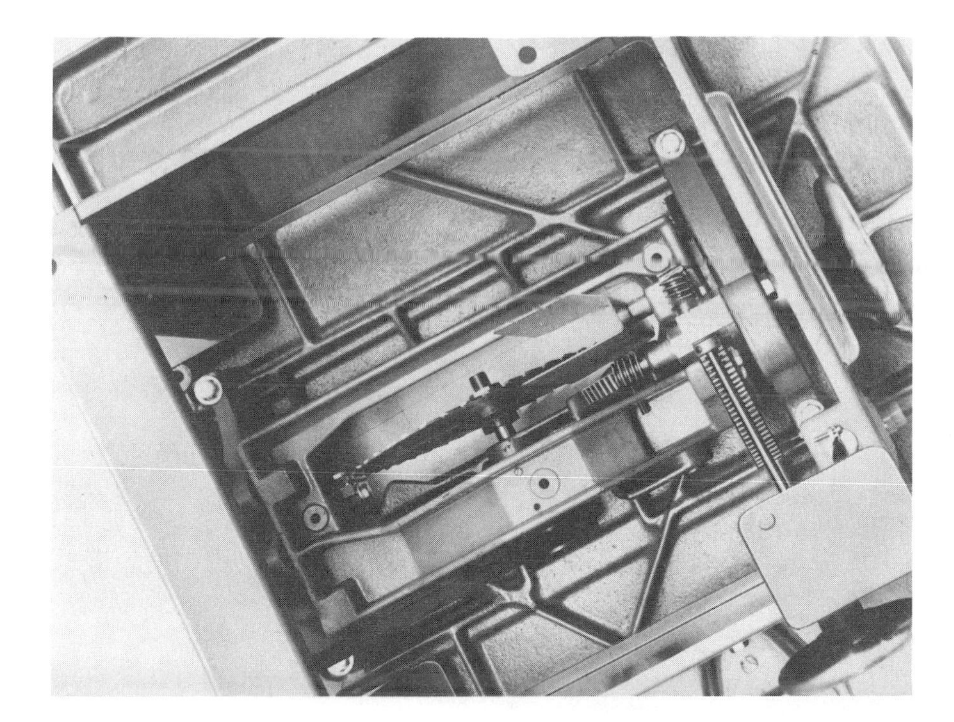

Illus. 1-7. A view from the bottom of the table saw allows you to see the worm gears that tilt the arbor and control its height.

Illus. 1-8. The power take-off on this table saw allows the saw to be used for mortising and horizontal boring. The auxiliary table makes complex setups possible.

arbor moves on a gearlike mechanism that is controlled by a handwheel or crank on the side of the saw (Illus. 1-7). On a tilting table saw, the stock is at an angle when it is fed across the table. Stock is not as easy to handle when the table is tilted. The operator must contend with the forces of gravity.

Most table saws with a tilting table have a power take-off on the end of the motor opposite the blade (Illus. 1-8). The power take-off allows the attachment of other accessories such as a mortiser or drill bit.

Tilting tables are not as common as they once were. They are still used on some combination machines such as the Shopsmith and the Kity K 5. The biggest problem with a tilting table occurs when beveling a sheet of plywood or bevel-ripping a long piece of 2-inch-thick stock. The force of gravity makes it difficult to control the workpiece during these operations. On a tilting arbor saw, the stock remains horizontal.

Sliding Table A sliding or rolling table is usually offered as an option on larger table saws and some smaller saws. It can be an integral part of the saw table (Illus. 1-9), or it can be an addition that attaches to the edge of the saw table (Illus. 1-10 and 1-11). In some cases, the attachment of a sliding table requires the removal of the extension wing (Illus. 1-12–1-14).

When the sliding table that is an integral part of the table saw is unlocked, it allows wider, heavier pieces of stock to be controlled easily. A miter head is attached to the sliding table to control the stock as it passes into the blade. The entire table glides forward with little effort (Illus. 1-15–1-17). This ensures a quality cut.

The sliding table also reduces the chance of the workpiece becoming scuffed through contact with the table. The work moves with the table; it does

Illus. 1-9. This rolling table is an integral part of the table saw. It makes control of wider or heavier pieces much easier.

Illus. 1-10. This add-on sliding table takes up slightly more floor space due to the rod extending beyond the table. The table rolls on this rod. Ball bearings reduce friction and make it roll easily.

Illus. 1-11. The operator saws a sheet of plywood easily without help.

Illus. 1-12. This add-on sliding table is mounted to a cabinet saw.

Illus. 1-13. The fence on this sliding table will move toward or away from the blade. A stop is included with the fence to control stock length.

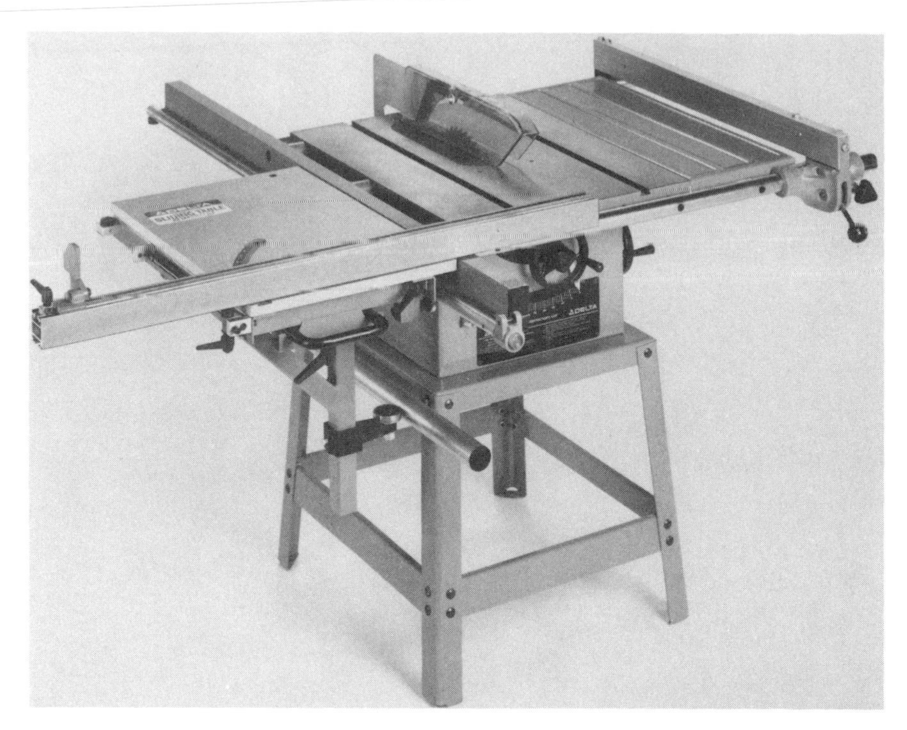

Illus. 1-14. This sliding table can be used on most contractor and cabinet saws. It can also be used on some shapers. (Photo courtesy of Delta International Machinery Corporation.)

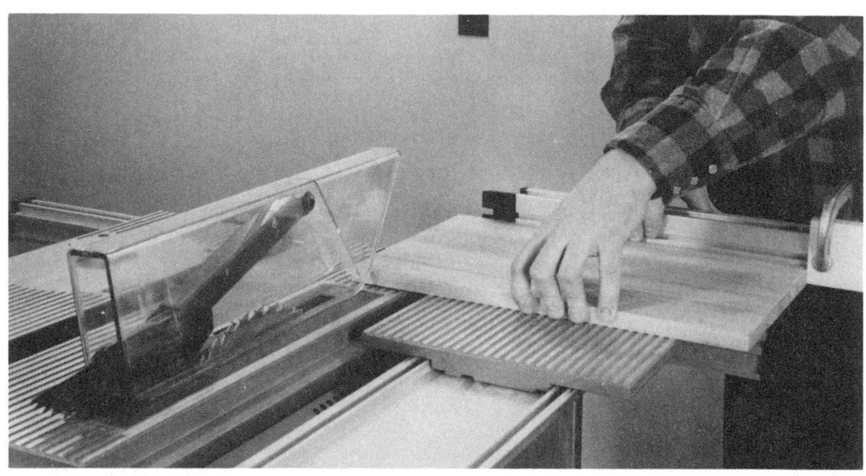

Illus. 1-15. This sliding table is an integral part of this contractor saw. Once the table is released, it can be moved.

Illus. 1-16. This crosscut is made using the sliding table. A head or fence is secured to the table to control the stock while it is being cut.

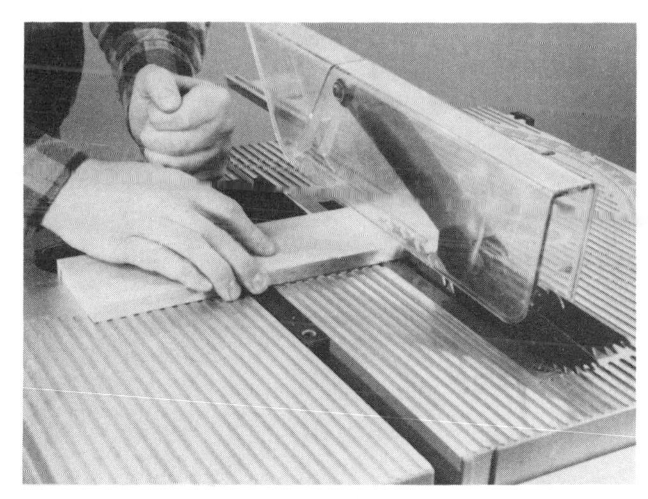

Illus. 1-17. A standard miter gauge may also be used on this contractor saw. The slot is formed betwen the table and moveable extension wing. This allows you to use jigs and fixtures which were designed for a saw with a miter slot.

Illus. 1-19. The extension wing is removed on this saw to accommodate the new sliding table. (Photo courtesy of Sears Craftsman.)

not slide across the table. A sliding table has stops or travel limits at both ends. This prevents the table from sliding out of its track. Most sliding tables have provisions for adjustment and alignment.

Some companies offer a sliding table as an add-on accessory for the table saw. These sliding tables do the same thing as the integral sliding table, but take up more floor space. Add-on sliding tables can be purchased to fit almost any table saw. They allow a single operator to handle larger stock (Illus. 1-18 and 1-19). Make sure the add-on table is compatible with the saw before you buy it.

Grades of Table Saw

Table saws are categorized in grades according to major design considerations. The most important grades are benchtop, contractor, cabinet, and industrial. Saws in each of these grades have certain features and are designed for specific purposes.

Benchtop Saws Benchtop table saws (Illus. 1-20) are designed for use in the home (Illus. 1-21) or in the field (Illus. 1-22). They are compact and can easily be clamped to a benchtop or a pair of sawhorses. Benchtop table saws are also available with a stand, but most operators buy these saws for

Illus. 1-18. This sliding table can be mounted to some contractor and cabinet saws. It is sold as an accessory. (Photo courtesy of Sears Craftsman.)

Illus. 1-20. This is a common benchtop table-saw design. It is small, lightweight, and motorized. (Photo courtesy of Sears Craftsman.)

Illus. 1-21. This benchtop saw is being used in a small hobby shop. It will handle most woodworking tasks. Note the dust-collection hookup. This will keep the shop air much cleaner. (Photo courtesy of Sears Craftsman.)

Illus. 1-22. This benchtop saw is being used in the field to rip dimensional lumber. It is bolted to a pair of sawhorses. Note the table extension, which is built into the saw. (Photo courtesy of Delta International Machinery Corporation.)

occasional use and are more concerned with storage and portability (Illus. 1-23).

Illus. 1-23. This benchtop table saw has a built-in carriage handle. All of the saw accessories clamp to the sides of the saw for transportation. (Photo courtesy of Delta International Machinery Corporation.)

Benchtop table saws have a small table and turn a blade from 7¼ to 10 inches in diameter. They are usually motor-driven; the motor is usually a universal motor which turns at 5,000 RPM and generates more noise than other motors. These saws use a 110-volt power source.

The benchtop table saw is suitable for small household chores (Illus. 1-24) or for use in the field for ripping stock for jambs, porches, and other routine construction tasks (Illus. 1-25). For constant use, the benchtop saw would not be the best choice.

Contractor Saws Contractor table saws are designed for continuous use and are often used in a shop. They are heavier than benchtop tools and are usually attached to a stand (Illus. 1-26 and 1-27). Contractor saws are also used on the job, but their setup requires more than one person. Contractor-grade table saws are usually motor-driven. The

Illus. 1-24. This shop workbench was designed for use with benchtop tools such as this table saw. Note how the height of the bench can be adjusted to accommodate any benchtop table saw. (Photo courtesy of Sears Craftsman.)

Illus. 1-25. This benchtop table saw will accommodate a dado head. The auxiliary throat plate must be used with the dado head. If you plan on making dado cuts, be sure the benchtop saw was designed for this purpose. (Photo courtesy of Delta International Machinery Corporation.)

Illus. 1-26. This contractor's saw is designed for use in a shop or the field. It is not as portable as a benchtop saw. (Photo courtesy of Delta International Machinery Corporation.)

motor extends out the back of the table saw on most models, but may be beneath the table on others (Illus. 1-28).

The trunion, which elevates and tilts the motor, is bolted onto the underside of the tables (Illus. 1-29). This design feature makes it difficult to align. This is also true for benchtop table saws. In some cases, there is not enough tolerance between the bolt holding the trunion to the table and the hole in the trunion to allow it to be moved into correct alignment. This topic is discussed further under Tuning Up a Table Saw.

Most contractor-grade saws also have an open base. This is because the motor is suspended from the rear of the saw. This makes dust collection more

Illus. 1-27. This contractor's saw has a metal base in a mobile machinery base. It can be moved on a garage floor. (Photo courtesy of Delta International Machinery Corporation.)

Illus. 1-28. This contractor's saw has its motor beneath the table in the enclosed cabinet. This makes dust collection easier. The trunions are still attached to the underside of the table. (Photo courtesy of Delta International Machinery Corporation.)

Illus. 1-29. The motor has been removed from this contractor's saw so you can see how much the trunion is bolted to the underside of the table. Note also how the back of the cabinet is open. This makes dust collection more difficult. (Photo courtesy of Delta International Machinery Corporation.)

difficult, although newer models have incorporated a dust shroud around the blade which connects it to the hose of a dust collector. Contractor saws

Illus. 1-30. This contractor's saw is motorized. It also has provisions for mobility. The fence has provisions for a 24-inch right rip cut. (Photo courtesy of Sears Craftsman.)

usually run on a 110-volt circuit, but draw more amps than a benchtop saw. The motors on most contractor saws can be converted to 220-volt operation if desired. This conversion greatly enhances the performance of the saw. Numerous accessory fences, switches, and stands can be attached to a contractor-grade table saw (Illus. 1-30–1-33).

Cabinet Saws Cabinet saws get their name from the metal cabinet which encloses the motor and trunion (Illus. 1-34–1-36). The tabletop is bolted to the cabinet as a separate piece. These saws are easy to adjust since alignment only requires movement of the top, which is connected by four bolts to the cabinet.

The totally enclosed base and motor cover (Illus. 1-37 and 1-38) also make dust collection easier. The base usually has a hose port of dust chute built in (Illus. 1-39). A hose port can be attached to the dust chute if necessary, and then the dust hose is

Illus. 1-31. This motorized saw has a 24-inch right and left rip fence. Note the grate-like extension wings. The fence has micro-adjustment and cam-locking features. (Photo courtesy of Sears Craftsman.)

Illus. 1-32. This contractor's saw has a substantial fence and stand. Note also the position of the push-button switch. (Photo courtesy of Jet Power Tools.)

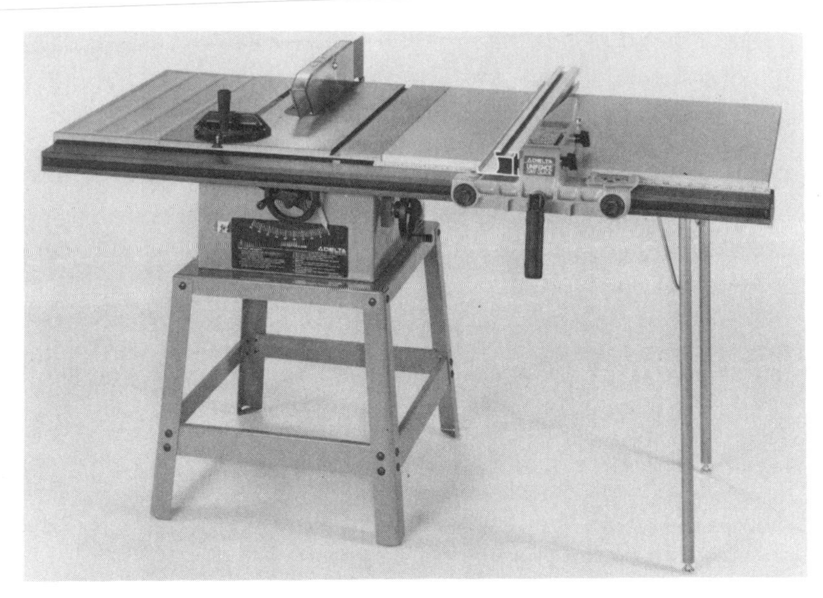

Illus. 1-33. This contractor's saw is designed for stationary use. The extension wing and Unifence extend the ripping capacity of the saw. (Photo courtesy of Delta International Machinery Corporation.)

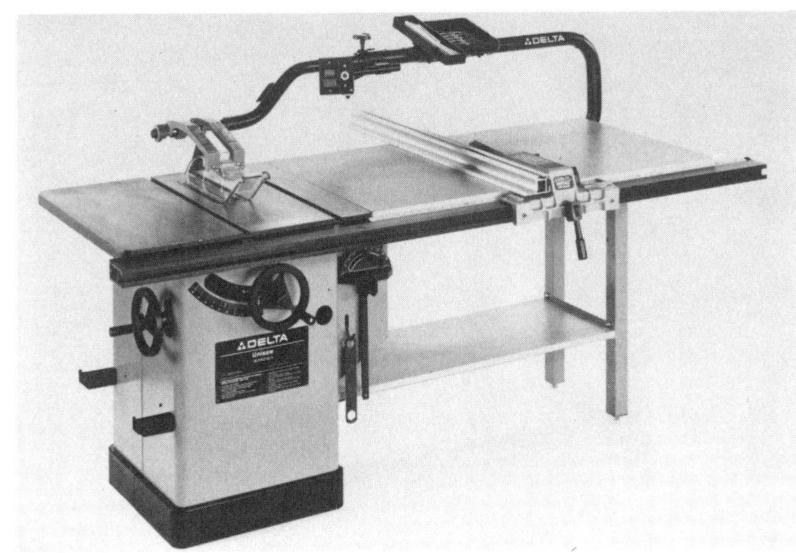

Illus. 1-34. This cabinet saw has a different accessory package. The extension allows wider ripping. (Photo courtesy of Delta International Machinery Corporation.)

Illus. 1-35. This cabinet saw has a metal cabinet and motor cover. The trunion is bolted to the top of the cabinet. (Photo courtesy of Delta International Machinery Corporation.)

Illus. 1-36. This cabinet saw also has a metal cabinet with a motor cover on the opposite side. The cabinet is on the opposite side of the motor. The dust port is above the motor cover. (Photo courtesy of Jet Power Tools.)

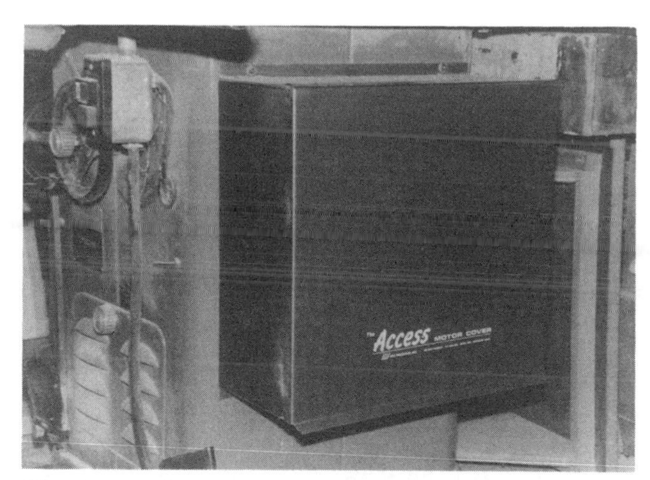

Illus. 1-37. This motor cover is an accessory for a cabinet saw. It makes dust collection easier. Until recently, motor covers were an accessory on cabinet saws.

Illus. 1-38. This motor cover has an easy-to-remove panel which makes access to overload resets easier.

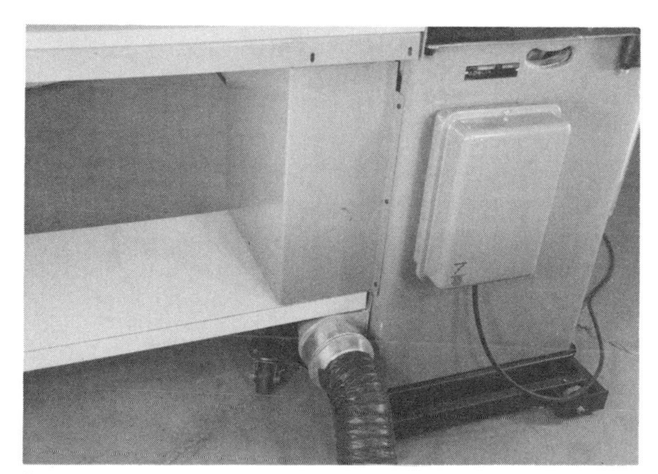

Illus. 1-39. The dust port on this cabinet saw is located beneath the motor cover.

connected. Dust collection is important in woodworking, and the cabinet saw lends itself to easy dust collection.

The cabinet saw is quite heavy and is rarely used outside the shop. In some applications, such as the total renovation or the building out of an entire floor of a building, you may see a cabinet saw on the job.

Cabinet saws run on 220-volt circuits. They can be either single phase or three phase. These saws range in horsepower from 1½ to 5, typically. Cabinet saws are usually equipped with 10- or 12-inch blades.

Industrial Saws Industrial table saws have blades 12 inches in diameter or greater. The arbor hole increases from the typical ⅝ to 1 inch. Industrial saws use 220- or 440-volt three-phase electricity and have horsepower ratings as high as ten.

An industrial saw is rarely moved after installation. These saws are used for processing lumber and large parts (Illus. 1-40). Some industrial table saws are categorized as universal table saws. A universal table saw has two arbors and motors; as the elevating handwheel is turned, the motors (and blades) make an orbit inside the saw. The motor on top is the one that goes on when the switch is turned on (Illus. 1-5).

Two blades can be permanently mounted on universal table saws. When the operator wishes to change blades, it is a matter of turning the elevating handwheel.

Determining Table-Saw Size

The size of a table saw is misleading. You can consider overall size, table size, blade diameter, and many other measures of size. The following discussion of table-saw size will help you determine what measures of sizes are important to your work.

Blade Diameter Blade diameter is the most common method of determining table-saw size. The largest diameter blade that the table saw will take is its size. For example, a table saw that will take a blade with a 10-inch diameter is a 10-inch table saw. The diameter of the blade affects the maximum stock thickness that the table saw will cut.

Most table saws have lugs near the blade's periphery. They limit blade size and eliminate the

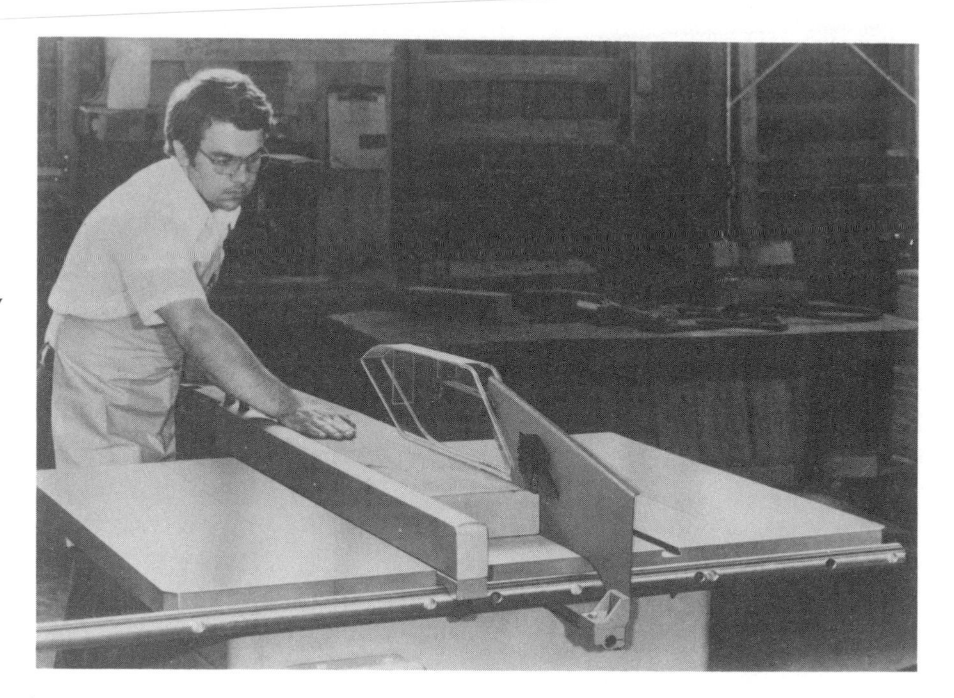

Illus. 1-40. This industrial saw uses a 12-inch blade and is designed for processing large parts and thick lumber.

chance of installing an oversize blade. Some people use an undersize blade on the table saw, but the largest blade that the saw will accommodate actually determines size.

Table Size The size of the table on a table saw is also important when you are considering table-saw size. It is much easier to balance and control large sheets of stock on a large surface. Not all 10-inch table saws have the same size table or work surface (Illus. 1-41).

It is possible to build a large wooden table around a bench saw or small table saw. This increases the working area and makes the table saw more versatile. Extensions can also be attached to the fence or the sides or ends of the table saw. This allows greater support and control when you are cutting long, wide, or thin pieces of stock.

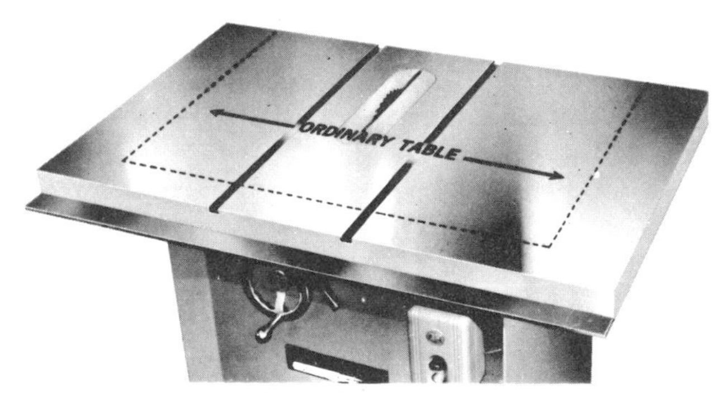

Illus. 1-41. Not all 10-inch table saws have the same size table. Some are larger (or smaller) than ordinary.

Maximum Ripping Width The widest piece of stock that can be ripped (cut with the grain) is another size determinant on the table saw. The length of the rails on which the rip fence travels determines the maximum ripping width (Illus. 1-42).

Most 10-inch saws have rails 28–30 inches long. These rails allow a 12-inch rip on the left and right of the blade. They can also be adjusted for a 24-inch rip on the right or left side. Some 10-inch saws allow for a 12-inch rip on the left side and a 24-inch rip on the right side of the blade. This is a desirable setup. It allows rip cuts to the center (width) of panel stock on the right side of the blade and provides for occasional cuts on the left side of the blade.

Other rails are offered for certain table saws. They allow for a 50-inch rip on the right side of the blade. They allow the saw to crosscut to the center (length) of 4-foot × 8-foot panel stock. Many manufacturers of table saws offer more than one length of rails. Usually the saw is sold with the shortest rails available. This is because the longer rails require a much larger working space. Consult the manufacturer's catalogue to determine what rails are available for your saw.

Illus. 1-42. The length of the rails on which the rip fence travels determines the maximum ripping width. The saw will rip 50 inches on the right of the saw blade. (Photo courtesy of Jet Power Tools.)

If the fence rails only allow a 24-inch rip cut and you want to make a larger cut in sheet stock such as plywood, you can subtract the desired width from 48 inches. The remainder is the distance from the left side of the blade to the fence. If you use the right side of the blade, the saw cut will be in the piece you wish to keep and will make it about ⅛ inch smaller than desired. Be sure to make an allowance if you use this method.

Distance from Table Front to Blade The distance from the front of the table to the front of the blade (at full height) is also an important measurement. The greater this distance, the greater the control over the work. This is important for cutting both with or across the grain.

It is much safer to balance a large piece of stock on the table before the cut begins. If the distance from the table front to the blade is minimal, cutting begins almost as soon as the stock touches the table. Greater strength and skill are needed to obtain a good cut under these circumstances. Large tables usually have a greater distance between the front of the table and the blade (Illus. 1-43).

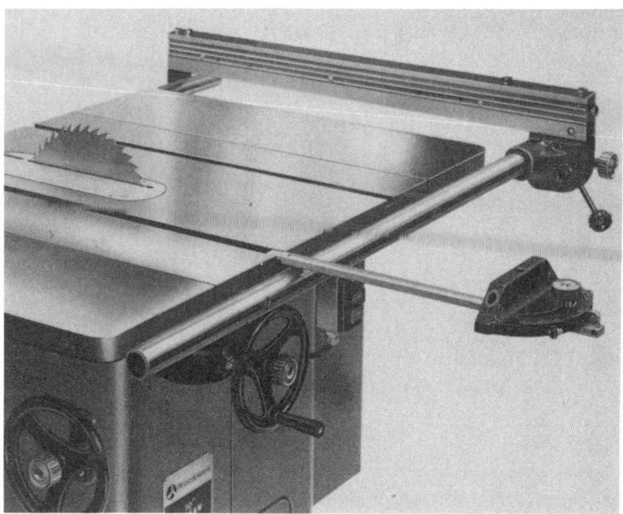

Illus. 1-43. This 10-inch table saw has great distance between the blade and the front of the table. It is easier to control stock on a table like this.

Horsepower Horsepower is an important table-saw-size consideration. Several motors of varying types and horsepower ratings can be used on the same table saw. The motors may even have the same outside dimensions, which makes selection more difficult. Comparing one type of motor such as a universal motor to another type such as an induction motor can make comparisons even more confusing. The following discussion will help you determine which size and type of motor your saw needs. It will also eliminate confusion between the terms *rated horsepower* and *peak horsepower*.

Motor Type The two designs or types of motors used on table saws are *universal* and *induction* motors. Universal motors are most common on benchtop saws, and induction motors are more common on contractor and cabinet table saws, but they can be used on any table saw.

A universal motor is physically smaller and lighter than an induction motor. For example, a ½-

horsepower universal motor weighs about 2½ pounds, and a ½-horsepower induction motor weighs about 25 pounds. This means that it offers the most horsepower per pound. It is also the reason it is favored for portable table saws such as the benchtop model. Universal motors are not as reliable as induction motors. Their operating life is generally shorter than that of an induction motor.

Universal motors are called universal because they can operate on either direct current or alternating current. Induction motors are designed to operate only on alternating current.

Induction motors are very rugged. They turn at lower speeds than universal motors, so they usually transfer power to the blade through a belt and pulleys. If your table saw is designed for belt drive, it is using an induction motor. Induction and universal motors are both used on motorized table saws.

Rated Horsepower versus Peak Horsepower Horsepower is a function of torque and rpms (revolutions per minute). Peak or developed horsepower is the horsepower of the motor when it has no load. This is also referred to as the *maximum developed horsepower*. Rated horsepower is the horsepower under load. It is lower than the peak horsepower.

Generally, the best comparison between motors is the amperage rating. The rule of thumb is that a 12-ampere, 110-volt motor has a rated or actual horsepower of one. This means that three additional amperes would raise the rating one-fourth of a horsepower. For example, a 15-ampere motor would actually be 1¼ horsepowers.

Universal motors are generally rated by amperes only. The universal motor is much more difficult to stall than an induction motor. This means that the rated horsepower will go higher on a universal motor.

Determining How Much Horsepower Is Needed Most table saws come equipped with a motor that ranges from ½ horsepower (rated) to 1.0 horsepower (rated). This is a considerable difference in horsepower. The ½-horsepower motor would be found on a 7½-inch table saw. This is because the saw turns a smaller blade and is not designed to cut thick stock.

A 16-inch table saw would have a 5–10-horsepower (rated) motor on it. A 10-inch table saw would have a 1–5-horsepower (rated) motor on it. The difference in horsepower between these saws is due to the different job these saws have to perform. If a 10-inch saw is used to cut framing lumber, a 4-horsepower (rated) motor would be selected. This is because the stock is not as dry or true as furniture lumber. The twist in the stock may put extra strain on a smaller motor. The extra moisture in framing lumber means that more horsepower is needed to throw or eject the heavier sawdust.

Table saws that are purchased for heavy ripping or dadoing operations should have the largest available motor installed. Ripping requires more energy than crosscutting. Turning a large dado head and making dado cuts also require more energy than general sawing.

In most cases, a 10-inch table saw is underpowered if it has a 1-horsepower (rated) or smaller motor. A 1½-horsepower (rated) motor should be the smallest motor installed on a 10-inch table saw for general duty. A 10-inch table saw with an 8-inch blade mounted on the arbor will have more power. More power is available to cut since less power is used to turn the smaller blade. When using a smaller blade, make sure that its rpm rating is correct for your saw.

Larger horsepower motors also have more energy to kick back (eject or kick stock towards you). I have taught many students table saw basics on a ½-horsepower, 7½-inch table saw. Stock that binds on this saw usually freezes the blade and does not kick back.

Remember, an oversized saw in the hands of a beginner is similar to a sports car with a beginning driver at the wheel. Select the saw size according to the work you do. A 10-inch saw may be too large for miniature work and too small for panel work.

Are You Using All of Your Available Horsepower? There are many instances when a powerful table saw is not performing up to capacity. In such cases, the first response is to blame the saw, but the electrical power source is often the problem. If your garage has only one circuit or the supply wire to the garage is lighter than 12 gauge, there is a good chance that the motor will overheat.

Extension cords should always be at least 14 gauge to do an adequate job. The lower the gauge number, the larger the wire. If your saw bogs down in a heavy cut, the first thing to check is the electrical supply. The second thing to check is the blade. A very-fine cutting blade will increase cutting friction and requires more electricity. Going to a tool steel blade will reduce cutting friction. The tooth set on a tool steel blade results in much less tooth friction than that on a carbide-tooth blade. The cut, however, will not be as smooth, and the blade will dull sooner.

—2—

Table Saw Controls and Accessories

Controls

There are three common controls on all tilting-arbor table saws: the power switch, the blade-elevating wheel, and the blade-tilting handwheel (Illus. 2-1–2-3). On tilting table saws (Illus. 2-4), there is a table-tilting mechanism and table-raising mechanism instead of a blade-tilting or blade-elevating mechanism. In addition, some table saws are equipped with a brake. The brake stops the blade as soon as the saw is shut off.

Power Switch There are many types of power switches in use on table saws. Some use a conventional light switch, while others are more specialized. Specialized switches are easier to turn off than on (Illus. 2-5). This makes accidental starting of the saw more difficult. Usually, these switches are color-coded for increased safety. Green is ON and red is OFF. The power switch should be positioned so that the operator can turn the saw on and off easily without reaching. The operator should be able to shut the saw off quickly in an emergency.

Some newer models actually have the switch on the arm of the blade guard (Illus. 2-6). This puts the switch in view at all times and puts it above the workpiece where it can be operated easily. The wiring can be attached to the blade-guard support. This support is a metal tube which attaches to the saw's table. This switch cannot be shut off with a

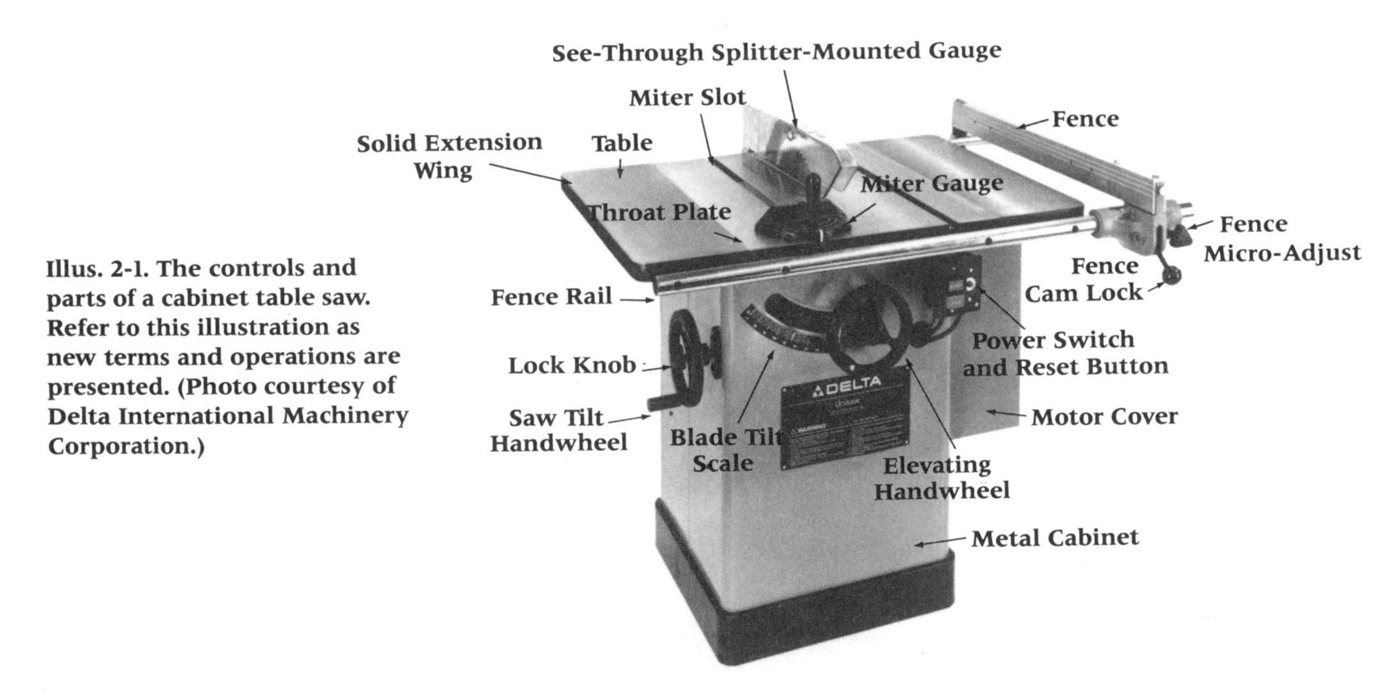

Illus. 2-1. The controls and parts of a cabinet table saw. Refer to this illustration as new terms and operations are presented. (Photo courtesy of Delta International Machinery Corporation.)

knee, as some of the lower-mount switches can. Your work application will determine switch placement.

Some power switches require that a key be inserted before the table saw can be used. This type of switch keeps inexperienced operators and curious children from operating the saw. Any table saw (or other power tool) in a home where children are

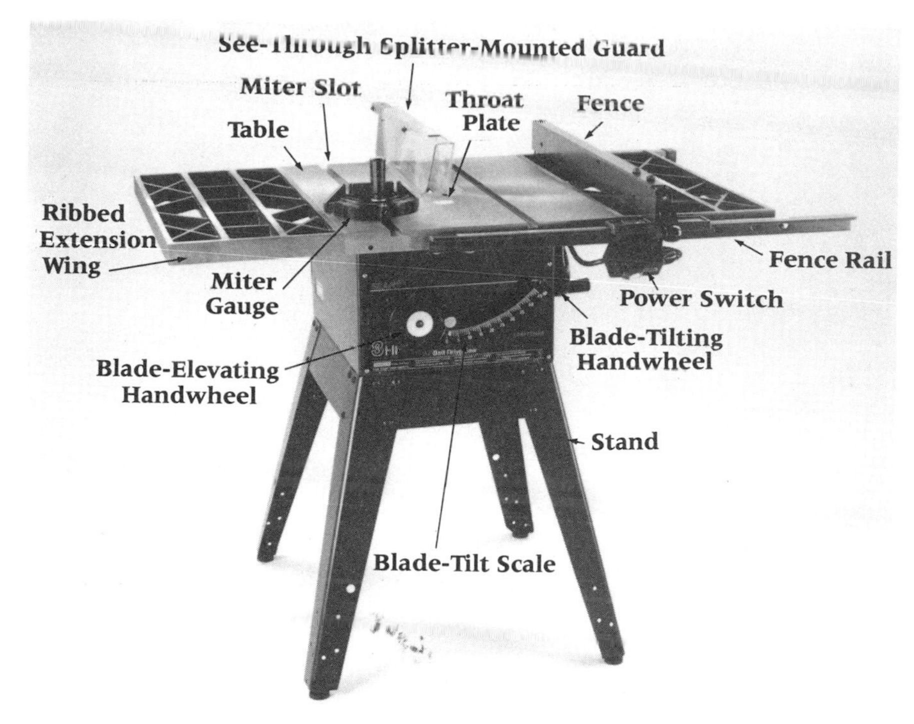

Illus. 2-2. This contractor saw has parts similar to those on the cabinet saw shown in Illus. 2-1. Familiarize yourself with its parts. (Photo courtesy of Sears Craftsman.)

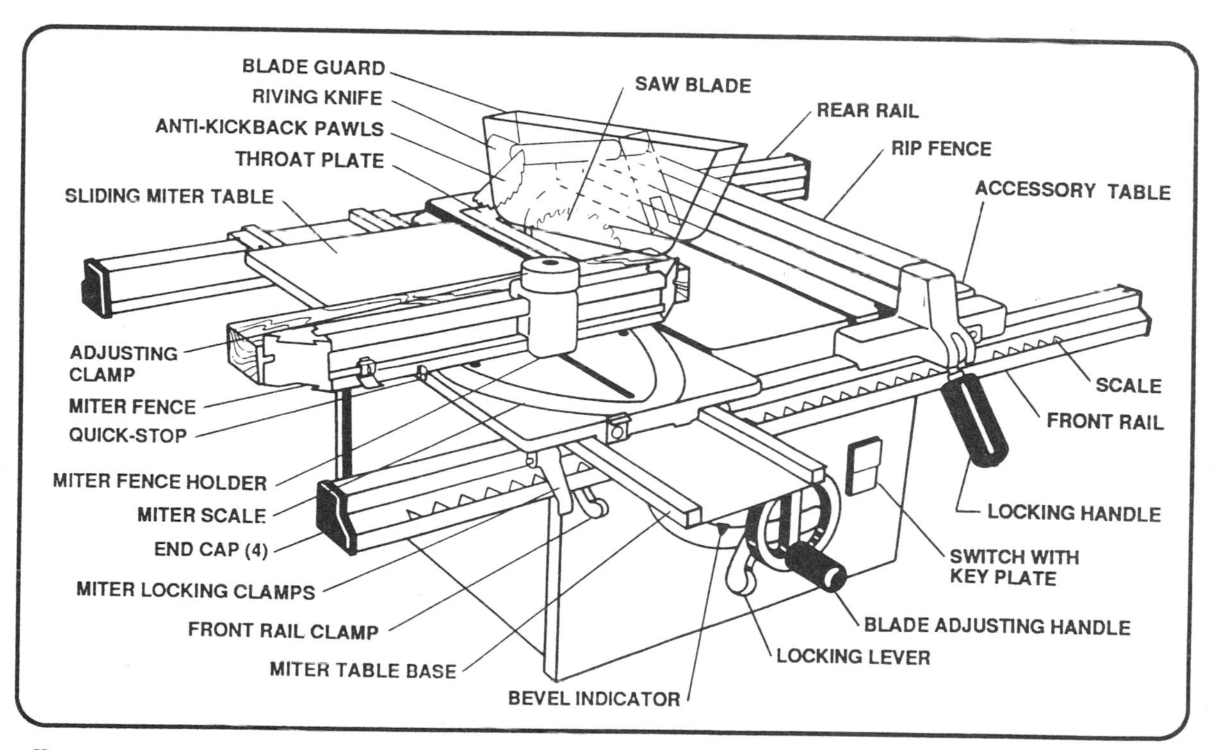

Illus. 2-3. This benchtop saw has a sliding table and some unique parts. (Drawing courtesy of Ryobi America Corporation.)

Illus. 2-4. This table saw has a table-tilting mechanism and a table-elevating mechanism. The blade does not tilt or move up and down. The table tilts in both directions, which allows easy cutting of dovetails.

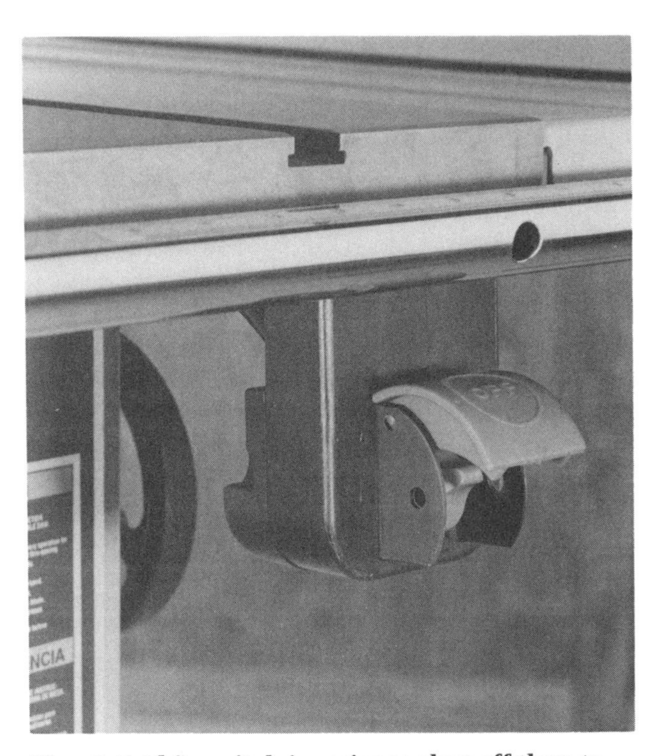

Illus. 2-5. This switch is easier to shut off than to turn on. This makes the saw safer if a problem occurs. (Photo courtesy of Delta International Machinery Corporation.)

Illus. 2-6. This power switch is mounted to the guard support above the saw. This makes it easily accessible. (Photo courtesy of Delta International Machinery Corporation.)

present should either have key-activated switches or tools that are kept behind a locked door, to prevent a mishap.

On high-voltage table saw motors, a low-voltage switching system is used The system uses a 24-volt circuit to the motor. This system activates a solenoid on the motor to the on or off position. The 24-volt circuit minimizes the chance of high-voltage electric shock to the operator. The saw will not restart after a power failure. This is a safety feature.

Blade-Elevating Handwheel The blade-elevating handwheel controls blade height through a worm-gear and rack-gear mechanism (Illus. 2-7). Most (but not all) handwheels are turned clockwise to elevate the blade. Most table saws have positive stops at full blade height and depth. Avoid over-cranking the handwheel, as the elevating mechanism can become jammed.

Illus. 2-7. The blade-elevating handwheel controls blade height. On most saws, the wheel is turned clockwise to elevate the blade.

There is usually a locking device (Illus. 2-8) to lock the blade at the desired height. Be sure to loosen this device before changing blade height. Raising or lowering the blade while the locking device is on may damage the saw. Always check the locking device before making any adjustment.

When adjusting blade height, make the final setting as the blade is being raised. This increases the accuracy of the setting. When the blade is raised, there is positive contact between the worm and rack gears. This eliminates slippage due to gear lash.

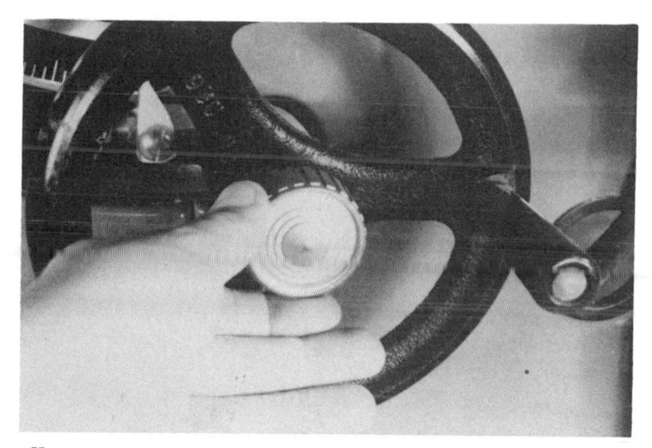

Illus. 2-8. The small knob in the center of the handwheel locks the blade height at the desired setting.

Blade-Tilting Handwheel The blade-tilting handwheel controls the angle of the blade. Table saws have a protractor-like scale on the front of the saw to help you determine the blade angle. This scale is helpful, but it is not very accurate. It is more accurate to measure the angle between the table and the blade. Use a sliding T-bevel or other device to measure the angle.

On some bench or variety saws, the blade is tilted at the front of the saw. First, the clamp is released (Illus. 2-9), and then the ring behind the blade-elevating mechanism is engaged. As the ring is turned, the blade is tilted (Illus. 2-10). Once the angle has been correctly set, the clamp lever is engaged. This holds the setting for all the bevel cuts.

Brakes Some table saws made today are equipped with brakes that stop the blade instantly after the power is shut off. The brakes may be mechanical or electronic. Mechanical brakes consist of a pad and a drum similar to those on a car. Some are activated by a solenoid, and others are operated manually. These brakes must be adjusted periodically, and the pads must be changed when they become worn. Electronic brakes stop the blade by sending current through the motor. The current counteracts the motion of the motor, causing it to stop. Electronic brakes can easily be installed on most table saws.

Brakes make the table saw easier to operate, and minimize setup time. The operator does not have to wait for the motor to coast to a stop before chang-

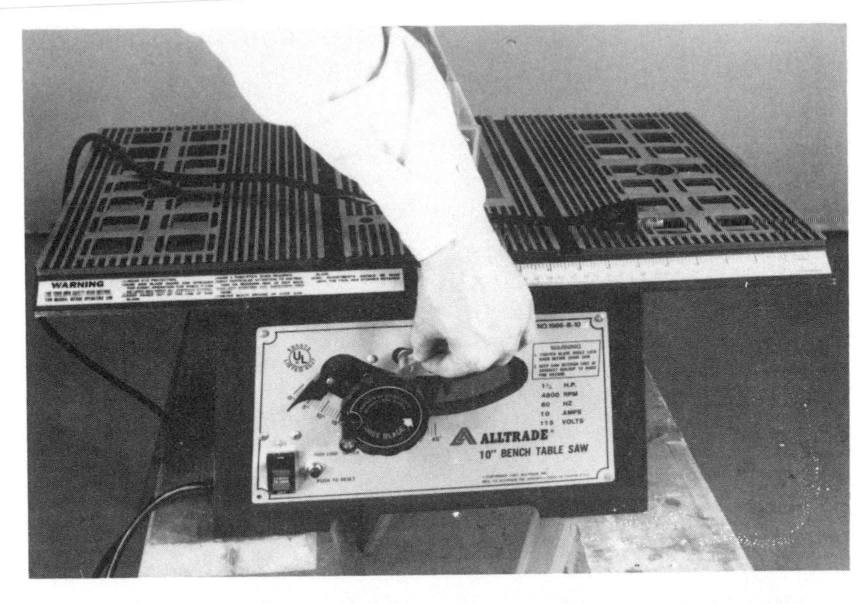

Illus. 2-9. To tilt the blade on the bench saw, release the clamp. Some clamps look like a lever.

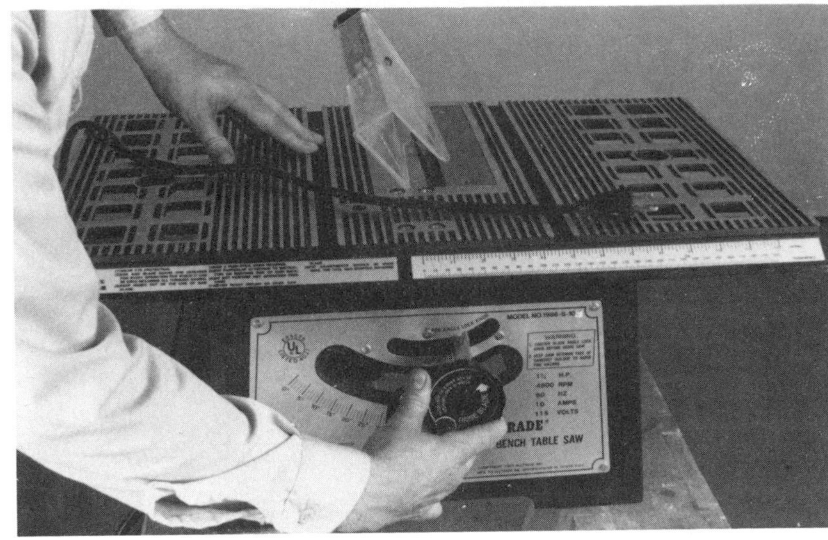

Illus. 2-10. Pushing in the elevating handwheel will engage the tilting mechanism. Once the blade is in position, lock the clamp again. Pull out the elevating handwheel to adjust blade height.

ing the setup. The electronic brake causes no appreciable wear on the electric motor.

Accessories

There are many accessories available for the table saw. Some come with the saw, and others are shop-made or sold as optional equipment. These accessories make the saw safer and easier to use.

Power-Feed Unit A power-feed unit is a motor-operated device that feeds stock into the blade (Illus. 2-11). Older units are often attached to the fence, but today's units are usually bolted to the table. A base is bolted to the table; this base supports a steel column. This column has a casting that moves vertically on it. Through the casting extends another steel column that moves horizontally. At the end of this column is another casting and pivoting mechanism. The feeding motor attaches to this casting.

The motor has a series of drive wheels (usually 3 or 4) or an endless belt mounted to it. These wheels or the belt can be moved either forward or backward and are used to drive the stock into the blade. The belt or wheels are made of a soft plastic which grabs the stock and drives it into the blade.

In addition to turning the wheels forward and backward, the motor is usually equipped with 2 to 4 speeds. The speed changes may be at the motor

Illus. 2-11. This power-feed unit is an accessory for larger table saws. The wheels feed the stock into the blade. There is little chance of kickback, and the power feeder acts as a barrier between the blade and the operator. (Photo courtesy of Delta International Machinery Corporation.)

switch, or they may consist of a gear change. Most power feeders have a low range of 10–12 feet per minute and a high range of 40–80 feet per minute.

The motors may use a 110- or 220-volt power supply, and some may use either power supply. Power-feed motors are rated at ⅙ to 3 horsepower. The smallest power feeders will handle most ripping, dadoing, and shaping operations in one- or two-inch stock at the lower feed rates. The varying feed rates allow you to compensate for stock of varying hardness or thickness, for the amount of stock being removed, or for the horsepower of the table saw.

Power feeders are used on table saws more frequently today for many reasons, but the chief reasons include the following:

1. *Power feeders reduce operator fatigue.* The constant lifting and pushing of stock into a table saw can generate fatigue. The power feeder reduces this fatigue.

2. *Power feeders reduce accidents.* The power feeder actually acts as a barrier between the blade and the operator. This reduces possible contact with the blade. The power feeder also helps reduce accidents caused by the monotony of production operations. There is less of a hazard if inattention to the job occurs.

3. *Power feeders reduce kickbacks.* The power feeder has a gear motor which provides positive feed and reduces the chance of kickback.

4. *Power feeders increase productivity.* The power feeder keeps stock in motion without any hesitation. It can feed stock faster than any table-saw operator. Setting up the power feeder for sawing is presented under Ripping Stock on pages 101–105.

Dust Collector A dust-collection system should be used on all table saws. Such a system collects most of the chips and dust produced by the table saw. It consists of fittings attached to the table saw, a collection hose, and a dust collector (Illus. 2-12 and 2-13).

A dust collector consists of an impeller or fan which generates air movement. On a single-stage dust collector, the chips and dust travel through the impeller. On a two-stage dust collector, the chips drop into a container in front of the impeller, and only the fine dust travels through the impeller into a dust bag. The advantage of the two-stage dust collector is that large chips or metal parts (such as

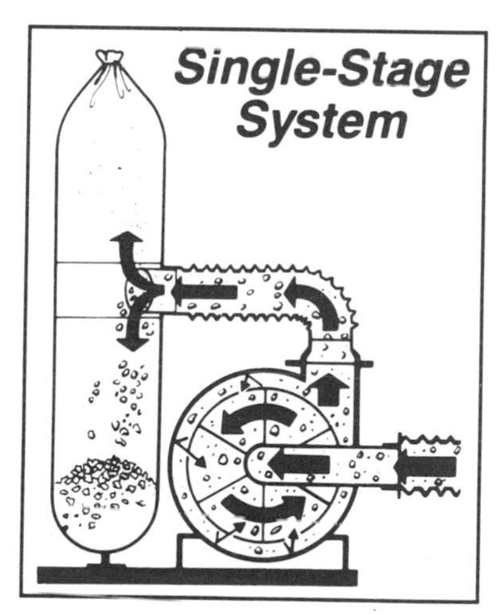

Illus. 2-12. This single-stage dust collector pulls all chips through the impeller. (Drawing courtesy of Delta International Machinery Corporation.)

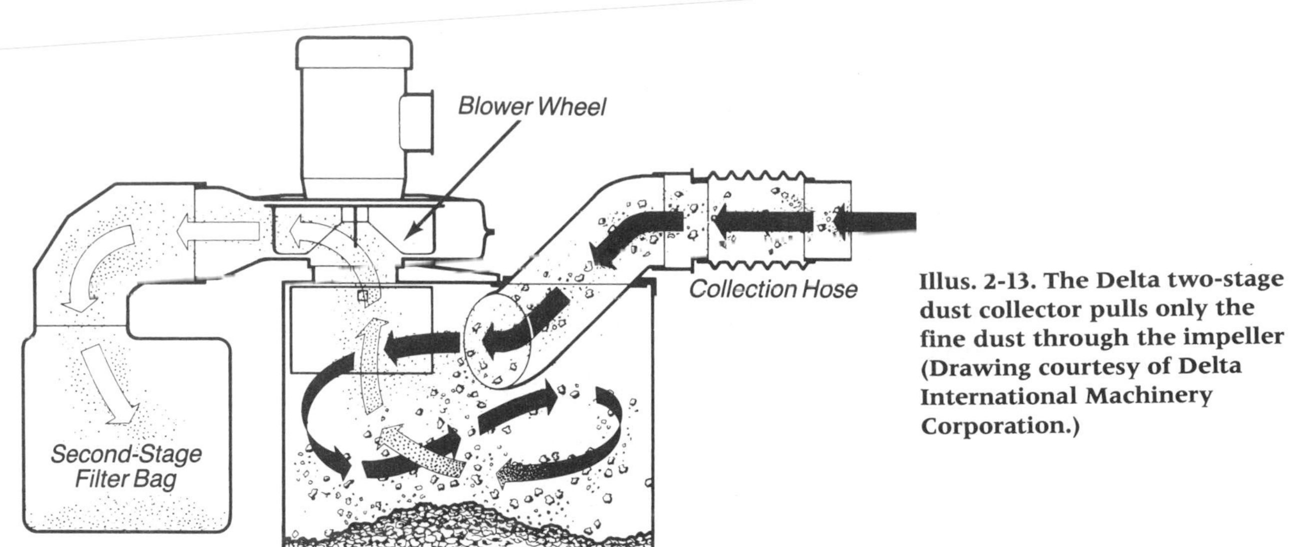

Illus. 2-13. The Delta two-stage dust collector pulls only the fine dust through the impeller (Drawing courtesy of Delta International Machinery Corporation.)

the arbor nut) do not contact the impeller. This eliminates damage to the impeller and reduces the chance of sparking and the resulting fire hazard.

Dust collectors are rated by their horsepower and the number of cubic feet of air they move per minute (CFM). Dust collectors range in speed from approximately 300 cubic feet per minute up to over 1,000 cubic feet per minute. A typical table saw using a dedicated dust-collection system could utilize a dust collector rated at 300 cubic feet per minute.

Dust collectors make the air cleaner to breathe and reduce fire and explosive hazards. Sawdust can explode in the same way as grain dust will, and should be treated as a hazard. Many of the treated woods and particleboards increase the breathing hazard of wood dust. Their additional chemicals are likely to be more hazardous than actual wood dust. Research has shown that wood dust has contributed to nasal cancer and upper respiratory problems in woodworkers.

Attaching a dust-collection system to a table saw may require some adapters to connect the hose (Illus. 2-14). It may also require motor covers or other box-like devices to contain dust at the saw. Cabinet-type saws lend themselves to dust-collection systems more easily than other types of saws. Contractor saws are more difficult to set up for dust collection. This is because the motor extends from the back of the saw. It is difficult to close this opening because the belt and motor must be able to pivot for bevel cutting.

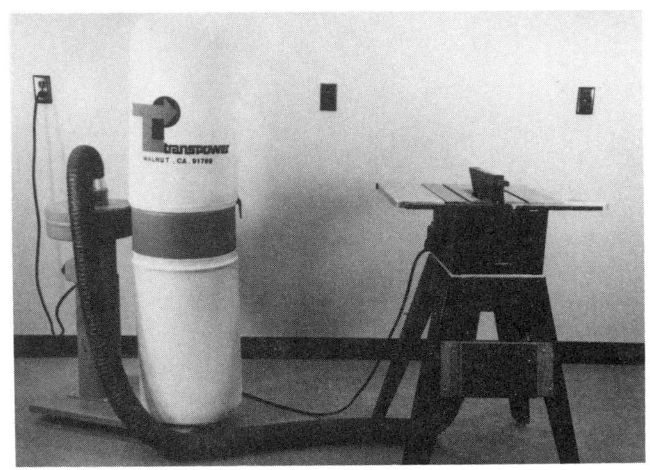

Illus. 2-14. This single-stage dust collector is connected to this benchtop table saw with a series of adapters and a three-inch flexible hose.

Fence The fence is an accessory that is standard equipment with all table saws. The fence clamps to one or two table rails or is bolted to the table. The fence is used to control stock when ripping (cutting with the grain) solid stock or when cutting strips from a piece of sheet stock. The distance between the fence and the blade determines the size of the strips being cut.

Some fences may be tilted to accommodate pieces with beveled edges. This feature is usually available only on expensive industrial saws. The same feature can be added to a common table saw with an angular wooden fence attachment. The unit attaches to the fence and will control stock with a beveled edge.

Some woodworkers attach a piece of stock to the fence. This protects the fence from contact with the blade. This piece of stock must be true, to ensure that the fence remains parallel with the blade.

Fence Alignment There are many theories on fence alignment and fence length. Some experienced operators feel that the fence should be exactly parallel with the blade. Others feel that the fence should be angled away from the blade at the far end, to minimize pinching and kickback. I have used table saws with both settings and found little difference.

If the fence is angled away on the right side of the blade, it will pinch when moved to the left side. Keep that in mind if you move the fence.

Fence length is also debatable. Some experienced operators use a short fence so there is no binding beyond the blade. The fence extends just beyond the blade's arbor. Other experienced operators prefer a fence that extends the entire length of the table. I prefer this type because it allows greater control over the wood.

Fence Adjustment Many fence-locking mechanisms do not always lock parallel to the blade or as they were adjusted. Periodically check the fence for correct alignment. Lock the fence and raise the blade to full height. Measure the distance to the fence at the front of the blade. Turn the blade so the same tooth is at the rear of the table, and measure the distance to the fence. If both measurements are the same, the fence is parallel. More information on table saw alignment can be found in Chapter 7.

Retro-Fit Fences Retro-fit fences are commercial fences which can be mounted on a number of different table saws (Illus. 2-15). These fences are designed to work more efficiently than the ones offered as standard equipment on most table saws. Once these fences are fitted to a table saw, they require much less adjustment and maintenance. Retro-fit fences hold their settings and accuracy, which consists of tolerances of plus or minus .002 inch.

Retro-fit fences come in many styles. Some of the features to consider when evaluating these fences include the following:

1. *A fence that locks to a front and a back rail.* When the fence locks to a front and a back rail, holding devices such as featherboards can be clamped to the rails (Illus. 2-16). If the fence does not lock to the front and back rails, a clamp may be furnished to secure the fence to the back rail. It is also possible to use a C clamp for this purpose.
2. *Ease of removal.* Can the fence be removed from any position on the fence rails? When it can, it is easy to remove or replace the fence (Illus. 2-17).

Illus. 2-15. This Exact-I-Fence is a retrofit fence for Sears Craftsman table saws. It is easy to position and use. (Photo courtesy of Sears Craftsman.)

Illus. 2-16. This Paralok retrofit fence locks to a front and back rail. It remains parallel to the blade with a cable system.

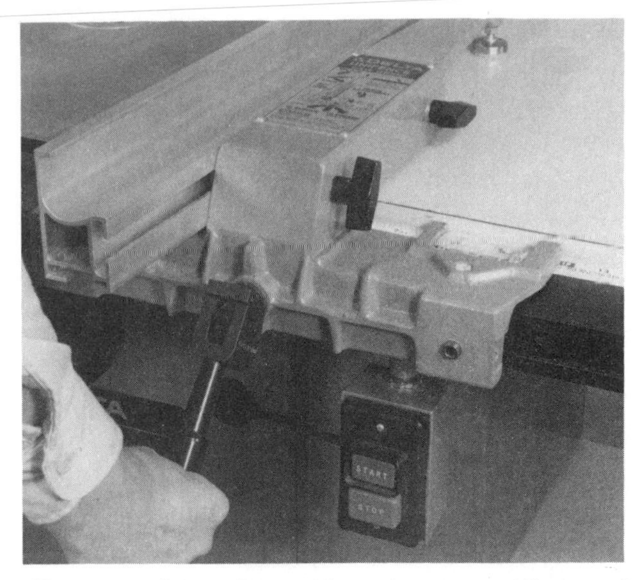

Illus. 2-17. This Delta Unifence is easy to adjust and use. It can be removed from any position on the fence rail.

When it cannot, it means extra time involved in moving the fence to the end of the rails for removal.

3. *Attachment of auxiliary fences.* Have provisions been made to attach auxiliary wooden fences or jigs to the fence? This means holes have been provided or can be easily drilled to accommodate screws or other fasteners.

4. *Availability of accessories.* Many fences are actually a system to which anti-kickback and pushing devices can be attached or incorporated. These accessories can enhance the fence's utility and contribute to the safe operation of the table saw (Illus. 2-18).

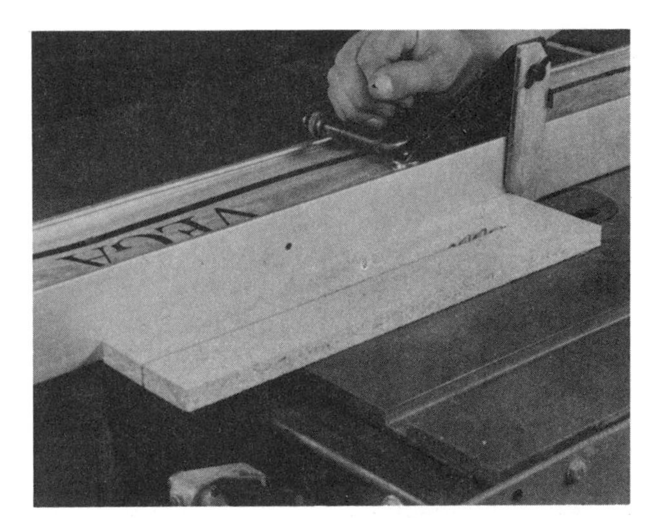

Illus. 2-18. This Vega fence has an accessory push block which rides in the grooves on top of the fence. It is the perfect accessory for narrow rip cuts.

5. *Smoothness or ease of operation.* Not all fences operate with equal smoothness. Do your homework before you invest in any fence. Try actual demonstration models in the showroom, and, if possible, try some which have been used in the field. Trying the ones used in the field will demonstrate how they hold up under actual working conditions.

6. *Ease of installation.* Not all fences install easily on all table saws (Illus. 2-19 and 2-20). Some actually require more layout and fastening time than others. In some cases, the directions are confusing, which can lead to a repeat of installation steps or the redrilling of holes. Be sure to look over the installation steps or ask someone who has installed one how long it took and how confusing the instructions were. If you are prepared for the confusion, it may actually be easier. Once you have made the purchase, help may not be as easy to find as you hoped.

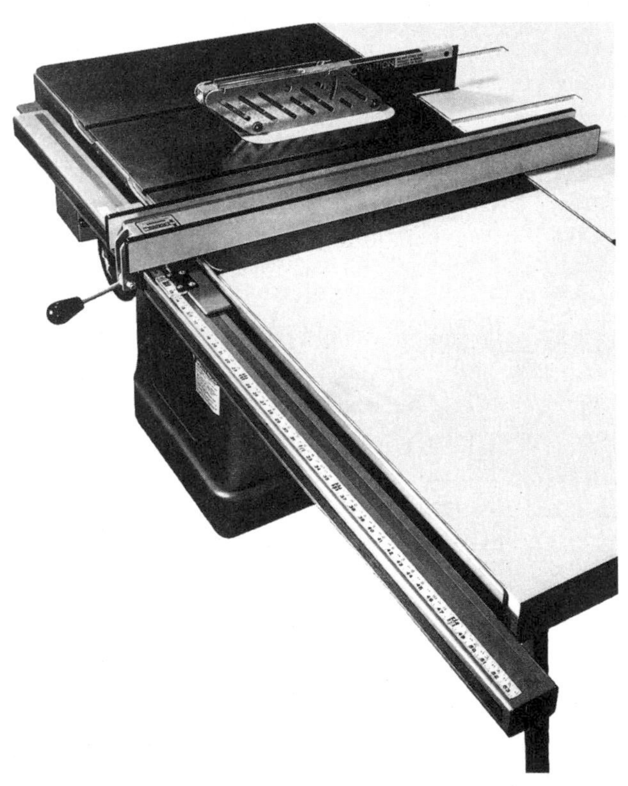

Illus. 2-19. This fence is called a T-Square. It is easy to mount on most table saws. It is easy to adjust and holds a setting quite well.

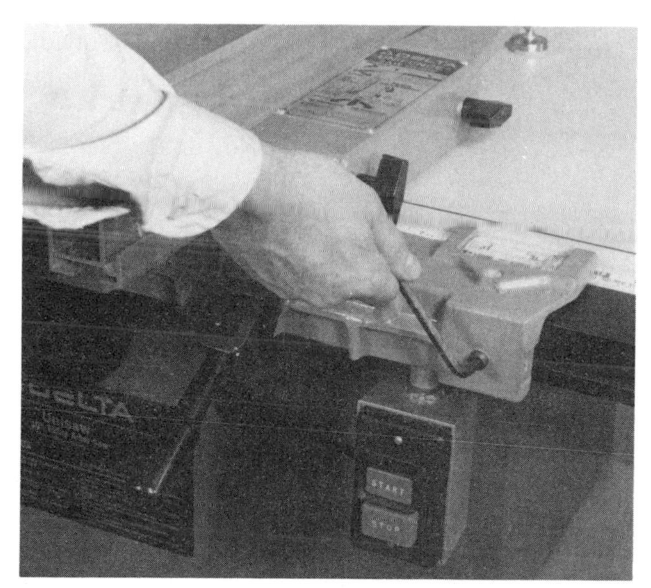

Illus. 2-20. Installing a fence on a table saw.

Illus. 2-22. The protractor scale and needle adjust this miter gauge. Note the adjustable stops for 90 and 45 degrees.

Miter Gauge The miter gauge controls solid stock when it is crosscut (cut across the grain) (Illus. 2-21). It is also used to trim small pieces of sheet stock and can be turned to make angular cuts such as miters on picture-frame stock.

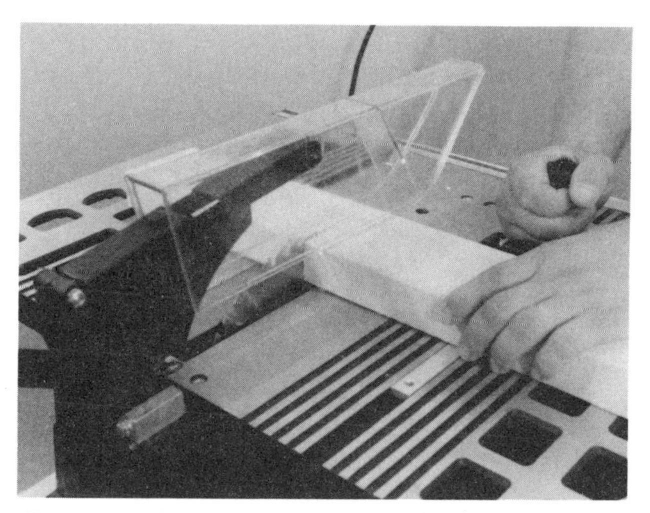

Illus. 2-21. The miter gauge controls stock when it is cut across the grain. (Photo courtesy of Skil Power Tools.)

Illus. 2-23. The most accurate measurement of the miter-gauge angle is between the head of the miter gauge and the blade.

The miter gauge has a protractor-like scale on it (Illus. 2-22), but it is more accurate to measure the angle between the blade and the head of the miter gauge (Illus. 2-23). To adjust the angle of the miter gauge, loosen the clamp knob that secures the head to the tongue. Turn the head of the miter gauge to the desired setting and lock it securely. Be sure to hold the head while tightening the clamp knob (Illus. 2-24).

The miter gauge is standard equipment on all table saws. Some are made of plastic, while others are made of metal. The miter gauge has a metal bar or tongue which slides in one of the two miter slots on the table. The miter slots are on both sides of the blade and are parallel to the blade when the saw is adjusted properly. On some table saws, the miter slot has a T shape. The T shape accommodates a

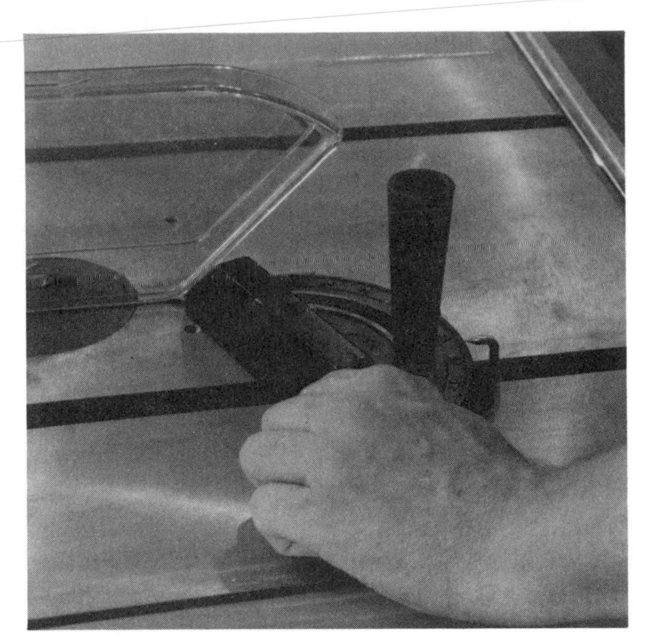

Illus. 2-24. When tightening the miter gauge, hold its head securely while tightening the clamp.

washer or shoulder on the metal bar or tongue of the miter gauge. The purpose of this design is to keep the gauge from falling off the saw when it is pulled toward the operator and released (Illus. 2-25).

Illus. 2-25. This miter gauge slides in a T-shaped slot. This keeps the miter gauge from falling off the saw. It also makes handling wider pieces more convenient.

Some miter gauges have an adjustable control surface. This surface can slide laterally in the head towards or away from the blade. This allows you to adjust the miter-gauge head for stock support no matter at what angle you set the miter gauge. It also allows you to accommodate a dado head. While this feature increases stock control, it is also possible to contact the blade with the head. Always check the setup to keep from damaging the miter gauge or saw blade and to protect against a mishap (Illus. 2-26).

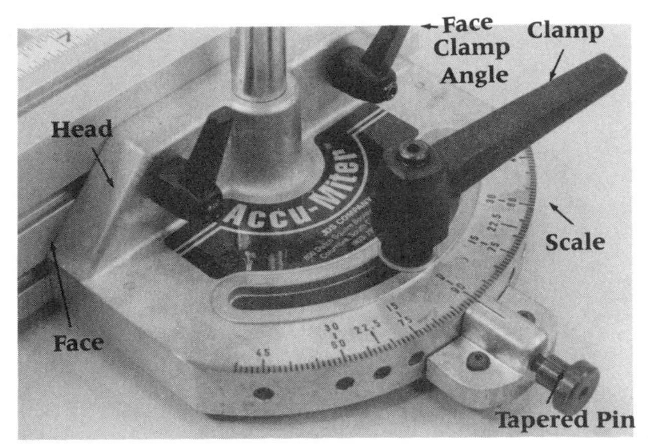

Illus. 2-26. The clamp on the head of the miter gauge allows the face to slide laterally toward or away from the blade. Be sure to keep the face out of the blade's path. (Photo courtesy of JDS Company.)

Many adjustable miter-gauge heads are also equipped with a stop (Illus. 2-27). The stop controls stock during a crosscut or miter cut. Some

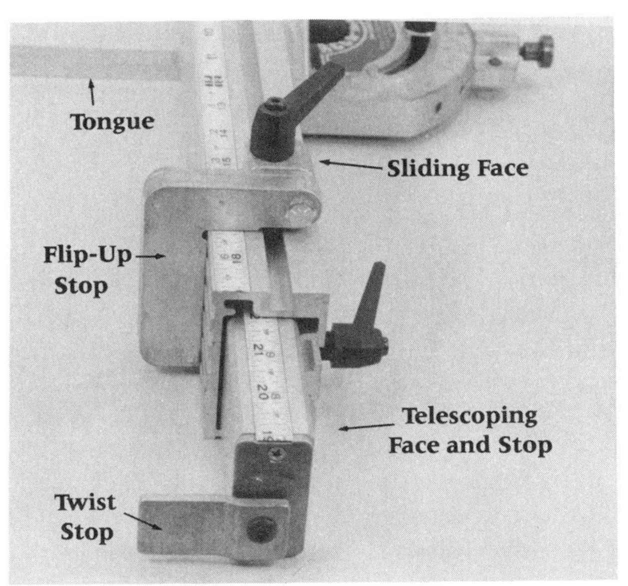

Illus. 2-27. The two stops and telescoping face enable this miter gauge to cut uniform lengths of stock at any angle. (Photo courtesy of JDS Company.)

standard miter gauges are also equipped with a hole in their heads to hold a pair of stop rods. These rods are also adjusted to control stock length. These rods can also contact the blade if they are not adjusted correctly. Always check the setup before cutting, to prevent damage or a mishap.

A clamping accessory is available for some miter gauges (Illus. 2-28). This clamping accessory secures the stock to the miter gauge so that it will not slip or get chipped during the cut. The clamping mechanism is usually secured to the miter gauge in one or more places. The clamping mechanism keeps your hands further from the blade during the operation and ensures an accurate cut.

Ordinarily, stock should not creep during the cut. If stock seems to creep when it is not clamped, there may be an alignment problem. Consult the table saw tune-up section in Chapter 7.

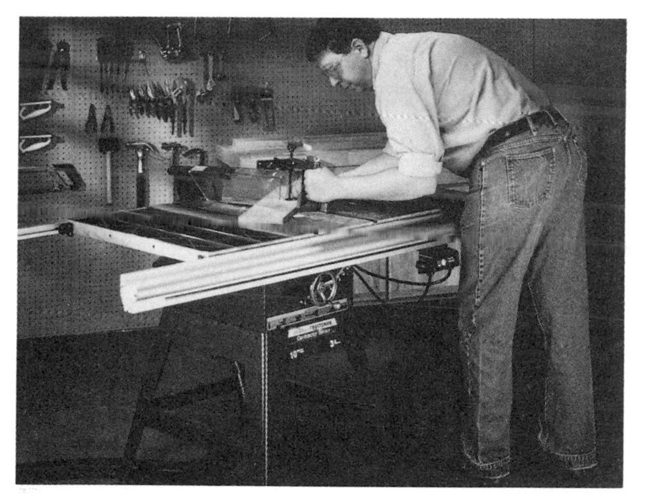

Illus. 2-28. The miter gauge used here has a clamping device attached to it. The clamp holds the stock securely between the head and tongue of the miter gauge. (Photo courtesy of Sears Craftsman.)

While most of the clamping devices and other features are not common with the typical miter gauge, this does not mean they cannot be adapted to it to improve its utility. In fact, the basic miter gauge can be modified a number of ways to make it fit the task at hand. Some woodworkers attach a piece of true solid stock to the head of the miter gauge using wood screws (Illus. 2-29). The solid-stock piece increases the length of the control surface, making the cut more accurate. In some cases, the solid stock extends past the blade (Illus. 2-30). This allows the cut to be backed to reduce grain tearing. It also acts as a scrap sweep which moves the cutoff past the blade, eliminating a possible kickback condition.

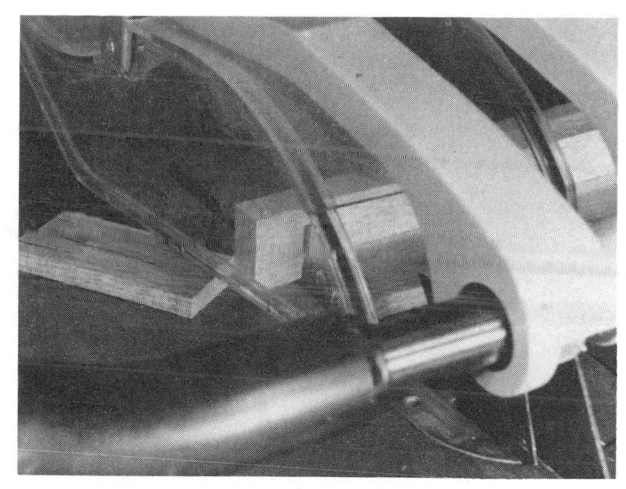

Illus. 2-29. This solid stock is attached to the miter-gauge head with wood screws. Be sure the stock is true and free of defects. The saw kerf tells you where the cutting line should be positioned.

Illus. 2-30. The auxiliary fence sweeps the scrap past the blade. This prevents the possibility of binding or kickback.

Some woodworkers glue abrasive stock to the wooden piece to increase friction and control between the stock and the miter gauge. This can enhance accuracy, but if slipping or chipping is evident, there may be an alignment problem. This is discussed in the tune-up section in Chapter 7.

Some woodworkers also devise clamping

methods (Illus. 2-31) to be used with the miter gauge and auxiliary wooden fence. With many clamps, stock is secured between the tongue of the miter gauge and the clamp pad. In some cases, an L-shaped piece is secured to the head of the miter gauge. The clamp secures the piece between the clamp and pad and the base of the L. This technique also protects finished or well-sanded wood from dragging on the table saw, and eliminates scratching or scuffing of the surface (Illus. 2-32).

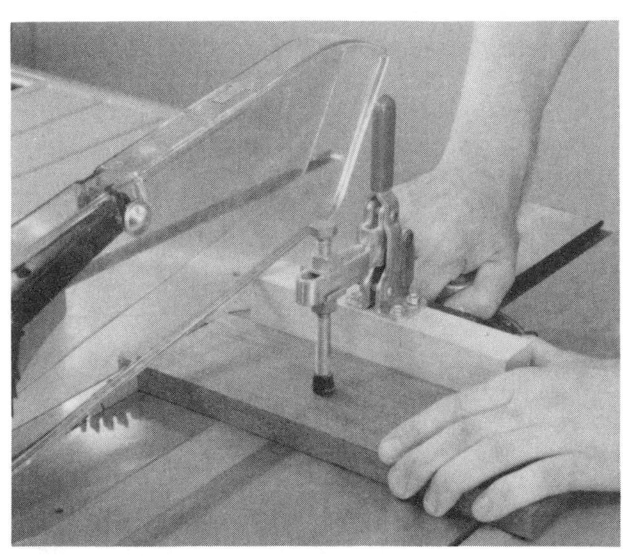

Illus. 2-31. This shop-made clamping system converts the conventional miter gauge into a clamping miter gauge. The clamp can be easily removed and used on other jigs or fixtures.

Illus. 2-32. This small shooting board can be used as a substitute miter gauge. This is very handy when the miter gauge is set up for a cut.

Stops can be used as auxiliary faces on miter gauges (Illus. 2-33 and 2-34). There are also many accessories which can be adapted to solid-stock fences. These include specialty miter gauges. These accessories are available at woodworking shows, woodworking supply houses, and through woodworking mail-order stores.

Illus. 2-33. This flip-up stop, which is a short piece of aluminum, can be used on a wooden auxiliary fence. The aluminum slides on the wood and clamps in place. The stop moves in the track and can be clamped in position. Note the microadjustment device.

Illus. 2-34. This aluminum extension can be cut to any convenient length and attached to a wooden fence. The stop moves in the extrusion. A microadjustment device can be used with it.

Specialty Miter Gauges Because of all the desirable features people like to see in miter gauges, numerous specialty miter gauges exist today. They incorporate extremely accurate machining features and numerous special features. Woodworkers who

Illus. 2-35. The Accu-Mitre miter gauge is a specialty miter gauge with extremely precise angle stops. Two clamping devices are available: a hand-actuated one and a pneumatic one. (Photo courtesy of JDS Company.)

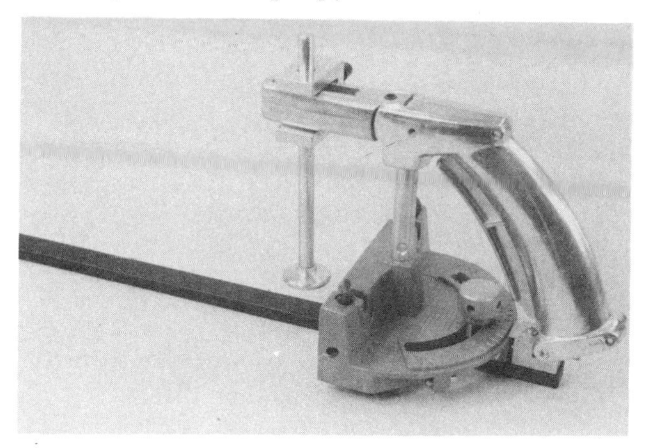

Illus. 2-36. This inexpensive miter gauge has provisions for stop rods and an adjustable clamping device.

use a miter gauge frequently may find one of these desirable. They may also find that it is a nice addition to the original miter gauge. Study Illus. 2-35–2-37 to see some of the many features commercial miter gauges offer.

Miter Square When a large number of miters must be cut for picture frames, door trim, or window trim, a miter square can be helpful. The miter square has a right triangle incorporated into its head as a part of the design. On dedicated models, the right triangle is oriented at a 45-degree angle to the blade. When you use both miter slots, one angle is cut on either side of the right triangle (Illus. 2-38–2-40). This means that if there is a slight error, it will not be obvious because the angles are complementary. All miters will fit snugly together.

Other miter squares can be used for crosscutting as well as mitering. They, too, have a right triangle as part of their design (Illus. 2-41 and 2-42). In order to use this model for mitering, the head has to be set at a 45-degree angle. This model uses only one miter slot, so the cutting is faster. A stop and sliding auxiliary fence are part of this design. Both of these models reduce setup and cutting time. They also eliminate the potential of error when you change a conventional miter gauge to cut miters at the opposite end of parts. Miter squares are not standard equipment and are sold as an accessory.

The dedicated miter square also has a clamping device (Illus. 2-43). The clamping device holds stock securely while the miters are cut and reduces

Illus. 2-37. The Kity miter gauge has a stop and a sliding face. It can be fitted to any table saw.

Illus. 2-38. This Sears Craftsman miter square is used in both miter slots. The wing nut clamps the stock to the triangle.

Illus. 2-39. These wheels secure the stock to the tongue of the miter square; the miter is ready to cut.

Illus. 2-40. The mating miter is now cut in the opposite miter slot. The stop rod controls the length of the piece. This jig was designed to be used with any guard.

Illus. 2-41. The head of the Kity miter square is turned to a 45-degree angle. With the 90-degree angle formed, both miters can be cut. The first miter is cut on the back of the miter square's head.

Illus. 2-42. The face is moved to back the mating cut and control the length of the mitered piece. This miter gauge will also work with any guard.

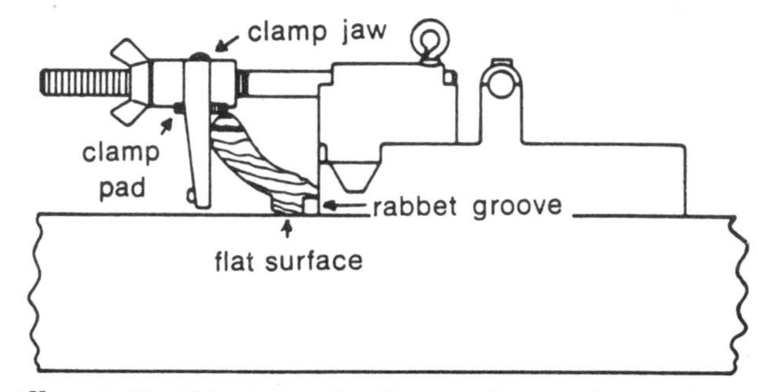

Illus. 2-43. This Sears Craftsman jig can be used to cut compound miters. The clamps secure the stock at the correct angle. (Drawing courtesy of Sears Craftsman.)

the problem of creeping. The dedicated miter square can also be used for cutting compound miters.

Tenoning and Universal Jigs The tenoning jig (Illus. 2-44) and the universal jig (Illus. 2-45) are designed to hold stock in a vertical or near-vertical orientation. The universal jig will also hold irregularly shaped pieces. When stock is cut on its end, it is usually cut for joinery purposes. These cuts require a tenoning jig because a fence does not provide enough control surface and even the slightest movement away from the fence can cause a kickback.

Since most joinery operations (such as making mortise-and-tenon and lap joints) are not through cuts, a guard cannot be used. The tenoning and universal jigs keep your hands farther away from the saw blade and provide greater control over the stock (Illus. 2-46–2-48).

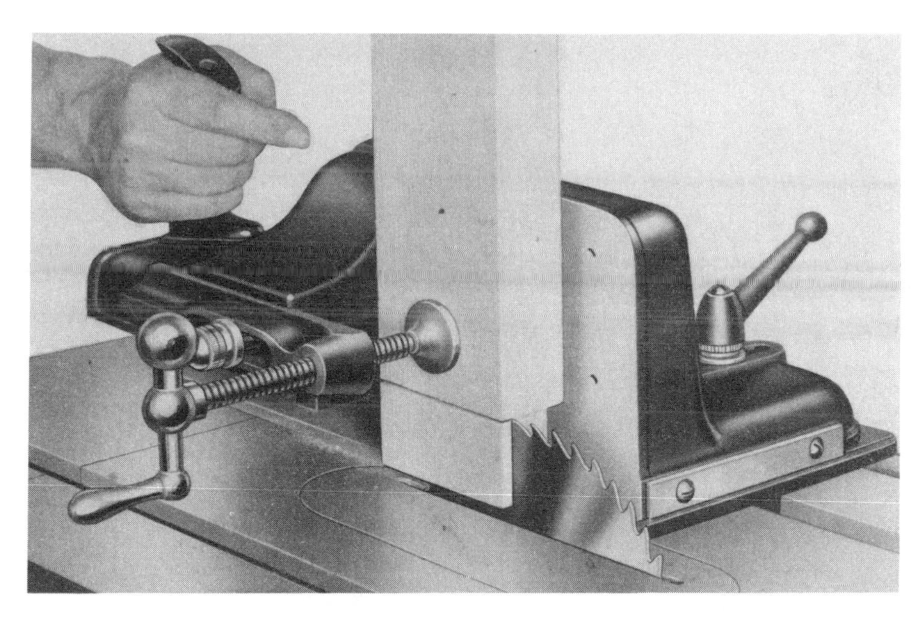

Illus. 2-44. This tenoning jig is designed to control stock that is cut or shaped on its end. The jig rides in the miter slot. (Photo courtesy of Delta International Machinery Corporation.)

Illus. 2-45. The universal jig is similar to the tenoning jig. It may be adjusted to make cuts on irregularly shaped pieces.

Illus. 2-46. This Delta tenoning jig can be turned at a simple or compound angle.

Tenoning jigs and universal jigs can be made of machined or die-cast metal. They can also be made of wood (Illus. 2-49 and 2-50). Plans for the jig in Illus. 2-49 can be found in Chapter 8. Some metal jigs have provisions for controlling the cut at a compound angle. These newer models increase the versatility of the jig.

Commercial tenoning jigs and universal jigs are controlled by the miter slot. They move towards and away from the blade to position the stock for cutting (Illus. 2-51). If you experience burning while using a tenoning jig, try using a coarser blade. This will reduce the heat of the cut. If you still

Illus. 2-47. Cutting the end of a piece of stock requires absolute control. This Delta jig provides control and keeps your hands clear of the blade. See Illus. 2-48.

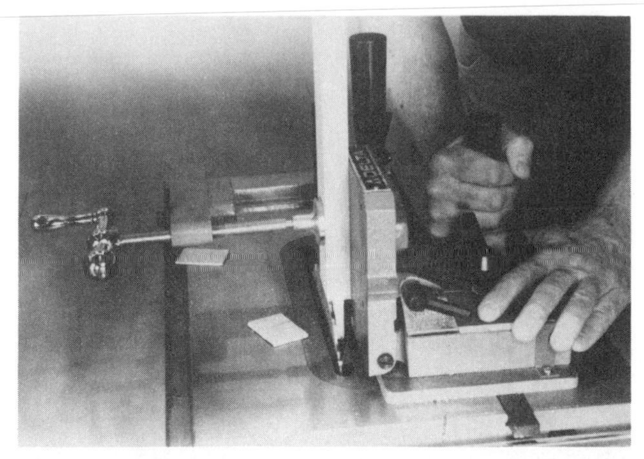

Illus 2-48. Cutting the end of a piece of stock.

Illus. 2-49. This shop-made tenoning jig can be adapted for other operations. Plans can be found in Chapter 8.

Illus. 2-50. This shop-made tenoning jig operates off the fence. It is adjusted by moving the fence.

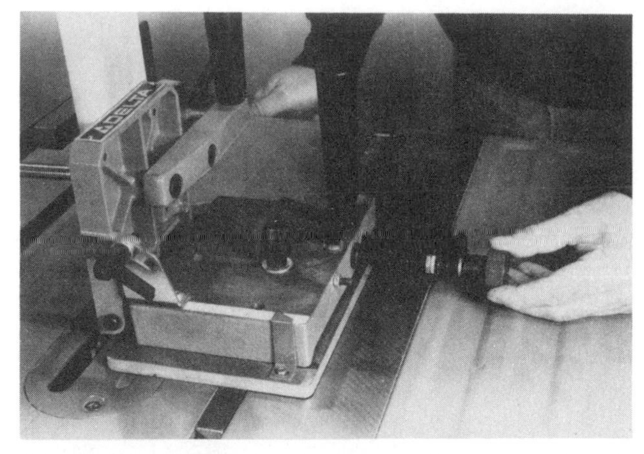

Illus. 2-51. The micro-adjustment features makes it easy to position the jig correctly.

experience burning, check the alignment of the miter slot to the blade. If they are not parallel, burning and possible kickback can occur. Refer to Table Saw Tune-Up in Chapter 7 to align your table saw. It is also possible that the tenoning jig is misaligned. The cutting face should be parallel to the bar which rides in the miter slot.

Box Joint Jig Many woodworking projects incorporate box or finger joints (Illus. 2-52). These joints are commonly made using a spacer device in conjunction with the fence or miter gauge. This box joint does the same job, but offers two additional features. First, it allows microadjustment of the spacing (Illus. 2-53). It also acts as a barrier guard during the operations (Illus. 2-54). The metal shields cover the blade or dado head during the

Illus. 2-52. The box joint shown here was cut using the spacer jig behind it. It is attached to the miter gauge.

Illus. 2-53. The Kity box-cutting jig has a micro-cutting adjusting wheel. This makes it easy to get perfect-fitting box joints.

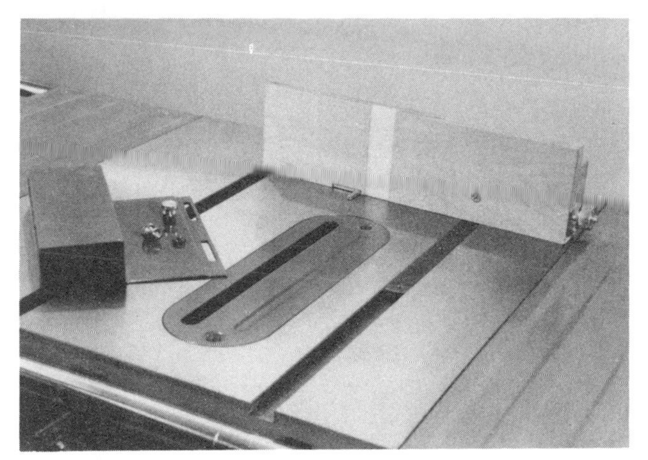

Illus. 2-54. The metal shield on the Kity box-joint jig acts as a barrier between you and the dado head.

cutting of the joint. This commercial accessory is available from Farris machinery and may also be used for mitering (see Illus. 2-41 and 2-42).

Throat Plate The throat plate (Illus. 2-55) is an insert in the table that allows access to the blade, arbor, arbor nut, and arbor washers. Some throat plates can be adjusted. They can be leveled with the tabletop. Others snap into place and are not adjustable. The arbor nut is removed to change blades. Two arbor washers sandwich the blade, and the arbor nut holds them securely to the arbor. Arbor nuts may have right- or left-hand threads. Inspect the threads carefully to determine which way the nut must be turned.

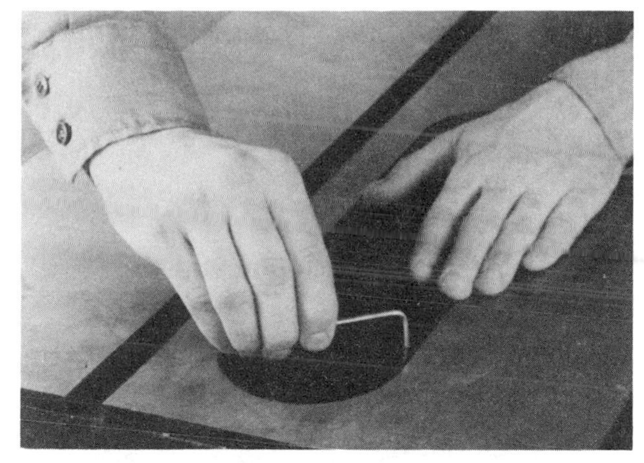

Illus. 2-55. The throat plate allows access to the blade, arbor, and arbor nut. Some throat plates may be adjusted so they are in the same plane as the table.

Throat plates are usually made of metal (Illus. 2-56), but they may also be made of wood or plastic. In some cases, a throat plate is custom-made for the job.

The size of the opening in the throat plate varies according to what blade or attachment is being

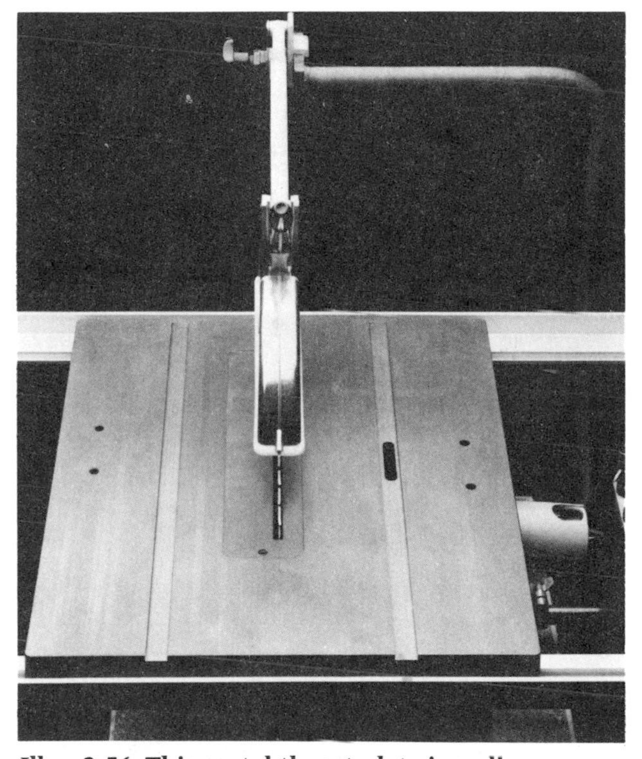

Illus. 2-56. This metal throat plate is well machined and is held securely with screws. Note the tight fit around the blade.

used. Be sure to select the correct or recommended throat plate for the operation you are performing. Avoid using a throat plate with an opening that is too large for the operation (Illus. 2-57). The workpiece could fall into the opening and cause a kickback or other mishap.

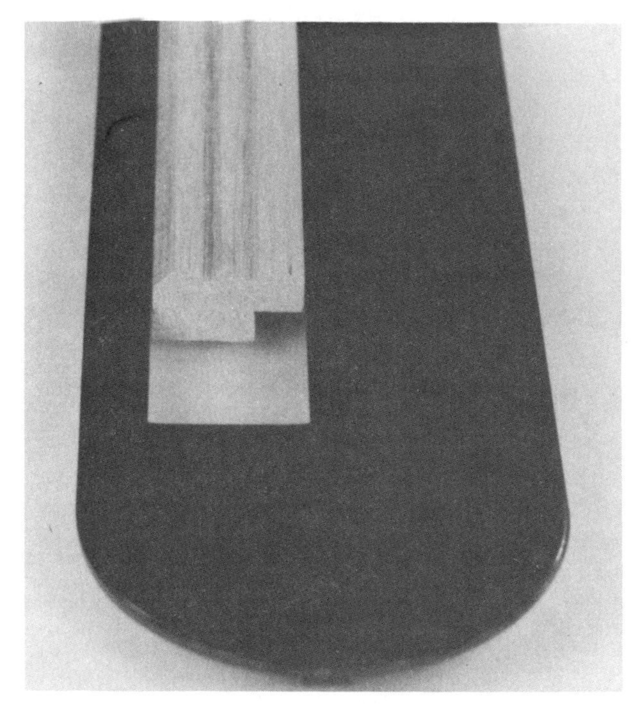

Illus. 2-57. The opening on some commercial throat plates may be too large for the work. This piece could easily fall into the cutter. A plywood throat plate was made to shape this stock.

When shaping stock with the molding head or sawing with a specialized blade, it may be necessary to make your own throat plate. Auxiliary throat plates are usually made of wood or plastic. Wooden throat plates are the easiest to cut, but plastic throat plates will resist wear better than wood.

Use any throat plate that fits the saw as a model. Select stock as thick as the throat plate or slightly thinner. Veneer-core plywood works well for throat plates. Rip the stock to the width of the throat plate. Lay out the curved ends with the throat plate (Illus. 2-58). Cut the curved ends with a band saw or saber saw. Disc sand the curves to your layout line (Illus. 2-59).

You may have to drill and tap holes to hold the throat plate in place (Illus. 2-60). Locate these holes

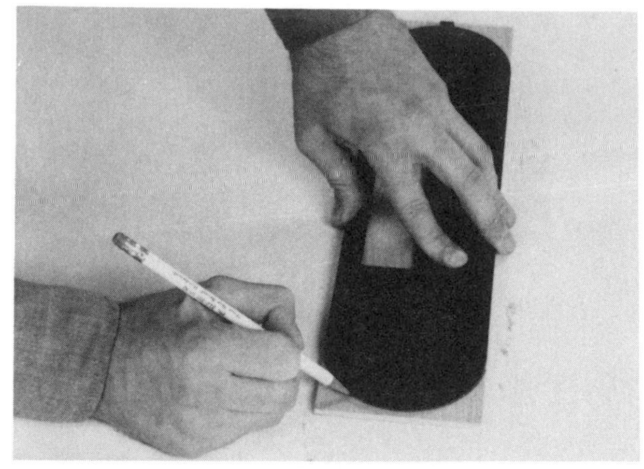

Illus. 2-58. When making an auxiliary throat plate, use the metal throat plate as a template. Rip stock to throat-plate width before laying out the ends.

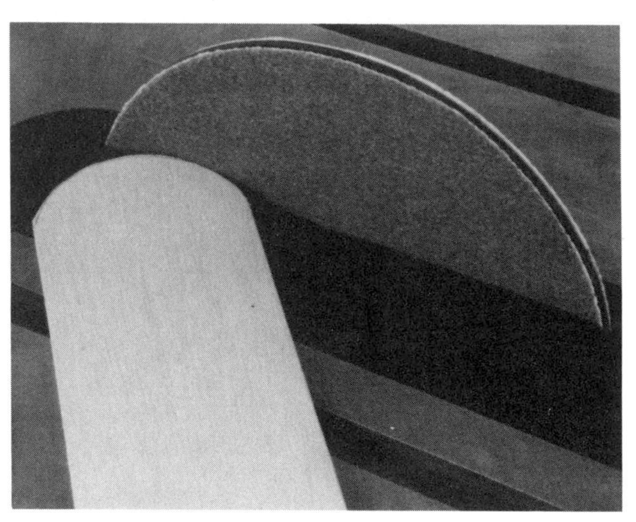

Illus. 2-59. You can use the sanding disc to shape the ends of the wooden throat plate.

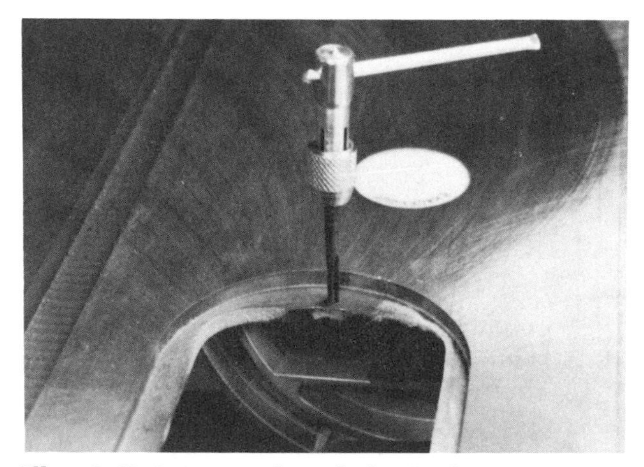

Illus. 2-60. Locate and tap holes in the support lugs of the table. These holes allow machine screws to hold the throat plate securely in place.

in the lugs that support the throat plate. Drill the throat plate to match these holes. Anchor the throat plate with flathead machine screws. If the throat plate is too low, use tape, paper, or veneer to raise it.

The hole in the throat plate is cut with the blade or shaper cutter. Mount the correct blade or shaper cutter and drop it beneath the table. Install the throat plate (Illus. 2-61), turn on the saw, and slowly raise the moving blade or shaper head into the throat plate. The hole made (Illus. 2-62) in the throat plate will match the blade or cutter perfectly. If the arbor is to be tilted, the blade or cutter must be lowered beneath the table, tilted, and then raised into the throat plate while it is moving.

It may be that the throat plate you have fabricated drops into the blade's space. This may require that you use a smaller blade to cut the hole in the throat plate. If the saw blade is in contact with the throat plate, the opening must be made with a smaller blade. It may also be possible to rout or chisel away stock from the underside of the throat plate to eliminate contact with the blade. This is an appropriate way of dealing with this problem.

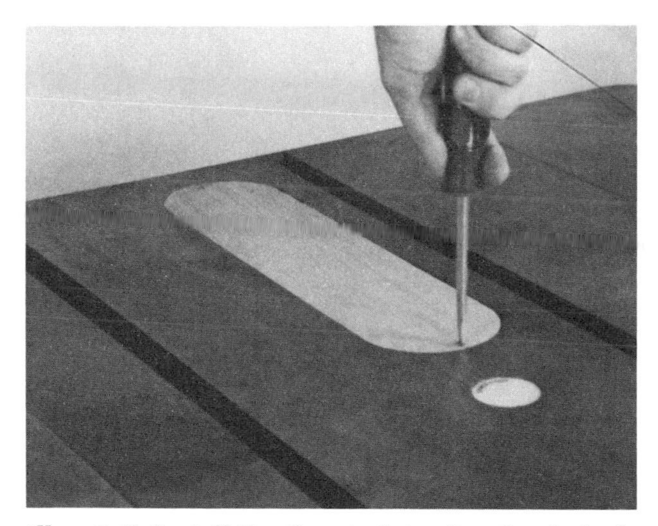

Illus. 2-61. Install the throat plate after the desired blade or shaper head is mounted on the arbor. Be sure to lower the arbor so the blade or cutter is beneath the throat plate.

Illus. 2-62. Slowly raise the turning blade or shaper head into the throat plate. The correct-size hole will be cut.

Remember that some materials like particleboard could actually dull a tool-steel blade or cutter before an opening is cut into a throat plate. Choose your stock for throat plates according to its abrasive qualities as well as its strength.

When using wooden throat plates with saw blades, the opening you cut has zero clearance; This reduces tear-out at the blade and increases the overall quality of the cut. When you make any cut in a throat plate, always raise the blade or cutter $\frac{1}{16}$–$\frac{1}{8}$ inch higher than needed. This way, when you drop the blade to actual cutting height, there is no friction between the rim of the blade and the throat-plate opening. This friction generates heat and causes premature dulling.

Today, many suppliers make auxiliary throat plates for most popular table saws. They are usually equipped with screws to adjust their height so they can be secured into the opening. Most of these throat plates are made from a synthetic such as plastic. This material is not abrasive to blades or cutters when the opening is cut.

When you cut into an auxiliary throat plate, be sure it is held securely in place with screws or some clamping device. *Never* use your hands to hold the throat plate in position while making this cut! An accident is certain to result. Clamp a piece of stock over the throat plate, or use the fence to secure it. Make sure you do not cut into the fence.

If the throat plate is not secured with metal fasteners, use wooden wedges to hold it in. When cutting an opening for a molding cutter, the opening must be close to the cutters. Too much space could generate an air current. This air current could lift the throat plate out of the opening. It is best to cover the molding-head cutters when holding the throat plate in place. You can get an idea of where the top of the molding head is by determining how many revolutions of the elevating handwheel will put the molding head in the desired position. This determination is made before you position the throat plate and cover it.

Saw-Blade Dampeners and Collars A saw-blade dampener (Illus. 2-63) is a flat disc of steel that goes next to the blade, usually closest to the arbor nut. Most saw vibration ends up at the blade, causing blade flutter and run-out. The dampener dampens or reduces this vibration. The reduction in vibration reduces noise, improves the quality of the cut, and reduces wear on the blade. Blade wear is reduced because the blade travels in a straighter line.

Saw-blade collars (Illus. 2-64) are discs that are also used to improve the quality of the saw cut and reduce noise and blade wear. They must be used in pairs. The collars are hollow ground, and the hollow-ground faces go against the blade. This causes the blade to be clamped in a truer orbit and makes the blade run smoother with less deflection. Saw-blade collars are also known as stabilizers and can be thought of as oversized arbor washers.

Illus. 2-63. A saw-blade dampener is a flat disc of steel that goes next to the blade. It is usually put nearest the arbor nut so that the blade remains centered in the throat plate. Saw-blade dampeners reduce blade vibration.

Illus. 2-64. These collars are hollow-ground and must be used in pairs. Collars reduce vibration and hold the blade in a truer orbit.

When using either collars or a dampener, be sure to check the position of the blade relative to the opening in the throat plate. The blade may rub against the throat plate. Remove the throat plate from the saw and file out the opening until it clears the blade. It is also possible to replace the metal throat plate with a wooden one.

In addition, be careful if you tilt or raise the blade. The collars or dampener could rub on the underside of the throat plate or touch the side of the opening. They could also rub on the underside of the wood. If you were to raise the blade under power, it could lift the throat plate from the table and throw it towards you (Illus. 2-65). Double-check the throat-plate opening and its relationship to the blade and dampener before doing any woodworking!

Illus. 2-65. Collars or a dampener could lift the throat plate out of position and throw it toward the operator. Always check for this problem with the power disconnected.

When you use a dampener or a pair of saw collars, you can no longer use the blade at its full height. A 10-inch-diameter blade with a 5-inch-diameter dampener is limited to a 2½-inch depth of cut. It may be necessary to remove the dampener or collars for full-depth cuts.

Most woodworkers use dampeners or collars to reduce noise and vibration at the blade. While that is the purpose of the dampeners and collars, you should make every effort to eliminate vibration at

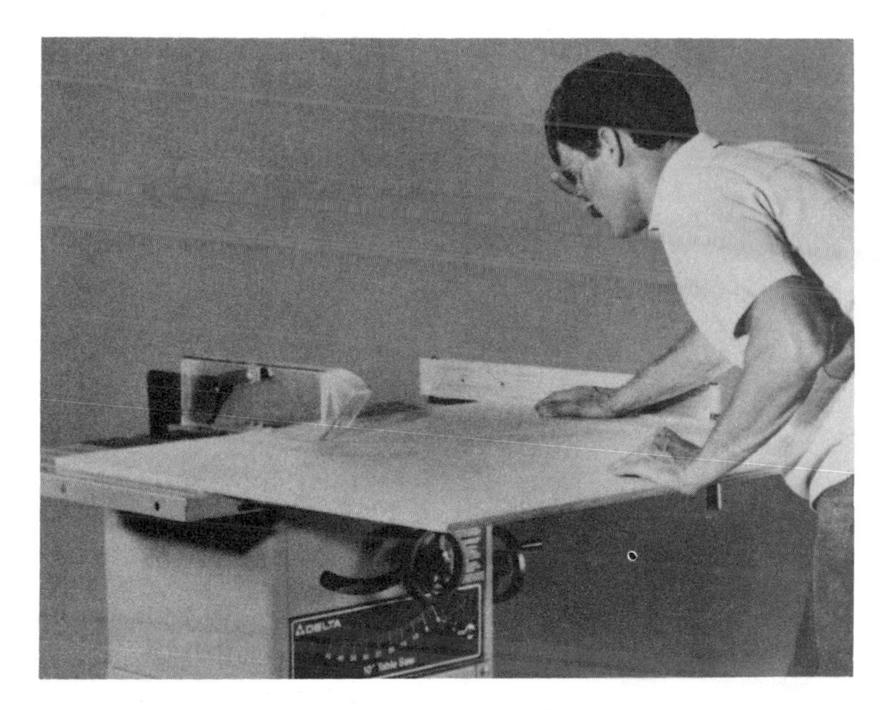

Illus. 2-66. This splitter-mounted guard provides protection for the operator during most operations. (Photo courtesy of Delta International Machinery Corporation.)

the saw. See the tune-up section in Chapter 7 for a discussion of table saw tune-up. Noise from a saw blade can also mean that the blade is cracked or defective. Be sure to inspect the blade periodically for cracks.

Always check the blade alignment with the guard when using collars or a dampener. If the blade's position has changed, the splitter will also have to change. See the following section for a discussion of guards and splitters.

Guards and Splitters Guards protect the operator from contact with the blade (Illus. 2-66). Some guards are held in position by the splitter. The splitter holds the saw kerf (the cut in the wood made by the blade) open while cutting proceeds (Illus. 2-67). The splitter keeps the saw kerf from closing on the blade, which can possibly cause a kickback. Stresses in the wood can cause pinching and binding against the blade (Illus. 2-68). The splitter limits the pinching action since it is only slightly thinner than the standard ⅛-inch saw kerf (Illus. 2-69).

Illus. 2-67. The splitter supports the barrier and keeps the saw kerf open. The anti-kickback pawls ride on the work and guard against kickback.

Illus. 2-68. Stresses in wood caused by grain structure, moisture loss, or the heat of cutting can cause the kerf to close on the teeth of the saw blade. The splitter keeps the kerf open and reduces the chances of kickback.

Illus. 2-69. The saw kerf is held open during the cut by the splitter, which is slightly thinner than the saw blade and saw kerf. (Photo courtesy of Sears Craftsman.)

Other guards are suspended from arms attached to the saw (Illus. 2-70 and 2-71) or from a frame attached to the floor, ceiling, or table saw. The splitter used with this type of guard is either the pop-up type (Illus. 2-72) or one of those that can be removed and replaced (Illus. 2-73). In either case, the splitter can be removed for non-through cuts such as dadoes and rabbets (Illus. 2-74). This allows the guard to be used.

Splitters are usually equipped with anti-kickback pawls or dogs. These pawls are made of steel with sharpened points on their lower edges. The pawls are spring-loaded and ride on the wood's upper surface during the cut. The anti-kickback pawls provide no resistance during the cut unless the stock starts to kick back. The pawls then grab the wood and slow or stop its kickback. To be effective, the anti-kickback pawls must remain sharp. Check them periodically and sharpen them if they become dull.

Guards are usually made of steel or clear plastic. Plastic guards offer more visibility (Illus. 2-75), but they tend to become scratched and blurred. Solid-metal guards limit the view of the cutting opera-

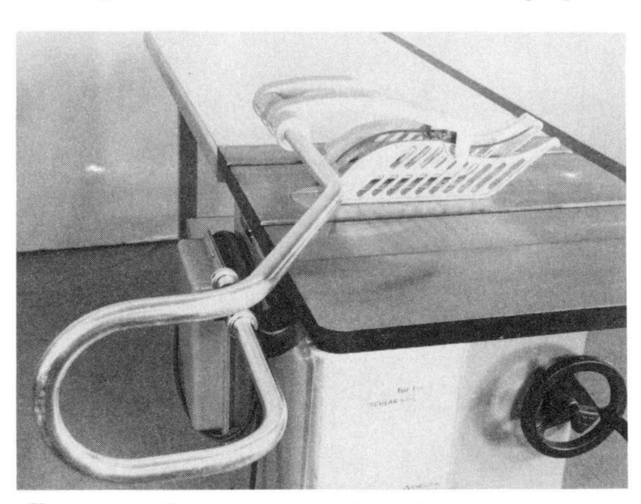

Illus. 2-70. This metal guard has sides which move separately. The splitter pops up through the throat plate. It stays down for dadoes and rabbets. The guard is mounted to the back of the saw.

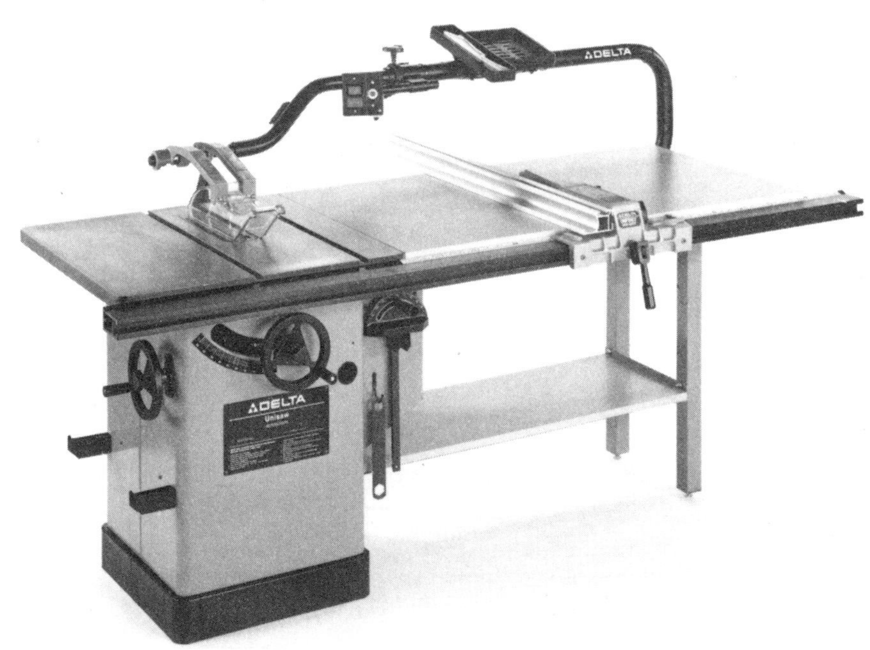

Illus. 2-71. This guard is mounted to a tube which is clamped to the back of the table. It contains a switch and a place for a push stick. The guard will accommodate large panel stock. (Photo courtesy of Delta International Machinery Corporation.)

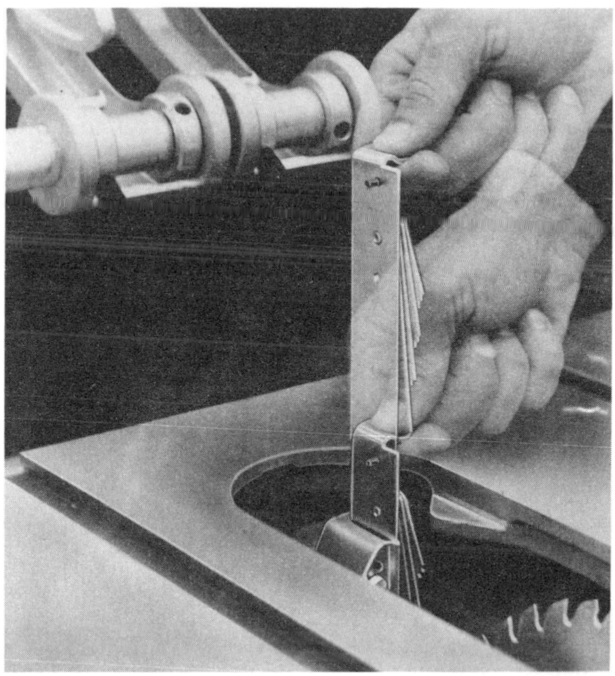

Illus. 2-72. This splitter and anti-kickback device pops up for use in through cutting. It is pushed below the table for non-through cutting. (Photo courtesy of Delta International Machinery Corporation.)

Illus. 2-74. Before making a non-through cut, remove the splitter. The splitter will not allow the cut to be completed. (Photo courtesy of Delta International Machine Corporation.)

Illus. 2-73. This splitter and anti-kickback device is held in place with a threaded metal fastener. When not in use, it is stored in a bracket on the guard. (Photo courtesy of Delta International Machinery Corporation.)

Illus. 2-75. This Brett Guard is sold by HTC of Huron, Michigan. It is made of a thick industrial-grade plastic which resists scratching. (Photo courtesy of Brett Guard.)

tion, but afford good protection (Illus. 2-76). Woven wire guards protect the operator almost as well and provide some view of the operation.

All guards which are suspended from the splitter must be removed for non-through cutting (Illus. 2-77). In those cases, featherboards or other accessories should be used in lieu of the guard to make the operation as safe as possible.

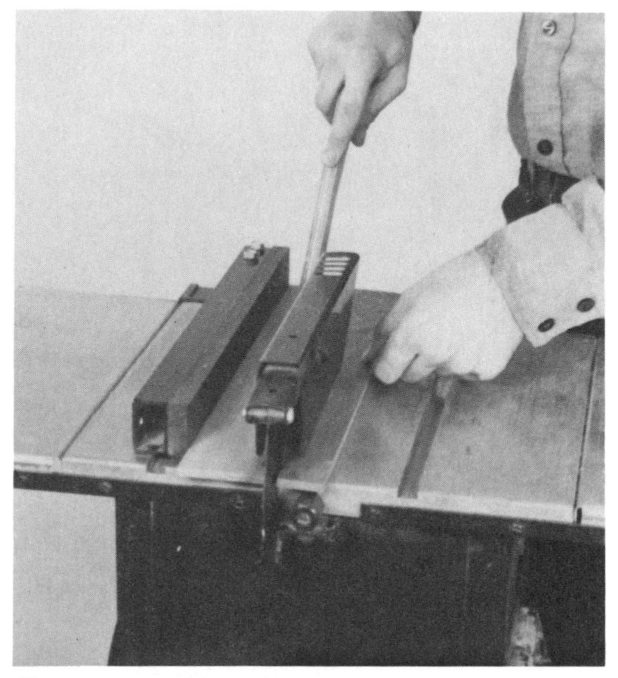

Illus. 2-76. Metal guards reduce vision, but afford good protection against flying debris.

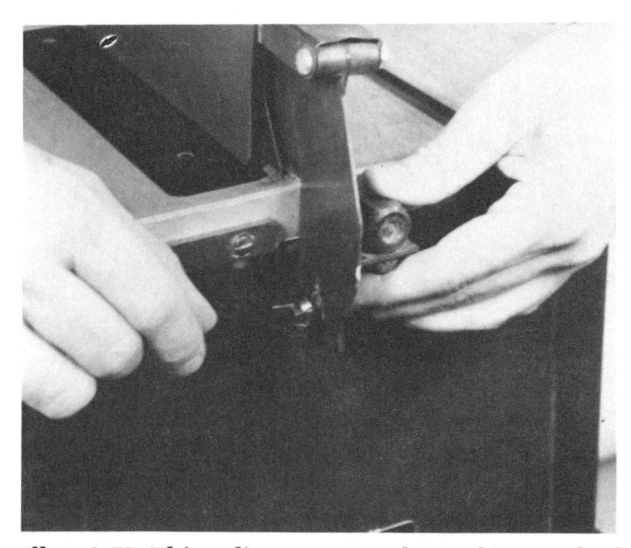

Illus. 2-77. This splitter-mounted guard is attached to a bracket on the back of the saw. It can be removed easily for non-through cutting.

Featherboard A featherboard (Illus. 2-78) is a shop-made device used to help control stock during hand feeding. The featherboard is a piece of solid stock with several kerfs equally spaced along or with the grain. The end of the piece is cut at a 30–45 degree angle. The featherboard is clamped to the table or fence, and is used to hold stock against the fence or table (Illus. 2-79). The featherboard acts like a spring. The feathers force stock against the fence or table. They help minimize kickback hazards.

Illus. 2-78. The featherboard is a shop-made device used to help control stock.

Illus. 2-79. These featherboards help guide stock and reduce the chance of a kickback. Featherboards should never pinch the saw kerf shut or bind against the saw blade.

The featherboard is an excellent table-saw project. Use two spacer sticks (Illus. 2-80) and the fence to space the kerfs evenly. One stick is as thick as the desired "feathers," and the other is as thick as one feather and a saw kerf. Select a piece of stock 3–4 inches wide and 12–18 inches long. Cut off the end of the workpiece at a 45-degree angle before making any kerf cuts (Illus. 2-81). Mark the feather length on the workpiece with a pencil.

Set the distance between the blade and the fence with the thinner stick (Illus. 2-82). Adjust blade height to slightly above stock thickness and make the first cut. When the blade reaches the layout line (Illus. 2-83), shut off the saw and let the blade coast to a stop. Do not move the workpiece.

With the work still over the blade, unlock the fence and insert the thicker stick between the fence and the work. Lock the fence in this position (Illus.

Illus. 2-80. Making a featherboard requires pieces of stock 3–4 inches wide and 12–18 inches long. The two sticks space the kerfs in the featherboard. One is as thick as a feather (about ¼ inch); the other is as thick as a feather and a saw kerf.

Illus. 2-81. The end of the work is cut off at a 45-degree angle. Feather length is then marked on the work.

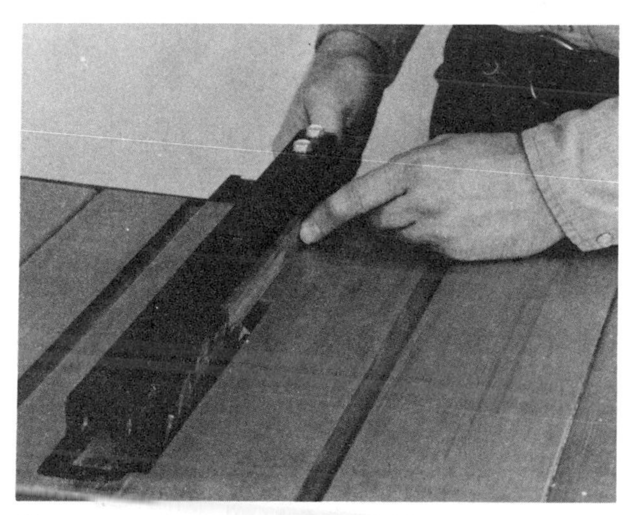

Illus. 2-82. Use the stick that is the thickness of one feather to set the fence for the first cut.

Illus. 2-83. Make the first cut. Set the blade slightly above the stock thickness and feed into the layout line. Hold the stock securely and shut off the saw. Do not release the stock until the blade stops turning.

2-84). Lift the work off the blade and move it over so that it is touching the fence. The second kerf can now be cut (Illus. 2-85). Let the blade coast to a stop when it reaches the layout line. Use the thicker stick to space the fence again (Illus. 2-86). The last feather can be wider than the others. It can be eliminated by moving the fence with the thick stick and cutting off the entire edge (Illus. 2-87). Sand the featherboard lightly, and it is ready for use.

In addition to shop-made featherboards, there are many commercial featherboards on the market. These devices are made of wood or plastic. Many of these featherboards clamp in the miter slot of the table saw (Illus. 2-88 and 2-89). As they are adjusted and fasteners are tightened, the bar in the miter slot expands and makes a secure fit. Some featherboards actually affix themselves to the table with magnetic force (Illus. 2-90 and 2-91). These devices can be easily removed with a horizontal sweeping motion, but remain in place once positioned.

Illus. 2-84. Leave the work in position on the blade and release the fence. Use the thicker spacer to set the fence. Lift the stock off the blade.

Illus. 2-85. Cut the second kerf. Stop the saw at the layout line. Do not release the stock until the blade stops.

Illus. 2-86. Continue moving the fence using the thicker stock to space the kerfs.

Illus. 2-87. If the last feather is narrower or wider than the others, simply cut it off. The featherboard is now ready to use.

Anti-Kickback Devices In addition to featherboards, there are many anti-kickback devices that can be used when hand-feeding stock on table

Illus. 2-88. The split-metal base of this featherboard fits into the miter slot of the table saw.

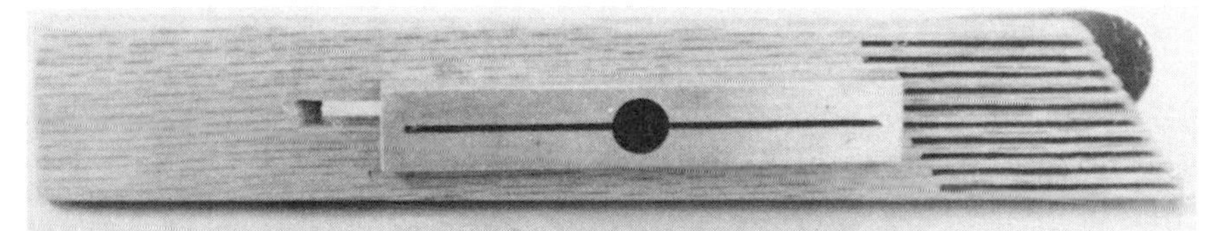

Illus. 2-89. As the wing nut is tightened and the metal bar expands in the miter slot, the featherboard holds the work against the fence.

Illus. 2-90. This block of wood has plastic feathers. It is held in place by a magnet glued into its base.

Illus. 2-91. The plastic feathers hold in the stock against the fence and table. This featherboard is easily secured on a ferrous surface.

saws. Most of these devices are commercially made and designed for many woodworking applications.

Shophelper wheels are urethane wheels that are attached to the fence or a wooden auxiliary fence (Illus. 2-92 and 2-93). These wheels have a one-way bearing and turn only in the direction of feed. The wheels are attached to a spring-loaded arm. The tension on the spring is adjustable, and the

Illus. 2-92. These Shophelper wheels or Board Buddies are mounted in a metal track or directly to an auxiliary wooden face which is attached to the fence.

Illus. 2-93. The urethane wheels have a one-way bearing which only turns in the direction of feed. They can be adjusted to any stock thickness.

spring tension holds the stock in and down. The arms attach to special brackets and gibs which are secured to the fence or an auxiliary wooden fence. By holding the stock against the fence and table, the Shophelper wheels reduce vibration. If a kickback occurs, the wheels lock and stop or reduce the velocity of the kickback.

Shophelper wheels can also act as a barrier between the operator and the blade. They can be adjusted for tension and can be moved in and out and back and forth on the fence. This means the wheels can be kept close to a molding head, dado head (Illus. 2-94), or blade regardless of cutter diameter or board width.

The Ripstrate is another anti-kickback device that can be used on the table saw (Illus. 2-95). It attaches to the fence or an auxiliary fence. It is spring-loaded and uses wheels equipped with a breaking device to stop a kickback.

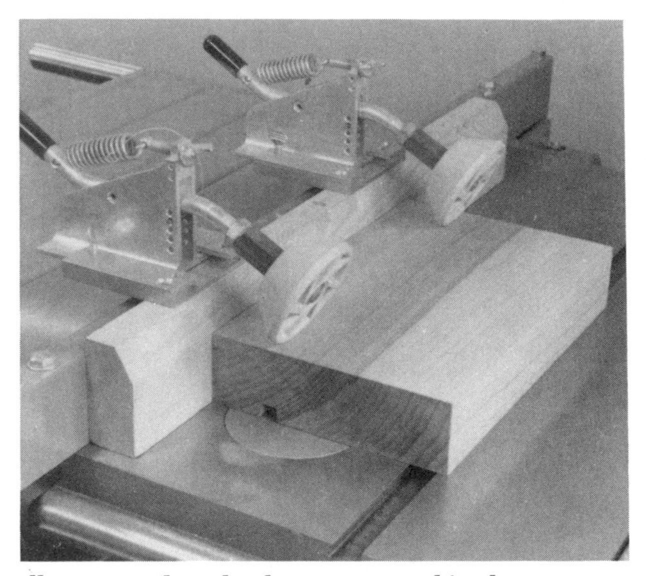

Illus. 2-94. The wheels are mounted in the brackets, which are screwed to the auxiliary face. These wheels hold stock securely during this dadoing operation.

A similar anti-kickback device is marketed by Leichtung (Illus. 2-96). It has a cog system which keeps the wheel from turning rearward in the event of a kickback.

Regardless of the type of work you are doing, it is a good practice to use featherboards or other anti-kickback devices when hand-feeding stock on a table saw. This will make the job safer and enhance the quality of your work.

Illus. 2-95. On wider rips, any common guard can be used with this Ripstrate ripping device. There is also a locking device built into the wheels so they only turn one way. This minimizes the chance of a kickback.

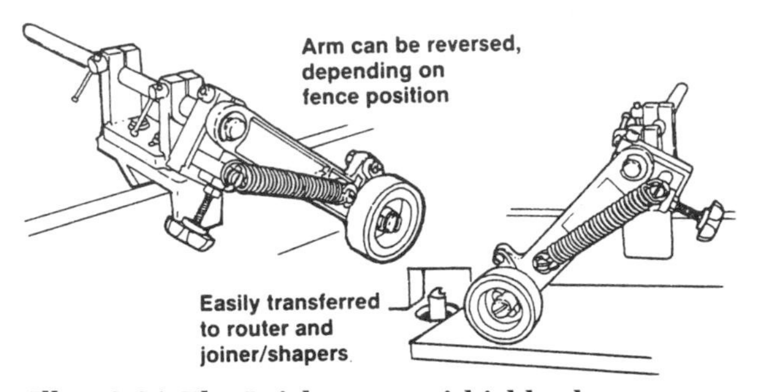

Illus. 2-96. The Leichtung anti-kickback system clamps to the fence. It is spring-loaded. (Drawing courtesy of Leichtung Workshops.)

Push Stick The push stick is usually a shop-made device (Illus. 2-97 and 2-98). It is used to feed stock through the blade of the table saw. The push stick keeps your fingers clear of the blade and allows you to cut thin or narrow pieces safely.

Push sticks take on many different sizes and shapes. They are cut for the job at hand. Since the push stick has many curves, it is not a good table-saw project. Use a saber saw or band saw to make a push stick.

Note: Before you do any sawing, cut several push sticks and keep them near the saw. Plywood scraps make good push sticks. Many serious accidents can be avoided by simply using one or two push sticks. Several push-stick patterns are furnished for your use (Illus. 2-99–2-102). Use these shapes or modify them to suit your needs. Be sure to round all edges

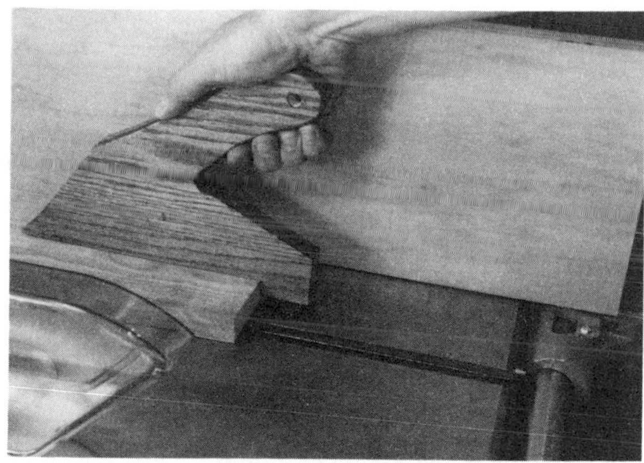

Illus. 2-97. A push stick is usually a shop-made device. It is used to guide and control stock during many operations. Note how this push stick holds down the stock and guides it forward. One or two push sticks can be used, depending on the job.

Illus. 2-98. This shop-made push stick has been cut into a shape that enables it to be used with this guard. The pushing shoe will move stock past the blade (at any height) before it contacts the overarm supporting the guard.

and avoid sharp corners on the push sticks you make. Sharp edges and corners can be easily split your skin if they are forced into your hand by a kickback.

Commercial push sticks are also available for use on table saws. They are usually made of some type of plastic or soft metal. Commercial push sticks come in many different shapes, and can be designed for special operations (Illus. 2-103 and 2-104). Commercial push sticks should have smooth, rounded handles and should grip wood positively.

Shooting Table A shooting table or board (Illus. 2-105 and 2-106) is a shop-made or commercial device that takes the place of the miter gauge for

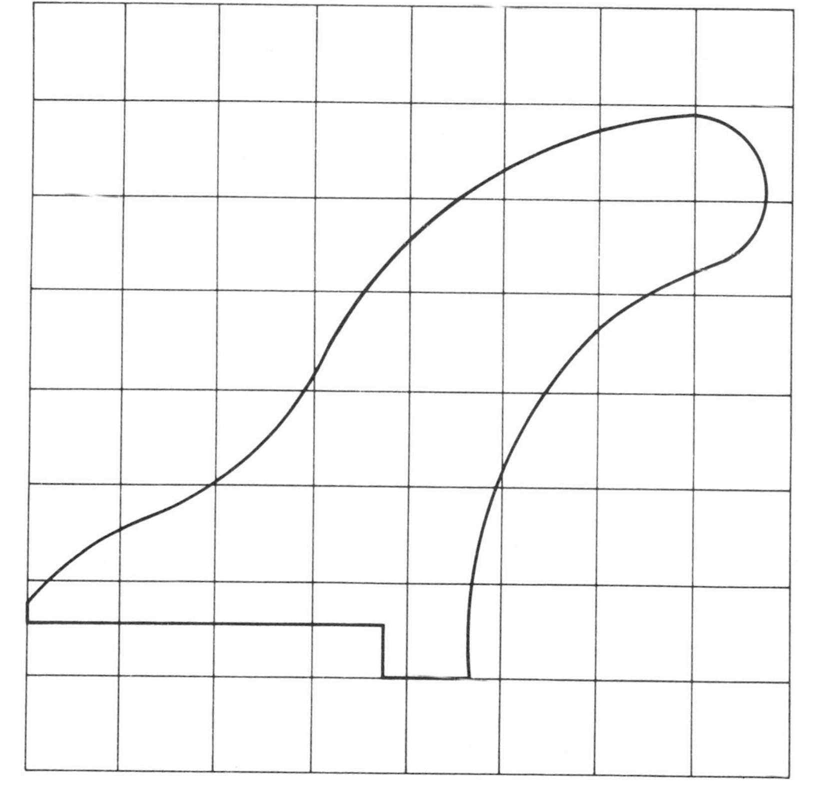

Illus. 2-99–2-102. Use the pattern shown here and those in Illus. 2-100–2-102 to make push sticks for your shop. Modify them to suit your needs, but avoid sharp corners and edges. The patterns are on a 1-inch grid. This pattern is half-size.

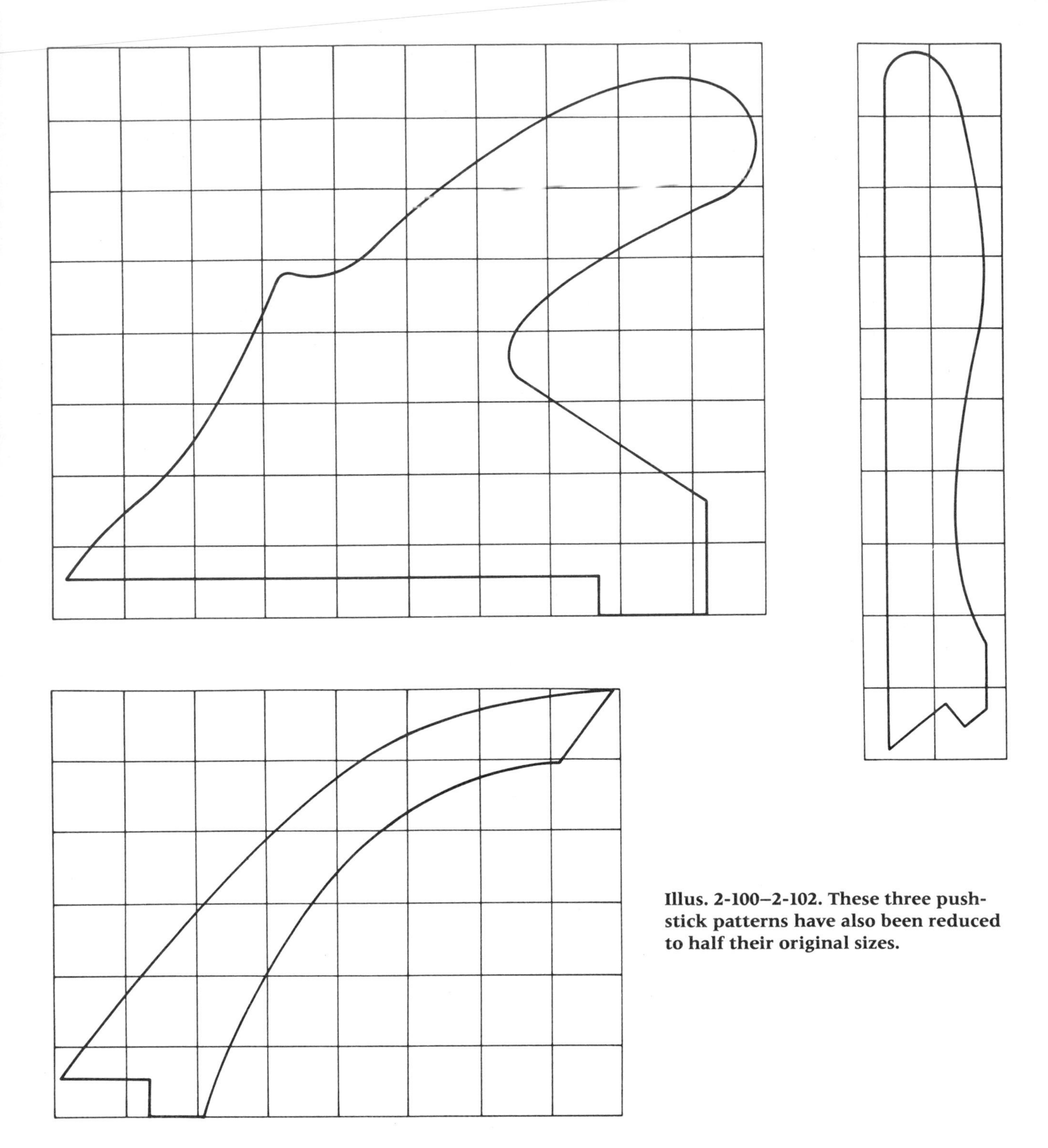

Illus. 2-100–2-102. These three push-stick patterns have also been reduced to half their original sizes.

crosscutting or mitering work. The shooting board is usually set for a 90-degree-angle cut. Shooting boards can be set at other fixed angles, but they are not adjustable.

The shooting board provides better control over a large piece because it is larger than the miter gauge. This increases the control surface. The stock also rides on the base of the shooting board. It does not touch the table. This eliminates contact between sanded boards that causes damage, and it also reduces the tendency of a board to turn as it drags on the table-saw surface.

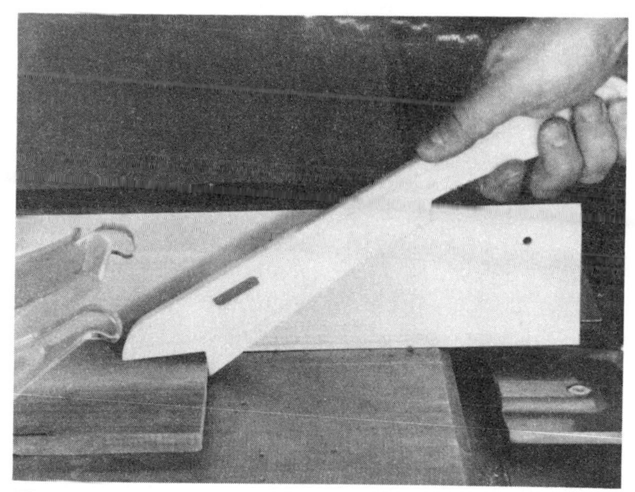

Illus. 2-103. This commercial push stick is made of molded plastic. It keeps your hands clear of the operation.

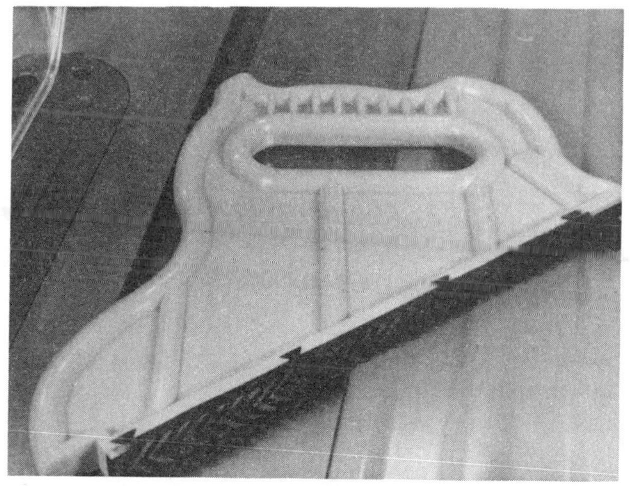

Illus. 2-104. This commercial push stick can be used on the face or corner of the workpiece. The large handle makes it easy to control.

Illus. 2-105. The shooting board takes the place of a miter gauge for cut-off work. Shooting boards are usually not adjustable.

Illus. 2-106. The shooting board has a plastic shield over the blade's path. A wooden barrier covers the blade when it exits the back of the shooting board. Some woodworkers box in the sides of the shielded area to further reduce the chance of contact with the blade.

The shooting board is a challenging table-saw project. The base is made out of sheet stock that is 3/8–3/4 inch thick. Sheet stock with a melamine face is the best type to use because it rides smoothly on the table. The guides that fit in the miter slots should be made from hardwood, plastic, or metal so they resist wear (Illus. 2-107). They can be screwed into the board or dadoed into it.

The vertical pieces should be true, and about 1½ inches thick. Make the pieces wide enough so that the blade does not cut them in half when elevated to full height. Put a plastic shield around the blade area, and a tunnel on the back to shield you from the blade.

Illus. 2-107. The guides that fit the miter slots should be made from hardwood, so they resist wear.

Commercial Shooting Boards The Dubby jig is a commercial shooting board (Illus. 2-108). It can also be adjusted to almost any angle for mitering. The backstop pivots off a point close to the blade. Because of the great length of the backstop, the miter angle is very accurate. This jig works very well for cutting hexagons, octagons, and other polygons.

The angle on this jig is easy to set precisely (Illus. 2-109). The jig also has a length stop to ensure that all parts are uniform in length. The angle between the blade and backstop can be adjusted precisely with the built-in angle stop.

There is a right- and a left-hand Dubby jig. The left-hand one works in the left miter slot. The right-hand one works in the right miter slot and is needed only for compound mitering, although it can be used for flat mitering. A piece of sheet stock is also furnished with the Dubby jig. This piece is affixed on the other side of the blade to support stock as it is cut off and to prevent it from dropping and getting into the blade.

Another commercial shooting board on the market is the Angle Pro. It also rides in the miter slot. It adjusts for various angles, and also provides clamping pressure to hold the stock in position while the cut is being made.

Dead Man The dead man or roller stand (Illus. 2-110 and 2-111) is a device used to support long or wide pieces of stock being cut on the table saw. There are many different types of supports. Some are commercial and others are shop-made.

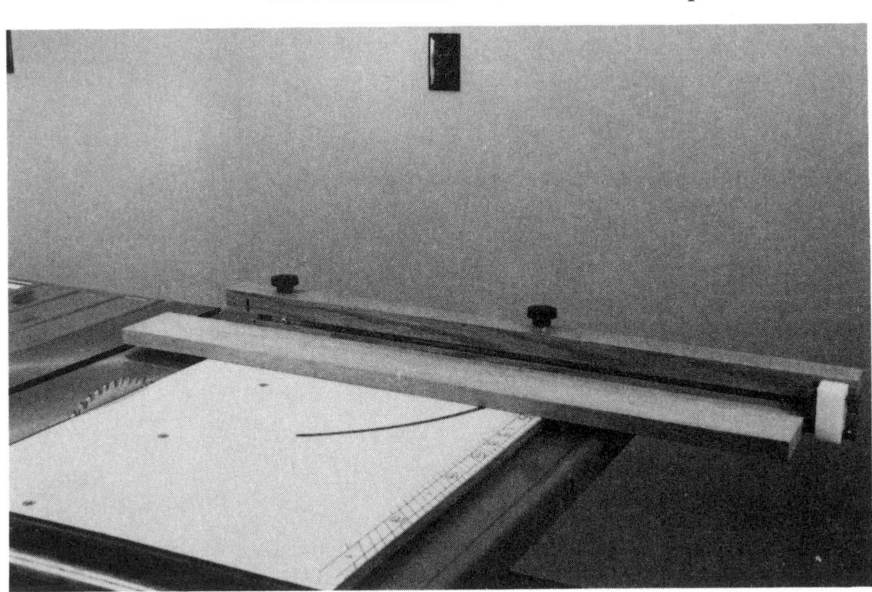

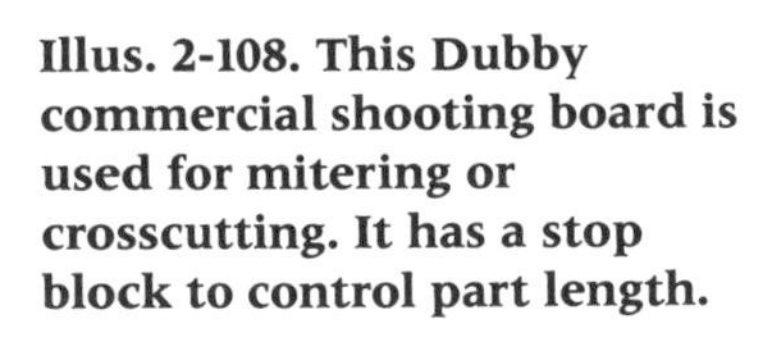

Illus. 2-108. This Dubby commercial shooting board is used for mitering or crosscutting. It has a stop block to control part length.

Illus. 2-109. This commercial shooting board is easy to adjust for mitering. Note the large scale on the edge of the board. This makes precise adjustment easy. A piece of sheet stock is affixed to the table on the other side of the blade to support the cut-off piece.

Illus. 2-110. This dead man, or roller stand, will support wide or long stock. It has convenient height adjustment and it folds flat for storage. (Photo courtesy of Delta International Machinery Corporation.)

Illus. 2-111. This roller stand has a larger surface area to control stock. It is more stable, but it takes up more space. (Photo courtesy of Delta International Machinery Corporation.)

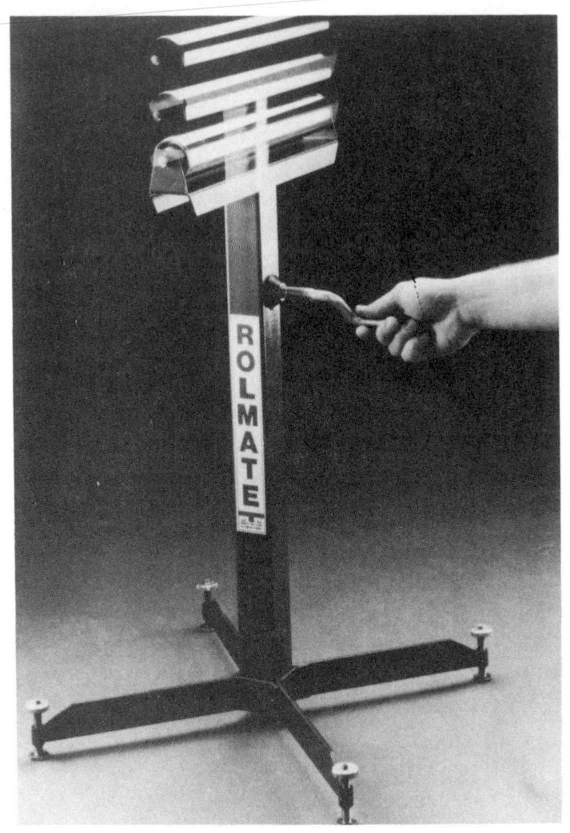

Illus. 2-112. The height on most commercial roller stands is adjustable. This one locks at the desired height.

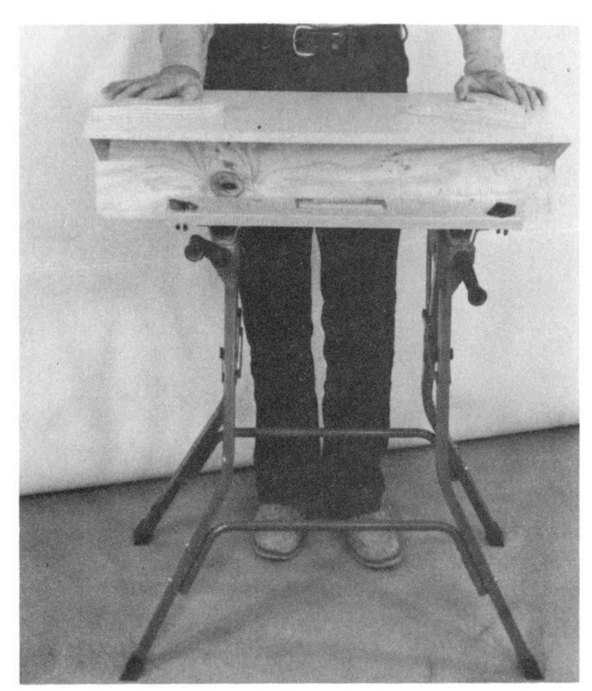

Illus. 2-113. A portable workbench sawhorse with a straight table clamped to it can be used as a dead man.

Commercial supports are usually metal. Their height is adjustable, and they have a rolling device to support the stock (Illus. 2-112). The rolling device makes travel smoother. Shop-made supports can also have a rolling device made of pipe, closet rod, or a rolling pin. The shop-made dead man can be adjustable or fixed. Some shop-made dead-man devices are much simpler. They use a portable workbench sawhorse with a piece of stock (Illus. 2-113) or a roller (Illus. 2-114) clamped to it. A sawhorse with a piece of stock clamped to it (Illus. 2-115) can also be used. The support or dead man is adjusted at the correct height to support the stock. For occasional use, the simple dead man is enough, but for frequent use a better one should be made or purchased.

Portable Bases Portable bases or rolling stands are a popular table-saw accessory. Portable bases fit between the table saw and floor. They are equipped with small wheels which make the table saw easy

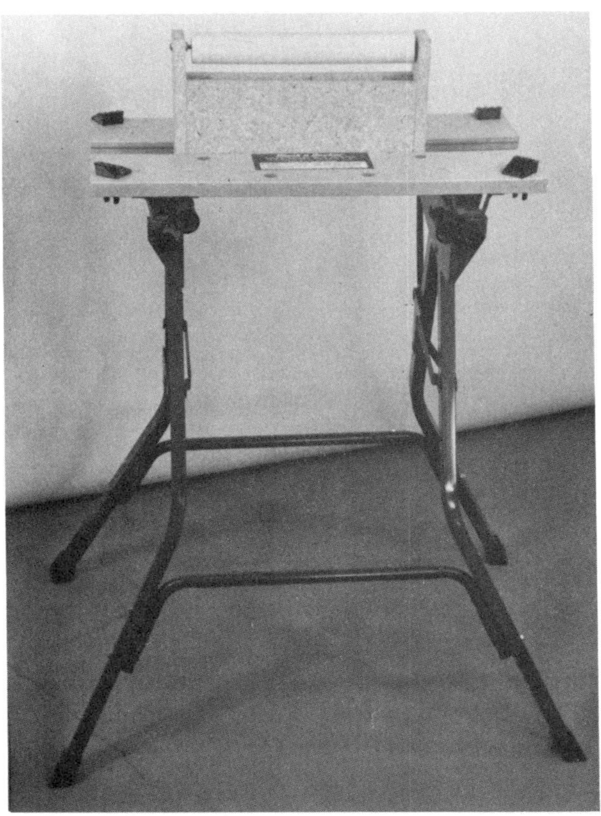

Illus. 2-114. The roller in this device is a piece of closet rod. It works well as a roller stand and is easy to store and transport.

Illus. 2-115. A sawhorse with a piece of stock clamped to it can be used as a dead man. When a dead man is needed frequently, a commercial one should be purchased.

to move. The wheels may be locked or lifted out of contact with the floor to keep the saw from moving once it is in position (Illus. 2-116 and 2-117).

The portable base raises the saw less than an inch. The easy-rolling wheels make it easier to move the saw, and reduce the chance that moving the saw will take it out of alignment or adjustment.

Some manufacturers offer wheels as an accessory. They attach to the saw legs and make it easier to move about. One pair of the wheels can be retracted to fix the saw in position.

Take-Off Table A take-off table is a device that butts or is attached to the out-feed side of the saw's table. The take-off table is usually even with the top of the saw or slightly lower. It supports the work as it is fed through the blade (Illus. 2-118). This keeps the weight of the workpiece from lifting it off the

Illus. 2-116. A portable base fits between the table saw and the floor.

Illus. 2-117. This HTC rolling base supports both the saw and the legs on its extension stand. To secure its position, tighten the clamps above the wheels.

blade. It also makes the work easier to control and reduces operator fatigue. Some of these tables fold against the table saw when they are not in use (Illus. 2-119). This reduces the footprint of the saw on the floor and makes it easier to move the saw if necessary.

Stationary tables take up a larger area, but may be favored for high-volume work stations.

In some small shops, a workbench or fence extension is used as a take-off table. This means that the bench must be clear when you are sawing. This setup may be more awkward, but for limited spaces it is very efficient.

Accessory Storage Table-saw accessories must be stored in a convenient and safe location (Illus. 2-120). The miter gauge should hang on or near the saw when not in use. This keeps it from being

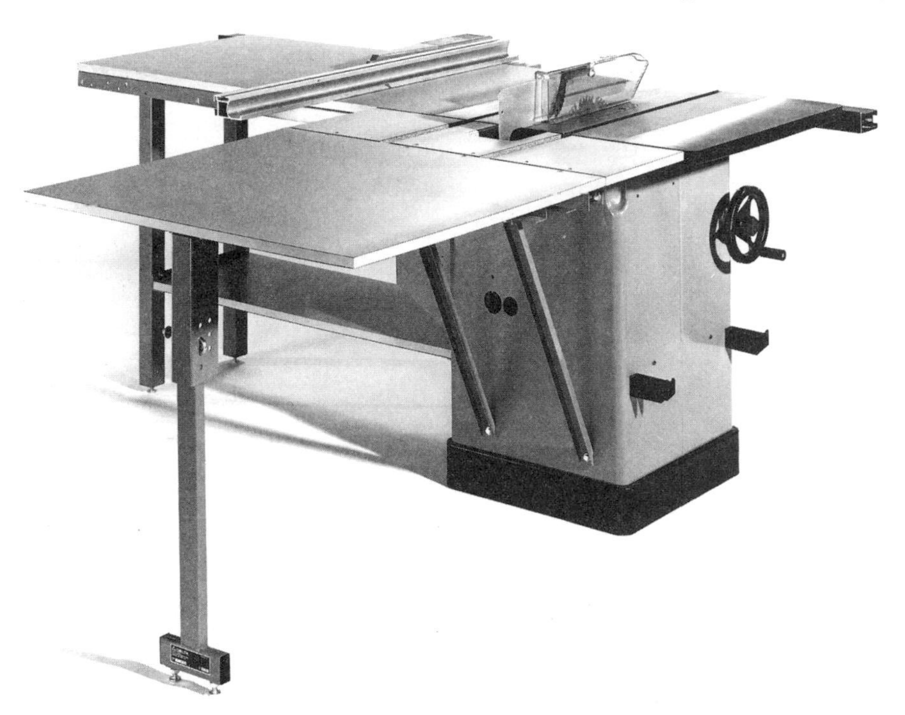

Illus. 2-118. This take-off table supports sheet rock or long pieces of solid stock. A take-off table makes it easier and safer to cut larger pieces of stock. (Photo courtesy of Delta International Machinery Corporation.)

Illus. 2-119. When this take-off table is not in use, fold it up against the saw. For smaller shops, this allows the space to be used for other purposes such as assembly. (Photo courtesy of Delta International Machinery Corporation.)

Illus. 2-120. Note how the miter gauge and arbor wrench are held on supports when not in use. A push stick could also be suspended from the wrench hook. The brackets on the right support the fence when it is not in use. Many fences are damaged when they are stored on the floor. (Photo courtesy of Delta International Machinery Corporation.)

dropped or misplaced. The fence should also be stored in a convenient place. Many fences are damaged when they are not being used. Damage to either the fence or miter gauge encourages the operator to use the table saw without these accessories. This is dangerous and unnecessary!

At least one push stick should be available at the saw. A hook, magnet or hook, or loop-fastening system can be used to hold the push stick against the saw. Having a push stick at the saw eliminates the temptation to work without one. Keep several extra push sticks stored in a handy spot. When a push stick gets damaged, cut it in half and throw it away. This discourages the use of an unsafe push stick.

Extra throat plates, arbor nuts, and arbor washers should be stored near or with the saw blades (Illus. 2-121). Mark the back of the throat plate so that you can match it to the correct blade or accessories.

Many accessories such as dado and molding heads come in a protective storage package. Use the package to store the accessory. In most cases, it can be stored in a shelf or drawer. Be sure to protect blades. Dado and molding heads rust. A damp environment can rust these accessories quickly.

Illus. 2-121. Keep accessories stored close to the saw in an orderly manner.

—3—
Circular-Saw Blades and Attachments

Wood is a stringy material. If you break a piece of wood, the stringy fibers make it difficult to get a clean break. If you split a piece of wood, the split is clean because the stringy fibers run parallel to the separation. When wood is crosscut (cut across the grain or stringy fibers), a crosscut blade is used (Illus. 3-1). The teeth are designed for crosscutting. Rip blades (for cutting with the grain or fibers) are designed for ripping only (Illus. 3-2). They do not crosscut efficiently.

The blade on a table saw is the most important link in the sawing process. It must be sharp and true. Blades should be checked frequently to make sure of this.

A saw blade is subjected to extreme forces. Imagine a thin disc with the force of 1½ horsepower at 3,450 rpm applied at the center, and the resistance of 2-inch-thick oak applied at the periphery. There is great power at the center and great resistance at the outer edge. This generates the stress, heat, and vibration that dull the blade. This is why many blades have small slots at their outer edges. These slots allow the blade to expand as the edge heats up. The slots prevent possible blade warpage.

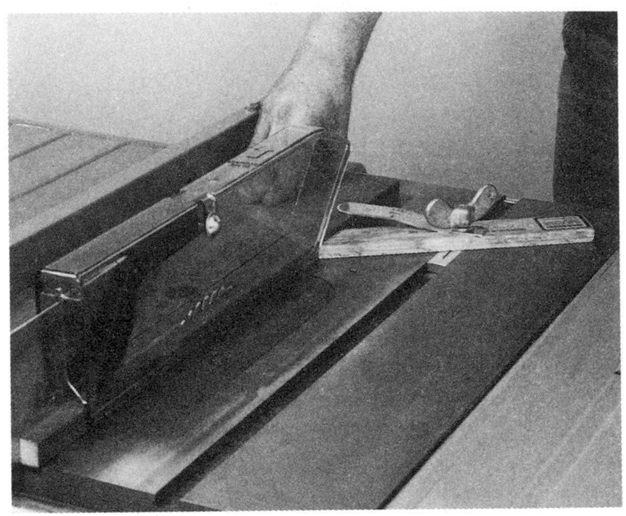

Illus. 3-2. Ripping is done with the grain or stringy fibers. A rip blade with chisel-shaped teeth is best for ripping.

Illus. 3-1. Crosscutting is done across the grain or stringy fibers. A crosscut blade with pointed teeth works best for this operation.

Circular Saw Terms

The cut made by a circular saw blade is called the kerf (Illus. 3-3). The kerf must be slightly larger than the saw-blade thickness. The tooth set or offset is the bend in the teeth (Illus. 3-4). This set allows the blade to cut a kerf that is larger than the

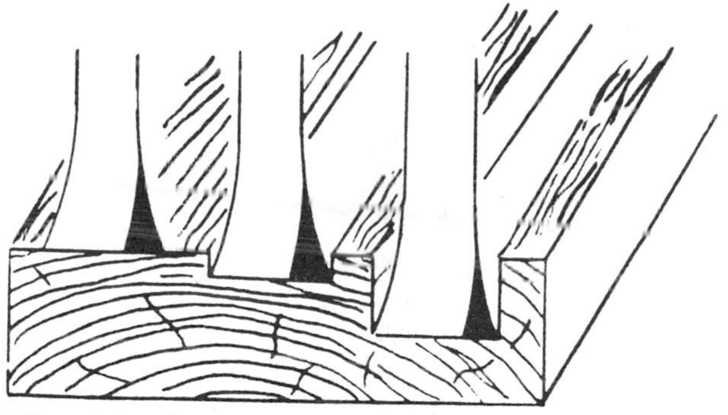

Illus. 3-3. The cut made by the blade is called the kerf. The kerf is slightly larger than the blade thickness due to the set of the teeth.

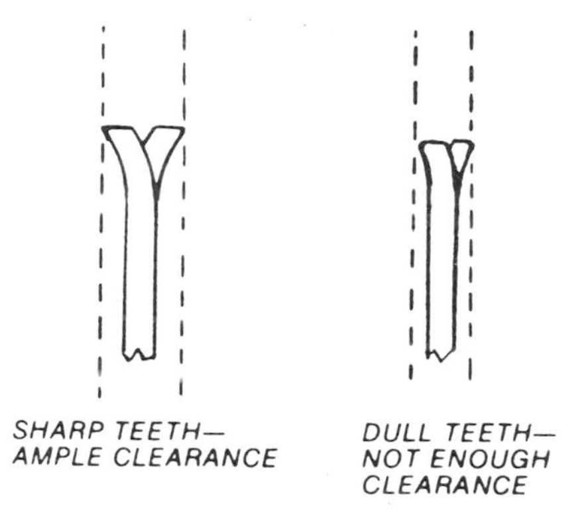

Illus. 3-4. The bend in the teeth is the set. Sharp teeth have more set than dull teeth. Set allows clearance for the blade as it travels through the kerf.

blade's thickness. The teeth on a circular saw blade are set in alternate directions.

The gullet is the area behind the cutting edge of the tooth (Illus. 3-5). It carries away the sawdust cut by the tooth. The larger the tooth, the larger the gullet.

The hook angle is the angle of the tooth's cutting edge as it relates to the centerline of the blade. Rip saws usually have a hook angle of about 30 degrees. Crosscut saws usually have a hook angle of about 15 degrees. The greater the hook angle, the bigger the tooth's bite (Illus. 3-6). Negative hook angles (Illus. 3-7) are sometimes used for tough cutting jobs. Some circular saw blades designed to cut used lumber have a negative hook angle. This allows them to cut nails or other metal in the wood.

Top clearance (Illus. 3-8) is the downward slope of the back of the tooth. This slope keeps the back of the tooth from rubbing on the wood. Without top clearance, the blade cannot cut.

Common Blade Types

Rip Blades Rip blades have deep gullets and a large hook angle. The tooth's cutting edge looks like a chisel. It has a straight cutting edge designed to cut with the grain. Rip teeth are usually quite large.

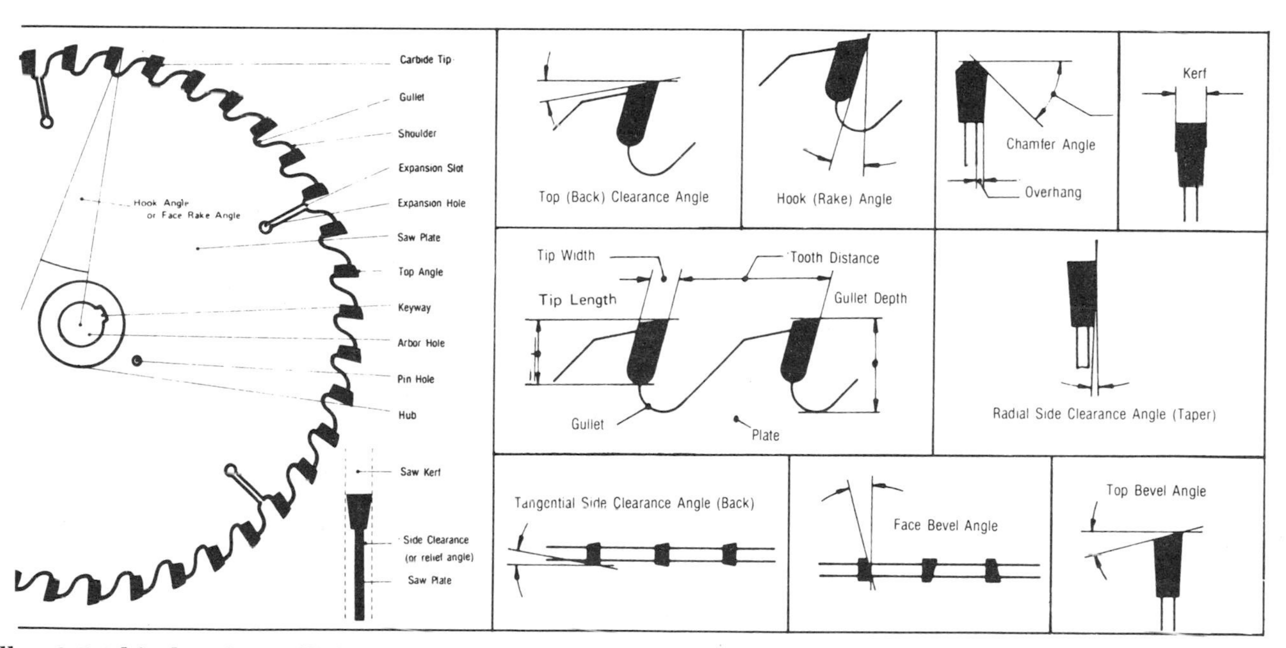

Illus. 3-5. This drawing will clarify saw-blade terminology. Refer to it as you read this book. (Drawing courtesy of Nordic Saw and Tool Manufacturing, Turlock, California.)

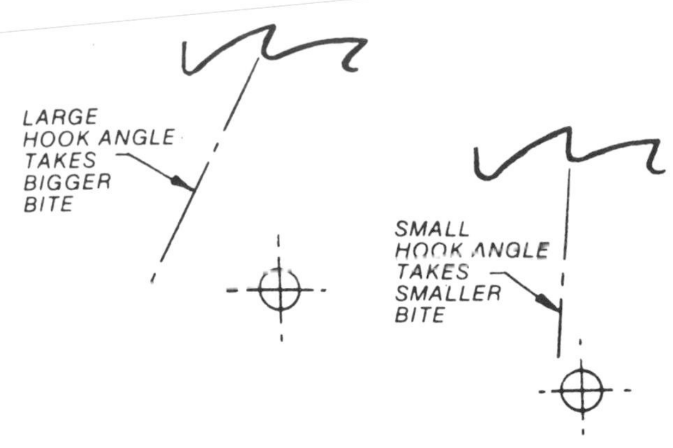

Illus. 3-6. The greater the hook angle, the bigger the tooth's bite. The larger the bite, the larger the gullet must be to clear the chips or sawdust.

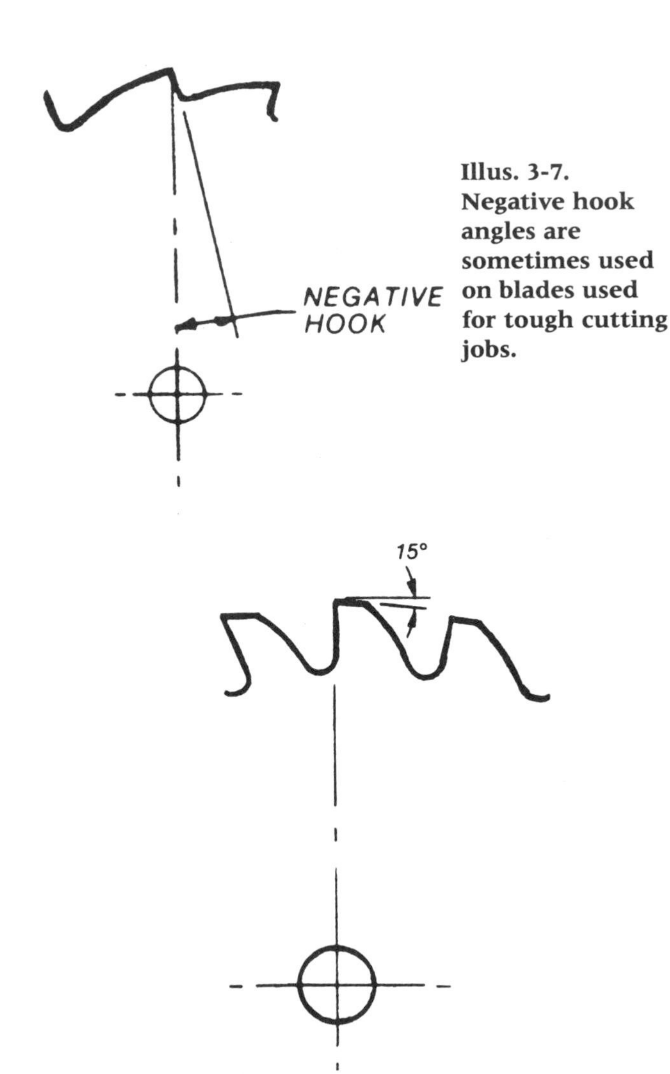

Illus. 3-7. Negative hook angles are sometimes used on blades used for tough cutting jobs.

Illus. 3-8. Top clearance is the downward slope of the back of the tooth. This clearance angle keeps the back of the tooth from rubbing or pounding on the wood as the cut is made.

Crosscut Blades Crosscut blades have smaller teeth than rip blades. The teeth on a crosscut blade come to a point, not an edge. This allows them to cut the stringy fibers in the wood.

Combination Blades Combination blades are designed for both ripping and crosscutting. They work very well for cutting wood fibers at an angle (miter joints). Some combination blades have teeth that come to a point, but have a rip-tooth profile. Others have a chisel edge and a smaller hook angle. These blades do not produce smooth cuts, but they are well suited to general carpentry on rough construction (Tables 3-1 and 3-2).

Smooth-cutting combination blades are sometimes called novelty combination blades. These blades have both rip and crosscut teeth. Novelty combination blades are preferred for cabinet and furniture work. This is because they cut smoothly with little tear-out (Table 3-2).

Hollow-Ground Blades Hollow-ground blades (Illus. 3-9) are blades with no set. The sides of the blade are recessed for clearance in the kerf. Some hollow-ground blades have sides that are recessed all the way to the hub (Illus. 3-10). Others are recessed only part of the way (Illus. 3-11). Blades with partially recessed sides cannot cut thick stock, but are more rigid.

Hollow-ground blades cause less splintering and tear-out in the wood they cut. The sides of the blade may burn and accumulate pitch (wood residue) if they are used for heavy cutting instead of finish cutting. Hollow-ground blades work best with very true stock.

Most hollow-ground blades have novelty combination teeth. Hollow-ground blades are sometimes called *planer* blades. This is because the wood is very smooth after being cut. It appears to have been planed.

Plywood Blades Plywood blades, sometimes called paneling or veneer blades, are designed to cut hardwood plywood with cabinet- or furniture-grade outer veneers. These blades have very fine crosscut teeth with little set (Illus. 3-12). Some of these blades are hollow ground. The fine teeth and small amount of set allow very smooth splinter-free cuts. These blades should be used only when appropriate. Using them for other purposes can ruin them quickly. Certain types of plywood cores (particle or fiber) can dull these blades quickly. Carbide-tipped blades would be a better choice for particle- or fiber-core plywood or other sheet stock.

Plywood blades can be useful when you have to resaw solid wood. They have a fine kerf which reduces the amount of wood wasted. In addition, because the teeth are offset, there is little friction during the cut. The small teeth also take a small bite and reduce the chance of kickback. These blades also work well for sawing the lid off a box.

Carbide-Tipped Blades Carbide-tipped blades have teeth made from small pieces of carbide. The carbide is brazed onto the circular blade. Usually, there is a little set cut in the blade. This is where the carbide is brazed. Most carbide tips are wider than the metal blade, so no set is required. Carbide is much harder than the steel used for conventional blades. Carbide-tipped blades stay sharp five to ten times longer than conventional blades. Because of its hardness, carbide is also quite brittle. Carbide will fracture easily if struck against a hard object. Carbide-tipped blades must be handled with care.

Carbide-tipped blades are more expensive than steel blades, but they require much less maintenance. Carbide-tipped blades are preferred for tough materials such as hardboard, plastic laminates, and particleboard.

Carbide-tipped blades come in rip, crosscut, combination, hollow-ground, and plywood categories. They do not always resemble their steel counterparts (Illus. 3-13—3-16). Usually, the type of teeth, the number of teeth, and the hook angle determine the blade's function. The teeth may be alternate top bevel, triple chip, rip, cut-off, or combination.

Blade Deflection A condition in which the circular-saw blade bounces away from the workpiece.

Carbide-Tipped Blade A blade with teeth made from small pieces of carbide. Carbide-tipped blades are much harder and more brittle than the steel used for conventional blades. They are also more expensive, but require much less maintenance. Carbide-tipped blades come in the following classifications: rip, crosscut, hollow-ground, and plywood.

Coarse Blade A blade with large teeth, designed for heavy, fast, or less delicate work.

Fine Blade A blade with small teeth, designed for more delicate work.

Crosscut Blade A blade that cuts across the grain. Crosscut blades have smaller teeth than rip blades. These teeth come to a point, not an edge.

Footprint (blade) Amount of blade engaged with the workpiece.

Friction The amount of resistance caused by contact between the sides of the blade and the saw kerf.

Hollow-Ground Blade (also called Planer Blade) A blade with no set. The sides of the blade are recessed for clearance in the kerf. Hollow-ground blades should be used to cut mitres and compound mitres, but not used for heavy ripping.

Kerf The cut made by a circular-saw blade. The kerf must be larger than the saw-blade thickness.

Particleboard Sheet material made from wood chips or wood particles.

Resins Material within the wood which can build up on sides of the blade.

Runout The amount that one surface is not true with another surface, or any deviation from a true orbit.

Rip Blade A blade with a straight-cutting edge that is designed to cut with the grain. Rip blades have deep gullets and large hook angles.

Tear-out (grain) When the blade rips or tears out the grain of a workpiece. Tear-out can occur on the back, top, or bottom of a workpiece.

Tooth Set The bend in the blade's teeth that allows the blade to cut a kerf that is larger than the blade's thickness.

Table 3-1. A clarification of the terms that are used in this chapter.

BLADES

A dull blade will cause slow, inefficient cutting and an overload on the saw motor. It is a good practice to keep extra blades on hand so that sharp blades are available while the dull ones are being sharpened. (See "SAWS—SHARPENING" in Yellow Pages.) In fact, many lower-priced blades can be replaced with new ones at very little cost over the sharpening price.

Hardened gum on the blade will slow down the cutting. This gum can best be removed with trichlorethylene, kerosene or turpentine.

The following types of blade can be used with your saw:

COMBINATION BLADE—This is the latest-type fast-cutting blade for general service ripping and crosscutting. Each blade carries the correct number of teeth to cut chips rather than scrape sawdust.

CHISEL-TOOTH COMBINATION—Chisel-tooth blade edge is specially designed for general-purpose ripping and crosscutting. Fast, smooth cuts. Use of maximum speed in most cutting applications.

FRAMING/RIP COMBINATION—A 40-tooth blade for fascia, roofing, siding, sub-flooring, framing, form cutting. Rips, crosscuts, mitres, etc. Gives fast, smooth finishes when cutting with the grain of both soft and hard woods. Popular with users of worm-drive saws.

CROSSCUT BLADE—Designed specifically for fast, smooth crosscutting. Makes a smoother cut than the Combination Blade listed above.

RIP BLADE—Fast for rip cuts. Minimum binding and better chip clearance given by large teeth.

PLYWOOD BLADE—A hollow-ground, hard-chromed surface blade especially designed for exceptionally smooth cuts in plywood.

PLANER BLADE—This blade makes both rip and crosscuts. Ideal for interior woodwork. Hollow ground to produce the finest-possible saw-cut finish.

FLOORING BLADE—This is the correct blade to use on jobs when occasional nails may be encountered. Especially useful in cutting through flooring, sawing reclaimed lumber and opening boxes.

METAL-CUTTING BLADE—Has teeth shaped and set for cutting aluminum, copper, lead, and other soft metals.

FRICTION BLADE—Ideal for cutting corrugated, galvanized sheets and sheet metal up to 16 gauge. Cuts faster, with less dirt, than abrasive disc. Blade is taper-ground for clearance.

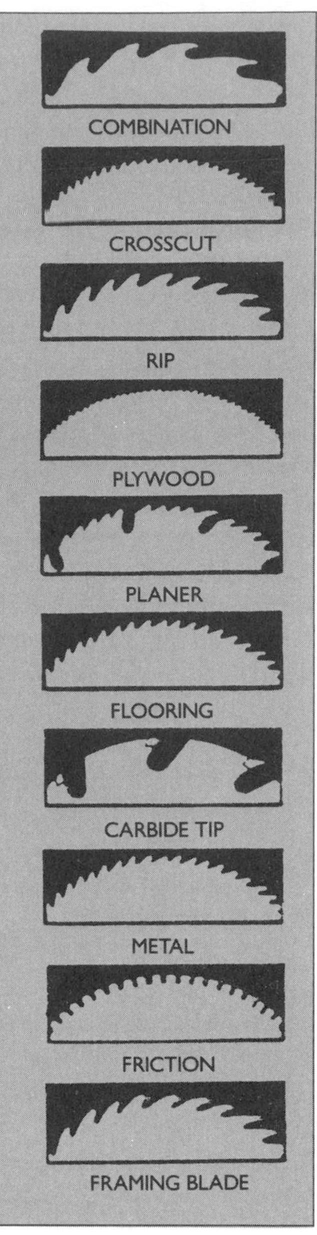

Table 3-2. Use this chart to select the proper tool-steel blade for the job you are doing. (Drawing courtesy of Sears, Roebuck and Company.)

Illus. 3-9. Hollow-ground blades have sides that are relieved or ground thinner than the teeth. The thinner sides provide clearance in the kerf. The teeth have no set and there is less tear-out.

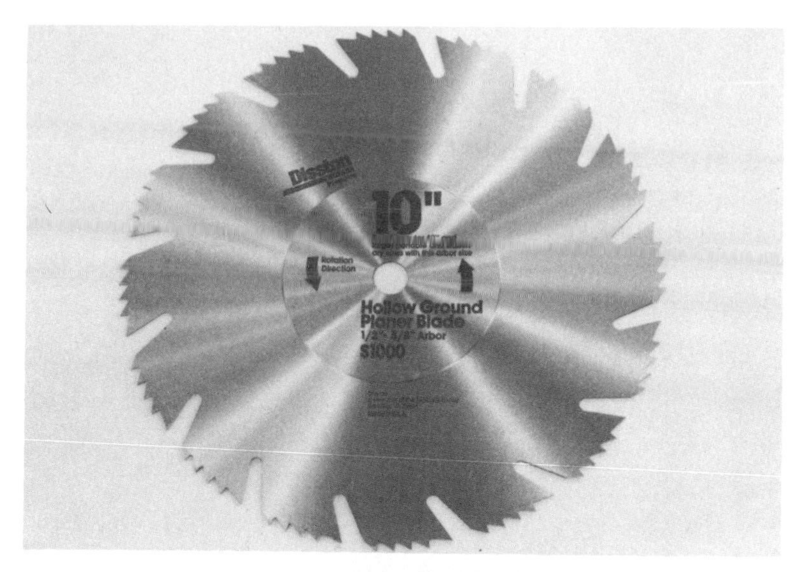

Illus. 3-10. This hollow-ground blade is ground back to the hub. It will cut through thick stock.

Illus. 3-11. This hollow-ground blade is only ground part of the way back to the hub. It is designed to cut through sheet stock and solid stock less than 1¼ inches. This blade has greater rigidity than those ground all the way to the hub.

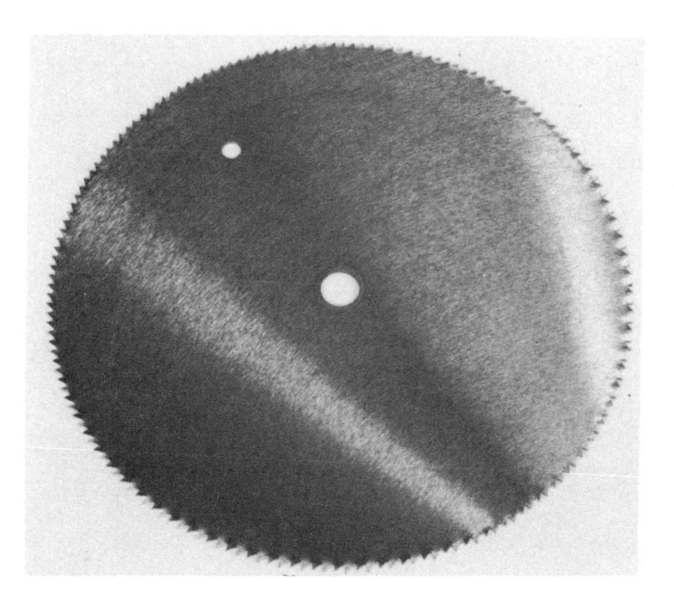

Illus. 3-12 (left). The plywood blade has fine teeth and very little set. Use these blades for finish cuts only. General use will dull the teeth quickly.

Illus. 3-13. This is a chip-limiting rip blade. The humps in front of each gullet limit the feed speed and the chip size when a cut is made. Limiting the sizes of the chips also reduces the likelihood of kickback.

Illus. 3-14. This 40-tooth, carbide-tipped combination blade is well suited to general cutting in stock up to 2 inches thick.

Illus. 3-15. This 48-tooth, carbide-tipped blade is designed for crosscutting and trimming plastic laminates.

Illus. 3-16. This 60-tooth thin-rim carbide-tipped blade is designed for very fine cutting in sheet stock, plastic laminates, and hardwood. Depth of cut is limited by the hub just below the expansion slots.

Four Popular Tooth Designs

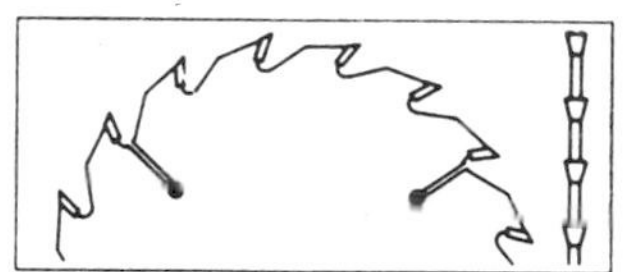

Flat Top Grind (FT). Generally, for cutting material with grain. Larger gullets on this type blade accept greater chip loads; permit higher feed rates. Excellent for ripping on either single or multi-rip machines where speed of cut is more important than quality of cut. Teeth with square or flat top shape act as chisels, cutting material with chisel-like action. Also serve as rakers to clean out the cuttings or chips.

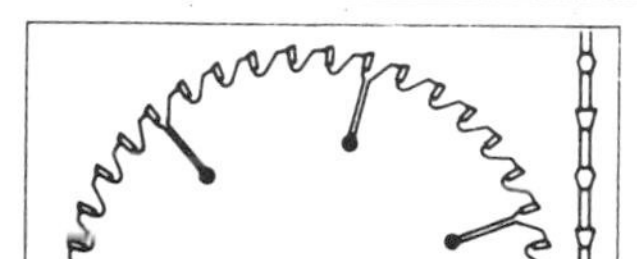

Triple Chip & Flat Grind (TC&F). Recommended for cutting brittle and/or hard, abrasive-type materials. Two shapes of teeth—alternate triple-edge and flat top design for dual action cutting. Triple-edge teeth chip down center of kerf; flat top raker teeth follow to clean out material from both sides. TC&F blades with negative hook angle are also recommended for cutting non-ferrous metals. Negative hook angle prevents climbing; gives you total control over the feed rate.

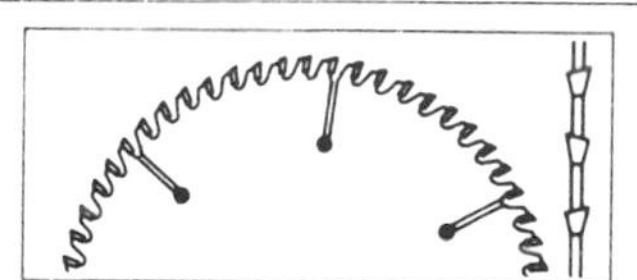

Alternate Top Bevel Grind (ATB). For across-the-grain cutting and/or cut-off and trimming operations on undefined grain work. Top bevel shaped teeth sever the material with shearing action alternately left and right. Given a choice, the ATB blade with the higher number of teeth will produce the higher quality of finish cut. Where finish is no concern, select the blade with fewer teeth.

Alternate Top Bevel & Raker (ATB&R). Excellent for cutting operations both with and/or across the grain. Achieves a fairly high level of quality over wide range of cuts. Two sets of shearing-action alternate left and right top bevel teeth followed by a raking action flat top tooth with large round gullet to facilitate chip removal.

Illus. 3-17. Note the common tooth designs used on carbide-tipped blades. Each tooth design is discussed under the illustration. (Drawing courtesy of Delta International Machinery Corporation.)

Refer to Illus. 3-17 and Table 3-1 to learn the terminology related to carbide-tipped circular-saw blades. They will help you to understand any discussion of these blades.

Carbide-Tooth Geometry The tooth geometry of carbide-tipped blades is designed to improve cutting quality (Illus. 3-17). There are four basic tooth configurations used on carbide-tipped blades: alternate top bevel (ATB), alternate top bevel and raker (ATB & Raker), triple chip (TC), and flat top (FT).

Alternate top bevel teeth are designed primarily for crosscutting, although they are also used for ripping. When they are used for ripping, feed speed drops somewhat. Alternate top bevel teeth come to a point on alternate sides of the blade. The points cut the edges of the kerf before the middle of the kerf is cut out. This reduces the chance of tear-out.

If you plan to do ripping and crosscutting, use a blade with alternate-top-bevel-and-raker teeth. The alternate top-bevel teeth ensure good results when you are crosscutting, and the raker teeth (which have a flat top) clean out the kerf during rip cuts. They actually rake out the chips and increase feed speed.

The flat top raker tooth is slightly lower than the alternate top bevel teeth. This prevents the raker tooth from causing tear-out during a crosscut. If you experience tear-out when crosscutting with an alternate-top-bevel-and-raker-tooth configuration, it is likely that the points have dulled and the raker teeth are in the same orbit as the alternate top bevel teeth.

The triple-chip tooth configuration is designed for cutting plywood, particleboard, and other wood-based sheet stock. One tooth has a flat top, and the next tooth looks like a flat-top tooth with the corners cut off. The tooth with its corners cut off separates the material, and the flat-top tooth planes the sides for a smooth tear-out-free cut.

The tooth's shape resists the abrasive glues and resins in sheet stock. This allows the blade to remain sharp after prolonged cutting of sheet stock. Blades with triple-chip teeth can also be used for cutting solid stock, but generally they are not as efficient as blades with alternate top bevel or alternate-top-bevel-and-raker teeth.

Flat-top, carbide-tipped blades have only one function: ripping. Since the wood fibers go the long way in the board, the flat-top tooth will rip the wood smoothly. The quality of the cut is diminished greatly when a flat-top blade is used for crosscutting.

Blade Noise Saw blades are not equal in the noise they generate. Blades with laser cuts through them which run parallel with the blade's rim tend to produce less noise (Illus. 3-18). This is because the noise does not resonate through the blade, but is stopped at each laser cut.

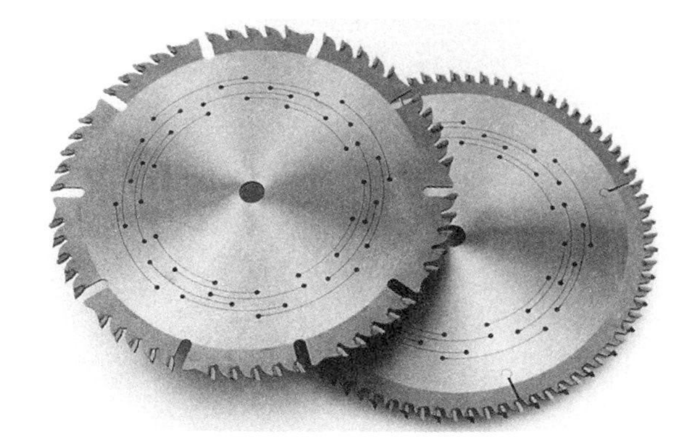

Illus. 3-18. The laser-cut slots in these blades reduce the transmission of noise while the blade is turning and/or cutting. (Photo courtesy of CMT Tools.)

Blade noise is a function of the blade design, the saw the blade is mounted on, and the material being cut. When buying blades, inquire about the noise level of the blade when it is coasting, and while it is cutting.

Blade dampeners and saw collars can reduce blade noise somewhat. A discussion of dampeners and collars is found in Chapter 2.

Chip-Limiting Blades Some carbide-tipped blades have a chip-limiting feature. The chip-limiting feature slows the feed speed somewhat because it limits the size of the bite any tooth can take. It also reduces the chance of kickback because each tooth has such a small grip on the wood. The blade's plate and rim stop the stock from feeding too quickly into the blade.

A chip-limiting blade is ideal for beginning woodworkers. They will have better control over the stock and will not be intimidated by the blade. This makes it easier for the beginner to succeed at the table saw. Experts will not notice any difference in blade performance except when power feeding.

Selecting Blades

When you select a saw blade, you reach a series of compromises concerning hook angle, number of

Illus. 3-19. The blades shown here have different tooth shapes and different numbers of teeth. Each blade is a compromise of design intended for a specific type of cutting. (Photo courtesy of CMT Tools.)

teeth, size of gullets, and a number of other design factors (Illus. 3-19). This is why one blade cannot do all things (Illus. 3-20 and 3-21). There are several factors you must consider when selecting a blade. In addition to tooth style and configuration, you must have an understanding of the relationships between the saw, its power and tolerances, the wood, and the type and diameter of saw blade. These all have an influence on friction (blade heat) and feed speed.

Illus. 3-20 and 3-21. These blades each have 80 teeth, but their tooth geometries are different. The one on top is used for melamine-faced particleboard, and the one below it is used for cutting miters in solid stock. (Photos courtesy of CMT Tools.)

Friction is a cause of most sawing problems. When you use a fine blade (a blade with many teeth), there are more teeth in the wood during the cut. Since the teeth are smaller, they take a smaller bite. This causes the feed speed to decrease, which means an increase in friction. Increased friction can overwork the motor and cause burning on both edges of the saw kerf. Regardless of how smooth the cut is, burning will ruin its appearance and reduce edge-gluing strength. When the motor is overworked, the tip speed of the blade decreases. This condition increases blade torque and could contribute to a kickback. If you find that the motor is being overworked, go to a coarser blade.

All things being equal, a carbide-tipped saw blade will generate more friction than its tool-steel counterpart. This is because the clearance on a tool-steel blade is obtained by bending or offsetting the teeth. This is known as set. The offset teeth touch a small area in the kerf, so there is not much friction. In thick materials, a tool-steel blade might reduce friction enough to improve the cut.

Tool-steel blades do not usually produce as high quality a cut as carbide-tipped blades, so they are used as a last resort to reduce friction on a thick cut. For example, a 24-tooth, carbide-tipped blade might burn when making a cut in material. A 24-tooth steel blade would have about one-fourth the friction, so it may handle the cut even on a light-duty table saw. Tool-steel blades are not appropriate for materials such as particleboard and fiber-core plywood.

As a guideline, try to keep three to five of the blade's teeth in the wood during the cut (Illus. 3-22–3-24). This will minimize the amount of friction and maximize feed speed. Remember, as the stock gets thicker there are more teeth in the wood. This reduces feed speed, which taxes the saw motor and increases friction. The solution is to replace the blade with a coarser one.

If you tilt the saw blade, friction will also increase. For example, if the blade has five teeth in the wood, and you tilt the blade to 45 degrees, there will now be seven teeth in the wood, and the stock will be 1.4 times as thick. This is because the hypotenuse of an isosceles right triangle is about 1.4 times as long as the other legs.

To reduce the number of teeth in the wood, some

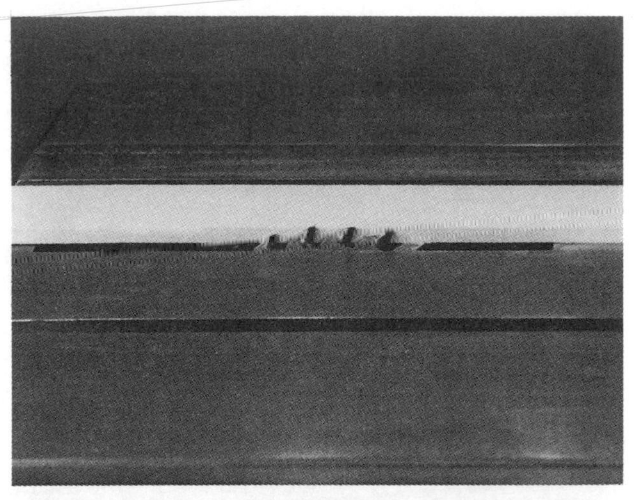

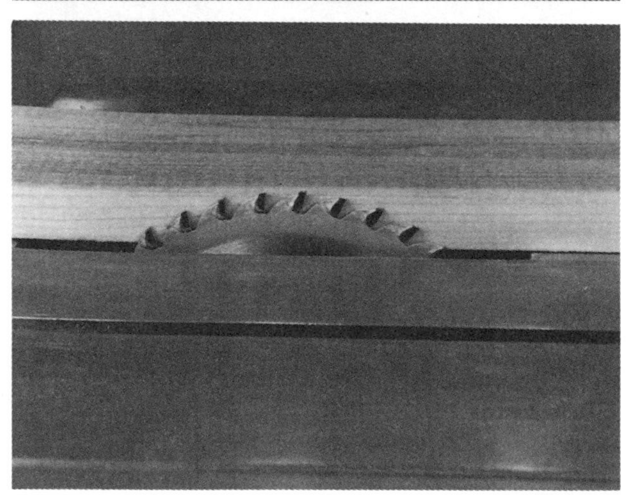

Illus. 3-22–3-24. The same blade on the same saw has been adjusted for ¼-, ½-, and ¾-inch stock. Note how the number of teeth in the work increases as stock thickness increases. The top photo shows ¼-inch-thick stock being cut. The middle photo shows ½-inch-thick stock being cut. The bottom photo shows ¾-inch-thick stock being cut.

woodworkers will raise the saw blade to full height. While the number of teeth in the wood decreases, the footprint of the blade in the wood is much greater. This increases the chance of a kickback. If the board twists slightly during a rip cut, this will actually cause binding, and possibly a kickback.

There is also a much greater chance of injury with the blade at full height. These injuries can be severe, so *keep the blade low and use the guard!* If the blade has too many teeth to do the job efficiently, change blades. Select a blade with fewer teeth; it will increase feed speed and reduce friction.

Table-saw horsepower is also a factor in detemining which blade to select. A table saw needs at least 1½ actual horsepower to cut efficiently. If your saw has less than 1½ horsepower, consider using a smaller-diameter blade. If you own a 10-inch table saw, consider mounting an 8-inch-diameter blade on the saw. A smaller blade requires less energy to turn, so there is more energy left to cut wood. The peripheral speed (rim speed) of the blade decreases, so you will be feeding the stock a little slower. Select a coarser blade to compensate for the slower feed speed.

A smaller blade will not cut as deeply, but most woodworkers rarely need to use the full depth of the blade. In those rare cases when you do, change to a larger-diameter blade.

One additional advantage of the smaller-diameter blade is reduced blade deflection. If the arbor of the saw has a .002-inch run-out, it will be more obvious at the tip of a 10-inch blade. The farther the tip of the blade is from the run-out, the more noticeable it becomes. Poorly toleranced saws actually work better with a smaller-diameter blade.

The following list contains generalizations concerning saw blades. Use this information to help determine which blade to use in a certain situation. Remember, this is *generalized* information. There are always exceptions to the rule.

1. Harder woods require a slower feed rate and develop more heat. Coarser blades or lighter cuts (less depth) increase feed speed.
2. Three to five teeth in the wood are ideal. Softer woods can tolerate more teeth because they have less feed resistance.
3. Smaller-diameter blades require less energy to

turn, so there is more energy to cut wood. Smaller blades also run truer because arbor run-out is not as pronounced.
4. Tool-steel blades generate less friction than carbide-tipped blades. This is because there is less metal contacting the sides of the saw kerf.
5. Tool-steel blades will become dull faster than carbide-tipped blades. Tool-steel blades cannot be used on materials with high-glue contact such as particleboard and fiber-core plywood. The glues in these materials are so hard that they actually take the edge off a tool-steel blade in one cut.
6. If you have two carbide-tipped blades with an equal number of teeth, remember that the blade with the largest gullets (openings in front of the teeth) will cut the fastest.
7. Friction in the saw cut is usually caused by the blade, but it can also be caused by misalignment. Make sure that the fence and blade are parallel to the miter slot. Any misalignment can cause friction.

There are ways to determine what is the cause of friction. If both sides of the saw kerf are burned, the blade is too fine. If only the fence side is burned, the fence is probably pinching the stock against the blade. If stock tends to creep along the fence of the miter gauge when you are crosscutting, the blade is not parallel to the miter slots. Check your owner's manual for alignment specifics.
8. Tilting the blade increases friction. The operation increases friction by making the cut deeper, engaging more teeth in the wood, and reducing feed speed.
9. Keep the blade no more than ¼ inch above the work. This will reduce the footprint of the blade in the work and minimize the chance of kickback.
10. For maximum efficiency, use the coarsest blade that produces adequate results.
11. Blades with larger teeth are best for ripping.
12. Use a rip blade when the job is strictly ripping.
13. Small teeth mean a smoother cut and a slower feed rate.
14. Hollow-ground blades and paneling blades should be used only for true, dry, cabinet-grade lumber.
15. Remove high-quality or specialty blades as soon as the job is done.
16. Green lumber and construction lumber require blades with more set than dry hardwood lumber. This is due to the increased moisture content.
17. Never use a dull blade. It is unsafe and produces poor results.

Always analyze the job using the general rules listed and any other information you may have. The time spent changing blades is time well spent. The correct blade does the most efficient and safest job. Dull blades waste time and energy.

Trial-and-error experience will help you select the best blade for every job you do. Make note of which blade does the best job. This provides a ready reference for future use.

Some blades have a knock-out arbor hole so that they may be used with more than one size of arbor. Be sure the knock-out is in securely when it must be used. The blade's arbor hole should just fit the arbor. A sloppy fit means the blade is incorrect for the arbor. Extra knock-outs or spacers can be purchased at most hardware stores.

A prick punch may be used to offset metal around the arbor hole. This holds the knock-out in more securely. Knock-outs are frequently removed when the blade is sharpened. Always check the arbor hole after your blades have been sharpened.

Evaluating and Selecting Carbide-Tipped Blades When selecting a carbide-tipped blade for your saw, select a blade 8–10 inches in diameter with 24 to 60 teeth. For general-duty work, use a 10-inch blade with 40 to 50 alternate-top-bevel or alternate-top-bevel-and-raker teeth (Illus. 3-25). As you become familiar with your saw and the type of work you are doing, select the saw blade best suited to your needs. Buy only what you need; add blades as the job presents itself. Review all information in this section before buying a blade.

Not all carbide-tipped blades are equal in quality. Before buying any blade, look it over and evaluate it carefully. The size of the carbide tips is important. The larger the tips, the more times they can be sharpened, but if they are too long, they can increase blade friction. Look at the braze joint between the blade and carbide tip. It often indicates blade quality. A quality braze joint will have no voids or pits, and all the braze joints on a blade will be the same size.

Illus. 3-25. This 50-tooth combination blade is considered a general-duty blade for a 10-inch table saw. It has chip-limiting features and laser-cut slots to reduce noise. (Photo courtesy of CMT Tools.)

Inspect the teeth; they should be ground smooth (Illus. 3-26 and 3-27). The smoother the surface of the carbide, the better the cut. The smoother the carbide, the longer the blade will remain sharp. This is because smooth grinding puts more carbide at the edges of the blade, where cutting occurs. More carbide increases the resistance to wear. Keep the carbide blade sharp. Use a reliable sharpening service that leaves no coarse grinding marks.

As you shop for blades, look very carefully at the tips. Some lower-quality blades are painted with a silver paint. This makes the blade look like an expensive alloy. In reality, all the paint does is hide the scratches in the carbide tips and the pits in the braze joints. High-quality blades are never painted; the manufacturer is pleased to show you the carbide tips and braze joints.

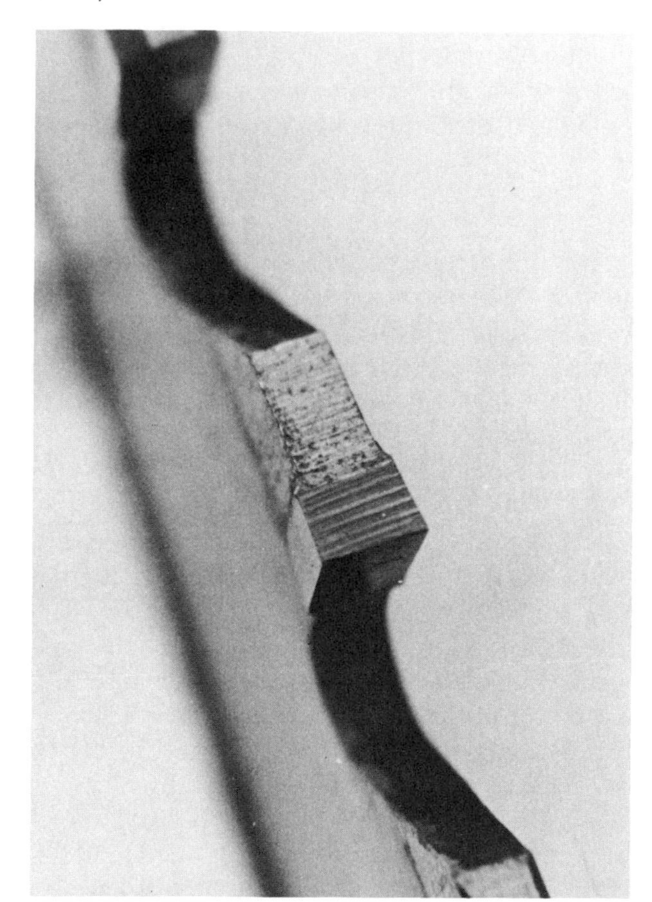

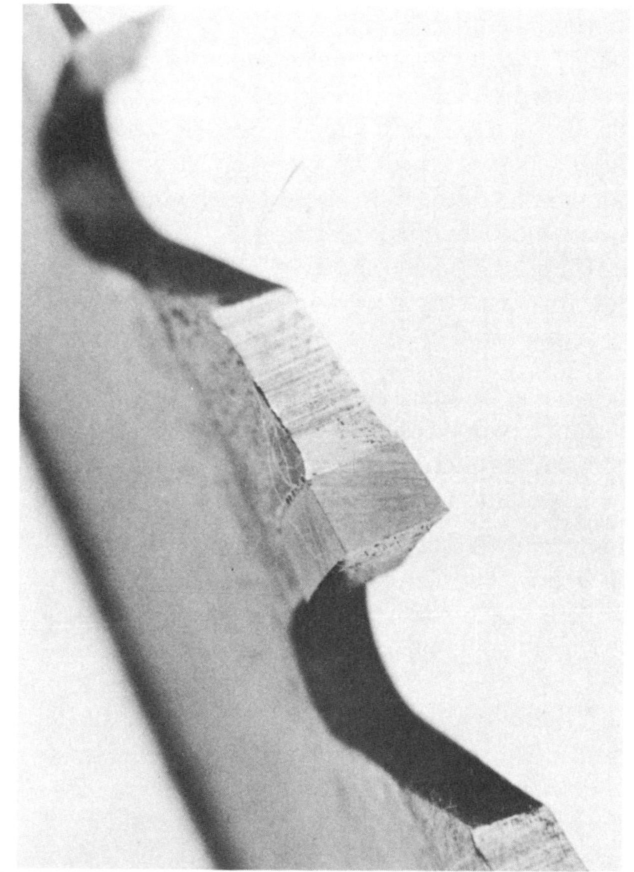

Illus. 3-26 and 3-27. Notice the difference in grinding quality from rough surface (shown on the left) to smooth surface (right). Smoother surfaces mean sharper teeth and greater longevity.

Blade Maintenance

Blades should be protected from damage when not in use. The teeth of blades in storage should not touch. Such contact can dull or break carbide teeth, and will dull steel blades. Hang blades individually or with spacers between them. This will keep them sharp. Protect blades from corrosion. Corrosion will deteriorate a sharp cutting edge.

Handle circular-saw blades carefully. A sharp (or dull) blade can cut you. Never lay a blade on the cast-iron surface of your table saw. The set of the teeth causes them to scratch the table and become dull. Lay the blade on a scrap of stock when changing blades (Illus. 3-28).

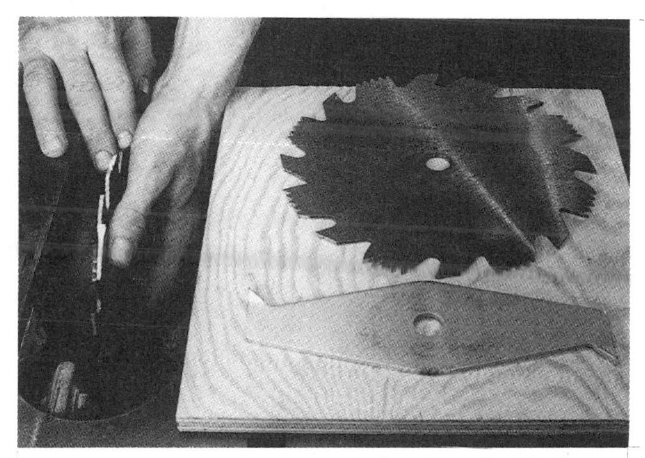

Illus. 3-28. When changing blades, lay the blade on a scrap of wood. Contact with the metal table can dull the blade quickly.

Pitch When a circular-saw blade becomes hot, pitch will accumulate on it. Pitch is a brown, sticky substance (wood resin) that looks like varnish (Illus. 3-29). As pitch accumulates on the blade, it acts as an insulator. This keeps the blade from dissipating heat and causes it to become dull faster.

Pitch is usually a sign of a blade with too little set for the job. It can also mean that the blade is too dull to cut. In some cases, the blade accumulates pitch and smokes when it is installed backward (teeth pointing the wrong way). Some blades are Teflon-coated to resist pitch accumulation, but the Teflon wears off after two or three resharpenings. Commercial pitch removers can be used to clean blades. Water-based hand cleaners, some commercial kitchen cleaners, oven cleaners, and hot water also work well. Avoid using abrasives to remove

Illus. 3-29. Pitch is a brown sticky substance that looks like varnish. Here it is accumulating behind the carbide tips on this blade.

pitch. Abrasives leave scratches that make it easier for pitch to anchor itself to the blade. Pitch accumulation does not always mean the blade is dull. Heat could increase pitch accumulation.

Pitch can be high in acid content. When it remains on carbide tips, it can actually etch the cutting edges. A dirty blade can actually dull in storage. Keep blades clean and store them in a clean condition.

Dull Blades Some indications of a dull blade include:

1. Stock tends to climb over the blade.
2. Blade smokes or gives off a burnt odor.
3. Increased effort is needed to feed the stock into the blade.
4. The saw no longer cuts a straight line.

Dull blades can also be identified by visual inspection. Look at the teeth. Rip teeth should come to an edge (Illus. 3-30). The edge should be a straight line and not rounded. Crosscut teeth should come to a point. The two cutting angles should form a straight line to the point of the tooth (Illus. 3-31).

Carbide teeth stay sharp longer than steel teeth, but they also become dull. If a dull carbide blade is left on the saw, the brittle teeth will crack or shatter. Drag your fingernail across the carbide tip (Illus.

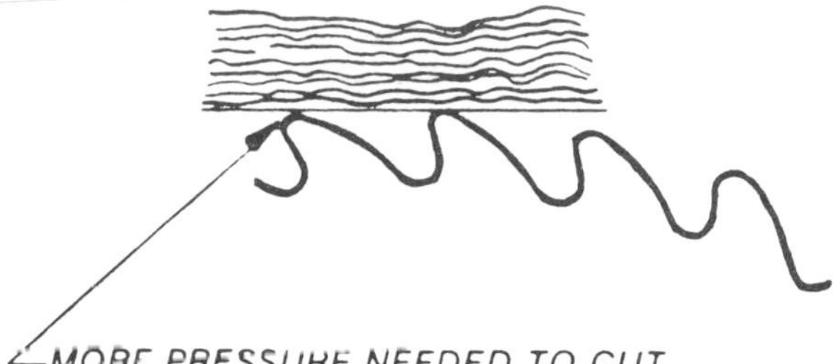

Illus. 3-30. The rip teeth shown here have rounded ends. This means they are dull. They should form a straight line or edge. More energy and feed pressure is needed to make a rip cut with a dull blade.

SHARP DULL

Illus. 3-31. Crosscut teeth also become rounded or flat on their ends. Sharp teeth come to a point.

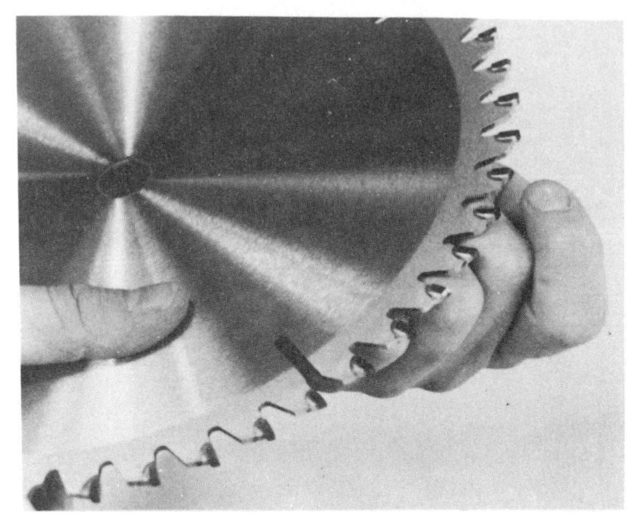

Illus. 3-32. If a carbide-tipped blade is sharp, it will raise a chip on your finger (you can see one on my index finger). If it is dull, your fingernail will slide across the tip.

3-32). It should cut a chip (remove a curl from your fingernail). If it does not (your fingernail slides across the tip), it is too dull to cut properly. Disconnect the saw to check a blade that is mounted. Replacing broken carbide tips is much more expensive than sharpening. Keep carbide blades sharp, and broken tips will not be a problem.

Getting Blades Sharpened In most cases, it is best to have your blades sharpened by professionals. The equipment they use is very accurate, but too expensive for the individual (Illus. 3-33). Find a reliable service and develop a good working relationship. Not all sharpening services are equal. Some do better work than others. When trying a new service, do not send them your best blades. Have them sharpen one or two general-duty blades first. Inspect the blades carefully (Illus. 3-34). If the

Illus. 3-33. Professional sharpening equipment is very accurate, but too expensive for the average woodworker. A quality sharpening job is a bargain. (Photo courtesy of Forrest Manufacturing.)

results are not satisfactory, try another sharpening service.

Make a board for transporting blades (Illus. 3-35). Put cardboard spacers between the blades. This will make the blades safer and easier to transport. It will also keep them well protected and sharp.

The board also indicates to the sharpening service that you take care of your blades and that you expect high-quality sharpening (Illus. 3-36). To encourage high-quality work, ask the sharpening service what is the finest-grit wheel they use on blades, and whether they will be grinding wet or dry. A 400–600-grit wheel is indicative of quality service. Wet grinding is also indicative of high-quality service. Wet grinding keeps the braze joint cool and improves the surface quality of the grinding.

Illus. 3-34. Inspect blades after they have been sharpened. Carbide-tipped blades ground as smoothly as the one shown here will stay sharp a long time.

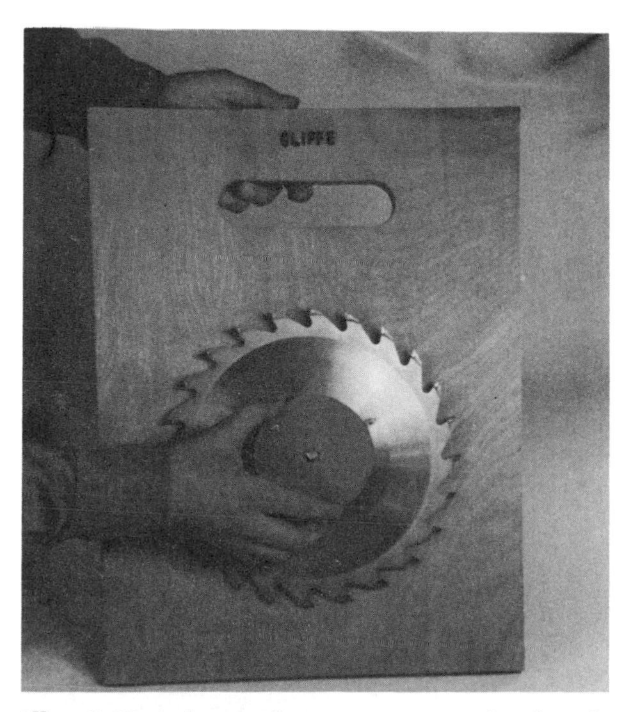

Illus. 3-35. A sharpening or transportation board like this one will keep blades sharp. Use a cardboard spacer between blades to keep them separated and sharp.

Illus. 3-36. This carrying board will accommodate a dado head and some blades. This carrier protects the blade during storage or transportation. (Photo courtesy of CMT Tools.)

Dado Heads

A dado head is used to cut dadoes and rabbets. Dadoes are square or rectangular channels in wood. Rabbets are L-shaped cuts along the edge of a piece of stock. The dado head is used for joinery cuts. There are three types of dado heads: the wobble type, the adjustable V-shaped type, and the stack, or blade-and-chipper, type. These types require a special throat plate when they are used.

Wobble Dado Heads Wooble dado heads have a single wobbling blade. The oscillation of the blade causes it to cut a dado (Illus. 3-37 and 3-38). The width of the dado is controlled by the position of the offset washers located on either side of the blade. The washers have registration marks to tell you the width of the dado (Illus. 3-39). The greater the incline of the blade, the wider the dado. The blade consists of a heavy-gauge plate with carbide tips. The wobble dado can be used on any material, including particleboard. The wobble dado and washers are a total set and should be used that way. *Never* attempt to use a standard saw blade for wobble dadoing. It is not designed for the internal stress.

Wobble dado heads are available with varying numbers of carbide tips on the blade. The larger the number of carbide tips, the smoother the cut usually is, but light cuts and slower feed speeds will also yield smooth cuts with fewer carbide tips.

Wobble dado heads do not produce a flat bottom. This is because the wobbling action causes the bottom of the dado to be slightly concave. The wobbling also promotes tear-out in the face of the stock due to the wobbling action striking the shoulders of the dado. For best results, take light cuts.

Adjustable V-Shaped Dado Head The twin-blade, or adjustable V-shaped, dado head has a large center hub with two 8-inch-diameter carbide-tipped saw blades mounted on it (Illus. 3-40). Each of these blades has 24 teeth. As the hub turns, the blades spread at one end only. This makes it look like the letter V. In each revolution of the dado head, the saw blades remove all the stock in their paths, thus forming a dado. The adjustable dado head is sold by DML and Sears. Sears calls its adjustable dado head the Excalibur.

The adjustable collar at the center of the adjustable V-shaped dado head tells you the approximate dado width. The blade is marked at its widest point to simplify setup. It also has a depth-of-cut scale to help you set dado depth.

The hubs on the adjustable V and the wobble dado heads are quite thick, and may not fit on the arbor of some table saws. Make sure that your saw will accommodate the dado head before you buy it.

The quality of the dado made by the adjustable

Illus. 3-37. These wobble dado heads can be used to cut dadoes on most table saws. The incline is achieved by turning the wedge-shaped washers on either side of the table.

Illus. 3-38. The number of teeth on a wobble dado head can have some impact on the quality of the cut, but so does feed speed and saw alignment.

Illus. 3-39. The highest tooth on this wobble dado head has been marked. This enables the dado head to be aligned with a layout line. The black rim has a scale of dado widths on it.

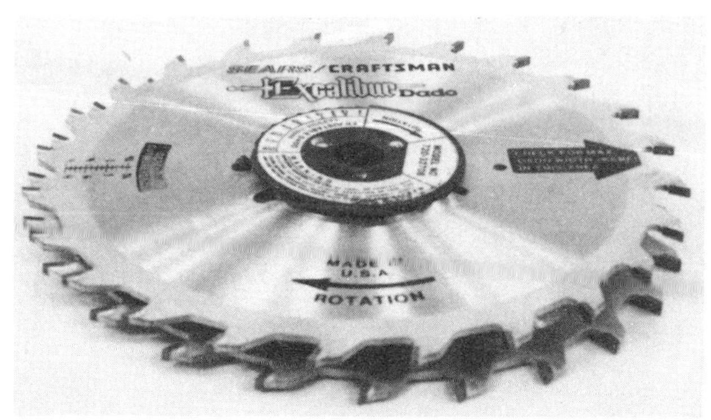

Illus. 3-40. The adjustable V-shaped dado head spreads two 24-tooth blades into a V shape to make a dado.

V-shaped dado head is generally superior to that of a wobble head. There will be less tear-out, but the bottom of the dado will not be even. Feed speed and depth of cut have a great effect on the quality of the cut.

Blade-and-Chipper (or Stack) Dado Heads

Blade-and-chipper dado heads come as a complete set. The two blades or cutters resemble a combination blade (Illus. 3-41 and 3-42). Each blade or cutter is designed to cut a 1/8-inch kerf. The chippers have two to eight cutting edges. They are mounted between the blades. Chippers are designed for 1/8- or 1/6-inch spacing. When cutters and chippers are used together, they appear as a stack; hence the name stack dado.

Blade-and-chipper dado heads are available as carbide-tipped or tool steel, but if you are purchasing one today, the best investment is a carbide-tipped set. Tool-steel stack dado heads can only be used in solid wood, and do not hold an edge long. Carbide-tipped stack dado heads can be used in any wood or remanufactured wood sheet stock for a long time without sharpening.

A complete dado set will cut dadoes from 1/8 or 1/4 inch to 13/16 inch when the number of chippers is varied between the blades. Two blades or cutters must be used for all dadoes except 1/8-inch dadoes. This requires one blade. A 1/4-inch dado would be made with two blades or cutters. A 3/8-inch dado would be made with the two 1/8-inch blades and a single 1/8-inch chipper between them. Chippers are never used alone. They must always be mounted between two cutters.

The blade-and-chipper dado head cannot be adjusted for odd-sized dadoes as easily as a wobble or adjustable V-shaped dado head (Illus. 3-43). With the use of paper, plastic, or metal shim rings, the stack dado can be adjusted to .001 inch. This is done by inserting the shim rings of various thick-

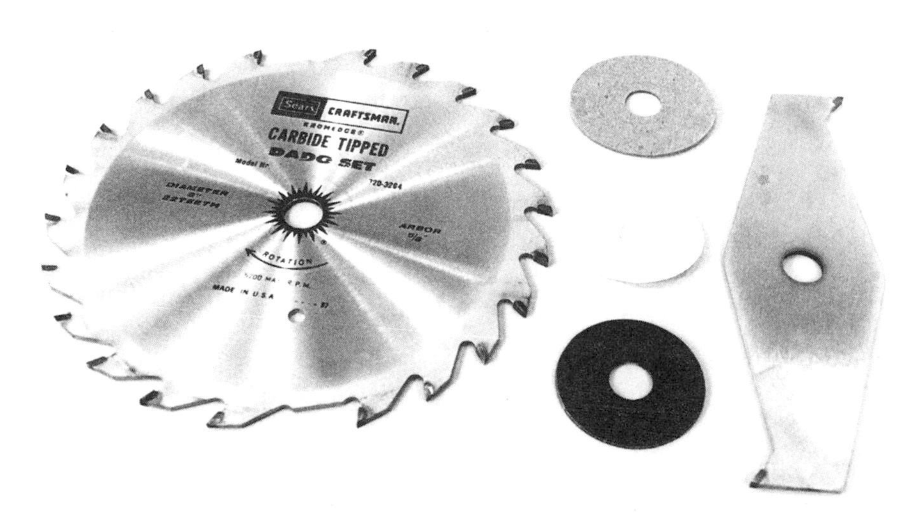

Illus. 3-41. This dado set includes cutters (left), spacing shims (center), and chippers (right). One or two cutters are always used. Spacers and chippers are used between cutters.

Illus. 3-42. The chippers in this set have four or eight cutting edges. Each revolution actually takes a series of smaller bites. This may improve the dado quality.

Illus. 3-43. Cutter-and-chipper dado heads can be spaced with paper washers to make an odd-sized dado.

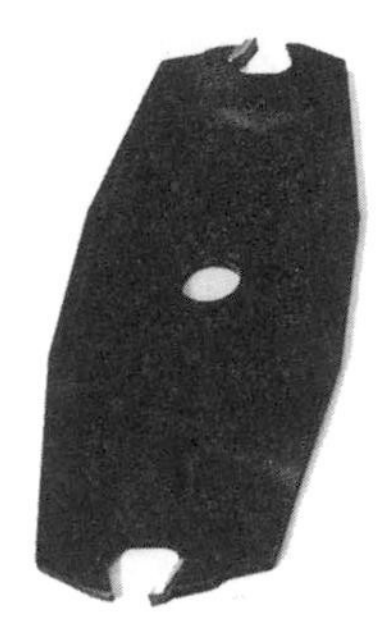

Illus. 3-44. This chip-limiting dado head has limiters on the chippers (left) and the cutter (right). This reduces the chance of kickback.

ness between the cutters and chippers. The shim rings spread the width of the dado head, and the width of the cutting edge of the chippers compensates for them. All of the area is cut cleanly, since the cutting edge of all chippers is actually wider than the plate or body.

Some stack dado heads are categorized as chip-limiting (Illus. 3-44). These dado heads have a small limiter in front of the cutting edges of the cutters and chippers. The limiter reaches both feed speed and the amount of bite each tooth takes. This reduces the kickback potential and kickback velocity because the engagement between the wood and the dado head is reduced. Chip-limiting dado heads were designed for hand-feeding, although they may be used for power-feeding.

Molding Heads

Molding heads are used to shape stock on the table saw. Stock can be shaped into molding, lipped doors, and joinery. The molding head mounts on the saw arbor. It has slots into which the molding cutters are fastened. A special throat plate is used with the molding head. Some molding heads have only one or two cutters, but most have a set of three cutters for each shape that is cut. The molding heads that use a set of three cutters are safest and cut smoother molding.

There are many molding cutter types and shapes. They are ground from flat steel and usually have a mounting hold. The mounting hole is used to attach them to the molding head. Molding cutter manufacturers have their own mounting designs. This means that cutters of different brands are not interchangeable. Follow manufacturer's directions for mounting molding cutters in the molding head (Illus. 3-45). Check them periodically during an operation to be sure they are tight. Be certain the

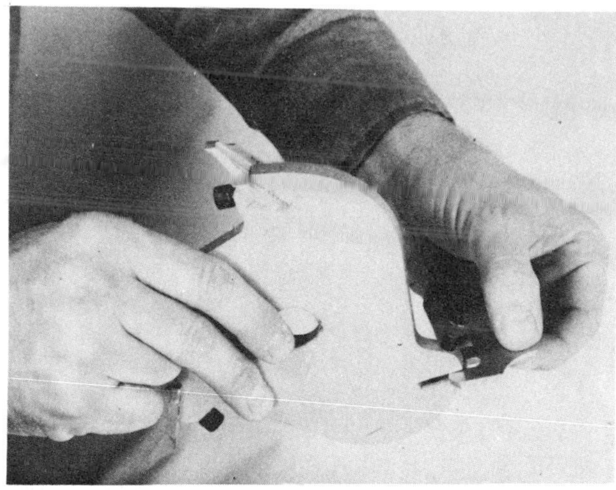

Illus. 3-45. When installing cutters in the shaper head, follow the manufacturer's instructions. Be sure the cutters are tightened securely; check them periodically.

cutters all face forward. The flat side of the cutter does the cutting.

There are also two types of molding heads. One is manufactured by Delta, and the other is manufactured by a number of suppliers. The chief difference between them is the way they are held in the cutter head. On the Delta molding head, the head of the fastener is secured to the molding head (Illus. 3-46). The others actually have the metal fastener going through the cutter to secure it in place (Illus. 3-47 and 3-48). Both heads hold the cutters securely in position.

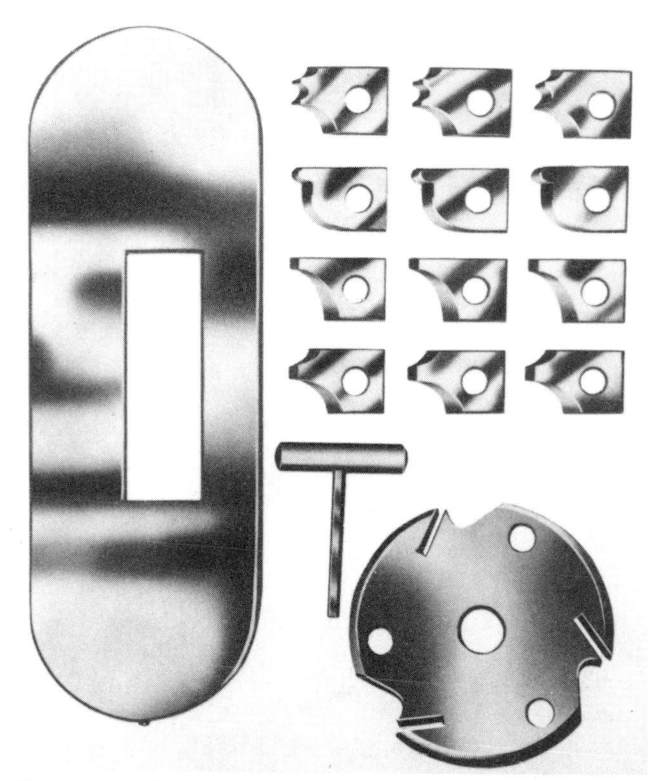

Illus. 3-46. This Delta molding head holds the cutters to the head with screws. The head of the screw locks them in place. (Photo courtesy of Delta International Machinery Corporation.)

Delta sells a smaller-diameter cutter head which uses the same molding cutters (Illus. 3-49). This enables you to use the cutters either on the table saw with the larger cutter head or on a shaper with the smallest cutter head. If you cut specialty or restoration molding, this could be an asset (Illus. 3-50).

When the cutters become dull, the flat side can be honed on an oilstone or waterstone (Illus. 3-51). Honing the flat side will cause the clearance angles to form an edge with the flat side. Never hone the clearance angles on the cutters. This could change the shape of the cut. If cutters have large nicks, discard them and buy a new set. It is important to keep shaper cutters sharp. Dull cutters tend to tear the wood and may cause a kickback.

With the development of the many router bits, router tables, and specialty routing devices, many people question the value of a molding head. Does a molding head have some unique advantages over these devices? First, each set of cutters is usually much cheaper than a router bit. Second, as you tilt the arbor of the table saw, each cutting profile actually will cut an infinite number of shapes in wood.

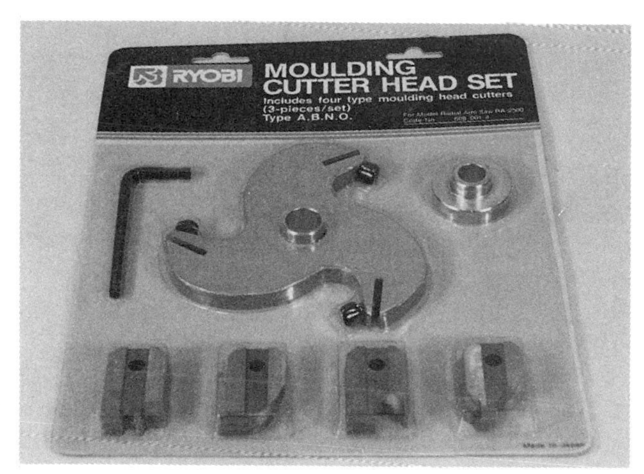

Illus. 3-47. This kit contains four profiles of cutters and a head. The adapter is used on some table-saw arbors.

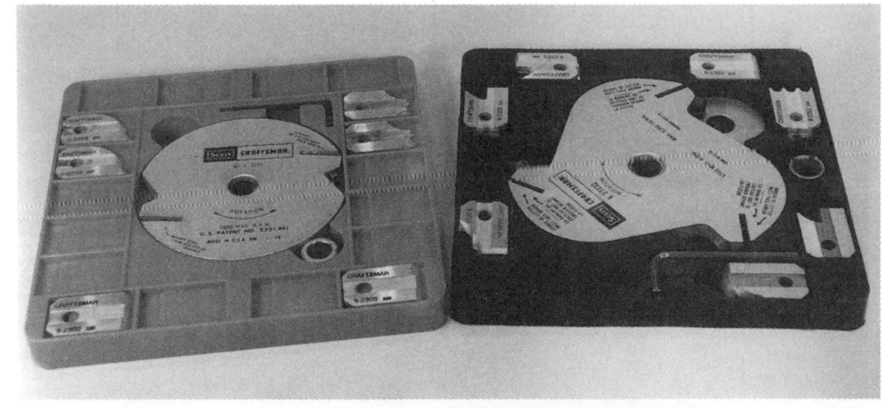

Illus. 3-48. These Craftsman heads use two (left) or three cutters. The two-cutter head is usually used on a smaller, low-powered table saw.

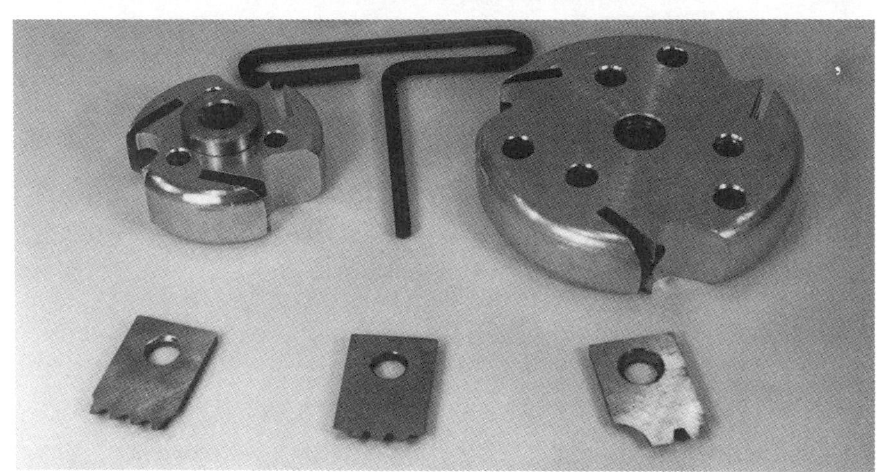

Illus. 3-49. This Delta head is smaller than the molding heads shown in Illus. 3-48, and can be used on a shaper. This enables you to use the insert cutters on a table saw or shaper.

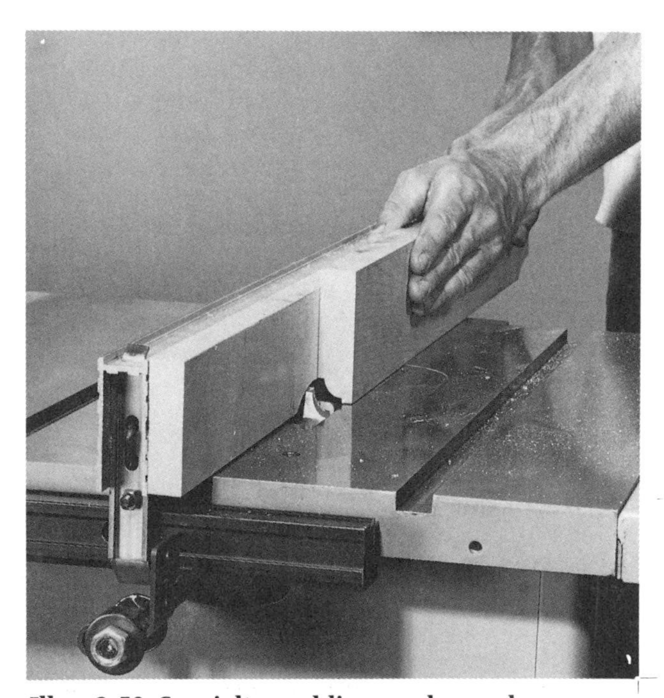

Illus. 3-50. Specialty molding can be made on a shaper or table saw if you use the Delta molding head. (Photo courtesy of Delta International Machinery Corporation.)

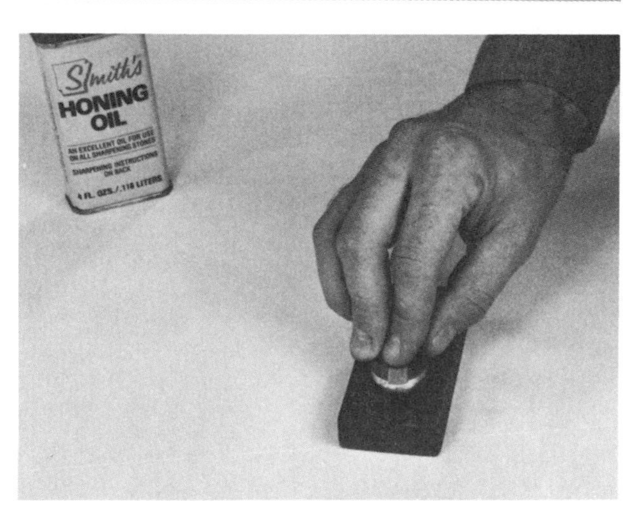

Illus. 3-51. Dull cutters can be honed on an oilstone or waterstone. Hone the flat side only. Keep the cutters sharp and free of rust.

Third, by combining various profiles and the tilt of the arbor, just about any profile may be cut. Finally, by using the cutters on both a shaper and table saw, many unique profile combinations may be developed.

Sanding Discs

Sanding discs for table saws are made from tempered steel or cast aluminum. They vary in size from about 6 to 10 inches in diameter. When a sanding disc is mounted on the arbor, the table saw can be used to disc-sand outside curves and straight edges. The disc can be tilted to sand chamfers and bevels.

The most common mistake made when disc sanding is to use too fine an abrasive. Because of the high rpms of the disc, fine abrasives cannot clear the wood chips fast enough. This causes heat and ultimately burns the abrasive. For general-duty sanding, 60- or 80-grit abrasives work best. Rougher work can be done with 40-grit abrasives, and fine work can be done with 100- or 120-grit abrasives. Avoid heavy feed or large cuts when using fine abrasives. Remove most of the stock with coarse abrasives. Then progress to a finer abrasive. Some discs carry abrasives on both sides. This makes it easy to go from a coarse abrasive to a fine abrasive quickly.

When abrasives wear out (Illus. 3-52), they must be replaced. If contact-type cement is used, the abrasive sheet peels off easily (Illus. 3-53). Other disc cements make disc removal more difficult. If

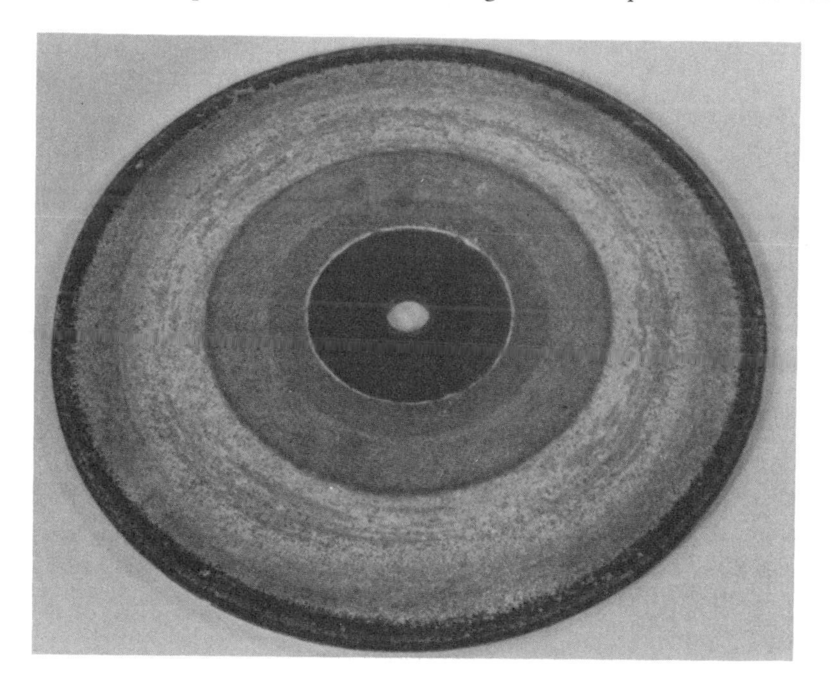

Illus. 3-52. When abrasives become worn or burned, they must be replaced.

Illus. 3-53. Discs anchored with contact cement peel off easily.

residue remains on the disc, it can be removed with a sharpened piece of hardwood.

Mount the disc on the table saw using the correct throat plate. Turn the saw on with the disc at full height. Use the sharpened piece of hardwood to scrape the disc. Press the wood lightly against the disc (Illus. 3-54). Work from the outside edge towards the center. Repeat the process until the disc is clean. Attach the new disc according to the directions furnished with the disc cement (Illus. 3-55 and 3-56). Cement and precut discs are available from most hardware dealers. Discs can also be made from heavyweight abrasive paper.

Illus. 3-54. Press the piece of stock against the turning disc. Work from the outside towards the center.

Illus. 3-55. Apply the contact cement liberally to the surface of the disc.

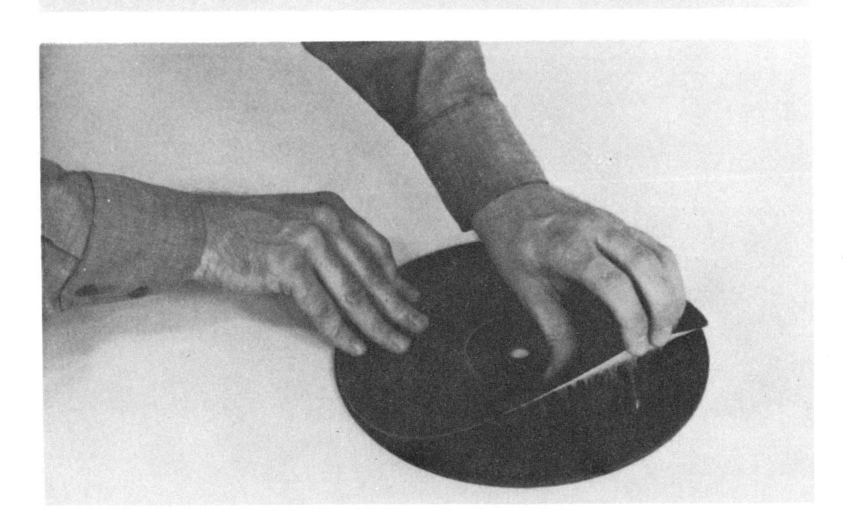

Illus. 3-56. Press the disc into the cement and lift up to allow the solvents to evaporate.

—4—
Safety Procedures

Factors Contributing to Accidents with the Table Saw

Accidents on the table saw can occur to both the novice and the experienced operator. The novice operator's accident is usually caused by a lack of knowledge of table saw safety. The novice operator may not be able to identify an accident-producing situation.

Illus. 4-1. If the factors listed above are not observed, accidents can occur. Any negative factors should be a warning to stop working. (Drawing courtesy of Power Tool Institute.)

The experienced operator's accident is usually caused by carelessness or an outright violation of the safety rules. When an experienced operator attempts and gets away with safety rule violations, they soon become common practice. This is when the accident is likely to occur.

All accidents have other contributing factors (Illus. 4-1), among which are the following:

1. *Working while tired or taking medication.* Whenever you are tired, stop or take a break. Accidents are most likely to happen when you are tired. Medication—as well as alcohol—can affect your perception and reaction time.
2. *Rushing the job.* Trying to finish a job in a hurry leads to errors and accidents. The stress of rushing the job also leads to early fatigue.
3. *Inattention to the job.* Daydreaming or thinking about another job while operating the table saw can contribute to accident potential. Repetitive cuts lend themselves to daydreaming. Be doubly careful when making them.
4. *Distractions.* Conversing with others, unfamiliar noises, and doors opening and closing are all distractions in the shop. Shut off the table saw before you converse or investigate an umfamiliar noise.
5. *General housekeeping.* A dirty or cluttered work area provides tripping hazards and excess dust that can be a breathing hazard. Keep the shop neat and clean (Illus. 4-2). It is more pleasant and safer to work in a clean area.

Kickbacks

A kickback occurs when a piece of stock is forced towards the operator at great speed. Usually the

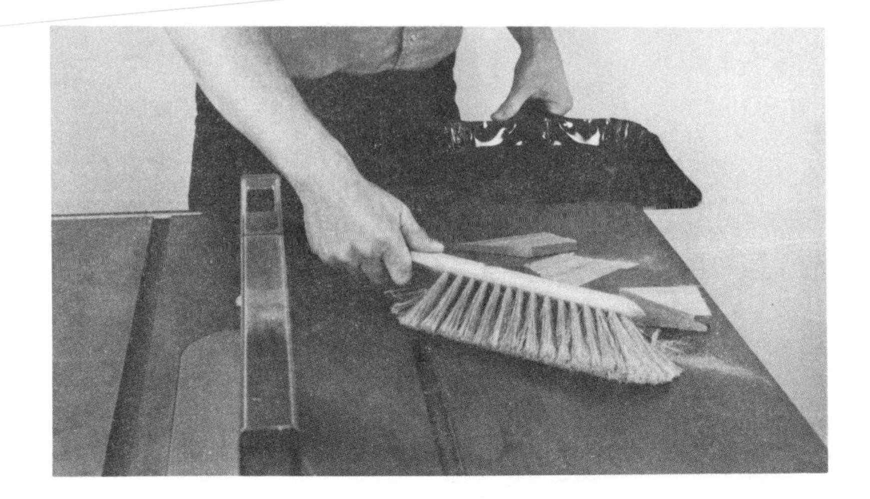

Illus. 4-2. Housekeeping is an important aspect of accident prevention. Pieces left on the table can be thrown by the blade or pinched between the blade and guard, causing a kickback. Scrap that accumulates on the floor can also be a tripping hazard.

stock becomes trapped between the rotating blade and a stationary object such as the fence or guard. In some cases, the saw kerf closes around the blade. This traps the blade and may also cause a kickback. Stock that is kicked back can have the velocity of an arrow. This is a serious hazard. Another hazard of the kickback is the fact that the operator's hand may be pulled into the blade as the stock kicks back.

Kickback hazards can be minimized by observing the following precautions:

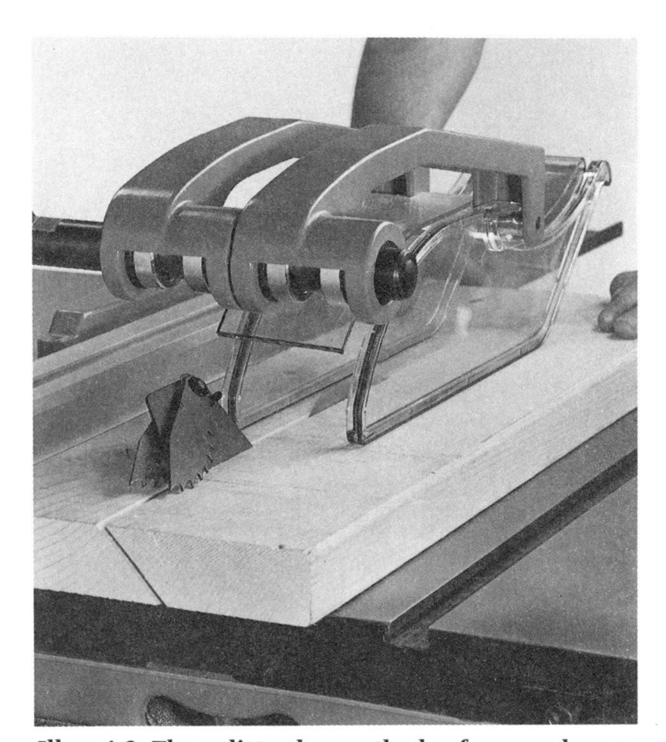

Illus. 4-3. The splitter keeps the kerf open when a piece is ripped. This minimizes the chance of pinching and kickback.

1. Cut only true, smooth stock that will not become twisted and pinched in the blade.
2. Use a guard equipped with a splitter. The splitter keeps the kerf open when the blade is cutting stock (Illus. 4-3).
3. Keep the anti-kickback pawls sharp. This allows them to dig into the wood if it begins to kick back.
4. Use only sharp, true blades. Dull or pitch-loaded blades lend themselves to kickbacks. Warped blades also tend to pinch in the kerf and cause kickbacks.
5. Avoid using the fence for crosscutting. Stock can get trapped between the blade and fence, and will kick back or kick up as the cut is completed.
6. Control all cuts with a miter gauge, fence, or jig. Never attempt to cut freehand (without any stock control). The stock will become twisted and kick back.
7. Make sure the rip fence is parallel to the blade. When the fence is not parallel, stock may be pinched.
8. Always feed the piece being cut completely through and past the blade when ripping. Never release the stock while it is still touching the blade and fence. A kickback may result. Use a push stick or push block for thin rip cuts.
9. Stand to the side of the saw when making rip cuts. If you stand behind the piece being ripped, you become the target of a kickback (Illus. 4-4).
10. When resawing (ripping a thick board into two thinner boards), raise the blade an inch at a time. This will reduce the strain on the motor, and reduce the chance of a kickback.
11. When dadoing, take a light cut. Avoid re-

Illus. 4-4. Standing to the side of the work when ripping keeps your body out of the kickback zone.

moving all stock in a single pass if the dado is larger than ⅜ inch × ¾ inch or when the wood is very hard.

12. When using a molding head, take a light cut. If there is a great deal of stock to be removed, saw away most of the waste so the cutter will have very little wood to remove. Heavy cuts are certain to kick back.

13. Reduce the kickback potential by using chip-limiting saw blades and dado heads. They will reduce the engagement between the wood and cutter and limit the kickback potential and velocity.

General Working Environment

The working environment can also be a factor in the safe operation of the table saw. The saw should be set at a comfortable height. Most operators prefer a height of 34–36 inches. Make certain the saw does not rock and has been leveled properly. When possible, it is good practice to anchor the saw to the floor.

Make sure a grounded outlet of the correct amperage is close by. This outlet should be below the saw so the cord does not interfere with the stock being cut. Adequate lighting makes operation of the saw much safer. Shadows and dim lighting increase operator fatigue and measurement errors.

The area surrounding the table saw should be ample enough to handle large pieces of stock. Traffic should be routed away from the back of the saw. In the event of a kickback, this is where the stock is most likely to go. Keep the floor around the saw free of cut-offs and debris. Cut-offs and other debris can be a tripping or slipping hazard.

Table Saw Operating Rules

1. *Protect yourself.* Always wear protective glasses when you operate the table saw. If the area is noisy, wear ear plugs or muffs to preserve your hearing and minimize fatigue. Gloves are all right to handle rough lumber, but *never* wear gloves (or other loose clothing) when operating the table saw (Illus. 4-5). Your hand could easily be pulled into the blade if the blade caught the glove (or other loose clothing).

Protect yourself whenever possible from dust. Collect dust at the saw (Illus. 4-6). This will reduce fire hazards and protect the air you breathe from fine wood dust. If no dust collection is available, be sure to wear a dust mask.

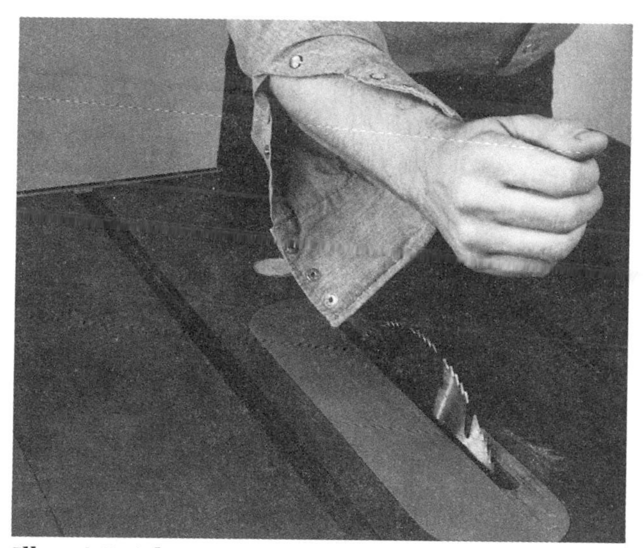
Illus. 4-5. A loose sleeve can cause you to get "wrapped up" in your work. Avoid loose sleeves and clothing.

2. *Use the guard.* Whenever possible, use the guard. The guard minimizes the chance of kickbacks with the splitter and anti-kickback pawls. It also makes contact with the saw blade very difficult (Illus. 4-7).

3. *Keep the blade low.* Set the blade height no more than ¼ inch higher than stock thickness (Illus. 4-8). This minimizes the amount of exposed blade. Less blade in the stock also reduces the possibility of kickback caused by pinching.

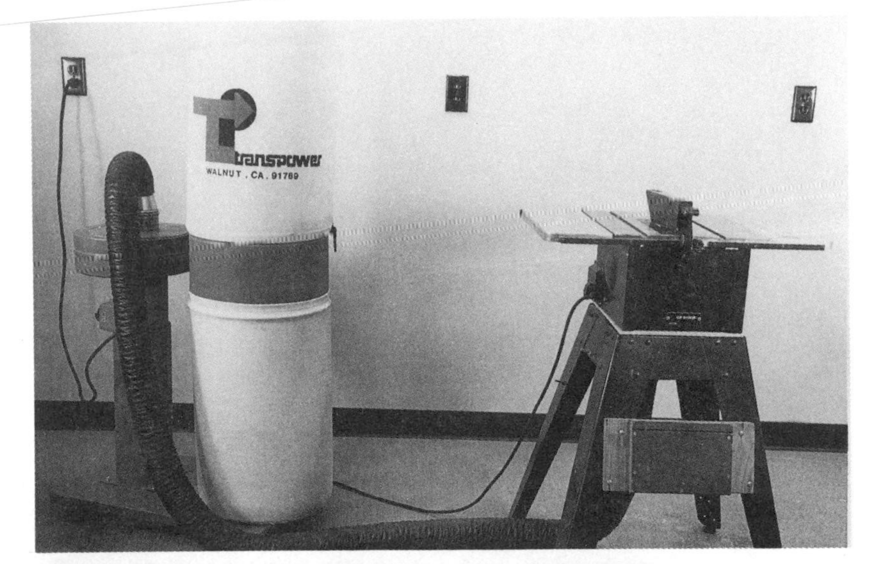

Illus. 4-6. Whenever possible, collect dust at the saw. This protects the air you breathe from fine wood dust.

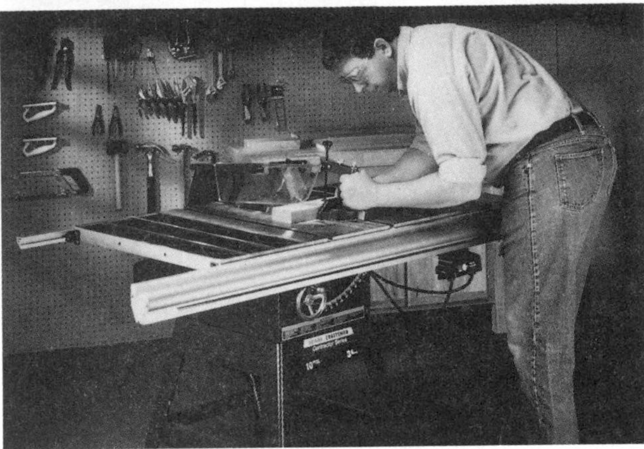

Illus. 4-7. The guard minimizes the chance of contact with the blade. The splitter and anti-kickback pawls minimize the chance of kickback. Note the dust-collection hose. (Photo courtesy of Sears Craftsman.)

4. *Keep the blade sharp.* A sharp blade makes the table saw much safer to use. A dull or an incorrect blade increases the chance of kickback. It also requires more cutting force. This excess force can throw the operator off balance and lead to an accident.

5. *Inspect your stock.* Before sawing any stock, look it over. Loose knots, twists, cupping (Illus. 4-9–4-13), and rough or wet lumber can mean trouble. Loose knots can be ejected by the saw blade. Rough, warped, or wet lumber can cause kickbacks. Small pieces can also mean trouble. Machining them puts your hands too close to the blade. If possible, machine large pieces and cut them into smaller pieces.

6. *Position yourself.* Stand to the side of the blade to avoid kickbacks. Make sure you have firm footing and balance when operating the table saw. Avoid overreaching and reaching over the blade.

Illus. 4-8. A low-set blade (¼ inch above the work) is important. This minimizes your chance of contact with the blade and reduces the kickback hazard.

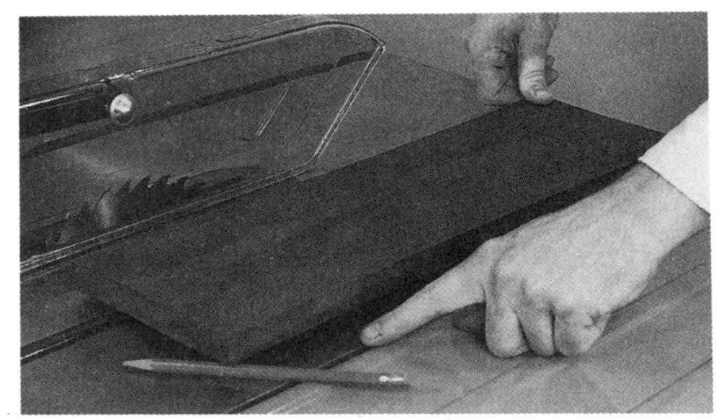

Illus. 4-9. This twisted piece of stock would get caught between the blade and fence if it were ripped. Stock must have a true face and edge.

Illus. 4-10. The true edge and face of this piece are indicated by the thumb and index finger. These perpendicular surfaces are the control surfaces. They must contact the table, fence, or miter gauge.

Illus. 4-11. One control surface (the face) is on the table, while the other control surface (the edge) is against the miter gauge. Stock must have a true edge and face to be machined at a table saw.

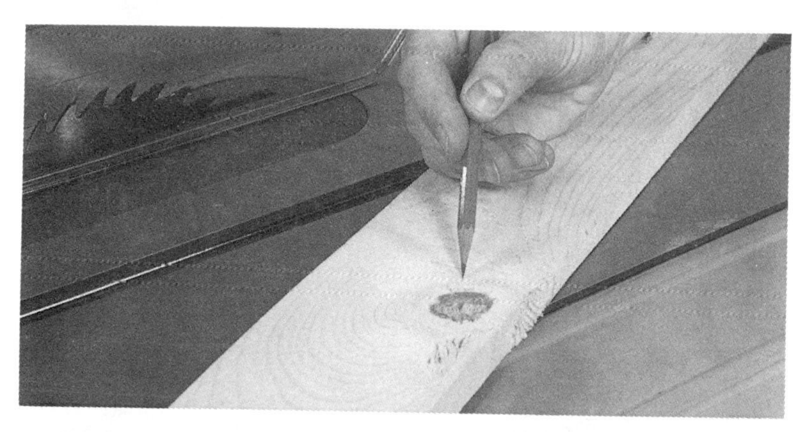

Illus. 4-12. This knot could be ejected if it were cut. It is best to cut knots out of the stock by cutting around them.

Illus. 4-13. When you cut knots out of the wood, there is no chance they will be ejected or cause blade damage.

7. Guard against accidental starting. When making adjustments to the table saw, do so with the power off. It is too easy to make an adjustment error that could cause an accident when the power is on. Make repairs, change blades, and install dado and molding heads with the power disconnected (Illus. 4-14). Otherwise, a serious accident could occur.

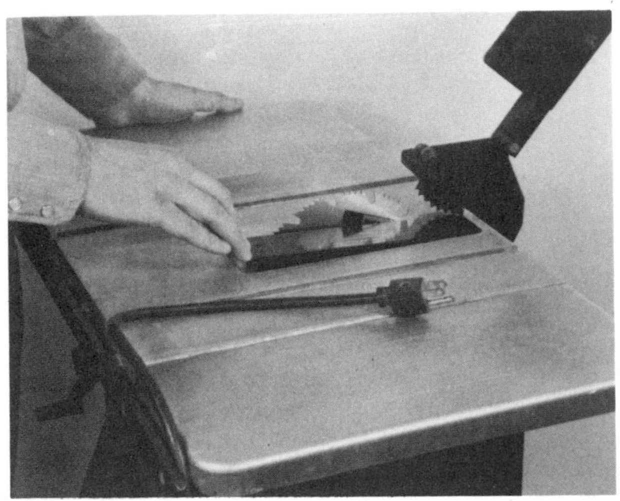

Illus. 4-14. Make sure the power is disconnected before you change the blade or make adjustments. Placing the plug on the table assures you that the power has been disconnected.

8. Use control devices. Devices like push sticks and featherboards make handling stock safer. These devices get in close and control the stock. Your hands are well away from the blade in a safe position (Illus. 4-15). Keep these control devices near the saw at all times. Patterns for push sticks can be found in Chapter 2.

9. Keep a safe margin. By keeping your hands a safe distance (4–6 inches) from the blade, you allow a margin for error. When your hands are a safe distance from the blade, there is always time to react to a hazardous situation.

10. Think about the job. When performing a new operation, think about the job before you begin. Ask yourself, "What could happen when I . . . ?" Questions of this nature help you identify and avoid an accident-producing situation. If you have a premonition of trouble, stop! Avoid any job that gives you a bad feeling. Try setting up the job another way, or ask some other experienced operator for an opinion.

11. Know your saw. Read the owner's manual and understand it before you operate the saw. All saws are different; make sure you understand the one you are using.

12. Be aware of the three most common errors woodworkers make. While conversing with woodworkers who have had an accident while using a table saw, I found that many were not using the guard, were using one or no push stick, or reached over the blade to pull the workpiece through the blade. As the workpiece began to kick back, they reacted by grasping the workpiece with their nondominant hand, which was cut by the blade.

You can avoid such an accident by using the guard. The splitter portion has anti-kickback pawls, and the hood provides a barrier between the blade and you. In addition, use two push sticks, one in each hand. If you work with two push sticks, you cannot grab anything. Your hands are already full. This eliminates the temptation to reach over the blade.

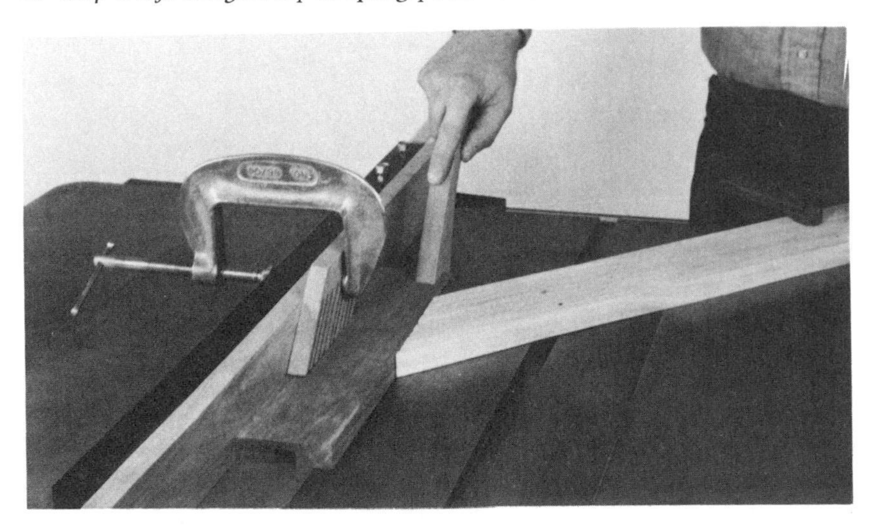

Illus. 4-15. The featherboards and push stick make contact with the blade or a kickback almost impossible. Strive for a safe setup whenever you operate the saw.

Part II:
Basic, Intermediate, and Advanced Operations

—5—
Basic Operations on the Table Saw

Basic operations include common table-saw cuts and maintenance. Careful planning and accurate measurements are a part of every table-saw operation. Always plan ahead. Think about the job before you begin. The job will be safer, and the results better.

Changing the Blade

Changing the blade is one of the most common table-saw operations. Select the correct blade for the job you are doing. Before you change the blade, disconnect the power. Unplug the saw or shut off the power at the main junction box.

Raise the guard and lift out the throat plate (Illus. 5-1). On some saws, it is easiest to change the blade when it is raised to full height. Look at the threads on the arbor. If they are right-hand threads, remove the arbor nut by turning it counterclockwise. Remove a left-hand arbor nut by turning it clockwise. It may be necessary to hold the blade stationary while the arbor nut is loosened. This is done by wedging a push stick or scrap against the blade (Illus. 5-2). Remove the outer arbor washer (and blade stabilizer, if one is used) and lift the blade off the arbor.

Inspect the arbor washers (and blade stabilizers, if used) for pitch or wood chips (Illus. 5-3). The bearing surfaces of the arbor washers should be clean. They should bear against the saw blade uniformly at their outer edge. Remove any pitch before replacing the arbor washers (and blade stabilizers).

Replace the inner blade washer (and blade stabilizer). On some table saws, the inner arbor washer is actually part of the arbor and cannot be removed. Install the desired blade over the arbor. The blade's

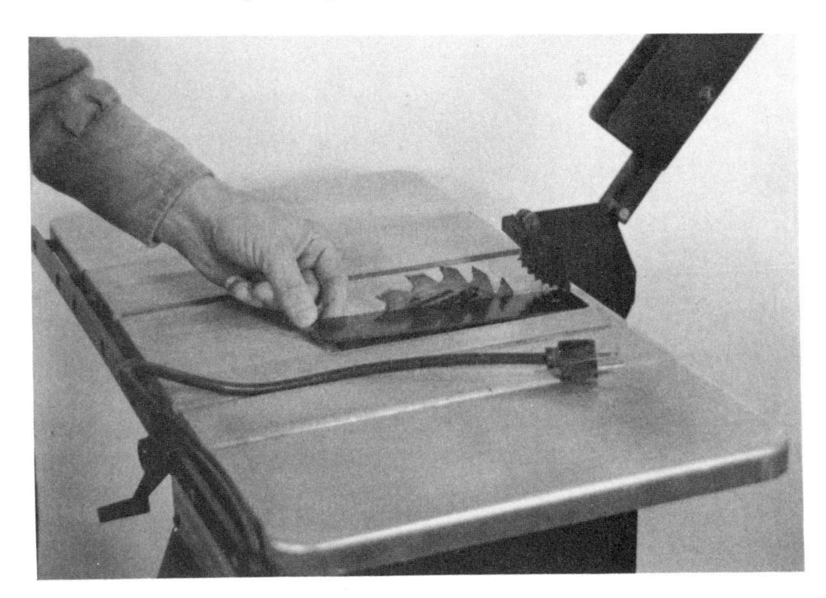

Illus. 5-1. Disconnect the saw and remove the throat plate. Some throat plates can be removed in only one way, so do not force them. The cord in clear view indicates to you that the saw is disconnected.

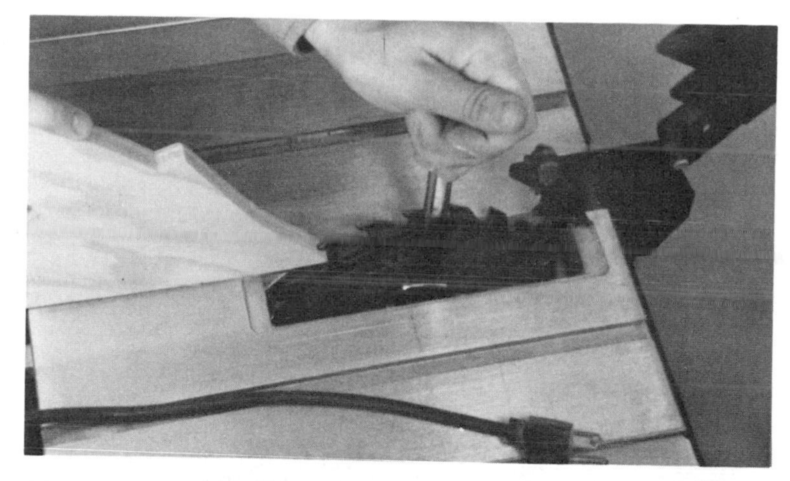

Illus. 5-2. Inspect the threads to determine which way to turn the arbor nut. Wedge a piece of scrap or push stick between the blade and saw to hold the blade while the nut is being turned. Do not force the arbor nut; you could be turning it the wrong way.

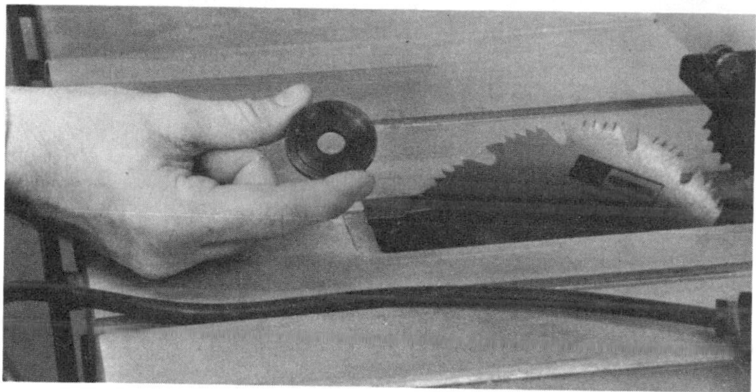

Illus. 5-3. Replace the blade. Make sure the teeth are pointing in the right direction. Inspect the arbor washers (and blade collars, if used) for pitch or wood chips. They can cause the blade to wobble instead of running true.

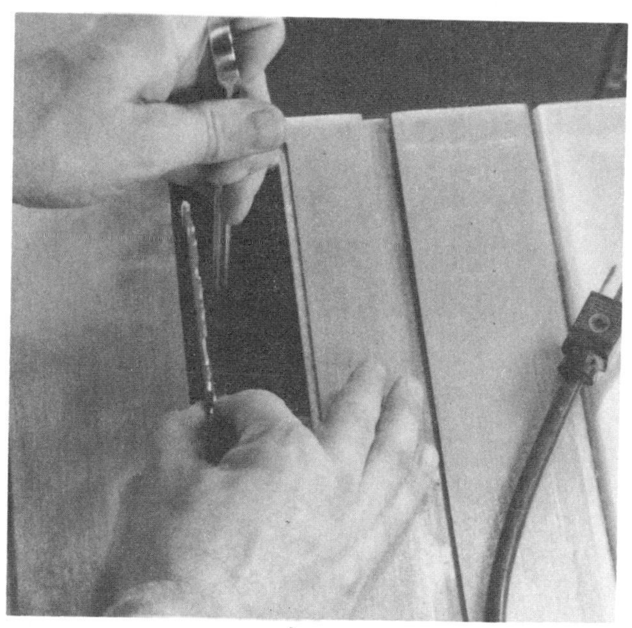

Illus. 5-4. When tightening the blade, pinch the blade between your thumb and index finger. Tighten the arbor nut until you can no longer hold the blade still. This is usually tight enough. Overtightening the blade makes its removal difficult.

teeth should point towards the front of the machine. The outer arbor washer (and blade stabilizer) is now placed on the arbor. Replace the arbor nut. Tighten it snugly against the blade, but do not overtighten it (Illus. 5-4). This can make removal very difficult.

Replace the throat plate (Illus. 5-5). Check the blade to be sure it is square with the table. Adjust the blade tilt if necessary. Replace the guard and proceed.

Common Table-Saw Cuts

The two most common table-saw cuts are rip cuts and crosscuts. Rip cuts are made with the grain and crosscuts are made across the grain.

Ripping Ripping is done using the fence as a guide. Set the distance between the fence and blade at the desired stock width. You may wish to allow extra width for planing off saw marks. This will depend on the type of blade and the quality of the

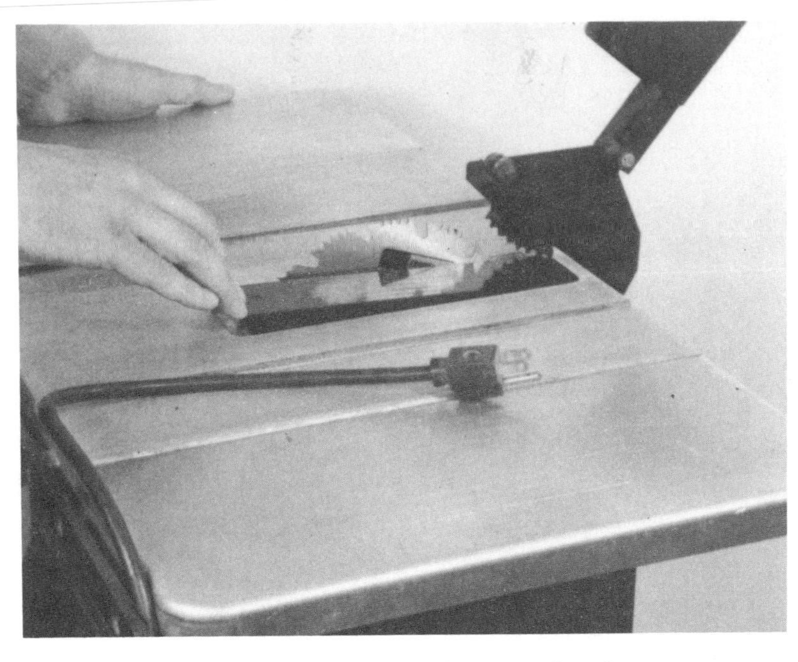

Illus. 5-5. Replace the throat plate. Make sure it is secured properly. Turn the blade over by hand to make sure it does not hit the throat plate.

cut. Measure the desired width from the face of a tooth on the blade (Illus. 5-6). The tooth should be one that is set or pointed towards the fence. This produces the most accurate measurement. On some fences, this setting can be made by using the scale on the fence. It is a good practice to check it for accuracy with a test cut. The cursor on the fence lines up with the scale on the fence rail to indicate the width of the rip. Lock the fence once the cursor is aligned.

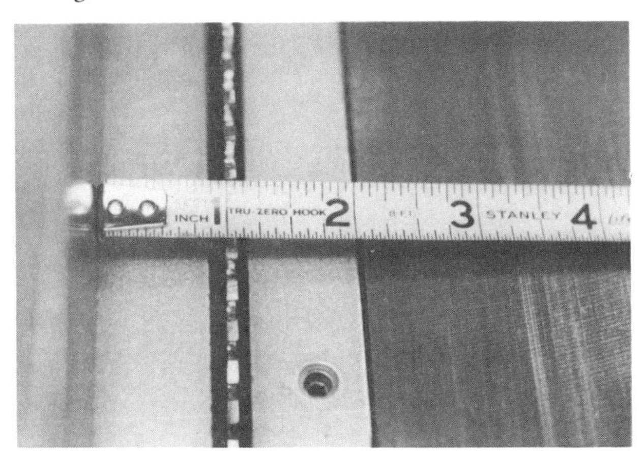

Illus. 5-6. Set the distance from the fence to a tooth that points toward the fence. This distance determines the rip dimension. The setup shown is for a 1-inch rip cut.

Set the blade height about ¼ inch above the stock and replace the guard and splitter. Inspect your stock. Place the truest edge against the fence. If the rip is narrower than 5 inches, be sure to use a push stick to guide the wood.

Turn on the saw and position yourself comfortably to the side of the blade. Right-handers usually stand to the left of the blade, and left-handers usually stand to the right. Guide the wood into the blade at a uniform speed (Illus. 5-7–5-12). If the blade slows down, you are feeding too fast. If the edges of your stock appear burned, you may be feeding too slowly, or you may be using a blade with too many teeth. Fine blades slow feed speed and generate more heat than coarse blades. This may also indicate a dull blade or blade binding.

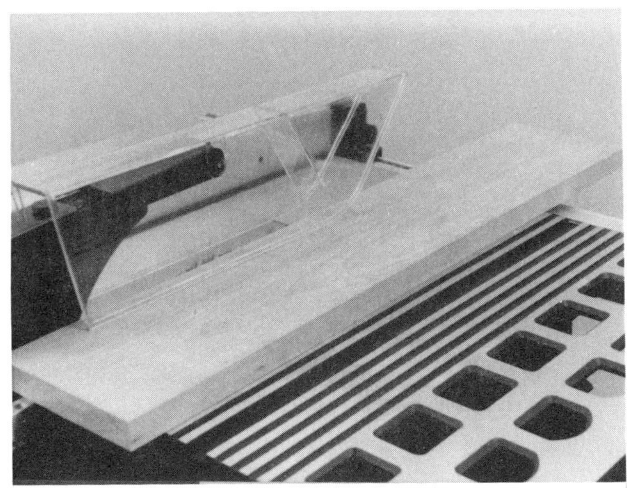

Illus. 5-7. Set blade height about ¼ inch above stock thickness. (Photo courtesy of Skil Power Tools.)

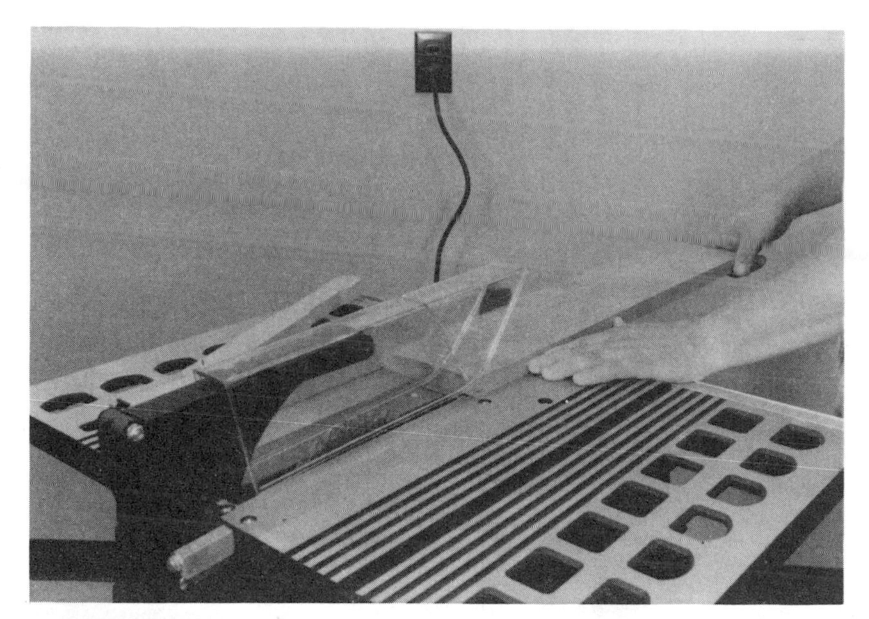

Illus. 5-8. Position the stock on the table and against the fence. Have your push stick in a convenient place. (Photo courtesy of Skil Power Tools.)

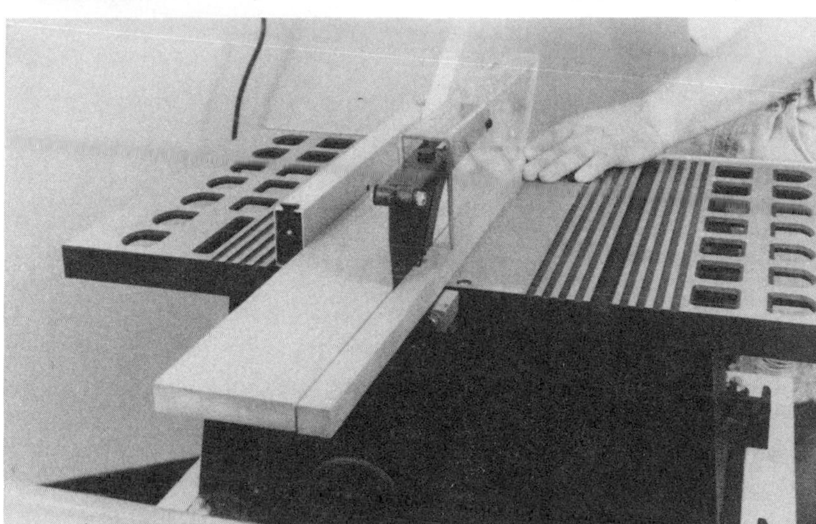

Illus. 5-9. Use the push stick to guide the piece as your hand nears the blade. (Photo courtesy of Skil Power Tools.)

Illus. 5-10. Stand clear of the kickback zone as you make the cut. Do not force the stock into the blade. (Photo courtesy of Skil Power Tools.)

Illus. 5-11. The dead-man roller will support the work as the cut is completed. It is set about ⅛ inch lower than the surface of the table saw.

Illus. 5-12. The workpiece exits the blade area before you stop. The cutoff stops next to the blade, but the anti-kickback pawl and guard hold the cutoff in place.

Illus. 5-13. This commercial device pulls stock toward the fence and acts as a guard on narrow rips.

Check the fence to be sure it is parallel to the blade. Some commercial devices can be used to hold stock against the fence (Illus. 5-13).

Guide the entire length of stock past the blade. Do not stop feeding the stock until its entire length is past the blade. If the piece stops while in contact with the blade and fence, a kickback could occur.

When ripping long pieces, use a dead man to support the wood (Illus. 5-14). Large, heavy pieces may require an extra person to handle and guide them safely (Illus. 5-15). Never try to rip stock that is too heavy for you to handle. When ripping strips off a piece of sheet stock, make the widest rip first. This allows most of the weight of the panel to balance on the table saw. This also minimizes the flexing in thin, lighter sheets and allows truer cuts. It may also be beneficial to cut the length of the panel in half before making the rip cut. This can be done on large table saws. It can also be done with a portable circular saw.

When working with large pieces, a helper or take-off person can make the job easier or more difficult. Communication is the key to making the job easier. If you are the take-off person, observe the following guidelines. If you are working with a take-off person, communicate these guidelines to him or her.

1. The operator of the saw is in charge. The take-off person follows his or her lead.
2. The take-off person supports the stock and may

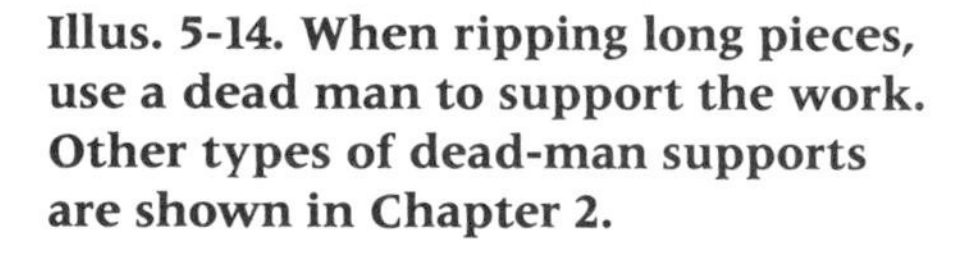

Illus. 5-14. When ripping long pieces, use a dead man to support the work. Other types of dead-man supports are shown in Chapter 2.

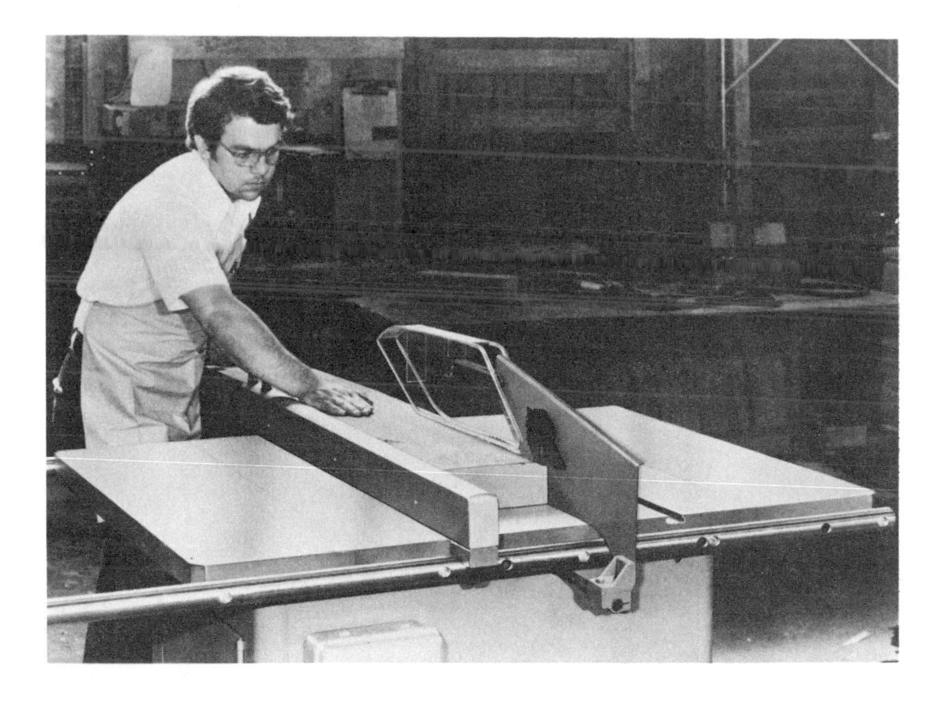

Illus. 5-15. Large, heavy pieces may require an extra person to support the stock on the way in or out. Avoid ripping heavy pieces of stock alone. They are difficult to handle, so control and guide them carefully.

lightly guide it. The operator is in control of the stock.
3. The operator feeds the work. The take-off person should not have to push or pull stock. If the take-off person causes the stock to bind, it could kick back and possibly injure the operator and/or the take-off person.
4. The take-off person must retain secure footing and balance, and avoid reaching or stretching. Reaching or stretching could cause additional problems if you were to fall toward the blade.
5. Keep a safe margin from the stock. The take-off person should not have to touch the stock until it is leaving the table. A kickback could pull you into the blade if you are too close.

Ripping Stock with Irregular Edges Stock with irregular edges can be ripped as long as a true edge guide is used. First, determine where you wish the rip cut to be, and then mark a line. Next, mark a line parallel to the line in the waste area (Illus. 5-16). Attach a straightedge to the line using nails or screws (Illus. 5-17). Position the rip fence, and make the rip cut (Illus. 5-18). Keep the straightedge

Illus. 5-16. Mark the rip line on the irregular edge, and then mark a parallel line on the opposite edge.

against the fence for the entire cut. Remove the straightedge and cut the opposite side. The first cut is now a true edge, and it will ride along the fence (Illus. 5-19).

Specialty devices can be clamped to a straightedge (Illus. 5-20) to do the same job. The clamps do not damage the stock. Cutting is done in the same way discussed above (Illus. 5-21).

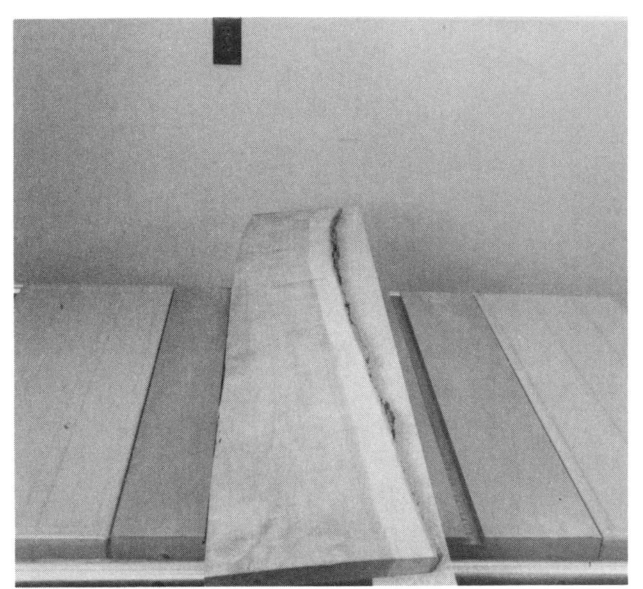

Illus. 5-17. This straightedge was nailed to the waste area on the layout line.

Illus. 5-18. The straightedge rides along the fence and controls the stock. The cutting line travels along the blade.

Illus. 5-19. The straightedge is removed, and the opposite edge is ripped parallel to the original cut.

Illus. 5-20. These metal clamps attach to a straightedge. The work is clamped to the opposite side.

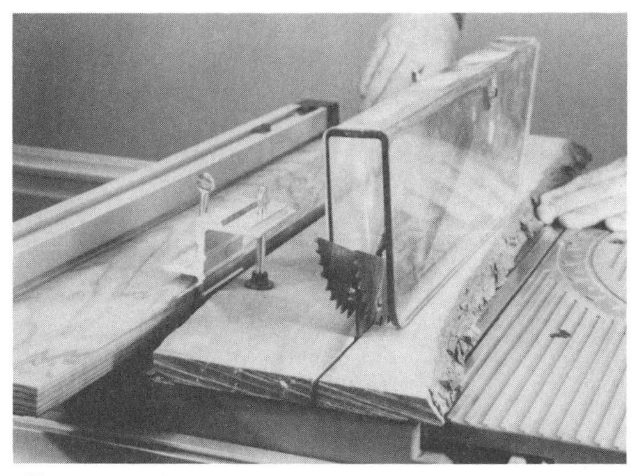

Illus. 5-21. The irregular edge is cut parallel to the straightedge. This device can also be used to cut a slight taper.

Ripping Narrow Pieces Ripping narrow pieces can be dangerous if not done carefully. Narrow pieces cannot usually be cut with the guard in position. This is because the push stick will not go between the fence and the guard. In addition, thin stock tends to climb the blade and bounce or kick.

A plywood fixture can be made to rip narrow pieces using the guard (Illus. 5-22). A notch cut along the edge leaves a heel that will grip the work. The fixture rides along the fence and allows clearance between the guard and fence (Illus. 5-23). Use a push stick to hold the stock against the fixture. Strips will be uniform in size (Illus. 5-24), and the operation will be much safer.

Thin stock that must be ripped into narrow pieces can be cut with the help of a featherboard. The guard is removed, and the fence is positioned. The featherboard is clamped to the fence. The blade must be beneath the table when this is done (Illus. 5-25). The blade is then turned on and raised into the featherboard. Stock may now be ripped. The featherboard acts as a guard and a hold-down (Illus. 5-26).

Also see Narrow Ripping Jigs and Narrow Rip Cuts by Subtraction on pages 105–108.

Ripping with a Power Feeder For production jobs, a power feeder can be used to rip stock to size. The power feeder will reduce operator fatigue and keep the operator's hands away from the blade. The

Illus. 5-22. A plywood fixture can be made to aid you in ripping narrow strips. This plywood fixture has a notch cut along one edge to grip the work.

Illus. 5-23. This fixture allows you to use the guard when you are ripping narrow strips.

quality of the cut will also be enhanced due to a uniform chip load.

The column which supports the power feeder is usually bolted to the saw to the operator's left on the out-feed side. The corner of the table is usually drilled for the base (Illus. 5-27–5-29). The space between the wheels may be immediately above the blade. The power-feeder motor is turned inward

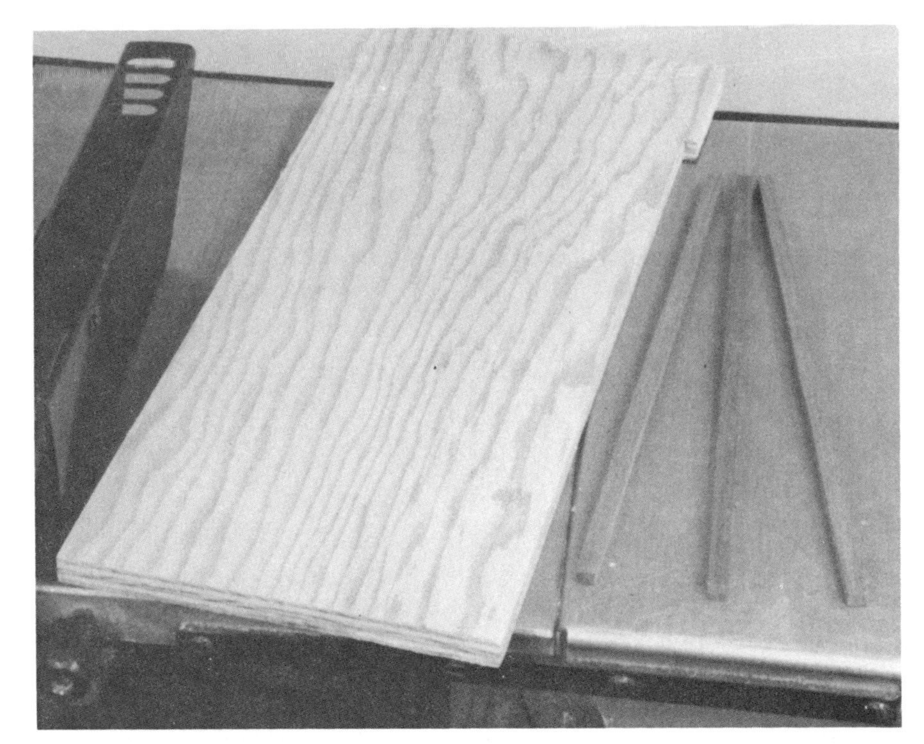

Illus. 5-24. The notch on the fixture grips the work for feeding, but it also minimizes the chance of kickback. Often, the anti-kickback pawls will not ride on a narrow strip of wood and function correctly.

Illus. 5-25. Thin, narrow strips tend to rattle and flutter when ripped. A featherboard can eliminate this problem. The featherboard is clamped over the blade's path. The blade is dropped below the table and elevated into the featherboard (while the table saw is running).

Illus. 5-26. As the thin strips are ripped, the featherboard eliminates rattle and acts as a guard by covering the blade.

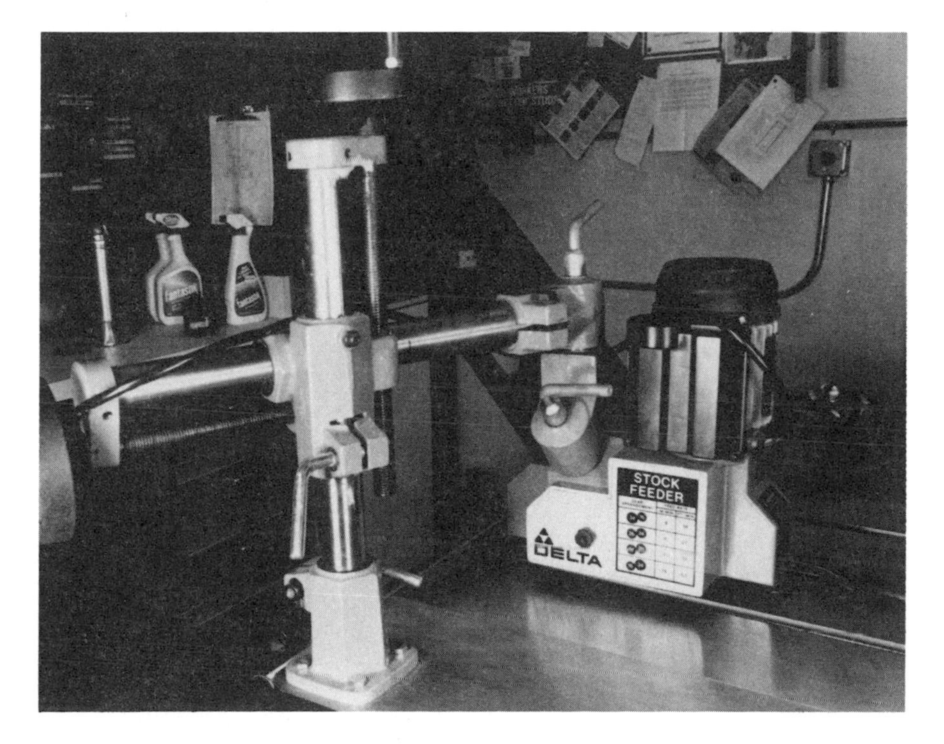

Illus. 5-27. The power feeder is mounted on the out-feed side at the operator's left. It should be bolted to the extension wing.

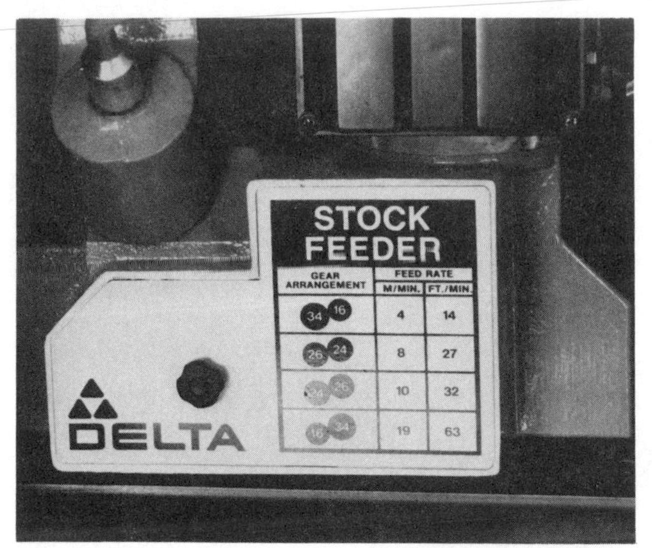

Illus. 5-28. This power feeder has four speeds. Speed changes are made by moving gears which are behind the plate.

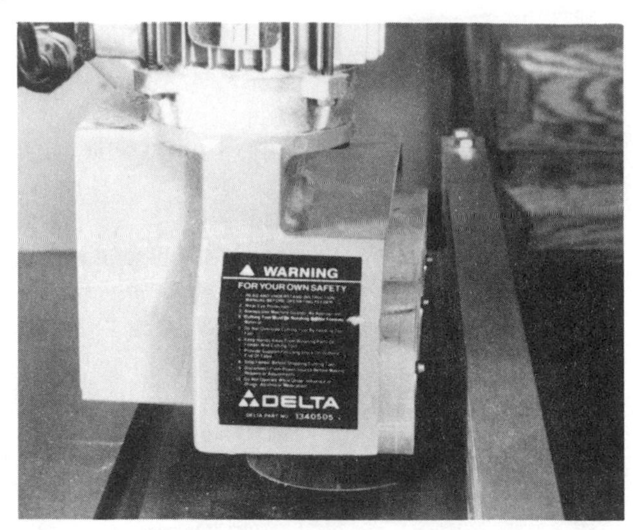

Illus. 5-30. When the power feeder is positioned for ripping, the wheel at the out-feed end is about ⅛ inch closer to the fence. This keeps the stock tight against the fence.

Illus. 5-29. The gears are moved to achieve different speeds. Make sure the power is disconnected when making these changes. Also be certain to replace this plate after making the changes.

Illus. 5-31. Note how the blade is positioned between the wheels of the power feeder. Make sure that the blade does not cut the wheels. The wheels are ¼ inch closer to the table than the top of the workpiece.

towards the fence at the out-feed end about ⅛ inch (Illus. 5-30). This will force stock against the fence as the cut is made. The wheels are ¼ inch closer to the tabletop than the thinnest piece of wood they are expected to feed. Once the height is set, the wheels are also checked to ensure that the entire wheel surface is parallel to the table and not in contact with the blade (Illus. 5-31). Secure all clamps in place and check for any movement.

Turn on the power feeder to be sure that it is turning in the correct direction. The feed speed should be the lowest possible speed for initial setup. Turn on the saw and guide stock against the fence and into the feeder (Illus. 5-32). Keep your hands and fingers in a safe position. As the power feeder begins controlling the stock, your fingers could be pinched between the tabletop and the underside of the board.

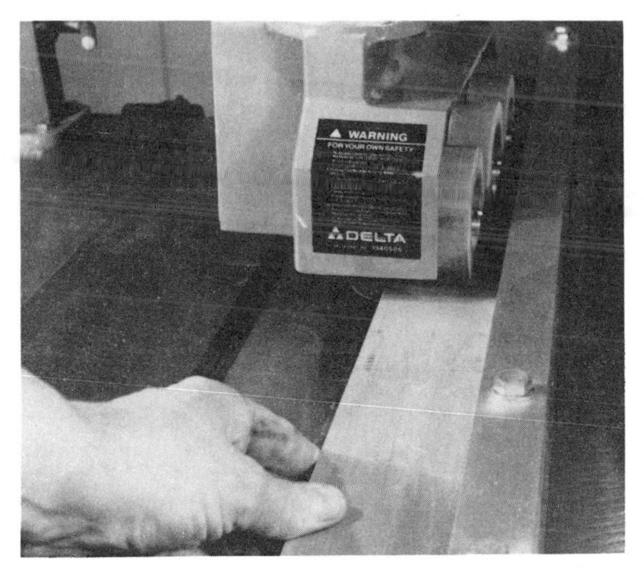

Illus. 5-32. Guide the work into the power feeder with the work's true edge against the fence. Keep your fingers away from the underside of the workpiece, where they could be pinched between the table and the underside of the work.

Illus. 5-33. Once the wheels are all engaged with the wood, they will guide the work past the blade.

The power feeder should guide the work through and past the blade with no problems (Illus. 5-33). If the feed speed is too slow, burning may result, so increase the feed speed. Feed speed is dependent on the number of teeth on the blade, the saw's horsepower, the hardness of the wood, and the wood's thickness. Feed speed is a matter of trial-and-error setting.

In order to work safely with a power feeder, be sure to follow these precautions:

1. Make certain that all the settings are correct and that all the clamps are tightened securely. Also make sure that the fence is positioned correctly and locked in position.
2. Make certain that the blade is not set too high. It could cut into the wheels of the power feeder.
3. Stand to the side when feeding a saw with a power feeder. A power feeder reduces, but does not entirely eliminate, the likelihood of a kickback.
4. Never allow stock to come into contact with the back teeth of the saw blade. The stock could get trapped between the power feeder and the saw blade. This could cause a kickback.
5. Beware of pinch points. The power feeder can pinch your fingers between the board and table. Never wear gloves. They could pull your hand into the blade.
6. Be sure to observe all other standard safety practices outlined for table-saw use as personal protective equipment.

Narrow Ripping Jigs The narrow ripping jigs described here consist of a fence (Illus. 5-34) and a push block (Illus. 5-35). Study the drawings and make a set if you are ripping long, narrow strips. The fence is attached to the metal saw fence with clamps or screws. The distance to the blade is set from the auxiliary wooden fence. Stock is then ripped in the normal fashion (Illus. 5-36). Once the end of the piece nears the table (Illus. 5-37), the push block is positioned. Stock is guided through

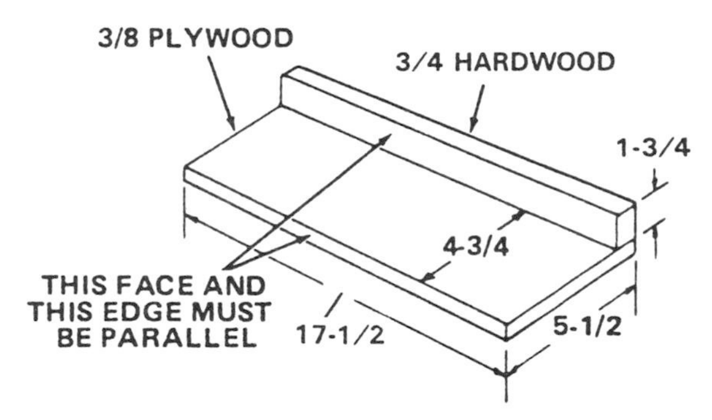

Illus. 5-34. A narrow rip requires a fence similar to the one shown here. The fence should be about as long as your table saw's table. (Drawing courtesy of Skil Power Tools.)

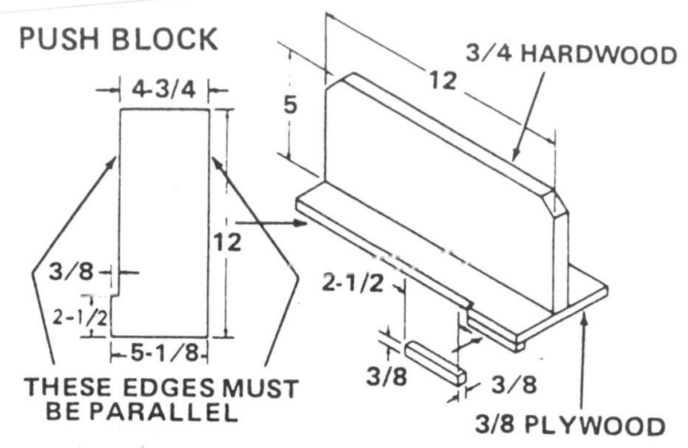

Illus. 5-35. The push blocks ride on the wooden fence. The parts are held together with glue and wood screws. (Drawing courtesy of Skil Power Tools.)

the blade using the push block (Illus. 5-38). The push block is designed to allow generous clearance for your hand between the fence and guard. This ripping method allows anti-kickback protection and makes contact with the blade almost impossible.

Narrow Rip Cuts by Subtraction The subtraction method can be used for short runs of narrow strips. Suppose, for example, that you wanted to cut ¾-inch-thick stock 18 inches long into ⅛-inch strips, and you needed about 20 of them. To make these pieces, subtract each piece from the edge of your workpiece.

The first step is to "zero" your fence with your

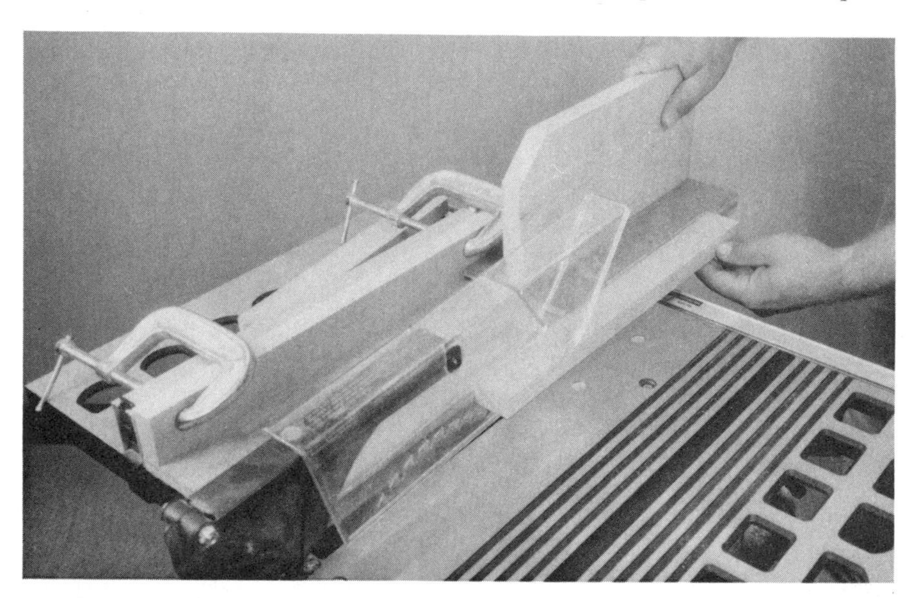

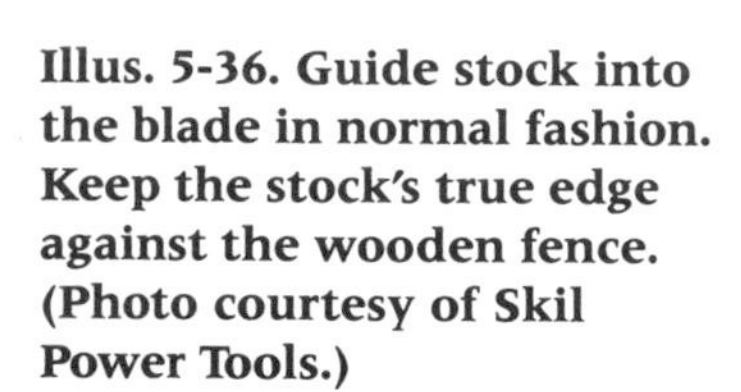

Illus. 5-36. Guide stock into the blade in normal fashion. Keep the stock's true edge against the wooden fence. (Photo courtesy of Skil Power Tools.)

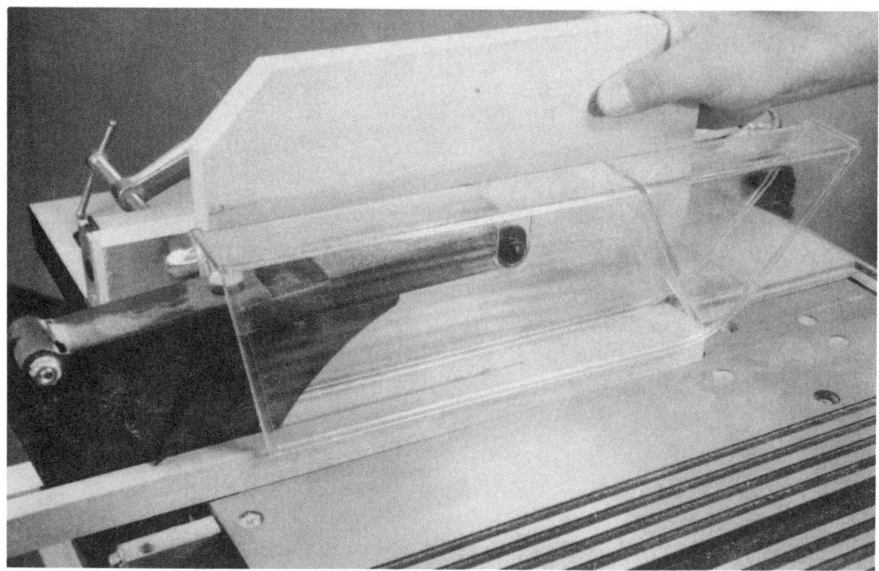

Illus. 5-37. The push block guides the stock past the guard and blade. (Photo courtesy of Skil Power Tools.)

Illus. 5-38. This fixture makes the ripping of narrow stock safe and efficient. The guard does the job it was intended to do. (Photo courtesy of Skil Power Tools.)

blade (Illus. 5-39). Do this by butting the fence to the blade and setting the fence cursor on the zero point. Do this with the power disconnected. Next, cut the pieces to a fixed widest width possible: 5 inches or so. Then move the fence in ¼ inch. This will produce a ⅛-inch strip and a ⅛-inch saw kerf

Illus. 5-39. When using the scale on your saw to set it to make narrow rip cuts, "zero" the blade to the fence. To do this, set the cursor to zero while the fence is touching the blade. Make this adjustment with the power disconnected. (Photo courtesy of Skil Power Tools.)

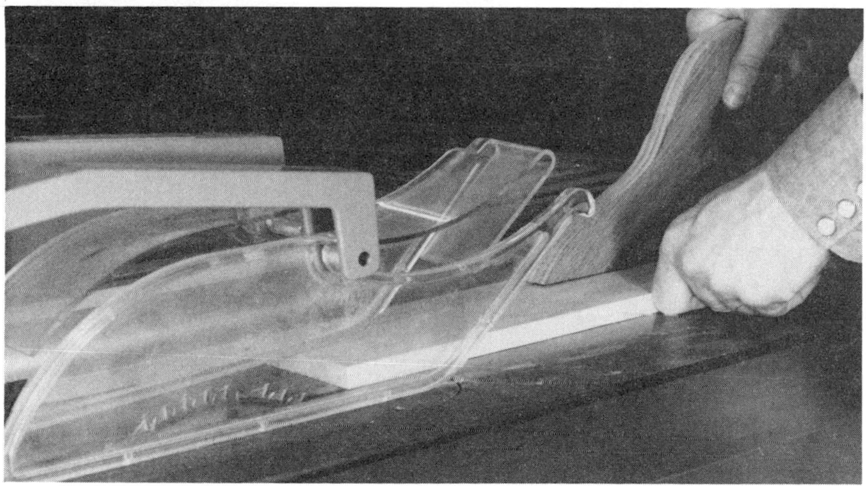

Illus. 5-40. The fence is moved ¼ inch toward the blade for the first thin rip. This accounts for the ⅛-inch saw kerf and the ⅛-inch strip.

Illus. 5-41. The thin strip is free when the cut is complete. A thin strip trapped between the blade and fence is more likely to kick back.

(Illus. 5-40 and 5-41). Keep cutting the strips and moving the fence towards the blade. You'll get four strips per inch of width; you'll need another inch to allow clearance for the fence on each piece. As you get close to the guard, you will need a push stick to get between the guard and fence (Illus. 5-42). There are other methods of ripping narrow strips, but they are not as quick as this method and they do not use guards during the entire operation (Illus. 5-43).

Crosscutting Crosscutting is usually done with the miter gauge. A shooting table or board may also be used (Illus. 5-44). When crosscutting an individual piece, the usual procedure is to mark and cut it along the layout line. A pencil line is most common, but a utility knife is sometimes used. The utility knife cuts the wood fibers and minimizes tear-out along the cut (Illus. 5-45).

To ensure that a square cut will be made, make sure the miter gauge is perpendicular to the blade (Illus. 5-46) and the blade is perpendicular to the table (Illus. 5-47). Use a square to check the angle. Raise the blade to full height and position the miter gauge across from the blade. Place the head of the square against the blade, and the blade of the square against the miter gauge. Check the angle, and adjust the miter gauge if necessary. Make sure the set of the blade does not tilt the square for an incorrect adjustment. Keep the square off the blade's teeth.

To make a crosscut, place the stock against the

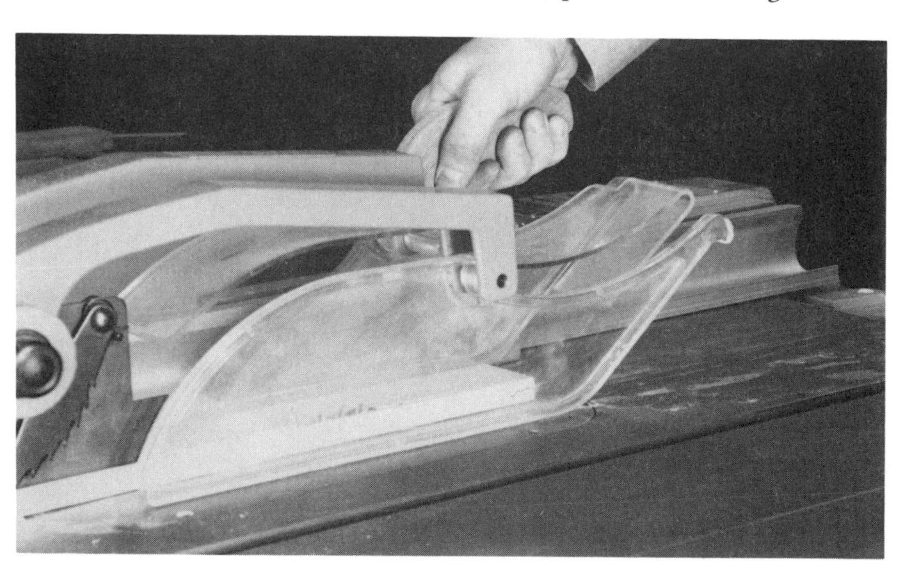

Illus. 5-42. As the workpiece gets narrower, a push stick could be used to guide the stock.

Illus. 5-43. These thin strips are identical in thickness. Care in setting the fence will ensure precise results.

Illus. 5-44. A shop-made shooting board can be used for crosscutting. The shooting board cuts stock at a fixed angle, while the miter gauge can be adjusted to different angles.

Illus. 5-45. Marking the layout line with a utility knife will reduce tear-out of the wood fibers when the cut is made. A pencil can also be used for less exact work.

Illus. 5-46. Before making a square cut, make sure the blade is perpendicular to the miter gauge.

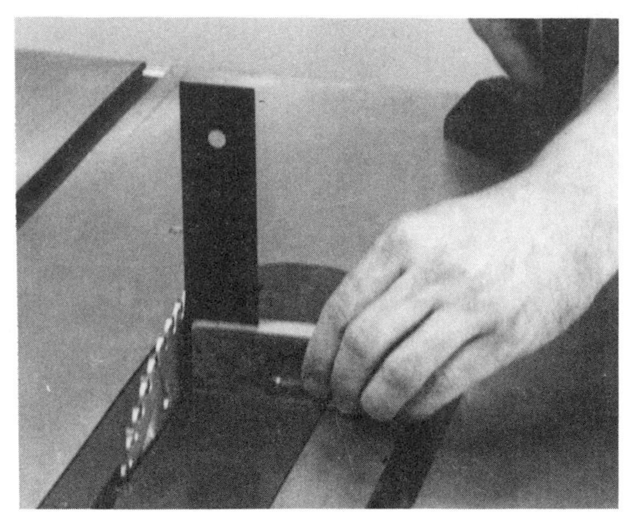

Illus. 5-47. In addition to being perpendicular to the miter gauge, the blade must also be perpendicular to the table.

miter gauge and move up to the blade. Your layout line should line up with a tooth that points towards the layout line (Illus. 5-48).

Move back from the blade with the stock held firmly against the miter guard, and replace the guard. Turn on the saw and advance the miter gauge, holding the stock firmly (Illus. 5-49 and 5-50). Feed the stock into the blade at a uniform speed. When the piece is cut, retract the miter gauge. Keep a firm grip on the stock until it is clear of the blade.

Note: When crosscutting, keep the fence well away from the blade. Any cut-off stock trapped between the blade and fence could kick back. Keep the table clear of scraps as you work; accumulated scrap can also be a hazard. Clear the scrap with the saw turned off.

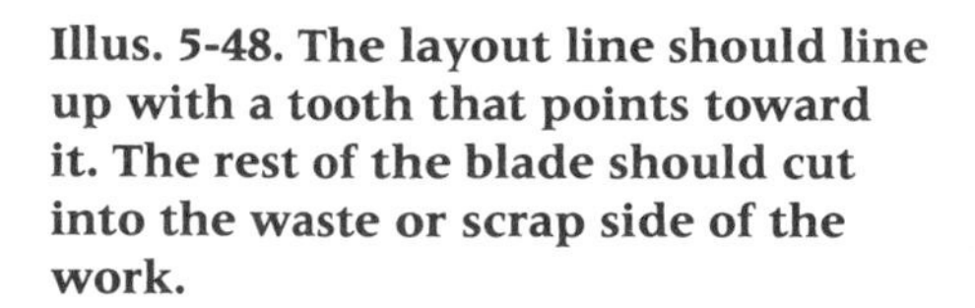

Illus. 5-48. The layout line should line up with a tooth that points toward it. The rest of the blade should cut into the waste or scrap side of the work.

Illus. 5-49. Advance the miter gauge into the blade at a moderate speed when crosscutting. Feeding too slowly wastes time, and feeding too quickly increases tear-out. Keep the good, or exposed, face of your work up so that any tear-out occurs on the back or unexposed side of the work.

Illus. 5-50. You can check your crosscut for accuracy with a square. Make any needed adjustments to the miter gauge if the setting is incorrect.

An auxiliary face attached to the miter gauge can also help you to make accurate cuts. After a saw kerf has been cut in the auxiliary face, a cutting line can be aligned with the kerf (Illus. 5-51). This ensures that the cut will be accurate and that tear-out

Illus. 5-51. The auxiliary face on this miter gauge has been cut by the saw blade. Align the crosscut line with the edge of the saw kerf for an accurate cut.

will be minimized. The piece of the face which extends beyond the saw kerf sweeps the scrap away from the blade, thus reducing the likelihood of a kickback (Illus. 5-52). The auxiliary face should be about 1 to 1½ inches higher than the stock you are crosscutting.

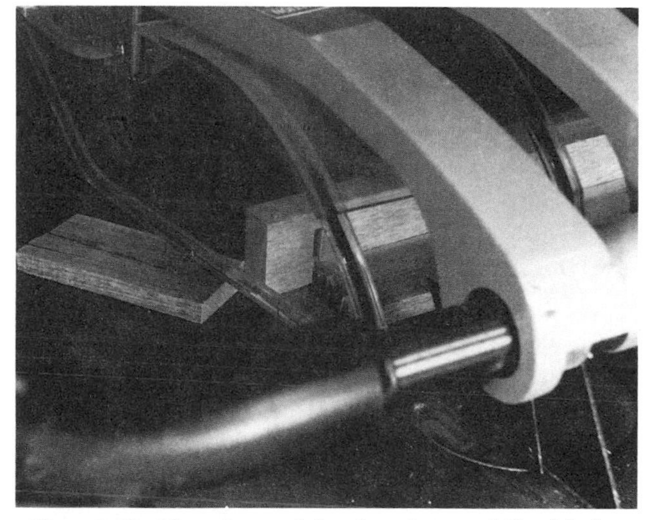

Illus. 5-52. The piece of the face beyond the blade on this auxiliary fence sweeps the stock away from the blade. This reduces the chance of a kickback. The auxiliary fence is about 1½ inches higher than the workpiece.

When crosscutting large panels, it may be necessary to reverse the miter gauge (Illus. 5-53) in the slot. This is because the tongue on the miter gauge is too short to reach the slot when located behind the stock. If the tongue will not stay engaged in the slot for the entire cut, shut the saw off midway into the cut. After the blade stops, reverse the miter gauge (Illus. 5-54), and proceed. It is also possible to clamp a straightedge on the panel (Illus. 5-55) and allow it to ride along the table edge. The straightedge becomes the control surface for the cut. Make sure that the end of the saw is parallel with the miter slot, or the cut may not be accurate, and there will be increased tear-out because the saw blade will not be parallel to the cutting line.

It is frequently necessary to crosscut several pieces to the same length. To eliminate layout of individual pieces, a stop rod or a stop block may be used. A stop block is a true piece of stock that is clamped to the table, fence, or miter gauge. It locates one end of the part. This end should already be square. The distance from that end to the blade is the length of the desired part. When the stop block is clamped to the fence (Illus. 5-56–5-60) or table (Illus. 5-61–5-64), it should not be near the blade. Keep the stop block towards the front of the table.

Illus. 5-53. Sometimes the miter gauge has to be reversed when wide panels are being crosscut. This is because the stock is wider than the tongue on the miter gauge. The miter gauge has to be reversed in the middle of a cut.

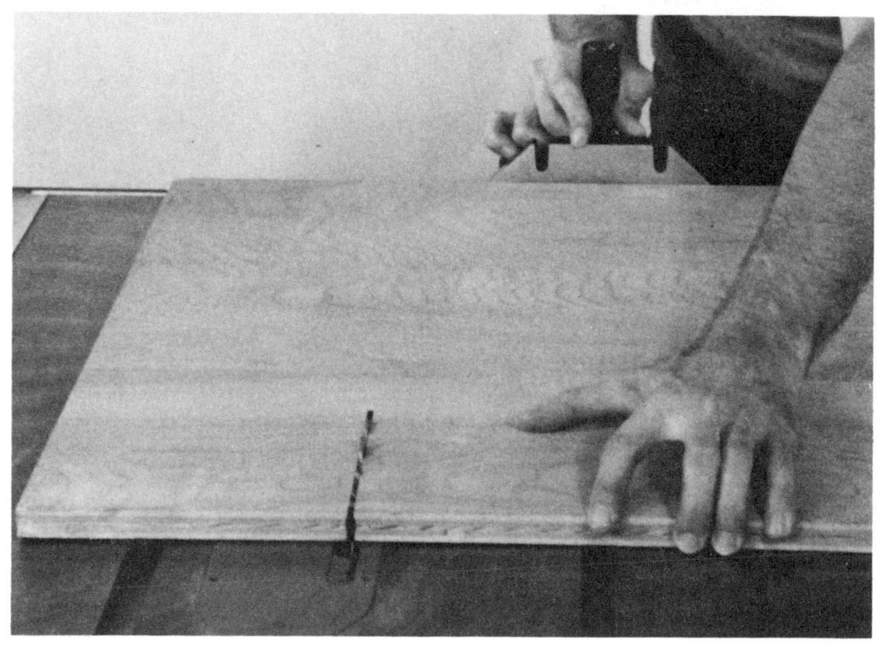

Illus. 5-54. When the stock is on the table, shut off the saw. Allow the blade to come to a complete stop. Reverse the miter gauge and proceed with the cut.

Illus. 5-55. A straightedge clamped to the work can be used as a fence on large pieces. The straightedge rides along the end of the table.

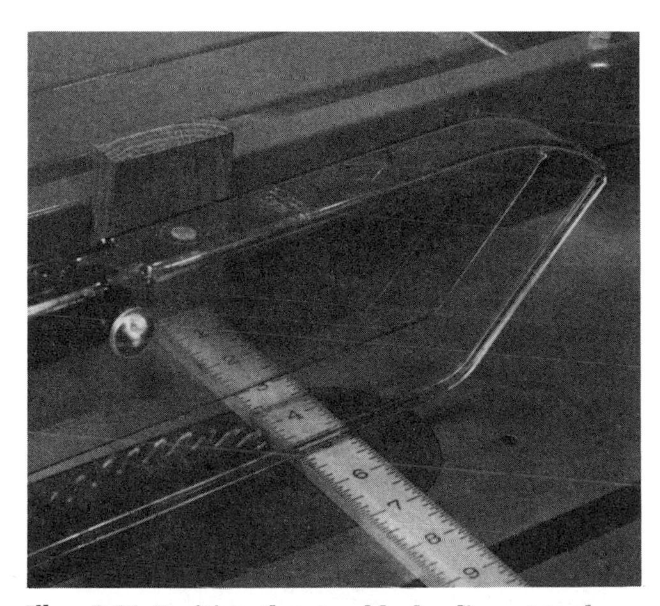

Illus. 5-56. Position the stop block adjacent to the blade to determine the fence position. Lock the fence at the desired setting.

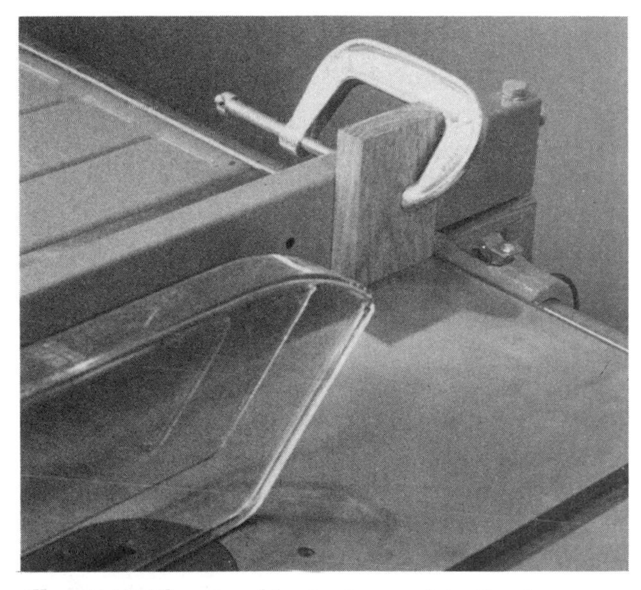

Illus. 5-57. The stop block clamped to the fence positions stock for cutting. All parts are cut uniformly and quickly.

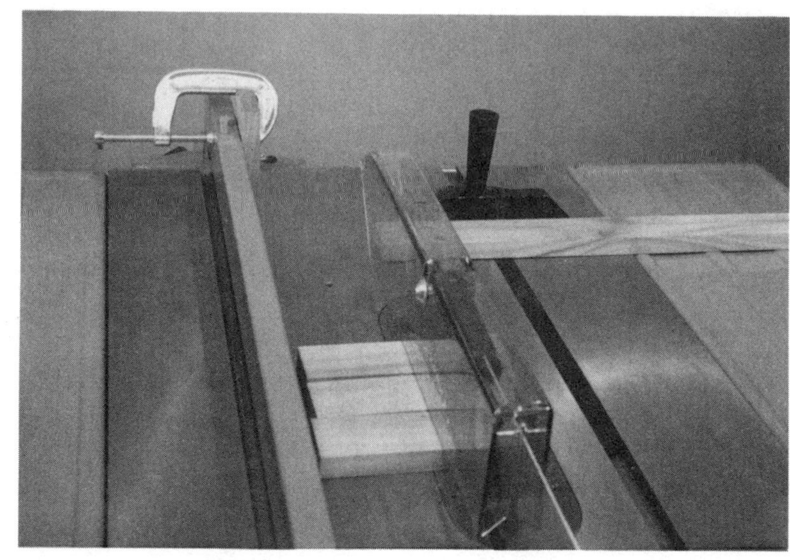

Illus. 5-58. The extra space between the blade and fence keeps the parts from being trapped between them. All parts are cut uniformly and quickly.

Illus. 5-59. The narrower piece here does not touch the blade and fence, but the wider piece does. The clearance varies according to the width of the workpiece.

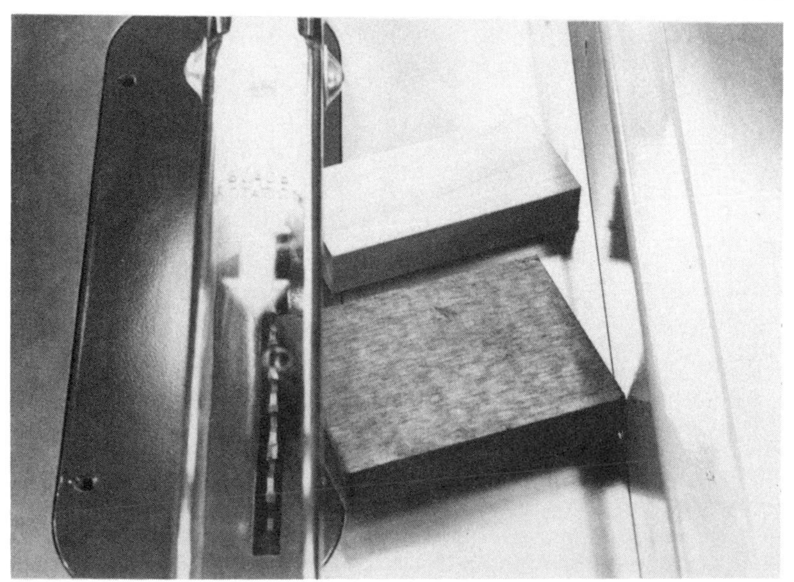

Illus. 5-60. Measure the diagonal distance across the cutoff. The clearance between the blade and the fence should be greater than the diagonal dimension of the cutoff.

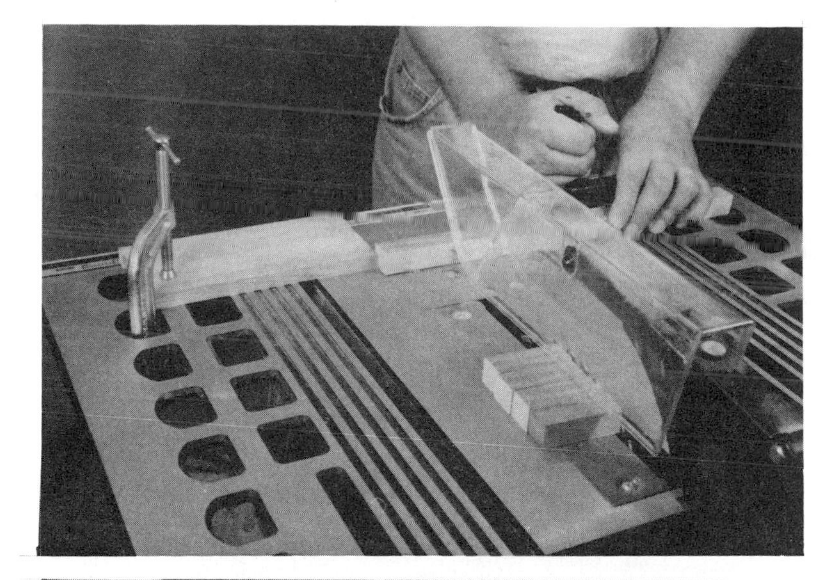

Illus. 5-61. A stop can be clamped to the table. Keep it well away from the blade so there will be no kickback. (Photo courtesy of Skil Power Tools.)

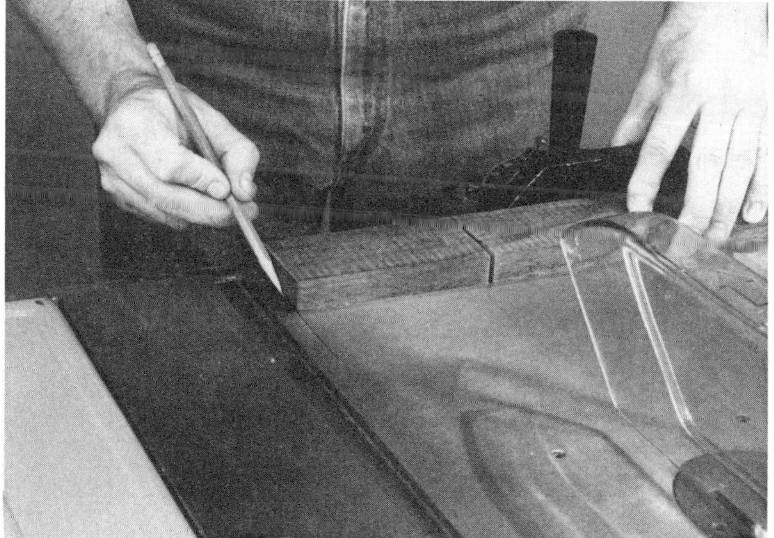

Illus. 5-62. The easiest way to position the stop block is to partially cut a setup piece on the layout line. The piece is then backed up and the table is marked.

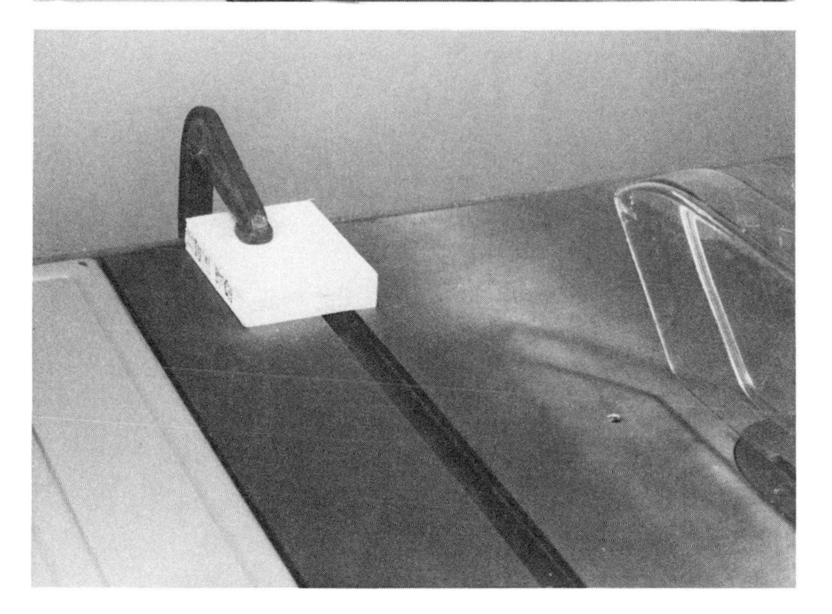

Illus. 5-63. The stop block is aligned with the mark and clamped securely in position.

Illus. 5-64. Complete the cut and check the piece for accurate layout.

This will eliminate a pinching problem and prevent kickbacks.

Note: The stop block used has to be big enough to ensure that the distance between the blade and fence is greater than the diagonal measurement of the parts you are cutting. If this distance is not greater, one corner could contact the blade while the other corner diagonally contacts the blade. This would result in a kickback. Clamping the stock block to the table and removing the fence eliminates the problem.

A stop block can be clamped to the shooting board (Illus. 5-65) or the miter gauge. It can also be clamped to a piece of stock attached to the miter gauge (Illus. 5-66). The clamp should be adjusted so that vision or movement is not impaired. A clamp of the correct size will minimize this problem.

Illus. 5-65. A stop block has been clamped to the shooting board to control the length of the parts being cut. The square end of the part is butted to the stop block.

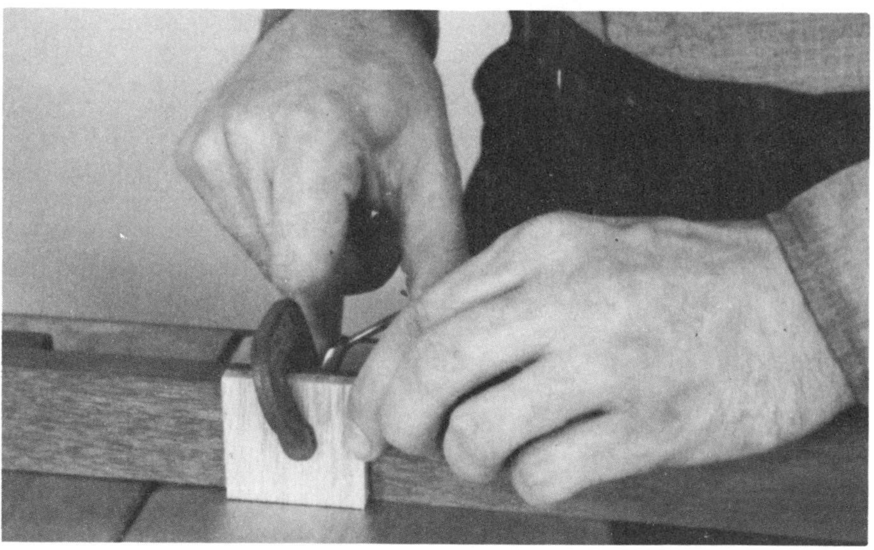

Illus. 5-66. For longer parts, the stop block can be clamped (or screwed) to a piece of stock that has been attached to the miter gauge.

Illus. 5-67. A stop rod can also be used to crosscut parts to length. The square end of the workpiece is butted against the hook, and the cut is made. Make sure to keep the stop rod out of the blade's path.

Illus. 5-68. Notice how all parts not being cut are stacked well away from the work area. All scrap has also been cleared away. This is a safe work area. Note the rolling table on this production saw.

The stop rod is an accessory made for the miter gauge. It attaches to either side of the miter gauge. The stop rod is adjusted to the correct stock length and locked in position. The stock is held against the miter gauge. One end of the stock touches the stop rod (Illus, 5-67). The other end is then cut to the desired length. Make sure that the end that touches the stop rod has been squared before you make the cut. A precision setup does little good when the stock is not square.

Note: The most common mistake made with the stop rod is to run it into the saw blade. Double-check the stop-rod position and blade height before you make a cut. Failure to do so could damage the stop rod or the saw blade.

When cutting several pieces, work carefully. Do not feed too fast, or grain tear-out will increase. Keep extra pieces well away from the blade (Illus. 5-68), and do not allow scrap to accumulate.

Cutting Plywood and Sheet Stock

Plywood and other sheet stock can be difficult to cut on the table saw in the home shop. The home shop table usually has little surface area to support a cut with the grain, and the fence does not extend far enough to allow a crosscut through the center of an eight-foot panel. In most cases, table saws with enough table area for cutting plywood are too large for the home shop. These table saws require so much floor area that there would not be enough room for any other tools or assembly of the objects being built.

Illus. 5-69. Keep an eye on the fence as you move forward with the sheet stock.

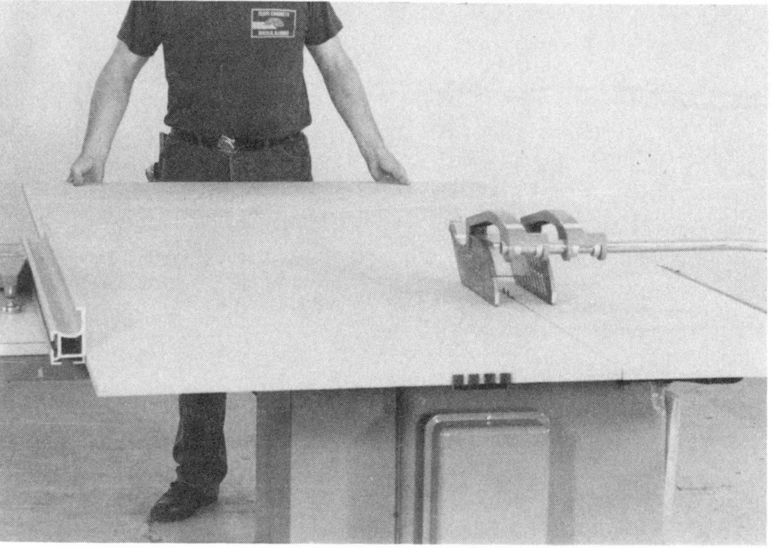

Illus. 5-70. If you stay aligned with the fence, the cut will be true and there will be less chance of binding.

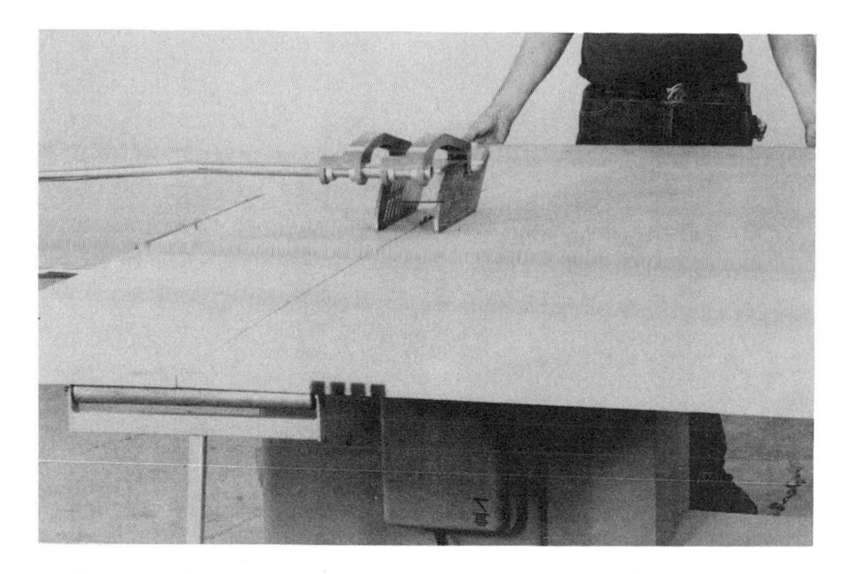

Illus. 5-71. A roller stand or other take-off device should be used to support both sides of the saw kerf as cutting progresses.

If you make rip cuts first, a temporary take-off table can be used to support the work as it is being cut. When making a long plywood cut, keep an eye on the fence as well as the cut (Illus. 5-69–5-71). Exert a slight force against the stock to keep it in alignment with the fence. It is recommended that you have someone help you handle the stock. An extra pair of hands will increase control over the panel and reduce physical strain. This person should review the rules for a take-off person in the section on ripping.

If the sheet stock must be crosscut first, most home woodworkers will cut the sheet into smaller pieces with a portable circular saw. The pieces are more manageable, and can be cut into parts with the table saw. There is less chance of tear-out at the table saw when stock control increases.

When crosscutting sheet stock with a portable circular saw, be sure to utilize the factory edges of the sheet. The factory edges are the edges at the perimeter of the sheet. These edges were cut at the factory and are smooth, true, and perpendicular to each other. Be sure to check them for damage from handling before using them.

After the sheet stock has been cut into manageable pieces with a portable circular saw, use these factory edges to control stock on the table saw (Illus. 5-72–5-77). The factory edges can ride against the miter gauge or fence. The parts can be cut using true edges or control surfaces.

Whenever you cut sheet stock to size, planning is an important element. Develop a stock-cutting sheet before you begin. Do this using graph paper with one-inch squares. Draw a rectangle around an area four squares wide and eight squares long. This becomes a model for a four- × eight-foot piece of sheet stock (Illus. 5-78). If you are working with plywood, you may wish to pencil in some grain on the rectangle. This will ensure that the grain direction is correct on the parts you are cutting.

The stock-cutting sheet helps you reduce waste and plan the most efficient cutting sequence. You can number the saw cuts to make the cutting operation more efficient. The cutting sequence is determined by the longest possible cut. Make the longest cut first, and then proceed to the next longest cut. For economy of motion, it may be more practical to

Illus. 5-72. The miter-gauge extension increases the crosscutting capacity of this saw.

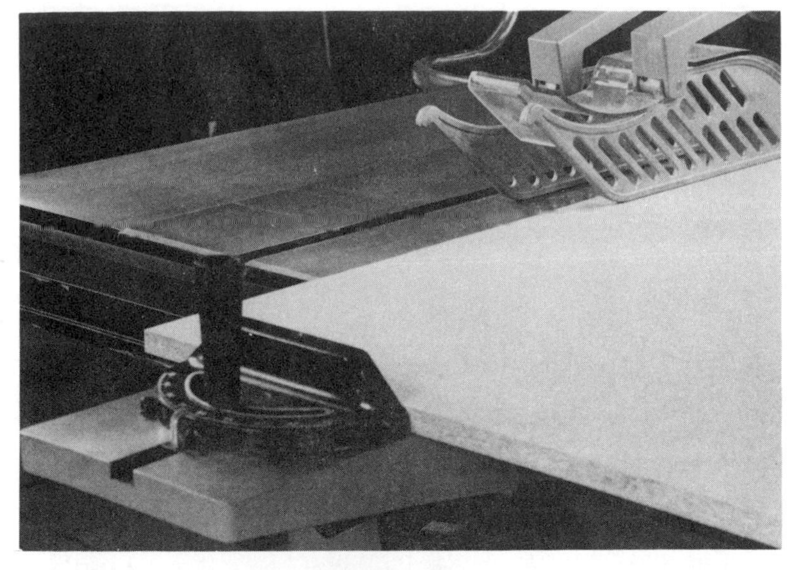

Illus. 5-73. The extension is secured to the fence with a clamping action. The slot in the casting is aligned with the slot in the table.

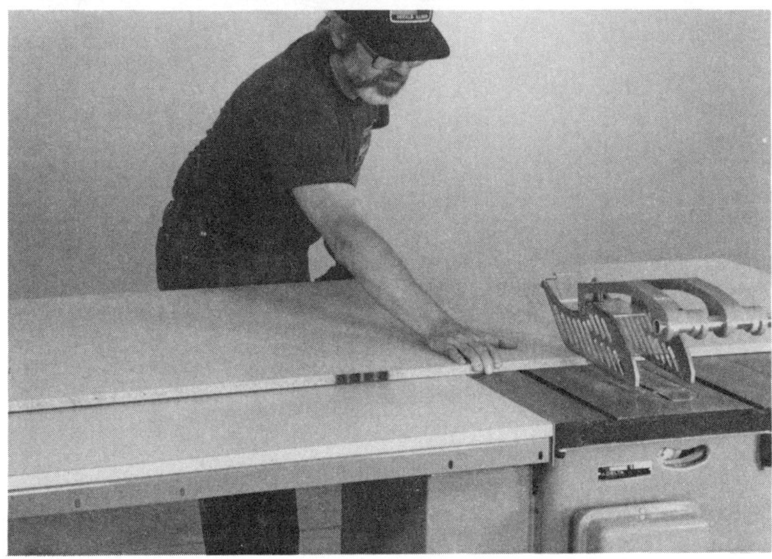

Illus. 5-74. With the extension in position, you can crosscut wider pieces of sheet stock, but not those 48 inches wide.

Illus. 5-75. This specialty miter gauge has a stop which enables you to cut pieces to exact length.

Illus. 5-76. With the stop retracted, shorter lengths can be cut to exact size.

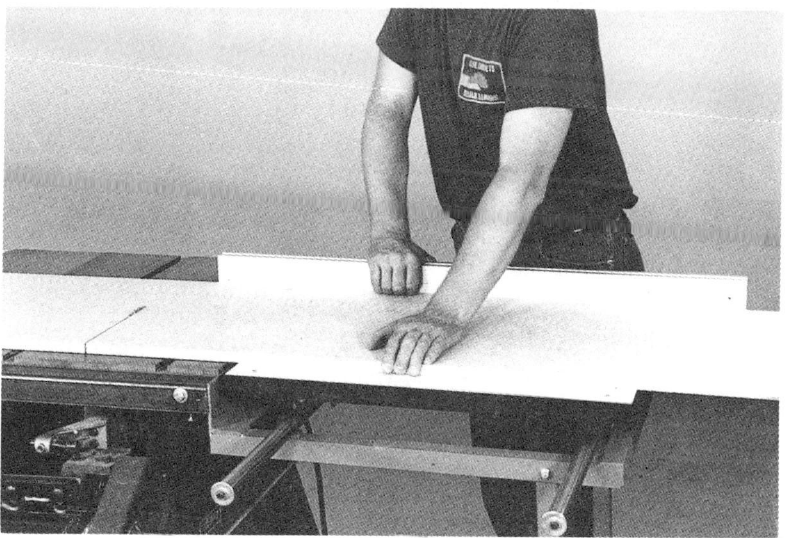

Illus. 5-77. This sliding table is a retrofit to most contractor or cabinet saws. It makes it easier to handle large pieces of sheet stock.

make all crosscuts first or all rip cuts first. Experience will help you to plan the best cutting sequence.

If you are cutting fine-veneer plywood, a carbide-tipped blade with alternate top bevel teeth will work the best. The points on the teeth cut away the edges of the veneer first, so that there is little chance of tear-out.

If you are cutting particleboard or other panel stock, a triple-chip blade will resist the resin and glue in the panel. An alternate top bevel blade would dull much faster in particleboard.

If tear-out is a problem in fine-veneer plywood, apply masking tape to the cutting line. The masking tape holds the veneers down on both sides of the blade while the cut is being made. When the cut is complete, remove the tape carefully. It can actually lift the veneer off the sheet if it is removed too quickly. Work slowly and carefully.

Another way of reducing tear-out is to cut through the face veneers with a utility knife. This cut weakens the veneers. When the blade cuts through, the veneers begin to tear, but they break evenly along their weakest point, the scored line. The other face of the plywood may tear out, but it will not be exposed.

If tear-out is visible only on one side of the kerf, there may be an alignment problem with the saw. Measure the distance from the miter slot to the blade where it goes through the throat plate. Do this at both the in-feed and out-feed sides of the blade. If the measurements are not the same, there

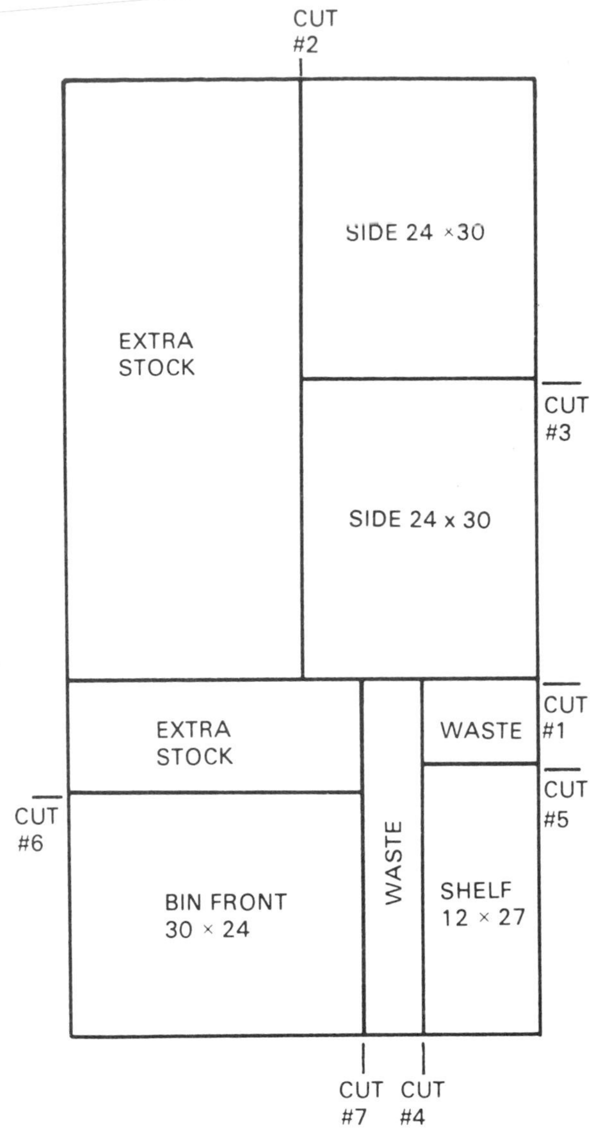

Illus. 5-78. The stock-cutting sheet is usually drawn on graph paper. It is a plan for cutting plywood or sheet stock. This plan saves time and reduces waste. The plan shown here is for a 4-foot-wide by 8-foot-long piece of sheet stock.

is an alignment problem. Also, check the fence to be sure that it is parallel to the miter slot. If it is not, the back of the blade could be binding on the work at the back of the blade.

It will be easier to cut sheet stock if your table saw is equipped with a rolling table. This is because control over the sheet stock is spread over a longer surface. Less energy is required to control the stock because the rolling table reduces friction and makes the feed more uniform.

Some home-shop woodworkers use a shooting board to control larger plywood parts. The shooting board provides a longer control surface and reduces the chance that the workpiece will twist or bind during a cut.

Cutting Miters

Miters are rip cuts or crosscuts made to any angle other than 90 degrees. The most common mitering jobs are crosscuts on picture frames and door or window trim. These jobs require a miter-gauge angle of 45 degrees. Rip-cut miters are discussed under Cutting Chamfers and Bevels (pages 128–132).

When cutting miters, begin by squaring the saw blade to the table. Any tilt in the blade can make miters more difficult to fit. The angle between the blade and miter gauge can be read off the protractor scale on the miter gauge. It is more accurate to set the desired angle with a drafting square (Illus. 5-79), combination square (Illus. 5-80 and 5-81), or a sliding T-bevel. For angles other than 45 degrees, copy the angle with a sliding T-bevel and adjust the angle between the blade and miter gauge to this setting. The included angle is the desired angle, regardless of the angle indicated on the miter gauge. The miter gauge's protractor is not always accurate.

If the stock you are mitering has the angle laid out, use it to adjust the miter gauge. Turn the miter gauge upside down and adjust it so its head is touching the edge of the stock (Illus. 5-82). Adjust its tongue so that it is parallel to the layout line. The miter gauge will not cut the desired angle.

A miter is cut in the same manner as a crosscut (Illus. 5-83–5-85). Because of the incline of the miter gauge, the stock may slide or creep as the miter is cut. Abrasives glued to the miter-gauge head can reduce creeping. The stock can also be held in place with a clamp to control creeping (Illus. 5-86). A stop rod can also be used to control sliding (Illus. 5-87). It works better when the miter gauge is turned the opposite way. This holds the stock in a trapped position and eliminates creeping. If the miter burns at one end when it is being cut in the trapped position, it usually means that the blade is not parallel to the miter slots.

A shop-made (Illus. 5-88) or commercial (Illus. 5-89 and 5-90) miter jig can be helpful when you

Illus. 5-79. A drafting square is one of the most accurate tools for setting the miter gauge or blade for miter cuts. Make sure that the blade set does not affect your setup.

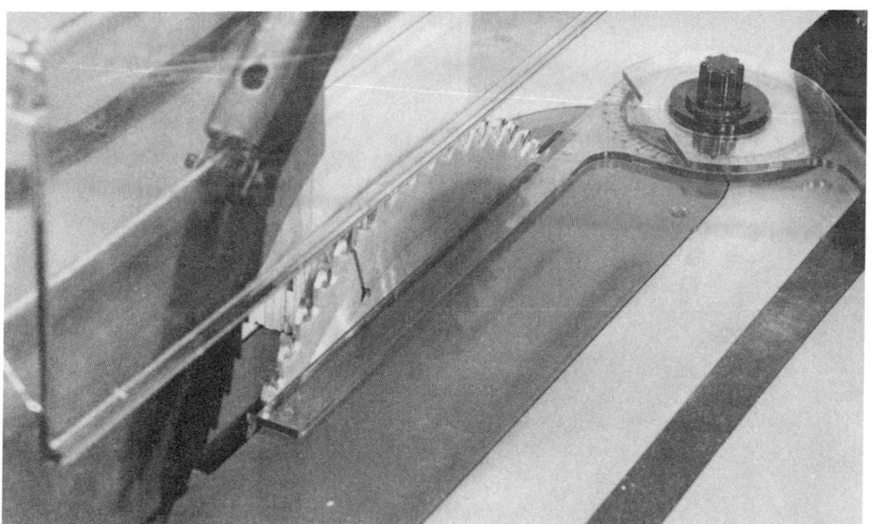

Illus. 5-80. This precision protractor can set any angle desired. Keep the blade off the teeth of the blade. The higher blade gives you a longer surface on which to measure.

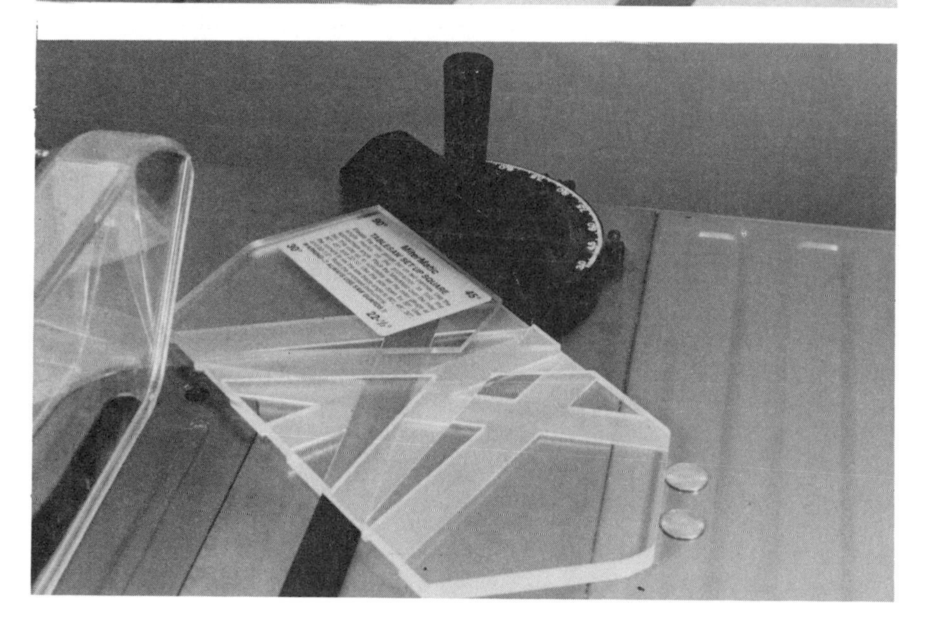

Illus. 5-81. This device sets precise angles between the miter-gauge head and tongue. Two pennies are put under the tongue to elevate it while the setting is being made.

Illus. 5-82. The miter gauge can be used to copy a layout line on your work. The head touches the edge of the work, and the tongue is turned to the desired angle. Copying the angle directly off the work reduces the chance of error.

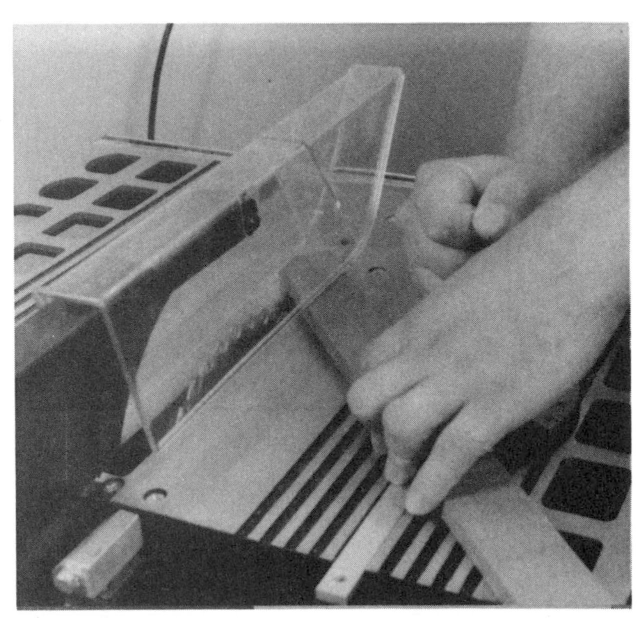

Illus. 5-83. The miter gauge is turned to the desired angle, and the stock is butted to the head of the miter gauge. (Photo courtesy of Skil Power Tools.)

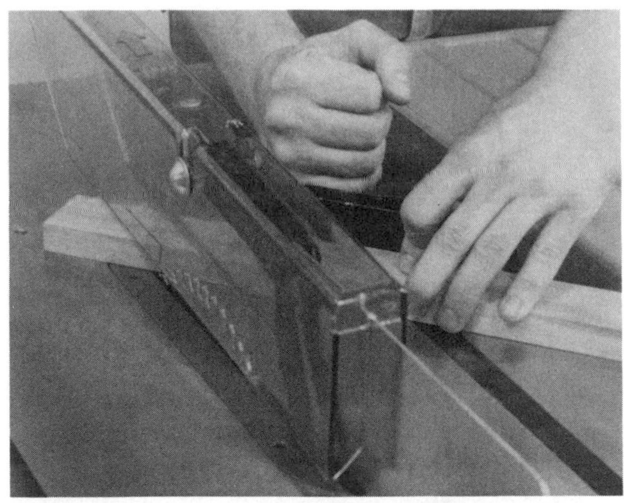

Illus. 5-84. The cutting line is positioned so that the blade is on the waste side of the line.

Illus. 5-85. Guide the stock into the blade, holding it firmly against the head of the miter gauge.

Illus. 5-86. Using a miter gauge with a clamp will reduce creeping or sliding problems.

Illus. 5-87. A stop rod will control stock length when you are making miter cuts. It will also reduce creeping or sliding problems.

are cutting several miters. The jig travels in the table slot or slots. It is inclined 45 degrees in both directions, and the included angle is 90 degrees. This ensures a 90-degree corner even when the 45-degree angles are not perfect. One end of every part is cut on the left side of the jig. The complementary angle is cut on the right side of the jig. This angle is on the other end of every part. As the two parts are fit together, the result is a 90-degree corner.

The same result can be achieved using two miter gauges. Set the miter gauge in the left slot to 45 degrees. Set the miter gauge in the right side perpendicular to it with a framing square (Illus. 5-91). One blade of the square is placed against each miter gauge. The result is a 90-degree included angle. Complementary miters will be cut (Illus. 5-92) if the setup is accurate. A stop rod can be added to this setup to control length. Check your framing square before this set-up. Make sure the blades are perpendicular to each other. It is common to find new framing squares on the shelf that do not have perpendicular blades.

Fitting miters can be more difficult than cutting them. When the angles are all correct, the frame can still appear to have poorly fitted miters. Following are some causes of poorly fitted miters:

Illus. 5-88. This shop-made jig can be used to cut complementary angles which total 90 degrees. Any error on one side is compensated for with the mating cut. Note the barriers that guard against contact with the blade. A stop block controls the length of the part.

Illus. 5-89. This commercial mitering jig is being used in the left slot to make the first cut.

Illus. 5-90. The complementary miter is cut using the right miter slot. A stop rod is added to control stock length. This device was designed to be used with a guard.

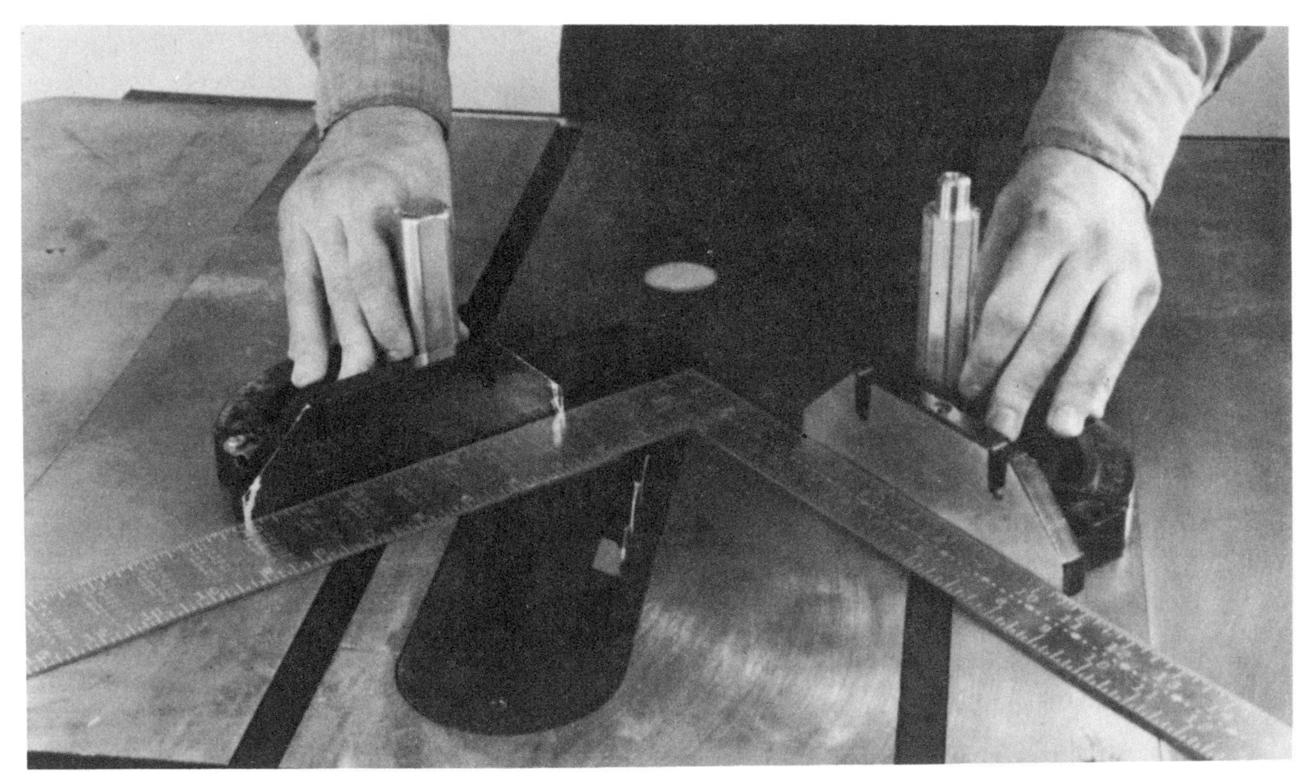

Illus. 5-91. With two miter gauges, you can cut complementary miters. The miter gauge in the left slot is set at 45 degrees. The miter gauge in the right slot is set perpendicular to it. A framing square is used to adjust the miter gauge in the right slot.

Illus. 5-92. These two miters will have an included angle of 90 degrees even if the two miters are not exactly 45 degrees. A stop rod can also be used to control stock length.

1. A thin blade that flutters while cutting. This causes the cut or miter to have some dips.
2. One piece of the frame is too long or short.
3. The blade is not perpendicular to the table.
4. The blade is dull and is tearing the miter.
5. The object being framed is not square—thus affecting the fit of the miters.
6. The framing stock does not have parallel edges.
7. There is slop in the miter-gauge slot, which causes the gauge to wander while the miter is cut.

Illus. 5-93. Small adjustments in a miter joint can be made with a piece of paper or veneer. The paper or veneer is placed between the work and the miter gauge. This alters the angle of the miter slightly, and may improve the fit.

Minor adjustments in a miter cut can be made by placing a piece of paper or veneer at one end of the miter gauge (Illus. 5-93). This changes the miter angle slightly. It may be enough to improve the fit. When fitting miters, work patiently and carefully. Make test cuts on a scrap to be sure of a proper fit. Well-fitted miters are the sign of a high-quality job.

When fitting miters, make note as to whether they are tight at their short or long points. This information will help you determine where the miter must be trimmed to improve the fit. If the miters fit well at assembly, and later open, it is generally a moisture problem. If miters on a frame open at its outer perimeter, the wood has taken on moisture. If the miters open at the inside, the wood has lost water and shrinkage has occurred.

Mitering Safety Procedures When cutting miters, you can encounter many hazards. It is important that you recognize the hazards before they lead to accidents. Be aware of the following situations:

1. During any mitering opeation, several cut-offs accumulate near the blade on the table. If the guard is in position, it is possible for these small cut-offs to become trapped between the blade and guard. This could cause a kickback. If the guard is not in position, the air current surrounding the blade at the throat-plate opening can lift a cut-off from the table and propel it towards the operator.

There is also the possibility that some cutoffs will get caught in the large gullet of the saw blade. As the tooth tries to go through the throat-plate opening, the cut-off is ejected with great force toward the operator. A fine-tooth blade with small gullets will eliminate these problems in most cases.

Many of the cut-offs have sharp points. If they are thrown, they can injure you or others in the shop. Shut off the saw periodically to remove the cut-offs before they accumulate and cause problems.

2. Long parts that are being mitered on a table saw can cause problems. The weight of the piece can cause the blade to bind or generate a kickback. Binding could cause the blade to start burning. It is suggested that you attach a long straightedge to the miter gauge, to provide more control over the workpiece as it is being cut. This reduces the chance of kickback or saw binding. It also moves the cut-off past the blade, where it can be removed easily.

3. Make sure that a cut-off is never trapped between the fence or other stationary object and the blade while you are making miter cuts. This is certain to cause a kickback and send a very sharp piece of wood back towards you. For maximum safety, remove the fence from the saw before you begin to cut end miters.

Cutting Chamfers and Bevels

Chamfers and bevels (Illus. 5-94) are cut with the blade tilted. Chamfers are inclined surfaces that go from a face to an edge. Bevels are inclined surfaces that go from face to face. End and edge miters are bevel cuts made at 45 degrees. The blade, instead of the miter gauge, is tilted for end and edge miters.

When chamfers and bevels are cut with the grain, the rip fence is used to guide the wood. Chamfers and bevels cut across the grain are guided with the miter gauge. The blade is tilted to the desired angle by turning the blade-tilting handwheel on the side of the saw (Illus. 5-95). Use the scale on the front of the saw or a sliding T-bevel (Illus. 5-96) to set the blade angle. A sliding T-bevel is the most accurate method.

Once the desired angle is set, lock the blade tilt in position. Set the blade height to no more than ¼ inch above the work. Make sure the guard works properly with the blade tilted (Illus. 5-97). Adjust it if necessary. Special devices can be used to make the cut when positioning the fence near the guard is difficult (Illus. 5-98 and 5-99).

When cutting with the grain, adjust the fence to the desired stock width. The piece being cut should be between the blade and fence. The cut-off should fall free on the other side of the blade (Illus. 5-100). Avoid cuts that pinch a triangular-shaped piece between the fence and the blade. A kickback is certain to result.

Make edge chamfer cuts or bevel cuts the same way you would make a rip cut. Push the stock completely clear of the blade at the end of the cut.

Some questions arise concerning the position of the fence when you are ripping bevels and chamfers. If the blade tilts toward the fence, the workpiece is between the incline of the blade and the fence. This condition could cause binding if the

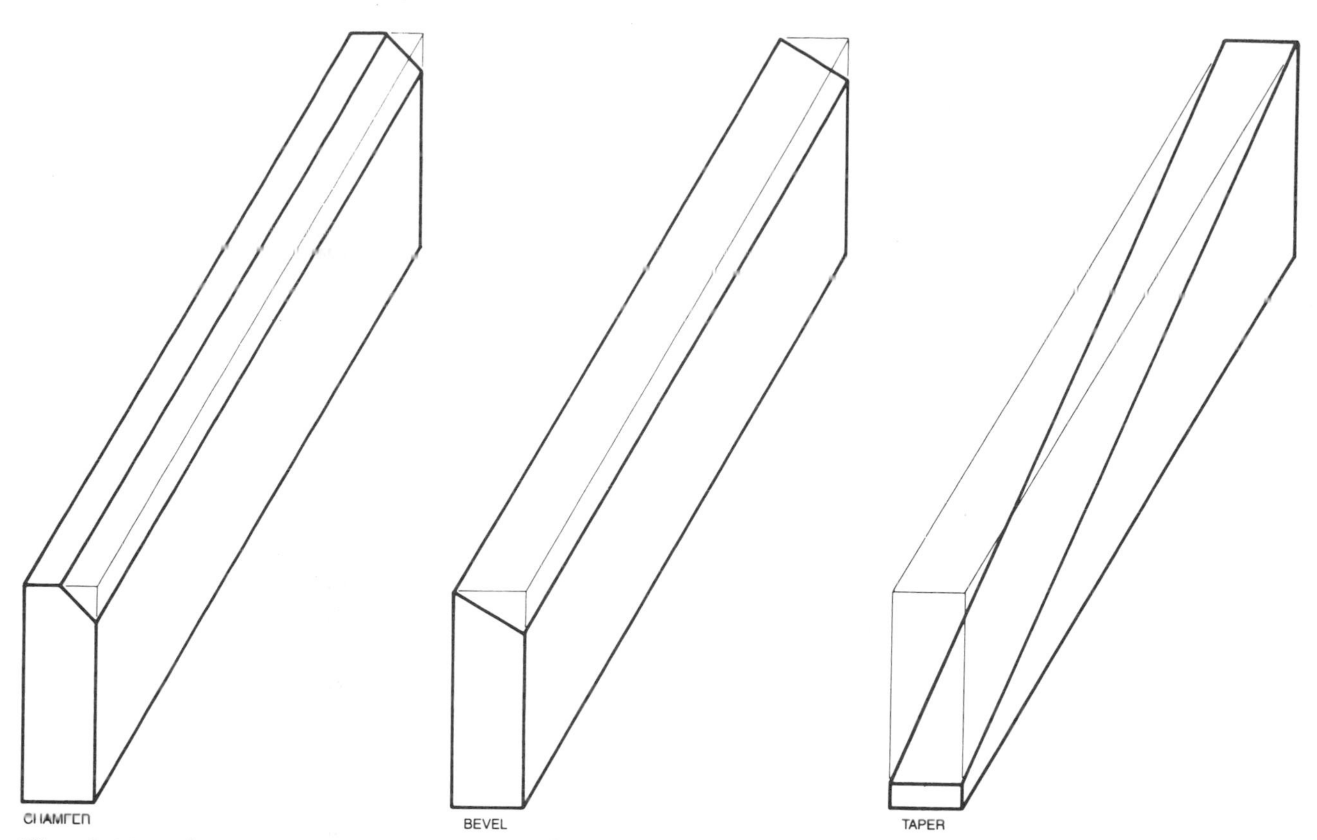

Illus. 5-94. A chamfer is an inclined surface that goes from a face on stock to its edge. A bevel is an inclined surface that goes from face to face. A taper is an inclined surface that goes from end to end.

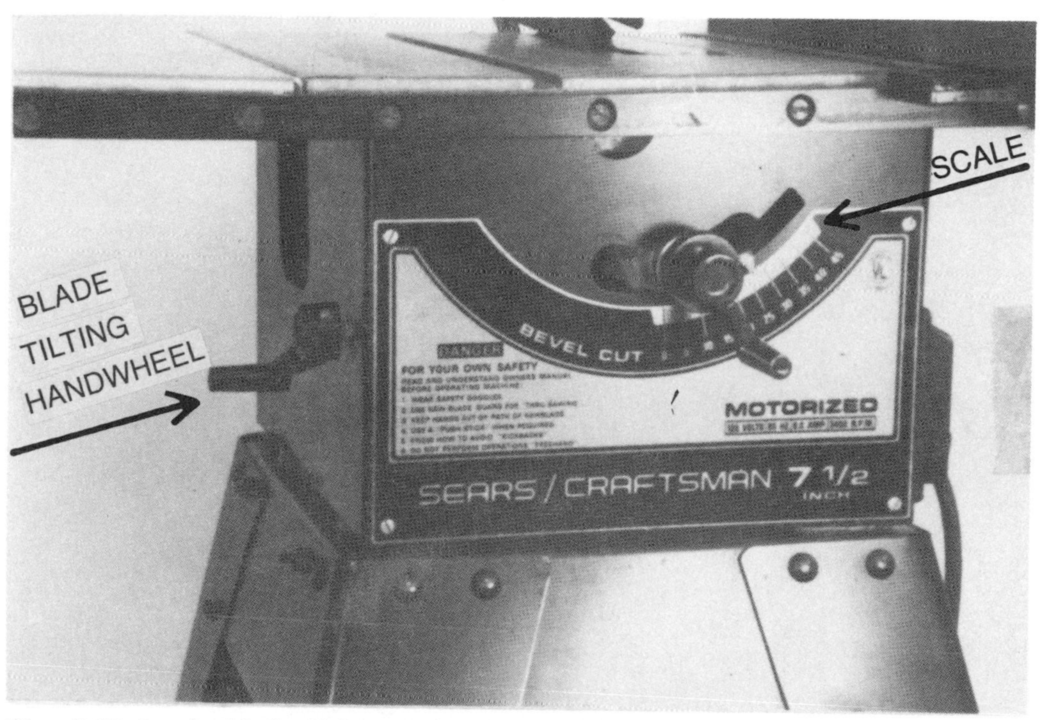

Illus. 5-95. Set the blade tilt by turning the handwheel on the side of the saw. Make sure any locking device has been released before you turn the handwheel. The scale on the front of the saw will help you determine the blade's angle.

Ills. 5-96. A sliding T-bevel will give you a more accurate setting than the scale on the saw. Use a protractor to set the sliding T-bevel.

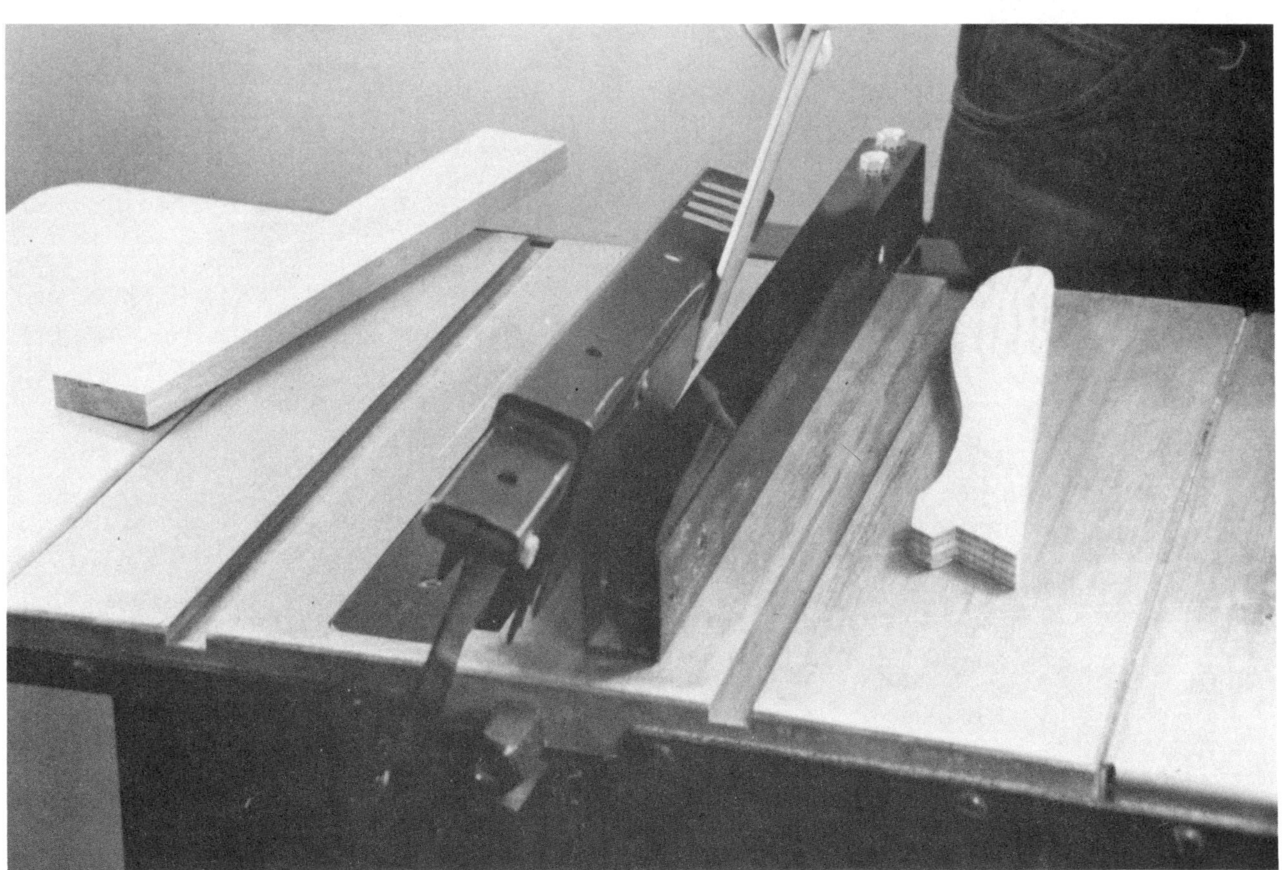

Illus. 5-97. Make sure the guard works properly with the blade tilted. Here the push stick will not go between the guard and fence.

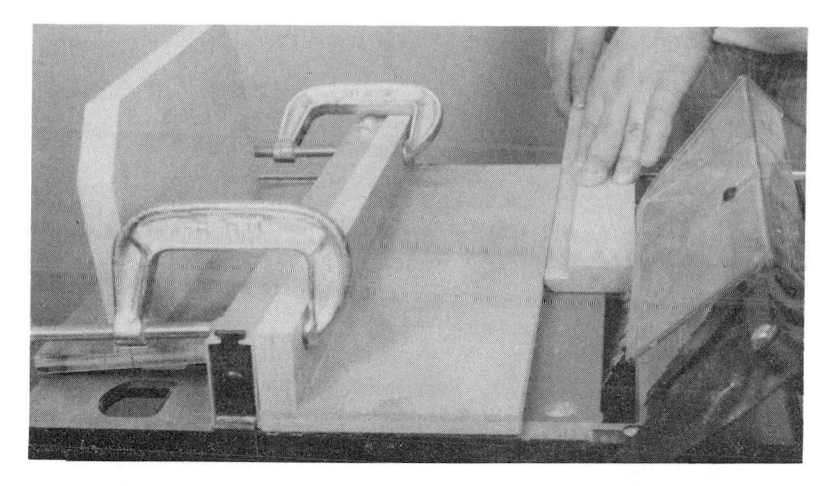

Illus. 5-98. This ripping device allows the fence and guard to be used in this chamfer cut.

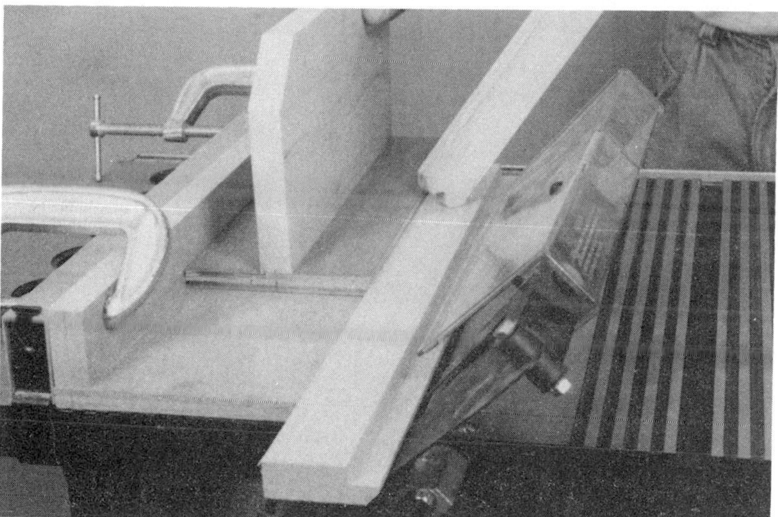

Illus. 5-99. The push block guides the stock through the last few inches of the cut. A push stick is also used to hold the stock down and increase control.

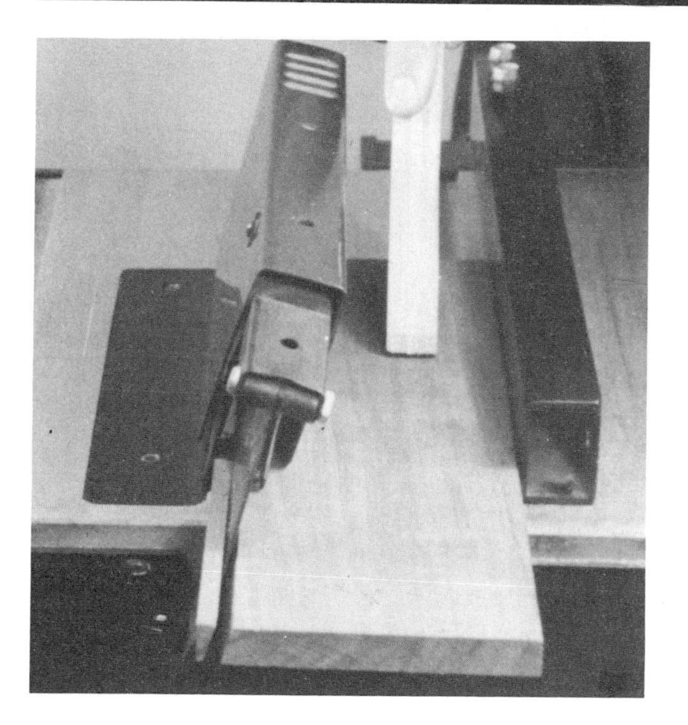

Illus. 5-100. Make sure the cutoff falls free when the cut is complete. When the scrap is pinched between the blade and fence, a kickback could result.

workpiece is warped. This could cause a kickback.

If the blade tilts toward the fence when the fence is on the operator's right, there is a chance of binding. Moving the fence to the other side of the blade eliminates the chance of this happening. Moving the fence to the left may be awkward for the operator and could pose a hazard of another sort.

It would seem that this condition will be improved if the blade tilts away from the fence when it is on the operator's left. But the operator's hands are then closer to the blade for bevel crosscutting in the left miter slot. The left miter slot is favored by most operators for this cut. There is no easy way to solve this problem. Make sure that your stock has a true edge against the fence and that it is free of warp, cup, or twist, if you have the blade tilted toward the fence for bevel-ripping.

Make end chamfer cuts and bevel cuts the same way you would make a crosscut (Illus. 5-101). Thicker stock (Illus. 5-102) will require slower feeding than thin stock. If several pieces are being cut, set up a stop block or stop rod.

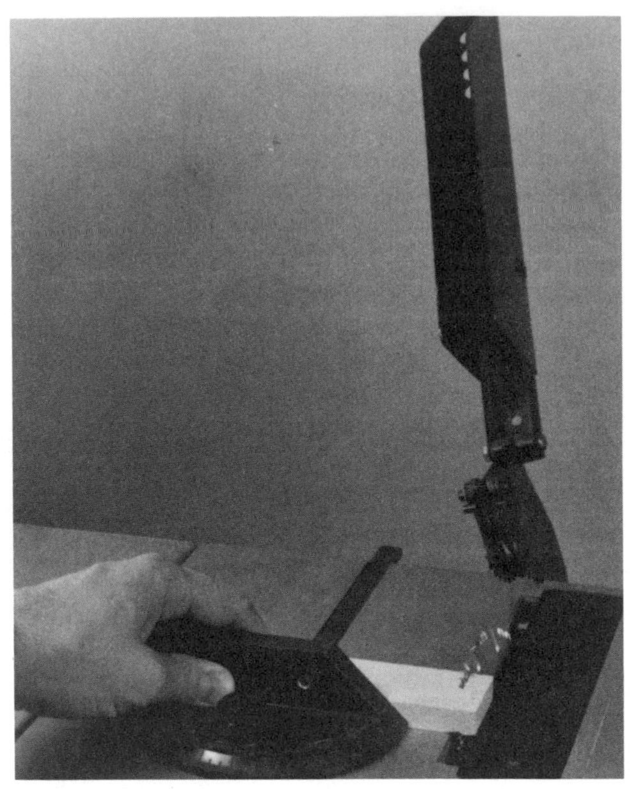

Illus. 5-101. A bevel or chamfer cut on the end of your work is made in the same way as a crosscut.

Cutting Compound Miters

Compound miters are usually made with both the blade and miter gauge tilted. A compound miter is cut when the mitered stock is angled or inclined from the true plane. The following charts give some of the common inclines and the correct settings for the blade and miter gauge. Practice these cuts on scrap until you master them.

When the blade tilts towards the left miter slot, the miter gauge has to be tilted clockwise for right-hand miters (left miter slot) (Illus. 5-103) and counterclockwise for left-hand miters (left miter slot) (Illus. 5-104). The setting remains the same. If the blade tilts toward the right miter slot, use the

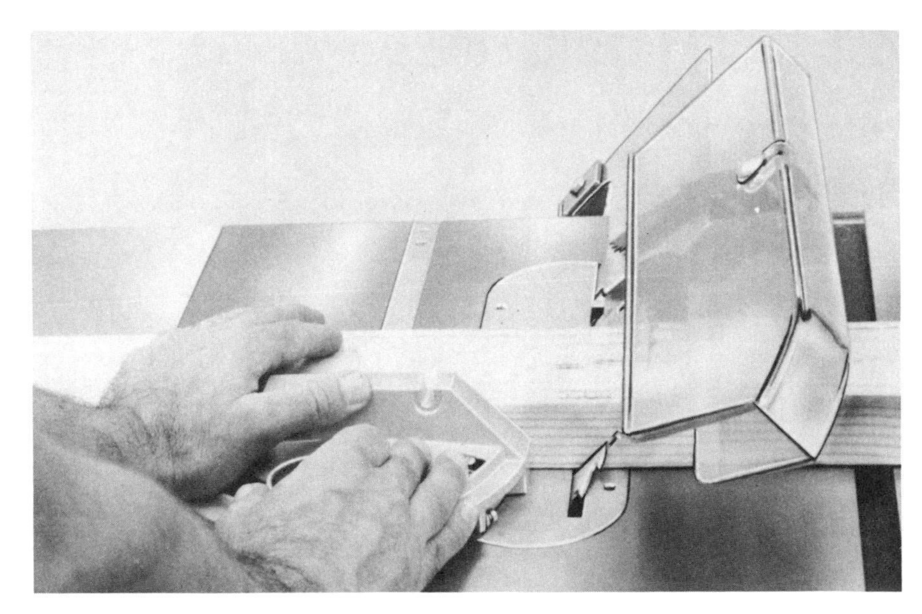

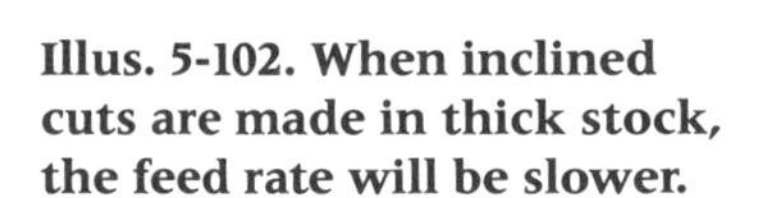

Illus. 5-102. When inclined cuts are made in thick stock, the feed rate will be slower.

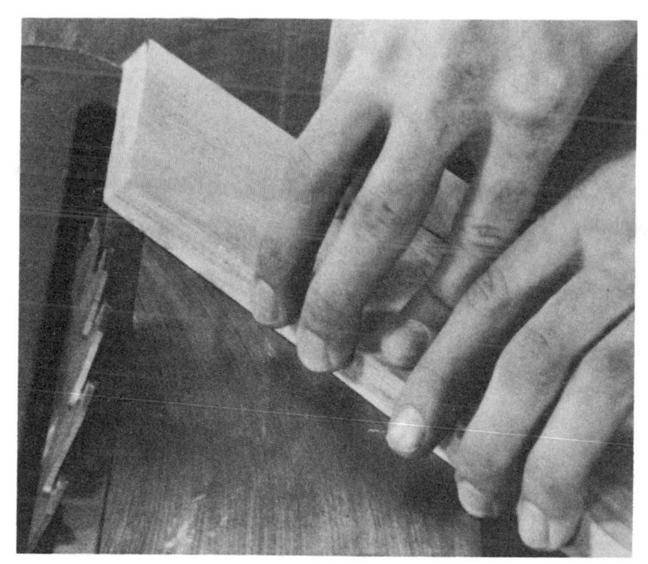

Illus. 5-103. The right-hand compound miter is cut in the left miter slot. The miter gauge is tilted clockwise.

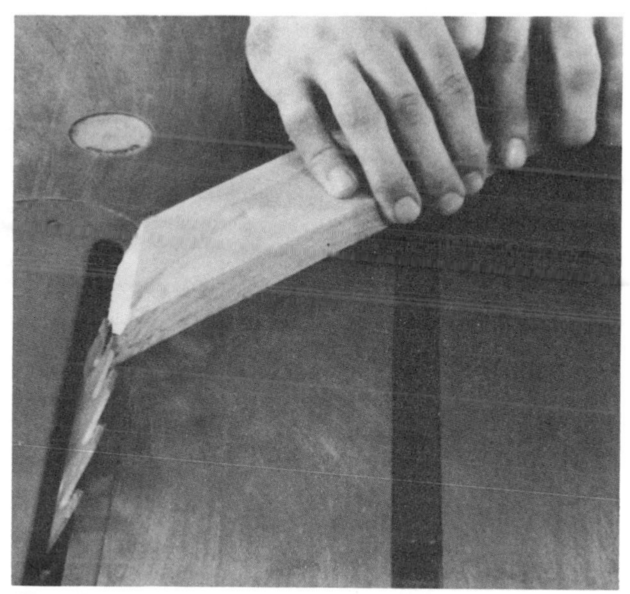

Illus. 5-104. The left-hand compound miter is also cut in the left miter slot. The miter gauge is tilted counterclockwise.

same procedure with that slot. Some miter-gauge angles with ¼-degree increments are difficult to set. Be sure to test the setup on scrap or oversized parts. Minor adjustments may be needed.

A stop block or stop rod can be clamped to the miter gauge when you cut the second compound miter. This will ensure uniform length. A mitering jig can also be used. Be sure to measure the length of the picture frame along the rabbet (Illus. 5-105). The picture frame must accommodate a piece of glass. The standard-size glass fits the frame's rabbet. If you measure the inner edge of the frame, the frame may be too small for the glass.

If the work is tilted to the desired angle, the blade may be set at 90 degrees, and the miter gauge set at 45 degrees. When the work is tilted (Illus. 5-106), the setup is easier to make and more accurate. On wide stock, the blade may not go high enough to cut through the stock. With extra blade exposed, this setup is not as safe as one with the blade and miter gauge inclined. Work carefully, and be sure

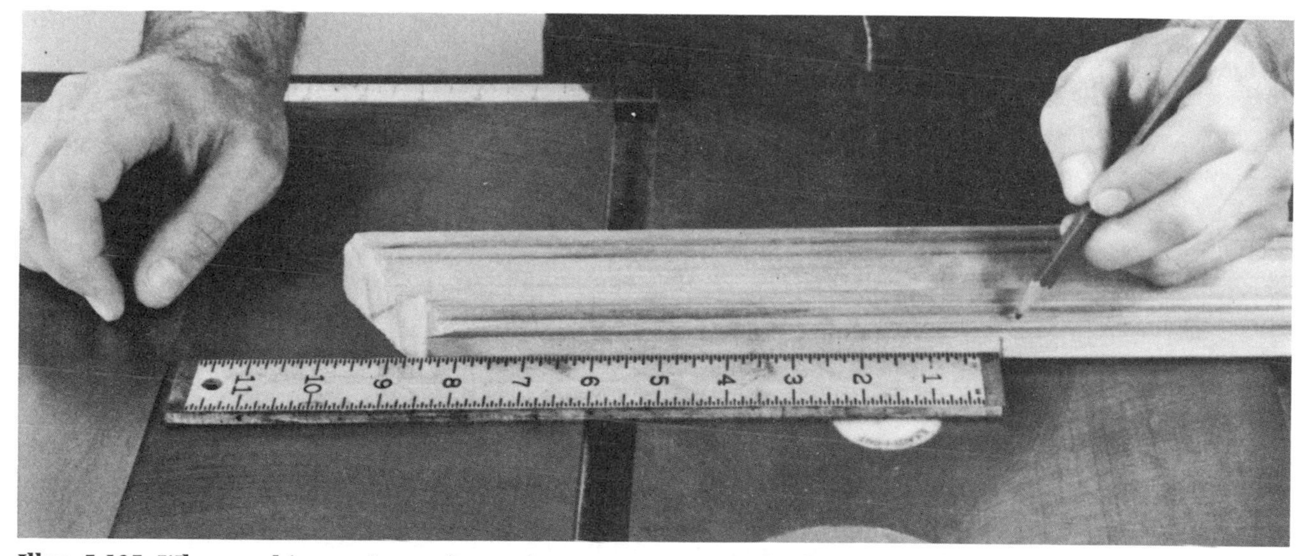

Illus. 5-105. When making a picture frame, be sure to measure the frame length along the rabbet. The frame has to be cut to the desired glass size, and the glass fits in the rabbet.

Illus. 5-106. Compound miters are sometimes cut with the work inclined to its intended angle. When cut this way, the blade is set at 90 degrees and the miter gauge at 45 degrees. More blade is exposed with this method, and it will not work on wide pieces.

the stock is tilted to the exact angle at which it will be used.

Cutting a Dado with a Dado Head

Dadoes are U-shaped channels going through a piece of stock. They can be cut with a single blade or a dado head. The information contained here describes cutting dadoes with a dado head. The information in the next chapter describes both methods.

When cutting dadoes, first disconnect the power and remove the blade from the arbor. Replace the blade with a dado head. Adjust the V-shaped or wobble dado head to the desired width, and bolt it to the arbor (Illus. 5-107). When using a stack dado head, select the correct combination of blades and chippers (Illus. 5-08–5-112). One or two blades (cutters) are always used. Chippers make up the rest of the combination; they are sandwiched between the two blades. A ½-inch dado head would use two ⅛-inch blades and two ⅛-inch chippers.

Mount the dado head carefully. Make sure its teeth point toward the front of the saw. The stack dado head should be tightened carefully, so that its head is balanced. The chippers closest to the blade should rest in the gullets of the blade. This keeps them from rocking, and ensures an accurate setup. Carbide tips can be broken if they are not positioned in the gullets. The pressure of the arbor nut will actually shatter them. Some cutters will look as if two teeth have been cut off the blade. This is to allow space for the chippers, which are positioned in the cutout area.

Make sure that the correct throat plate is used with the dado head (Illus. 5-113). It is good practice to turn the dado head over by hand to make certain

Illus. 5-107. Before installing the dado head, disconnect the saw from its power source and remove the throat plate and blade.

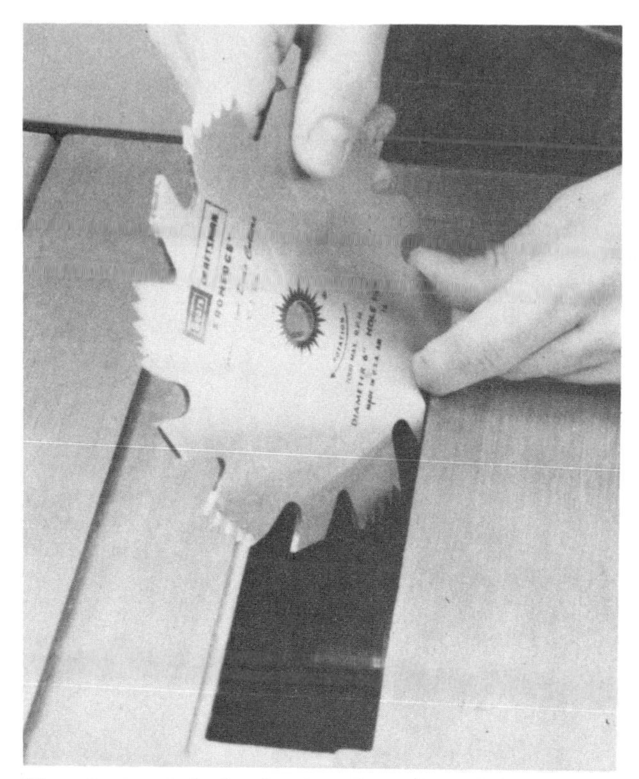

Illus. 5-108. A dado size is selected, and the cutter is placed on the arbor. Cutter teeth should point toward the front of the saw. Make sure the power is disconnected before you begin.

Illus. 5-109. The chippers are added after the cutter is mounted. Be sure to stagger the chippers so the dado head is balanced.

Illus. 5-110. Paper washers can be added for slight adjustments in dado width.

Illus. 5-111. The dado head is set up and ready to be tightened. Chippers are in the gullets of the cutters and staggered around the head. Make sure the dado head does not hit the throat plate.

Illus. 5-112. A test cut is made after the dado head is set up.

that it does not hit the throat plate. *Make all setups and preliminary checks with the power disconnected.*

The species of wood used, horsepower of the saw, and the dado head will determine the appropriate dado depth. As you become more familiar with dado operations, you will become aware of your table saw and dado head. However, as a general rule, a ⅜-inch dado depth is suggested for each pass or cut. If a ¾-inch dado depth is required, make one cut ⅜ inch deep and one cut ¾ inch deep (Illus. 5-114–5-116). Generally, harder woods such

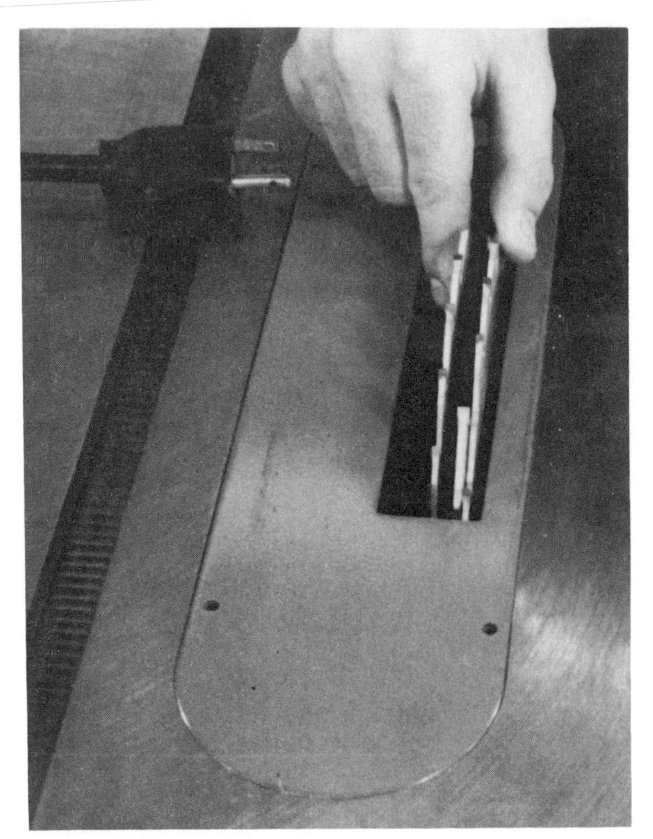

Illus. 5-113. A throat plate must be used with the dado head. Turn the dado head over slowly to be sure it does not hit the throat plate. Make this check again if you tilt the dado head.

as oak and beech require lighter cuts than softer woods such as pine or basswood.

Cut a dado in scrap stock and check its width. If the width is correct, set up the depth. Turn the

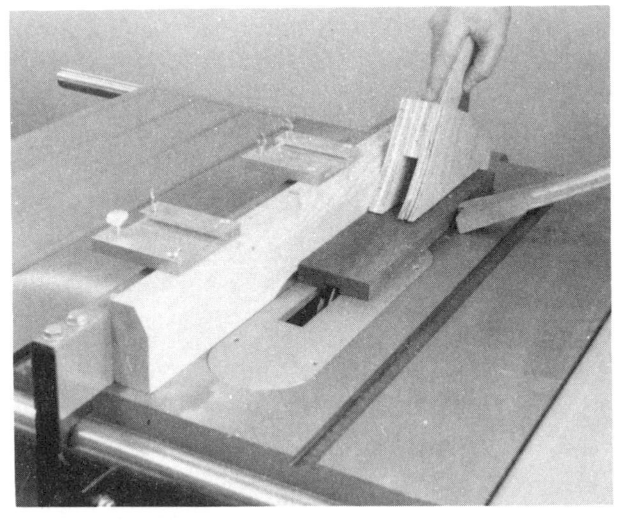

Illus. 5-114. Make the first cut ⅜ inch deep and ⅝ inch wide.

elevating handwheel to adjust dado depth. Proceed with the cut (Illus. 5-117).

To change the width of an adjustable V-shaped or wobble dado head, you have to turn the hub or offset washers. To do this, disconnect the saw, remove the throat plate, and loosen the arbor nut. Turn the hub or offset washers and tighten the arbor nut.

To change the width of the stack dado head, you have to add or subtract chippers or spacers. To make the dado head 1/16 inch larger, add a 1/16-inch chipper. For smaller adjustments, paper or cardboard spacers can be placed between the cutters and chippers.

As with the V-shaped and wobble dado heads, first disconnect the power. Add (or subtract) the chippers and spacers. Replace the arbor nut, and tighten it securely (Illus. 5-118). Be consistent in how you tighten the arbor nut; this can affect the dado width. *Note:* Most dado heads are used without the outer arbor washer because its extra width makes it impossible to fasten the arbor nut. If this is not possible, do not use the dado head on the saw (Illus. 5-119 and 5-120).

If you are using a stack dado head, you can remove some chippers so that all the threads on the arbor are engaged. In such a case, it may take two separate cuts with the dado head to cut the dado to the appropriate width. This is a much safer way of working, however.

Not all dadoes are perpendicular to the stock. The dado head (Illus. 5-121) and/or miter gauge can be tilted to cut the desired dado. Make sure the dado head does not hit the throat plate when tilted. When working with dado heads, several problems can occur. Common problems are tear-out and

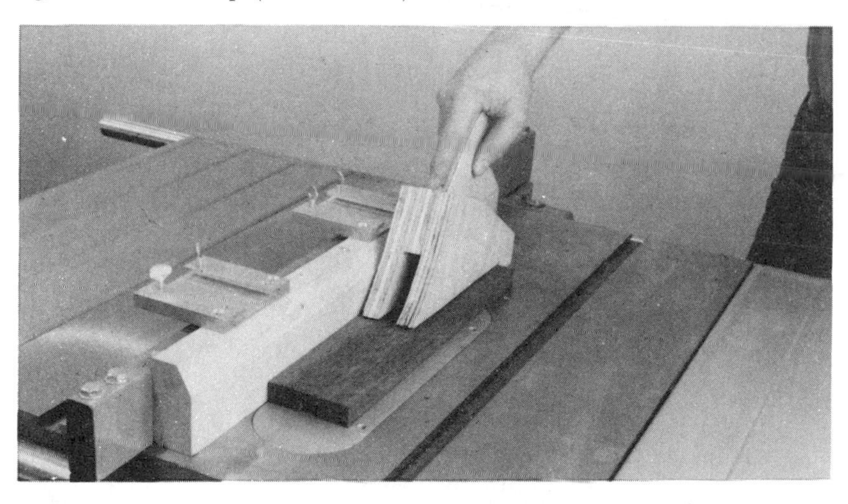

Illus. 5-115. Make the second cut 3/4 inch deep and 5/8 inch wide. Make sure you keep the same edge of the piece against the fence for both cuts. Light cuts produce better dadoes and reduce the chance of a kickback.

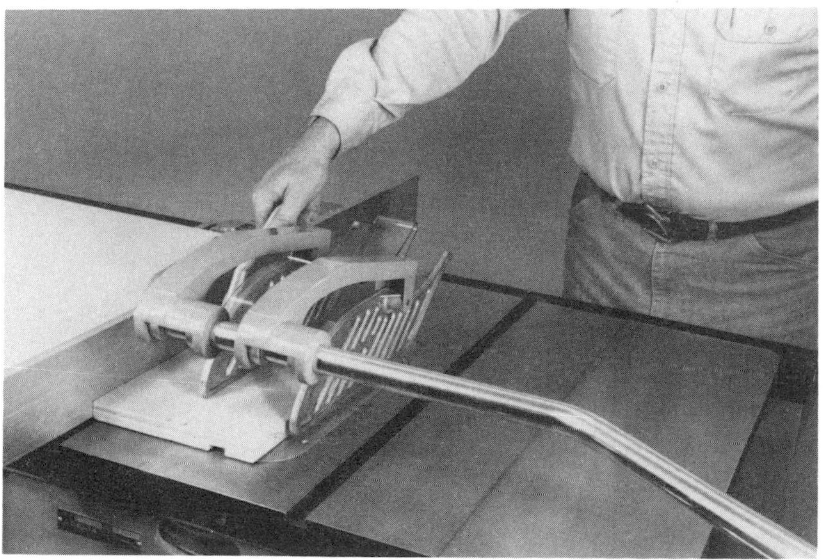

Illus. 5-116. Some guards can be used with the dado head, but each setup is different.

Illus. 5-117. Shophelper wheels help control this piece during the dadoing operation. The wheels hold the stock against the fence and table with spring tension. Also use push sticks to guide the stock.

Illus. 5-118. Be consistent in how you tighten the dado head. It can affect dado width slightly.

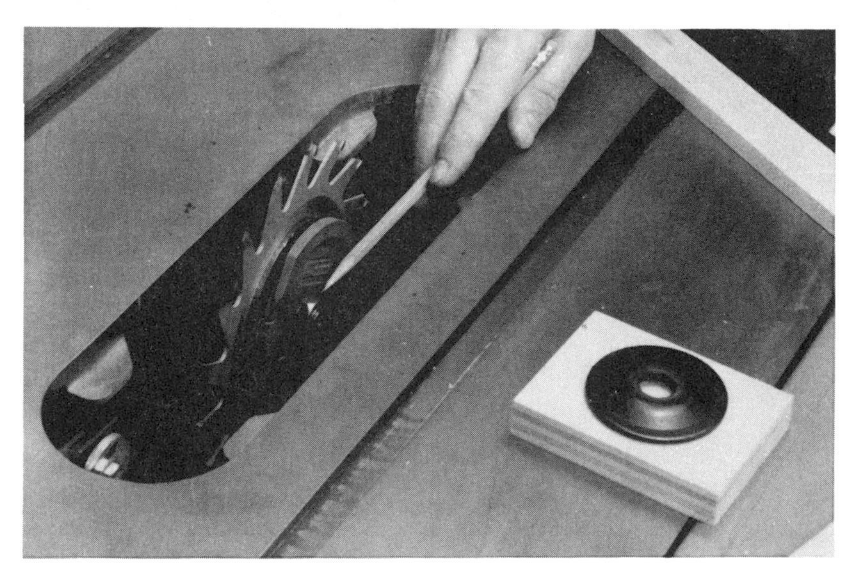

Illus. 5-119. In some cases, the arbor washer cannot be used with the dado head. Make certain that all of the threads on the arbor washer are engaged with the threads on the arbor. If this is not possible, do not use the dado head on the saw.

Illus. 5-120. This chip-limiting stack dado head is set for a ⅝-inch cut. On this arbor, the arbor washer and arbor nut can be used. A larger dado head would require removal of the arbor washer.

Illus. 5-121. The dado head can be tilted for an inclined dado. The miter gauge can also be tilted for a dado cut at an angle.

dadoes of irregular depth. Tear-out can occur at the end of the cut or on the face of the cut.

Tear-out on the face of the cut can be caused by a lack of set or clearance on the outside cutters. This pinches the dado head and tears out the face of the stock. A dull dado head will also cause face tear-out.

Feeding the stock across the dado head too fast can also cause tear-out (Illus. 5-122). Vary your speed and compare the results. Cutting a dado too deeply in one cut may also cause tear-out. Take a lighter cut to see if the tear-out stops.

Tear-out at the end of the cut is caused by the force of the dado head pushing against the stock. A piece of stock attached to the miter gauge can be used to back the cut (Illus. 5-123). The tear-out then occurs in the stock attached to the miter gauge. It is also possible to cut the dadoes in oversized stock. Trim away the tear-out as you cut the piece to finished size.

Dado heads with cutters and chippers are designed to cut the dado slightly deeper under the cutters. The cutters scribe the two sides of the dado, and the chippers remove the stock in between. The

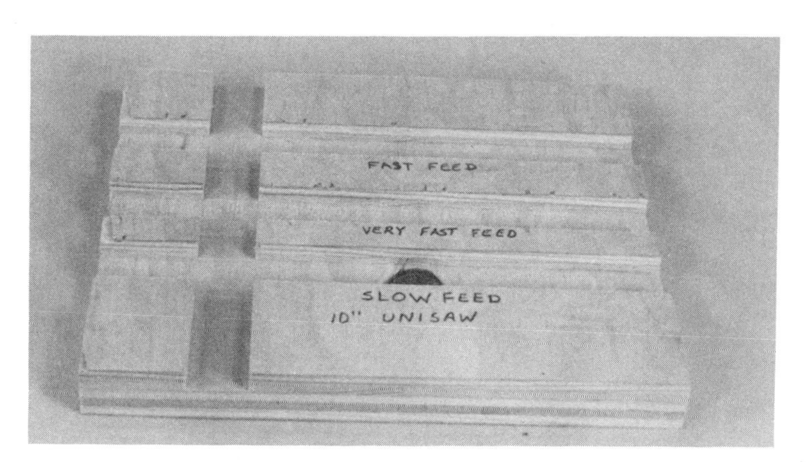

Illus. 5-122. The speed at which you feed the stock into the dado head will have some effect on tear-out and the quality of the cut. Misalignment of the saw can also reduce the quality of the dado cut.

Illus. 5-123. Always check your setup in scrap stock. If the width is correct, set the desired depth of cut. Note the piece of stock backing up the work. This eliminates tear-out.

extra dado depth at the cutters allows the stock cut by the chippers to break off evenly. With large-diameter wobble dado heads, the bottom of the dado may appear concave or convex. This is a result of the wobble in the blade. On wider dadoes, it cuts deeper in the center of the dado than at the edges (Illus. 5-124). Blade-and-chipper dado heads may also have an irregular bottom (Illus. 5-125).

A sharp chisel (Illus. 5-126) or router plane can be used to true up the dado. If the dado is not visible, the slight irregularity will not affect gluing. Work carefully when trimming a dado. Take light cuts. Heavy cuts can leave the bottom of the dado more irregular than it was.

Keep the dado head sharp. A dull dado head produces poor results. Extra force is needed to cut with a dull dado had. This makes it unsafe. Make sure all the sheet stock is dadoed with a carbide-tipped dado head. Steel dado heads become dull rapidly in all materials except solid wood. The glue and other additives are hard. They take the edge off steel tools quickly.

Power Feeding A power feeder can be used to cut dadoes with the grain or on the long edge of sheet stock. The feed speed of a power feeder used to cut dadoes will be slower than when it is used for ripping. This is because the amount of stock removed and the cutting volume has increased considerably.

The power feeder is a good choice for dadoing. It keeps the operator's hands clear of the dado head, and it reduces operator fatigue (Illus. 5-127). The quality of the cut also increases because the chip load is uniform throughout the cut.

To set the power feeder up for dadoing, follow the procedures outlined for ripping with a power feeder. Never raise the dado head under power. It could come into contact with the power feeder. Check the dado throat plate to be sure it is even with the table. If it is not, the work could be stopped by the irregular surface. Use paraffin wax to lubricate the table on long runs. The wood will move more easily, and it will not cause any finishing problems.

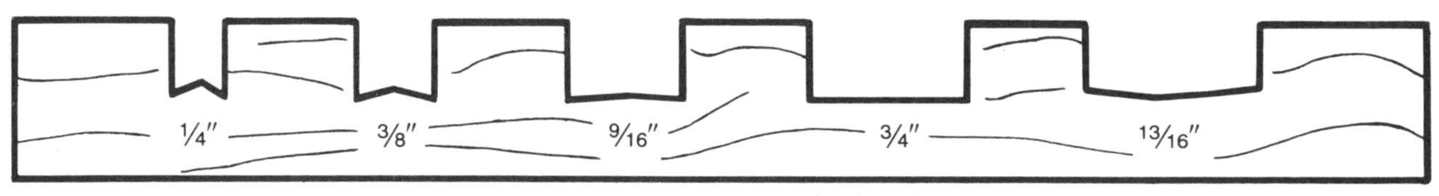

Illus. 5-124. Dadoes cut with a wobble head may have a concave or convex bottom.

Grooves at corners should be slightly deeper than middle of cut

Illus. 5-125. Dadoes cut with a cutter-and-chipper dado head will be slightly deeper under the cutters. This allows the chippers to break out the center of the dado evenly.

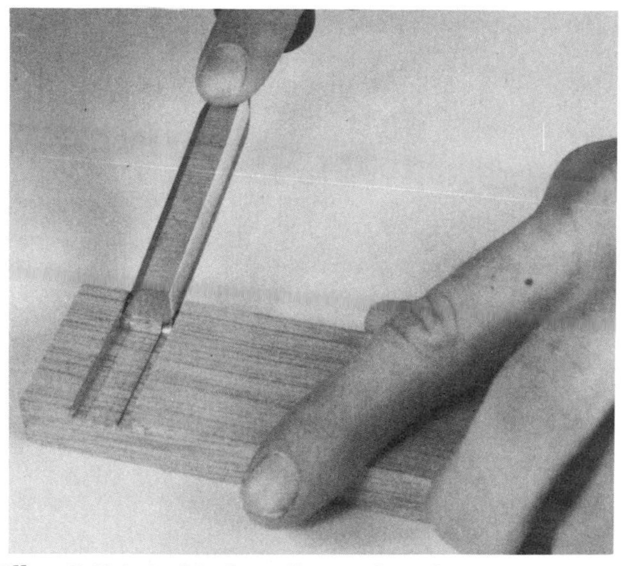

Illus. 5-126. A chisel can be used to clean up a dado. A router plane can also be used.

Illus. 5-127. A power feeder can be used for production dadoing on pieces which are longer than they are wide. The fence is always used with the power feeder.

Cutting Molding

Cutting molding on the table saw requires careful attention to detail. Molding cutters can cause kickbacks and serious injuries if you make contact with them. Light cuts must be taken, and all adjustments and setups must be carefully checked before you begin. Install the desired cutters in the molding head (Illus. 5-128 and 5-129). Follow the manufacturer's instructions to install them. Make sure that all the cutters are identical. A combination of tongue and groove cutters in the molding head would actually remove the entire edge. Inspect the molding head to make sure all the cutters are facing the same way. The fasteners should be tightened securely, and they should be checked periodically (Illus. 5-130).

Disconnect the power to the saw and mount the cutter head. The flat side of the cutters should face the front of the saw (Illus. 5-131). Select the correct throat plate for the molding head and set it in position. Turn the cutter head by hand to be sure it does not hit the throat plate. Also be certain that the stock will not drop into the hole in the throat plate (Illus. 5-132). Make a new throat plate if necessary (Illus. 5-133).

Mount an auxiliary fence against the left side of the fence. This auxiliary fence should be made on one-inch-thick stock which is as wide and as long as the metal fence. Use wood screws or metal fas-

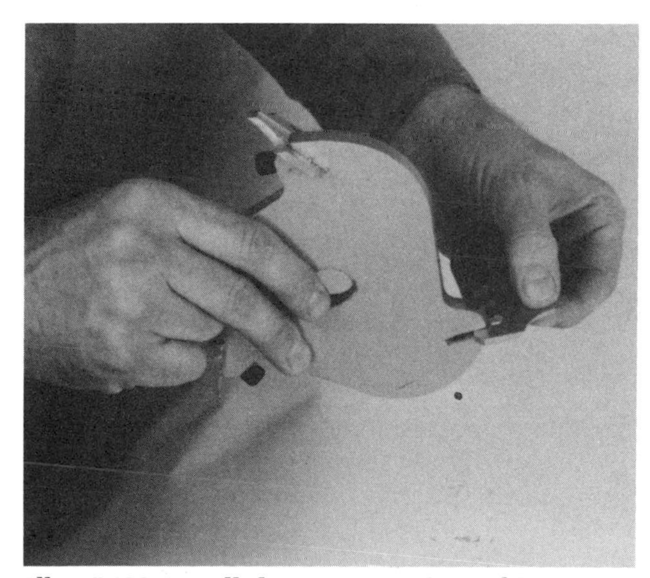

Illus. 5-128. Install the cutters in the molding or shaper head with the flat side pointing toward the operator or direction of rotation.

Illus. 5-129. The fastener's head holds these cutters in place. Make certain that all the profiles are the same and that they point in the same direction.

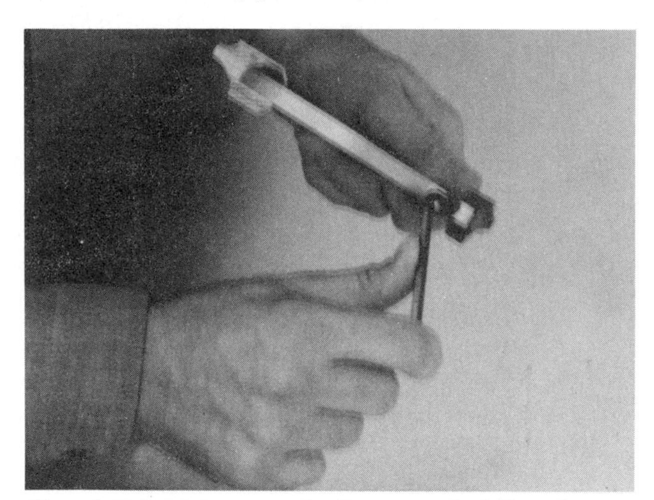

Illus. 5-130. Make sure the fasteners holding the cutters are locked securely. Check them periodically to be sure they remain tight.

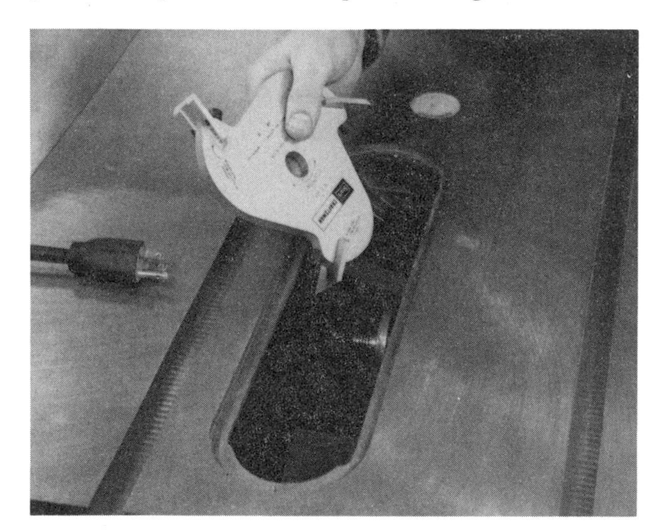

Illus. 5-131. Install the shaper head so the flat side of the cutters faces the operator. Be sure to use the appropriate spacers and bushings with the shaper head.

teners to secure the auxiliary fence in place. The wood you select should be made of true, dense solid stock with no knots or defects (Illus. 5-134).

Adjust the fence and the cutter height. Cuts of ⅛–¼ inch, depending on species hardness, are

Illus. 5-132. Make sure that the throat plate used with the shaper head is the correct size. If not, the work will fall into the throat plate.

Illus. 5-133. The wooden throat plate shown here is better suited to the work than the standard throat plate. The method of making auxiliary throat plates is discussed in Chapter 2 (pages 43–45).

best. Deeper cuts should be made in two or more passes. Keep the final pass light (1/16 inch) for best results. Use featherboards to help hold and guide the stock (Illus. 5-135–5-137). Use a push stick or push sticks to feed the stock. All shaping should be done with the cutter under the auxiliary fence or right next to the fence. This allows greater control of the stock and minimizes the chance of kickback.

Illus. 5-134. A wooden auxiliary fence is attached to the metal fence. Use a straight-grained hard wood for this purpose. Part of the fence will be cut away by the shaper cutter shown here.

When shaping, always control your stock. Use the fence for edge shaping. The miter gauge (Illus. 5-138) or a tenoning jig (Illus. 5-139) can be used for end shaping. The splitter-mounted guard cannot be used for shaping operations. Work carefully. Keep your hands clear of the cutter head and kick-back zone. Stand to the side of the stock as you feed

Illus. 5-135. Light cuts with the help of a featherboard and push stick are safest. Avoid heavy cuts. They tear the wood and cause tear-out.

it into the cutter. Take light cuts for smoother shaping and less chance of kickback. Feed stock slowly when shaping. This minimizes surface tear-out. If the motor slows down, take a lighter cut. Make sure the stock is true and free of defects. Shaping operations can destroy pieces containing loose knots, shakes, and honeycombs. When in doubt, do not shape the piece.

Back the piece with scrap stock to minimize tear-out. You can also shape oversized pieces and saw off the tear-out in some applications. Shape end grain first when doing all four sides of a piece (Illus. 5-140). Any tear-out at the ends will be

Illus. 5-136.

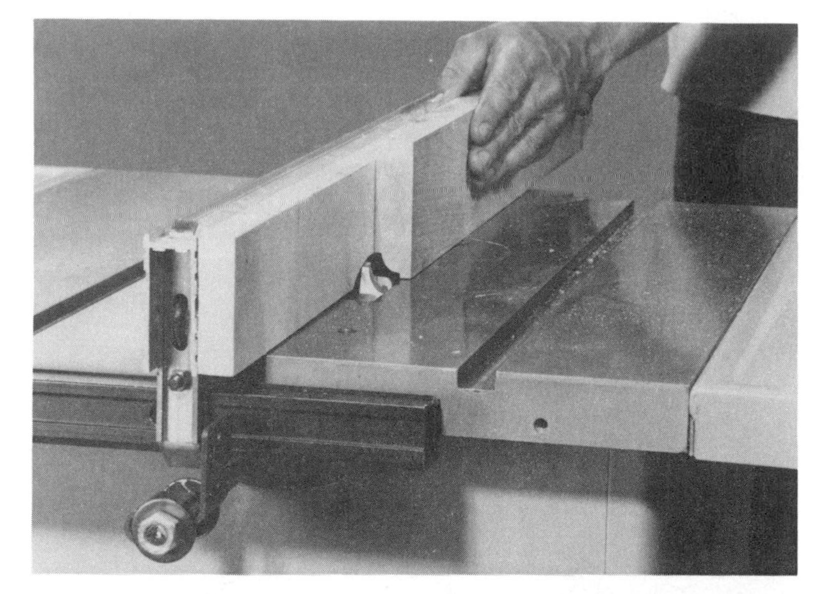

Illus. 5-137. Some molding cuts are done with the stock on edge. A featherboard could have helped control this piece. (Photo courtesy of Delta International Machinery Corporation.)

Illus. 5-138. The fence controls the depth of cut, and the miter gauge controls the work. Shaping is safest when the cutter is next to the fence.

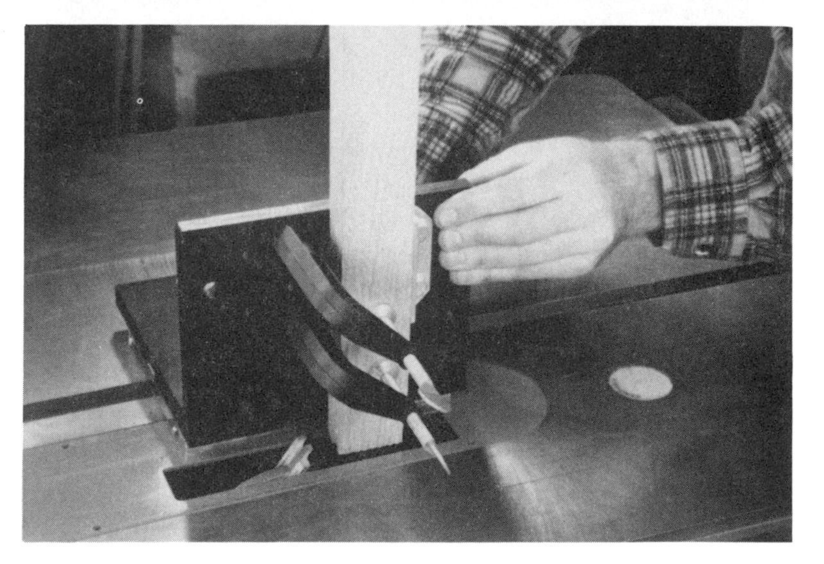

Illus. 5-139. Here the tenoning jig controls the work. The depth of cut is controlled by the cutter height.

removed when the edges are shaped (Illus. 5-141–5-144).

Fancy pieces of molding can be made by shaping stock with two or more cutters. Remember to retain two true surfaces to control the stock. One surface should rest on the table, and the other should be held against the fence or miter gauge.

When the arbor is tilted, additional shapes can be cut. After tilting the arbor, make sure it does not touch the throat plate. Before you turn on the power, turn the shaper head over by hand. Change the setup if it touches the throat plate. *Note:* This check should be made with the power disconnected!

Some small pieces of molding are safer and easier to cut when they are part of a larger piece. Both edges of a wider piece of stock are shaped. The molding is then ripped from both edges of the wider piece (Illus. 5-145). Use a fine-cut rip or hollow-ground combination blade to rip the molding from the wider piece. This will keep the edge smooth. No planing should be needed.

In addition to taking light cuts with a molding head, you can saw away a triangle of wasted wood before shaping the stock. This leaves just enough wood to make the molding in a single light cut (Illus. 5-146). This reduces the wear on the cutter head and allows the cutters to remain sharp longer. The lighter cut will also reduce the chance of kickback.

Illus. 5-140. Shape end grain first when shaping all four sides of a piece. This tear-out will be removed after edge-grain shaping.

Illus. 5-141. Note how the tear-out was removed when the edge was shaped.

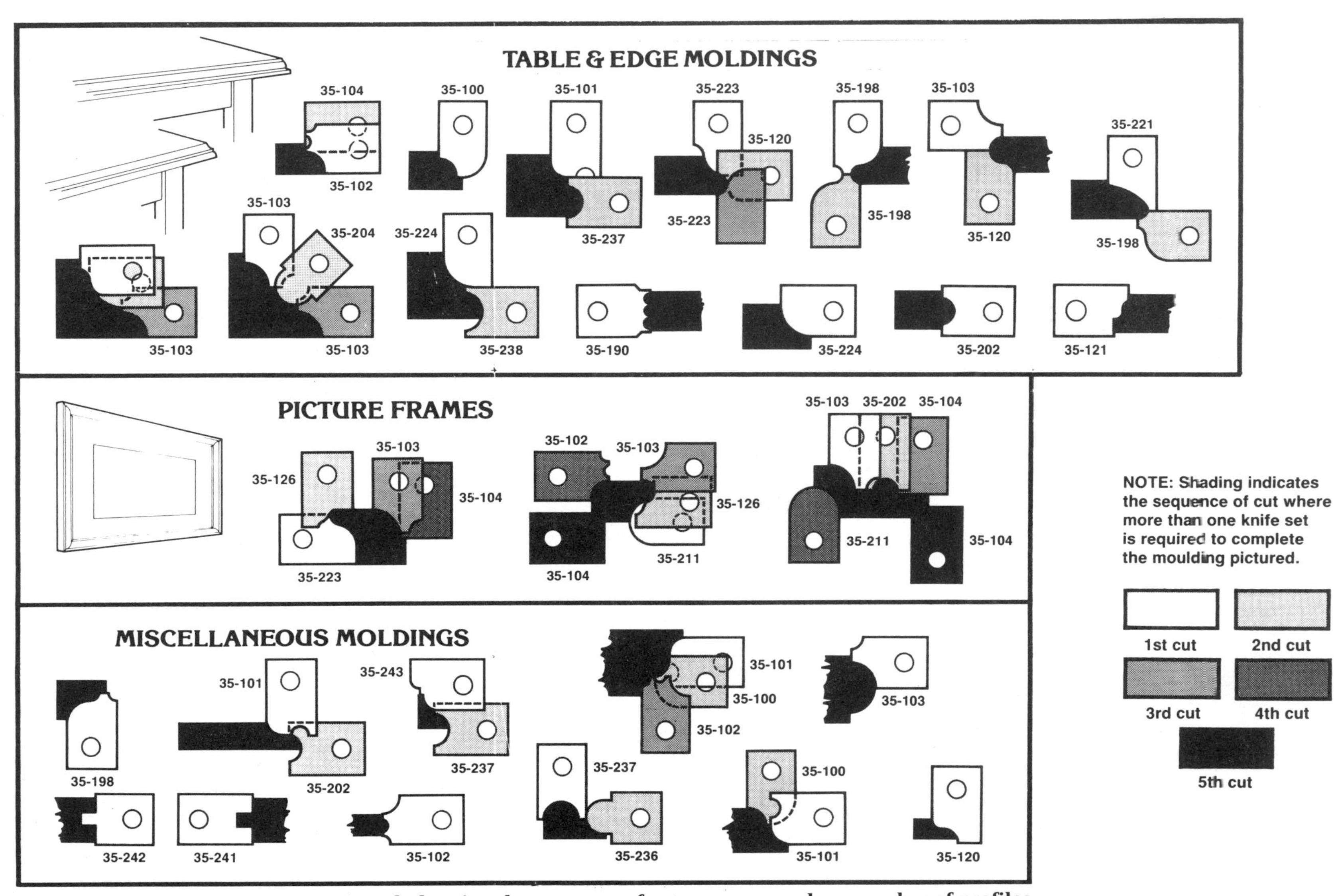

Illus. 5-142. By using various cutters and planning the sequence of cuts, you can make a number of profiles with the molding head. (Drawing courtesy of Delta International Machinery Corporation.)

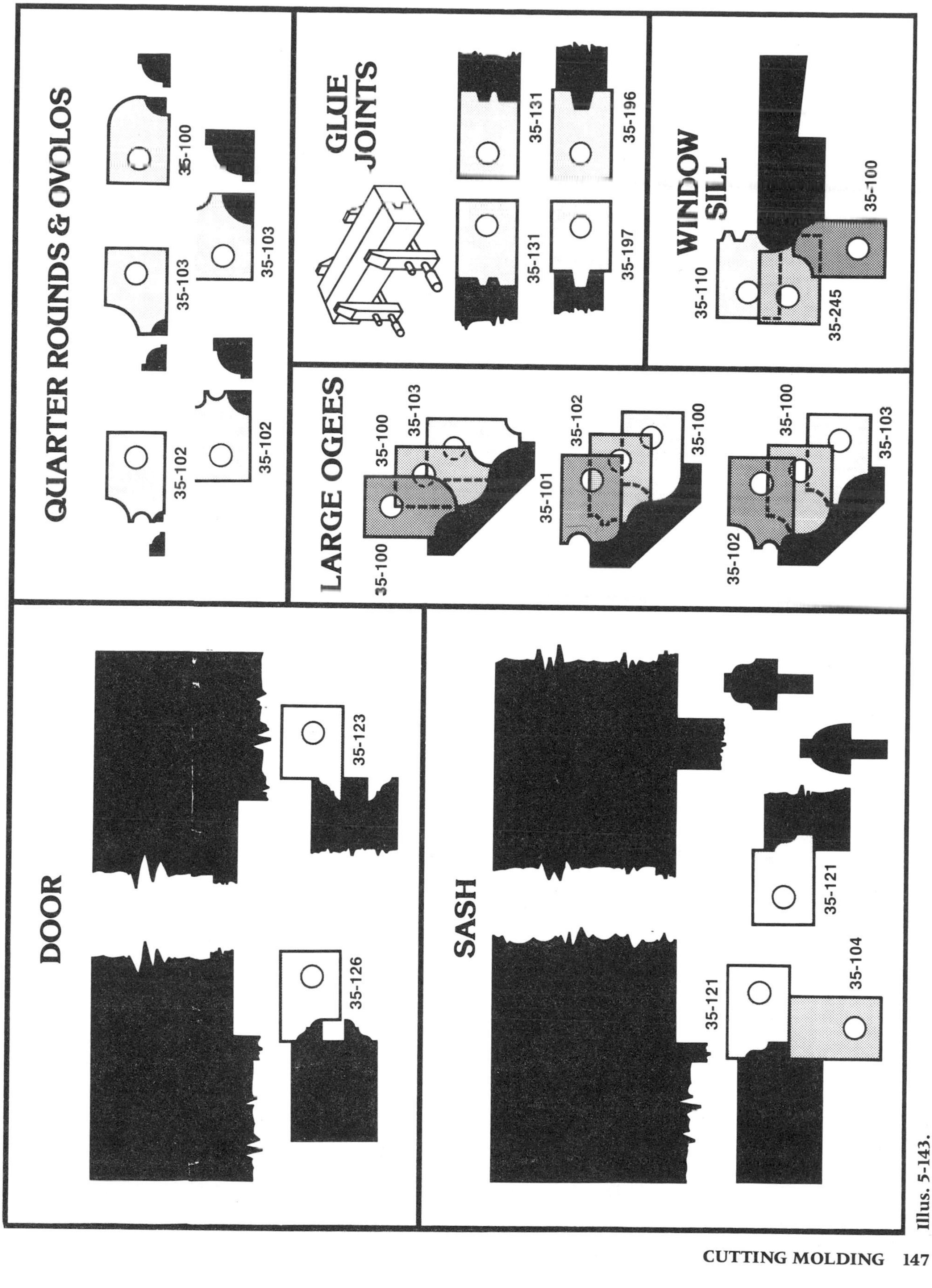

QUARTER ROUNDS & OVOLOS

35-100

35-103

35-103

35-102

35-102

GLUE JOINTS

35-131

35-196

35-131

35-197

WINDOW SILL

35-110

35-245

35-100

LARGE OGEES

35-100

35-100

35-103

35-101

35-102

35-100

35-102

35-100

35-103

DOOR

35-126

35-123

SASH

35-121

35-104

35-121

Illus. 5-143.

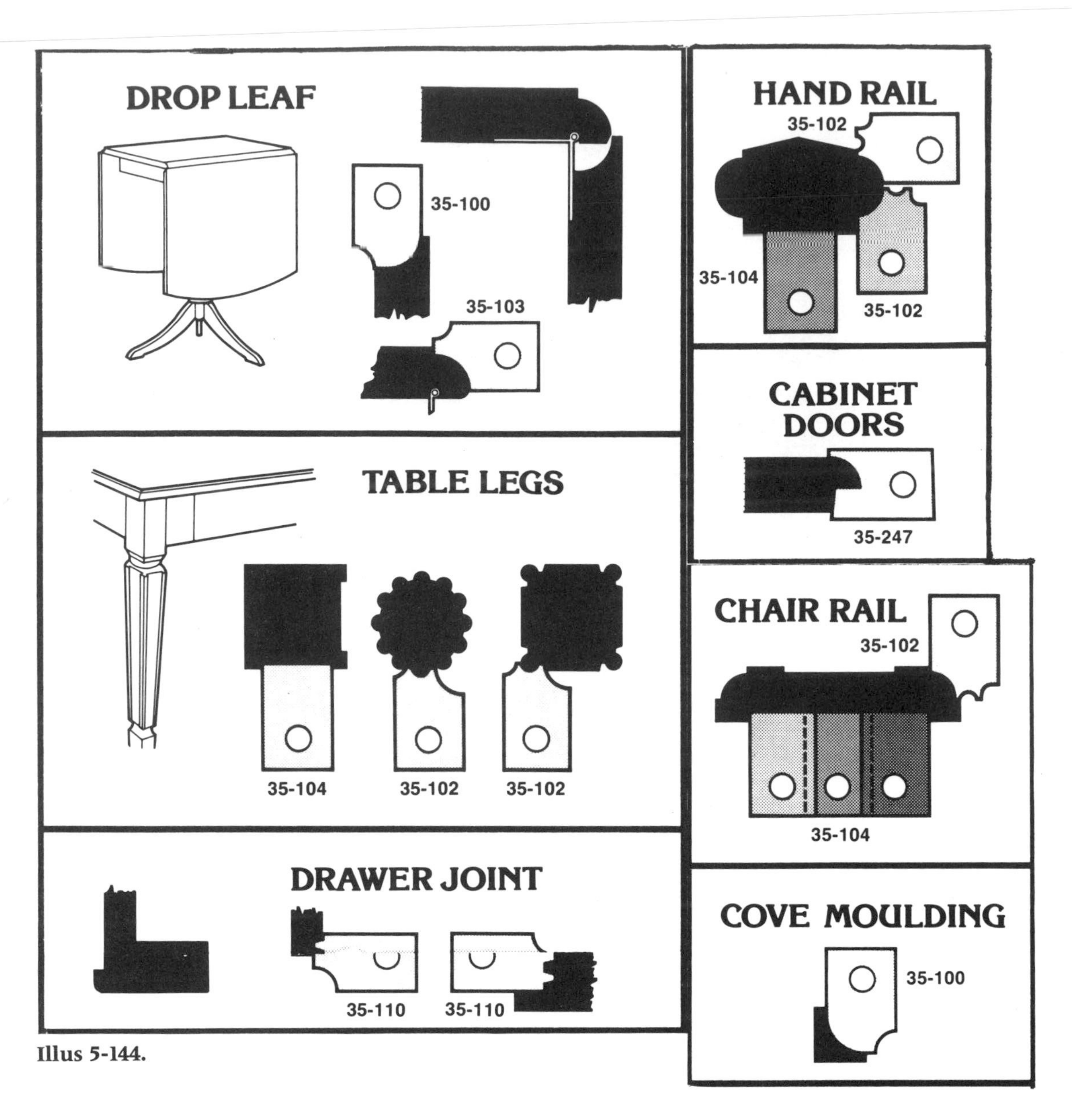

Illus 5-144.

Illus. 5-145. Small pieces of molding should be ripped away from a large piece. Small pieces tend to break or shatter when shaped.

Illus. 5-146. If the waste stock is cut away before the molding cut is made, the cutter does not have to work as hard. This reduces the number of cuts and the chance of kickback. The quality of the cut is usually better with this method.

The term "light cut" is a vague one when cutting molding is discussed. A groove cutter works one-half as hard as a tongue cutter when this two-part joint is made. It may be necessary to take two cuts when making the tongue. Light cuts are a function of the following: the hardness of the wood, the power of the saw, the amount of wood being removed, and the sharpness of the cutter.

Experience has shown that accidents with molding heads fall into two categories: kickback and/or contact with the cutters. Review the following causes for accidents before doing any shaping:

1. A kickback which hits the operator or pulls the support hand into the cutter head. Make a barrier guard whenever possible (Illus. 5-147–5-149).
2. Taking too heavy a cut, resulting in a kickback or the feeding hand making contact with the cutter.
3. A throat plate with an opening larger than the workpiece. This could result in a kickback or cutter breakage.
4. Working on short or narrow stock. This puts the operator's hands too close to the cutter head and could cause stock to shatter or kickback.
5. Trapping the workpiece between the fence and cutter head can cause kickback and expose the entire cutter head, even when only a portion of the cutter head is used.
6. Contact between the cutter head and metal fence can cause cutter breakage and possible injury from flying metal pieces.

Illus. 5-147. The barrier guard is clamped over the cutter head after the setting has been made. A spacer is used to put ⅛ inch clearance between the barrier and the work. This will reduce the chance of binding.

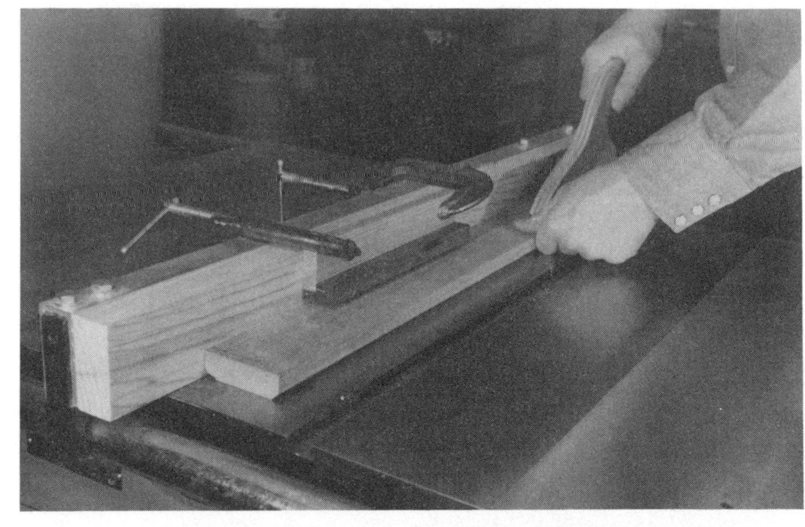

Illus. 5-148. A push stick is used in conjunction with the barrier to make the cut. Very little wood is actually being removed.

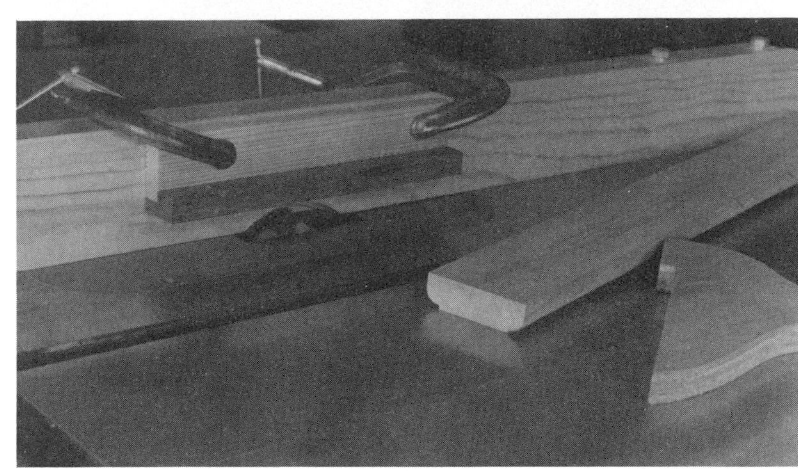

Illus. 5-149. Both cuts are complete. The cuts are high in quality, and the operation has been made safer because a barrier was used and because the saw blade was used to remove waste wood.

Using a Power Feeder A power feeder can be used to cut molding with the grain. Power feeders must be set up in the same way they are for ripping (Illus. 5-150 and 5-151). Feed speed may be lower for molding operations than for ripping. This is because more material is being removed. When in doubt, feed slowly and increase the feed slowly. Do not strain the motor of the power feeder or the table saw.

Power feeders reduce the likelihood of injury and increase the quality of the cut. The feed speed is uniform and the cut is smoother.

Power feeders can be turned 90 degrees so that they push the stock along the fence rather than the table. This position would be used for edge-shaping. If you are edge- or face-shaping, the throat-plate opening must not catch on the workpiece as it passes by (Illus. 5-152). Make sure the throat plate is level with the saw table. It may be necessary to make an auxiliary throat plate of wood to reduce the opening size and make shaping with a power feeder easier. Whenever possible, use a power feeder for shaping operations. Make sure the setup is done correctly (Illus. 5-153–5-156).

Illus. 5-150. A power feeder can be used to feed stock across the molding head.

Illus. 5-151. The power feeder reduces the likelihood of kickback and produces a smooth cut.

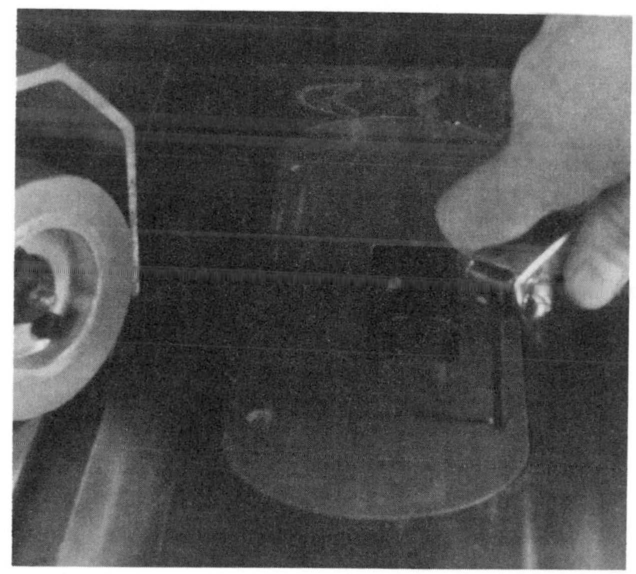

Illus. 5-152. Make sure the throat plate is flush with the top of the table, or the power feeder may not be able to guide the stock properly.

Illus. 5-153. The molding head is set up to take a cut along the edge. Part of the cutter is hidden inside the auxiliary wooden fence.

Illus. 5-154. The cut has been set up, and the fence is locked in position. Be sure to secure the blade height.

Illus. 5-155. Position the power feeder so that it is over the cutter head. This makes contact with the cutter head almost impossible.

Illus. 5-156. The power feeder reduces vibration and increases the quality of the cut while reducing the chance of kickbacks.

Disc Sanding

An outside curve is sanded against disc rotation. Turn on the power and feed the work into the disc (Illus. 5-157). Let the abrasive do the cutting. Take a light cut and keep the work moving. This will keep the abrasive from burning the wood. Always work on the half of the disc that is moving downward toward the table. If you work on the half of the disc moving upward, the disc has a tendency to lift the work.

If the edge of the curve is chamfered or beveled, the arbor or the stock can be tilted. This allows the disc to sand at the exact angle of the bevel or chamfer (Illus. 5-158). A miter gauge can be used for control, if desired (Illus. 5-159).

A circle-sanding jig can be used on the table saw (Illus. 5-160). The jig allows you to sand a perfect circle. The stock is first rough-cut to a slightly oversized circle. The rough-cut blank is then placed over the center pin on the jig. The blank is advanced into the moving disc (Illus. 5-161). When it touches, the disc is spun around the center pin until the entire edge is sanded.

Continue advancing the blank until you hit the stop on the jig. Back the circle away from the disc and remove it from the center pin. The edge of the disc is sanded to desired size. The circle-sanding jig works well for wheels, clock faces, and other circular objects. Straightedges can also be disc-sanded.

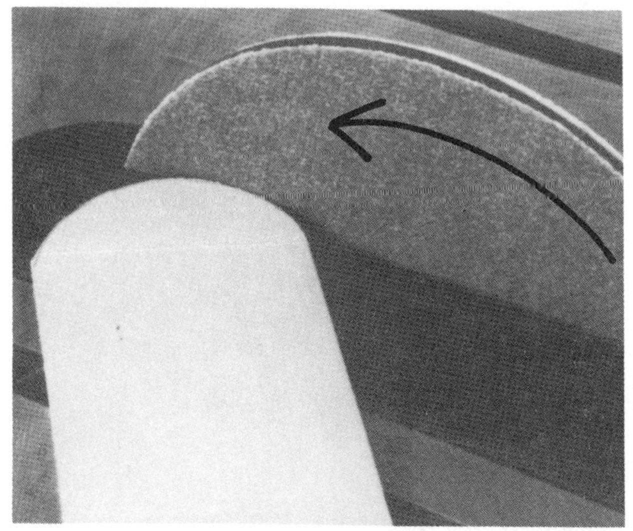

Illus. 5-157. An outside curve is sanded against disc rotation. Take light cuts and keep the work moving.

Some are sanded free-hand, and others are sanded with a guide such as the fence, miter gauge, or tapering jig.

When pinching a piece of stock between the fence and disc, take a light cut. A heavy cut can burn the wood and cause a kickback. Some discs require a slight offset (2 degrees) for edge-sanding with a fence. This reduces the stress on the disc and makes the sanding marks run parallel to the edge.

The most common error made when disc sanding is to burn the disc. The disc gets hot and fills up

Illus. 5-158. A bevel or chamfer can be moved to the desired angle and sanded. The arbor could also be tilted for this operation.

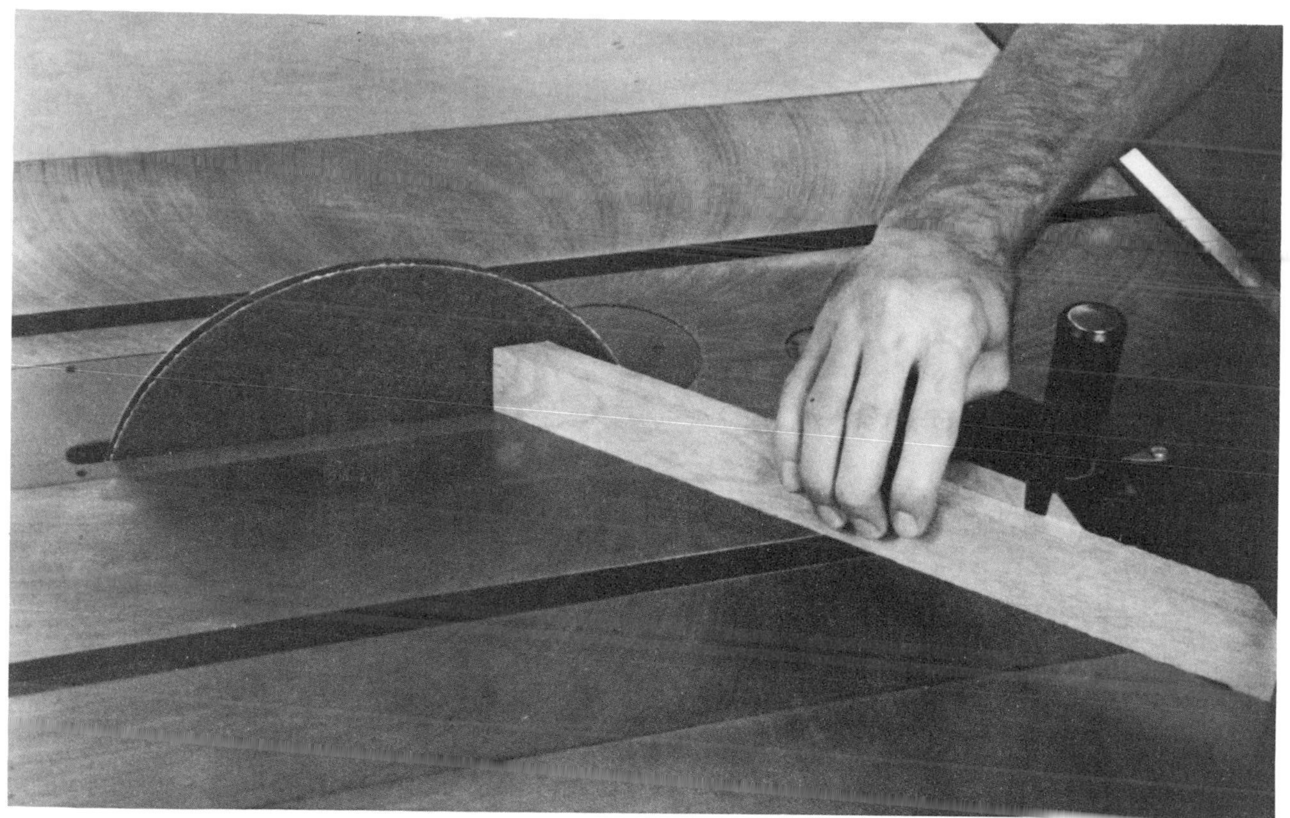
Illus. 5-159. For some sanding operations, the angle can be set on the miter gauge. The miter gauge also provides greater control over the work.

Illus. 5-160. This sanding jig allows you to sand a perfect circle. Stock is roughed out to a slightly oversized circle before sanding.

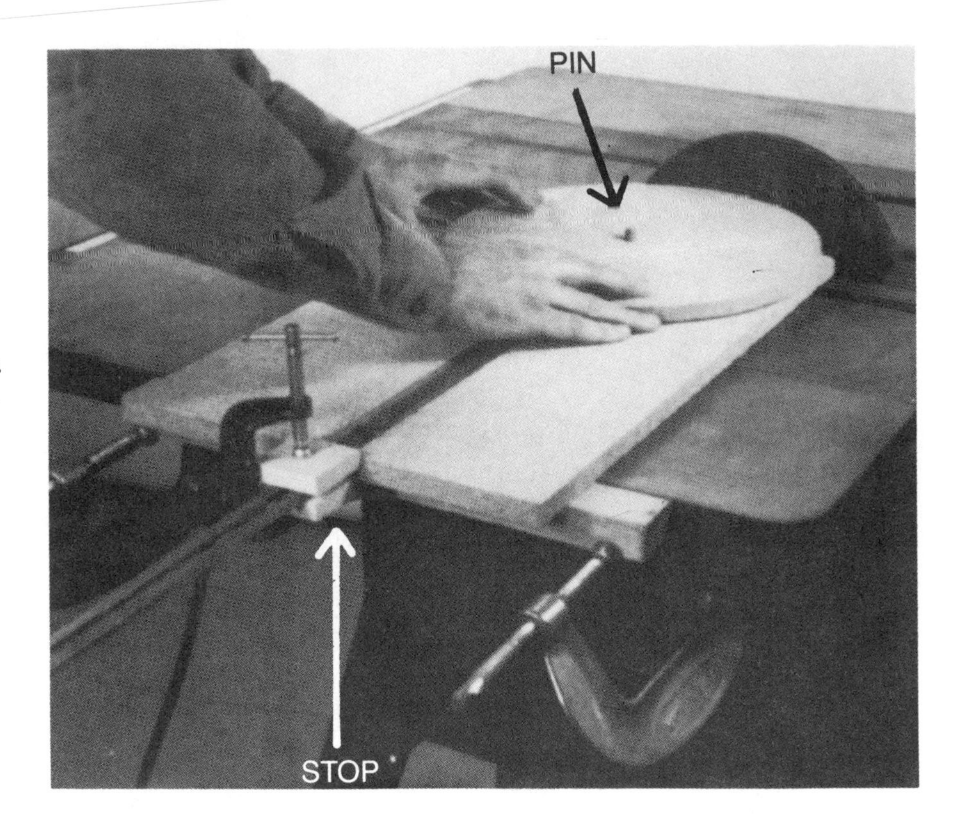

Illus. 5-161. The work turns around the pin in the center. The stop clamped to the pin controls the diameter of the circle.

with sawdust and pitch. A burned disc will not cut. Burning is caused by one of two things. The first is using too fine an abrasive for the job. The second is not moving the part as it is sanded. Keeping the part stationary causes heat buildup on the disc and the wood. Move the wood and use the entire downward-moving half of the disc. This spreads the heat over the wood and disc.

Remember, sanding operations cause a lot of dust to fly. Wear a dust mask, and make provisions for dust collection at the table saw. Because a sanding disc does not have teeth, some people feel that it is not as dangerous as a saw blade. A sanding disc is full of abrasive particles, which are small teeth. These teeth make smaller bites, but cut just the same. Keep your hands clear of the disc and throat plate. If your finger becomes pinched between the disc and throat plate, a serious injury can occur.

—6—
Intermediate and Advanced Operations

As you gain experience with the table saw, you will want to try some of the intermediate and advanced operations. Practice these operations on scrap stock. Save your expensive wood until you master the operations.

Remember, new experiences can present new hazards! Review Chapter 4 before you attempt any new operation. The information in Chapter 4 will help you identify an accident-producing situation and suggest ways of avoiding it.

Cutting Rabbets and Dadoes

Rabbets are L-shaped channels along the edge. Dadoes are U-shaped channels going through a piece of stock. These can be cut with a dado head or a single blade. For one or two rabbets or dadoes, it may be faster to use a single blade. It may take longer to set up a dado head than it takes to make the cut with a single blade. For multiple cuts, the dado head is much faster.

Single-Blade Rabbets and Dadoes A single-blade edge rabbet consists of two cuts. Set the distance from the fence to the blade for the rabbet width. Use a tooth that points away from the fence for this setting. Raise the blade to the rabbet height or slightly less. Turn on the saw and make the first cut on all pieces (Illus. 6-1). *Note:* The guard with the splitter cannot be used for this operation. Be sure to feed the stock with a push stick.

The second cut is now set up. With the stock on edge, adjust the fence. The piece being cut away should fall free as the cut is completed (Illus. 6-2). The distance between the blade and fence equals

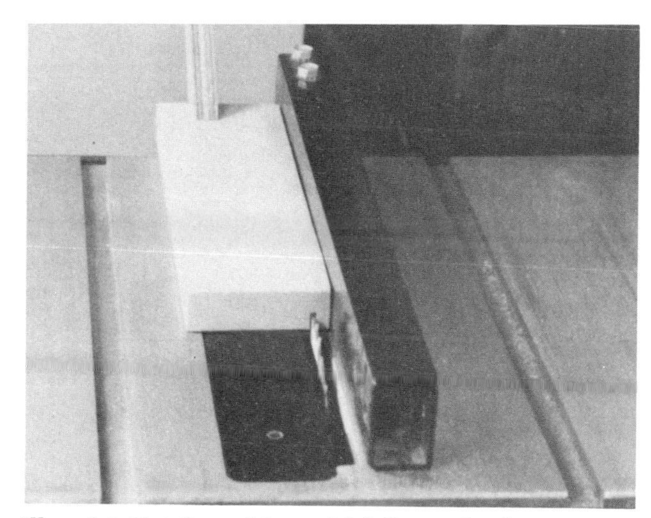

Illus. 6-1. Set the rabbet width from the fence to a tooth pointing away from the fence. Elevate the blade to rabbet height or slightly less. Guards having a splitter cannot be used for this cut.

Illus. 6-2. The thickness of the stock minus the rabbet determines the distance from the fence to a tooth that points toward the fence. Blade height should be set to meet the first kerf.

the thickness of the stock minus the rabbet. Use a tooth that points toward the fence. Set the blade height so that it meets the other kerf in the corner of the rabbet. Check the setup, and make the cut. A solid piece will be cut away (Illus. 6-3).

End-grain rabbets can be cut in a different way.

Illus. 6-3. A solid piece will be cut away when the rabbet is made. Notice how it falls free. If it were between the fence and blade, there could be a kickback.

Illus. 6-4. A series of saw kerfs can be used to make an end rabbet, which is the distance from the fence to the far side of the blade. Blade height determines rabbet height.

Set the distance from the fence to the far side of the blade at the desired rabbet width. Set the blade height to the desired rabbet height. Place the edge of the work against the miter gauge, and the end against the fence.

Turn on the saw and make the cut (Illus. 6-4). Now, move the stock one saw kerf away from the fence and make another cut (Illus. 6-5). Continue moving the stock (Illus. 6-6) until the rabbet is completed (Illus. 6-7). The top of the rabbet may be rough or irregular. Smooth it with a chisel or plane.

In some cases, a wooden fence is attached to the miter gauge. The end of the workpiece is positioned to its pencil line (Illus. 6-8), and a cut is made. The

Illus. 6-5. The work is moved away from the fence for the second cut.

Illus. 6-6. The final kerf is cut into the work.

Illus. 6-7. The completed end rabbet. The slight roughness on the rabbet face can be trimmed away with a chisel.

Illus. 6-9. By moving the workpiece away from the blade and making additional cuts, you will form an end rabbet. (Photo courtesy of Skil Power Tools.)

workpiece is moved one saw kerf away from the line, and another cut is made. This continues (Illus. 6-9) until a complete rabbet is formed.

The series of saw cuts used to form an end-grain rabbet is safer than turning the end grain down on the table to make a second cut. It is much more difficult to control the piece while it is in a vertical position, and it is possible for the rabbeted end to drop into the throat-plate opening. A tenoning jig can be used to make the second cut safely (Illus. 6-10).

Illus. 6-10. A tenoning jig can be used to hold the workpiece vertically while the mating cut is made. Make sure the stock is perpendicular to the table and clamped securely.

Illus. 6-8. The end of the workpiece aligns with the pencil line. The wooden face attached to the miter gauge reduces tear-out and supports the work while the rabbet is being cut. (Photo courtesy of Skil Power Tools.)

This procedure for cutting a rabbet can also be used to cut a dado. Set the fence to the near side of the blade for the first setting (Illus. 6-11). Use the distance from the end or edge to the top (the part of the dado closest to the fence) of the dado. Make this cut in all pieces (Illus. 6-12). Use the miter gauge to control cross-grain cuts.

Set the fence to the far side of the blade for the second setting. Use the distance from the end or edge to the bottom of the dado (the part of the dado farthest from the fence) (Illus. 6-13). Make this cut in the piece. If the dado is a cross-grain dado, move one saw kerf away from the fence and make another cut (Illus. 6-14). Continue until you meet the

Illus. 6-11. A single-blade dado is similar to a single-blade rabbet. Set the blade height to dado depth and adjust the fence so the blade cuts the top of the dado.

Illus. 6-12. Make the first cut in all pieces before changing the setup. Control stock with the miter gauge.

first kerf (Illus. 6-15). For a dado with the grain, the fence must be moved one saw kerf toward the waste stock. Another cut is made in all the pieces. Continue moving the fence until you meet the first saw kerf (Illus. 6-16).

Single-blade rabbets and dadoes are sometimes called lazy dadoes. This implies the operator is too lazy to set up a dado head. For a few rabbets or dadoes, the single-blade method may be best. When several dadoes or rabbets must be cut, the dado head should be set up. This reduces handling and setup time.

Cutting Rabbets with a Dado Head The best way to cut rabbets with the dado head requires the use of an auxiliary fence. The dado head is mounted and set up. The dado head should be wider than the rabbet. A ¾- or 1-inch-thick auxiliary fence is then attached to the fence (Illus. 6-17). The dado head is dropped below the table, and the auxiliary fence is

Illus. 6-13. Set the fence so the blade cuts the bottom of the dado. Do not change the blade height.

Illus. 6-14. Make the cut and move the piece away from the fence. Continue cutting until you meet the first kerf.

Illus. 6-15. The dado produced shows some irregularity. This can be smoothed with a chisel.

placed over the throat plate and locked in position. Mark the fence at the desired dado height (Illus. 6-18). Turn on the saw and raise the dado into the auxiliary fence (Illus. 6-19). Make sure the dado head only cuts into the wooden auxiliary fence. Stop the dado head at the mark on the fence. Shut off the saw and readjust the fence. The amount of dado head exposed should equal the rabbet width. Make a test cut on a piece of scrap.

Illus. 6-16. When a dado is cut with the grain, the fence must be moved one saw kerf toward the waste stock. Make sure you cut all parts before moving the fence.

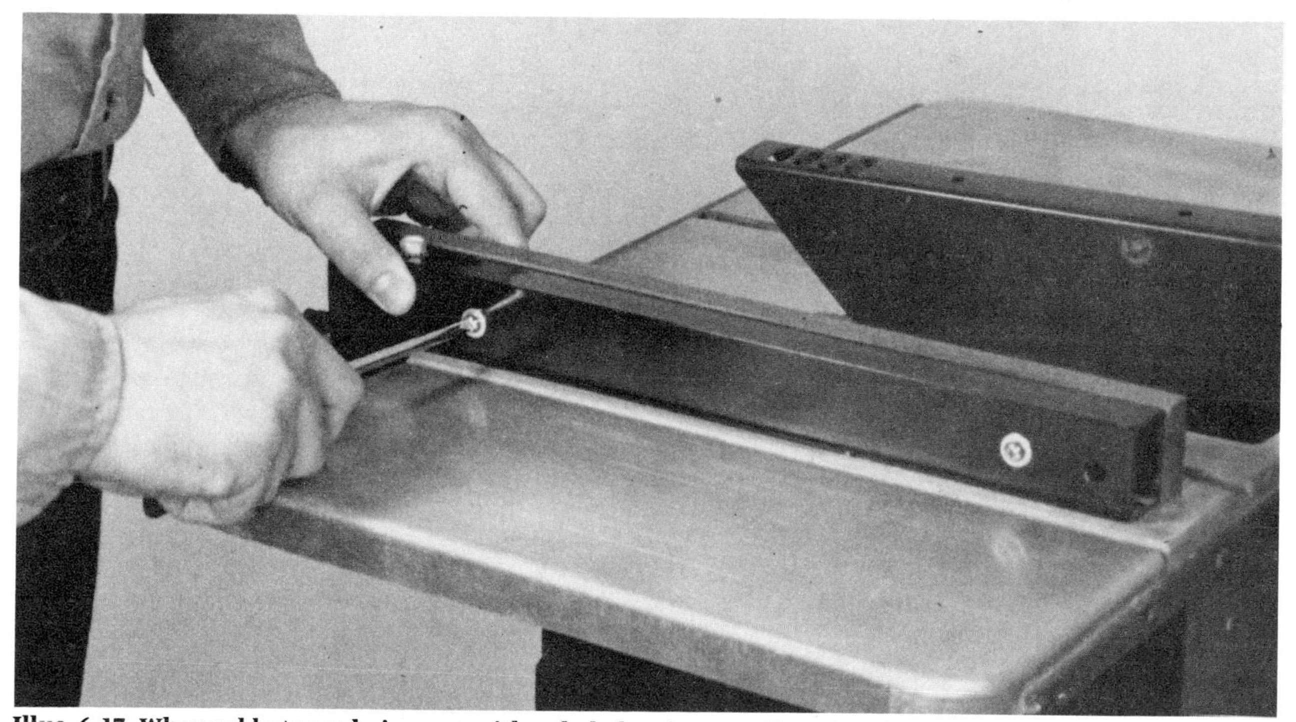

Illus. 6-17. When rabbets are being cut with a dado head, an auxiliary head must be attached to the fence. Attach it to the side closest to the dado head.

Illus. 6-18. Mark the desired height of the dado head on the auxiliary fence.

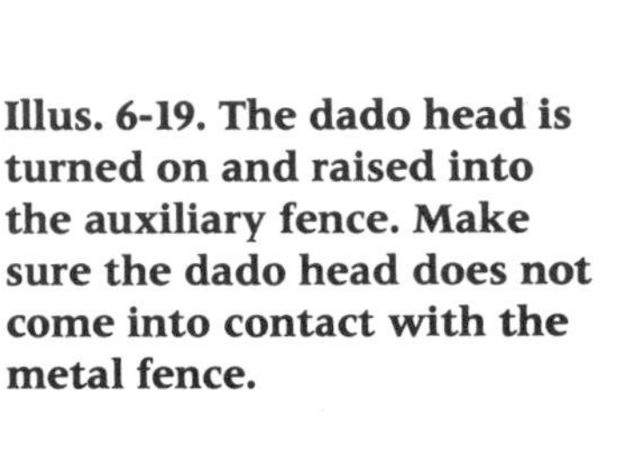

Illus. 6-19. The dado head is turned on and raised into the auxiliary fence. Make sure the dado head does not come into contact with the metal fence.

When edge rabbets are being cut, the stock can ride along the fence (Illus. 6-20). Use a push stick for narrow pieces. End rabbets should be controlled with the miter gauge (Illus. 6-21). If you are rabbeting sheet stock, it is best to use a carbide dado head. Steel dado heads dull rapidly.

A shaper or molding head equipped with jointer cutters can also be used to cut rabbets. The molding head is raised into the auxiliary fence in the same way as the dado head. The setup and cutting procedures are the same (Illus. 6-22). Shaper cutters are made of high-speed steel and should be used on solid stock.

Rabbets cut in the manner described here are faster to cut since you handle the stock only once. If you are cutting one or two rabbets, setup time will slow you down, and two saw-blade cuts would be faster. A power feeder can be used to guide stock into the dado head for edge-rabbeting. Set it up in the same way you would for ripping or dadoing.

Cutting Blind Dadoes Blind dadoes are dadoes that do not go through the piece. They stop somewhere in the part. Blind dadoes are often used in cabinetwork. A blind dado joint looks like a butt joint from the front. A blind dado shows no tear-out, and a loose fit is not visible from the front. It is cut in the same way as a regular dado except that it is not fed completely through.

After the dado head is set up correctly, you can

Illus. 6-20. The stock rides along the auxiliary fence for edge rabbets. Feed the stock with a push stick.

Illus. 6-21. When cutting end rabbets, butt the stock against the auxiliary fence. Use a miter gauge to control and feed the stock.

Illus. 6-22. A shaper head equipped with jointer cutters can also be used to cut rabbets. An auxiliary fence covers the portion of the cutters not in use.

locate stops or stop marks. These help indicate where to stop the dado. If the table is long enough, clamp a stop to the table or place a piece of masking tape on the table. If the dado is longer than the table, mark the end of the cut on top of the stock. Mark the end of the dado on the fence using masking tape (Illus. 6-23). When the lines meet, the dado is cut (Illus. 6-24).

Cut a blind dado as you would a regular dado. When you hit the stop or the stop marks line up, turn off the saw (Illus. 6-25). Let the dado head come to a complete stop before you move the stock.

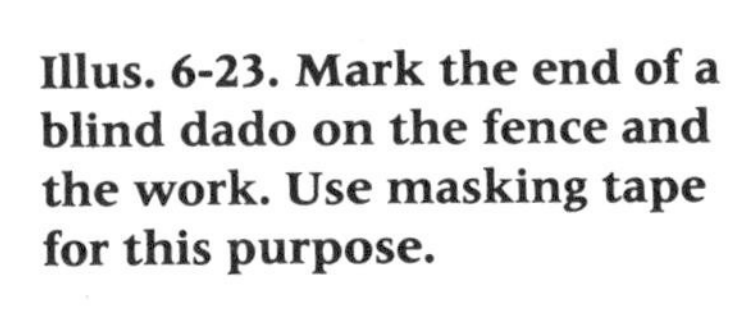

Illus. 6-23. Mark the end of a blind dado on the fence and the work. Use masking tape for this purpose.

Illus. 6-24. Feed the stock into the dado head as you would any other piece.

Illus. 6-25. When the marks line up, shut off the saw. Do not release the stock until the dado head stops.

Lift the stock off the dado head and check the end of the cut (Illus. 6-26). Make sure you have cut far enough into the stock. You may wish to make the end of the dado square with hand tools (Illus. 6-27). It is also possible to cut an arc on the mating piece so that no hand tool work is needed.

Illus. 6-26. The end of the cut will be curved due to the shape of the dado head.

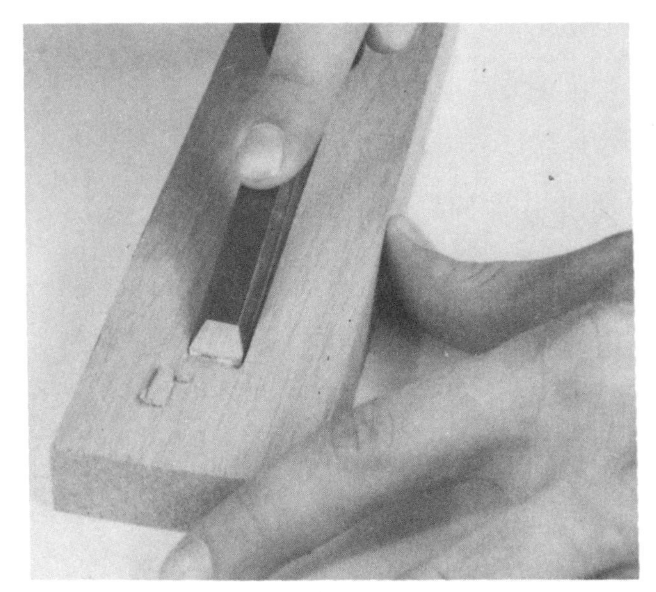

Illus. 6-27. The end of a blind dado can be squared with a chisel.

A dado which is blind at both ends should not be cut on a table saw. A plunge router is a safer tool for this job. Never attempt to set a piece down on a dado head to begin a blind dado! This is an inv ta-tion to tragedy and will almost surely cause a kick-back with your fingers very close to the dado head. A plunge router makes the cut safer; the stock is clamped, and your hands are on the router away from the cutter.

Cutting Lap Joints Lap joints are corner or cross joints where one piece laps over the other. They are commonly used on cabinet faceplates. The lap joint can be cut with a dado head. Set the height of the dado head to one-half the stock thickness. Chapter 7 shows you an easy technique to find the center of a board when using a dado head. For end lap joints, use the stock width to set the fence (Illus. 6-28). The distance from the far side of the dado head to the stop should equal the stock width.

Mark your pieces. One-half of the pieces will be cut on the good or exposed face (Illus. 6-29). The other half will be cut on the back. Use the miter

Illus. 6-28. Position the stock against the outside of the dado head. Position a stop between the fence and the stock. The fence is locked into position.

Illus. 6-29. Clamp the stop to the fence behind the position of the dado head. Note that the stock has been marked so that the lap is formed on the correct side of the workpiece.

gauge to control your stock (Illus. 6-30). You will have to make several cuts to make the lap joint (Illus. 6-31). The fence will mark the end of the joint. *Note:* If your pieces tear out as they are cut, you may wish to back the cut with a piece of scrap attached to the miter gauge (Illus. 6-32). Careful layout and setup will produce a good-fitting lap joint (Illus. 6-33).

Illus. 6-30. Butt the stock to the stop and turn the saw on. Guide the work into the dado head.

Illus. 6-31. Move the work away from the stop and continue making cuts. Note that the work and the operator's hands are moving away from the dado head.

Illus. 6-32. After making the last cut, test-fit the work to another piece. Make any needed adjustments to the dado height. Extra pieces should be prepared and used as test pieces.

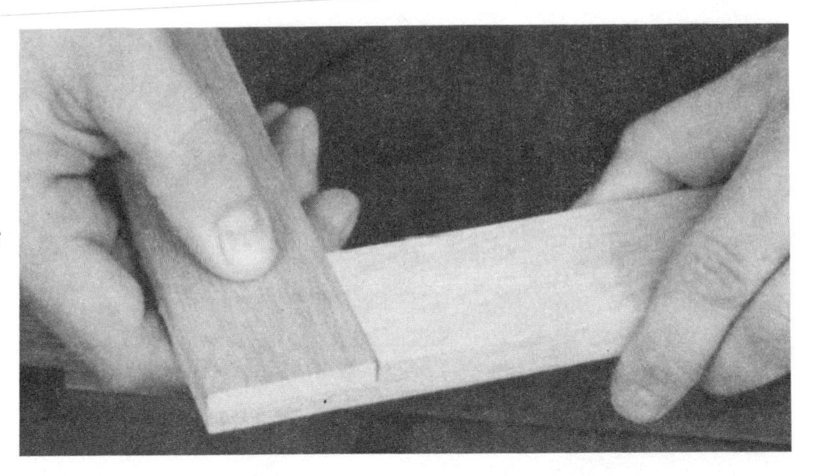

Illus. 6-33. A careful layout will produce a good-fitting lap joint.

End lap joints can also be cut using a miter gauge. A specialty miter gauge or a standard miter gauge with an auxiliary wooden fence can be used. The stock is marked, and the layout line is aligned with the dado head (Illus. 6-34). A stop is then secured to the miter gauge to position the stock (Illus. 6-35). Cut all of the parts using this setup (Illus. 6-36). If you are using a specialty miter gauge, make sure the metal face does not contact the dado head. Make additional cuts with the stop removed. Move the stock away from the dado head and make a cut. Continue this process until the joint is cut (Illus. 6-37).

Cross lap joints require two marks or stops. This

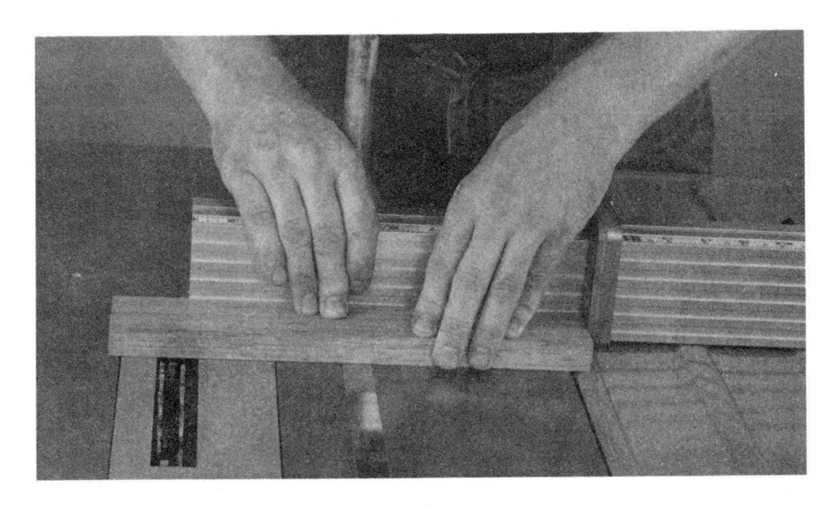

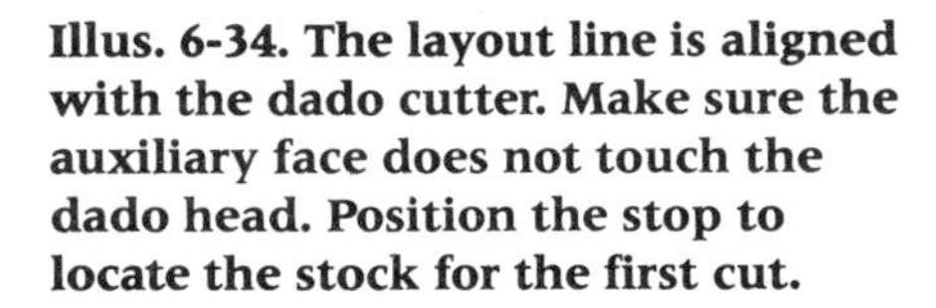

Illus. 6-34. The layout line is aligned with the dado cutter. Make sure the auxiliary face does not touch the dado head. Position the stop to locate the stock for the first cut.

Illus. 6-35. Butt the end of the workpiece to the stop and guide the miter gauge close to the dado head.

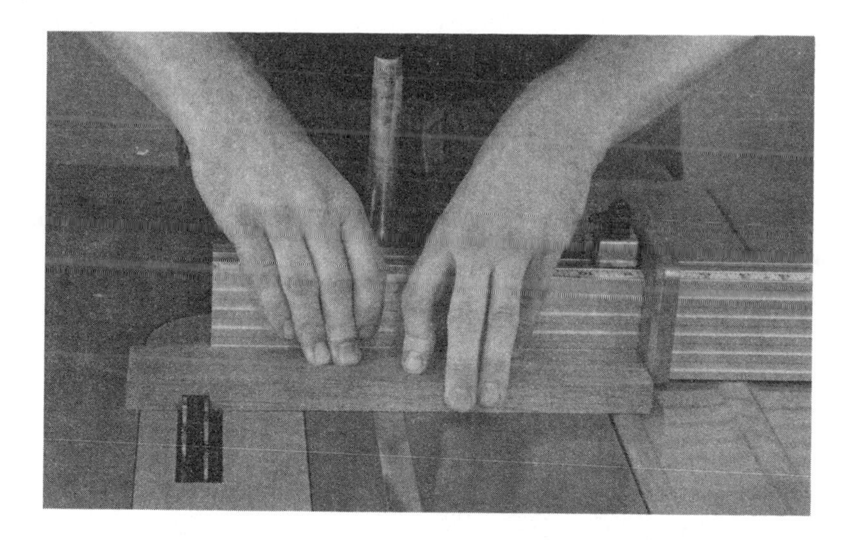

Illus. 6-36. Turn on the saw and make the cut in all of the pieces. Turn the pieces end for end if both ends get a lap joint.

Illus. 6-37. Lift the stop and continue making cuts until all of the stock is removed. This should produce a good-fitting joint.

is because they are not on the end of the piece. You can clamp two stops to the table. Each stop marks one end of the lap joint. Masking tape can also be used to mark the ends. Butt the work to the first stop and make a cut (Illus. 6-38). Use the miter gauge to control the work (Illus. 6-39). Use the second stop to make another cut (Illus. 6-40). Both ends of the lap joint are now cut (Illus. 6-41). If

Illus. 6-38. The stop clamped to the table marks both ends of a cross-lap joint. Butt the work to the first stop.

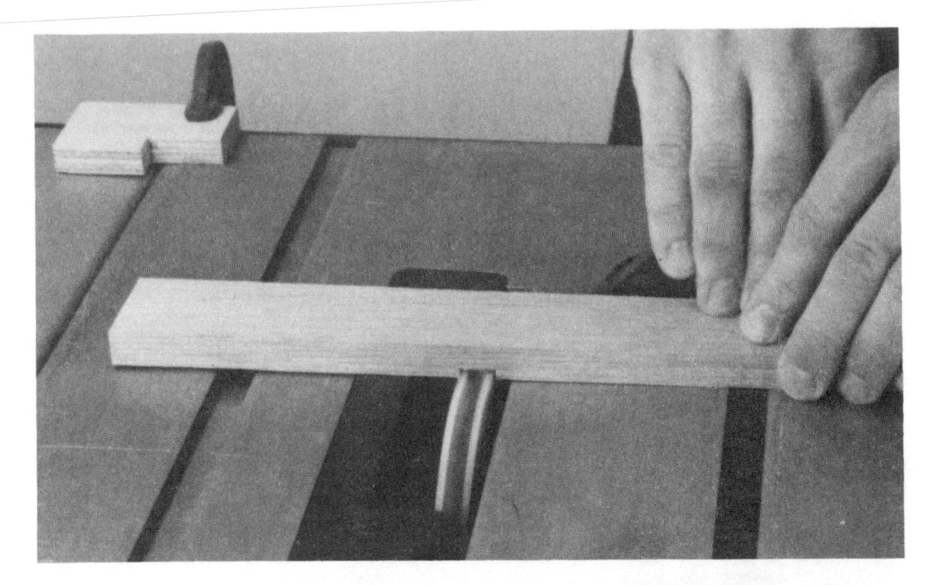

Illus. 6-39. Make the first cut. Control the stock with the miter gauge.

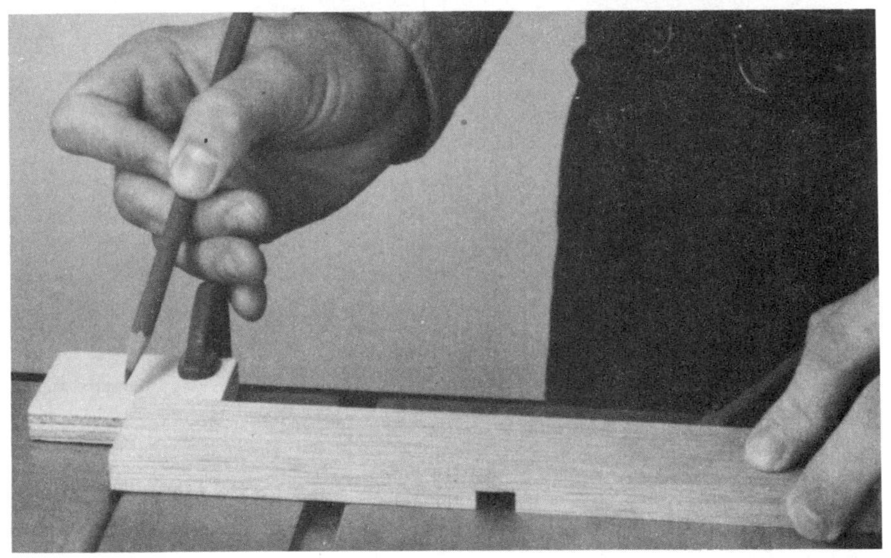

Illus. 6-40. Butt the work to the second stop.

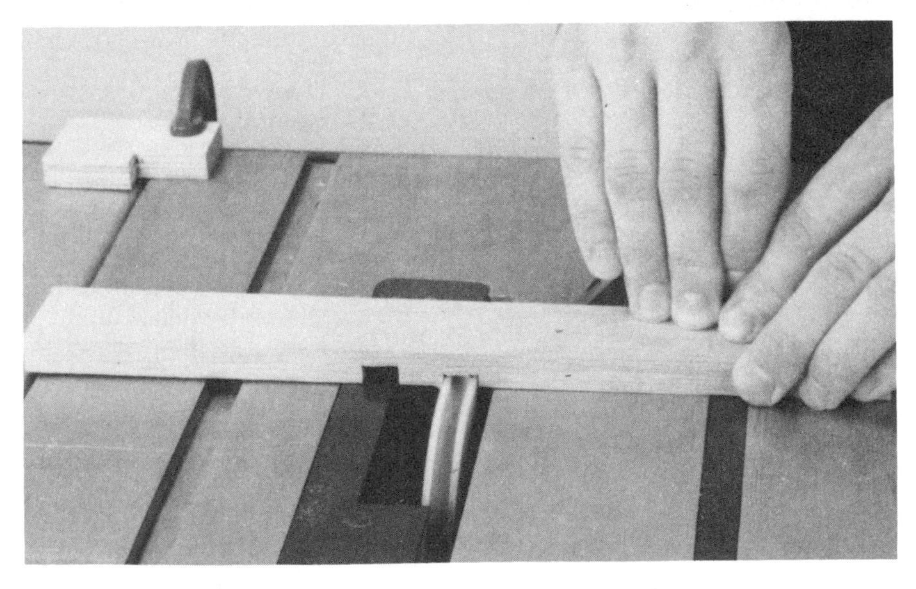

Illus. 6-41. Make the second cut. This cut marks the other end of the cross-lap joint.

more stock remains between the two cuts, continue cutting until it is gone (Illus. 6-42). Several identical cross lap joints can be produced quickly with this method (Illus. 6-43).

Cutting a Series of Dadoes Often, a series of equally spaced dadoes is needed. Pigeon holes are a good example of this (Illus. 6-44). After the dado head is set up, a stop is clamped to the table or a jig is fitted to the miter gauge. This stop should be slightly smaller than the dado. The distance from the stop to the dado should be the desired distance between dado cuts (Illus. 6-45).

Make the first dado cut (or rabbet), and butt this cut to the stop. This locates the next dado (Illus. 6-46). Proceed with the cutting. Control your stock

Illus. 6-42. Make additional cuts to remove the remaining stock.

Illus. 6-43. Tight cross-lap joints can be produced easily with this method.

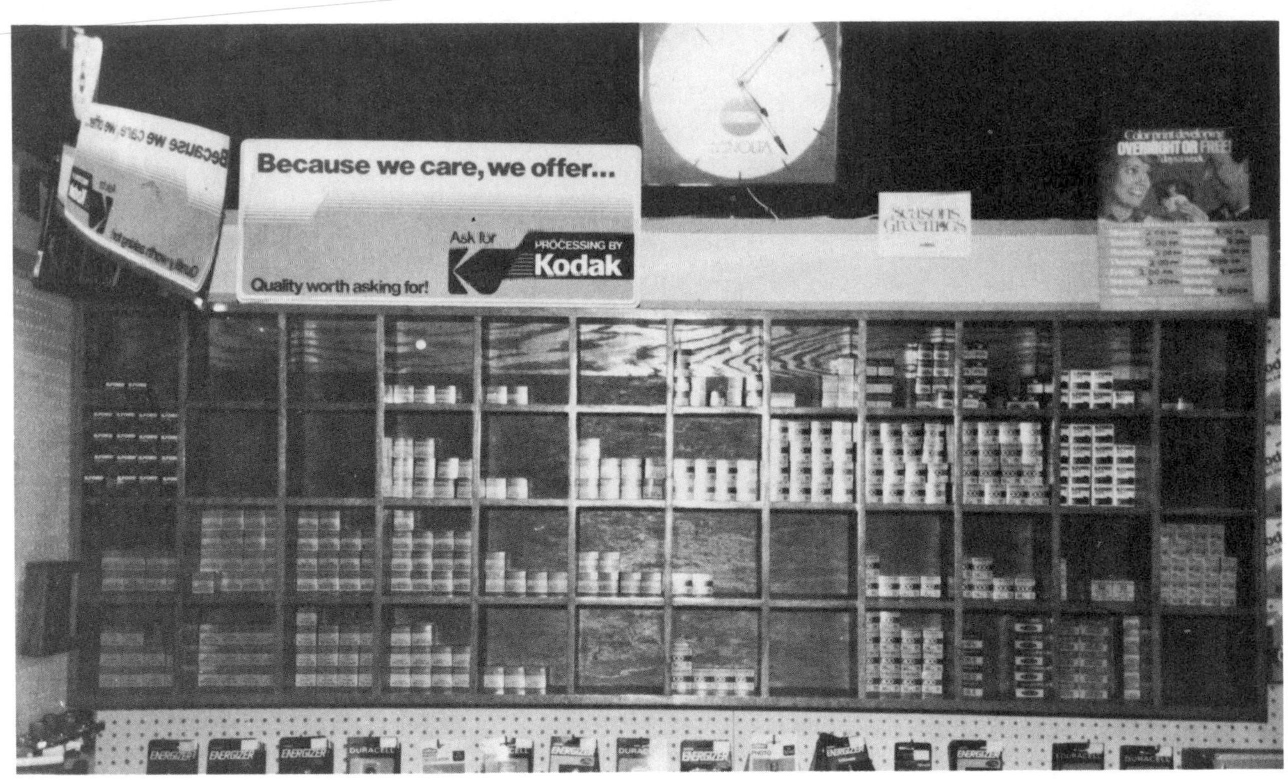

Illus. 6-44. These pigeon holes required several series of dado cuts. The cabinet was built in my shop.

Illus. 6-45. A stop attached to the miter gauge is used to locate dadoes in a pigeon-hole setup. The distance from the stop to the dado head controls dado spacing.

Illus. 6-46. The rabbet butted against the stop locates the first dado.

with the miter gauge (Illus. 6-47). The fence can also locate dadoes (Illus. 6-48). The stop clamped to the table is used for blind dadoes (Illus. 6-49).

When dadoes go with the grain, the fence has to be moved for each successive cut. A piece of stock has to be laid out for this, to be used to mark and set up the cuts. Always test the setup on a piece of scrap before cutting your parts.

Cutting Mortises and Tenons

A mortise-and-tenon joint is a two-part joint. The mortise is a slot or hole cut into one piece. The tenon is a mating tongue that fits into the mortise. The three most common mortise-and-tenon joints are the open, blind, and haunched joints. The open mortise-and-tenon joint can be cut completely on

Illus. 6-47. The stop is under the first dado as the second one is cut. The miter gauge controls the feed of the work.

Illus. 6-48. The fence can also locate dadoes. The stop clamped to the table is used to make blind dadoes.

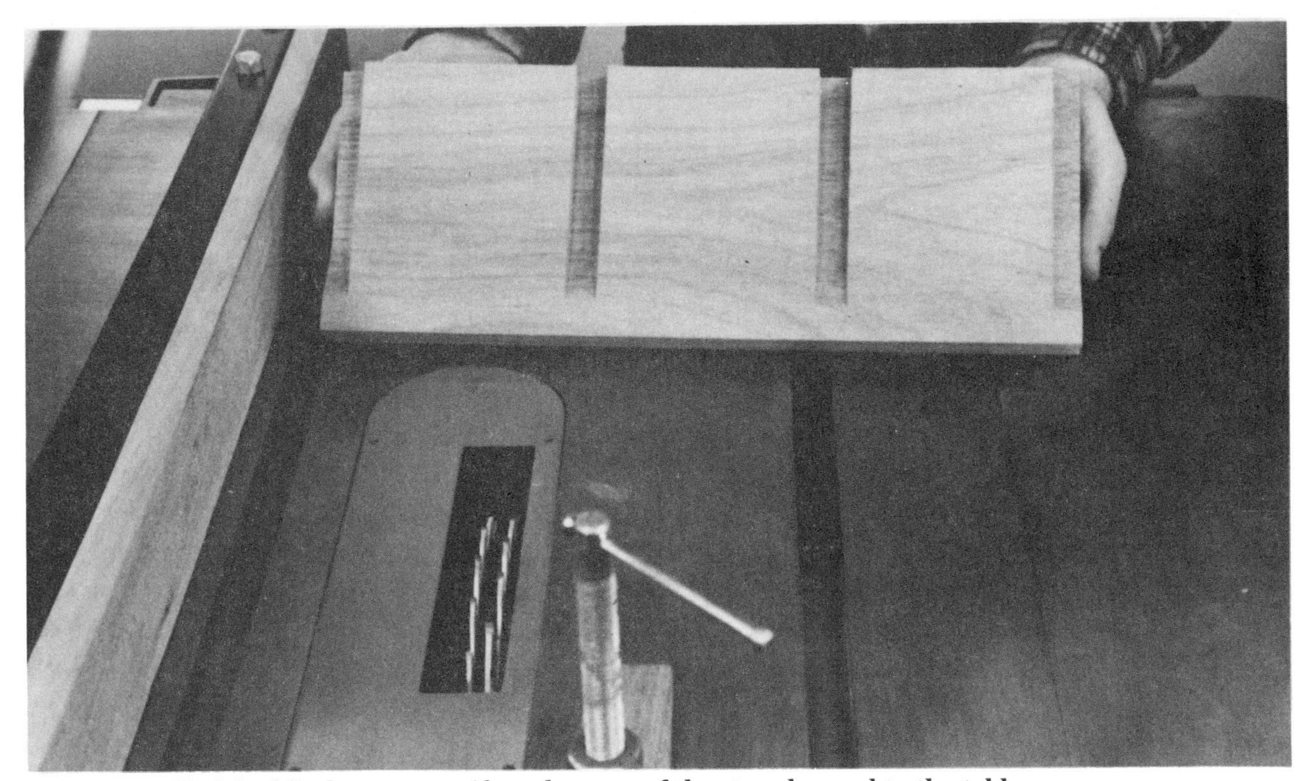

Illus. 6-49. All of the blind cuts are uniform because of the stop clamped to the table.

the table saw. The tenons on blind and haunched mortise-and-tenon joints can be cut on the table saw, but the mortises must be cut elsewhere.

Using a Tenoning Jig A tenoning jig is a device used to control stock while the tenon is cut (Illus. 6-50). It may be shop-made or commercially manufactured. Some tenoning jigs ride on or along the fence (Illus. 6-51) and others ride in the miter slot.

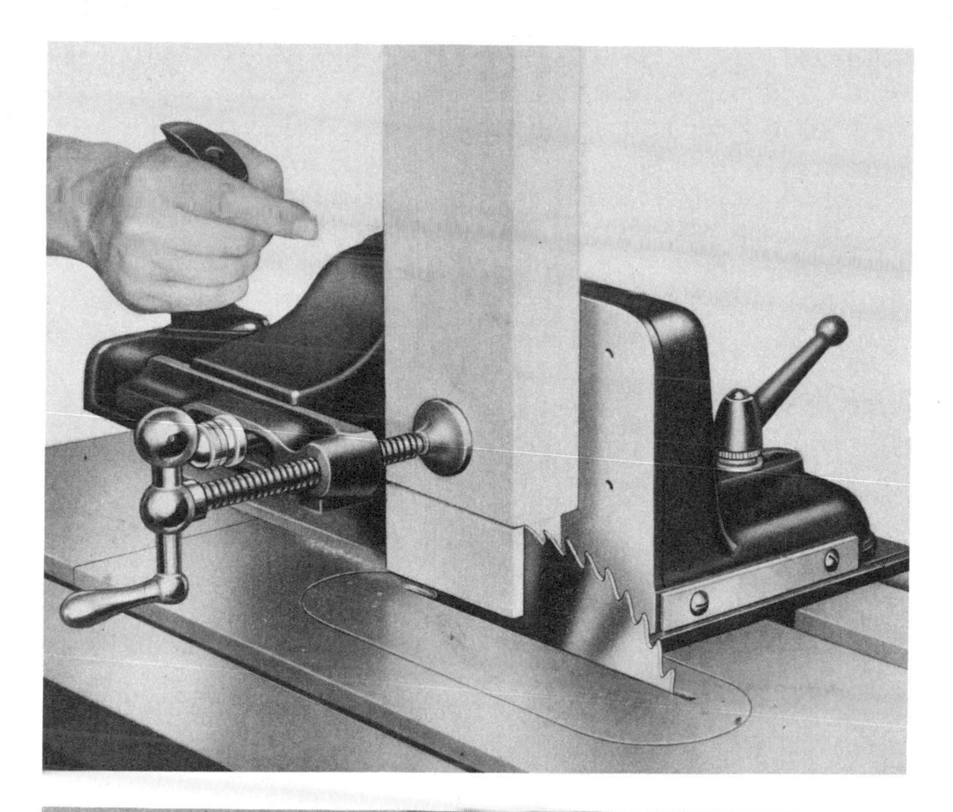

Illus. 6-50. The tenoning jig is a device used to control stock while the tenon is being cut. This one is commercially manufactured and rides in the miter slot.

Illus. 6-51. The tenoning jig makes the cheek cuts. This tenoning jig is shop-made. It rides on the fence.

The chief job of the tenoning jig is to hold stock in a vertical position while the cheek cut is made.

The shoulder cuts are made on the tenons first. Set the blade height to the layout line. Set the fence to the length of the tenon. Use the far side of the blade. On open mortise-and-tenon joints, this will be equal to stock width. On haunched and blind joints, it will be less than stock width. Make the shoulder cuts on both sides (faces) of all pieces (Illus. 6-52).

Set up the tenoning jig to make the cheek cuts. Adjust the tenoning jig so that the blade cuts a kerf that meets the shoulder cut (Illus. 6-51). The kerf should be in the waste portion of the cheek. Make sure the stock that is cut away during the cheek cut is not pinched between the fence and jig. This may cause a kickback. Make all cheek cuts (Illus. 6-53). The tenon can now be used to lay out the open mortise.

The tenoning jig can also be used to cut the open

Illus. 6-52. When a through tenon is made, the shoulders are cut on both faces of the stock.

Illus. 6-54. The first cheek in the open mortise is cut using the tenoning jig.

Illus. 6-53. Make the second cheek cut on all of the parts. Make sure the kerf is in the waste portion of the stock. Use the tenon to lay out the open mortise.

Illus. 6-55. Reversing the piece allows the second cheek cut to be made. Any stock between the cheeks should now be removed.

mortise. The open mortise is a series of cuts that match the tenon. Lay out the open mortise and set up the tenoning jig. The tenoning jig should make a cheek cut in the mortise area of the piece (Illus. 6-54). When the piece is reversed (Illus. 6-55), the tenoning jig will cut the other cheek of the mortise. Readjust the tenoning jig to remove the rest of the mortise. Check the fit of the mating parts (Illus. 6-56).

A chisel may be needed to true up the bottom of

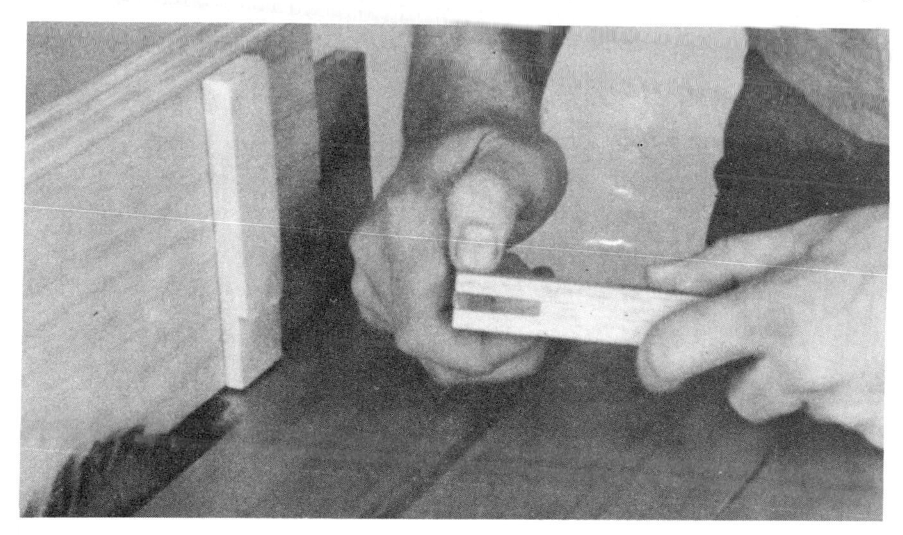

Illus. 6-56. Check the fit of your open mortise and tenon to ensure accurate setup.

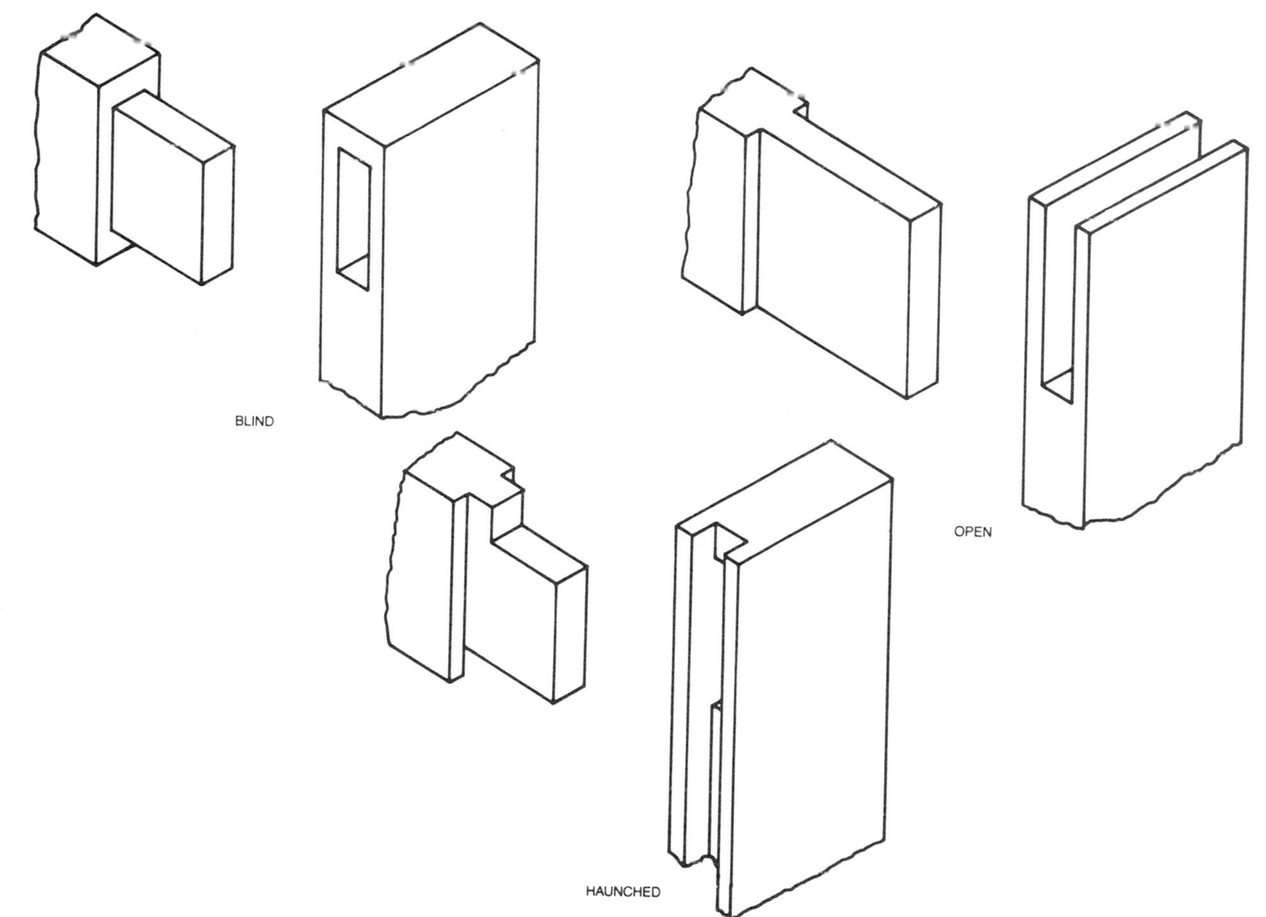

Illus. 6-57. Three types of mortises. A haunched mortise has a step (or haunch) cut into it. This allows it to fit the groove made on the vertical parts.

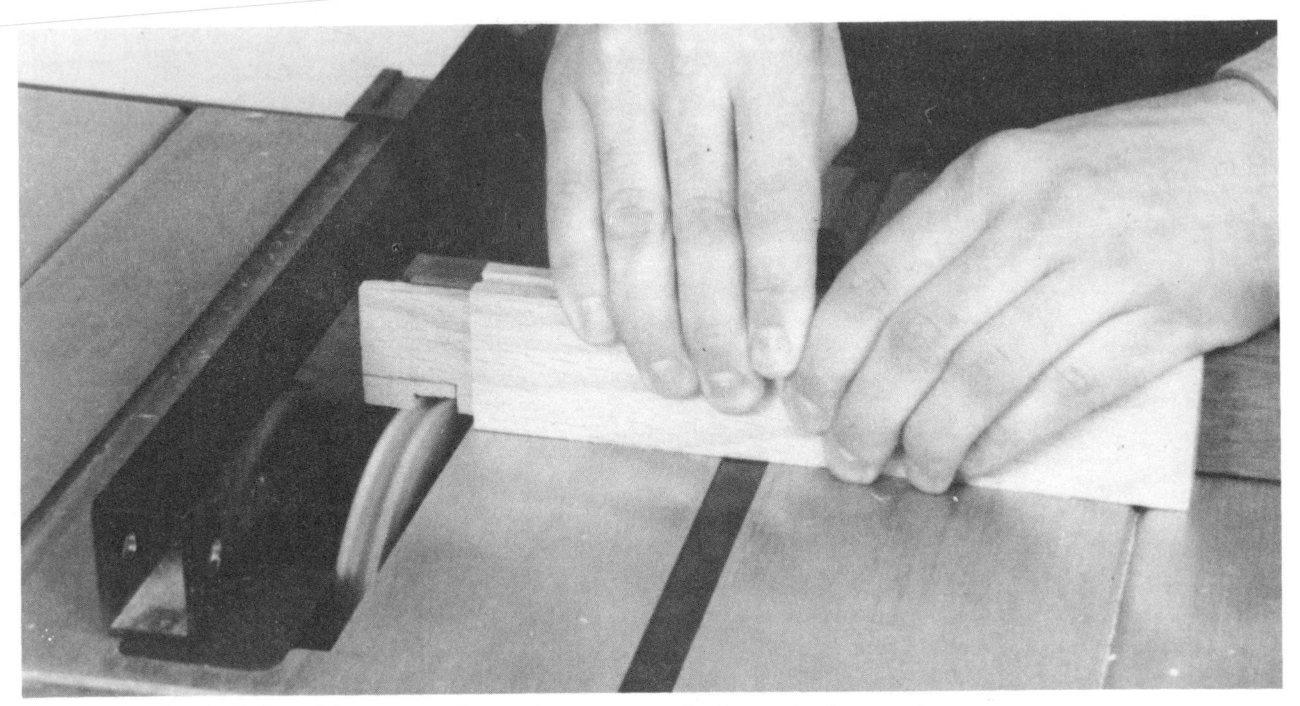

Illus. 6-58. The dado head is commonly used to cut out the haunched area of a tenon.

the mortise or improve the fit between the mortise and tenon. Work carefully and take light cuts. Removing too much stock will ruin the fit.

The haunched mortise-and-tenon joint is a joint preferred for door construction. The door frame has a groove cut around the inside edges of the rails (horizontal parts) and stiles (vertical parts). The rails have a haunch or step cut on the tenons (Illus. 6-57). This haunch fills the groove so it cannot be seen when the door is assembled. The groove around the inside edge of the frame accommodates a panel of plywood or solid wood. In some cases, a raised panel is used with this frame.

When the haunch is cut, it is as long and wide as the groove depth and width. The haunch takes a step of ½ inch or greater. This increases the strength of the door and ensures that the mortise cavity will not be opened with a rabbet cut of ⅜ inch. The ⅜-inch rabbet cut is common on ⅜-inch lip doors. Haunches are usually cut on the tenon with the dado head (Illus. 6-58). Use the haunched tenon to determine and lay out the mortise position (Illus. 6-59). The mortise can be drilled or routed out and squared with a chisel. It can also be cut with a mortising machine. Mortising machines cut mortises of a nominal size, such as ¼, ⅜, and ½ inch, etc. Keep this in mind when you lay out the grooves

Illus. 6-59. The haunched tenon can be used to lay out the mortise. Note the slight angle of the haunch. It fits tight at the surface, but there is no interference beneath.

on the inside edges of the parts. Odd-sized grooves (and tenons) make the mortises more difficult to cut.

Blind mortises are also laid out with the tenon. The tenon usually has four shoulders. The tenon is easiest to cut with a dado head if all its shoulders are of equal depth. On thinner stock (1 inch or less), two different shoulder depths are used. Shoulder depth on the faces is usually one-quarter to one-third of the stock thickness. Shoulder depth on the outer edge is at least one-half inch (Illus. 6-60). This keeps the joint from being fragile.

The mortises must be held at least ½ inch away from the end of the stock. Mortises closer to the end of the stock put too much stress on the end-grain fibers of the wood. This produces a weak joint. A blind mortise is cut in the same way as a haunched mortise.

Illus. 6-60. Shoulder depth on the outer edge is ½ inch. This keeps the joint from being fragile.

The tenoning jig can also be used to cut lap joints. The shoulder cut for the lap joint is made the same way as the shoulder cut for a tenon. Shoulder-cut depth for a lap joint equals one-half of stock thickness. The fence is set to the width of the stock. Use a tooth that points away from the fence. Mark all pieces so you know which face must be cut away.

Set up the tenoning jig to make the cheek cut. The cheek cut is made in the waste stock, and meets the shoulder cut. The two cuts should form a right angle (Illus. 6-61). Make a few practice cuts to be sure the pieces fit together correctly. Tenoning jigs are a challenge to make. A shop-made tenoning jig can be as accurate as a manufactured jig if it is built carefully. All the parts for a tenoning jig can be made on the table saw. Small pieces of sheet stock work well for most parts because they are less likely to swell or warp.

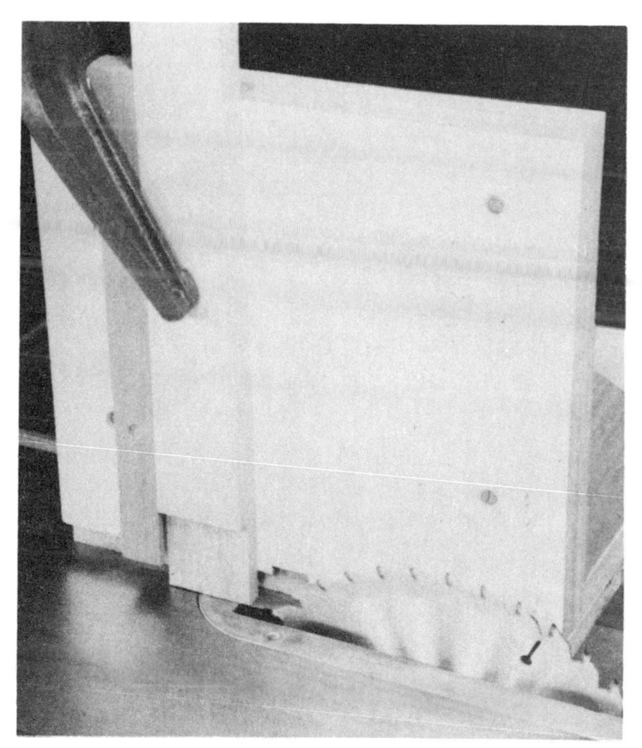

Illus. 6-61. The tenoning jig is used to make the cheek cut on a lap joint. The cheek cuts meets the shoulder cut squarely.

Cutting Tenons with a Dado Head Tenons made with a dado head require no more handling than tenons cut using a tenoning jig. This is because the dado head makes the shoulder cut and part of the

Illus. 6-62. Tenon length is the distance from the far side of the dado head to the fence.

cheek cut in one pass. Set the tenon length from the fence to the far side of the dado head (Illus. 6-62). Adjust the height of the dado head to meet the face of the tenon. Test the fence and dado height adjustments on a piece of scrap. Make any minor adjustments needed, and test the setup again.

On a tenon with edge shoulders, a different dado height may be needed. Cut the faces first (Illus. 6-63), and then readjust the dado height for the edge shoulders (Illus. 6-64). Test the setup on a piece of scrap. Readjust the setup if necessary.

Face and edge shoulders are cut in the same way. Stock is controlled with the miter gauge. The fence limits the length of the tenon. After the first cut, the stock is moved away from the fence so another cut can be made (Illus. 6-65). Repeat the process until all stock is removed. Cut the opposite side of the stock in the same manner.

Illus. 6-63. Both faces are cut before the setup is changed to cut edges.

Dado heads cannot be used to cut mortises. Lay out and cut the mortises using the same procedures listed under the section Cutting Mortises and Tenons: Using a Tenoning Jig (pages 174–179).

Resawing

Resawing is the process of ripping a thick piece of stock into two thinner pieces. Resawn pieces are often glued together to make wider panels for cabinet sides or doors (Illus. 6-66). The grain of the two thinner pieces is often matched at the glue line to give a book effect. This is commonly known as a book match. Stock to be resawn should be true. Its edges and faces should be parallel to each other. There should be no knots or other defects.

Choose a fine-cutting rip or combination blade. Its teeth should have a moderate set. This will minimize pitch accumulation and the chance of kickback.

Select a piece of stock that is thick enough to yield pieces of the desired thickness. For example, a ¾-inch-thick piece of stock cannot be resawn into two pieces ⅜ inch thick. This is because the saw blade will turn ⅛ inch or more of the thickness into the saw kerf. A ¾-inch piece will produce two pieces of ¼-inch stock with no trouble. This allows ¼ inch for a saw kerf and sanding or planing of the sawn surfaces.

Set the distance from the fence to the blade at the

Illus. 6-64. After the height of the dado is readjusted (if necessary), the edge shoulders are cut.

Illus. 6-65. The second edge shoulder is being cut. Stock is moved away from the fence for consecutive cuts.

Illus. 6-66. Resawn pieces are often glued together to make wider panels for cabinet sides or doors. Can you see the book-match line down the center of the panel?

desired stock thickness. Allow a little extra thickness for sanding or planing the stock. Set the blade height at slightly less than one-half the stock width or no more than 1 inch. With the stock's face against the fence and an edge on the table, make a rip cut through the piece. Place the other edge on the table and make another rip cut (Illus. 6-67). Keep the same face against the fence. On narrow stock, there will be a thin strip separating the two pieces. In most cases, the pieces will split apart

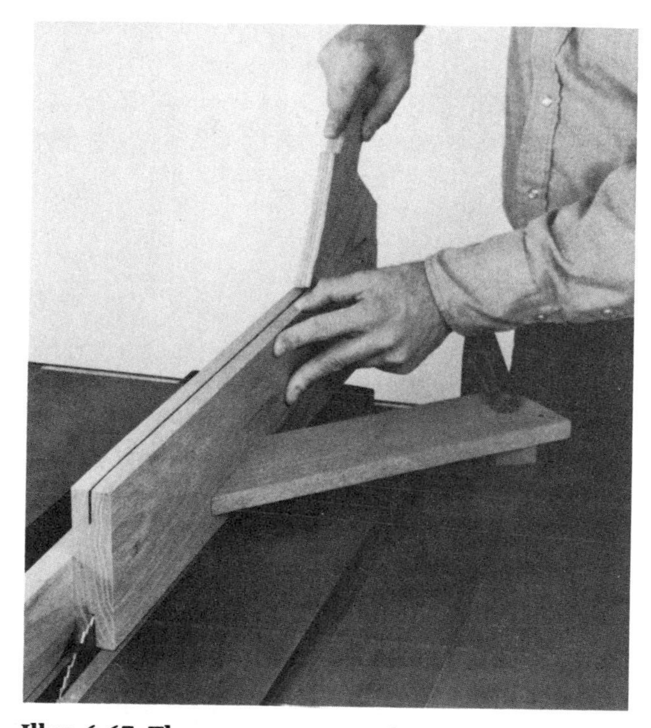

Illus. 6-67. The resaw cuts are about one inch deep. Keep the same face of the stock against the fence for both cuts.

easily (Illus. 6-68). They can then be sanded, planed, or glued together.

In other cases, the parts can be sawn apart with a band saw. This approach works well because the

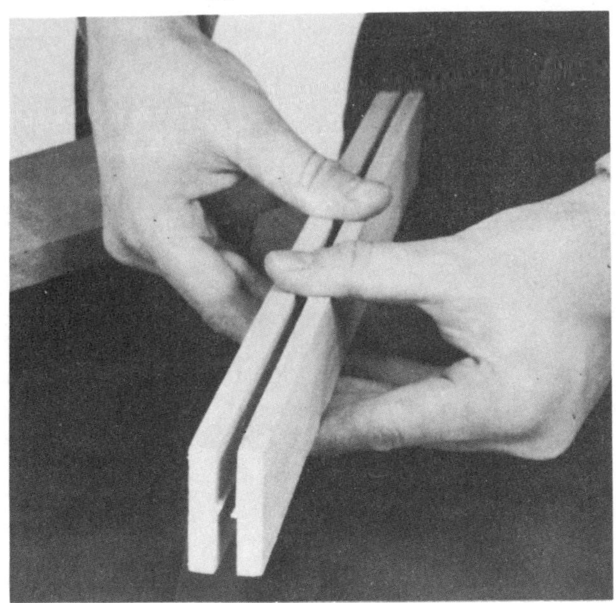

Illus. 6-68. The thin strip separates or splits easily. The split surfaces can be sanded or planed.

band-saw blade will follow the kerf made on the table saw. This will be almost as accurate and much safer than the previous method discussed.

In every example so far, a featherboard has been used to hold stock against the fence. A table-saw guard could not be used because of the stock width and because the cut was not a through cut. However, there is another method in which a barrier can be used between you and the blade, but in which a featherboard is not used. An L-shaped block about the same height as the fence is clamped to the table after the fence is positioned for resawing. The L-shaped piece cannot touch the work; there should be enough clearance so that there is no binding (Illus. 6-69). Next, the blade is raised to less than one-half of the stock width, and the cutting begins (Illus. 6-70). After all the cuts are made, the blade is raised again to slightly less than one-half the stock width and another cut is made (Illus. 6-71). The pieces can be split or cut away with a band saw or chisel after the cutting is complete (Illus. 6-72). The L-shaped block makes contact with the blade much less likely, but there is some loss of control. A push stick can help you maintain control, however.

On wider stock, the blade will have to be raised another inch or to slightly less than one-half the stock width (Illus. 6-73). Make another rip cut from each edge. Be sure to keep the same face against the fence. Separate these pieces when a thin strip remains (Illus. 6-74).

The blade is set at one inch for each cut, to reduce the stress on the blade and minimize the chance of kickbacks. The stock hardness and the horsepower of the saw may allow a slightly higher (or lower) setting. Experience will tell you the correct setting for your saw.

When resawing some pieces, you may wish to make cuts with both faces touching the fence (Illus. 6-75). This will make the saw kerf wider, and en-

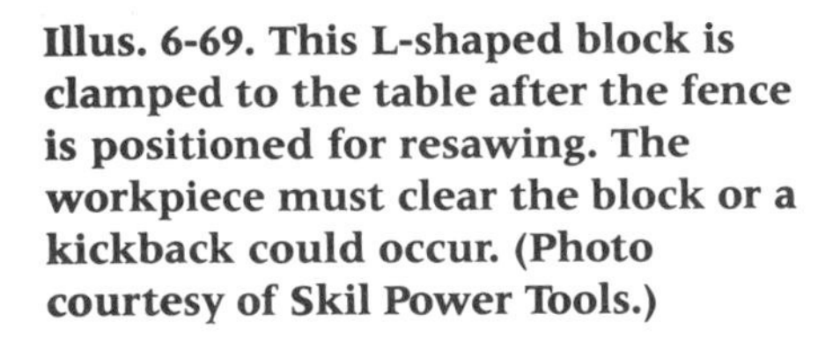

Illus. 6-69. This L-shaped block is clamped to the table after the fence is positioned for resawing. The workpiece must clear the block or a kickback could occur. (Photo courtesy of Skil Power Tools.)

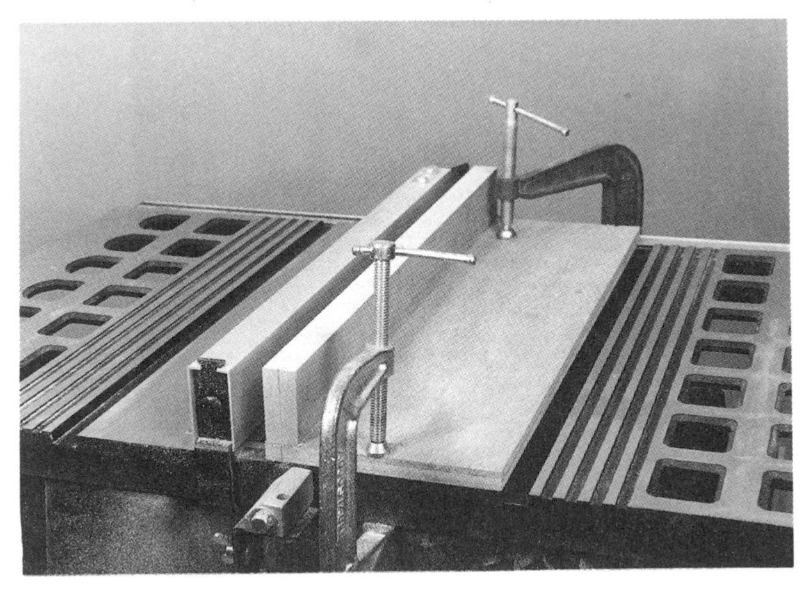

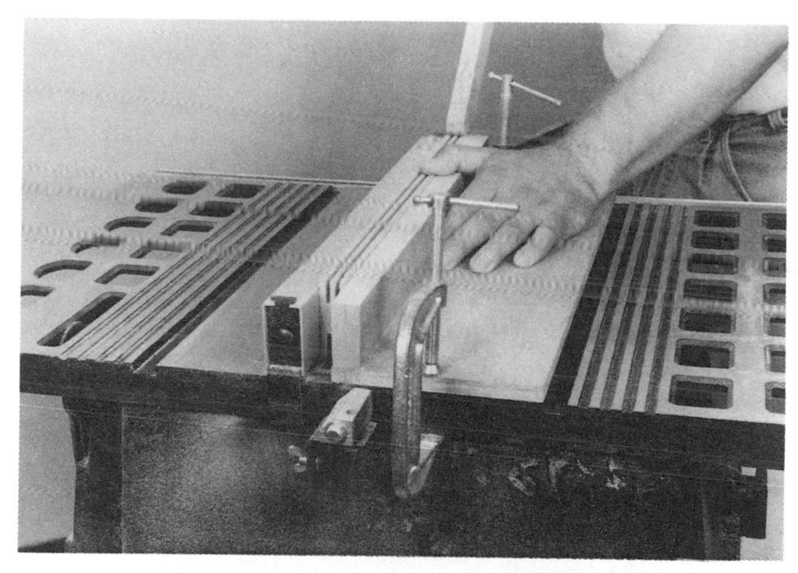

Illus. 6-70. Cuts are made from both edges of the two faces. Blade height is about one inch. (Photo courtesy of Skil Power Tools.)

Illus. 6-71. Blade height is raised for the final cut, but a small amount of stock remains uncut. This keeps the workpiece together and makes it easier to handle. (Photo courtesy of Skil Power Tools.)

Illus. 6-72. A chisel has been used to separate the pieces. A plane or belt sander can be used to smooth the sawn fences.

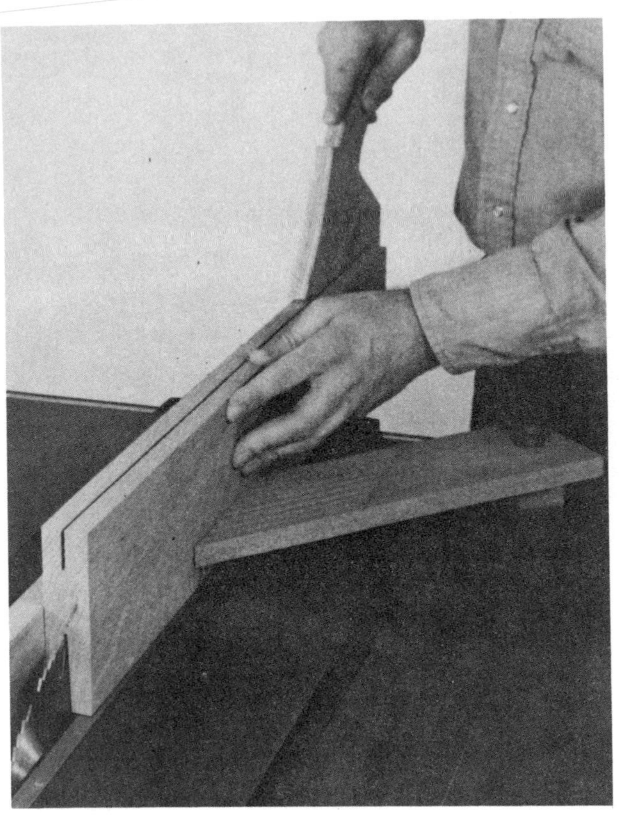

Illus. 6-73. On wider stock, a second cut is necessary.

Illus. 6-74. The wider stock in Illus. 6-73 was book-matched and glued into this panel. The knot was inside the stock.

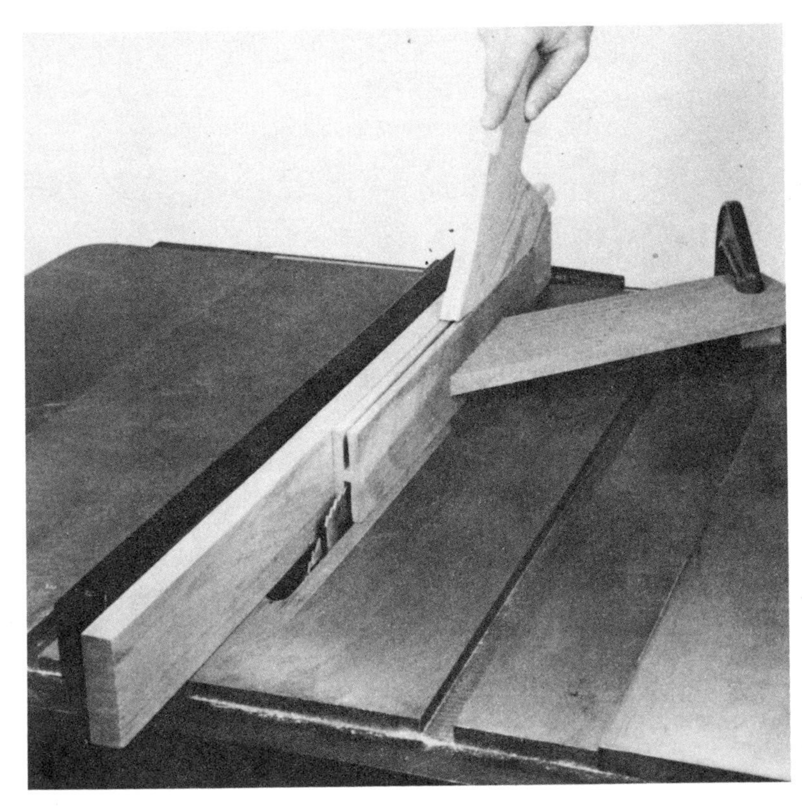

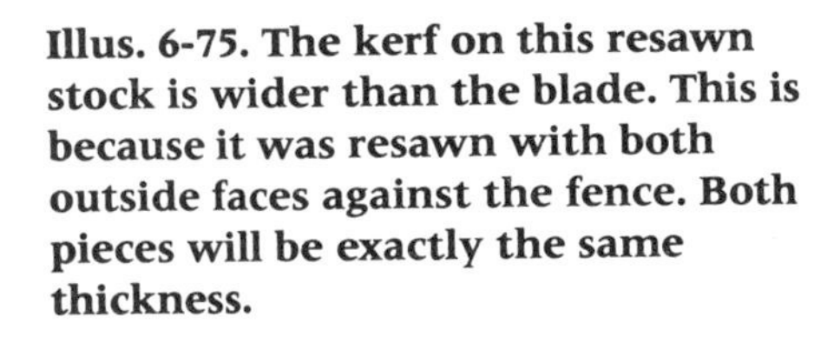

Illus. 6-75. The kerf on this resawn stock is wider than the blade. This is because it was resawn with both outside faces against the fence. Both pieces will be exactly the same thickness.

sure that the resawn pieces are the same thickness. It will be easier to glue up panels when the resawn pieces are the same thickness.

Cutting Keys and Keyways

Keys are reinforcing members added to miter joints. Miter joints are end-grain joints. They are

Illus. 6-76. This key-cutting jig rides on the fence. The V-shaped cradle holds the stock while the key is cut.

Illus. 6-77. This key-cutting jig rides in the miter slot. A test piece is in the cradle. The test piece ensures that the setup is correct before the work is cut.

the weakest type of wood joint. When a key is added to the miter joint, it becomes stronger. This is because the key is glued face-to-face in the two parts of the miter joint. Face-grain joints are the strongest type of wood joint.

A keyway is cut into the miter joint after it has been assembled and the glue has cured. The keyway or key-cutting jig is similar to the tenoning jig (Illus. 6-76). It has a V-shaped cradle instead of a vertical stop (Illus. 6-77). The V-shaped cradle

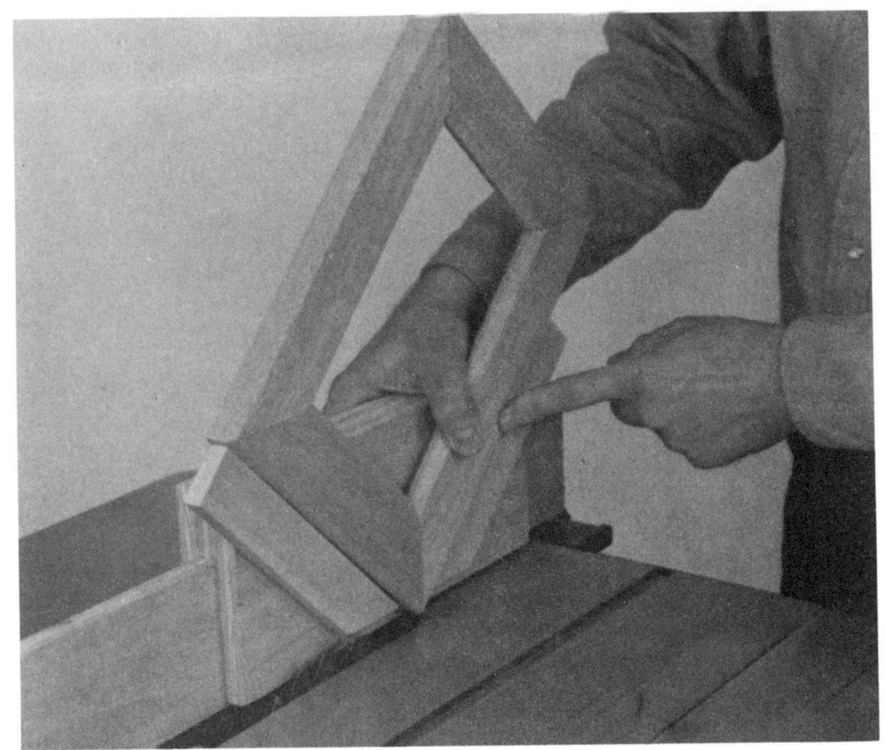

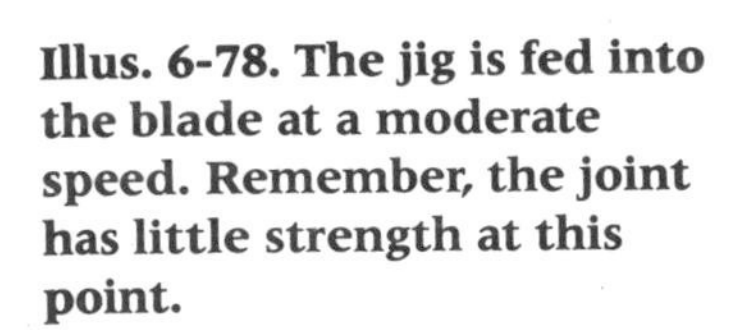

Illus. 6-78. The jig is fed into the blade at a moderate speed. Remember, the joint has little strength at this point.

Illus. 6-79. Make a trial fit of the keys. Make sure they fit correctly. Allow some space for glue.

holds the miter joint while the keyway is being cut.

Adjust the key-cutting jig to the desired position over the blade or dado head. A blade is used for thin keys, and a dado head is used for thicker keys. Set the height of the blade or dado head to the desired key depth. Place the miter joint in the cradle (Illus. 6-78), and feed it into the blade. For a frame, this process has to be repeated for each corner.

Rip some stock to fit the keyways. The stock is going to be glued into place, so allow some space for the glue. A key that is too thick for the keyway could break the joint during installation. Make a trial fit of the keys (Illus. 6-79). Mark them and cut them slightly long. Apply glue to the key and keyway. Insert the key and allow the glue to cure (Illus. 6-80). It is difficult to clamp the keys in place. If they do move around, secure them with a piece of masking tape. Sand the key flush with the stock when the glue has cured (Illus. 6-81).

Keys can also be cut the entire length of the miter joint. A universal jig is also used to cut the dado along the face of the miter joint (Illus. 6-82). Keep the exposed face of all parts facing the same direction when you make this cut.

Illus. 6-81. After the glue cures, sand the keys flush with the frame.

Illus. 6-80. Glue the keys in place and allow them to cure. Use masking tape to hold them if necessary.

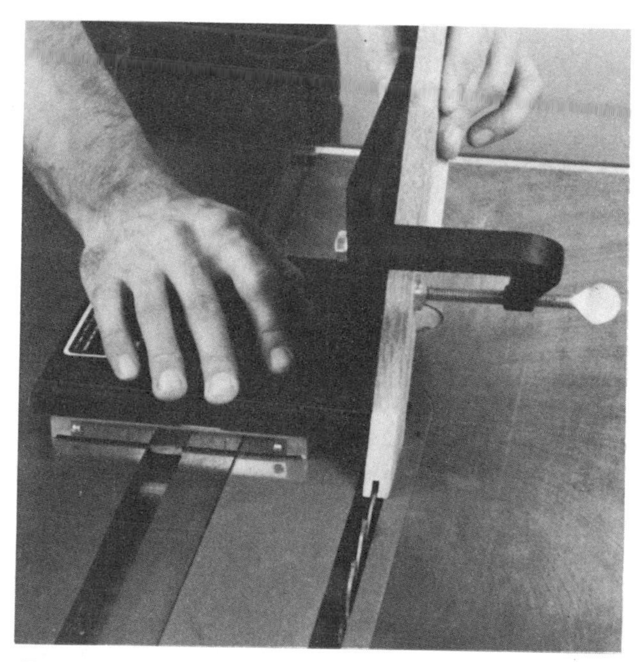

Illus. 6-82. Keys can also be cut the entire length of the miter. A commercial jig is being used for this purpose. This joint is sometimes called a spline miter joint.

Cutting Coves

A cove is a curved recess cut into a piece of stock. Most simple cove cuts are made with the molding head (Illus. 6-83). Some coves, however, do not

Illus. 6-83. Most standard coves are cut with a shaper head. Large coves cannot be cut with the shaper head.

Illus. 6-84 Top: This partial cove was cut with a saw blade and an inclined fence. Above: After a few more operations, this stock became the base molding used in my restored kitchen.

follow the arc of a machined cutter. These coves must be cut using a saw blade and an inclined fence. The blade and inclined-fence method can also be used for simple coves, but they are usually cut with the molding head. Many objects require this method of cutting coves. Restoration work (Illus. 6-84) often requires cove cuts to reproduce some type of molding. The brush shelf shown in 6-85 has a coved base. This keeps hairpins, combs, and brushes from being easily knocked off the shelf. Many picture frames with graceful coves are also

Illus. 6-85. This brush shelf has a coved base.

cut with a saw blade and inclined fence.

Begin by laying out the cove. Determine the arc of the cove and its relative location in the piece of stock. This layout can be photocopied and then glued to the ends of the stock (Illus. 6-86). Patterns can also be made to trace the profile on your work (Illus. 6-87).

Remove most of the stock in the cove area with straight cuts (Illus. 6-88). Adjust the fence and

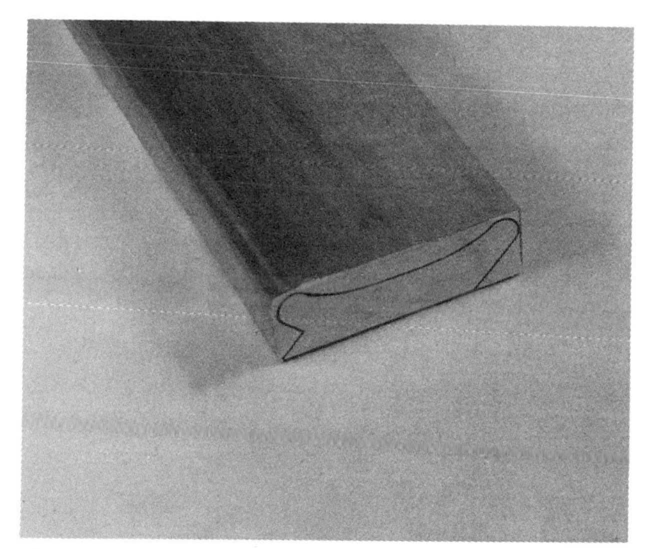

Illus. 6-86. The cove design has been glued to the end of the setup piece. This makes setup much easier.

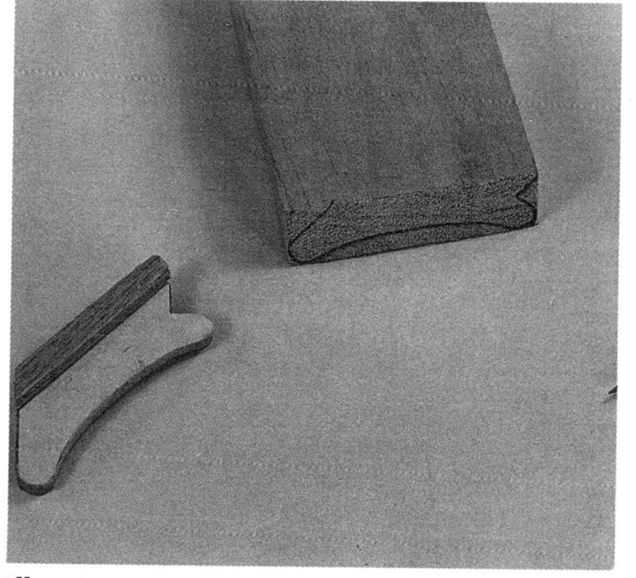

Illus. 6-87. Patterns can also be made to trace the profile on both ends of the work. Both ends of the piece can now be used for this layout.

Illus. 6-88. Straight cuts can be used to remove most of the stock in a cove. Adjust the fence and blade height for each cut.

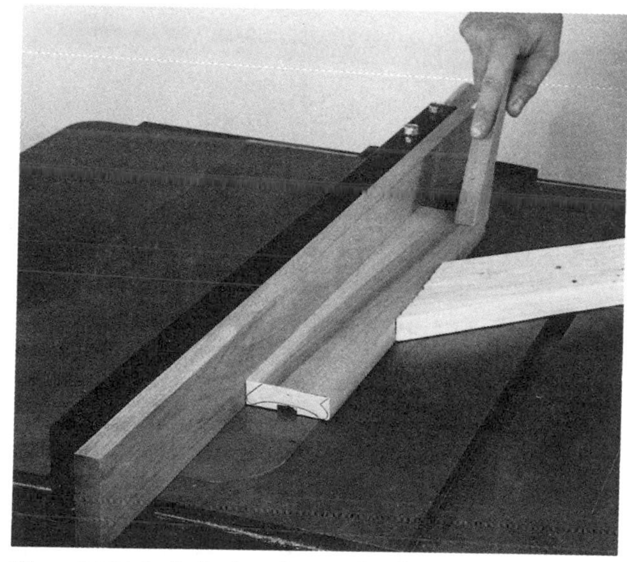

Illus. 6-89. A dado head can also be used to remove the stock in a cove.

blade height for each cut, or use a dado head if several parts are to be made (Illus. 6-89).

Select the appropriate blade for cove cutting, and install it. For thin, wide coves, a blade with a diameter of at least 10 inches works well. For more circular-shaped coves, a blade with an 8-inch diameter works well. Make sure the blade you select has fine teeth. This will reduce the amount of sanding required. Adjust the blade height to the deepest portion of the cove (Illus. 6-90). Set the parallel guide to the cove width (Illus. 6-91), and place the parallel guide over the blade. Turn the guide so that

Illus. 6-90. The first step in the cove setup is to adjust the blade height to full cove depth.

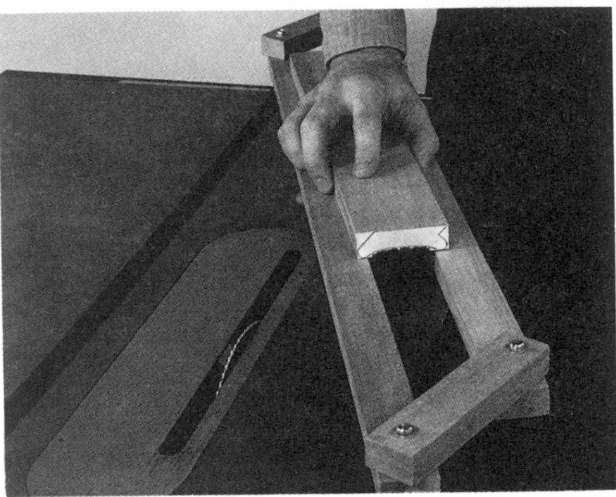
Illus. 6-91. Next, set the parallel guide to the cove width.

Illus. 6-92. The parallel guide is turned so that one edge touches each side of the blade.

one edge touches each side of the blade (Illus. 6-92).

The parallel guide is now resting at an angle to the blade. This angle is the angle at which the fence must be adjusted for cove cutting. Copy the angle with a sliding T-bevel (Illus. 6-93). Select a stiff, true piece of stock to use as your auxiliary fence. Set the fence to the angle of the sliding T-bevel. Make sure the fence is between the front of the saw and the blade (Illus. 6-94). This allows the thrust of the blade to force the work against the fence.

Illus. 6-93. A sliding T-bevel is used to copy the angle established by the parallel guide.

Illus. 6-94. Use the sliding T-bevel to set the fence at the correct angle.

Adjust the fence with reference to the stock being cut. The edge of the cove should just touch a tooth that points toward the fence (Illus. 6-95). Clamp the fence securely in place. Make certain the clamps do not block the control side of the fence. *Note:* For partial coves (Illus. 6-96), the fence actually covers a portion of the blade. The fence is adjusted with the blade beneath the table. The blade is then raised while it is running. It makes a cut in the wooden fence.

Illus. 6-95. The fence should be adjusted to the correct place on the cove with the blade adjusted to full cove depth. The fence should be between the blade and the operator.

Illus. 6-96. When a partial cove is cut, the fence actually covers part of the blade.

Lower the blade. About ⅛ inch of the blade should be above the table for the first cut. Light cuts produce the best results. Clamp two featherboards to the table (Illus. 6-97). These will hold the stock against the fence. Mark the fence side of your stock. Do this on the bottom of each piece. Marking the stock should keep you from reversing pieces. This is very important if the cove is not centered.

Turn on the saw and feed pieces across the blade. Keep them held firmly against the inclined fence. Push sticks keep hands clear of the blade and improve control of the stock (Illus. 6-98 and 6-99).

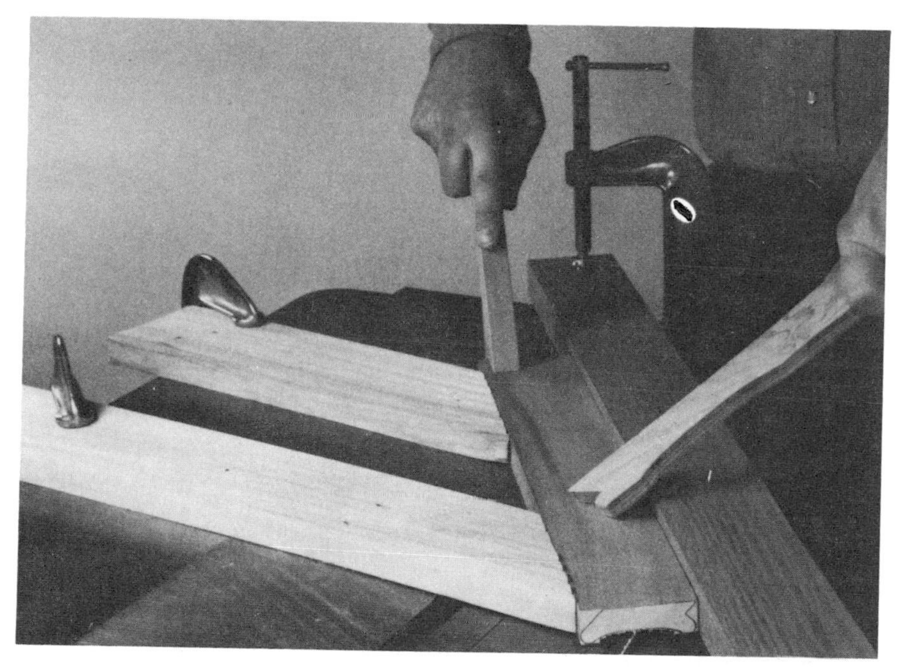

Illus. 6-97. Two featherboards can be used to hold the work against the fence. Push sticks should be used to feed stock across the blade.

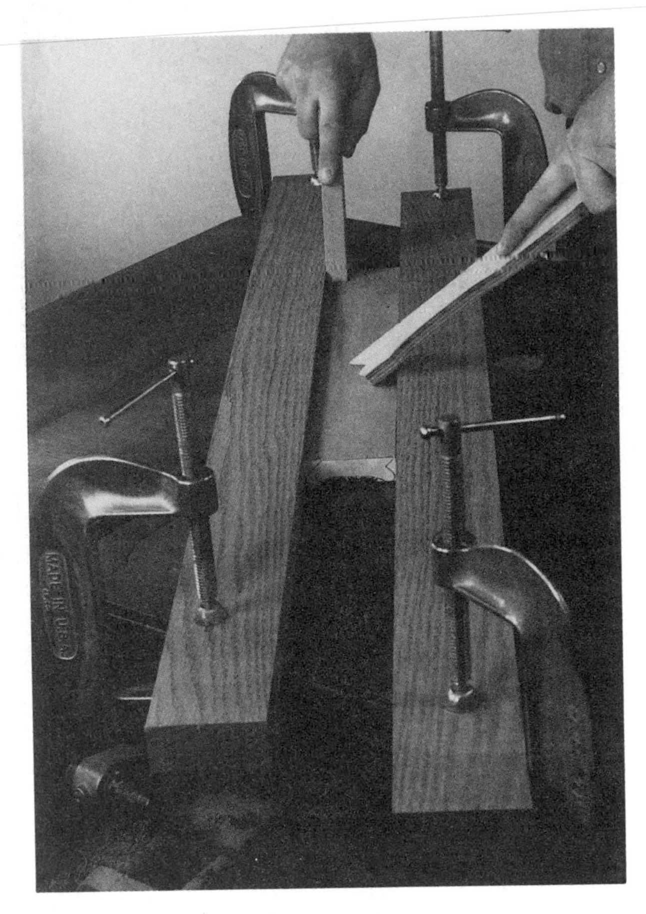

Illus. 6-98 (left). A second fence can be used instead of featherboards to hold stock in place. Illus. 6-99 (above). Light cuts should be taken. There is a great deal of side thrust on the blade when a cove cut is made.

Note: If you encounter resistance as you feed your stock across the blade, the blade may be too high. Lower the blade and try again.

After all the parts have been cut, raise the blade 1/32–1/16 inch. Make the second cut and repeat the process. Remember, as the blade is raised, more teeth come in contact with the blade. This means the blade has to work harder and is more likely to kick back. As your cove cut gets deeper, take lighter cuts—no more than 1/32 inch.

As you near the desired shape, take light cuts. This will reduce the amount of sanding needed. Feed the stock slowly on the final pass to make it smoother. Sometimes two passes at the final setting make the cove smoother. The cove must be sanded after machining (Illus. 6-100). Begin with 60- or 80-grit abrasives and work up. A dowel or a piece of stock cut to the shape of your cove can be used as a sanding block (Illus. 6-101).

As you work with coves, you may wish to make a parallel guide (Illus. 6-102). The guide is 5½ inches wide and 29½ inches long. Accurate layout and drilling are all that are necessary to complete the project. Use T nuts to hold the pieces together. The T nuts allow you to lock the parallel guide at the desired setting. More information is provided in Chapter 8 (Illus. 8-22–8-24).

If you frequently cut the same cove, you may want to make a layout guide (Illus. 6-103). This will make cove setup faster. Remember to use the same blade and fence with the layout guide. You may want to list this information on the guide.

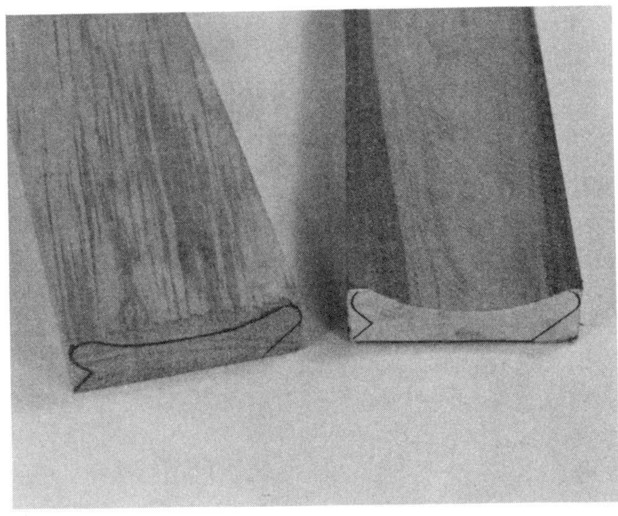

Illus. 6-100. Note the saw marks in the cove. A coarser blade would leave much larger saw marks. These marks have to be sanded.

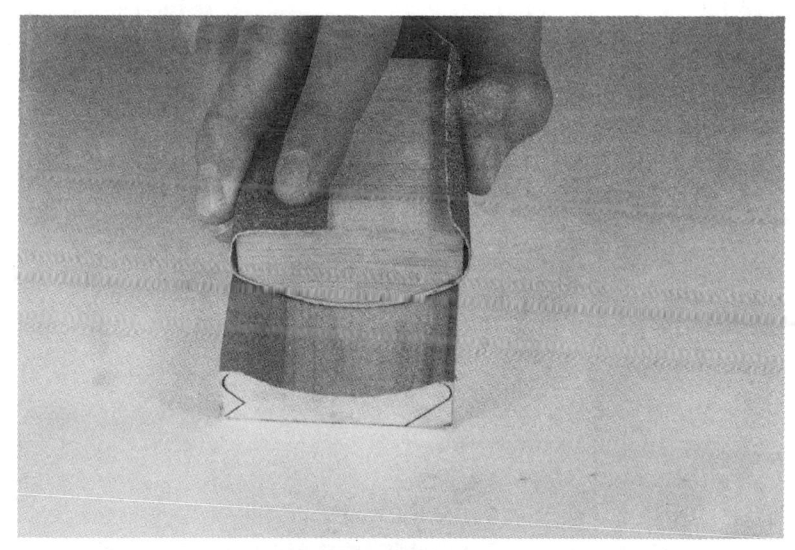

Illus. 6-101. A sanding block can be made to follow the contour of the cove.

Illus. 6-102. A parallel guide is a handy accessory to have when working with coves. A drawing and details for construction of a parallel guide appear in Chapter 8 (Illus. 8-22 and 8-23).

Illus. 6-103. This layout guide has the correct fence angle cut on one edge. This accessory is desirable if the same cove is made frequently.

If you wish to experiement with the cove-cutting process, try using a molding head with a cove cutter installed. It can also be used with an inclined fence. If you experiment with the process, remember the following points:

1. Remove most of the stock in the cove area with straight cuts.
2. Set up the inclined fence carefully. It is more difficult to set up the fence using the molding head.
3. Take light cuts! Heavy cuts can cause kickbacks, and may damage your work.
4. Stand to the side of the kickback zone. With the inclined fence, that zone is directly behind the auxiliary fence.
5. Use push sticks to control the stock.
6. Do not reach across the blade to retrieve parts.
7. Chip-limiting blades can reduce the possibility of kickbacks.

Cutting Finger Joints

Finger or box joints are corner joints made up of mating fingers (Illus. 6-104). The corners slip together to form a strong joint. Each finger exposes extra edge grain, which increases the amount of gluing surface. Finger joints are cut with a jig. Usually the jig is attached to the miter gauge, but some are designed to be attached to the fence. Fingers are usually no wider than the stock thickness. Fingers cut in ½-inch stock would be ½ inch wide or less. Narrower fingers look nicer, but take longer to cut.

After you decide on a finger width, set up the

Illus. 6-104. The corner joint on this box is called a finger or box joint. It is quite strong and very attractive. Complete plans for this box appear in Chapter 8 (pages 308–313).

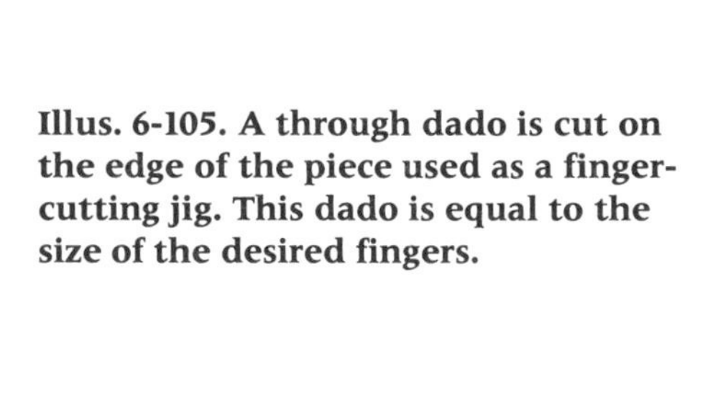

Illus. 6-105. A through dado is cut on the edge of the piece used as a finger-cutting jig. This dado is equal to the size of the desired fingers.

saw to cut that width. Use a dado head or a single saw blade. When using a single saw blade, use a combination or rip blade. These blades usually leave the end of the finger cut flat. Adjust the blade height to stock thickness or slightly more. By cutting fingers slightly deeper than stock thickness, you can sand a small amount of stock off the fingers after assembly. This ensures flush joints.

Select a true piece of stock about 4 inches wide and 8–12 inches long. Cut a dado through the edge of the piece near one end (Illus. 6-105). Measure the kerf or dado width. Mark off a space that size right next to the kerf. Insert and glue a piece of stock into the kerf (Illus. 6-106). The piece of stock should be equal to the kerf size and about 1 inch long. This piece of stock (the spacer) controls spacing between the fingers. Attach the finger jig to the miter gauge (Illus. 6-107). There should be a space equal to the finger size between the kerf and spacer.

Lay out the pieces. Set them on edge in the way they will fit together. Mark the pieces and determine which ones start with a finger and which ones start with a cutout. One way of keeping organized is to start the long pieces with a cutout. Mark the pieces accordingly (Illus. 6-108). Cut the pieces that begin with a finger first.

Place the stock against the jig with the stock's edge next to the spacer (the piece of stock in the right kerf) (Illus. 6-109). Push the piece of stock across the blade. Hold the stock firmly against the jig as the cut is made. Place the cutout area over the spacer and make another cut (Illus. 6-110). Con-

Illus. 6-106. A piece of stock is glued in the dado or kerf. It acts as a spacer when the fingers are cut.

Illus. 6-107. The finger jig is now attached to the miter gauge. There should be a space equal to the finger size between the kerf and spacer.

Illus. 6-108. Mark the pieces so that two begin with cuts and two with fingers. These pieces have been marked with letter C's and F's to keep them in order.

Illus. 6-109. Cut the pieces, starting with the fingers first. Butt the piece against the spacer and make the cuts.

Illus. 6-110. The first kerf goes over the spacer as the second cut is made.

tinue cutting until all fingers have been cut (Illus. 6-111).

Pieces beginning with a cutout are now cut. Start the cut by placing a finger between the spacer and the left kerf. Use a piece of stock that has already been cut. The first finger goes between the kerfs, and the first cutout goes over the spacer (Illus. 6-112). Butt the stock to be cut against the finger and the jig. Hold it firmly and make the first cutout.

After all of the cutouts have been made, remove the piece of stock with a finger over the spacer. Make the rest of the cutouts using the spacer as a stop (Illus. 6-113). After all cuts have been made (Illus. 6-114), test the fit between the parts (Illus. 6-115). If the fingers are too big, the parts will not fit together. This indicates that the space between the kerfs is too great. Too little space between the kerfs makes the fingers too small. This produces a sloppy fit. Adjust spacing or blade size to produce a satisfactory fit. Remember, glue must be added between each finger, so a little clearance is desirable. Other factors that can affect the fit of finger joints include the following:

1. Slop in the miter slot or jig that affects the spacing of the cuts.
2. A blade that is not perpendicular to the table or miter gauge.
3. Slippage between the jig and the miter gauge.
4. Failure to hold parts securely while they are being cut.
5. If the jig is off .002 inch, and if eight cuts were

Illus. 6-111. Continue moving the stock until all the fingers have been cut.

Illus. 6-112. Place the first finger of a piece between the spacer and kerf to cut pieces, beginning with a cutout. Make the cutout on all pieces first.

Illus. 6-113. Continue making the cuts using the spacer for control.

Illus. 6-114. Cut both ends of all pieces before changing the setup. Work slowly and carefully.

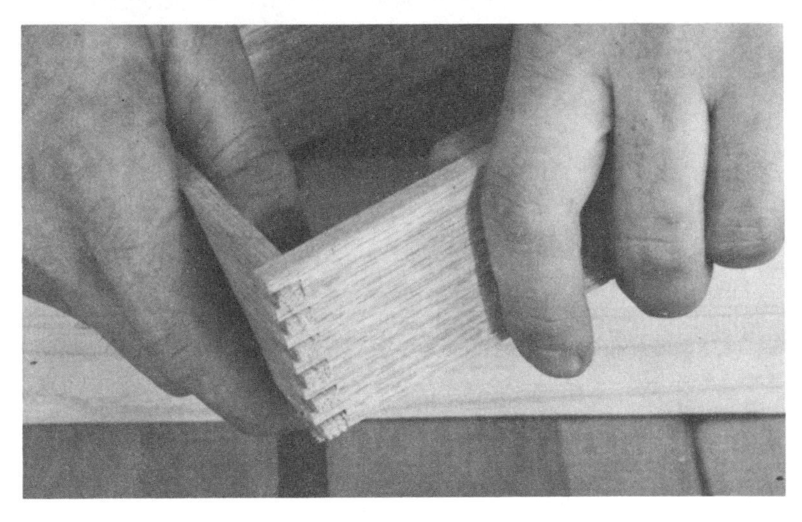

Illus. 6-115. This test fit shows that careful setup is worthwhile. There is just enough clearance for glue.

made, the eighth cut will be off approximately $\frac{1}{64}$ inch. This will make assembly difficult to impossible.

6. If the dado head is not tightened as securely as it was for a previous run, the dado may actually be a few thousandths of an inch wider. This will present a problem similar to that described in #5 above.

Tear-Out Sometimes tear-out will occur on the back side of the finger joint. This usually occurs if the opening in the backing board is too large. Add a piece of thin plywood to the face of the backing board and try again. You can also score the cutting line with a utility knife. This will cause the wood fibers to break on the score line, thus minimizing tear-out. If all else fails, take the parts to a thickness planer and plane away the tear-out. Your box will be a little smaller, but the tear-out will be gone.

Safety Practices Since finger joints are not through cuts, using guards is not easy. Make the backing board as wide as practical. This will keep your hands farther away from the blade or dado head. Clamps can also be used to hold the stock in place during the cut. This will keep your hands clear of the blade's path. Remember that the blade will exit through the back of the jig, so keep your hands clear of the blade's path.

If you wish to make finger-joint-cutting safer, try the approach shown in Illus. 6-116–6-129. In this technique, the blade is guarded as well as possible. Try this technique on the Kity finger-joint jig discussed below.

Illus. 6-116. This box joint is similar to the one in Illus. 6-106 except that it has a ¼-inch plywood base glued to it. This keeps the stock from dipping into the throat-plate opening.

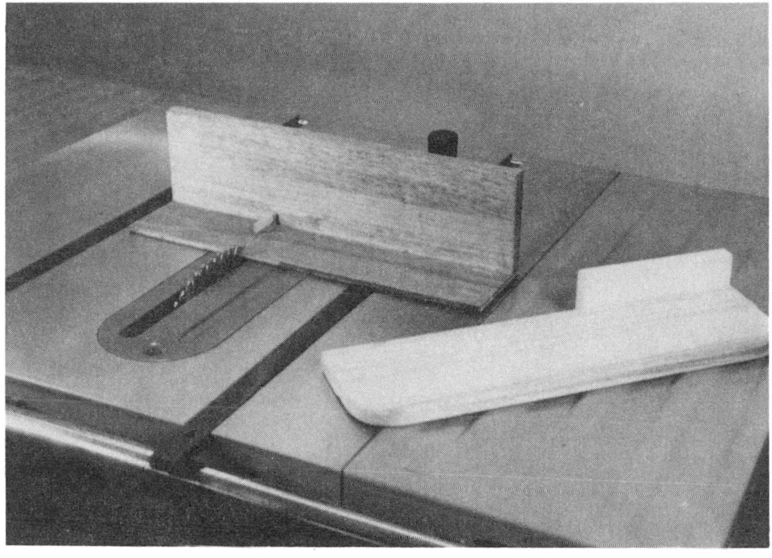

Illus. 6-117. This wood barrier guard is designed for use with the jig.

Illus. 6-118. The barrier clamps to the jig. It makes contact with the blade more difficult. The workpiece fits in the opening.

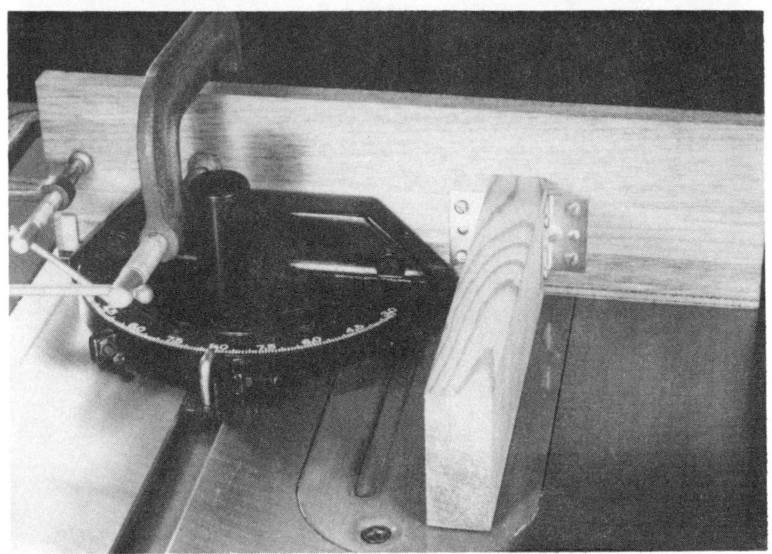

Illus. 6-119. The block of wood on the back of this jig will prevent the jig from coming into contact with the blade as it exits the workpiece. Two metal brackets hold it in place.

Illus. 6-120. A test piece can be butted to the pin and cut. Do this to two pieces.

Illus. 6-121. Make the test cuts with the guard clamped securely in position.

Illus. 6-122. Test the fit between the two pieces you cut. If the pieces fit snugly without being forced together, you are ready to make the cut.

Illus. 6-123. Mark the pieces with the letters F and C. Pieces with the letter F begin with a finger, and those with the letter C begin with a cut.

Illus. 6-124. Start by butting a piece with a letter F against the pin and making the first cut. Hold the stock securely as you guide the jig forward.

Illus. 6-125. Put the kerf you cut over the pin and make another cut.

Illus. 6-126. Continue cutting the end until the entire end has been cut.

Illus. 6-127. Put the first kerf you cut over the pin with the letter F, and the first finger near the blade. Butt the end of the mating piece with the letter C against it and make a cut.

Illus. 6-128. This will form a cut on the end of the piece. It will mate with the first cut against the pin and continue cutting the end.

Illus. 6-129. The fingers and cuts will fit together to form a perfect box after all the parts have been cut.

Kity Finger-Joint Jig The Kity finger joint jig is distributed by Farriss Machinery of Missouri. This jig allows for the use of guards and allows for the adjustment of pin size. This makes it easy to make pins and sockets that are the same size.

Once the dado head is set up to width (Illus. 6-130) and height, the backing board is positioned. It should be the distance from the pin to the dado width. The guard is then positioned, and a trial cut is made.

Illus 6-130. Once the dado width has been determined, the dado height is matched to the stock thickness. Set the dado head about 1/32 inch above the stock thickness.

If the parts match up, cut the rest of the parts (Illus. 6-131–6-144). If they do not, adjust the backing board. Make another trial cut, and then proceed with cutting.

Illus. 6-131. Mark the end of your stock near the end. The pieces with the letter F will be cut first.

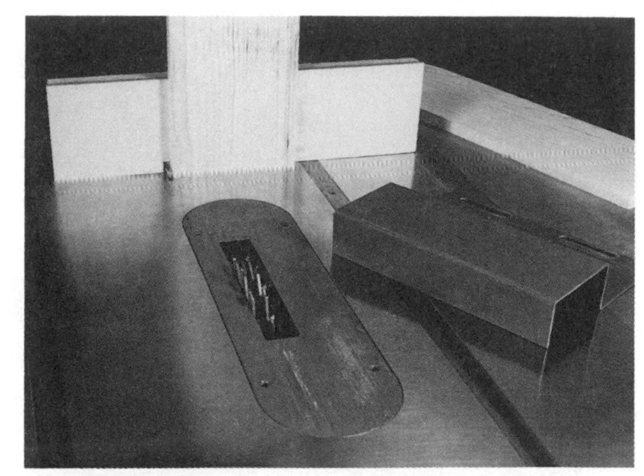

Illus. 6-132. Position the end with the letter F against the pin. This will position the first finger and first cut.

Illus. 6-133. Install the front guard and tighten the threader fasteners. Keep the space between the guard and the work under 1/4 inch.

Illus. 6-134. Grip the workpiece firmly as you guide the jig into the dado head.

Illus. 6-135. The first finger and cut have been made. Additional cuts are made by moving the cut onto the pin.

Illus. 6-136. The pin controls the position of the finger and the new cut. A series of cuts completes the end.

Illus. 6-137. The original finger is positioned between the pin and dado head. This sets the spacing for the end of a piece that begins with a cut.

Illus. 6-138. Make the cut by holding the pieces together firmly. No cutting will occur on the piece on your left.

Illus. 6-139. Once the cut is complete, the successive cuts are made the same way.

Illus. 6-140. Continue cutting until the end is complete.

Illus. 6-141. A uniform, snug-fitting joint is made when all adjustments are correct.

Illus. 6-142. Pieces of different widths can be joined with this method if all cutting begins from the bottom. This tea tray will require additional machinery.

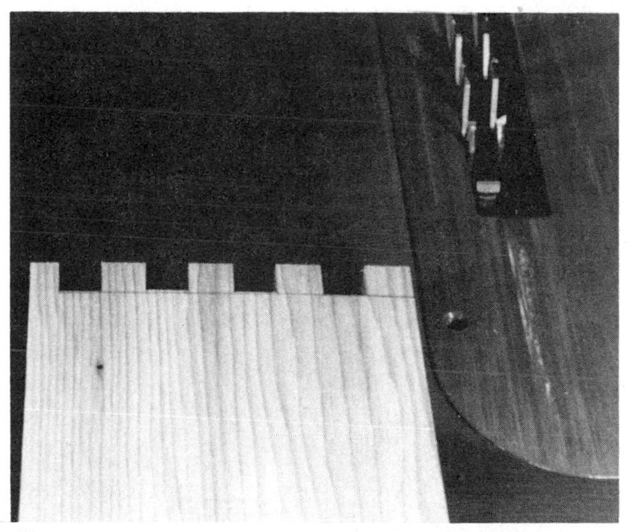

Illus. 6-143. When all cuts are not uniform in depth, check the throat plate for height.

Illus. 6-144. Tear-out like this is caused when there is no wood to back up the cut. A piece of plywood on the back of the jig could prevent this.

Cutting Edge Joints

Edge joints are often just glued together without any reinforcement. For certain edge joints, a spline or tongue-and-groove reinforcement improves the joint. Splines are commonly used when the edges of plywood are banded with solid stock. Tongue-and-groove joints are used to line up pieces that are not perfectly true. Gluing and clamping pieces with a tongue-and-groove joint usually makes the glued panel much truer.

Tongue-and-Groove Joint Tongue-and-groove joints are best cut with the molding or shaper head. Install the groove cutters in the shaper head, and then mount the shaper head on the table saw. Adjust the fence so that the center of the groove cutter is aligned with the center of the work (Illus. 6-145). Make sure the auxiliary fence is attached to the fence before making any adjustments. In most woods, the groove can be made with one cut (Illus. 6-146). Very hard wood may require two cuts to shape the groove.

Set up a featherboard to help you control the stock. Make a trial cut and any minor adjustments before you begin. Cut the groove on one edge of all pieces. *Note:* If you are making a panel, the first

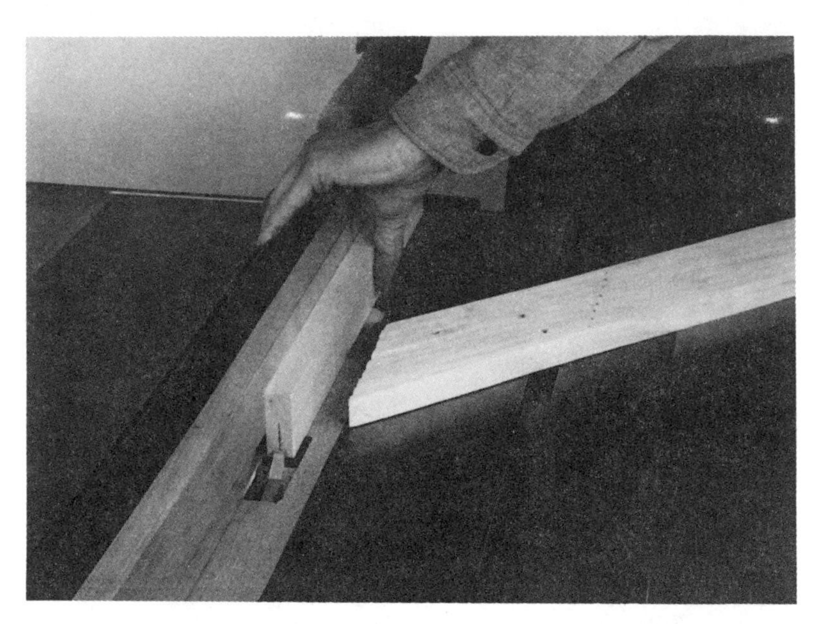

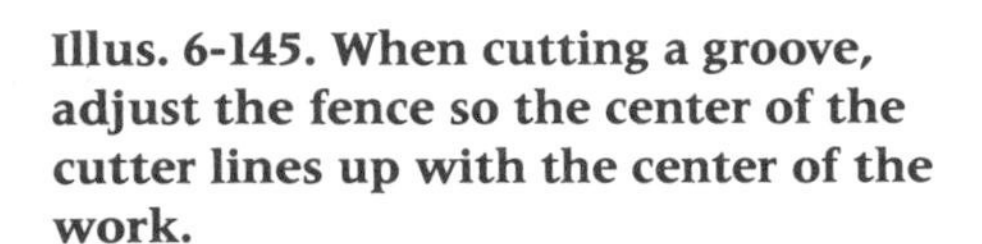

Illus. 6-145. When cutting a groove, adjust the fence so the center of the cutter lines up with the center of the work.

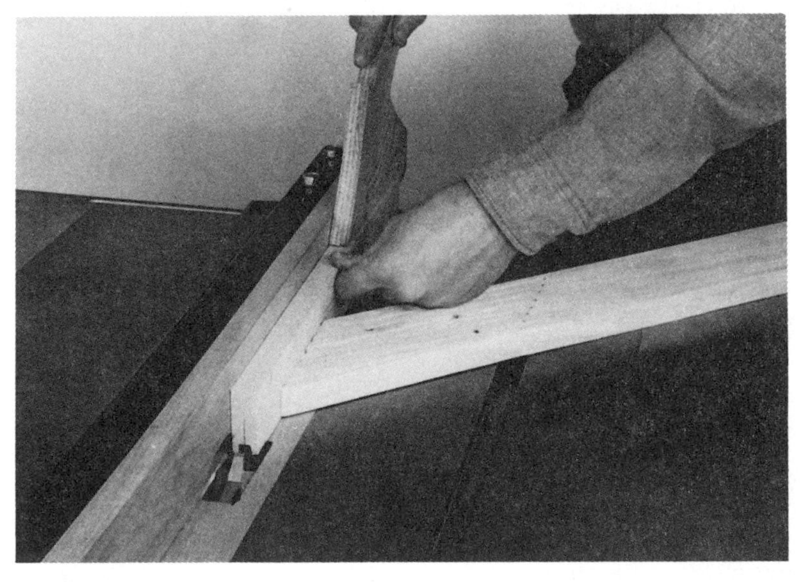

Illus. 6-146. A groove can usually be made in one cut. Very hard wood may require two cuts.

piece should not have a groove, and the last piece should not have a tongue.

After all grooves have been cut, remove the shaper head. Remove the groove cutters and replace them with the tongue cutters. Mount the shaper head and readjust the fence (Illus. 6-147). Tongues may require two successive cuts (Illus. 6-148). This is because twice as much stock is removed. Make a trial cut to determine correct depth of cut. Make sure the tongue lines up with the groove before cutting any parts (Illus. 6-149).

Work slowly and carefully when shaping tongue-and-groove joints. Guide the stock with featherboards and push sticks. Avoid defective pieces or pieces with loose knots. Straight-grained pieces shape easily; pieces with slanted grain may kick back. Lighter cuts minimize the chance of kickback.

A tongue-and-groove joint can also be cut with a dado head (Illus. 6-150). Set up the dado head and make a test cut (Illus. 6-151). Generally, tongue-and-groove joints on ¾-inch-thick stock require a groove that is ¼ inch wide and ¼ to ⅜ inch high. Make a test cut at the end of a piece and check the position of the groove (Illus. 6-152). The piece must be centered in the piece. Cut the groove on all but

Illus. 6-147. The tongue cutters are mounted, and the center of the work is lined up with the center of the tongue.

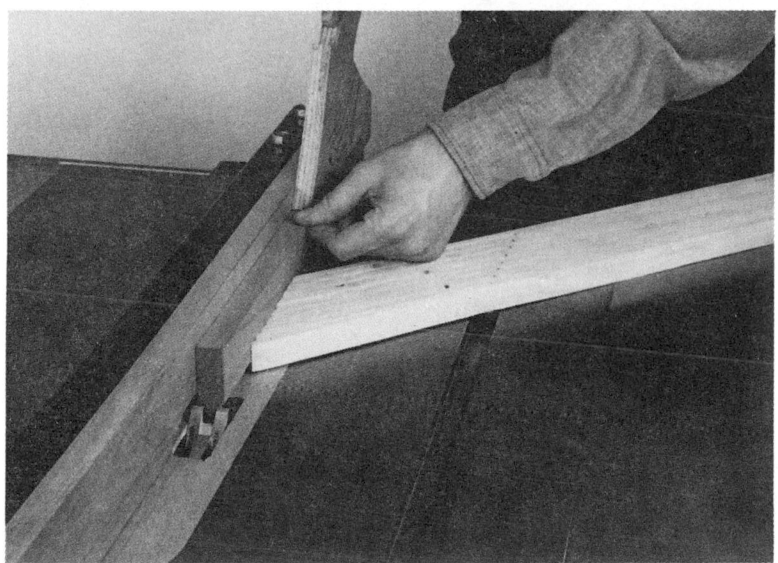

Illus. 6-148. Tongues usually require two successive cuts. This is because twice as much stock is removed.

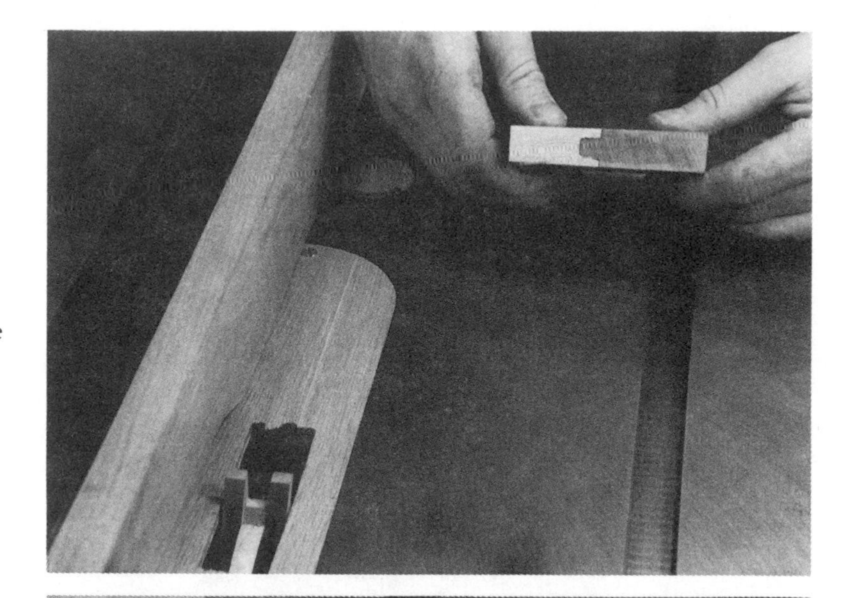

Illus. 6-149. Make sure the tongue and groove line up before cutting your parts. The practice stock should be the same thickness as the work.

Illus. 6-150. This tongue-and-groove joint has straight sides. It was cut with a dado head.

Illus. 6-151. Set the dado width at ¼ inch. Make a test cut and check the width. Set the height to ⅜ inch.

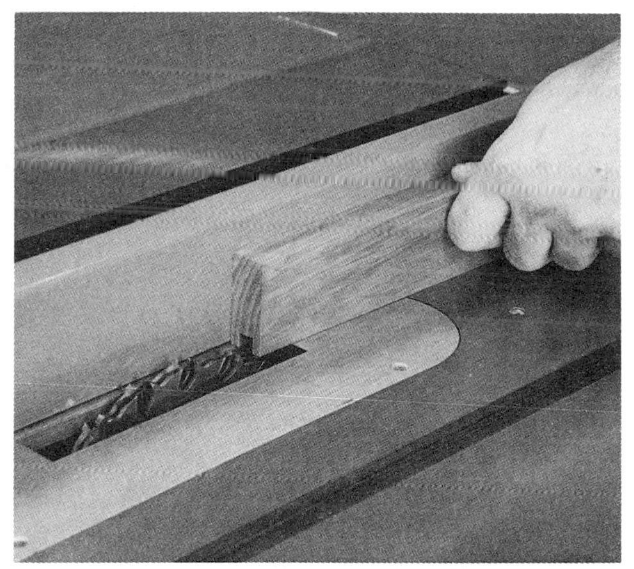

Illus. 6-152. Make the test cut in the edge of the stock. Make sure that it is centered on the edge.

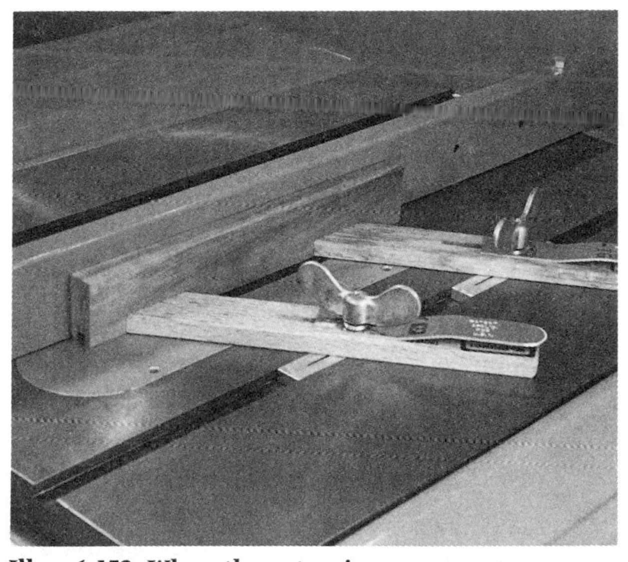

Illus. 6-153. When the setup is correct, cut a groove in all but one of the pieces. The starting piece does not need a groove. Use featherboards to hold the stock against the fence.

one of the pieces (Illus. 6-153). The one part not cut will be the starting piece in the panel.

The tongues can now be cut. Set up for a ½-to-⅝-inch dado and attach an auxiliary wooden fence on the metal fence (Illus. 6-154). Mark the fence at the bottom of the groove. Raise the dado head into the wooden fence until the line has been removed (Illus. 6-155). Adjust the top of the dado head with the bottom of the groove (Illus. 6-156), and then adjust the fence to the width of the groove

Illus. 6-154. Fasten an auxiliary wooden fence to the metal fence and mark the bottom of the groove.

Illus. 6-155. Cut away about ½ inch of the ¾-inch plywood thickness with the dado head. Raise it slightly above the pencil line.

Illus. 6-156. Adjust the dado height to the bottom of the groove. This line is also the bottom of the tongue.

(Illus. 6-157). The dado head will now remove the wood that is equal to one side of the groove. Position the featherboards and make the first rabbet cut. Make the second rabbet cut (Illus. 6-158) to form the tongue. Cut all but the end piece of the assembly (Illus. 6-159). The tongue is formed by two rabbet cuts. For more information, consult the section on cutting rabbets on pages 155–162. Be

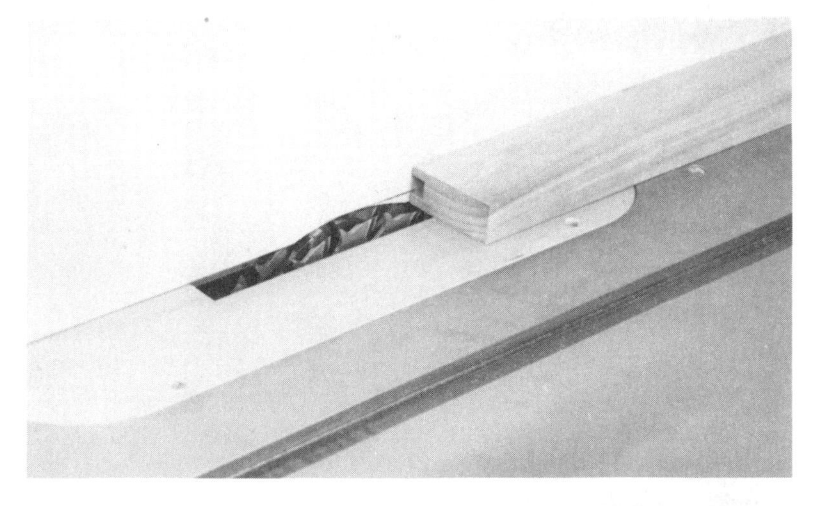

Illus. 6-157. Reposition the fence so that the dado exposure is equal to the depth of the groove.

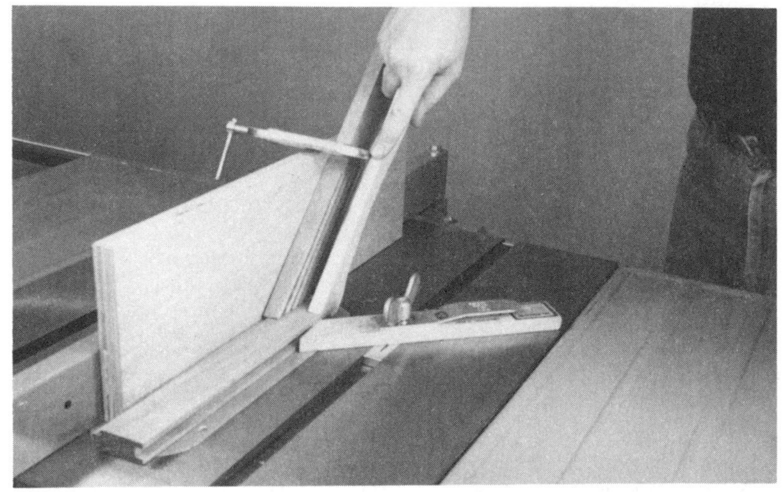

Illus. 6-158. Make two cuts on the edges of all but one grooved piece. The two rabbets actually form the tongue.

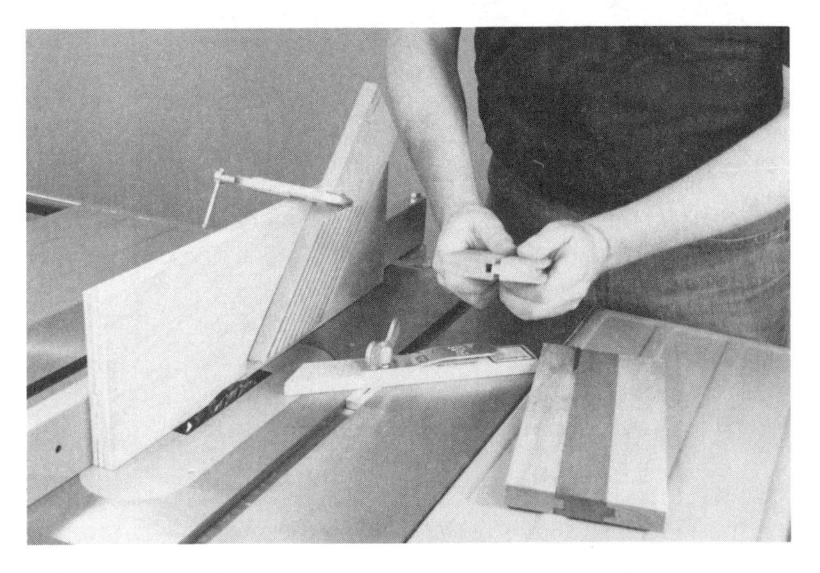

Illus. 6-159. The pieces slide together without being forced. If you are planning to glue them together, they should fit a little more loosely.

sure to use only straight, true stock. Rabbets can also be used to make a ship-lap edge joint. The same rabbeting technique is used to cut a rabbet in the center of the piece (Illus. 6-160–6-162). Use the same procedures outlined above.

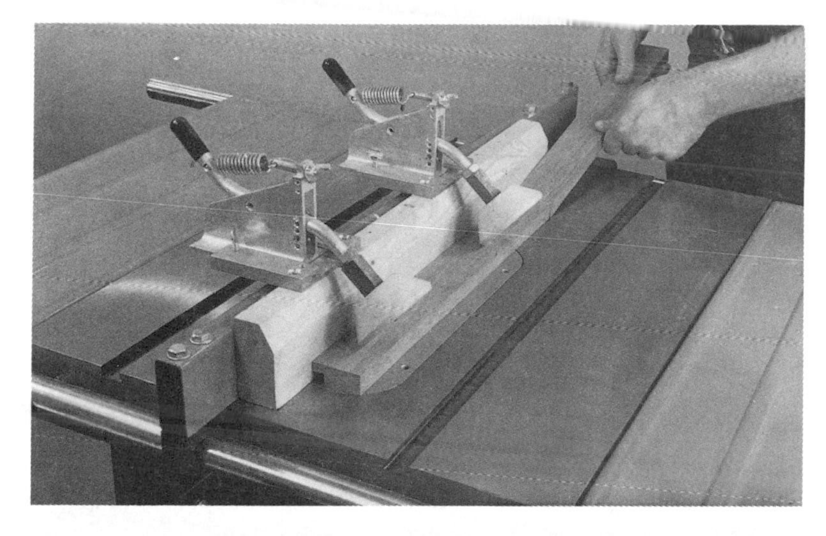

Illus. 6-160. The rabbeted edge goes to the center of the stock thickness. Cut both edges of all pieces except the beginning and end pieces. They are cut on one end only.

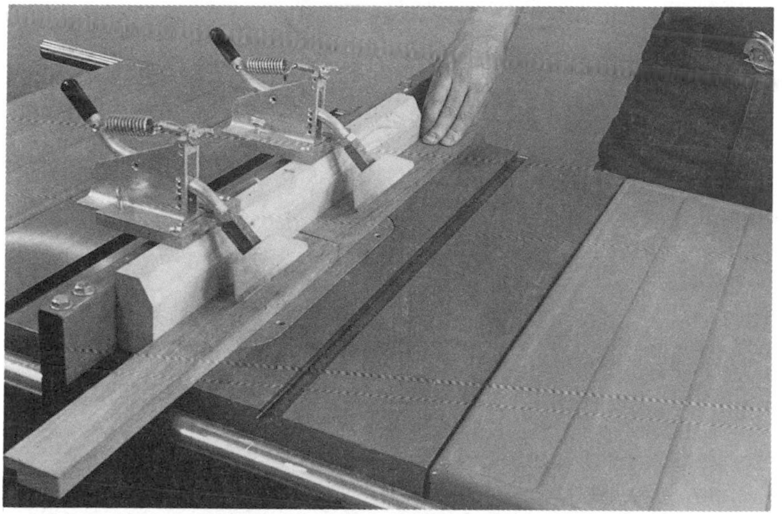

Illus. 6-161. Use one piece to guide the next across the dado head. A piece of scrap can be used to guide the last piece through.

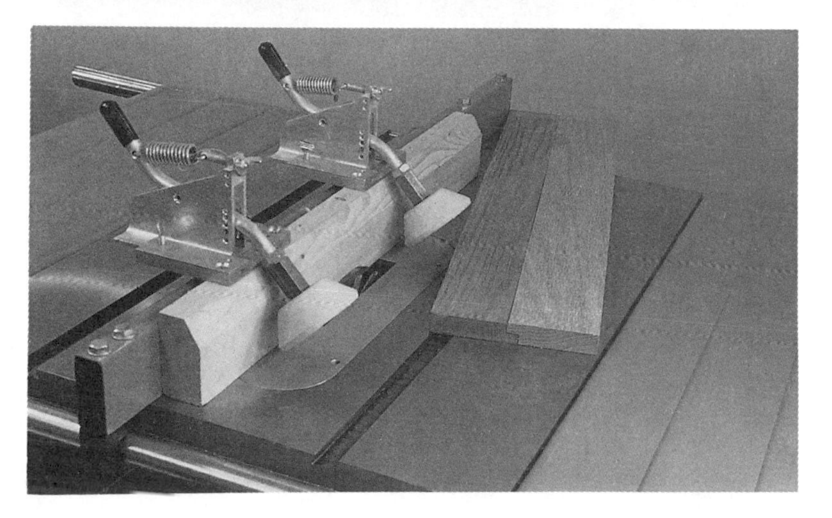

Illus. 6-162. Be sure to cut the good face of one piece and the bad face of the matching piece if only one is cut. When both edges are cut, one is done on each face.

Glue Joint A glue joint is a type of edge joint similar to a tongue-and-groove joint. It is cut with a shaper head. The center of the cutter is lined up with the center of the work (Illus. 6-163). All parts are cut with this setup. This is because the cutter is a mirror image of itself from the centerline.

Feed stock slowly across the cutter head (Illus. 6-164). Use a featherboard to hold the stock against the fence. Check your setup in scrap stock before you cut your work (Illus. 6-165).

Illus. 6-163. Line the center of the glue-joint cutter up with the center of the work.

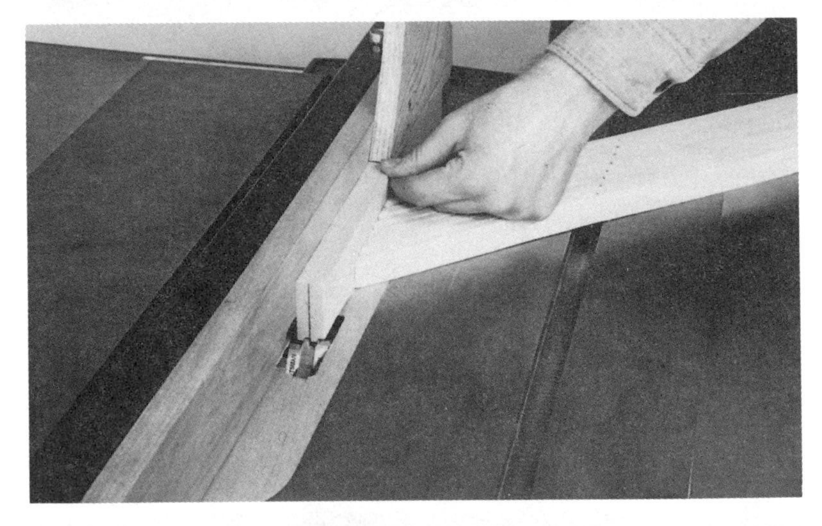

Illus. 6-164. Feed stock slowly across the cutter head. All parts are cut on this setup.

Illus. 6-165. Test your setup in scrap stock before you cut your work.

Safety Techniques When Cutting Tongue-and-Groove Joints with a Molding Head

When glue joints or tongue-and-groove joints do not fit well, the first impulse is to blame the cutter head. While this is a possibility, it is more likely that the saw has an alignment problem. Check the fence to be sure that it is parallel to the miter slot. Also check to see if the blade is parallel to the miter slot. Any misalignment will make the tongue smaller and the grooves bigger. Alignment is presented in Chapter 7.

Spline Joint Spline joints use a thin piece of stock as a tongue. It fits into a groove cut on both pieces. Splines line up the two parts and provide increased gluing surface. Splines can be cut with a dado head or a single blade. The groove should be centered in the piece and should be no wider than one-third of the stock thickness. The groove must be slightly larger than the spline. This is to allow for glue.

Cut a spline joint the same way you would cut grooves (Illus. 6-166). The spline should be slightly deeper than it is wide. Remember to keep all exposed faces pointing toward (or away from) the fence when cutting the grooves (Illus. 6-167). Any error is doubled when all parts are not cut uniformly (Illus. 6-168). This will make it difficult to align the pieces when fitting them together (Illus. 6-169).

Illus. 6-166. Spline cuts are cut the same way as a groove. A spline cut is slightly deeper than it is wide.

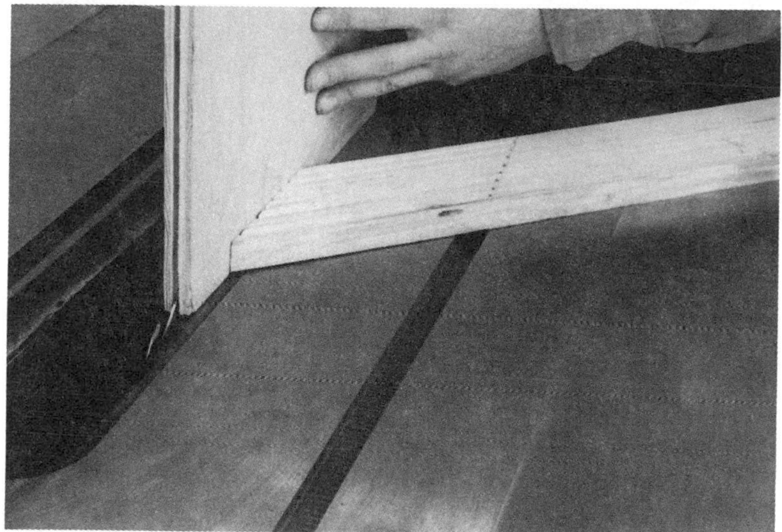

Illus. 6-167. Keep all exposed faces pointing toward (or away from) the fence. Any error is doubled if the parts do not all point the same way.

Illus. 6-168. The exposed side of this spline joint lines up perfectly. Plywood has been used for a spline.

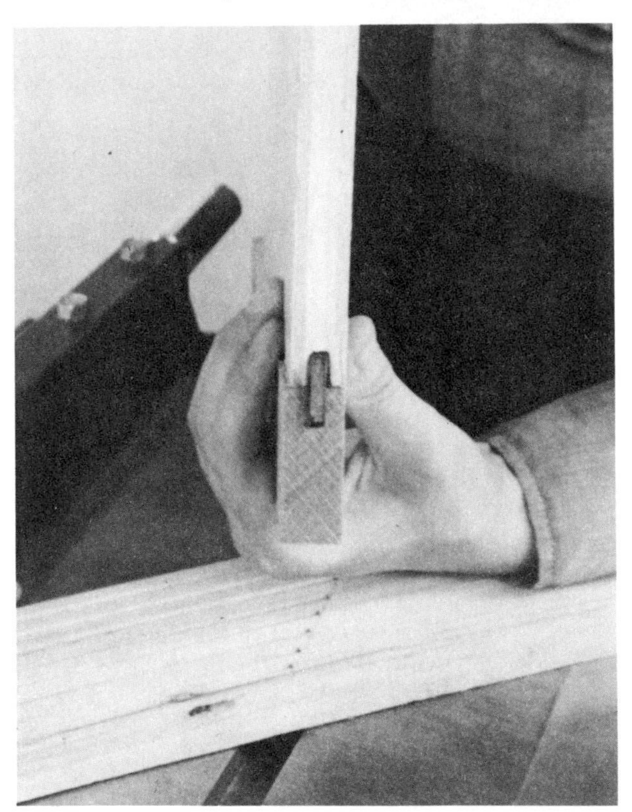

Illus. 6-169. The plywood and solid stock are not the same thickness, but the exposed-side pieces line up.

Kerfing Stock for Bending

Cutting kerfs in the back of a piece of solid stock allows it to be bent easily. The apron for a round table is one application of kerf-bending. The depth of the kerfs is about ¾ to ⅞ of the stock thickness. Shallow kerfs make the curve or arc appear to have flats opposite the kerf.

Kerf spacing is important. The kerfs must be uniformly spaced to produce a smooth arc. To determine spacing, use a piece of scrap that is about 5 inches longer than the radius of the bend. Cut a kerf about 3 inches from the end of the piece. Mark a line parallel to the kerf. The distance from the line to the kerf should equal the radius of the bend. Clamp the layout board with the kerf up to a true surface. Clamp the board to the short side of the kerf. Raise the long side of the board until the kerf closes. Measure the distance from the surface to the bottom of the board at the radius line. This distance equals the kerf spacing (Illus. 6-170).

These kerf cuts can be laid out on the stock, or a spacing jig can be attached to the miter gauge. To space the cuts, make a jig similar to the finger-cutting jig. The jig will ensure uniform spacing.

The pieces can now be bent to shape (Illus.

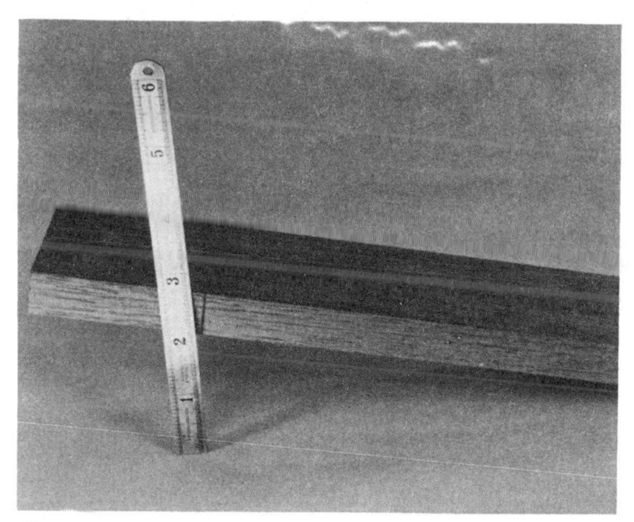

Illus. 6-170. In this example, the spacing between the kerfs is two inches.

6-171). Usually, glue is applied to all of the kerfs so the piece will hold the bend (Illus. 6-172). Some woodworkers glue a veneer to the kerf side of the bent piece to hide the kerfs (Illus. 6-173). Clamp the stock to a form until the glue cures (Illus. 6-174). *Note:* When kerfs are cut at an angle, the stock can be bent into a spiral.

Using Jigs and Patterns

Jigs and patterns are commonly employed when wedges, tapers, and polygons are cut. The jigs and patterns are designed for special purposes. Each of these purposes is discussed separately.

Pattern-Cutting For some shapes such as pentagons, hexagons, and octagons, pattern-cutting

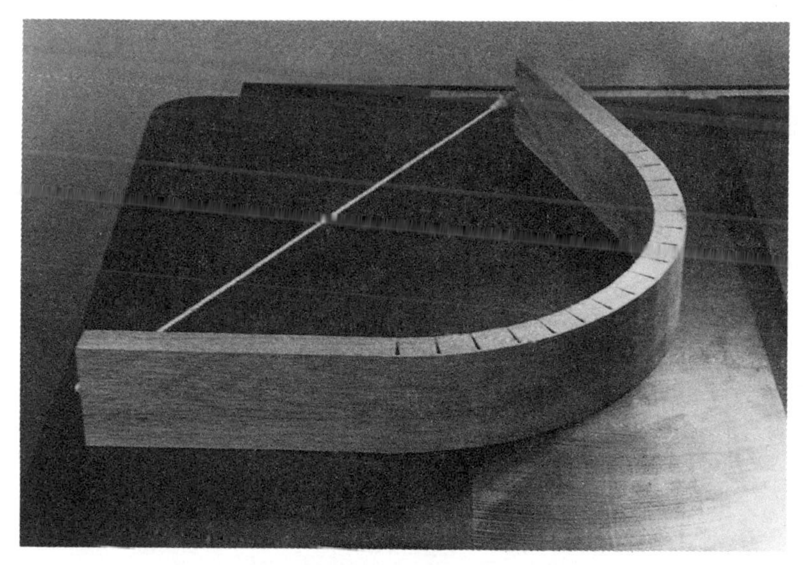

Illus. 6-171. In this scrap setup, the bend appears smooth. Note the flats that form on the face of the work. They are sometimes removed by sanding. The kerf width and depth can affect spacing. They will also affect the flats, and how obvious they are.

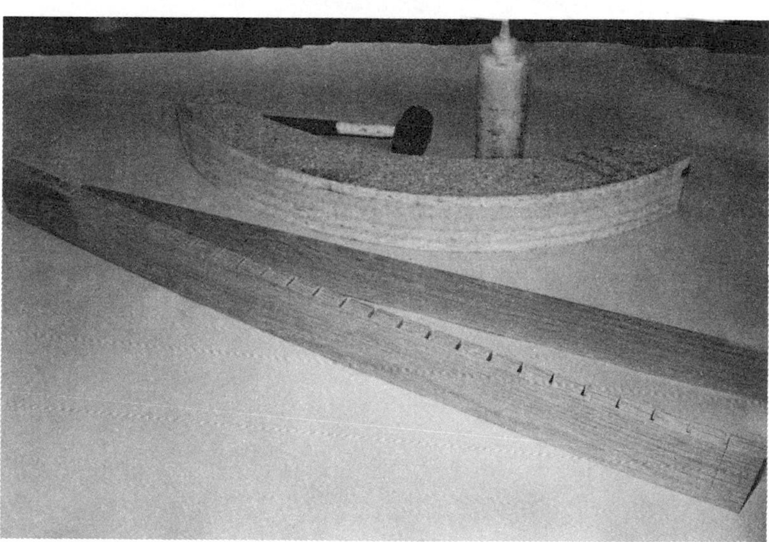

Illus. 6-172. This oak has been prepared for kerf-bending. A layer of veneer will go on the inside to hide the kerfs and add strength.

Illus. 6-173. Glue is spread carefully on the veneer and the kerf side of the bent piece.

Illus. 6-174. Both pieces are clamped to a form. They will remain clamped until the glue cures.

works well. The pattern can be the same size or smaller than the desired part. It is attached to the back of the workpiece with screws or nails (Illus. 6-175). The pattern is controlled by a guide that is attached to the auxiliary fence (Illus. 6-176). The workpiece slides under the guide and is cut to pattern shape by the blade.

The distance from the face of the guide to the blade must be subtracted from each side of the pattern. Lay out the pattern carefully and cut it precisely. Use dense hardwood, plywood, or particleboard for pattern stock.

The pattern must be anchored securely to the workpiece. Nails or screws should be used for this purpose. On thin stock, double-faced tape can be used. Usually, the pattern is attached to the back of the work so that the nail or screw holes are not visible.

Feed stock slowly into the blade, with one side of the pattern in full contact with the guide (Illus. 6-177). Avoid twisting the pattern; this could cause a kickback. Make sure the pieces trimmed from the workpiece do not get caught between the fence and the blade. This could also cause a kickback. Make the workpiece size as close as possible to the desired size, because this minimizes the amount of cutting needed and the scrap size or waste. Remove scraps frequently. Avoid pattern-cutting stock greater than ¾ inch thick.

Illus. 6-175. Patterns are usually attached to the back of the work with screws or nails.

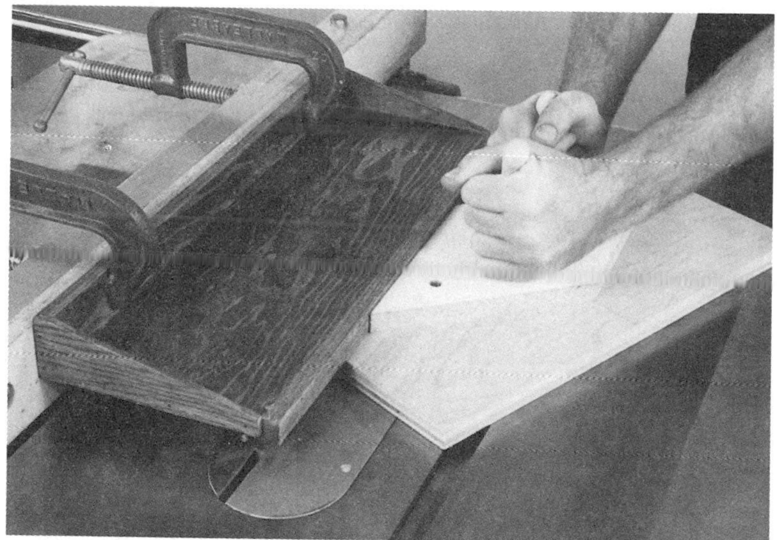

Illus. 6-176. The pattern is controlled by a guide that is attached to the fence. The accuracy of the work depends on the accuracy of the pattern and guide.

Illus. 6-177. Feed the stock slowly into the blade. Keep the pattern in contact with the guide. Avoid twisting the pattern.

Cutting Wedges Wedge cutting is done with a jig (Illus. 6-178). The jig is made for a specific wedge size. Wedge-cutting jigs ride along the fence. The jig is made of sheet stock or solid stock. A wedge-shaped notch is cut out along the blade size of the jig. The narrow end of the wedge is cut first. Fasten a piece of clear plastic or thin plywood over the notch. This will prevent the notch wedge from being thrown out of the jig as the cut is completed.

The throat-plate opening is also a consideration when cutting small wedges. If the opening is too large, the point of the wedge could fall into the opening near the back side of the blade. As the piece falls, it will bind between the blade and throat-plate opening. This could cause a kickback. A zero-clearance throat plate is best to use when cutting small wedges.

Keep the base of the jig wide enough so that your hands are always clear of the blade. A shop-made handle or the handle from a hand plane can be mounted on the jig. This will make it easier to use and control.

Place the jig on the table and move the fence into position. The stock is placed in the jig and fed into the blade (Illus. 6-179). After the first wedge is cut, turn the workpiece over. The wide side of the workpiece will now face the wide end of the notch. Push it into the jig and make another cut. Turning the work over between cuts allows more wedges to be cut from the workpiece. It also keeps the grain running straight in all of the wedges (Illus. 6-180). Long, thin wedges can be used as an inexpensive clamping device (Illus. 6-181).

The miter gauge equipped with an auxiliary face

Illus. 6-178. This jig is designed to cut small wedges. The notch holds the wedge as it is cut.

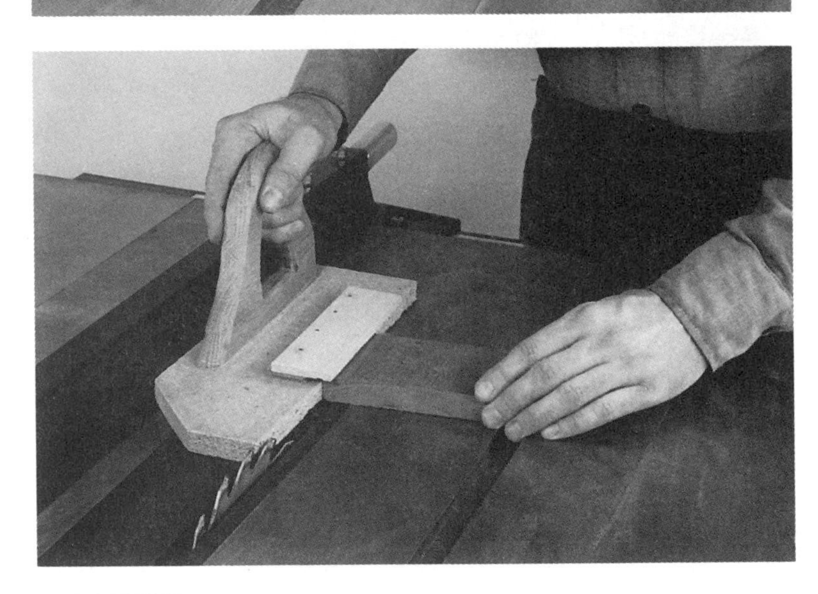

Illus. 6-179. Stock is fed into the blade while it is in contact with the jig. The strip of wood over the jig prevents the wedge from being forced upwards.

Illus. 6-180. The wedges have straight grain if the work is flipped over after each cut.

Illus. 6-181. These thin wedges make an inexpensive clamp that can be used when you are gluing several projects.

can also be used to cut wedges. The miter gauge is set at a shallow angle (Illus. 6-182). The first cut makes an incline on the one edge. The work is turned over and cut again (Illus. 6-183). A pencil line indicates where the stock should be positioned. The completed cut releases a wedge tapered on both sides (Illus. 6-184). Wide pieces work best for this operation. They keep your hands away from the blade.

Illus. 6-182. The square edge is cut away using the miter gauge with an auxiliary face attached. (Photo courtesy of Skil Power Tools.)

Illus. 6-183. The piece is turned over and the end of the stock is aligned with the pencil mark. A cut is then made. (Photo courtesy of Skil Power Tools.)

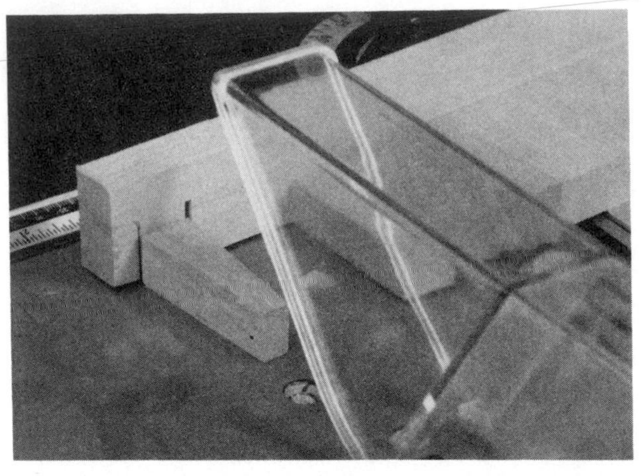
Illus. 6-184. A wedge-shaped piece is produced by the second cut. Wide pieces make this operation safer. (Photo courtesy of Skil Power Tools.)

Cutting Tapers Tapers are inclined surfaces along the edge of a board. A jig is used to cut a taper. Some jigs are used for a single purpose, and others are adjustable. A taper is measured or laid out by the amount of incline in a foot. A taper of ⅜ inch per foot would equal a ¾-inch incline on a board 2 feet long.

A single-purpose jig can be made from a piece of sheet stock (plywood or particleboard). Select a piece one to two inches longer than the stock that will be used. Square up the piece you will be using. Lay out two steps on the edge of the piece. One step is equal to the taper per foot. The other step is equal to twice the taper per foot.

On a piece 18 inches long, with a taper of ½ inch per foot, the first step would be ¾ inch. The second

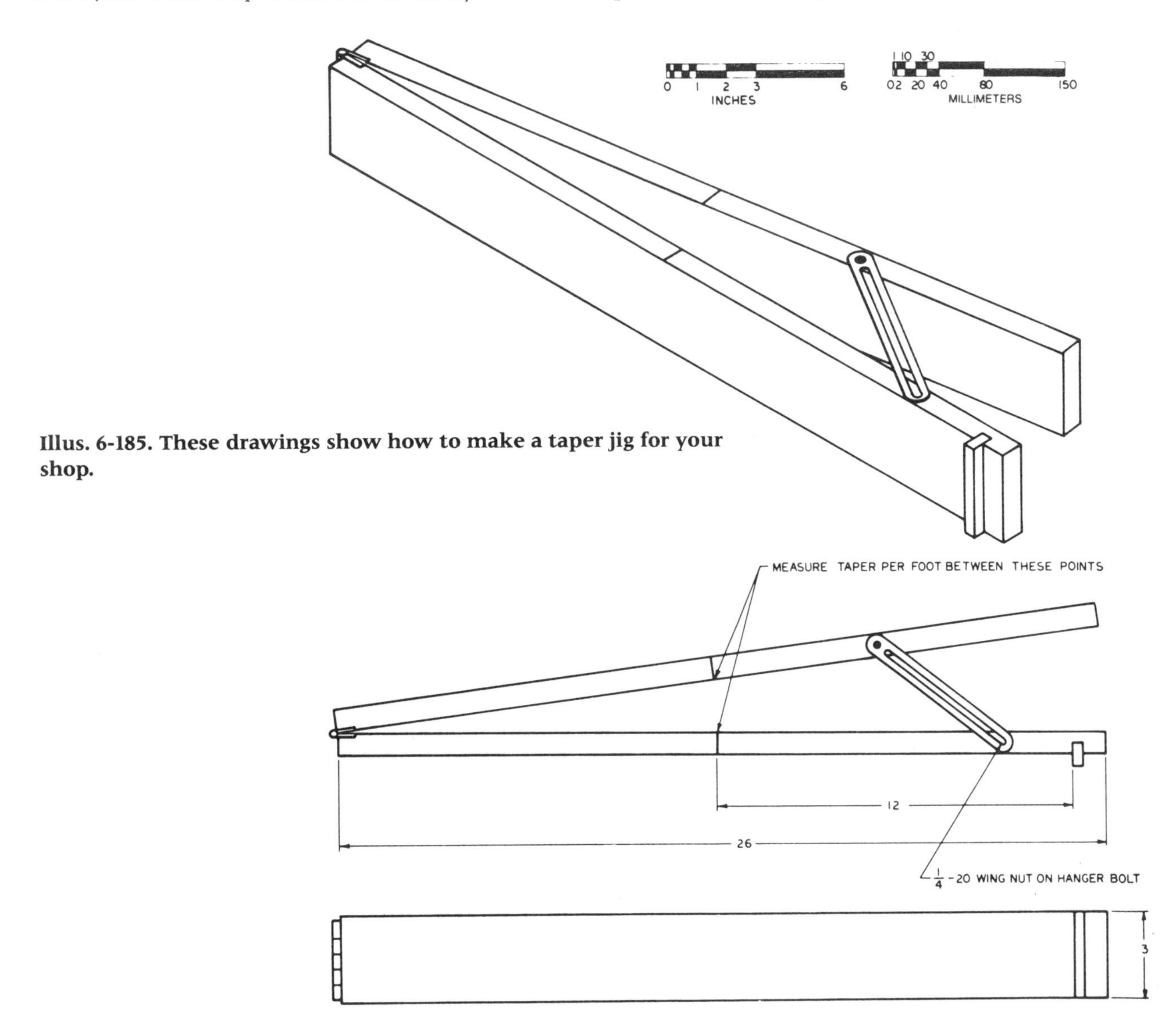

Illus. 6-185. These drawings show how to make a taper jig for your shop.

step would be 1½ inches. The single-purpose jig will be capable of cutting a single- or double-edge taper.

To make this jig, cut away the stock along the layout line using the rip fence. Finish up the cuts with a handsaw or band saw. The jig is now ready to cut tapers.

Adjustable taper jigs can be purchased or built in the shop (Illus. 6-185). Shop-built jigs are made from solid stock 3 inches wide and 24 inches long. Two pieces are needed. Cut a dado at one end of each part for the hinge (Illus. 6-186). Join the parts with a butt hinge (Illus. 6-187). A cleat is fastened to the opposite end of one piece (Illus. 6-188). With the hinge pointing away from you and the cleat on your left, fasten an adjusting mechanism at the

Illus. 6-186. Make a small dado at the ends of both parts of the taper jig. Smooth the bottom of the jig with a chisel.

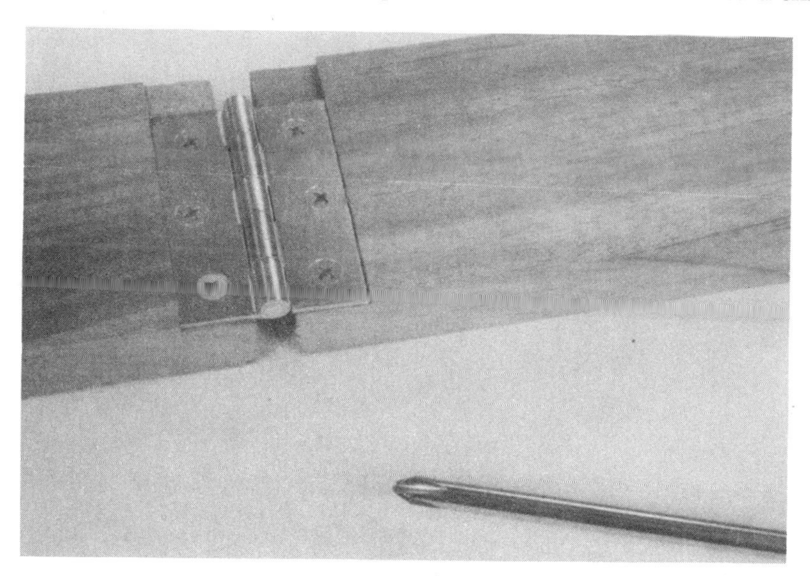

Illus. 6-187. Locate and install a butt hinge in the dado.

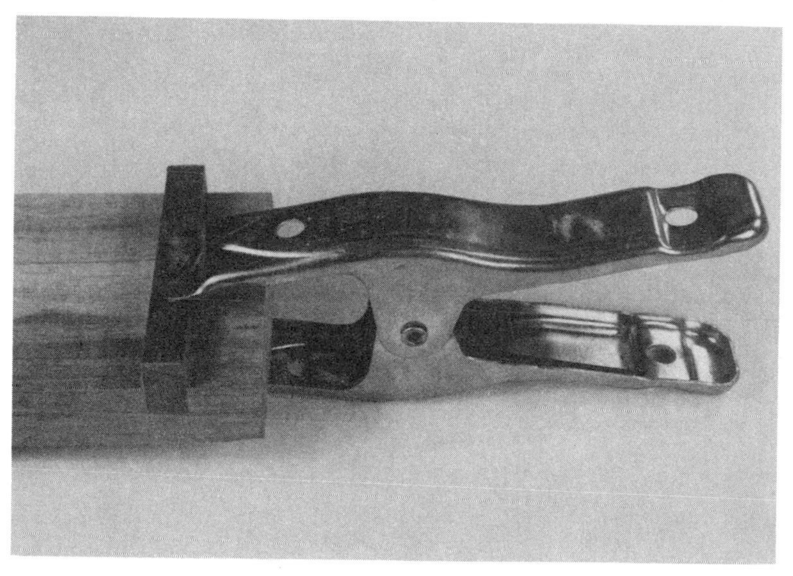

Illus. 6-188. Fasten a cleat in the opposite end of one piece. Cut a small dado and glue it in.

back of the jig. The mechanism can be part of a lid support (Illus. 6-189).

Screw the stationary end to the top of the right wing of the jig. A hanger bolt is installed in the left wing of the jig. The sliding part of the lid support is placed over the hanger bolt. A washer and a wing nut provide the clamping force that holds the jig at the desired setting.

Measure back from the hinge end of the jig exactly one foot. Scribe a line across both wings at this point (Illus. 6-190). The distance between the wings at this point is the taper per foot. Any taper-per-foot adjustment is made at this point. The taper jig is now ready for use.

Either taper jig rides along the fence (Illus. 6-191). The starting point of the taper is lined up with the blade. The fence is adjusted so that the jig is touching the fence while it holds the work in position. The fence is locked in place, and the taper can be cut (Illus. 6-192).

When both sides of the work are to be tapered, the second edge is cut using the second step of the single-purpose jig (Illus. 6-193). The adjustable jig must be opened to twice the taper per foot. Make this adjustment at the one-foot line scribed on the jig.

For production-tapering, a jig with a base is the safest jig to use (Illus. 6-194–6-203). The clamping mechanism holds the work against the ¼-inch base of the jig. As the cut is made, the stock is held securely and cannot lift. This provides for greater safety and control. The jig is positioned against the fence, and the cut is made.

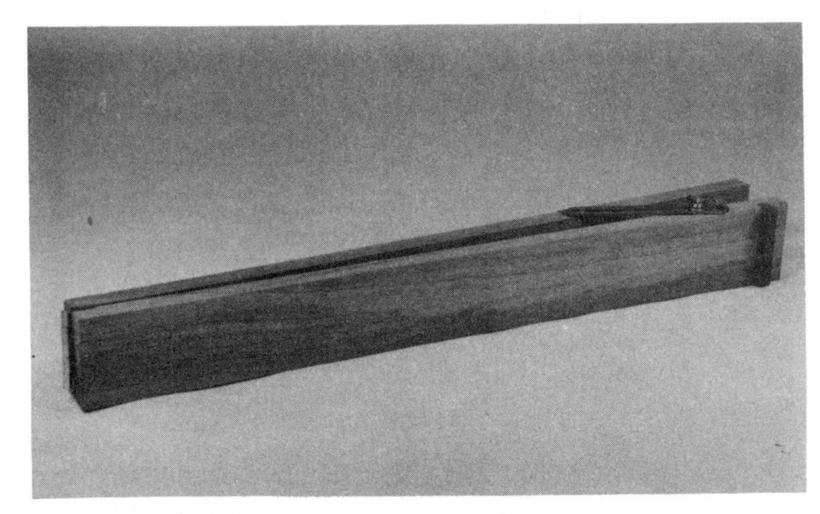

Illus. 6-189. The mechanism on this tapering jig is part of the lid support. A hanger bolt and wing nut lock the moving end of the lid support.

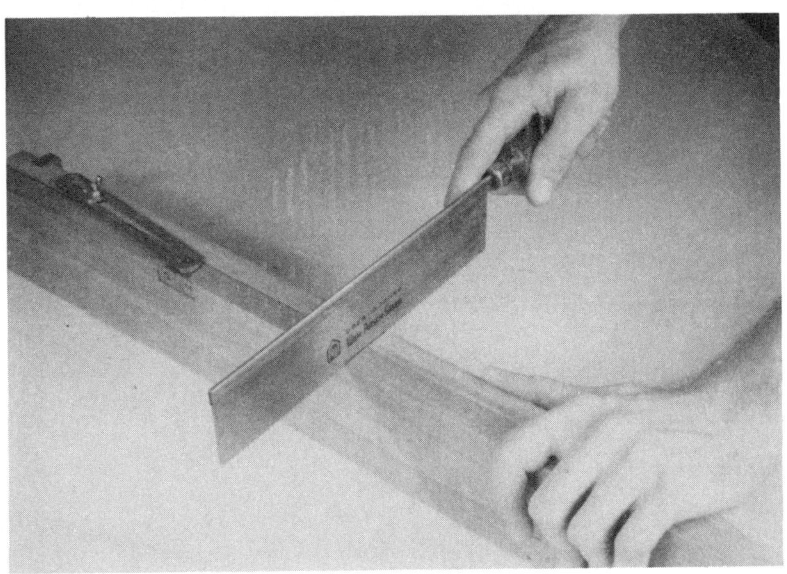

Illus. 6-190. A small kerf is cut in both pieces 12 inches from the cleat. Measurements at this point give the taper per foot.

Illus. 6-191. This commercial taper jig is being used to make a simple taper cut.

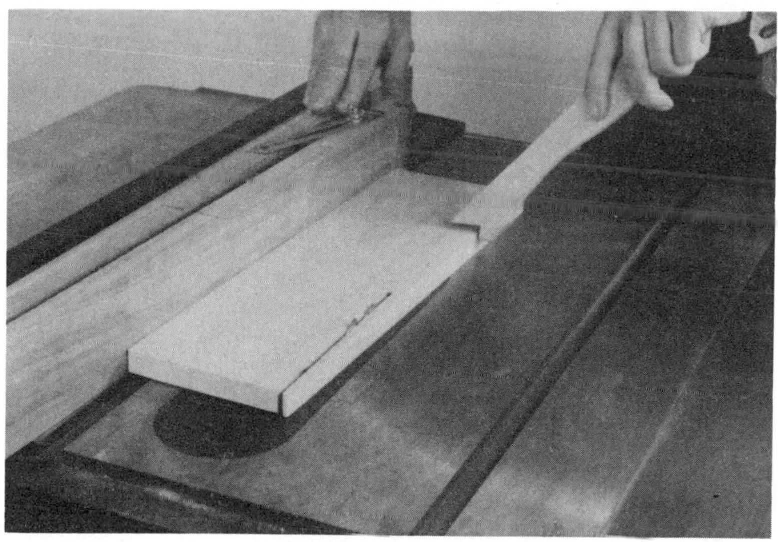

Illus. 6-192. This shop-made taper jig is being used to cut a similar taper. Make sure the jig is set correctly and locked securely before you begin.

Illus. 6-193. This taper jig is next used to cut a second taper on the work. Note the comfortable handle on the jig.

Illus. 6-194. This two-step tapering jig has a ¼-inch plywood platform glued to it.

Illus. 6-195. The clamps secure the stock in the jig. This provides greater control.

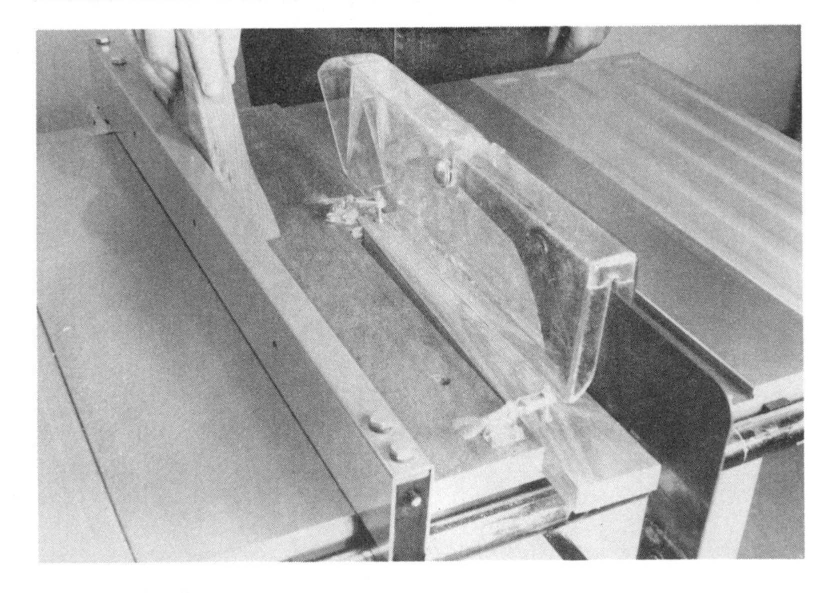

Illus. 6-196. The first edge is tapered with ease. The stock is held securely as it passes under the guard.

Illus. 6-197. A smooth cut was produced using the jig. No burning or fluttering was evident.

Illus. 6-198. The cut edge is put in the second step so the opposite edge can be tapered.

Illus. 6-199. Two identical edges were produced with this jig. Production runs are more efficient with jigs like this one.

Illus. 6-200. This single-taper production jig clamps the stock in two places.

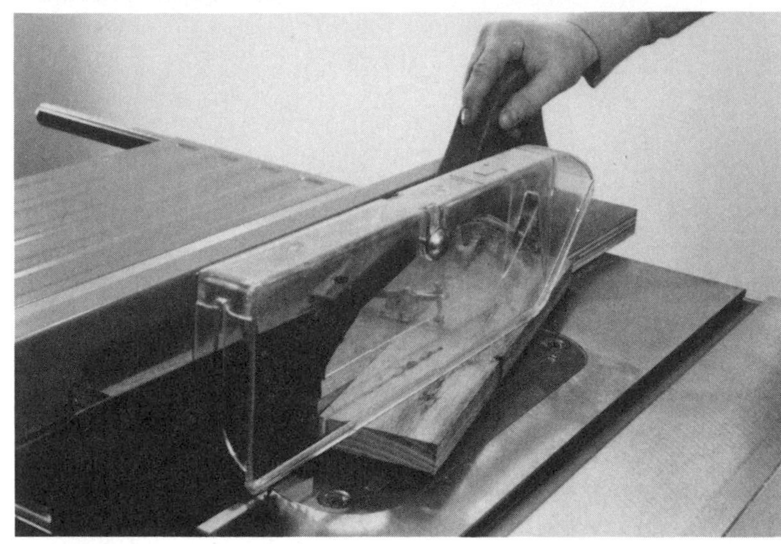

Illus. 6-201. The blade exposure is low, and the edge of the jig rides along the fence.

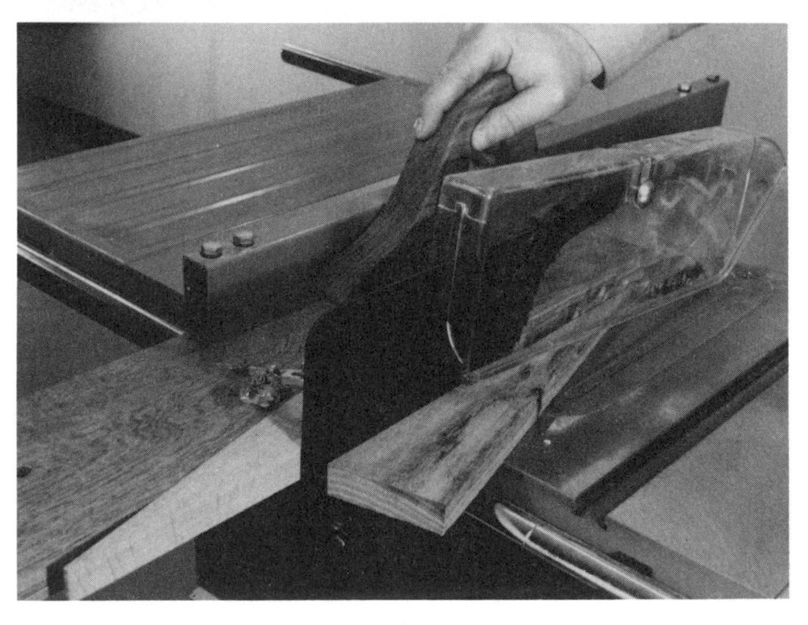

Illus. 6-202. As the cut is completed, the guard holds the cutoff in position until the blade coasts to a complete stop.

Illus. 6-203. The quality of the cut produced is consistently high. Production jobs are best done with these types of jig.

Cutting Circles Circles can be cut on the table saw with a special sawing fixture (Illus. 6-204). This fixture has a center pin on which the work pivots, and a clamp to hold the pieces while the cut is made. There are two positions for the clamp. The outer position is used until the piece becomes an octagon. Then the clamp is shifted to the inner position.

The procedure is simple. First place the work over the pin. A blind hole is drilled in the back of the work. This hole fits over the pin (Illus. 6-205). The piece is clamped in place, and the four corners are cut off (Illus. 6-206). The clamp is now moved to the inner position, and the cutting continues (Illus. 6-207). By turning the work a few degrees between cuts, it will become a circle. The tangent cuts make a smooth edge. Use a sanding disc to make it smoother.

All circle-cutting fixtures must be cut custom-

Illus. 6-204. This sawing fixture is used to cut circles on the table saw.

Illus. 6-205. The blind hole in the work fits over the pin on the fixture. The wing nut exerts the force needed for clamping.

Illus. 6-206. The first step is to cut off the four corners. The stock is clamped securely while the cut is made.

Illus. 6-207. The circle begins to appear as more cuts are made. The clamping device was moved closer to the work for these cuts.

made for the work being done. The distance from the center of the pin to the blade determines the radius of the work you cut. The clamping device must be mounted in relation to that radius.

Cutting Irregular Parts on the Table Saw Parts with an irregular shape cannot be guided or controlled easily with the fence or miter gauge. Parts of this type must be controlled with a fixture designed specifically for the part. Cutting a diamond shape (Illus. 6-208) would be difficult without the fixture. The steep angle of the sides would make control of the miter gauge difficult. The clamping mechanisms are located to hold the part in all four cuts. The part is turned over for the third and fourth cuts (Illus. 6-209).

Whatever the shape of the work, it can be held against a similar fixture for cutting. Consider the shape of the part when you make the fixture. Locate the clamping devices where they will do the most good. Remember, irregularly shaped parts *must* be held securely while they are cut.

Cutting Plastic Laminates In small shops, plastic-laminate sheets are cut on the table saw. A fine-cutting carbide blade works best for cutting plastic-laminate sheets. Since the laminate is very thin, an auxiliary fence is often clamped to the fence. This keeps the laminates from sliding under the fence.

Plastic laminates are very hard. This causes them to resist cutting. They climb over the saw blade. A featherboard can eliminate this problem. It holds the laminate in place while the cut is made (Illus. 6-210).

When long sheets of plastic laminates are being cut, the counter blank can be used to support the laminate while it is cut. Lay the counter blank on two sawhorses in front of the saw. The laminate can rest on the counter blank while the cut is made. This process eliminates the need to unroll the laminate as it is fed into the saw. This approach also minimizes any chance of breakage.

Sometimes laminated counters are cut on the saw. Again, a fine-cutting carbide blade works best.

Illus. 6-208. This diamond shape would be difficult to cut without a fixture. Steep angles on the work require a fixture like this.

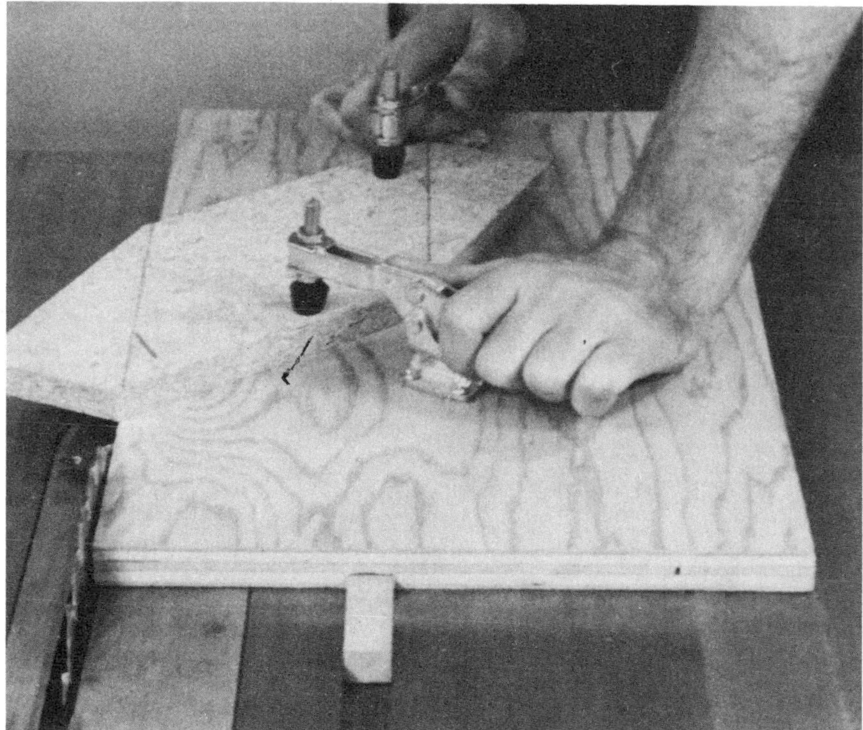

Illus. 6-209. The diamond shape is flipped over for the third or fourth cuts. Placement of these industrial clamps is determined by the shape of the work.

Illus. 6-210. The auxiliary fence keeps the plastic laminate from creeping under the fence. The featherboard holds the laminate down and acts as a guard.

When a counter blank is laminated on both sides, the bottom laminate tends to chip or tear out when it is cut.

A take-off person can be used to make it easier to cut sheet stock. If you are cutting several pieces of plastic laminate, a specialty jig may be useful (Illus. 6-211). The saw blade comes up through the sheet-stock base. The barrier above it keeps the operator's hands from contacting the blade (Illus. 6-212) and the laminate from lifting off the blade. A specialty metal extrusion can also be used to hold stock down and to prevent it from creeping under the fence (Illus. 6-213). It is attached to a wooden auxiliary fence, and can be used with any table saw. One thing to be aware of is that as the stock comes under the anti-kickback pawls, it may be scratched (Illus. 6-214). For more information on plastic laminates, consult *Working with Plastic Laminates*, by Roger Cliffe and Marc Adams.

For cabinetmakers who cut laminated blanks

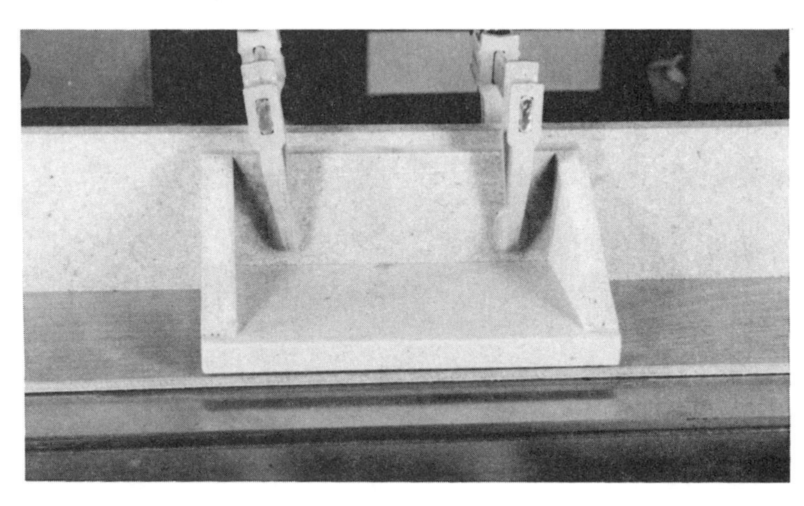

Illus. 6-211. Clamp the sawing guide to the fence and raise the moving blade up through the ¼-inch base and slightly into the guard strip.

Illus. 6-212. Feed the laminate into the saw-guide opening. Keep the laminate against the wooden fence as you make the cut.

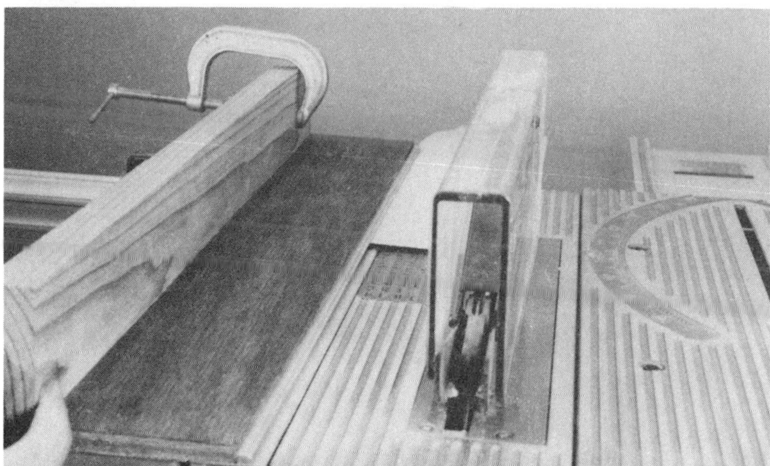

Illus. 6-213. This metal extrusion keeps the laminate from lifting or sliding under the fence. It is attached to a piece of plywood and clamped to the fence.

Illus. 6-214. The anti-kickback pawls can scratch the plastic laminate. Cut the stock wider than necessary or put some tape over the pawls.

frequently, a scoring table saw is desirable. It is designed to eliminate tear-out. The scoring table saw has two circular saw blades. The smaller blade at the front of the table scores the bottom laminate. The larger blade then cuts through the piece. Both blades cut in the same plane. This means that the larger blade exits through the kerf made with the scoring blade. Tear-out is eliminated with the scoring saw.

Making Cabinet Doors

Most cabinet doors consist of a frame around some type of panel. The panel may be glass, cane, solid stock, or plywood. The joinery and the panel differ from the door style.

Frame-and-panel doors can be flush, ⅜-inch rabbet, or overlay (Illus. 6-215). Flush doors sit in the door frame. Rabbeted doors have a ⅜-inch rabbet on all their edges. The door sits inside the door frame. The door is actually larger than the opening. Overlay doors are also larger than the door frame. They simply cover the opening.

Flush doors are the most difficult to fit. This is because the door frame and the door must both be square for a nice fit. When the door and door frame are out of square, hand-fitting and planing are required.

Rabbeted doors are easier to fit. The door is cut ½ inch longer and wider than the opening. A ⅜-inch rabbet is cut on all the edges. The rabbeted length and width of the door is reduced ¾ inch. This allows ¼ inch in width and length for adjusting the door in the frame.

Overlay doors are the easiest to fit. They are cut ¾–1 inch wider and longer than the opening. They are located over the opening and hinged. Hand work is rarely required on overlay doors.

Cope Joints Cope joints are two-part joints (Illus. 6-216). They are cut with the molding head. The panel edge of the vertical pieces (stiles) and horizontal pieces (rails) is shaped with a panel door cutter (Illus. 6-217). This cutter grooves the edges of the stock and leaves a decorative radius in front of the groove (Illus. 6-218).

The groove accommodates the panel. The radius gives the exposed side of the door a decorative shape. The door rails have to be shaped with a rail-end cutter. The rail ends are held vertically for shaping. A tenoning jig is used to guide the part. The complementary shape of the edge is cut on the ends of the rails (Illus. 6-219). The panel is then fitted to the frame, and the door is assembled.

When shaping the door edges, make sure the pieces are marked so their best sides become the door front. Set up the table saw in the manner discussed in Chapter 5 (pages 141–152). When edge-shaping, feed the stock with push sticks. Use a featherboard to hold the stock securely to the fence. Use the tenoning jig to shape the rail ends. Make certain you back the pieces with scrap. This will eliminate tear-out on the rails.

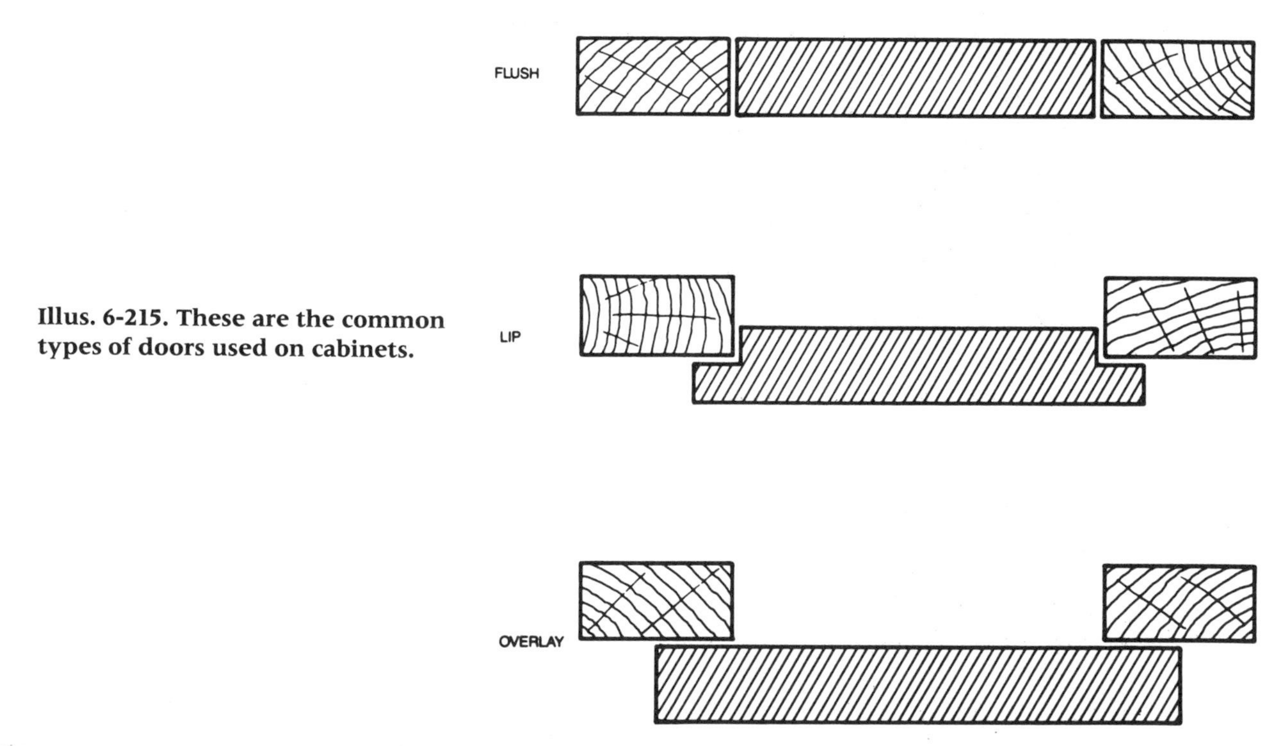

Illus. 6-215. These are the common types of doors used on cabinets.

Illus. 6-216. Cope joints are two-part joints used on door corners.

Illus. 6-217. The panel door cutter shapes the inside edge of the rails and stiles.

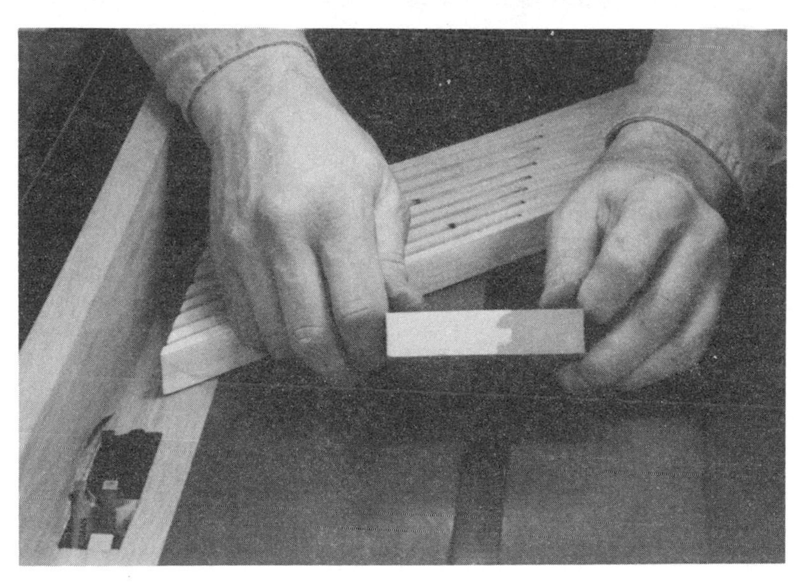

Illus. 6-218. The panel door cutter shaped the stile on the right. The rail end was shaped with the rail-end cutter.

Illus. 6-219. The rail-end cutter cuts the mating shape on both sides of the rails.

Lap Joints Lap joints work well for doors. The stiles are completely exposed. The rails go behind the stiles and are not completely exposed. Lap joints appear to be blind mortise-and-tenon joints when the door edge is rabbeted. This is because the rabbet hides the lap joint. The easiest way to make a lap-joint door is to glue up the frame and then rout a rabbet for the door panel. the rabbet is routed from the back of the door (Illus. 6-220). The panel is then slipped in from the back. Molding can be made to hold the stock in place.

This door works quite well for glass panels. The glass can be held securely with molding. The molding also allows the panel to be changed easily in the event of breakage.

Lap joints can be cut with the tenoning jig or the dado head. This process is discussed on pages 166–171. Make sure you mark the stock before you cut the lap joints. Remember, the stile is completely visible. Lap joints are cut on the back of the stile. Part of the rail is hidden by the stile. The lap is cut on the front of the rail.

Open mortise-and-tenon joints can also be cut with the tenoning jig. These doors frames are also glued up, and then routed for a panel. The stiles of these frames are completely visible, and part of the rails is hidden. The technique for cutting open mortise-and-tenon joints is discussed on pages 173–180. Mark your stock carefully before cutting the joints.

The strongest corner joint for cabinet doors is the haunched mortise-and-tenon joint. The parts actually trap the panel in a groove (Illus. 6-221). The gluing surfaces in the corners make the door very strong, and the door is not likely to sag or turn into a parallelogram. The haunch on the tenon actually fills the groove (Illus. 6-222).

Most of the joint is made with a saw blade or a dado head. The mortise has to be drilled out. This

Illus. 6-220. A rabbet is routed on the back of the lap-joint frame. A wood or glass panel can be held in the rabbet with molding. Square out the corners with a chisel.

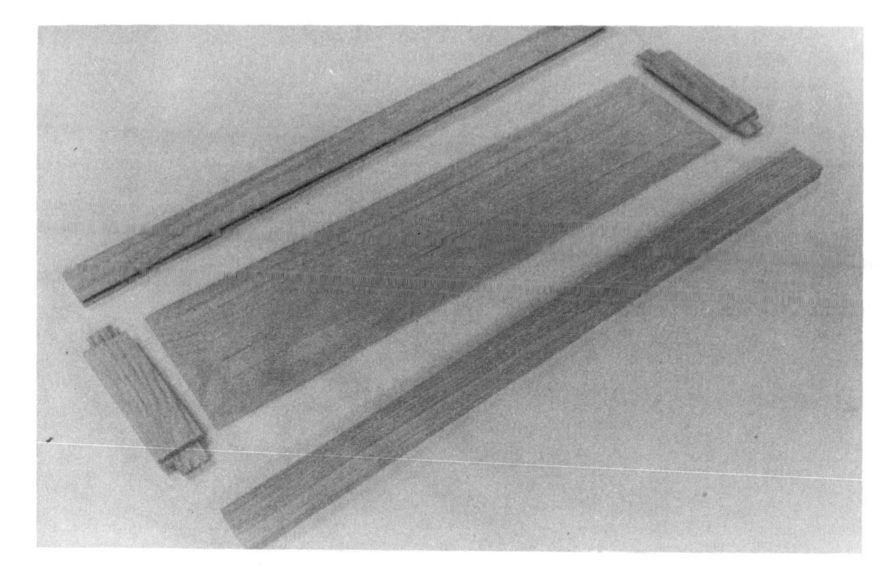

Illus. 6-221. Make a trial assembly of the door parts before gluing them together. Sand the panel completely. It will be difficult to sand in the assembled door.

Illus. 6-222. Make sure the door is square and the panel is centered when you glue up the door. Pin the center of the panel from the back side.

can be done with a drill bit, router bit, or mortiser. In any case, there will be some hand work that must be done with a chisel to fit the joint properly. (Study detail D in Illus. 8-142, which consists of plans for a Hall Chest.) Mortise-and-tenon joints are also discussed on pages 173–180.

Raised Panels Many doors use plain hardwood or plywood panels. These panels are usually ¼ inch thick. Raised panels are ½–¾ inch thick. They have edges that taper to ¼ inch and appear to be raised in the center. Raised panels are more decorative than plain panels (Illus. 6-223). The raised panel is first cut to the desired width and length. The typical panel is ½ inch thick. This thickness makes the panel even with the front of a ¾-inch door frame when assembled.

Begin by cutting a kerf on the face of the panel. Set the distance from the fence to the blade at about 1½ inches. Raise the blade to cut a kerf ⅛ inch deep. Make a cut along both ends and edges (Illus. 6-224–6-239). There will be four kerfs that cross in the corners (Illus. 6-240).

Set the distance from the fence to the blade at slightly more than ¼ inch. Raise the blade and tilt it so that it cuts up the kerf. The tilt angle will be about 6 degrees. Clamp a straightedge to the back of the panel before making any cuts. The straightedge

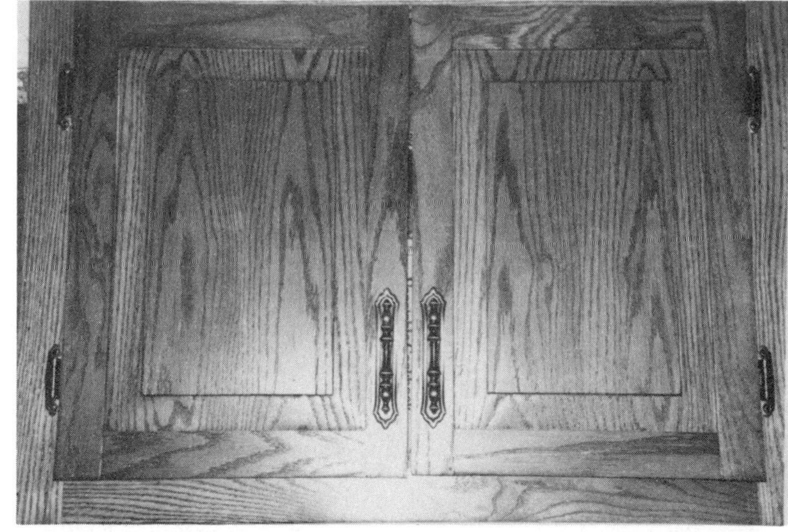

Illus. 6-223. Raised panels are much more decorative than plain ones.

Illus. 6-224. The panel stock is kerfed on all four edges. Start with the edges.

Illus. 6-225. The blade is 1½ inches from the fence and ⅛ inch above the table. These dimensions are appropriate for a 10-inch blade. For an 8-inch blade, set the fence 1¼ inches from the fence.

Illus. 6-226. When making the end-grain cuts, use the miter gauge to control the work.

Illus. 6-227. Keep the stock down on the table when making the saw kerfs. The cuts must all be the same depth.

Illus. 6-228. Inspect the intersection of the kerfs for uniform depth. If the kerfs are not the same depth, cut them again.

Illus. 6-229. An auxiliary fence about 8 inches high has been screwed to the metal fence. The work is clamped in position, and the fence is moved into approximate position. The power is disconnected.

Illus. 6-230. The tilt of the blade is about 6 degrees. You can eyeball the position of the blade to the stock. The bottom edge of the panel should just fit the groove in the frame. Notice how little support the panel has over the throat plate.

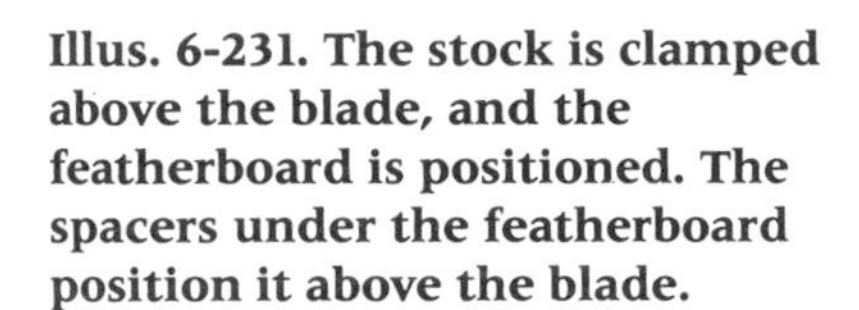

Illus. 6-231. The stock is clamped above the blade, and the featherboard is positioned. The spacers under the featherboard position it above the blade.

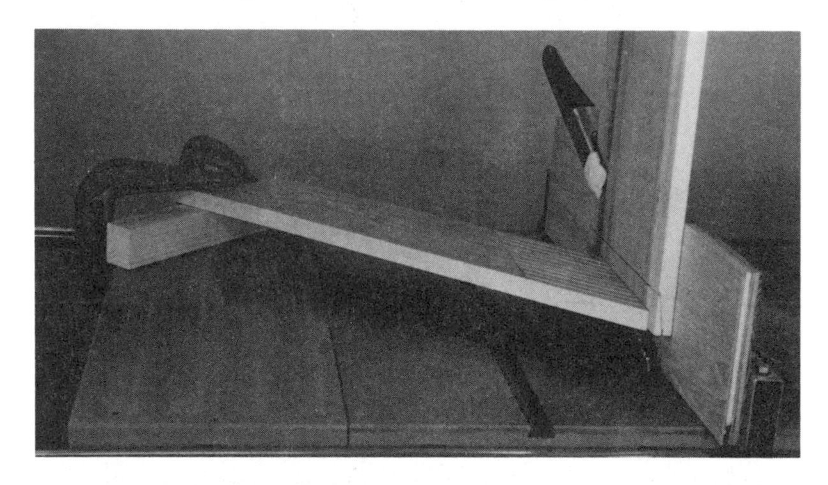

Illus. 6-232. A straightedge has been clamped to the panel. It will ride on the auxiliary fence as a miter gauge.

Illus. 6-233. In addition to being a miter gauge, the straightedge removes any warp from the panel and keeps the panel from dropping into the throat-plate opening.

Illus. 6-234. The edge is now ready to be cut. These cuts are rip cuts, and a chip-limiting rip blade was used.

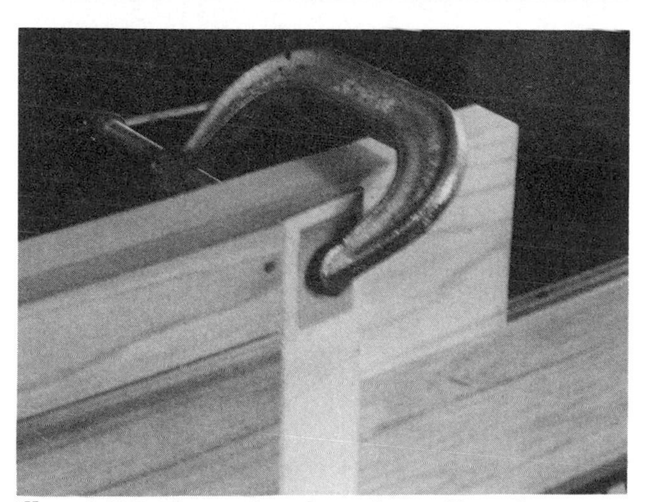

Illus. 6-235. The wedge-shaped cutoffs make great clamp pads when you are making the edge cuts.

Illus. 6-236. Notice how the featherboard holds the stock against the fence and also acts as a barrier guard above the blade.

Illus. 6-237. Notice the quality cut on this stock. The inclines form almost perfect miters between the raised and panel corners.

Illus. 6-238. Notice that the edge on this panel is true even though it is warped. The straightedge clamped to the panel pulled the warp out of it during the cut. Once again, there are no burn marks.

Illus. 6-239. A sanding frame like this one can make sanding easier and more comfortable. A small cleat holds the panel to the sanding jig.

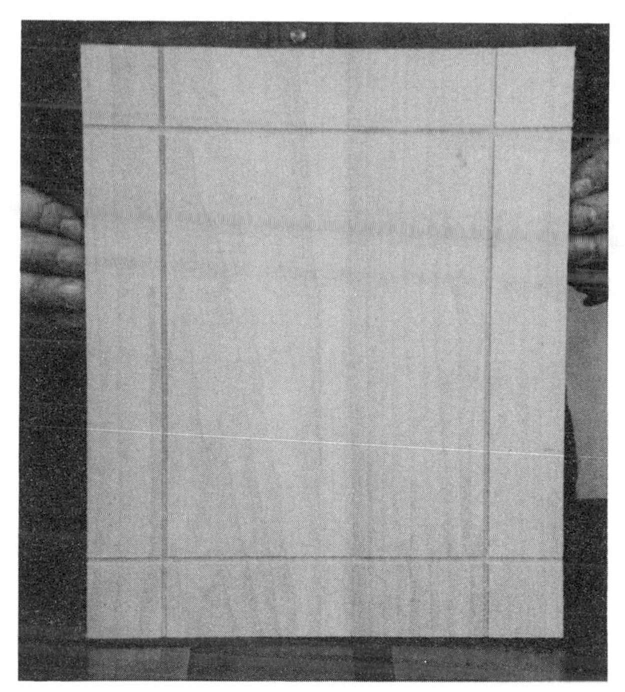

Illus. 6-240. The four kerfs cross in the corners. These kerfs form the shoulders of the raised panel.

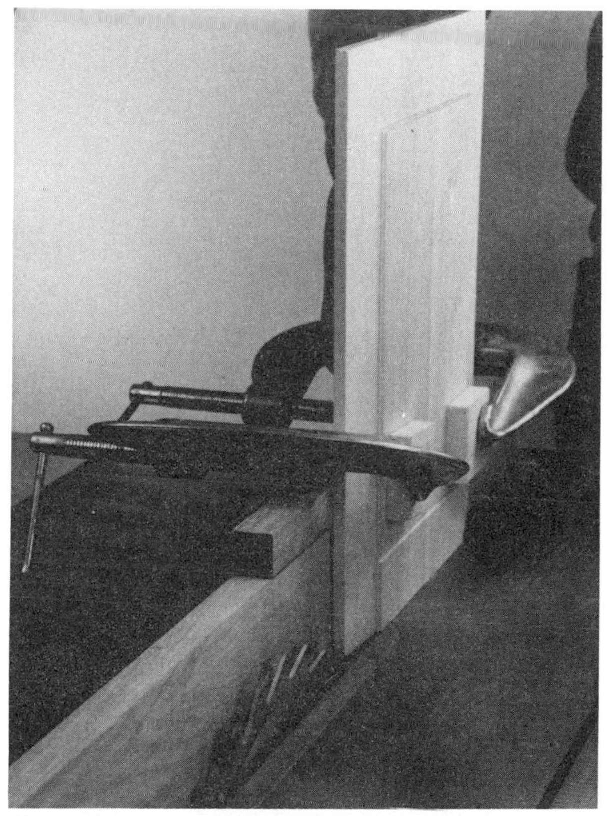

Illus. 6-241. A straightedge is clamped to the panel when the bevel cuts are made. If the panel is warped slightly, the straightedge pulls it into a true plane.

rides along the fence and keeps the piece from pinching (Illus. 6-241). It also keeps the piece from dropping down through the throat plate. Make all four cuts with the help of a straightedge. To minimize sanding of the inclined surfaces, a fine-cutting blade should be used. Sand the surfaces completely before installing the panel in a door.

Raised panels can be used in almost any type of door frame. Coped joints and haunched mortise-and-tenon joints are used in the highest-quality frames for raised panels. Lap joints, open mortise-and-tenon joints, and miter joints also make a nice frame for raised panels.

When using solid panels in a door frame, be sure to allow for expansion and contraction. Make the grooves in the rails and stiles about ⅛ inch deeper than the panel width and length. This allows for panel movement in the frame.

Raised panels are sometimes used as lids. The decorative shape of the panel makes it appealing as a box top (Illus. 6-242). Cut the panel slightly larger than the box. Trim it after it is glued to the box. Box tops can be thicker or thinner than the raised panel used in a door. Adjust your cutting plan accordingly.

Illus. 6-242. Raised panels are sometimes used as box tops. This one will be trimmed to size after the glue dries.

Miter Joints Doors using miter joints give the door panel a wrapped look. The frame wraps around the panel (Illus. 6-243). All frame parts are grooved and shaped before the miter joints are cut (Illus. 6-244). The mitering jig or two miter gauges

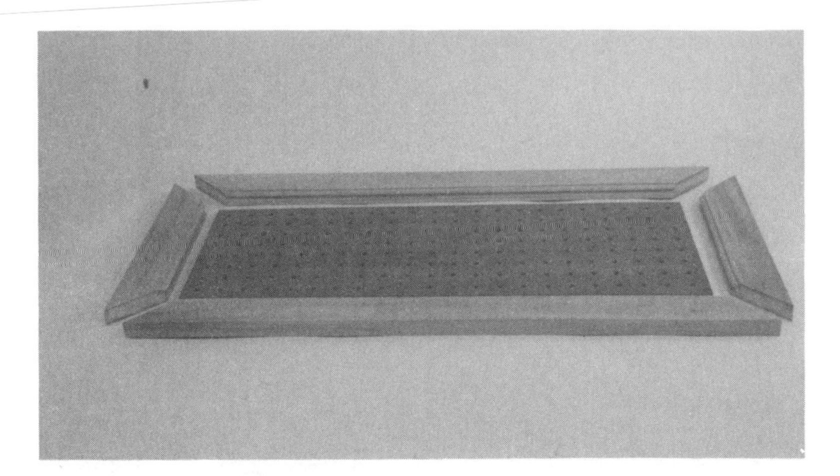

Illus. 6-243. The miters give the center panel a "wrapped" look.

can be used to cut the miters. It is a good idea to cut keys in the miter joints after the door is assembled. This increases the strength of the door.

Miter-trim doors look like mitered frame doors, but require less work to make. The trim is purchased in random lengths (Illus. 6-245). It is mitered and glued and/or nailed around a ¾-inch panel (Illus. 6-246). The rabbet butts against the panel and leaves a ⅜-inch × ⅜-inch offset. This offset is the ⅜-inch lip that is common on lipped doors. After the trim is installed, the door is ready for hinges. Similar trim can be made using a shaper head on the table saw.

Illus. 6-244. This stock was shaped before the miters were cut. Miters on large doors and doors with glass panels require reinforcement.

Shaping Door Edges Most lip doors have a rabbet cut on all four edges. This rabbet is usually ⅜ inch × ⅜ inch. The rabbet can be cut with a single blade, a dado head, or a molding head. Straight or jointer shaper cutters are used in the molding head. Follow the procedures outlined on pages 155–173 for cutting or shaping rabbets.

Some door frames have a decorative edge cut on their exposed edge. These shapes can be made with various shaper cutters. Roundover cutters and

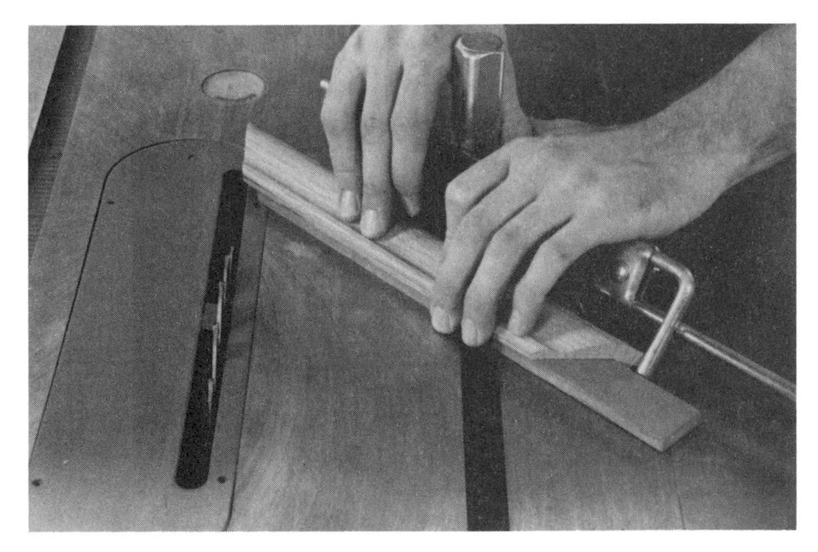

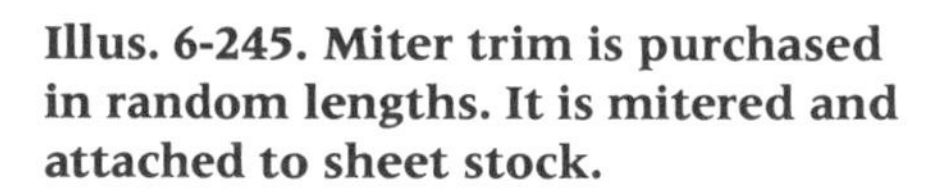

Illus. 6-245. Miter trim is purchased in random lengths. It is mitered and attached to sheet stock.

Illus. 6-246. This door front has miter trim attached to it. It is ready for hinges and fitting.

cabinet-door lip cutters can be mounted in the molding head for shaping the edges.

The cabinet-door lip cutter cuts a rabbet on the back of the door and a radius on the front of the door edge in one cut. Be sure to review shaping procedures before making this cut. Remember, harder woods will require two or more light cuts to shape a door edge because there is a great deal of material being cut.

Cutting Drawer Parts and Joints on the Table Saw

Cutting drawer joints and drawer parts on the table saw are common operations. Drawers, like cabinet doors, can be flush, lip, or overlay. The joinery differs with the type of drawer, but the drawer sides and back are all made about the same way.

Making Drawer Parts Most drawer parts are made from ½-inch-thick stock. Drawer parts usually have a groove cut near the edge to hold the drawer bottom in place. The drawer bottom is usually ¼ inch thick, but may vary according to the drawer size and purpose.

The groove is at least ¼ inch from the edge (Illus. 6-247). This minimizes the chance of splitting or breakage. With some types of drawer guide, the drawer bottom must be higher to accommodate the drawer guide. The drawer guides should be selected before any drawer parts are cut.

Grooves can be cut with a dado head, molding head, or a saw blade. The dado head allows easy adjustment to slightly more than ¼ inch. The increased size makes it easy to drop the drawer bottom in position. Always check the groove size with a piece of the stock used for drawer bottoms (Illus.

Illus. 6-247. Use a dado head or a single blade to cut the groove for the drawer bottom. The depth of the groove should be about one-half the drawer thickness.

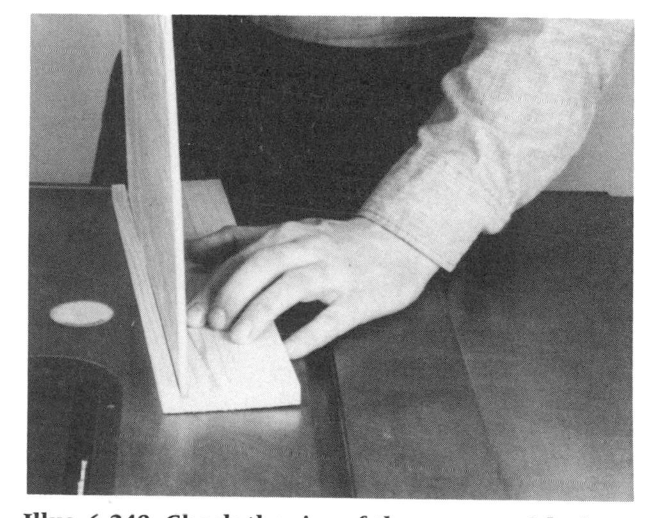

Illus. 6-248. Check the size of the groove with the stock being used for drawer bottoms. A loose fit means the bottom may rattle. A tight fit can make drawer assembly difficult.

6-248). Too large a groove causes excess drawer rattle when it is opened or closed.

After the groove is cut, the top can be "radiused." This makes the drawer sides less likely to catch on clothing or other articles. Some pieces are radiused from end to end. Others are radiused to within one inch of the end or ends (Illus. 6-249). This is common with flush drawers. The square end helps guide the drawers into position and makes the joint between the side and front look neater.

To "radius" drawer sides, set up a roundover cutter in the shaper head. Use a stop block (Illus.

Illus. 6-249. High-quality drawers usually have square ends and a radius in the center of their length. This radius can be cut with the shaper head.

6-250) to prevent a kickback. Position the stop block so the drawer side extends about one inch above the cutter. With the face of the drawer side against the fence, slowly lower it onto the molding head (Illus. 6-251).

Feed the piece across the cutters with a push stick (Illus. 6-252). Now, with the piece's edge against the fence and its end against the stop block, slowly lower the drawer side onto the molding head (Illus. 6-253). Feed the work with a push stick (Illus. 6-254). The finished drawer side will resemble the one in Illus. 6-255. Remember, if you have already cut the groove for the drawer bottom, you will have to make right- and left-hand sides.

Overlay Drawers Overlay drawers usually have two drawer fronts. The decorative front is larger than the opening. It is screwed to the false front. The false front is part of the drawer assembly (Illus. 6-256).

The joints on an overlay drawer can be as simple as butt joints. Butt joints are glued and nailed together. A rabbet dado joint on the drawer front and a dado joint on the back make a stronger drawer (Illus. 6-257). Drawers made with these joints are easier to glue and assemble.

The dadoes at the back of the drawer are wide enough to accommodate the drawer back (Illus. 6-258). The depth is one-half the thickness of the side. Make sure you mark the sides as right and left. The sides are not the same. They are mirror images of each other.

The dadoes at the front of the drawer sides are narrow (Illus. 6-259). They should be about one-third of the drawer-side thickness. A saw kerf is often wide enough. The depth of these dadoes is equal to those at the back of the drawer. When

Illus. 6-250. A roundover cutter and a stop block are used to "radius" drawer sides.

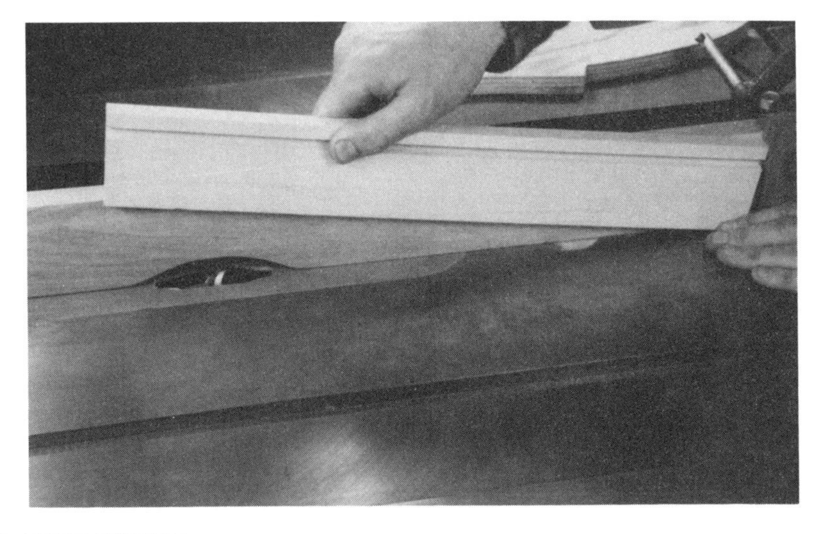

Illus. 6-251. Lower the drawer side slowly into the molding head. The back of the drawer should be butted to the stop block. The face of the drawer should be against the fence.

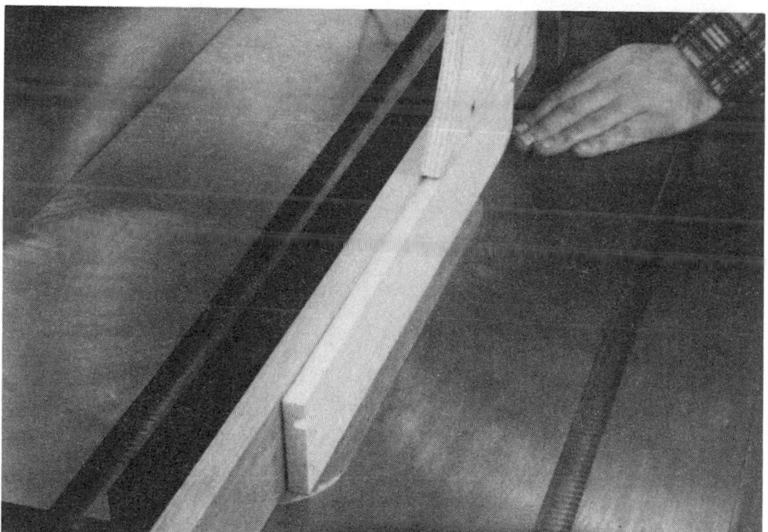

Illus. 6-252. Feed the work across the cutters with a push stick.

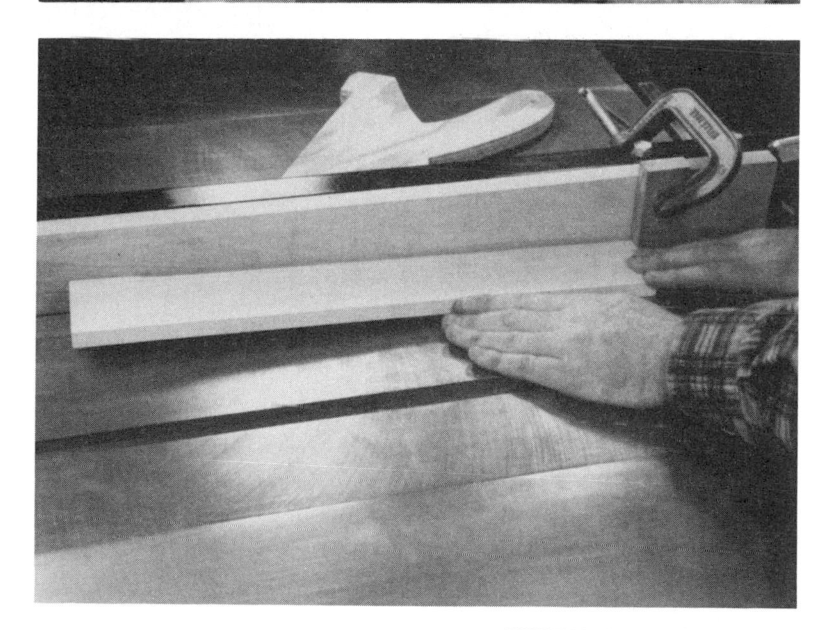

Illus. 6-253. Follow the same procedure for the second radius. This time, the drawer edge is against the fence.

Illus. 6-254. Use a push stick to feed the work. Feed the stock slowly and uniformly to reduce the chance of tear-out.

Illus. 6-255. The finished drawer side is square at its front and "radiused" at the back.

Illus. 6-256. Overlay drawers usually have two fronts: a decorative front and a false front. The decorative front is usually screwed to the false front.

Illus. 6-257. A rabbet dado joint is used between the drawer side and false front.

Illus. 6-258. Cut the dadoes at the back of the drawer sides large enough for the drawer back.

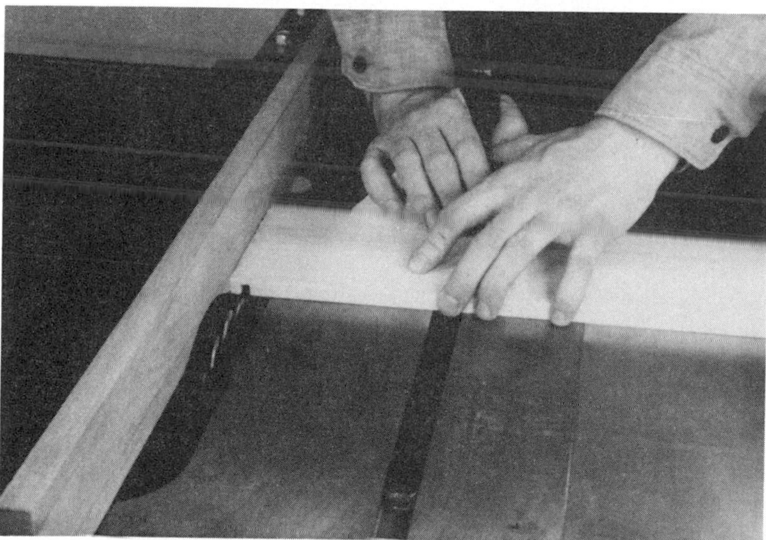

Illus. 6-259. The narrow dadoes at the front of the drawer sides can be cut with a saw blade.

Illus. 6-260. The dado head cuts the rabbet, which produces a tongue on the drawer front.

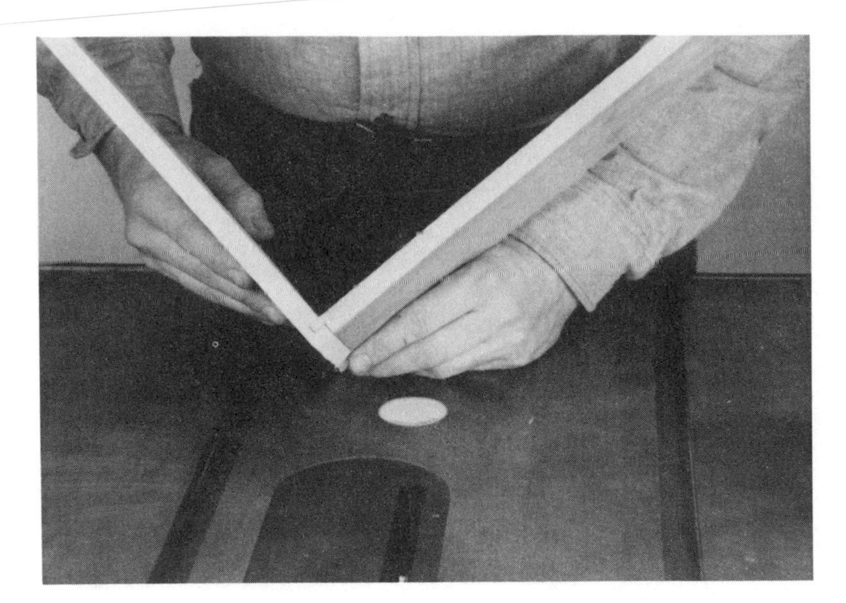

Illus. 6-261. Test the fit of the drawer joints and make any needed adjustments.

cutting this dado, the distance from the fence to the far side of the blade should equal the thickness of the false front.

Drawer backs need no dado work. They are ready to install. The false front must have a tongue cut on each end. This tongue fits the dado on the drawer side. An auxiliary fence is attached to the fence. The dado head is adjusted to cut the tongue (Illus. 6-260). Some of the dado head will be under the auxiliary fence.

Mark the pieces before you cut the tongue. The groove for the drawer bottom should be up when the tongues are cut. Test the fit of the drawer joints (Illus. 6-261). Make any needed adjustments. After the drawer is assembled, the exposed front can be attached. Screws are usually driven through the false front into the exposed front.

Lip Drawers Lip drawers usually have a rabbet joint at the front and a dado joint at the back. The drawer front is usually ¾ inch thick. The rabbet is ⅜ × ⅜ inch on the top and bottom. The sides have a wider rabbet. It is ⅜ inch plus the drawer-side thickness.

The rabbets can be cut in many different ways. The sides are glued and nailed to the rabbet joint. The drawer front must also have a groove cut for the drawer bottom. Use a drawer side to determine where the groove should be cut.

Flush Drawers Flush drawers can be joined with many different types of drawer joints. The rabbet joint is probably the simplest joint. Rabbets are cut on both ends of the drawer front. These rabbets are slightly wider than the drawer sides to allow some

Illus. 6-262. A dado is cut on both ends of the drawer front. A tenoning jig could also be used to control the work.

clearance for fitting. The depth of the rabbets should be at least one-half the thickness of the drawer front. The sides are dadoes, so the back can be joined to them.

A drawer corner is similar to a rabbet joint except the drawer front has a tongue that goes into the sides for added strength. A dado is cut on both ends of the drawer front (Illus. 6-262). The dado is about ¼ inch wide (on a ¾-inch-thick drawer front). The depth is slightly greater than the thickness of the drawer side. The dado can be centered in the stock or off-centered so that the tongue on the drawer back is slightly smaller than the one on the front.

A mating ¼-inch dado is then cut in the drawer sides (Illus. 6-263). This dado should be about ¼ inch from the end. Remember, the right and left sides are not the same. Mark your pieces carefully before you make any cuts. The side should now fit the tongue and dado on the drawer front (Illus. 6-264). The tongue will now have to be trimmed so the side can be butted against the drawer front (Illus. 6-265–6-267).

A lock corner is another variation of the drawer corner. The lock corner has a tongue on the drawer front and a tongue on the drawer side. This joint must be slid together. The back slides into dadoes in the sides. The back is not grooved. It rests on the drawer bottom. The sides and front are grooved to support the drawer bottom.

With the exception of one dado, drawer fronts with a drawer corner joint or a lock joint look alike. They are cut in the same way. The first dado cut on

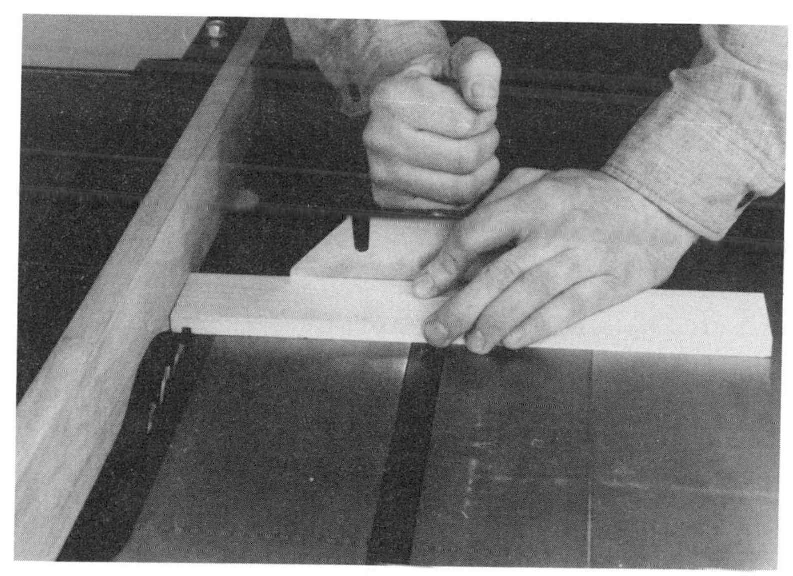

Illus. 6-263. A mating dado is cut into the front of the drawer sides.

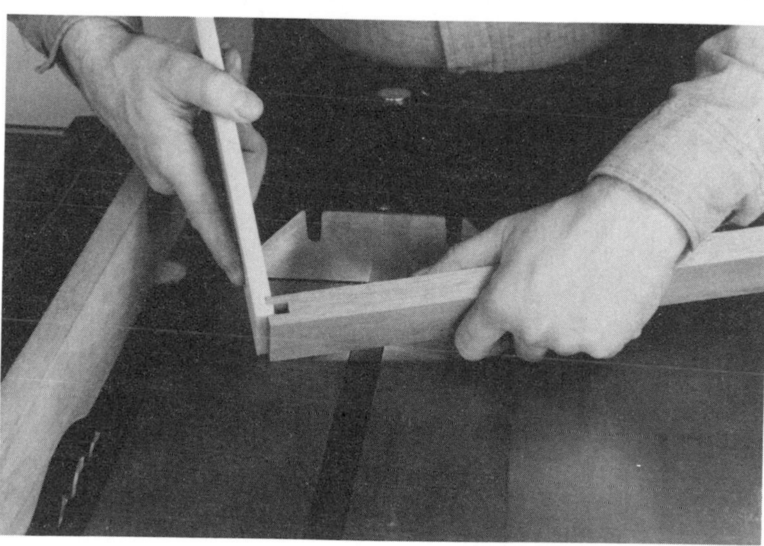

Illus. 6-264. The dado and tongue should fit correctly. Mark the tongue length with the drawer side.

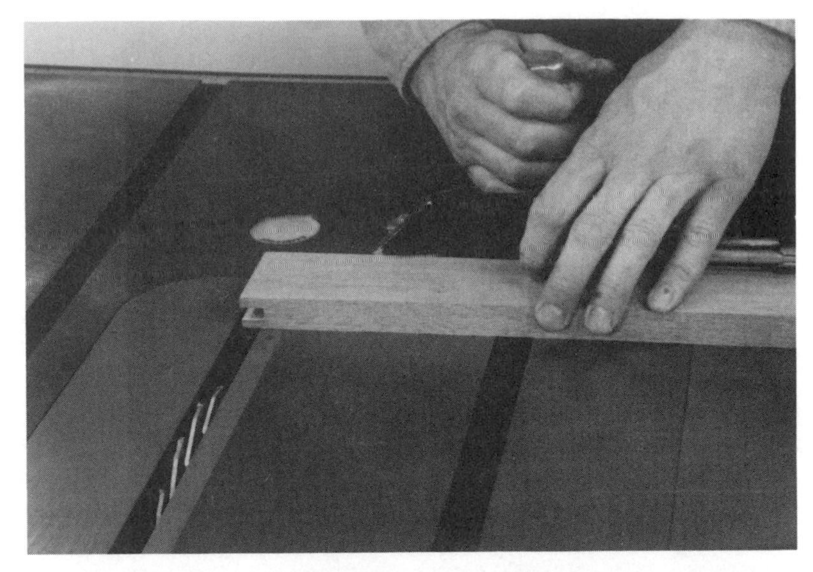

Illus. 6-265. Saw the tongue to correct length. A stop rod can be used to control the work.

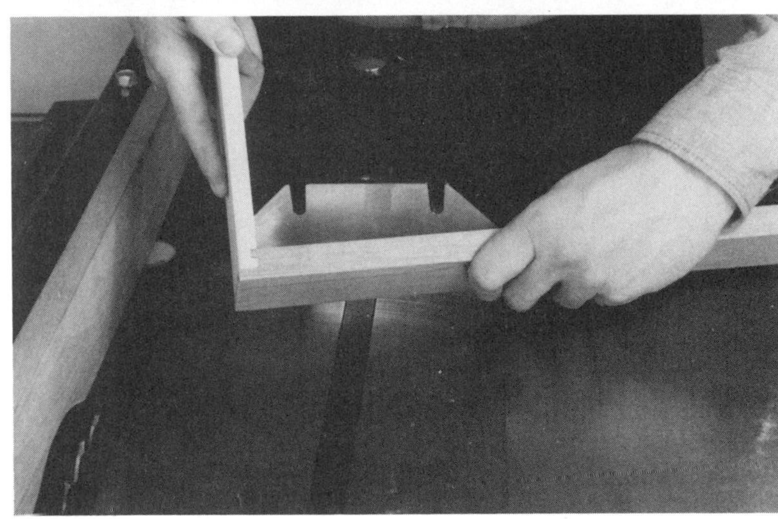

Illus. 6-266. The drawer-corner joint fits correctly. Careful layout makes the work rewarding.

Illus. 6-267. This bird's-eye maple drawer has drawer corner joints. Note the dado on the drawer side. This is for a drawer guide.

the ends of the drawer front is closer to the back (Illus. 6-268). The second dado cut trims the tongue and puts a dado in the front (Illus. 6-269).

The drawer side is then cut to fit the front. A tongue is cut on the front of the side (Illus. 6-270), and then a dado is cut on the inner side (Illus. 6-271). The pieces should slide together without force. If the pieces must be forced together, the glue will make it impossible to put the parts together (Illus. 6-272).

Flush drawers using metal side guides can be joined with through dovetails. The drawer front is dadoed to accommodate the sides. Determine where the drawer sides should be placed. Mark the centerline and cut a ¼-inch dado ½ inch deep (Illus. 6-273). Lay out the dovetail over the dado. Use a saw blade to cut the dovetailed sides (Illus.

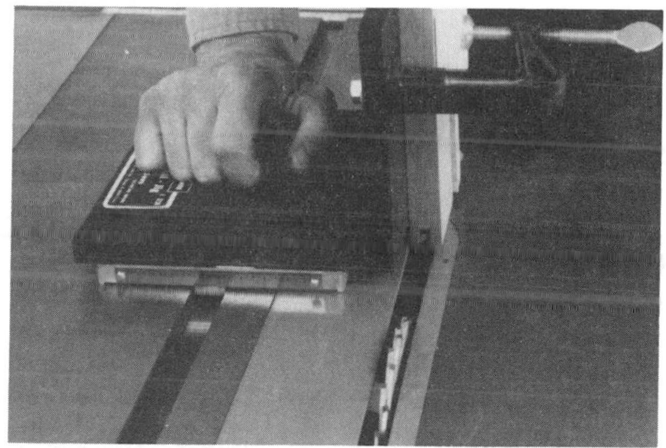

Illus. 6-268. The dado cut on the ends of the drawer front is closer to its back. A tenoning jig is being used to hold the work.

Illus. 6-269. The second dado cut trims the tongue as it makes the dado. A stop rod can be used to locate the cut.

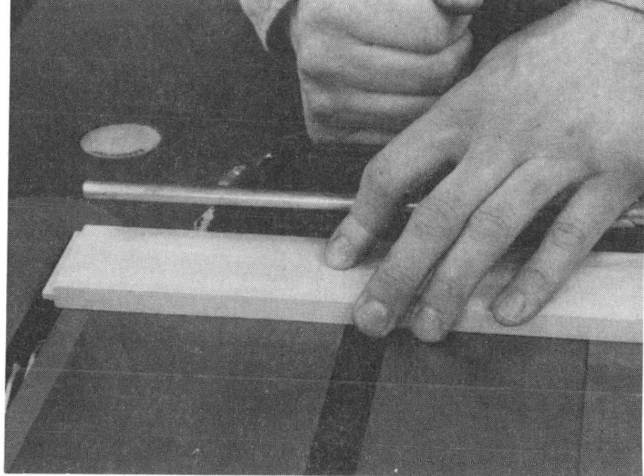

Illus. 6-270. A tongue is cut on the front of the drawer side. The stop rod is used to locate the tongue, but the fence could also be used.

Illus. 6-271. A dado is cut on the inside of the drawer side. This dado matches the tongue on the drawer front.

Illus. 6-272. Check the fit of the pieces. The pieces should slide together easily. A tight fit will be impossible to assemble when the glue is applied.

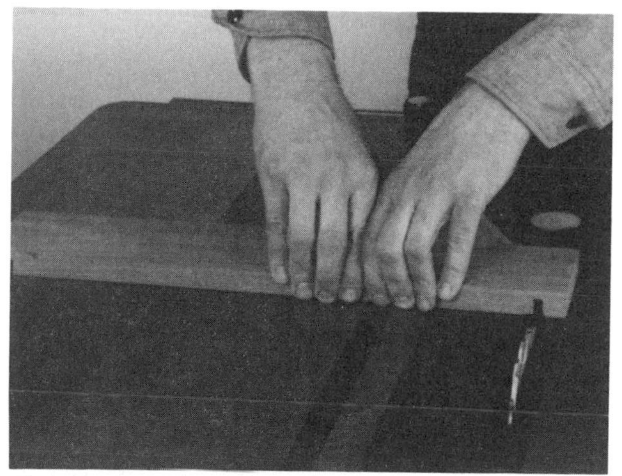

Illus. 6-273. A straight dado is cut in the drawer front first when a dovetail dado joint is being made.

Illus. 6-274. The blade is tilted to the desired angle when the angled sides in the dovetail dado joint are being cut.

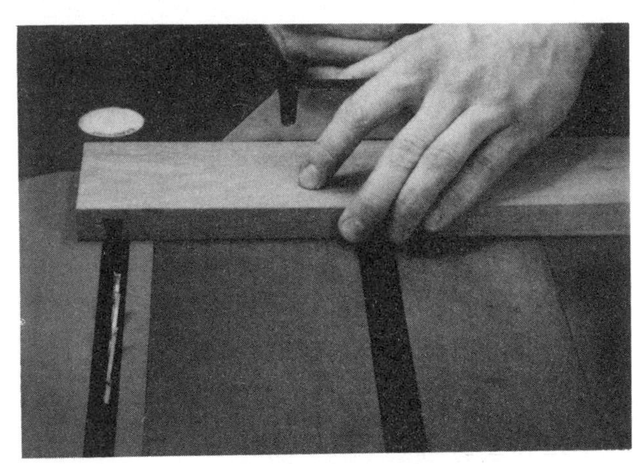

Illus. 6-275. The angled sides are being cut on the dovetail dado. The widest part of the dado should be ½ inch. The narrowest part should be ¼ inch. Overall dado depth is ½ inch.

6-274). The bottom of the dovetail dado should be ½ inch wide (Illus. 6-275).

Cut a kerf 1/16 inch deep on each face of the ½-inch-thick drawer side (Illus. 6-276). The distance from the fence to the far side of the blade should be ½ inch. Tilt the blade so that the sides of the dovetail can be cut.

Use a tenoning jig or straightedge to hold the pieces while the angular cuts are made on both faces (Illus. 6-277). Check the fit of the mating parts. They should slide together easily (Illus. 6-278).

The drawer back should be fitted to a dado. The drawer back will rest on the drawer bottom. It could not be installed if it were grooved.

Illus. 6-276. Both sides of the drawer fronts are kerfed. This kerf becomes the shoulder of the dovetail.

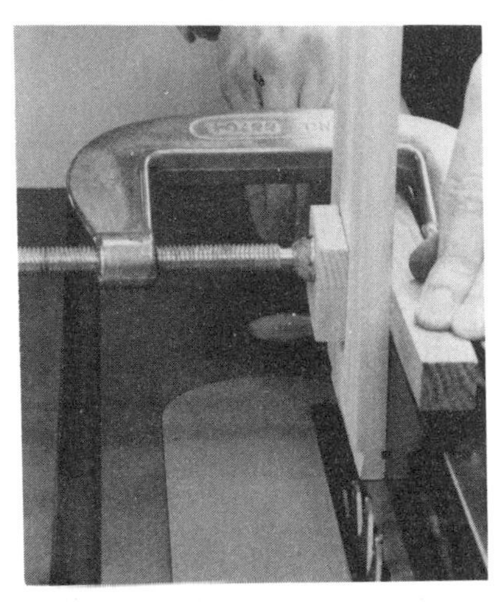

Illus. 6-277. A straightedge clamped to the work controls the cut. A tenoning jig could also be used to control the cut. Angular cuts are made on both sides.

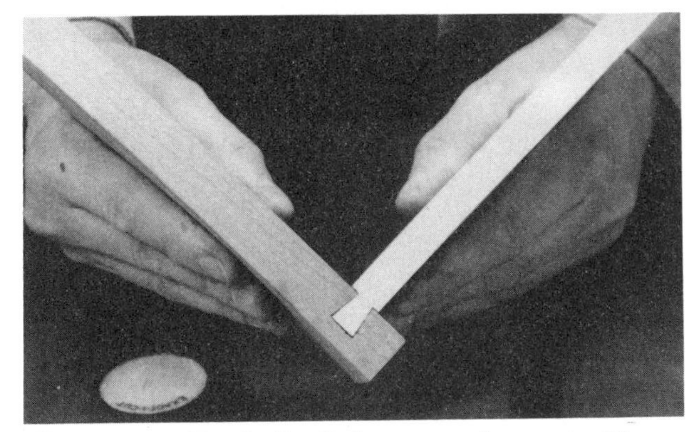

Illus. 6-278. Check the fit between the parts. The parts of the dovetail dado joint should slide together easily.

Part III:
Table Saw Guidelines

—7—
Useful Information about Table Saws

The more you use your table saw, the greater your desire becomes to do a better, safer, more accurate job. This chapter discusses topics that will help you improve the job you do.

General Maintenance of Your Table Saw

Maintenance of your table saw is important. A saw that is out of adjustment makes the job more difficult and usually yields poor results. The most common maintenance area on a table saw is the blade. Keep the blade sharp and free of pitch. Review Chapter 3 for blade-maintenance procedures.

Keep the table clean and protected. A light coat of paste wax reduces friction between the table and the work (Illus. 7-1). On cast-iron tables, the wax will also inhibit corrosion.

Illus. 7-1. Paste wax reduces friction on the table and inhibits corrosion.

Clean the table saw frequently. Keep chips and sawdust from accumulating under the motor and elevating and tilting mechanisms (Illus. 7-2). When sawdust gets packed around the motor or control mechanisms, problems can result. The motor can overheat or the chips and sawdust can become packed in the control mechanism. This will make it difficult to operate, and can cause the failure of gears or their teeth. Changing gears on a table saw is time-consuming and unnecessary. The parts are usually quite expensive. Often their cost equals the down payment on a new table saw.

Surface rust can be removed with steel wool or autobody rubbing compound. In most cases, rust is the result of humid air condensing on the cool metal parts. Putting a layer of clear plastic over the saw when it is not in use will reduce condensation on the cast iron. A layer of paste wax on the clear surface will reduce rusting too, but it will not eliminate it. If the saw is to be stored for any length of time, lightly oil any surface that may rust beforehand. The oil can be removed later with mineral spirits or other solvents. Oil is much easier to remove than rust.

When lubricating the control mechanisms, check them for sawdust accumulation. Use pitch remover and a wire brush to remove any accumulated sawdust.

A visual inspection of the saw during lubrication can identify potential problems. Look at the cord and electrical supply lines. Make sure they are not cut or frayed. Check the castings and stand for loose nuts and bolts. They increase saw noise and vibration, and can cause increased wear between two loose parts.

Illus. 7-2. Clean the motor housing and the control mechanisms frequently. Chips can become packed around the motor or control mechanisms and cause problems.

Surface rust can be removed from an iron table with auto rubbing compound and a wool bonnet (Illus. 7-3). Work slowly and carefully; use the rubbing compound liberally. After the table is clean, apply a coat of paste wax. If the saw is to be stored for any length of time, lightly oil any surface that may rust before storing the saw. The oil can be removed later with mineral spirits or other solvents. Oil is much easier to remove than rust.

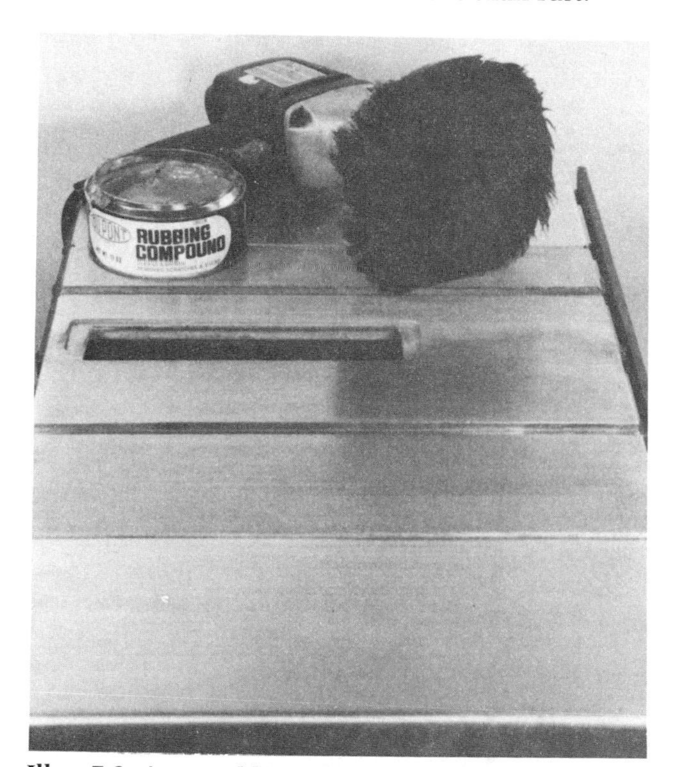

Illus. 7-3. Auto-rubbing compound and a wool bonnet can restore an oxidized table.

Table Saw Tune-Up

One of the worst situations in a workshop is a table saw that does not perform as expected. The quality of the cut or its accuracy are usually the problem. Many woodworkers try in vain to improve the cut by changing blades, adjusting angles, or realigning the saw. They fail because they do not do the procedure in an organized and efficient manner. The following discussion of table-saw tune-up is broken down into four steps: vibration, alignment, adjustment, and cleaning. The steps should be followed in this order; if you follow any other order, you may have to back up to previous steps. Review this entire section before you undertake the tune-up process. Remember to disconnect the saw from its power source before making any adjustments or beginning the tune-up.

Vibration Vibration is the first consideration in the tune-up of any table saw. All table-saw vibration ends up at the blade. This causes a poorer quality of cut. The saw may also start "walking" across the floor.

There are many reasons for vibration, but the first remedy attempted by most woodworkers is the addition of saw collars or a dampener. While both of these devices will reduce blade vibration, they do not eliminate saw vibration. Until saw vibration is reduced or eliminated, the quality of the cut will still be less than perfect. Saw collars and dampeners are discussed in Chapter 2.

The blade should be checked first. If the blade is

poorly manufactured or if the arbor hole is too large for the arbor, the blade will vibrate. Try replacing the blade first. Blades with a rigid plate are much less likely to vibrate. Some inexpensive blades have a plate with run-out. You can check for these problems in a couple of ways (Illus. 7-4–7-6). Experiment with your blades to see if this is the problem.

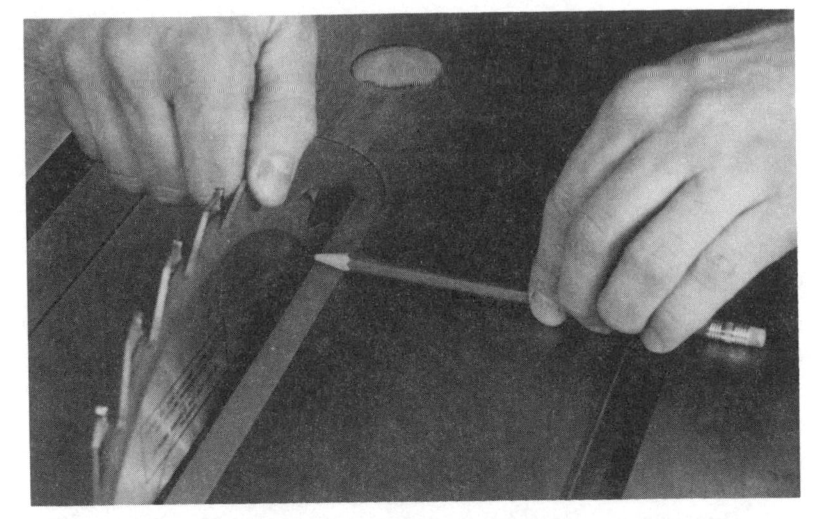

Illus. 7-4. A pencil can be used to check for a warped blade. Rotate the blade slowly. Make sure the power is disconnected.

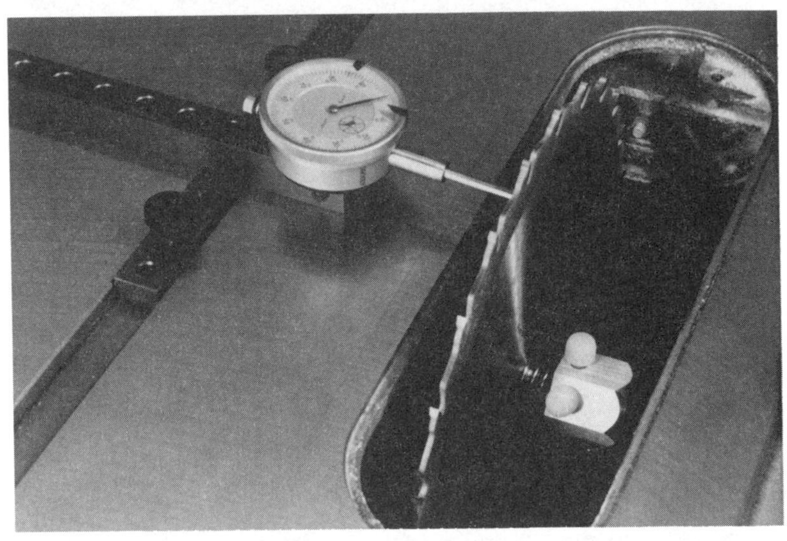

Illus. 7-5. Spring-loaded fasteners hold the blade to the arbor. You can turn either the arbor or the blade. This will help you isolate the cause of the run-out.

Illus. 7-6. The pencil lines represent a starting point. Turn the arbor one revolution and record the run-out. Then turn the blade on the arbor and record the turn-out. Some blades have considerable run-out in their bodies. They will produce poor cuts.

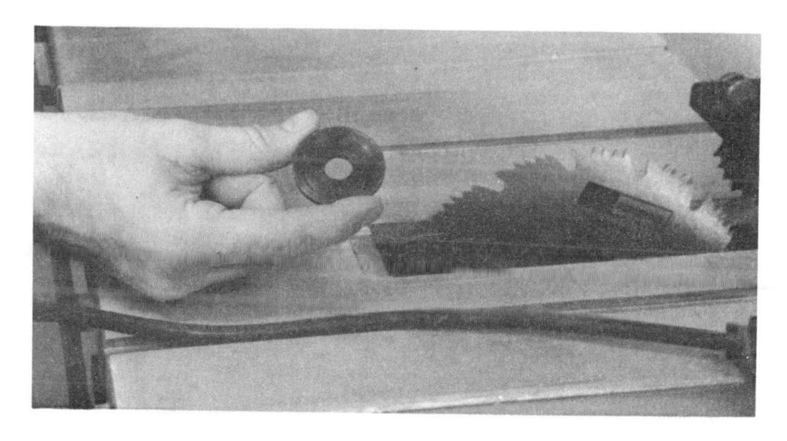

Illus. 7-7. When you are replacing the blade, make sure the teeth are pointing in the right direction. Inspect the arbor washers (and blade collars, if used) for pitch or wood chips. They can cause the blade to wobble instead of running true.

While you are changing blades, check the arbor washer for any irregularities (Illus. 7-7). It is possible that the arbor washer has been dropped on the floor, causing a "bump" or "blister" of steel along the edge of the washer. When this arbor washer is clamped against the blade, it contracts the blade at only two points. This can make the saw blade act like a wobble dado.

If you notice any irregularities along the edge of the arbor washer, you should remove them. Use a flat sharpening or honing stone to clean up the bearing surface. Work the washer back and forth on the sharpening stone until it appears smooth and shiny.

Illus. 7-8. Align the pulleys to the belt so there is a straight line between them. Any misalignment will contribute to vibration problems.

Another vibration problem can rest with the drive belt and pulleys. In some cases, just changing the belt can help decrease vibration. Many inexpensive belts have a joint in them that causes a bumping. This generates vibration and is sometimes referred to as "belt slap." Belt slap can also occur when the pulleys are misaligned. The belt is actually trying to climb off the pulley. This, too, causes vibration. Aligning the pulleys can also reduce vibration (Illus. 7-8).

Check the pulleys as you align them. If the pulleys are made from die-cast metal, it is possible that the drive pulley has an opening larger than the shaft on the motor. This is usually caused when the pulley loosens slightly and begins to wear. The opening in the drive pulley enlarges, and the pulley wobbles on the shaft, causing vibration.

It is good practice to replate the die-cast pulleys with steel pulleys (Illus. 7-9). Steel pulleys resist wear much better. Steel pulleys have been machined around the shaft opening, so the sheave on the pulley is concentric with the drive shaft. This will also reduce vibration.

When you replace the pulleys, make sure they are aligned. A straightedge can be used to check alignment. Installing a good drive belt is very important in reducing vibration. Belts sold for automobiles do not have the appropriate V shape for electric motor pulleys. Make sure the belt is correct for the pulleys. Pulleys and belts can usually be purchased in electric motor shops or from woodworking suppliers. Woven belts are also substituted by some table-saw operators. These belts have less

Illus. 7-9. The machined steel pulley on the left will turn truer than the die-cast pulley on the right. Die-cast pulleys are subject to wear and wobble. The truer the pulley, the less vibration you can expect.

"slap" and transmit less vibration. Woven belts are an aftermarket product sold by woodworking suppliers.

Now is the time to level the table saw. It is not absolutely necessary to "split the bubble" in the level, but it is important that the saw is bearing uniformly on all four legs or all the way around the base. Adjust the legs to bear uniformly on the floor, if possible. If not, use veneers or shim singles to spread the saw's weight uniformly (Illus. 7-10). A saw that rocks is sure to cause vibration.

A rocking saw is most common in the two-car garage. Many woodworkers back their cars out of the garage, and drag the saw out into the middle of the floor. Their anxiety to cut boards is greater than their urge to level the saw, so the saw rocks and causes vibration. It is important to level the saw when it is moved into position.

Illus. 7-10. Shim the low leg on the table saw to prevent rocking. Any rocking of the saw ends up as a vibration at the blade.

After all possible causes of vibration have been eliminated, it is time to consider a pair of saw collars or a dampener. Both are very effective in reducing run-out and vibration. While they are effective on all blades, they improve the running qualities of inexpensive blades in a more obvious manner. Higher-quality blades have a harder plate and are less likely to vibrate.

Some considerations when using collars or dampeners include guard alignment, throat-plate opening, and lifting. The use of collars causes the blade to move over approximately ⅛ inch on the arbor. This means that the blade is no longer aligned with the guard or centered in the throat-plate opening. This will require realignment of the splitter. While most throat-plate openings are large enough to accommodate this shift in position, they may not accommodate the blade when it is tilted for a bevel or miter cut. The teeth may scrape on the sides of the throat plate. Always turn the blade over by hand with the power to the saw disconnected. If the blade contacts the throat plate, enlarge the opening with a file.

A dampener goes on only one side of the blade. If it is put on the side closest to the arbor, no alignment problem will result, because the blade does not change position.

There is one hazard when using a dampener or a pair of collars: If you raise the saw blade while it is under power, the collars or dampeners could contact the underside of the throat plate and lift it off the table. Do not take chances when using a collar or dampener (Illus. 7-11).

Finally, if after exhausting all of the techniques listed above you still experience vibrations, the problem may be worn bearings or lateral move-

Illus. 7-11. The blade is close to the edge of the throat-plate opening. This could be a problem when the blade is tilted. Always check for contact between the blade and throat plate before restoring power to the saw.

ment in the arbor. These conditions are not common, but they may exist on an older saw.

You may be able to feel side-to-side or vertical arbor movement when you grasp the arbor and try to move it by hand. It may only be visible with a dial indicator. A precision measuring device can detect even a slight amount of run-out or side-to-side movement (Illus. 7-12).

Illus. 7-12. To check for movement or run-out with a dial indicator, place it on or against the arbor.

Correcting run-out or side-to-side movement may mean you have to replace the bearings. Consult the owner's manual or the manufacturer if these adjustments are necessary.

Alignment Once you have eliminated all vibration, it is time to turn your attention to alignment. Alignment problems show up in a manner of ways. The following conditions suggest an alignment problem between the blade and the miter slots:

1. During a crosscut in a wide piece of stock, the work tends to move toward or away from the blade. The work slides along the head of the miter gauge.
2. During a rip cut, the blade throws sawdust back toward the operator.
3. When you are crosscutting very high grade veneer plywood, the cut begins very well, but, when the entire blade is in the work, the veneer tends to lift off the face of the plywood adjacent to the teeth on the out-feed side of the blade.

If you have experienced any of these conditions, the cause may not have been obvious, but it is almost always a problem between the blade and the miter slot. This condition is commonly known as "heel." The blade is not parallel to the miter slot, which means that the front teeth of the blade do not follow the back teeth. The back teeth cut a second time, which causes chips to be thrown toward the operator in example 2 and the veneer lifting in example 3. The problem in the first example is caused by the nonparallel condition of the blade. The board creeps to the right when the back teeth are misaligned to the right of the front teeth.

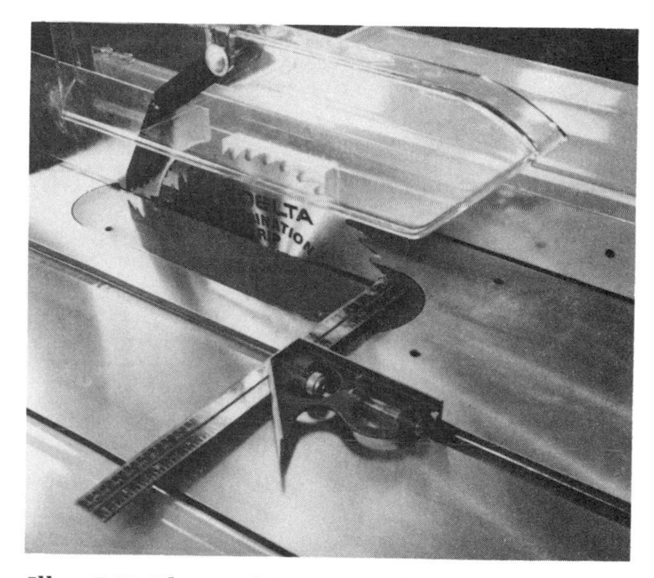

Illus. 7-13. The combination square is being used to check for alignment. The head touches the miter slot, and the blade touches the tip of the tooth pointing toward it. Lock the combination square at this setting.

To determine if there is a heel condition, first disconnect the power to the saw and raise the blade to full height. You can prove heel exists using a combination square or other measuring device. Choose a tooth close to the table, mark it with a pencil, and measure the distance from that tooth to the miter slot.

Next, hook the head of the combination square over the miter slot and extend the blade until it touches that tooth. Record the dimension or lock the setting (Illus. 7-13). Rotate the blade to the other end of the table and measure from the same miter slot to the tooth (Illus. 7-14). If the measurements are different, then you have a heel condition. There are other measuring techniques for heel conditions (Illus. 7-15—7-24).

Illus. 7-14. Roll the blade to the back of the table and check the dimension using the same tooth. If the dimension is the same, the saw is in alignment.

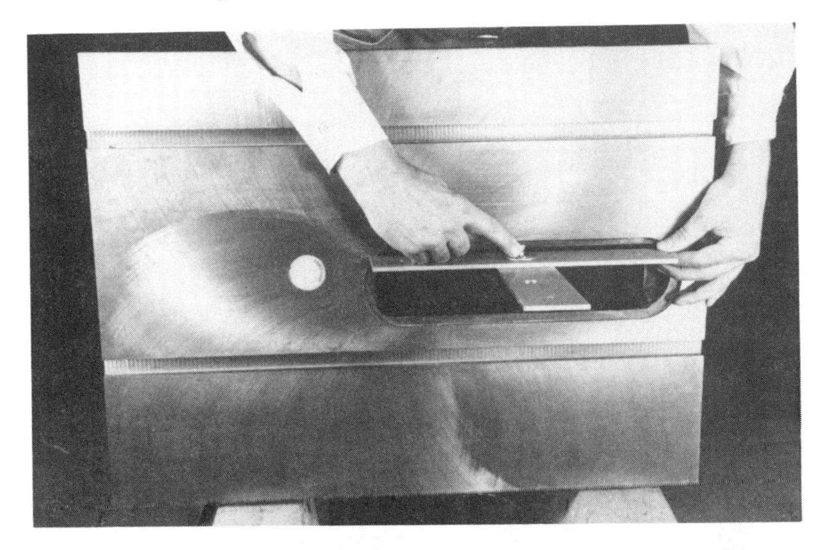

Illus. 7-15. This metal device attaches to the arbor. A second bar is attached, and alignment can be checked. These pieces are very true, so the measurements will be accurate.

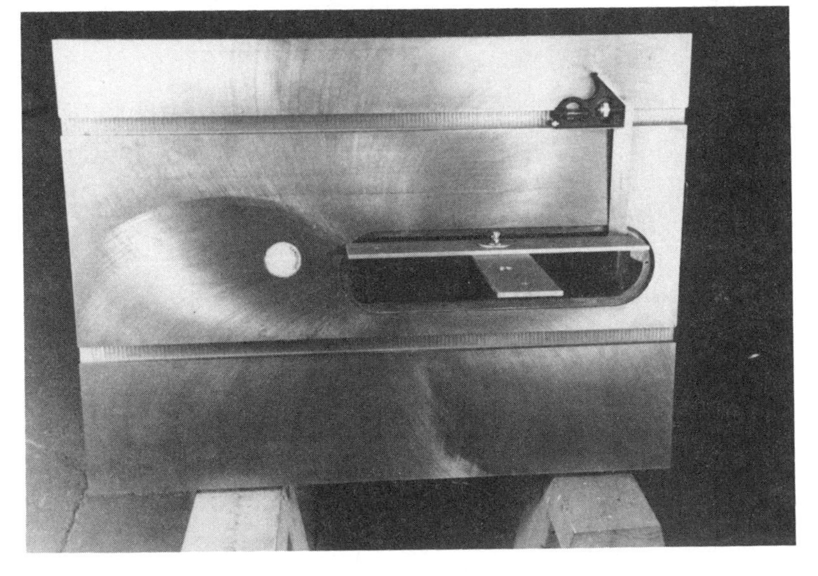

Illus. 7-16. A combination square is used here to check the dimension.

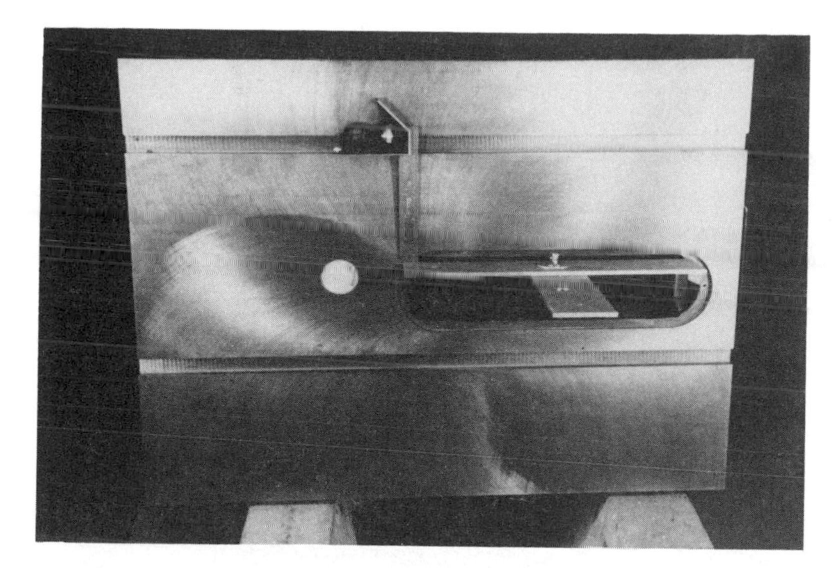

Illus. 7-17. Check the dimension at the other end of the bar. If the dimension is different, the trunion must be realigned.

Illus. 7-18. A long, true straightedge butted against the plate of the blade reveals the error.

Illus. 7-19. Use a combination square to check the dimension at one end of the table.

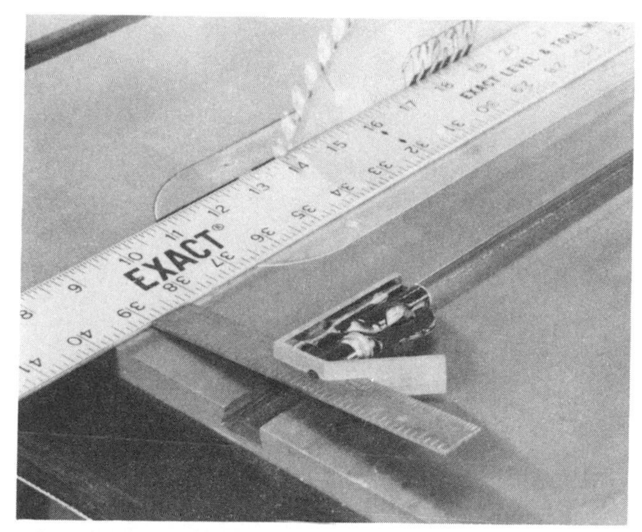

Illus. 7-20. Check this dimension at the other end of the table. By increasing the distance, you can measure a smaller error.

Illus. 7-21. A vernier can be used in place of a combination square for an exact measurement.

Illus. 7-22. Use the same tooth on the blade. This will give an exact measurement.

Illus. 7-23. The dial indicator is attached to a bar which travels in the miter slot. The indicator measurement is within .002 inch of the zero mark.

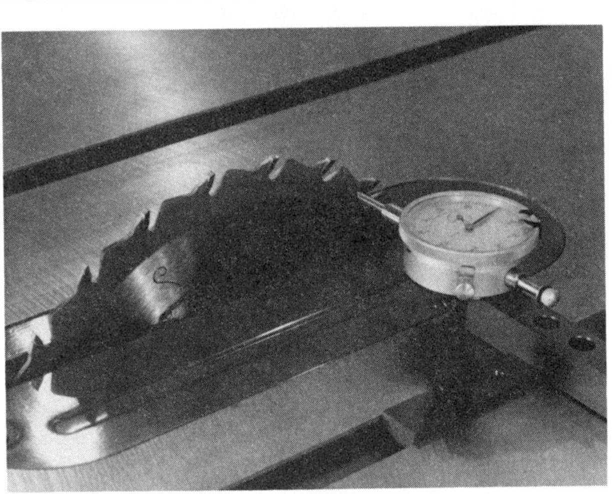

Illus. 7-24. When the dial indicator's position is changed, the measurement is zero, a .002 inch change. This alignment should produce very good results.

Many people want to know how much tolerance there can be between the two dimensions before heel becomes visible or impairs cutting. The answer is that this tolerance varies, but the blade should be realigned if it is over .015 inch or if it is causing problems.

In some cases, heel will not be obvious with an inexpensive blade, but when a quality blade is mounted, heel is apparent. The rigid plate of a quality blade will not deflect very much. This means that it will not bend to follow the stresses of the heel condition. Inexpensive blades have softer plates that will deflect easier and not show the heel condition.

The type of saw you own will determine how to eliminate heel. The cabinet saw is easiest to align, so let's begin there. The table is bolted to the metal cabinet after all the other parts are assembled. Four bolts hold the cabinet to the top. Once those four bolts are loosened, the top can be turned into perfect alignment. Check the alignment as you tighten the bolts. The act of tightening them could cause the table to creep out of alignment. Once the bolts are tightened, the saw is ready for the second stage of alignment.

When a cabinet saw goes out of alignment, it is usually caused by saw movement. Someone has moved the table saw using the fence rails as handles. This force is capable of twisting the tabletop on the cabinet. While cabinet saws are usually the easiest to align, those with long side tables or rear tables attached are more difficult to align because the hardware supporting the side or the rear table may be tied into the cast-iron table on the table saw (Illus. 7-25). This makes it more difficult to turn the table. To adjust the saw in this instance, some or all of the mounting hardware must be loosened.

To align contractor saws, loosen the bolts which secure the trunion to the underside of the table. The trunion is then turned into position. For best results, the bolts should only be loosened slightly (Illus. 7-26 and 7-27). The mechanism can then be tapped into position with a rubber mallet or a block of wood driven by a hammer.

Check the alignment frequently as you move the trunion. As you tighten the trunion, there will be some chance of creeping. Work slowly, to ensure accuracy. There have been contractor saws which were made to very poor specifications. It may not be possible to turn the trunion into alignment because there is not enough tolerance in the mounting holes. When this problem occurs, the mounting holes can be enlarged using a rattail file. This will allow the trunion to be turned correctly. It should be noted that the process of enlarging the holes is difficult and time-consuming. You will quickly realize why you "saved" money on the saw you bought.

The fasteners used to hold contractor trunions in place may not be hard enough to hold the setting. Replace the bolts with grade-five machinists' bolts. This will ensure that once adjusted, the contractor saw will stay adjusted. This also applies to the washers and lock washers (if any) used to hold the setting.

Benchtop saws can be aligned in the same way,

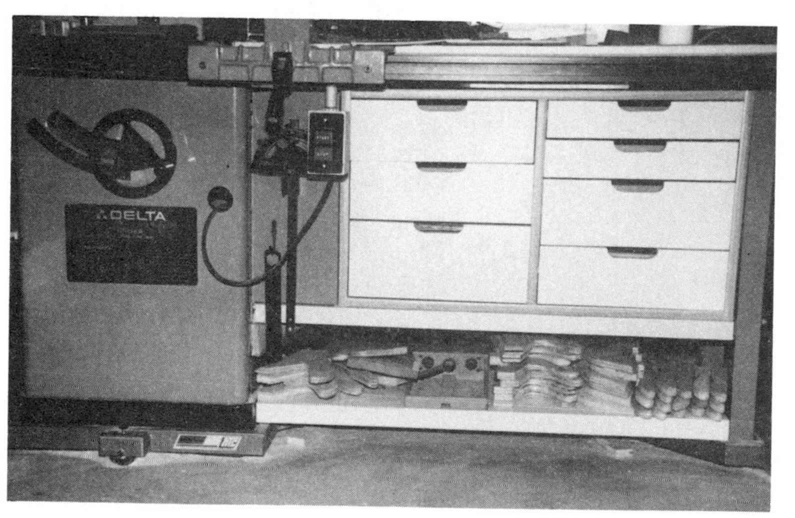

Illus. 7-25. Because of the built-ins, realignment of the table will be more difficult. Make sure your saw is aligned perfectly before adding built-ins.

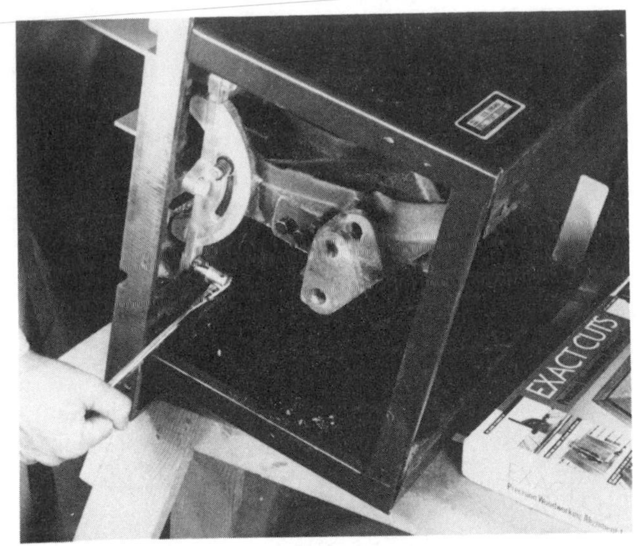

Illus. 7-26. A contractor saw has the trunion attached to the underside of the table. This saw has been stripped down to make it easier to align.

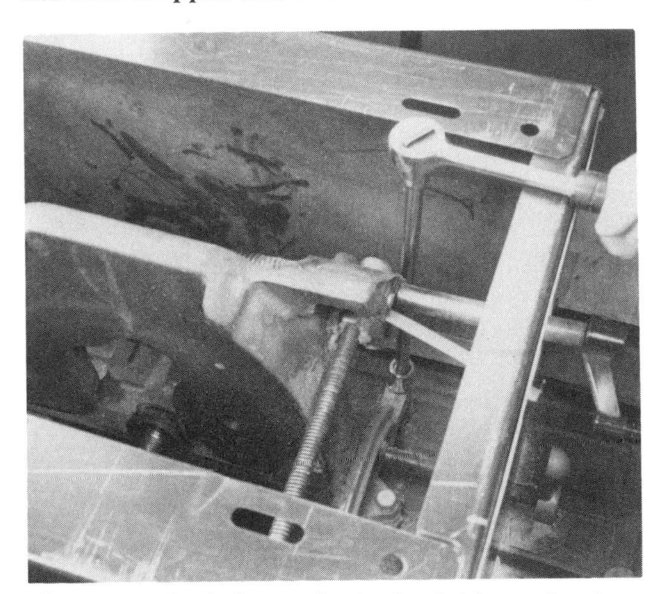

Illus. 7-27. The bolts on the in-feed side are harder to reach. A socket wrench with an appropriate extension makes them easier to tighten and loosen.

but some will have adjusting screws on the tables. The bench saws which have screws on their tables are easier to adjust because the saw does not have to be inverted to be adjusted. The screws are loosened, and the alignment is adjusted by tightening or loosening the screws.

Most benchtop saws have a light-duty trunion, which means that the saw may not hold alignment as well. Check the benchtop saw periodically to make sure it stays in alignment. Most woodworkers use benchtop saws for their portability. The constant movement of the benchtop saw can cause it to become misaligned.

Step two in aligning a table saw is fence alignment. It is step two because the fence could be aligned parallel to a misaligned blade and rip cuts could still be made accurately. By ensuring that the blade is aligned correctly first, the fence will be set one time, not two times.

When a fence is misaligned, the board may pinch and burn or there may be no obvious sign of misalignment. When the out-feed end of the fence is closer to the blade, the board will bind and pinch, possibly causing a kickback.

When the out-feed end of the fence is farther away from the blade, it may be more difficult to hold the stock against the fence. It is also possible that wood chips will be thrown back toward you when you are ripping with the fence misaligned this way.

Most standard fences can be aligned easily. There are one or two bolts on top of the fence (Illus. 7-28). When they are loosened, the fence can be moved into alignment. Begin by moving the fence over to the right miter slot. Check its alignment

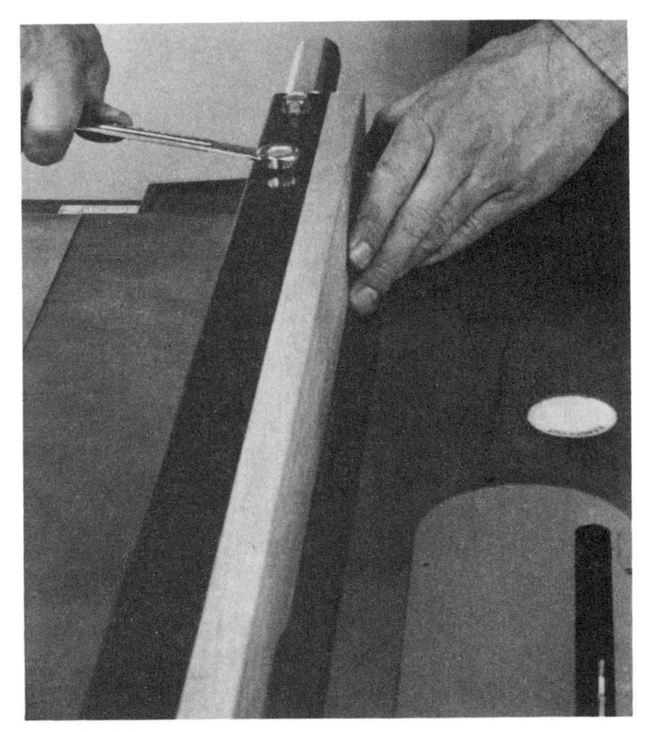

Illus. 7-28. The fence is adjusted parallel to the miter slot. The bolts on the fence lock it to the desired setting.

with the miter slot while it is locked in place. Some woodworkers prefer the precision of a measuring instrument to check alignment (Illus. 7-29–7-32). These approaches work equally well. If the fence is not in perfect alignment, it must be adjusted.

Loosen the clamping mechanism that clamps the out-feed end of the fence to the fence rail. There may be a threaded device on the end of the fence that must be loosened. When you use the Jet Lock fence on Delta saws, push the lock knob as far

Illus. 7-29. A vernier can be used on the in-feed end of the fence to check alignment.

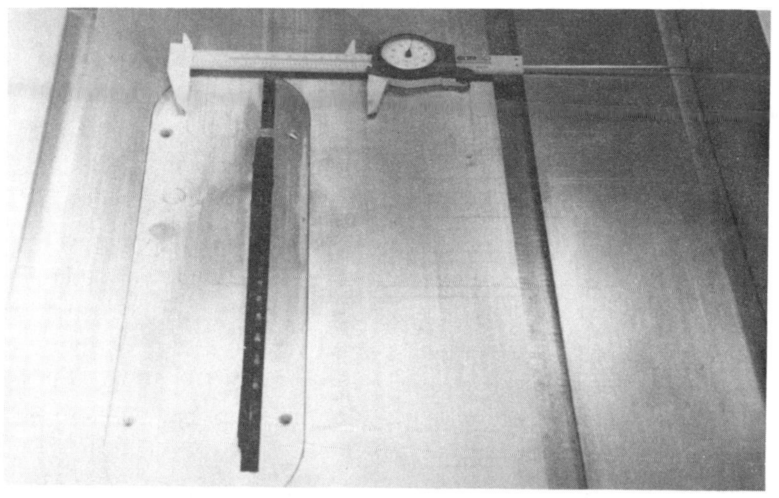

Illus. 7-30. The measurement at the out-feed end must be identical if the fence is in correct alignment.

Illus. 7-31. This dial indicator is very sensitive. It can check the entire face of the fence for absolute alignment.

Illus. 7-32. A comparison of the measurements along the fence reveals that the fence deviates from a straight line by within only .002 inch over its 24-inch length. This is an acceptable tolerance.

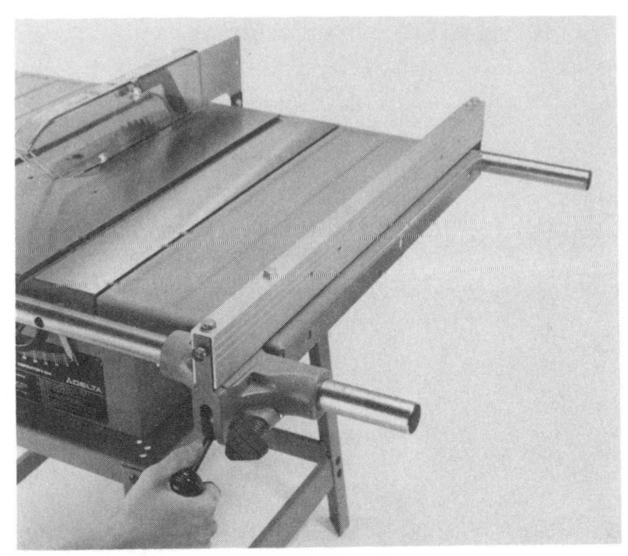

Illus. 7-33. When adjusting this type of fence, you must align its in-feed end and lock it before locking the out-feed end. (Photo courtesy of Delta International Machinery Corporation.)

down as possible and clamp the out-feed end. This adjusts the fence properly.

Check the Jet Lock fence (or similar adjusting mechanism) at the out-feed end after pushing the lock knob all the way down. Move it from side to side to see if it is clamped securely. Then tighten the threaded screw or knob above the clamp knob until the out-feed end is clamped in position.

Once the out-feed end is clamped, lift the clamp knob until the out-feed end is loose. All other fences should only be clamped on the in-feed end. Move the fence until it is parallel to the miter slot, and lock it into position. Watch the fence as you tighten the bolts. Test the setting at the other miter slot and then again at the fence's original position.

It is important that the fence be aligned and locked at the in-feed end before it is locked at the out-feed end. If the out-feed end locks first, the fence cannot be aligned (Illus. 7-33).

Many of the new fences have provisions for adjustment in the carriage that rides in the in-feed fence rail. By turning these adjustments in or out, fence alignment can be completely parallel to the miter slot.

Some woodworkers like to adjust the out-feed end of the fence so that it is 1/64 inch farther from the miter slot than the in-feed end of the fence. This adjustment would be on the right side of the blade. The rationale is that there will be no chance of friction or heat buildup as stock is ripped. It also compensates for stresses in the board which might cause it to bind on the fence during the ripping operation.

There is some merit to this adjustment, but if the fence is ever moved to the left side of the blade, then it is misaligned and the board will bind and pinch. There is sure to be some burning or kickback. If you adjust the fence with some additional clearance on the out-feed side, do not move the fence to the opposite side of the blade without readjustment.

Another way of compensating for stresses in the wood is to attach a wooden auxiliary fence to the metal fence. This wooden fence should stop at the centerline of the blade. This allows the stock to be controlled until the cut is complete. If stresses build up, there is 1½ inches of compensation. This approach is best when you are cutting green lumber or stock predisposed to stresses.

One final check of the fence is to determine that the face of the fence is perpendicular to the table. In most cases, a slight angle between the table and fence will be of no consequence, but if you plan to use an auxiliary fence for cutting raised panels or tenons, the error will be tranferred to the workpiece (Illus. 7-34). It may be necessary to shim the auxiliary fence to obtain a right angle between the fence and table.

The final part of the table saw you check for

Illus. 7-34. Check the face of the fence to make sure it is perpendicular to the table. If it is not, you can adjust the fence rails or put a wooden face on the fence and shim it in place.

alignment is the splitter. Some splitters work independently (Illus. 7-35–7-38), while others support the guard (Illus. 7-39). The splitter is anchored on one or two positions on the saw. The purpose of the splitter is to keep the saw kerf open. It is most important during ripping because that is when stresses in the wood are most likely to build up. When the splitter is misaligned, the saw blade binds in the kerf. This causes burning and possibly a kickback.

In most cases, the antikickback pawls are mounted to the splitter. They are used to reduce the chance of kickback. The pawls ride on top of the work while it is being cut. If the board begins to kick back, gravity or spring tension pushes the pawls into the wood. The sharp edges on the pawls dig into the wood and stop the kickback. This presupposes that the pawls are sharp. As wood travels under pawls, it can cause the pawls to become dull.

Check the pawls. If they are dull, sharpen them with a file. A thin block of wood can be clamped between the pawls to hold them in place while they are sharpened. It is a good practice to check them periodically to make sure they are sharp.

To align the splitter, raise the blade to full height. Place a framing square against the plate of the blade. Make sure the square is not touching any teeth. The blade of the square should extend toward

Illus. 7-35. This splitter mounts behind the blade and beneath the table. Alignment adjustments are made at the mounting plate.

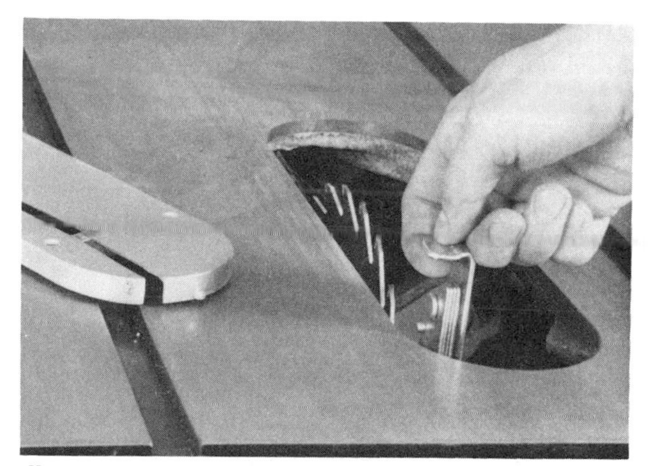

Illus. 7-36. This pop-up splitter also mounts beneath the table. It is lifted into position for use.

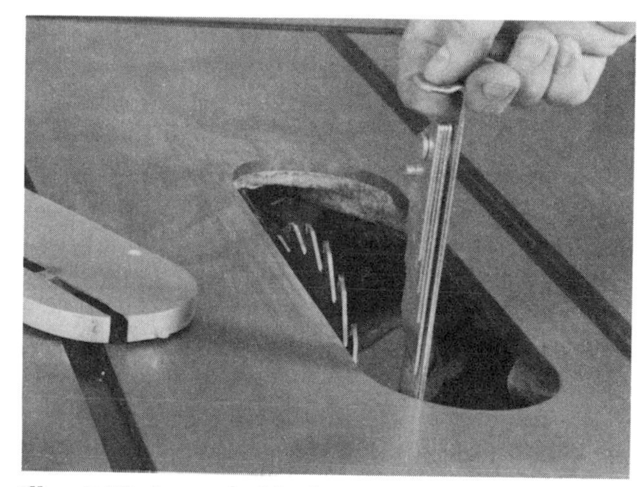

Illus. 7-37. A stop holds the splitter in position. A slot in the throat plate has been cut for the splitter. A mounting plate has provisions for adjustment.

Illus. 7-38. This splitter is used in conjunction with the Uniguard. It keeps the saw kerf from binding on the saw blade. (Photo courtesy of Delta International Machinery Corporation.)

Illus. 7-39. This is a splitter-mounted guard. The guard and anti-kickback pawls are supported by the splitter. (Photo courtesy of Skil Power Tools.)

the splitter. Check the position of the splitter relative to the blade (Illus. 7-40 and 7-41). It should not touch the framing square. Make the same test cut from the opposite side of the blade. The splitter should not touch the blade on the opposite side either.

The splitter is actually thinner than the typical ⅛-inch saw kerf, so it is possible to align the splitter with little difficulty. Independent splitters are aligned by moving the assembly where it mounts to the trunion. Access to the mounting bolt is beneath the throat plate. Double-check the alignment as you tighten the fasteners.

On most contractor saws, splitters have two connection points. One is behind the blade on the trunion. It is adjusted in the same way as the independent splitter. The out-feed end of the guard is mounted to a plate or rod (Illus. 7-42). If it is mounted to a plate, the screws attaching the splitter to the plate can be loosened to adjust the splitter. If it is attached to a rod, the bolts in the splitter bracket are loosened and the rod is turned until the splitter is aligned. The rod is mounted eccentrically from its threaded end. As the rod is turned, it moves the splitter. Secure the rod and the mounting bolts when the alignment is complete.

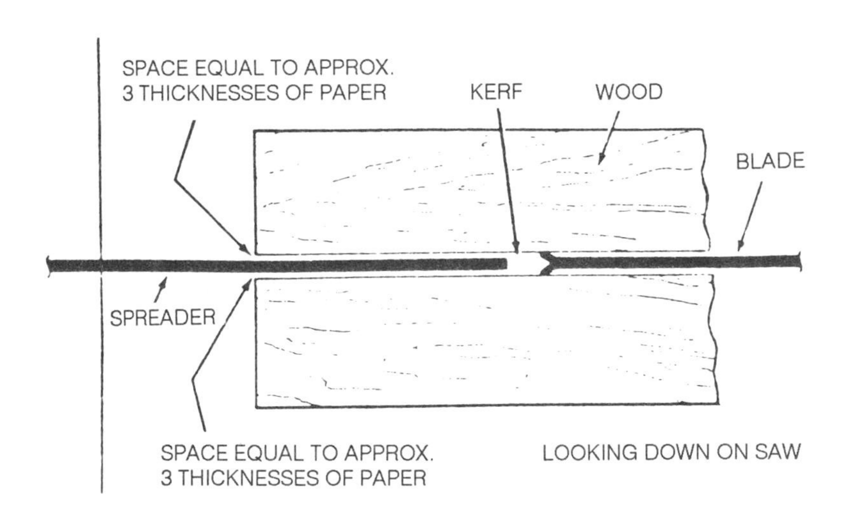

Illus. 7-40. The splitter, or spreader, keeps the kerf open while the cut is made. This reduces the strain on the blade. (Drawing courtesy of Sears Craftsman.)

Illus. 7-41. Make sure the splitter is aligned with the blade. If it is not, it may push the work away from a straight line. It could also cause blade binding. (Drawing courtesy of Sears Craftsman.)

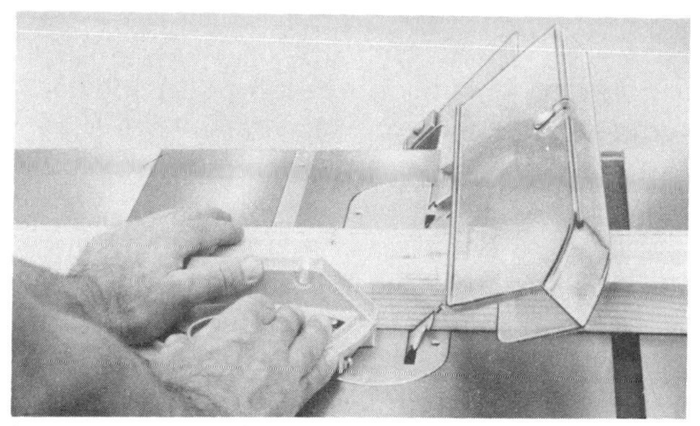

Illus. 7-42. The contractor's table saw usually has a splitter which is mounted in two places. This provides increased contact with the stock, but requires more careful alignment. (Photo courtesy of Delta International Machinery Corporation.)

Illus. 7-43. A high or low throat plate can sometimes affect accuracy. Check it to be sure it is even with the table.

Adjustment Adjustments make the table saw run smoother, but do not impact on actual alignment. The miter gauge, throat plate, and the legs of a table saw are adjusted. The miter gauge is the first concern. If you have realigned a cabinet saw, the miter gauge's 90-degree setting is no longer correct. Readjust the miter gauge by loosening the threaded rod(s) which bear against the stop. Use a square to adjust the single rod between the blade and the head of the miter gauge. Lock the 90-degree setting and adjust the threaded rod(s) to the stop. Repair the process for the 45-degree stops using any measuring device which has an accurate 45-degree angle.

On many table saws, there is slop or movement between the blade of the miter gauge and the miter slot. Some woodworkers want a tighter fit, to control the accuracy of the cut. You can tighten the fit between the tongue of the miter gauge and the slot using common metalworking tools.

Place the tongue of the miter gauge on a scrap of 2 × 4 with an edge up. Position a prick punch on the edge of the tongue near the front and strike it with a ball-peen hammer. Be sure to wear protective glasses. Repeat the process at the back of the tongue and test the fit. If the fit is still too loose, make the "bumps" larger by striking them a second time. If the fit is too tight, you can use a mill file to reduce the height of the "bumps."

Check the face of the miter-gauge head to see if it is flat and square to the table. Use a straightedge to see if the face is flat, and a try square to see if the face is perpendicular to the table. If there is a problem with the face of the miter gauge, a wooden auxiliary face can be attached to the miter gauge.

Shims can be used to square and true up the auxiliary face. Use a true piece of hardwood for the auxiliary fence. It can extend beyond the blade if desired. As it is cut, it will become a backing board. This will reduce tear-out in the cut and sweep the cut-off past the blade.

The throat plate must also be adjusted. Its top surface should be even with the top of the table saw (Illus. 7-43 and 7-44). If it is too high, it will obstruct the work or force the work off its intended path. If it is too low, it will allow the workpiece to vibrate during the cut. Vibration will decrease the quality of the cut significantly.

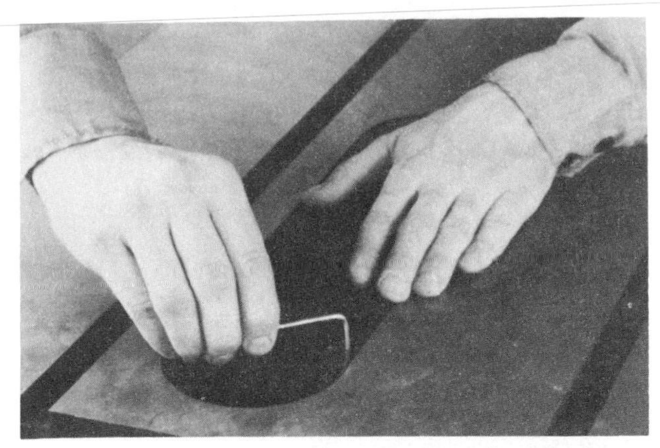

Illus. 7-44. The splitter must be aligned with the blade at full height for best results. Any twist in the splitter could cause binding.

Most throat plates have setscrews which allow them to be adjusted even with the tabletop. Work slowly, until all four screws are supporting the throat plate in position without rocking it.

If there are no adjusting screws, the throat plate can be raised by putting masking tape on the underside of it. If it is too high, it may be possible to file some material off the bottom. Since there are so many types of throat plates, each situation will require a different solution, but stock removal is usually the answer. In some cases, the throat plate may be twisted. It is possible to straighten the throat plate by clamping one end in a vise. A parallel clamp is attached to the other end. By twisting the parallel clamp, you can bring the throat plate into a true plane.

If your saw has extension wings, be sure to check their alignment with the saw table. If the wings are too high or too low, they will affect accuracy or encourage vibration. Bolts secure the extension; loosen them to make adjustments. A C-clamp can be used to hold the extension wing and table in alignment while you are tightening the bolts.

Adjusting the legs or base of the table saw is also important to saw operation. If the saw rocks, it can cause vibration. Make sure the entire cabinet base is in contact with the floor. Use shims or wedges to improve contact between the saw and the floor. Use a level to help determine where shims need to be added.

The level can be used to help adjust contractor saw legs. Loosen the nuts that allow the rubber feet to be raised and lowered. Make the needed adjustments, so that all four legs support the saw. Tighten the nuts at the desired setting.

As long as the saw is not moved, the feet will hold the saw in place and reduce saw vibration. Noise levels may go down as vibration is eliminated.

Cleaning To operate smoothly, the table saw must be clean inside and out. Remove any accumulation of sawdust from the elevating and tilting mechanisms (Illus. 7-45). Use a stiff wire or bristle brush. An old paintbrush works well. Cut the bristle length in half and brush the gears and threaded rods. Lubricate them with a non-petroleum product such as paste wax. Petroleum-based products such as motor oil attract dust. As the dust builds up on the gears, it is possible to break teeth off the mechanisms.

On inexpensive saws, the motor will have ventilation holes to allow it to cool off. These are found on contractor and benchtop saws. Keep the holes free of sawdust. Sweep or blow them clear. A sawdust buildup could restrict cooling. Avoid heat buildup by avoiding sawdust buildup.

Cabinet saws have the motor in the cabinet. These motors are totally enclosed and fan-cooled (TEFC), so they do not need cleaning. Dust is sealed

Illus. 7-45. A paintbrush with the bristles cut short works well for cleaning the elevating and tilting mechanisms on a table saw.

out, but the cabinet should not be allowed to fill with sawdust. Check it periodically.

The tabletop should also be kept clean. Rust or oxidation can build up on the surface. This can discolor the workpiece and make it more difficult to feed it across the table. The best products to clean the table with are Scotch Brite pad and autobody rubbing compound. The Scotch Brite pads will remove rust rings and most oxidation. After this treatment, the autobody rubbing compound can be used to polish the metal surface. You can use a wool bonnet on a buffer to rub the compound into the surface (Illus. 7-46). It can also be done by hand.

Illus. 7-46. Autobody rubbing compound works well for cleaning cast-iron machined surfaces. This can be done by power or by hand.

Remove the throat plate for the polishing operation. Make sure you protect the elevating mechanism with newspaper or paper towels. After polishing, clean the surface with mineral spirits (Illus. 7-47). You may have to wipe the surface two or three times to remove all the residue. Wipe the table dry and wax its surface with furniture paste wax or a machined surface treatment (Illus. 7-48 and 7-49).

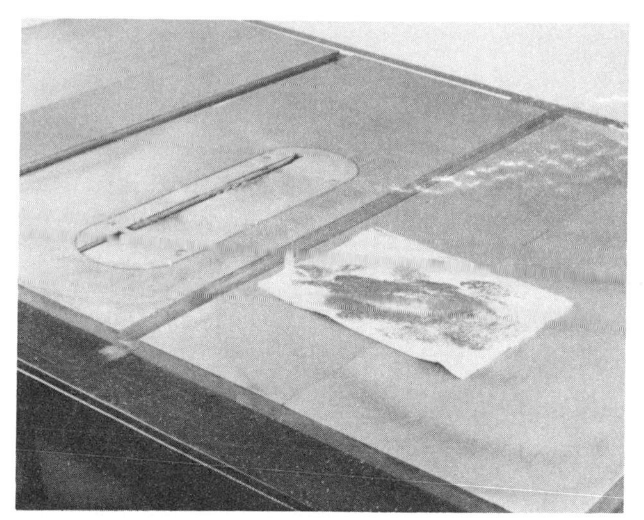

Illus. 7-47. Use mineral spirits and a soft cloth to clean the table after using the rubbing compound.

Illus. 7-48 and 7-49. Paste wax can be used to protect and lubricate the table after it is cleaned.

Illus. 7-49.

Layout Techniques at the Saw

Many errors in measurement are caused by an incorrect layout or setup at the saw. For example, when a rabbet is cut, the fence is set to the thickness of the piece that fits in the rabbet. First, the thickness of the piece is measured, and then the fence is set to this measurement. A ruler is used twice. This means that there are two opportunities to make a measurement error.

A better approach would be to set the fence using a piece of stock (Illus. 7-50). The stock thickness is placed over the blade and against the fence. The fence can be moved into exact position without the use of a ruler. Two chances for making an error have been eliminated.

Cutting lap joints or other joints where the blade must be cut to the center of the piece provides several chances for measurement error. Use two scraps of the correct thickness to set the blade height. No measurement is needed.

Illus. 7-50. Using a piece of stock to set the fence ensures an accurate setting.

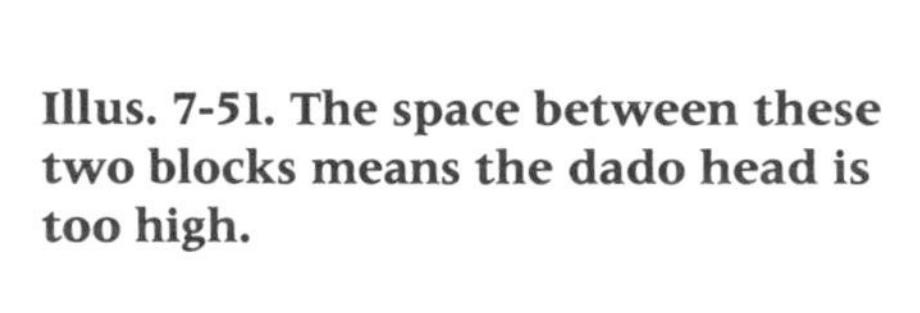

Illus. 7-51. The space between these two blocks means the dado head is too high.

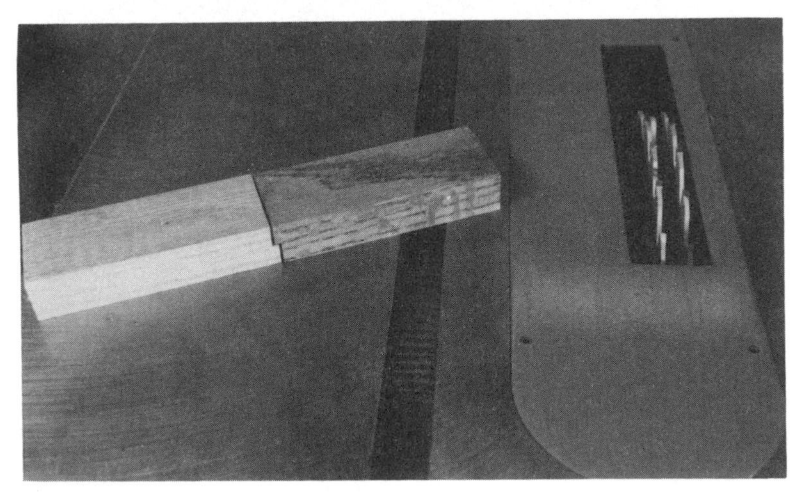

Illus. 7-52. The interference between these two blocks means the dado head is too low.

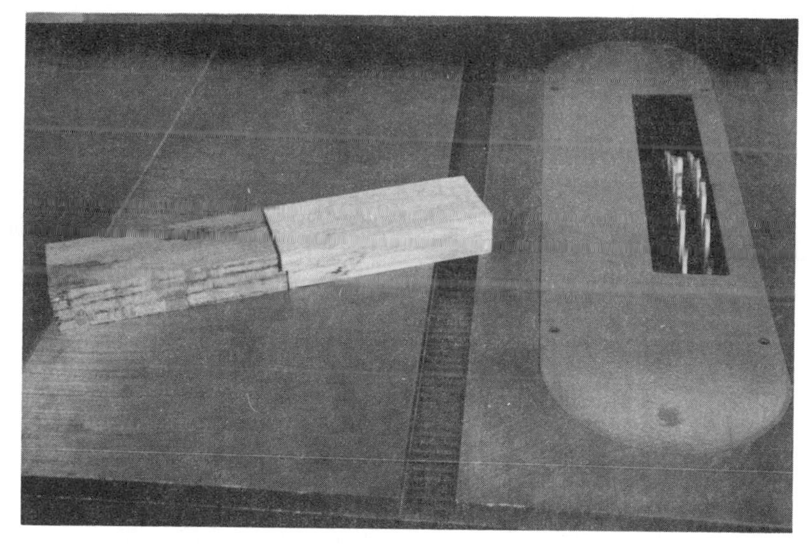

Illus. 7-53. The blocks fit together correctly. The dado head is set correctly.

Set the blade slightly below the center of the pieces and make a cut on the end of both pieces. Flip one piece over and push the cut ends together. The interference between the two ends is exactly twice the distance that the blade must be elevated.

Raise the blade slightly and check the pieces. Continue this process until the blade is adjusted (Illus. 7-51–7-53). It is important that the blade be elevated only during the process. Lowering the blade may cause creep. The slop or lash in the gears will allow the elevating mechanism to slowly drop from its adjusted height. As you practice this method of setting blade height, you will find it to be easier and more accurate than any measuring method.

Some table saws have a plastic circle set in the table. This circle is used to mark the blade's path. A line scribed on this circle can be matched to the layout line on your work. This will ensure an accurate cut and will be very helpful when the guard blocks your vision. The scribed lines may not be accurate when the blade is changed or saw collars are added. Additional marks will have to be scribed.

To scribe marks on any saw, clamp a piece of scrap to the miter gauge. Cut a kerf into, but not through, the scrap. Move the miter gauge toward the front of the table and scribe both sides of the kerf (Illus. 7-54). Use a scratch awl for a permanent line, and a pencil for a temporary line.

You can achieve similar accuracy without seeing the blade, in two ways. First, you can use a stop on the miter gauge (Illus. 7-55). This will control length and position stock for cutting. Second, you can kerf a backing face with the saw blade (Illus. 7-56). As long as the cutting line is positioned correctly with the kerf in the backing board, the cut will be correct.

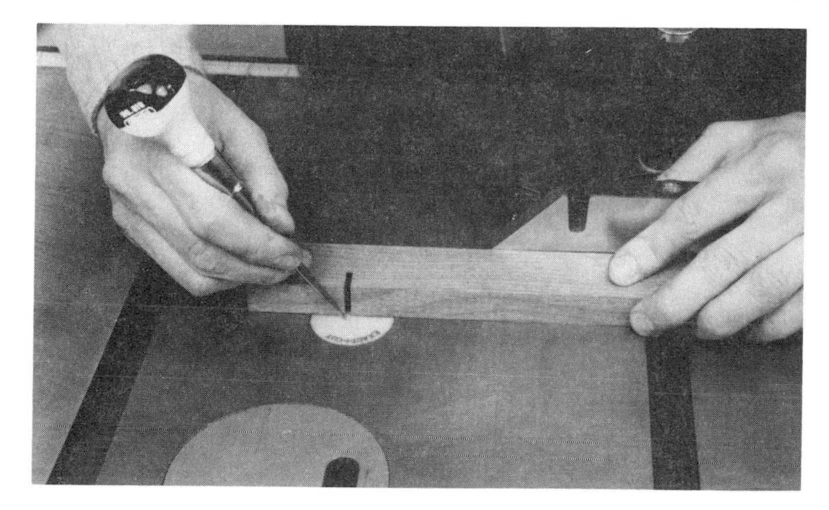

Illus. 7-54. A scratch awl can be used to mark the table for the path of the saw blade. Changing blades or adding blade stabilizers will affect the accuracy of these marks.

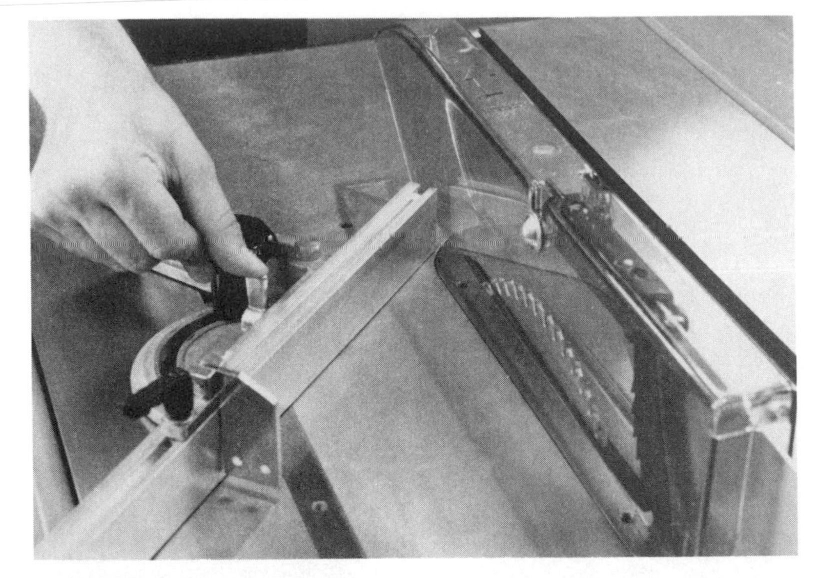

Illus. 7-55. The stop on this miter gauge makes cutting and stock positioning more accurate.

Illus. 7-56. Any pencil line positioned at the saw kerf will be cut precisely even if the blade's path is not visible.

Minimizing Tear-Out Problems

Grain tear-out is an annoying problem at the table saw. Tear-out can occur at the back, top, or bottom of the piece. If the wrong blade or a dull blade is used, tear-out is sure to occur. A rip blade will usually cause tear-out when you are crosscutting. Dull blades pound through the wood and cause tear-out. Feeding too fast can also cause tear-out. Moderate feeding speed will reduce tear-out.

One of the best methods of eliminating tear-out through the back of your work is by placing a piece of stock behind it. The tear-out occurs in the stock behind the workpiece. Attach a true piece of stock to the miter gauge. Stock butted firmly to this piece will not tear out through the back.

Tear-out through the top and bottom can be controlled by taping or scoring the stock. Tape applied over the area to be cut holds the wood fibers in place. The blade cuts through the tape, and the tape holds the fibers down on both sides of the kerf (Illus. 7-57).

Scoring the layout line with a utility knife will cause the wood fibers to break evenly at the line (Illus. 7-58). A sharp utility knife must be used. The wood should be scored to a depth of 1/16 inch or greater. Scribe both faces and edges to completely control tear-out.

Some tear-out problems may seem excessive (Illus. 7-59). If you inspect the blade, you will see that one tooth is out of alignment (Illus. 7-60 and 7-61).

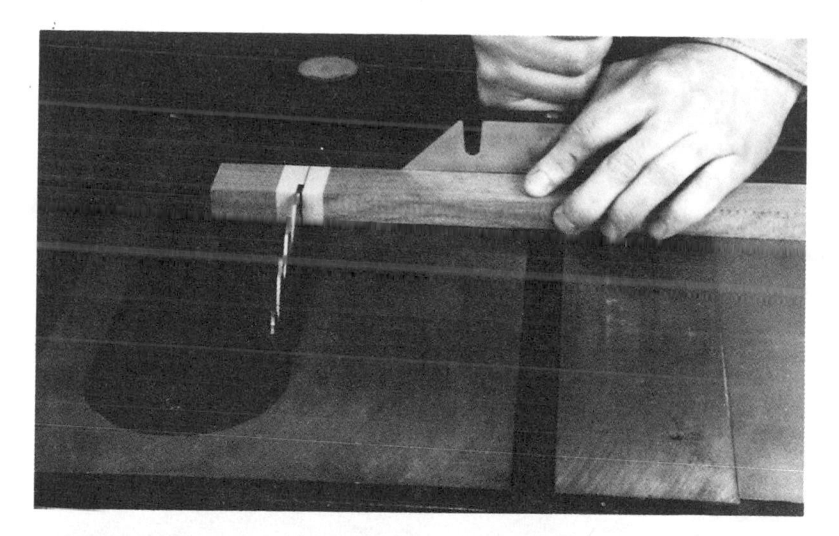

Illus. 7-57. Taping the work with masking tape will prevent grain tear-out. The tape holds the fibers in place while the blade cuts through it.

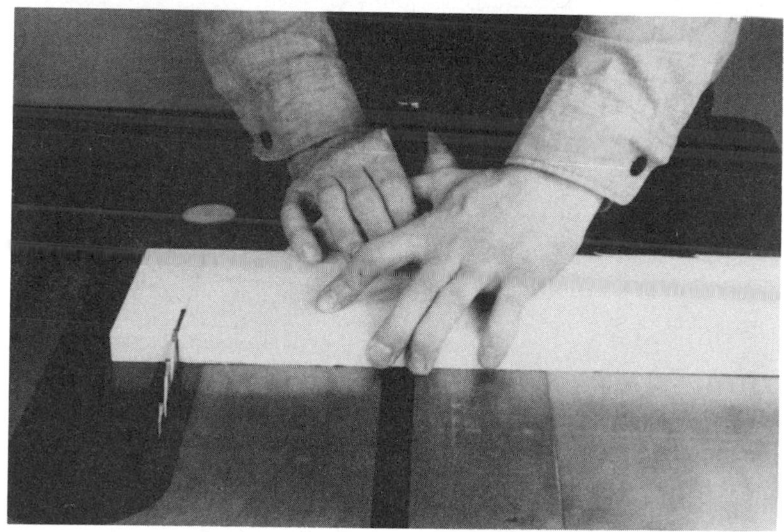

Illus. 7-58. Scoring the faces and edges of the work with a utility knife will also prevent tear-out. Make sure the cut goes into the wood about $\frac{1}{16}$ inch.

Illus. 7-59. The tearing on these cuts is excessive and suggests a problem.

Illus. 7-60. This tooth is the problem. It is misaligned by about .020 inch.

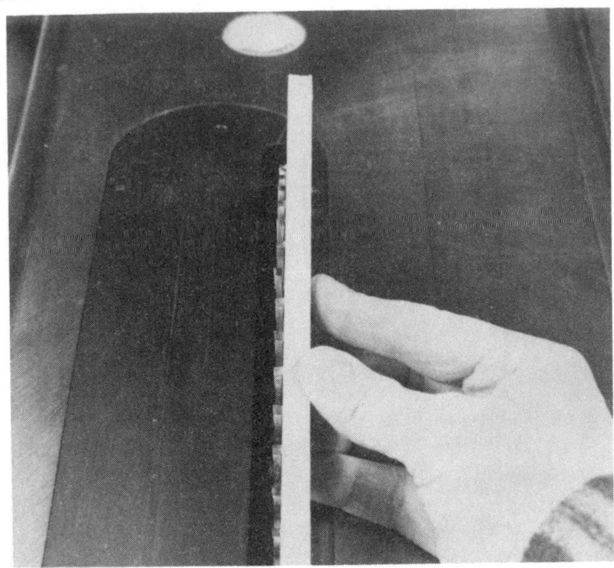

Illus. 7-61. Notice the tooth deflection. The tooth was probably bent by a loose knot or a piece of stock trapped beneath the tooth gullet and the throat plate.

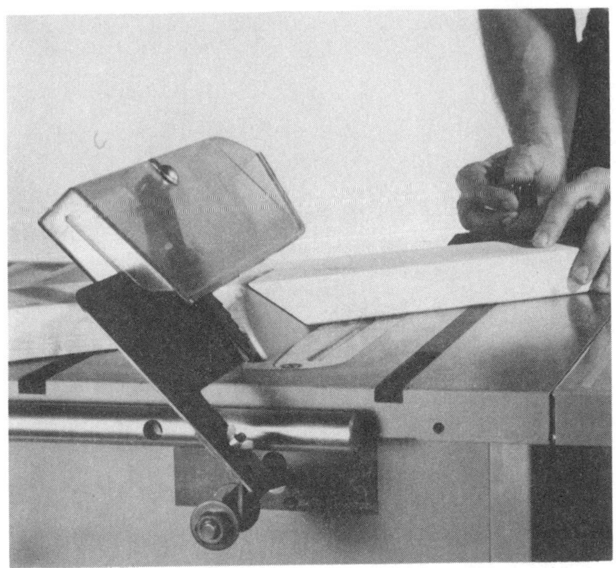

Illus. 7-62. A splitter-mounted guard can be used when you are making any through cut, including this compound miter. (Photo courtesy of Delta International Machinery Corporation.)

The tooth will have pitch on one side; the other side will be perfectly clean since it has done no work. Be sure to disconnect the power before making this check.

How Safe Is a Guard?

It is very difficult to cut yourself when the guard is in place. The guard covers the blade and minimizes the chance of contact with it. The splitter and anti-kickback pawls protect the operator from a kickback. The guard is a valuable, safe accessory for any table saw.

A guard is not perfect, however. While most through-cutting jobs can be done with a splitter-mounted guard (Illus. 7-62), some intermediate and advanced operations cannot be done with the guard in place. This is because the wood does not have a kerf. A dado or rabbet cut does not have a kerf in which the splitter can travel. In this case, many operators remove the guard for the advanced operation and never replace it. Some experienced operators feel that the guard is an added hazard. This group has three complaints about guards:

1. They limit vision.
2. They can be a kickback hazard (Illus. 7-63).
3. They make it difficult to do accurate work.

For extremely accurate work, the guard makes it difficult to cut along a layout line or trim a "hair" off the piece. Also, if a cutoff gets pinched between the blade and guard, it can kick back. This is a common problem with most guards. One other problem is that the removal and replacement of the guard throws it out of alignment. The splitter then pulls the piece off a straight line cut.

Illus. 7-63. When the cutoff is released from the board, it is trapped between the guard and the blade. In some cases, these pieces will kick back.

Some newer types of guards can be used for intermediate and advanced operations. These guards can be barriers for most advanced operations even if they do not have a splitter and anti-kickback pawls in back (Illus. 7-64–7-66). The guards can be used for almost all operations (Illus. 7-67–7-69). I have found these guards to be safe devices. I have used both extensively and have never had an injury occur when either of these guards was used.

It is good practice to use a guard whenever possible. If the setup cannot accommodate a guard, use featherboards and/or push sticks to make the cut safer. If you are not sure, consult an experienced woodworker. Keep a cautious attitude. If you have a premonition of danger, stop! Try some other method or tool.

Also do the following when using a table saw: keep the blade exposure low; quit working at the first sign of fatigue; and never work while under the influence of drugs, medications, or alcohol. Other procedures are covered in Chapter 4. Review the chapter occasionally; make it part of your work philosophy, and your risks will be minimized.

Illus. 7-64. This guard can be added to most table saws. The guard does not have a splitter, but it is the most effective guard for advanced operations.

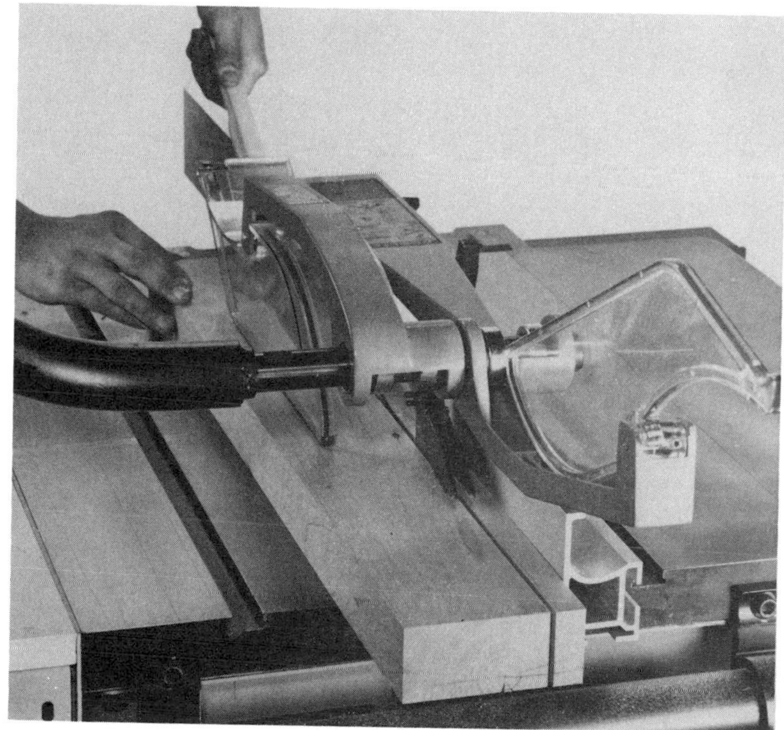

Illus. 7-65. For this rip cut, the Uniguard is being used with the removable splitter. This is a typical through cut. (Photo courtesy of Delta International Machinery Corporation.)

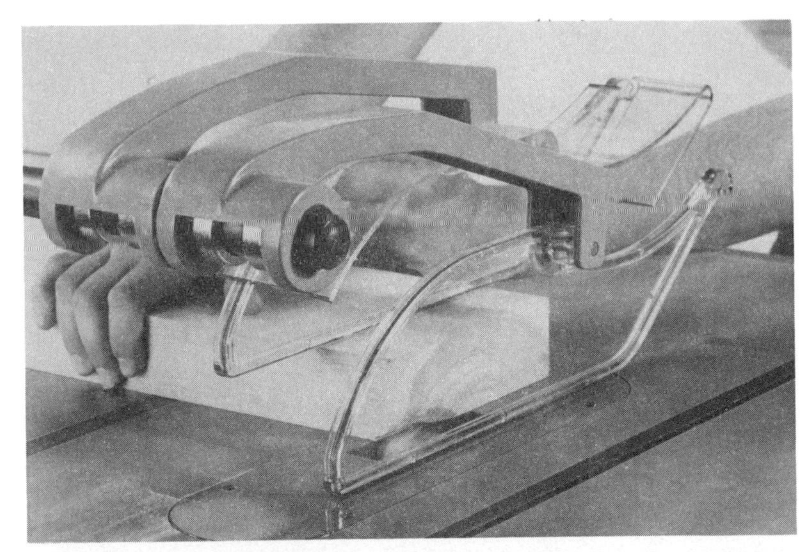

Illus. 7-66. The splitter has been removed for this non-through shaping cut. The guard still acts as a barrier between the cutter head and the operator. (Photo courtesy of Delta International Machinery Corporation.)

Illus. 7-67. The mitering jig is being used with the guard. The operator cannot contact the blade with this setup.

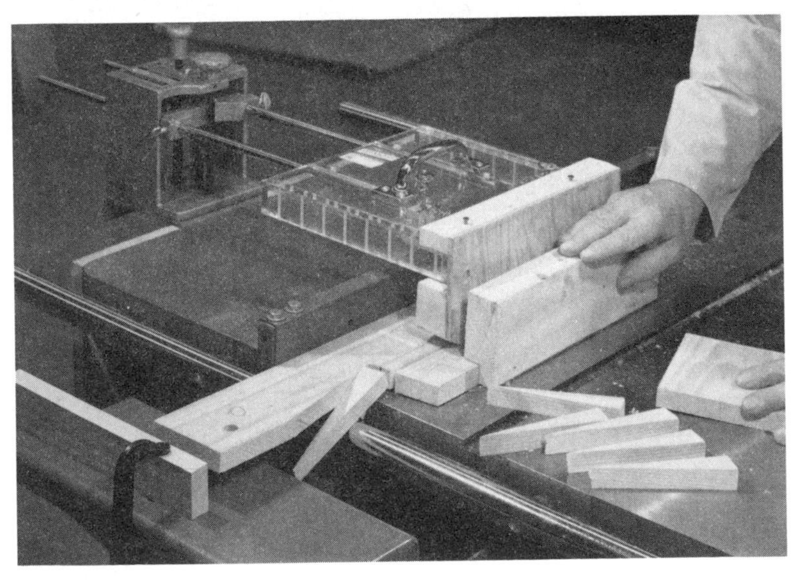

Illus. 7-68. This wedge-cutting setup also guards against contact with the blade. (Photo courtesy of The Foredom Electric Company.)

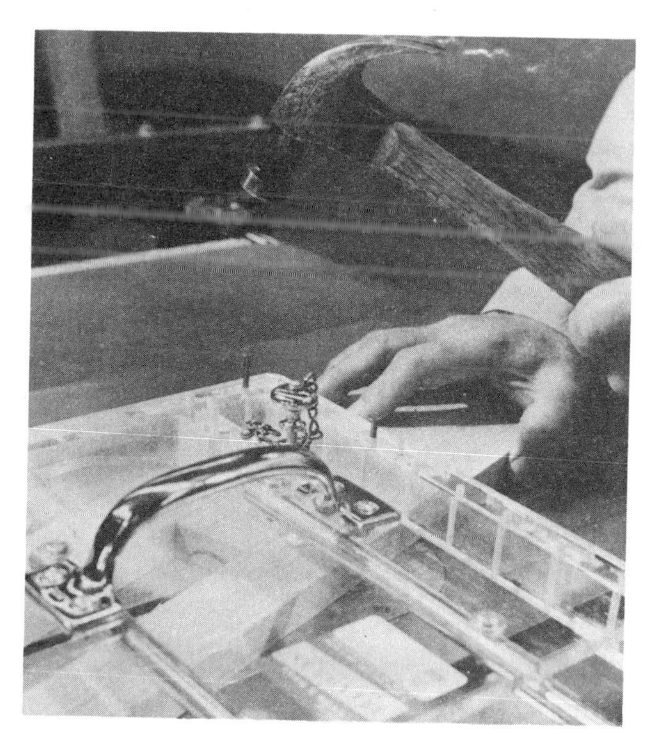

Illus. 7-69. The guard is being used to cut coves. The auxiliary fences are nailed to the guard. (Photo courtesy of The Foredom Electric Company.)

Bringing the Table Saw to the Job

Ever since my Uncle Irven mounted his table saw to the base of an old wheelbarrow, I have realized the importance of portability. Rolling casters (Illus. 7-70) may be more convenient than a wheelbarrow, but both are mobile.

Illus. 7-70. Rolling casters make this table saw more portable.

The small table saw featured in Illus. 7-71 and 7-72 breaks down into two parts: the base (Illus. 7-71) and the saw (Illus. 7-72). The wooden base

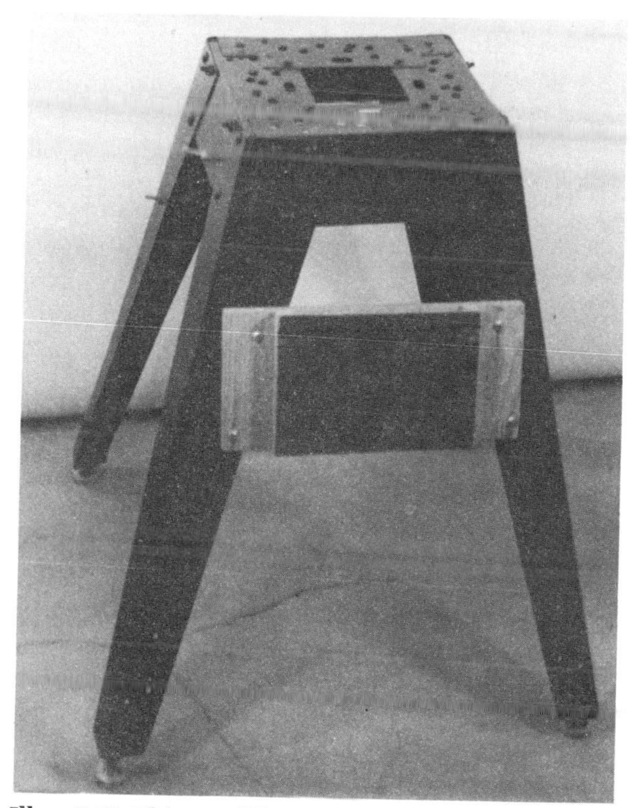

Illus. 7-71. This small base is easily moved to the job.

Illus. 7-72. This small saw is easily moved by one person. It can be attached to the base at the worksite.

protects the mounting bolts and stores the cord (Illus. 7-73). These bolts (Illus. 7-74) secure the saw to the base. The guard is then attached (Illus. 7-75), and the saw is ready to be leveled and used.

This small saw can be carried easily to the job. It also fits nicely in the back seat of an intermediate-sized car. For long rip cuts on the job, an extension is attached to the fence (Illus. 7-76). This allows support when no help is available on the job (Illus. 7-77).

Illus. 7-73. The wooden base holds the cord inside the saw and protects the bolts from damage.

Illus. 7-74. These bolts are used to secure the saw to the base.

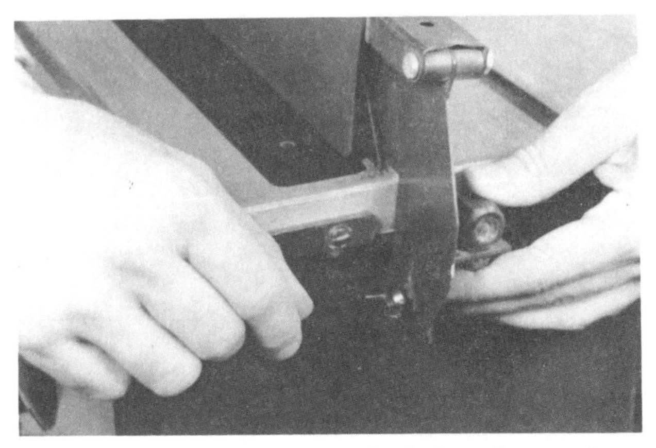

Illus. 7-75. The guard is attached after the saw is set up.

Larger saws are sometimes needed on the job. The one in Illus. 7-78 was brought up by elevator to the third floor of a bank. A shop was set up to remodel the entire floor.

When working on the job, make sure the electrical supply is compatible with your saw. I burned up a motor using a circuit that was fused too high for the motor. The fuse attached to the motor (Illus. 7-79) protects me from another expensive error.

Buying a Table Saw

Buying a table saw is similar to buying a car. When buying a new car, you know what options you want and how much you are willing or able to pay. When you buy a used car, your choice is limited to what is available. You may not get exactly what you want, but you save money.

The same is true of a table saw. A new saw can be equipped to suit your needs. Everything is under warranty, and no one has abused the tool. A used table saw, however, is like a used car. You must take the previous owner's word about the condition of the saw and how it was used. There is no warranty, and most repairs will be made by the owner.

A New Saw When you decide to buy a new table saw, the saw should fit your needs. Some of the following questions will help you determine what type of table saw fits your needs:

1. What type of stock will I be cutting? What is the thickest, widest, and longest piece I will cut?
2. How large a table and blade will be needed to handle the stock I will be cutting?
3. Is the shop space large enough to accommodate the table saw? A clear space 8 × 16 feet long is desirable. Smaller areas can be used, but stock size will be limited.
4. What type of electrical service is available? What voltage, amperage, and phase? For home use, a 110-volt circuit of 20 amps is needed. A 220-volt circuit of 10 amps will also work. A single phase is used exclusively in the home. A three-phase system is available for industrial use. It is used at voltage of 220 and above.

Illus. 7-76. This extension can be attached to the fence for long rip cuts.

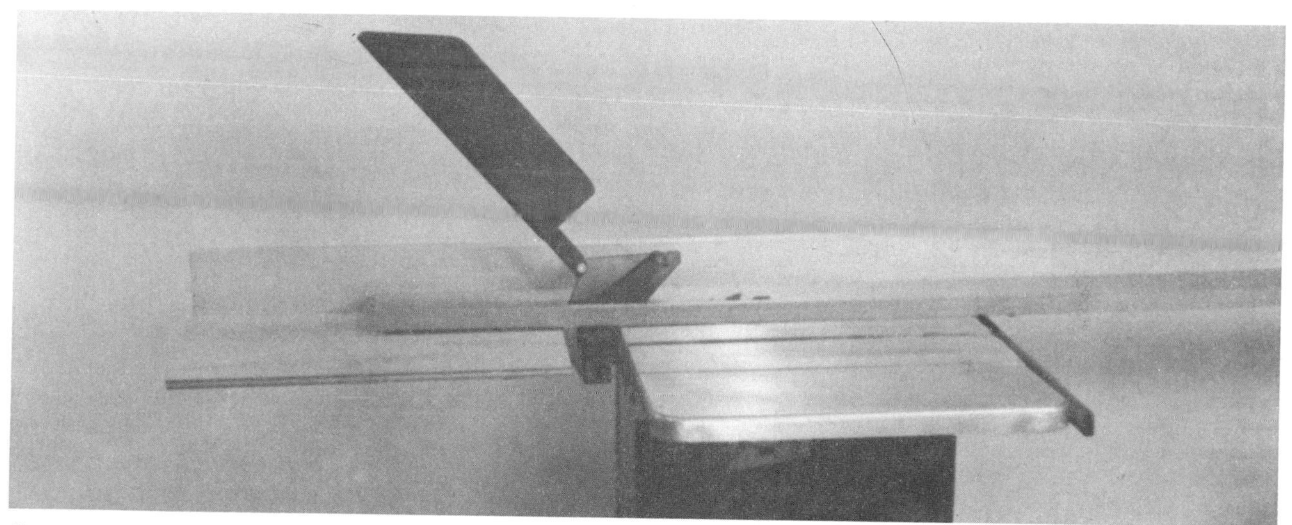

Illus. 7-77. This extension supports the stock when no helper is available.

Illus. 7-78. This table saw was transported to the third floor of a bank for a remodeling job. The office space became our workshop for the entire job.

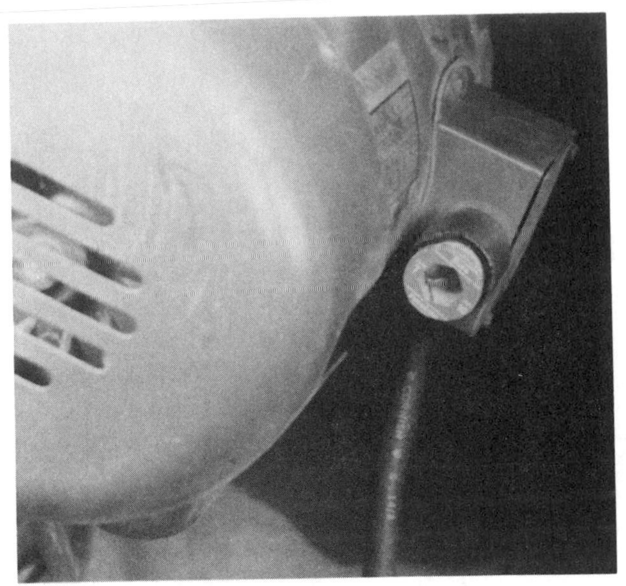

Illus. 7-79. The fuse attached to the motor protects it from burning up when connected to a high-amperage circuit.

5. Under what budget constraints am I working? What price range is desirable? Could options be added later to keep the initial price lower?
6. Should the table of the saw be cast iron, cast aluminum, stamped steel, or a composition material? Generally, cast iron minimizes vibration best, but in a damp basement cast aluminum may be better because it does not rust. Many of the composition materials resist rust and work as well as cast iron or aluminum.
7. Should the table saw be motorized or motor driven? Generally, motorized saws will not cut as deeply as motor-driven saws with the same blade diameter. This is because the motor limits the blade elevation. Motorized saws are usually louder than motor-driven saws. Motor-driven saws usually have less vibration than motorized saws, but the mass (weight) of the elevating mechanisms can also affect this (Illus. 7-80 and 7-81). More mass usually means less vibration. More than one belt (Illus. 7-82) also means more power and less chance of slippage.
8. What accessories are standard, and what other accessories will I need? Most table saws come with a guard (Illus. 7-83 and 7-84), a fence, miter gauge, and throat plate. A sliding table may be standard on some table saws (Illus. 7-85).

Accessories such as a molding head, dado head,

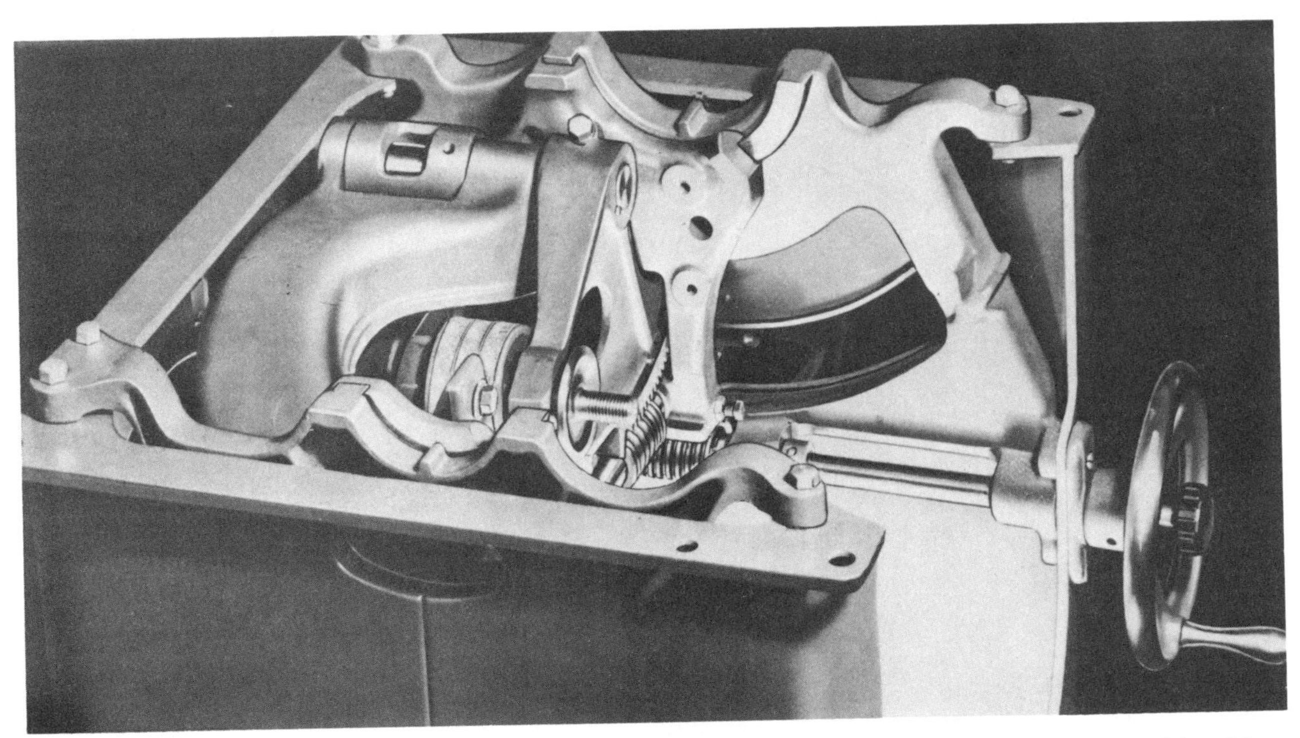

Illus. 7-80. The massive castings in the elevating mechanism dampen vibration and resist wear. This table saw is considered an industrial-grade table saw.

extra throat plates, and additional miter gauges will raise the initial cost of the saw. It is nice to have an extra miter gauge. The convenience of two miter gauges is worth the slight cost increase. One miter gauge can be left at 90 degrees, while the other can be set at any desired angle. The two may be used as a team when you are cutting miters.

9. What horsepower is needed to power the table

Illus. 7-81. The castings in this table saw are fewer and lighter than those in the one shown in Illus. 7-80. This table saw is considered a contractor table saw.

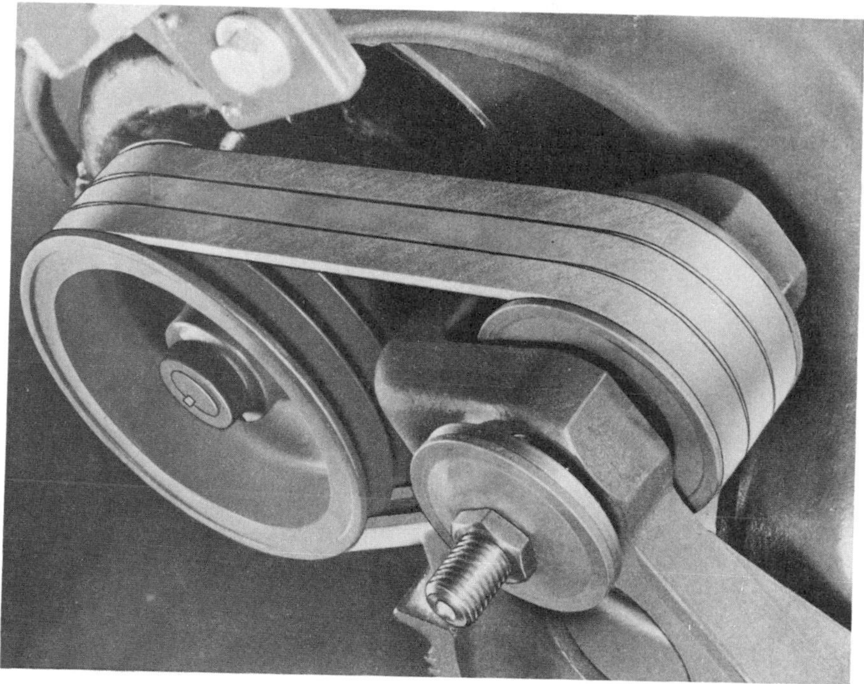

Illus. 7-82. The three belts driving the arbor mean more power and less chance of slippage. These belts must all be replaced at the same time, to ensure that they are the same length.

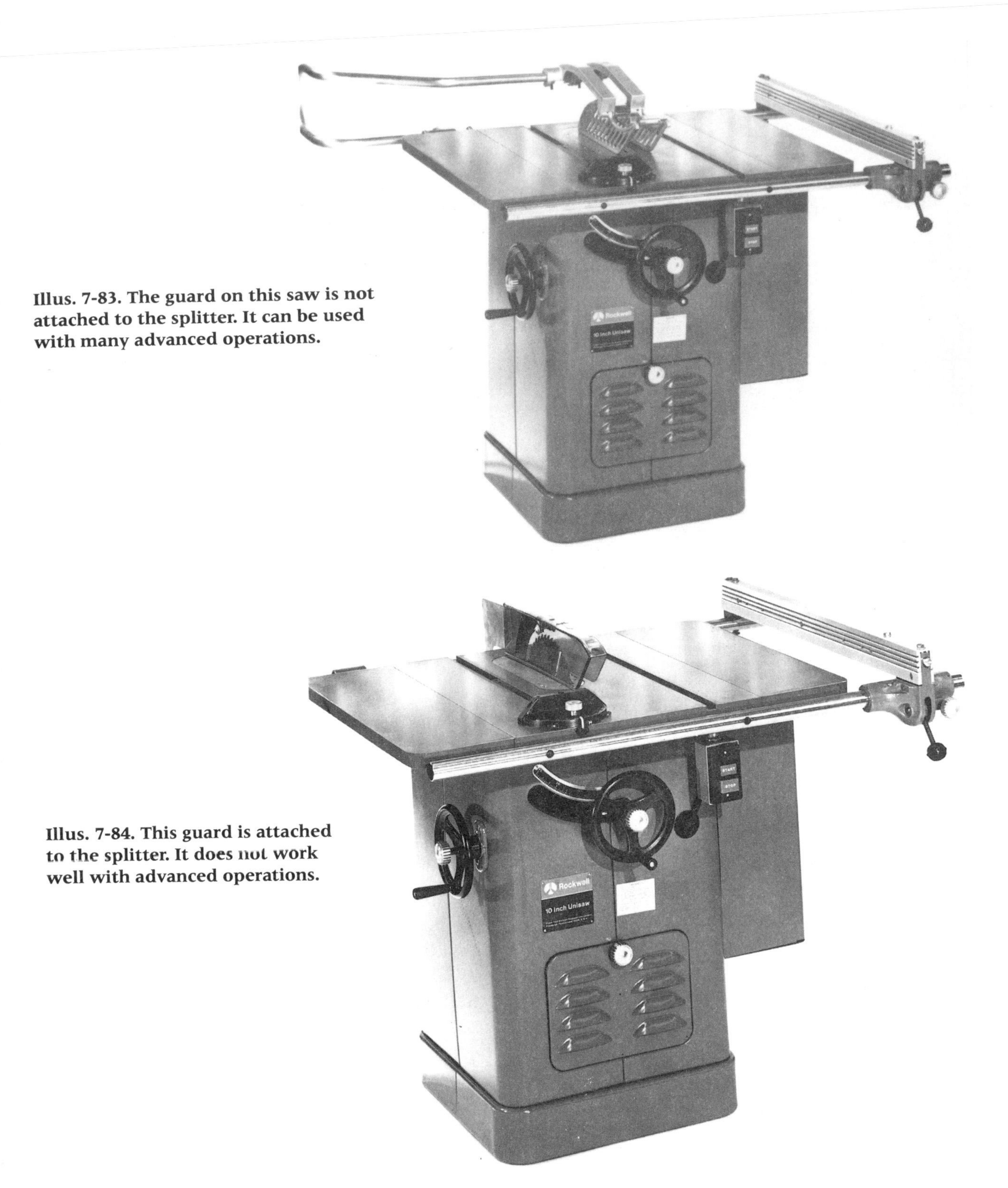

Illus. 7-83. The guard on this saw is not attached to the splitter. It can be used with many advanced operations.

Illus. 7-84. This guard is attached to the splitter. It does not work well with advanced operations.

saw adequately? This will depend on the stock you will be cutting and the blade diameter used on the saw. The discussion in Chapter 1 (pages 23–25) will help you determine the needed horsepower.

10. How does the fence lock to the table? Some work easier and are more accurate than others. How about the miter gauge; does it fit tightly to the table? Miter slop also means accuracy problems.

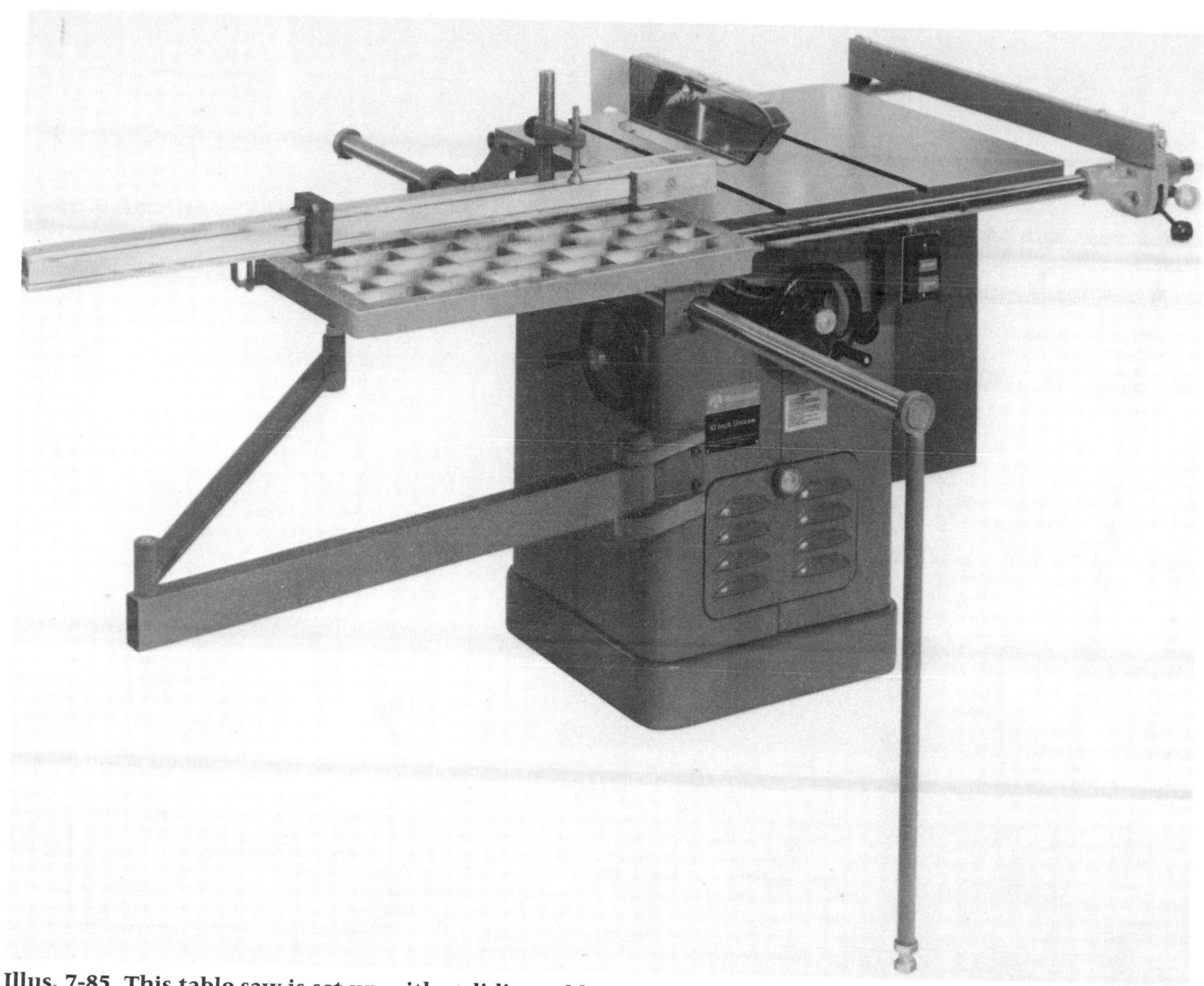

Illus. 7-85. This table saw is set up with a sliding table as standard equipment. The table could be added to the saw at a later date. This will keep the initial cost of the saw lower.

Constant adjustment of a table saw is irritating. You cannot use the saw if you are adjusting it.

11. How easy is it to realign the saw if it comes out of alignment? The more difficult the saw is to align, the less you'll be able to use it. You want to be a woodworker, not a wood watcher.

12. How long is the arbor? Will it accommodate a dado head or a molding head?

13. Are you locked into the manufacturer's system? Unusual threads, motor mounts, or miter slots lock you into the manufacturer's accessories only. This limits the number of accessories available and usually increases the cost of accessories or replacement parts.

14. How close to the blade are the miter slots? The closer they are to the blade, the closer your hands will be to the blade for all crosscutting and mitering.

15. What provisions are in place for dust collection? If you have to add dust-collecting accessories to the saw after purchasing it, its cost will increase significantly and you may not have gotten a bargain on your purchase.

16. What are the fit and finish like? How well-machined are the table, fence, and miter gauge? Poor fits and deviation in the tabletop can affect accuracy.

The planning sheet (Illus. 7-86) will help you put your needs on paper. You can fill in motor and saw specifications. The saw weight is included here because some woodworkers feel that the weight of the saw can be an indicator of quality. This tends to

Planning Sheet

Desired Motor

_____Volts _____Amps _____Horsepower

_____Phase _____24-volt Switch

_____T.E.F.C. (Totally Enclosed Fan-Cooled, Dust Proof)

_____Motorized _____Motor Driven

Desired Saw

_____Blade Diameter _____Sliding Table

_____Table Width _____Table Length

_____Enclosed Base _____Open Base

_____Tilting Table _____Tilting Arbor

_____Weight _____Table (Cast Iron, Cast Aluminum, etc.)

Desired Options (List)

__________ __________

__________ __________

Brand	List Price	Comments
1.		
2.		
3.		
4.		

Illus. 7-86. This planning sheet will help you determine your table saw needs on paper.

favor cast iron, but this should not be the only consideration.

At the bottom of the planning sheet you can list table saws that meet your specifications. The list price can be noted and any general comments, such as accessories included, or how the fence locks to the table.

After you determine which table saw(s) will meet your needs, ask some experts for their opinion of the saw. People who use the saw will be able to tell you about adjustment problems, ways to repair the saw, and general operation techniques. Cabinetmakers, carpenters, and woodworking teachers are usually willing to share their knowledge of woodworking equipment. This knowledge will help you make a wiser purchase.

The list price is a guideline of price. Not all sales agents hold that price, so it pays to shop. Also consider shipping charges and sales tax when comparing prices. Sales tax varies in cities and states. A 30-mile ride could mean two percent less sales tax.

Picking up the table saw at the factory or a distribution center can also reduce the actual cost of the table saw. Be ready to bargain; table saw suppliers will recognize an informed buyer. They may be willing to compromise to make the sale.

A Used Saw The cost of a new saw may be beyond your means. In this case, a used table saw may be more appealing. Though the planning sheet will still help you focus in on your needs, the used table saw evaluation sheet (Illus. 7-87) can help you determine the value of any table saw you consider buying. It will help you compare two or more used table saws when shopping.

The brand and age of the saw are important indicators of value. Some table saws have higher resale value because of the manufacturer's reputation. The fact that parts are still available for the table saw is important, too. It is very costly and sometimes impossible to have parts custom-made for a used table saw. The part could cost more than the saw is worth.

Electrical information is also important. A three-

Used Table Saw Evaluation Sheet

Name of Seller
Address
Phone
Table Saw Brand ______
Model Number ______ Year Manufactured ______
Company Still Makes Saw Yes No
Repair Parts Available Yes No
Owner's Manual Included Yes No
____Volts ____Amps ____Phase
____Table Width X ____Table Length
Options, Features, Accessories Included (List and Estimate Value)
______
______
______
______
Today's List Price of Same or Similar Saw ______
Asking Price of the Seller ______
Difference ______
General Condition of Saw (List descriptions of condition and cost of repair if damaged)
______
______
______

Illus. 7-87. With this used table saw elevation sheet, you can determine the value of a used saw.

phase motor would have to be replaced when you want to operate the saw where only one phase of electricity is available. Make sure you can use the saw before you buy it

Listing accessories helps determine the value of a used saw. A saw that has extra blades, a dado head, and a molding head is worth more than a basic table saw. Features like a sliding table or tenoning jig can also add to the value of the saw. Be sure to list all options, features, and accessories offered for sale with the table saw.

Comparing today's list price with the seller's asking price helps determine the value of the table saw. If the saw is 10 years old and the price difference is small, the value may be questionable. Consider this information carefully before you buy a table saw.

The general condition of the saw is usually obvious. Check the condition of the table and look for rust, cracks in the castings, and any signs of repair. If the saw is five to 10 years old and the owner still has the manual, the saw has probably been well-maintained. The manual should show some signs of wear. Pencil marks circling replacement parts or oily thumb prints indicate the manual was used on the job. If the table saw needs repair, estimate the cost of the repair. Make sure the seller's price reflects that repair, and that replacement parts are available.

Inspect the arbor, arbor nut, and arbor washer for wear and abuse. Try to move the abor from side to side. If there is movement, it can mean wear in the bearings. This can be an expensive replacement.

When buying a used table saw, decide on a fair price before making the seller an offer. Some woodworkers refuse to pay more than 60 percent of retail price for any woodworking tools regardless of age or condition. Their rationale is that if you can buy much more with the extra 40 percent, then the used tool is not worth the gamble. The 60 percent rule does not fit all sales, but it is another guideline.

When you shop for a used table saw, there are many places to look. Suppliers of new table saws often take used saws as trade ins. These saws are usually reconditioned and sold. Sometimes a warranty is included. Used saws from a supply house are usually more expensive and in better repair.

The want ads in newspapers and tabloids often

have table saws for sale. Price and quality will vary with each ad. You must inspect and compare the merchandise to determine value.

It is also possible to advertise for a table saw in the "Wanted to Buy" section of the want ads. A person who wants to sell a table saw will find it easier to call you than to place an ad. This gives you a better bargaining position because the seller does not have other buyers coming to inspect the saw. The seller has only one offer—yours!

Auctions often advertise table saws. An estate auction or a woodworking shop auction might have a table saw that fits your needs. Be careful when buying at an auction. Sometimes the excitement of the auction will cause the bidding to reach a price close to that of a new saw. Decide on your top bid before the auction begins, and stick with it. Auction-bought tools are not always a bargain.

Part IV: Projects

—8—

How to Build Table-Saw Accessories and Items for Your Home

The projects in this chapter can be divided into two groups. The first group consists of jigs or accessories. These are devices you can make for your table saw. The second group consists of projects for general use. These projects make nice gifts or accessories for your home or shop. They have been designed to help you hone your table-saw and woodworking skills.

This project chapter is last for good reason. You must digest the information in the first seven chapters before you begin building projects. If you begin a project without a full understanding of table-saw operations, you could waste material or incur an injury. Plan projects carefully and review unfamiliar operations before you begin.

Tips for Building Projects

When you start a project, consider the following tips. These tips will help you do a better job with fewer mistakes.

1. *Study the plans carefully.* Check the dimensions or the scale on the plans to be sure all parts will be cut correctly. Make allowances for joints or for trimming on all parts. Remember, some jigs are designed for a particular saw. Their dimensions may have to be changed to fit your saw.
2. *Develop auxiliary sketches when needed.* When plans are modified or an assembly is complex, develop an auxiliary sketch that you can take to the table saw. Sketches of picture-frame profiles can be glued to the stock. This makes the table-saw setup much quicker and more accurate.
3. *Develop a bill of materials.* A bill of materials is a list of all parts needed to build the project. The list includes the parts' dimensions (thickness, width, and length). The bill of materials helps in stock selection and table-saw setup.
4. *Write a plan of procedure.* The plan of procedure is a list of steps one should follow to build a project. The list is an orderly series of events. For example, the drawer opening would be made before the drawer front was cut to exact size. It is not considered good practice to make the drawer and then build the opening.
5. *Think before making any cuts.* Plan your cutting to reduce the chance of error. When cutting parts, cut the longest parts first. Any parts cut too short can be used for shorter parts on the bill of materials.

Before making a cut in your work, test the setup on a piece of scrap. Make sure it is correct before you begin. Mark complex cuts. Drawers and cabinets have a right and left side. The sides are not identical! They are mirror images of each other. Cut them carefully.

When several operations are being performed on a number of parts, mark the control edge. The control edge is the edge on the parts that always rides along the fence or against the miter gauge. This mark will minimize the chance of reversing the parts after a few operations have been performed. The mark is important on parts such as molding, picture-frame components, and cabinet sides.

6. *Check the fit of all parts before assembling them.* Fit the parts together before gluing them. Tight fits can

cause problems when glue is applied. Both parts will swell, and the parts may not fit together. It is much easier to trim parts and make minor adjustments when there is no glue on the parts.

7. *Plan ahead for finishing.* Sand all internal surfaces before assembling a box or cabinet. The surfaces may be difficult or impossible to sand after assembly. It may also be easier to stain and finish these surfaces before assembly.

Watch for glue smears on the wood. They can make your stain and finish appear blemished. Scrape or sand away these smears before applying stain or finish.

Table Saw Devices

Basic Design of Table-Saw Jigs Most jigs designed to be used on a table saw are controlled by the miter slot (Illus. 8-1) or the fence (Illus. 8-2). Jigs used in the miter slot are often adjustable. They move toward and away from the blade on a track. Jigs that are controlled by the fence are usually not adjustable. All adjustments are made by moving the fence toward or away from the fence.

The jig shown in Illus. 8-2 is easy to construct. A piece of plywood is attached to the fence, and jigs are built to ride on the plywood. A piece of plywood the same thickness as the piece attached to the fence separates the two sides of the jig. This makes a perfect fit. Sometimes a piece of paper is added to the center strip to make movement of the jig easier.

Illus. 8-2. This jig is guided and controlled by the fence. Moving the fence moves the position of the jig.

Illus. 8-1. This miter jig is controlled and guided by the miter slot. A cleat on the jig fits snugly in the miter slot.

The jig shown in Illus. 8-1 appears to be painted white. It actually has a plastic coating bonded to it. This coating resists wear and slides easily. When making a jig, select stock carefully. Most sheet stock resists warping, swelling, and wear. Sheet stock is a good material for jig construction.

Make the cleats that ride in the miter slot out of dense, hard wood. This will prevent the cleat from wearing and getting sloppy. Use quarter-sawn stock for cleats whenever possible. A quarter-sawn cleat will have annular rings running parallel to the saw blade. Quarter-sawn cleats will not swell across the miter slot. This means the jig will still operate well even with a moisture change.

Always consider safety when designing a jig for the table saw. Many times the table-saw owner builds the jig carelessly because it is regarded as a means to an end rather than an end itself. A well-made jig will be an accurate tool that can be used for many different operations. A poorly made jig may be dangerous, yield poor results, and be used only once.

A safe jig is planned carefully. The miter jig shown in Illus. 8-3 has a hook on the miter-slot cleat. This hook prevents the operator from sawing through the jig. This is easily done when you are doing repetitive cuts. The piece of wood behind the miter fence acts as a guard (Illus. 8-4). When the blade cuts through the work, it is housed inside the wooden guard. This prevents the blade from cutting the operator's thumb, which is also a common mishap when repetitive cuts are being made.

This jig could be made if a piece of clear plastic covered the blade's path on the front side of the jig. It would minimize contact with the blade without impairing vision.

Any jig you build can probably be improved or made safer, but careful planning will help you begin with a safe, accurate jig. Follow the basic safety rules in Chapter 4 when operating any jig on the table saw.

Building Basic Jigs and Accessories Many jigs and accessories were presented in the first seven chapters. You may wish to make some of them for your table saw.

In Chapter 2 (pages 56–59), some shooting boards were presented. These allow greater control of stock when you are crosscutting it. A small one can be made to be used as an extra miter gauge (Illus. 8-5), or a large one can be made to be used to crosscut large parts (Illus. 8-6).

Make sure the cleats are installed accurately and screwed down accurately (Illus. 8-7). The size of the

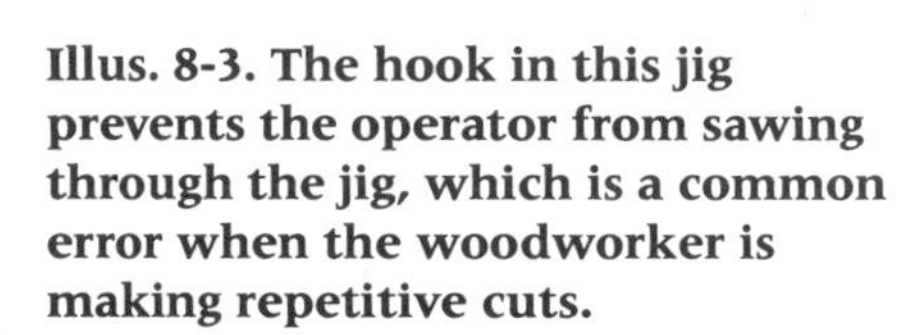

Illus. 8-3. The hook in this jig prevents the operator from sawing through the jig, which is a common error when the woodworker is making repetitive cuts.

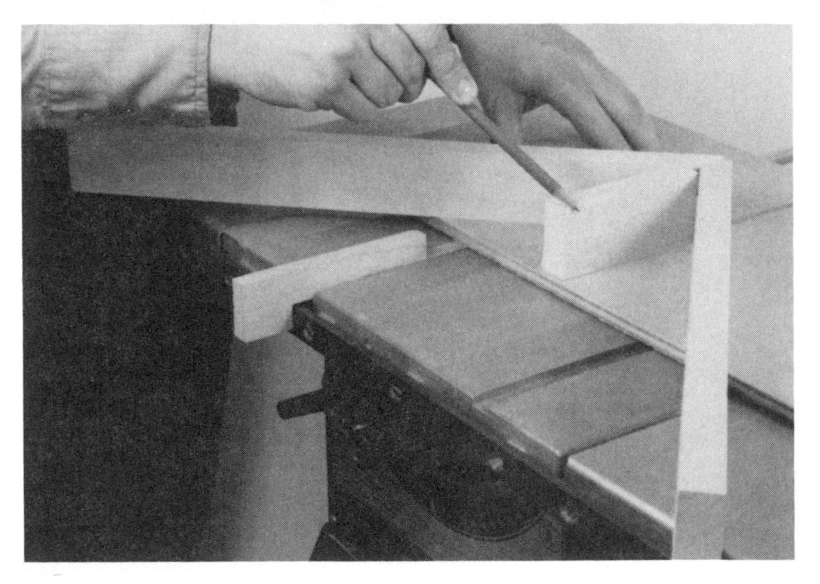

Illus. 8-4. This block of wood acts as a guard when the jig cuts through the work. The operator is protected.

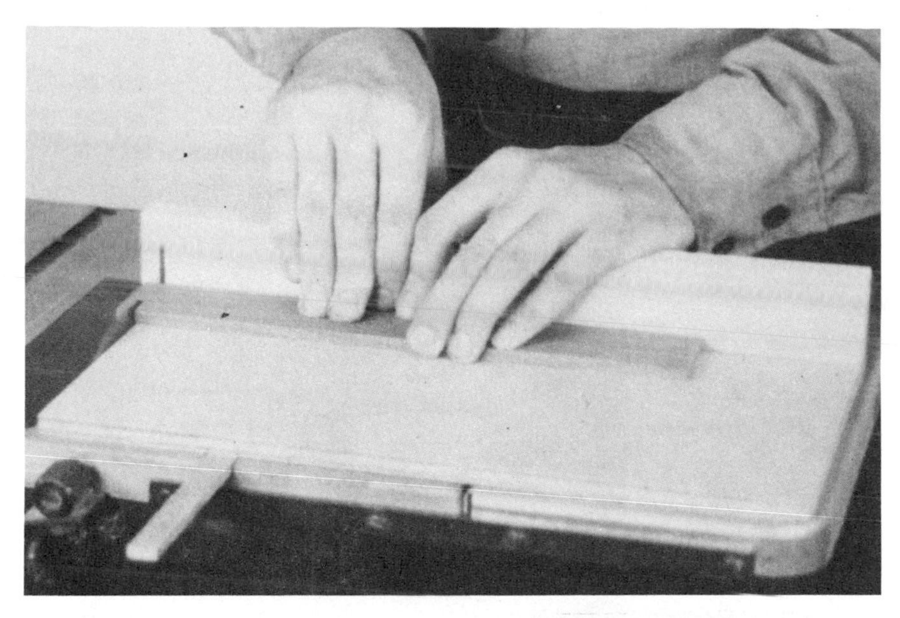

Illus. 8-5. This small shooting board can be used as a substitute miter gauge. It is very handy when the miter gauge is set up for a cut.

Illus. 8-6. This shooting board is ideal for crosscutting large parts. Make sure the control surfaces are taller than the highest blade setting.

Illus. 8-7. The cleats on a shooting board should be installed accurately and screwed down securely.

shooting board will depend on the size of your table saw. Make sure the control surface (fence) is higher than the blade.

A mitering jig (Illus. 8-3 and 8-4) is quite similar to a shooting board. Cut the board the same size as the table of your saw. Attach cleats and cut a kerf to the center of the board. Lay out one miter from the kerf and attach a fence. Use a framing square to lay out the other miter. Place one leg of the square against the 45-degree fence. The other leg determines placement of the other fence. Add a hook and a blade guard and test the jig.

If the framing square is not 90 degrees, the jig will be off. Check the square before using it. A piece of tape on the fence can compensate for minor errors.

Wooden extensions for your miter gauge can also be made. Glue a strip of abrasive to them to reduce slippage between the work and the miter gauge. Prepare for complex operations by making some auxiliary throat plates (Illus. 8-8). Trace them on sheet stock and cut them to fit. See Illus. 2-57–2-62 for more details on making and fitting auxiliary throat plates.

For advanced table-saw operations, a few featherboards (Illus. 8-9) would be helpful. A featherboard holds stock down or against the fence. This allows greater control of the work and reduces the chance of a kickback. See Illus. 2-78–2-87 for details on laying out and cutting a featherboard.

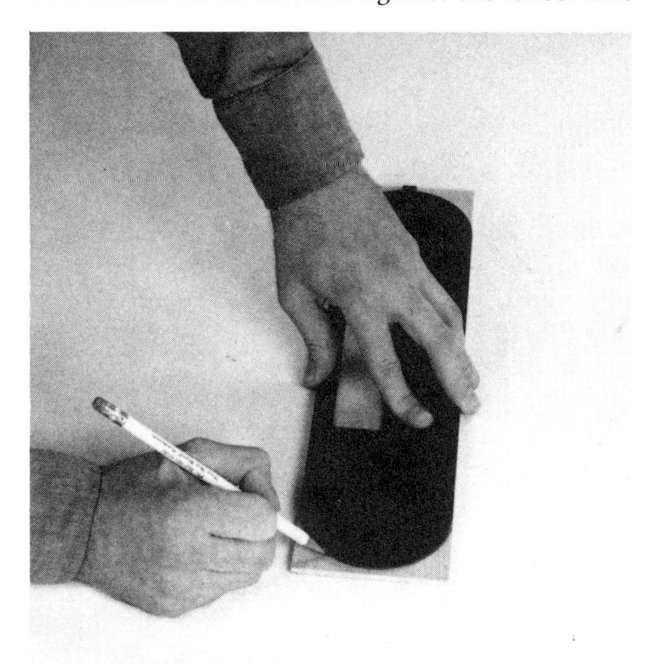

Illus. 8-8. Prepare for advance setups by making additional throat plates. See Chapter 2 (pages 43–45) for more details.

Illus. 8-9. A featherboard is a helpful accessory for complex setups. The featherboard makes it easier to control stock. See Chapter 2 (pages 50–53) for more details on making a featherboard.

Be sure to make some push sticks for your table saw. Use the templates shown in Illus. 2-99–2-102. Drill a hole in them so they can be hung on the table saw. Make some hooks that can be mounted on the table saw (Illus. 8-10). These hooks ensure that a push stick will be where it is needed at all times.

For long rip cuts, you may wish to make a dead man (Illus. 8-11) or a fence extension (Illus. 8-12). The dead man is a simple roller used in a portable

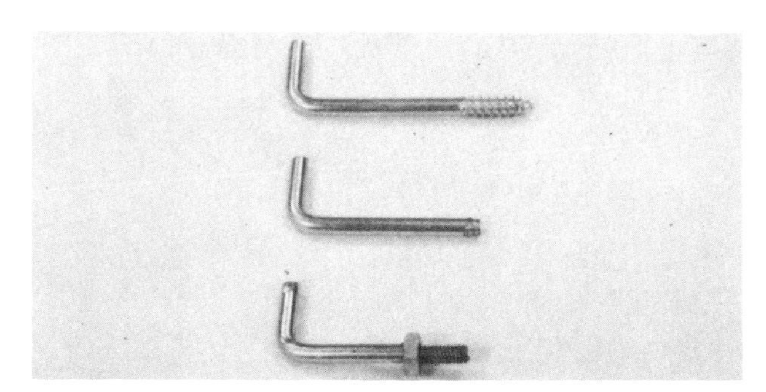

Illus. 8-10. Hooks like these can be used to hang push sticks on the table saw. Cut the wood threads off the hook, and cut machine threads with a die to replace them. Anchor them to the table with two nuts, or thread the table and use one nut.

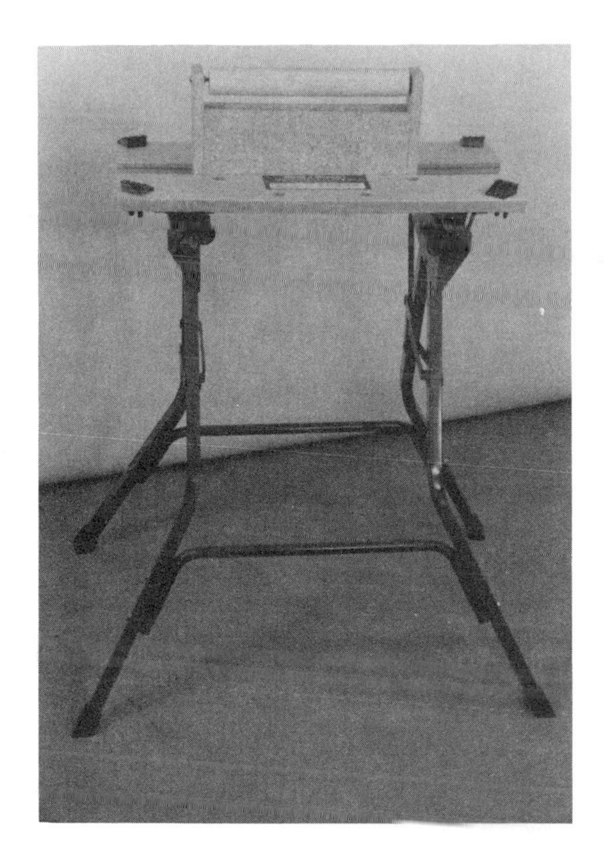

Illus. 8-11 (left). This dead man is a handy device for long rip cuts. The roller is held in place with nuts and bolts. Illus. 8-12 (above). This fence extension extends the fence and table for long rip cuts. Use a true piece of stock for the fence.

sawhorse. The roller in Illus. 8-11 is a piece of closet rod. It is available at most lumberyards. Study Illus. 8-13 and modify it to suit your needs or sawhorse. It can be assembled with glue and nails or screws.

The fence extension attaches to the fence and extends the fence and table. The piece attached to the bottom of the fence extension supports the work during long rip cuts. Study 8-14 and modify it to fit your table saw. Use screws and glue to assemble the two pieces. Remove any glue that squeezes out of the joint.

For cutting irregular pieces, you may want to make an auxiliary fence for pattern sawing (Illus. 8-15). The size of this auxiliary fence will be determined by the size of the part you are cutting. Use a dense, hard wood for the edge on which the pattern rides.

A jig for cutting irregular parts can also be made easily. Install a cleat onto the plywood base. The distance from the cleat to the end of the base should exceed the distance from the miter slot to the blade. The base is then sawn to size (Illus. 8-16). Use the same blades for this operation as the one you intend to use when cutting parts. Anything clamped on that edge will be cut to true size (Illus. 8-17). Before making the cut, make sure the blade is set at the desired angle.

The circle-cutting jig (Illus. 8-18) is similar to the

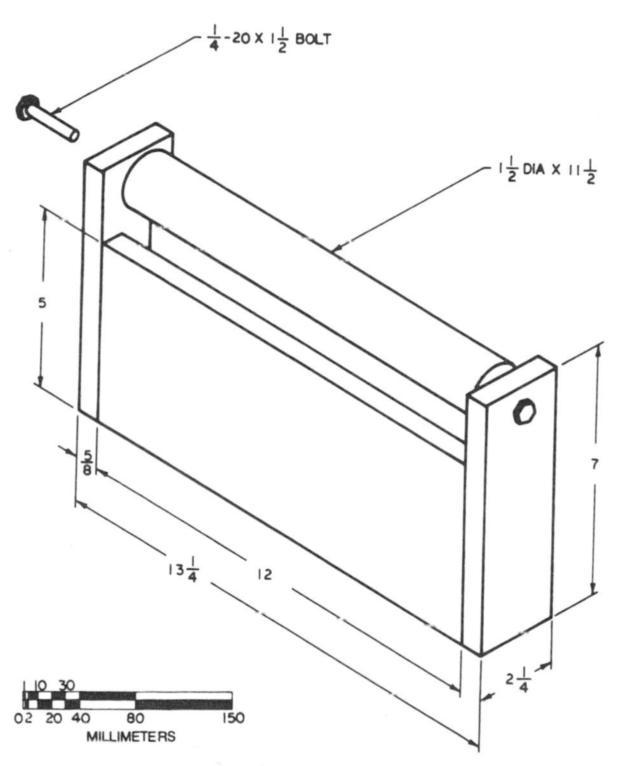

Illus. 8-13. Use this guide to make a dead man. Modify the dimensions to suit your needs.

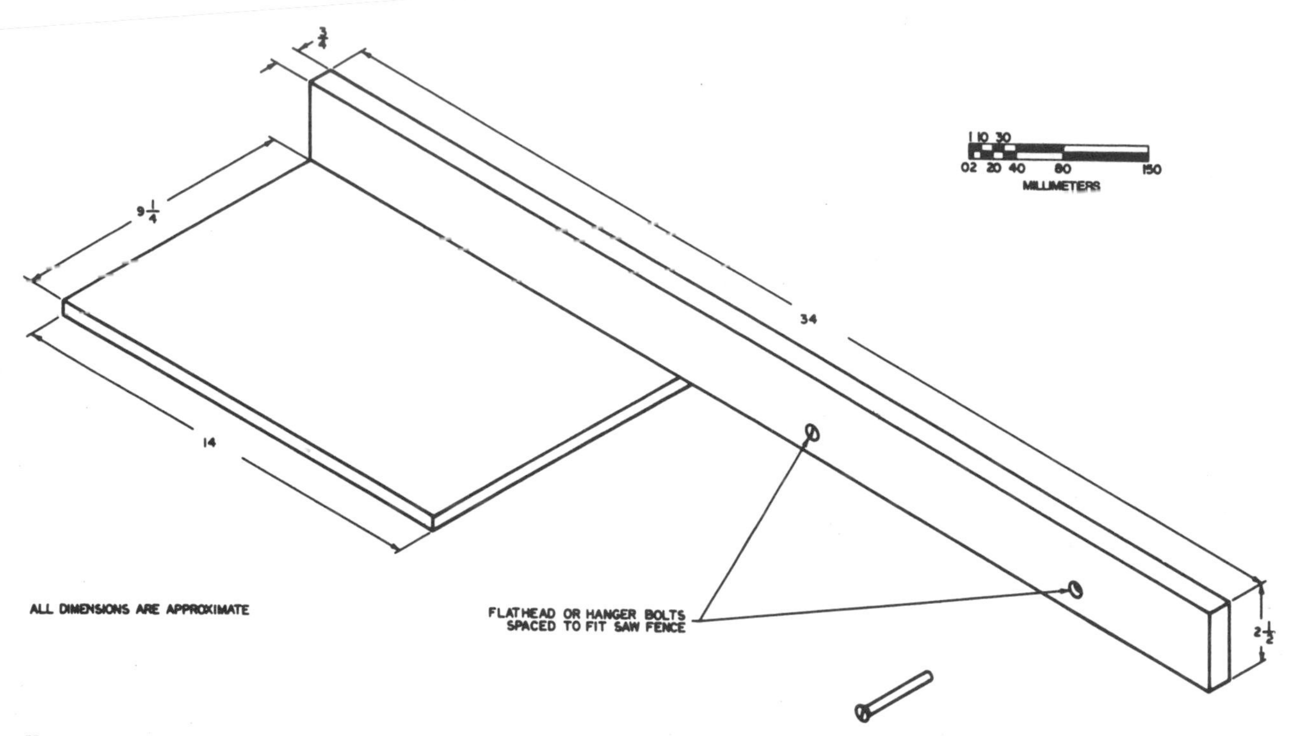

Illus. 8-14. Use this guide to make a fence extension. Modify the dimensions to suit your needs.

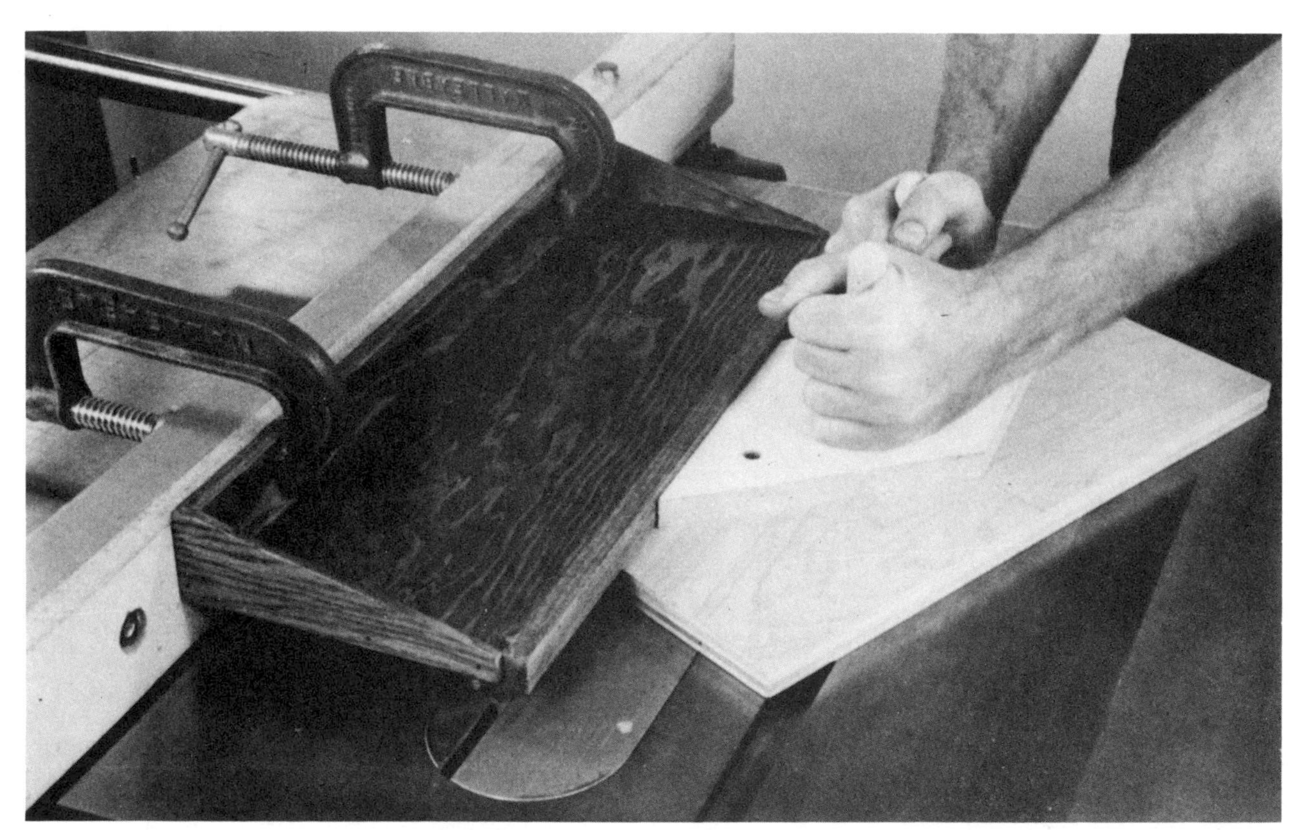

Illus. 8-15. This auxiliary fence is handy for pattern sawing. Use a dense, hard wood for the edge on which the pattern rides.

Illus. 8-16. The base of the irregular cutting jig is cut to size after the cleat is installed. When cutting parts, use the same blade used to cut the base.

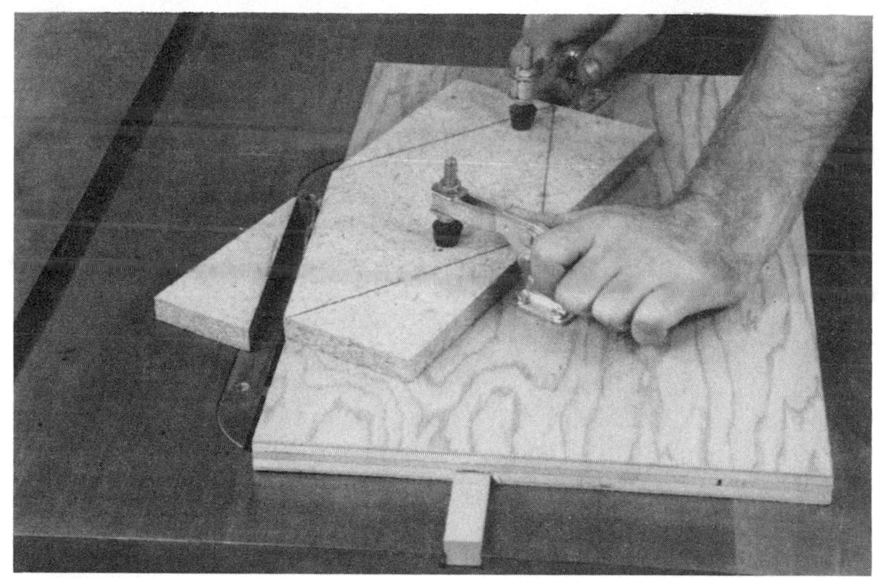

Illus. 8-17. Any object clamped along the ege of the irregular cutting jig will be cut on the line.

Illus. 8-18. This circle-cutting jig is an accessory that can be made for your table saw.

jig used to cut irregular parts. The size of the jig is determined by the diameter of the circle being cut. The jig is about four inches larger than the diameter of the circle. Attach the clamping device (Illus. 8-19) in the correct location for the circle diameter being cut. More information can be found in Chapter 6 (pages 229 and 230).

For pieces with inclined edges, a wedge-cutting jig (Illus. 8-20) or a taper-cutting jig (Illus. 8-21) can be built. The size of the wedge determines the layout of the wedge-cutting jig. A detailed look at the tapering jig appears in Chapter 6 (pages 222–229).

Illus. 8-19. This clamping device is used to hold stock against the circle-cutting jig. It can also be used on other shop-made jigs.

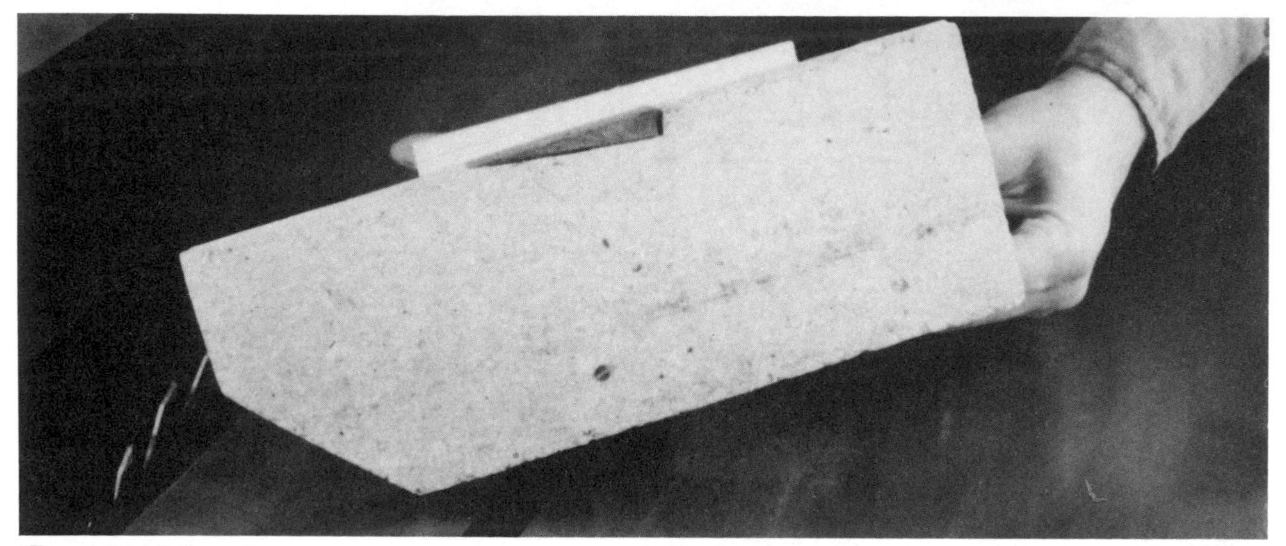

Illus. 8-20. This wedge-cutting jig is a project you may wish to make for your table saw.

Illus. 8-21. This tapering jig is a handy jig for your table saw. See Illus. 6-185 for a detailed drawing.

The parallels used for laying out a cove (Illus. 8-22) can also be made in the shop. Study Illus. 8-23, and then rip your stock to 1¼ inches. Cut your parts to length and lay out the holes. Drill the ¼-inch holes through all the parts. Counterbore the bottom holes to accommodate T nuts (Illus. 8-24). Assemble the parts and test for accuracy.

Building a Universal Jig The universal jig (Illus. 8-25) is actually several jigs in one. It has several work faces that can be attached to it. Each work face does a different job, such as tenoning, cutting feathers, or cutting splines. These work faces can also be made for specialty operations and attached

Illus. 8-22. These parallels are helpful when you are laying out a cove.

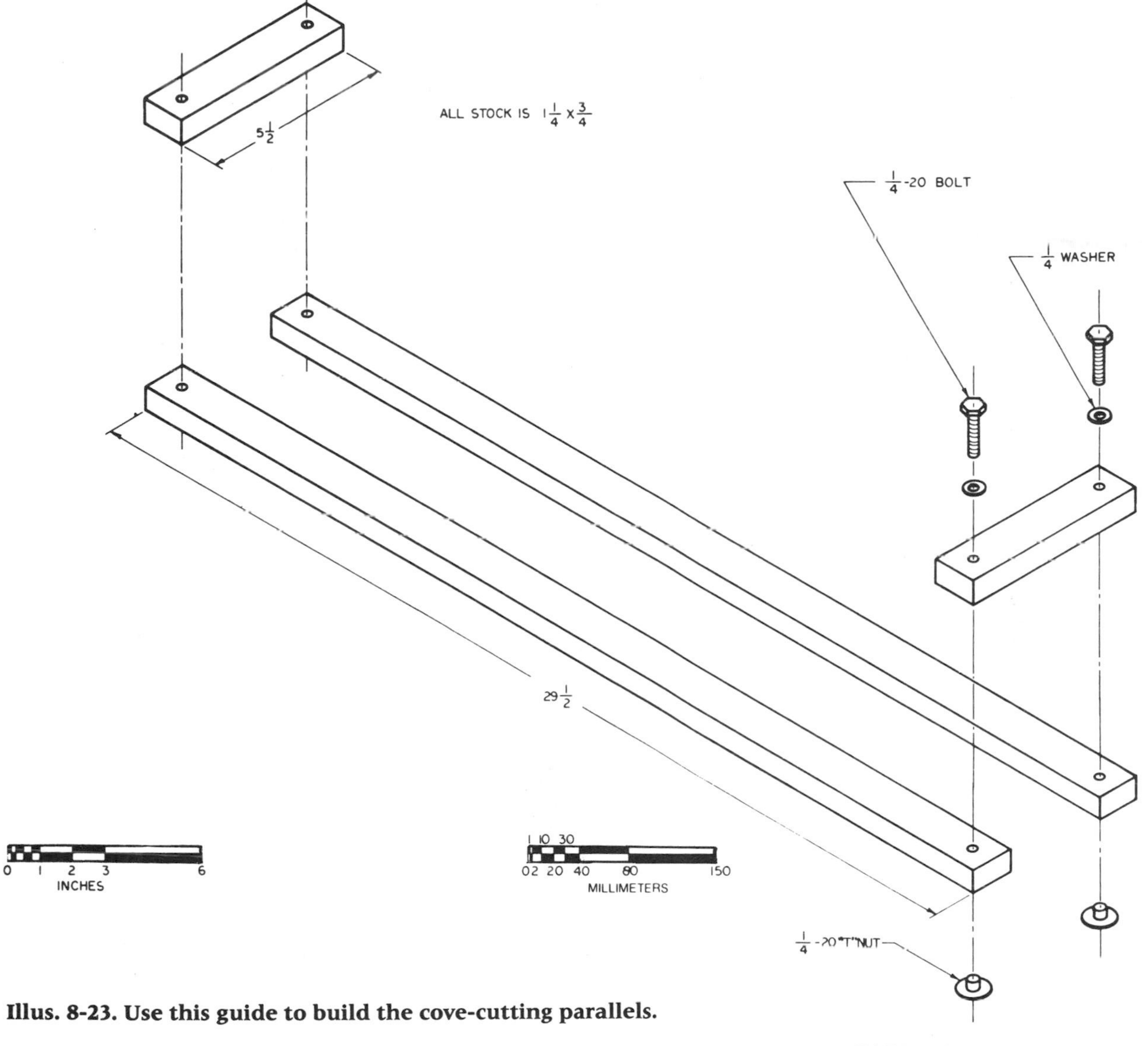

Illus. 8-23. Use this guide to build the cove-cutting parallels.

Illus. 8-24. Counterbore the bottom holes to accommodate the T nuts.

Illus. 8-25. This universal jig is several jigs in one. It is controlled by a cleat that rides in the miter slot.

to the sub-face of the jig. Only one jig is made. A new work face is made for different operations.

The subbase of the universal jig rides in the miter slot. A lock knob (Illus. 8-26) controls movement of the base on the subbase. The base is actually two pieces connected to form a right angle. The work faces are attached to the vertical part of the base. They are held in position with flathead machine screws and T nuts.

Begin this project by studying Illus. 8-27. Study this assembly drawing until you can name the parts and understand how they work.

Study the subbase drawing (Illus. 8-28) and develop a bill of materials. Cut the base to size, and cut the dado for the cleat that rides in the miter slot. The distance from the cleat to the edge of the subbase should be slightly less than the distance from the blade to the miter slot. Glue the cleat in position (Illus. 8-29).

Study the base drawing (Illus. 8-30), and develop a bill of materials. Cut the bottom of the base to size. Cut a dado in the bottom of that part and a matching dado in the top of the subbase. This dado must be perpendicular to the cleat dadoed into the bottom of the subbase.

Glue a cleat in the dado cut in the subbase. Remove any excess glue. Test the fit of the bottom of the base and the subbase. The parts should slide smoothly, but should not be loose. Install the flathead bolt through the subbase. Cut a matching hole in the bottom of the base and test the movement. See Illus. 8-28 and 8-30 for placement of the bolt.

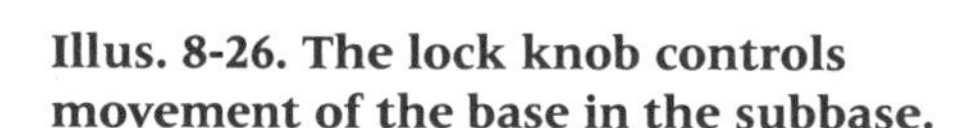

Illus. 8-26. The lock knob controls movement of the base in the subbase.

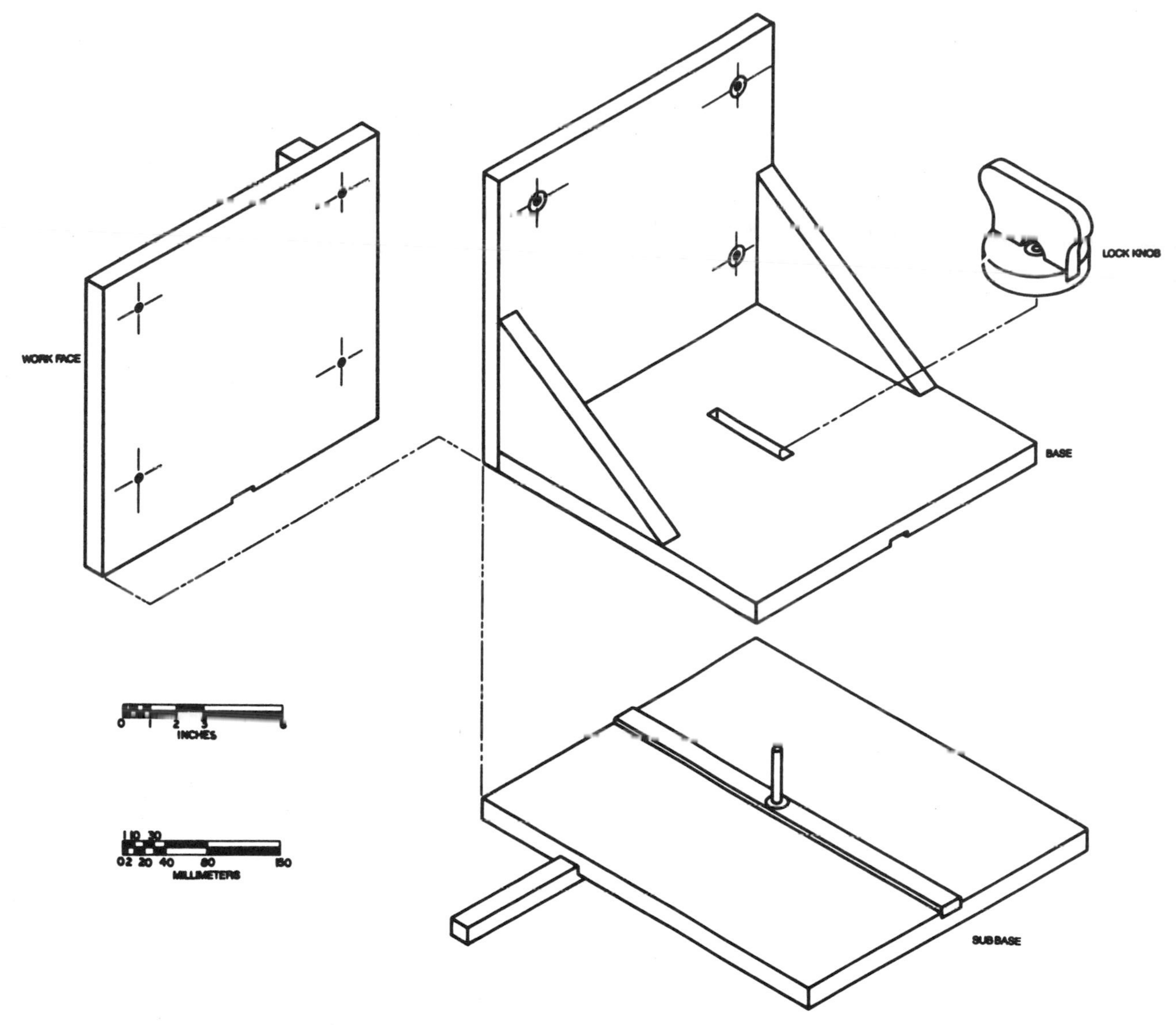

Illus. 8-27. This assembly drawing will help you identify the parts and undersand how they fit together.

Assemble the rest of the base. The subface is attached to the bottom of the base. Make sure these parts are perpendicular to each other. Attach the triangular braces to anchor the base assembly parts. Use glue and screws for assembly. Remove any excess glue before it cures.

Cut a notch in the subface to accommodate the cleat on the subbase. Do this with hand tools. The base and subbase should slide smoothly on each other.

Study the drawings for the work faces (Illus. 8-31 and 8-32) and develop a bill of materials. Cut the actual faces first. Cut some extra faces for specialty work you may do later.

Lay out the screw pattern for anchoring the work face to the subface on a template. Mark all the work faces and subface. Drill the holes. Install T nuts in the subface and countersink the holes in the work face. Test the fit. Make any needed adjustments. Attach the appropriate cleats to the work faces. See Illus. 8-31 and 8-32 for details.

Study the drawing for the lock knob (Illus. 8-33) and develop a bill of materials. Begin by laying out circles on a plywood scrap (Illus. 8-34). Drill a

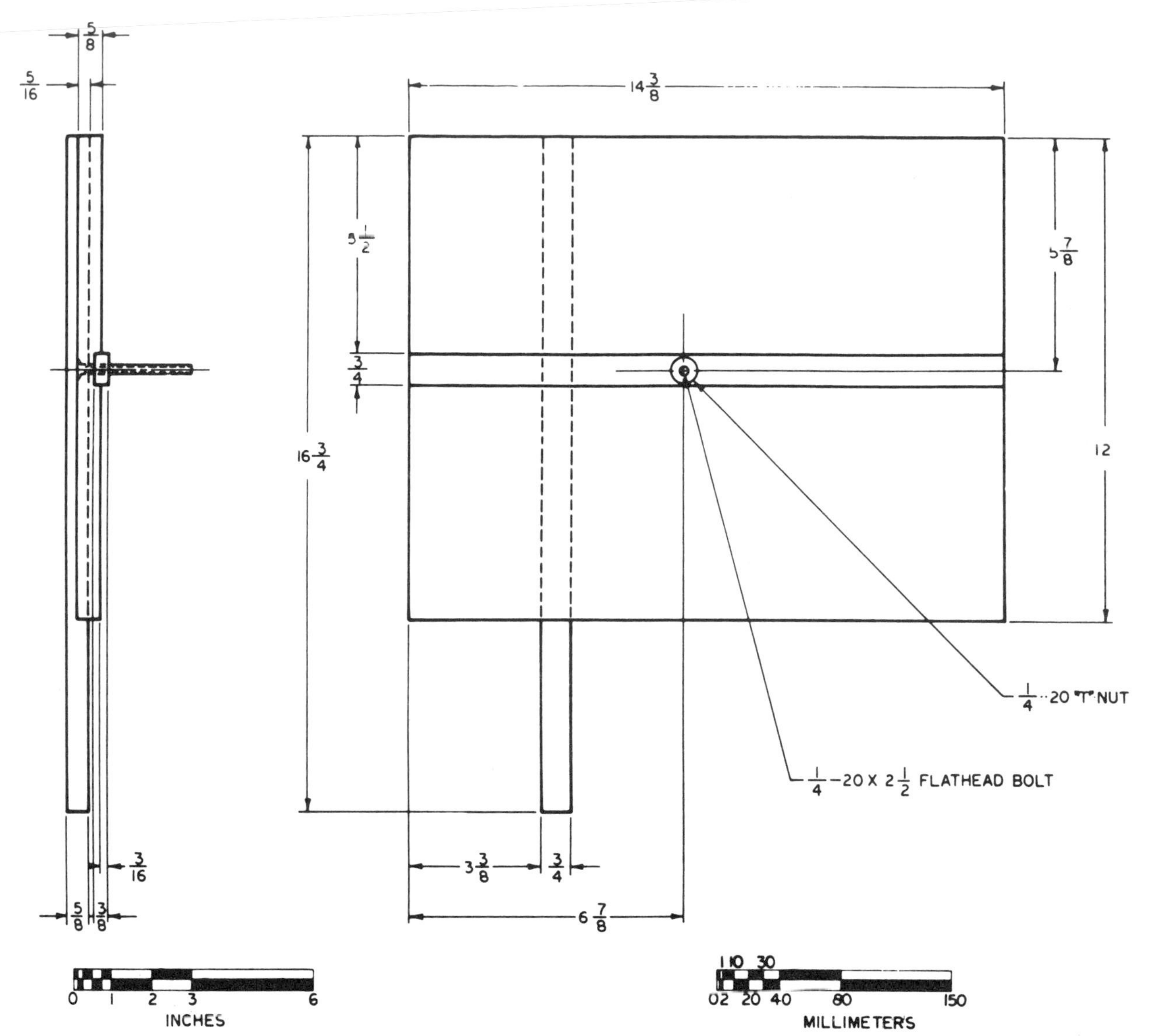

Illus. 8-28. This drawing of the subbase will help you build it accurately. Cleat position will vary according to table-saw make and model.

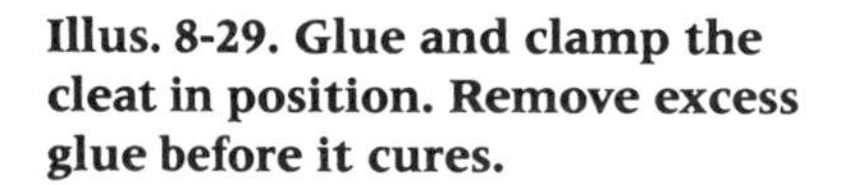

Illus. 8-29. Glue and clamp the cleat in position. Remove excess glue before it cures.

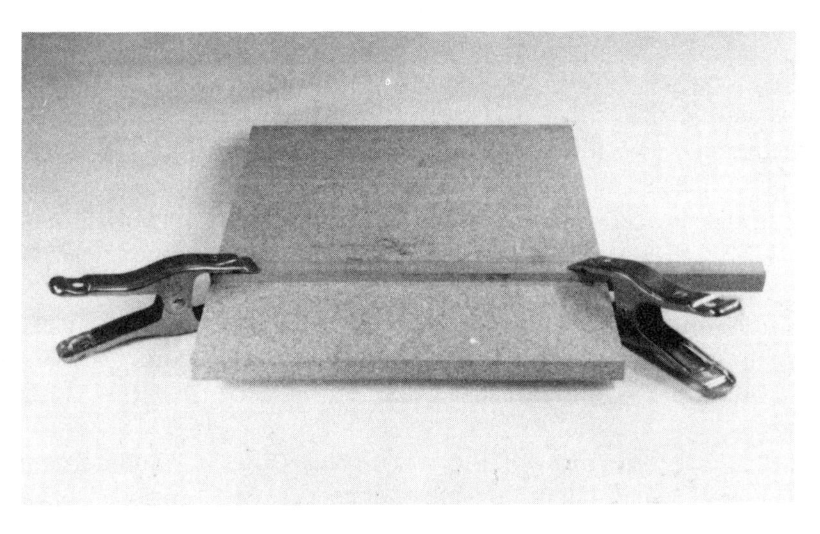

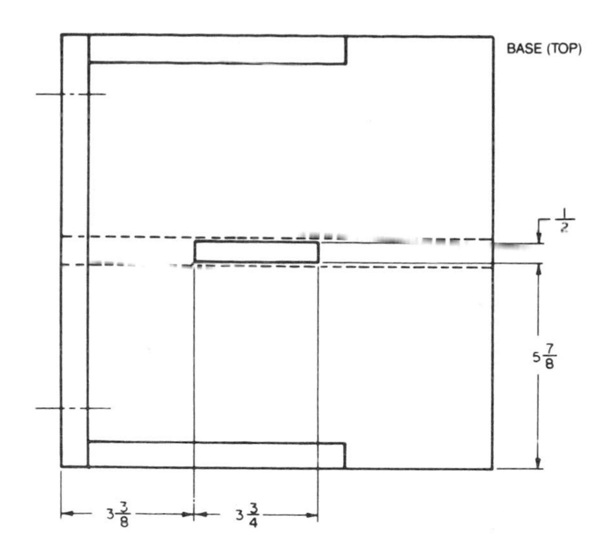

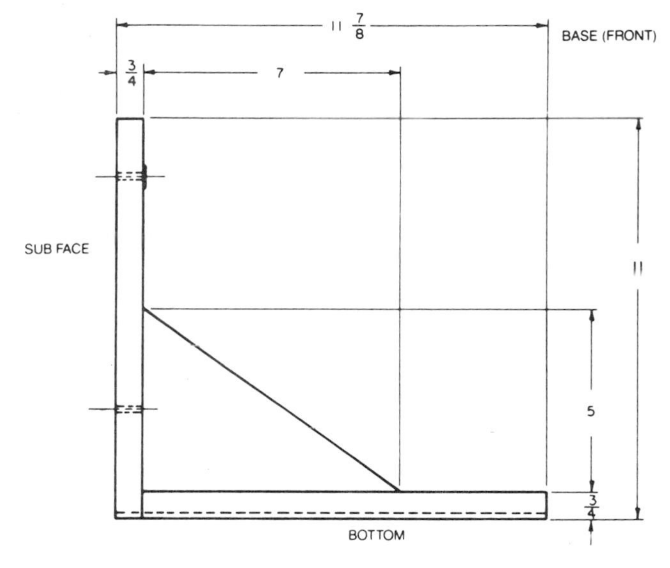

Illus. 8-30. Study this drawing of the base before cutting or assembling the parts.

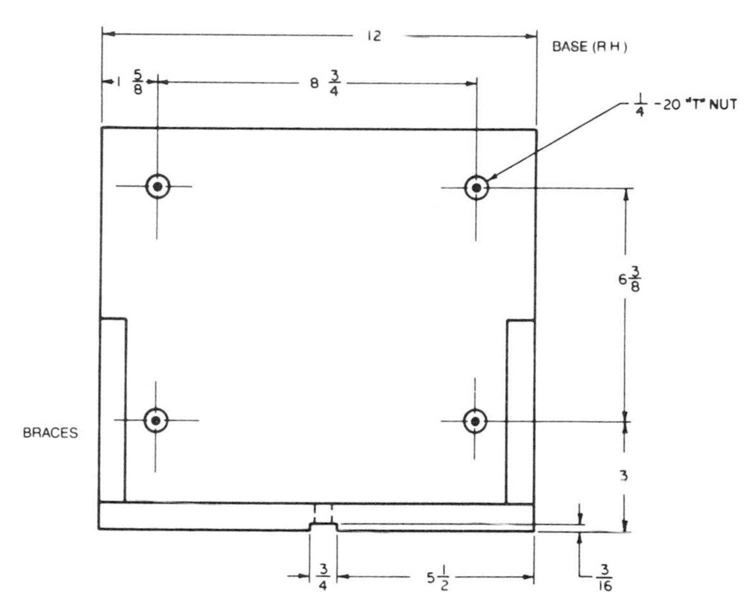

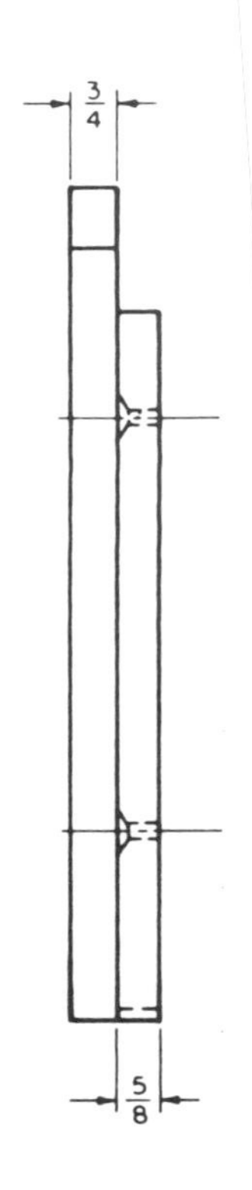

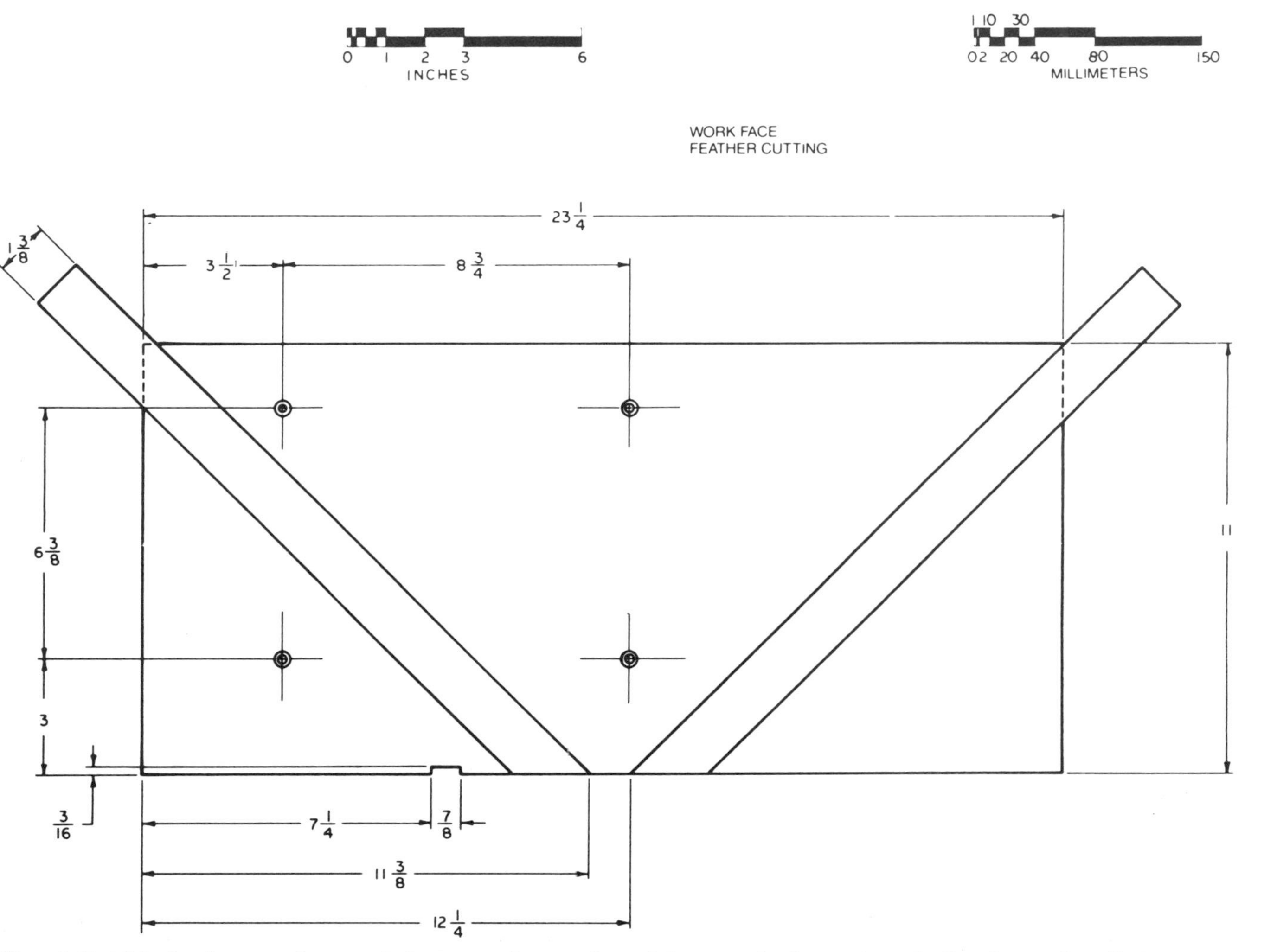

Illus. 8-31. This feather-cutting work face attaches to the subface on the base. Attach the cleats after fitting the work face to the subface.

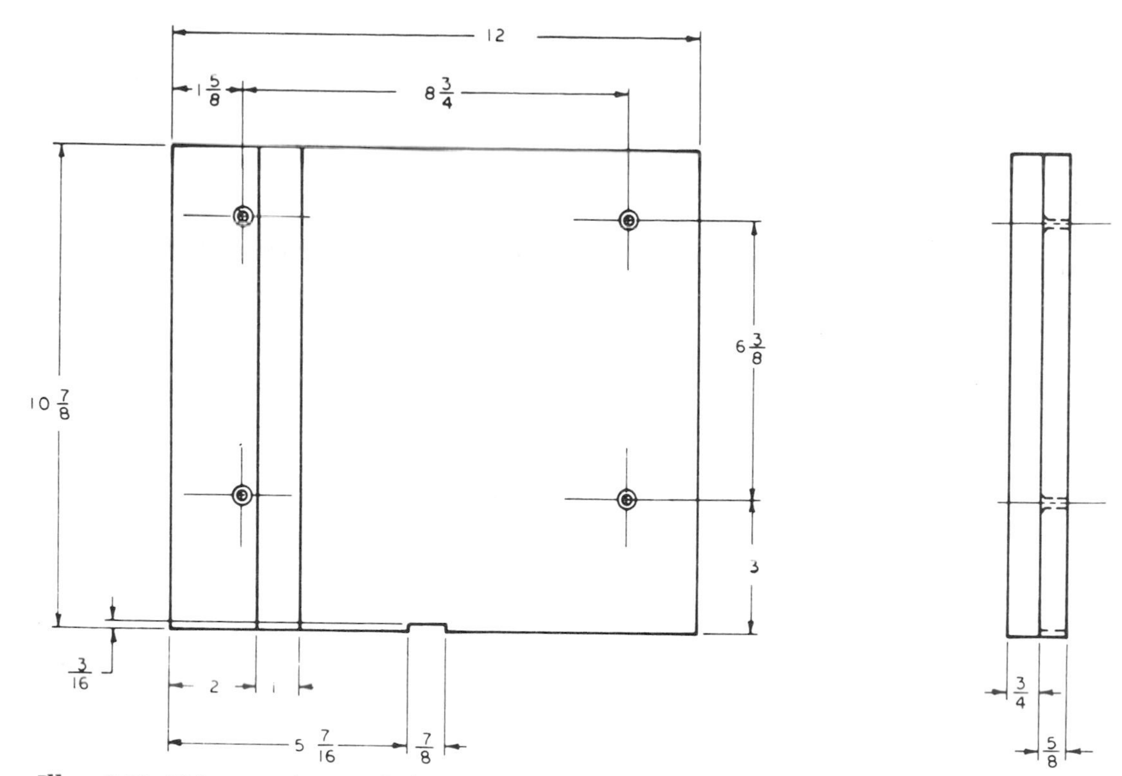

Illus. 8-32. This tenoning work face attaches to the subface on the base. Attach the cleats after fitting them to the work face.

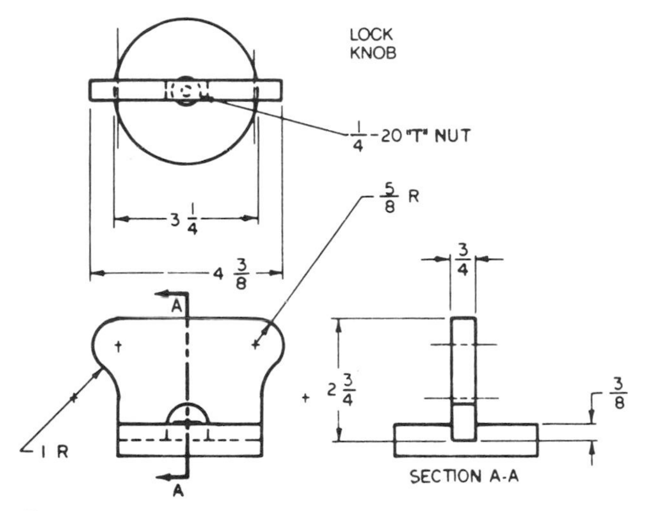

Illus. 8-33. Study this drawing and Illus. 8-34–8-39 before making the lock knob.

small hole through the center of the circles. Dado through the center of these circles (Illus. 8-35). Make the dado one-half the depth of the stock. The dado should be enough for the handle.

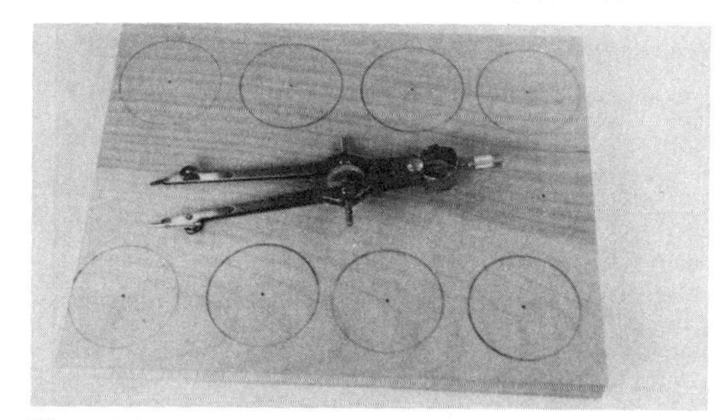
Illus. 8-34. Lay out circles for the lock knobs on plywood. Drill small holes through the center of the circles.

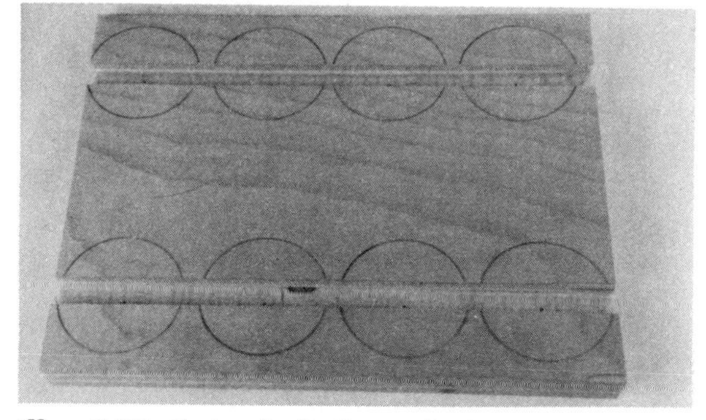
Illus. 8-35. Cut a dado through the circles. The handle fits in this dado.

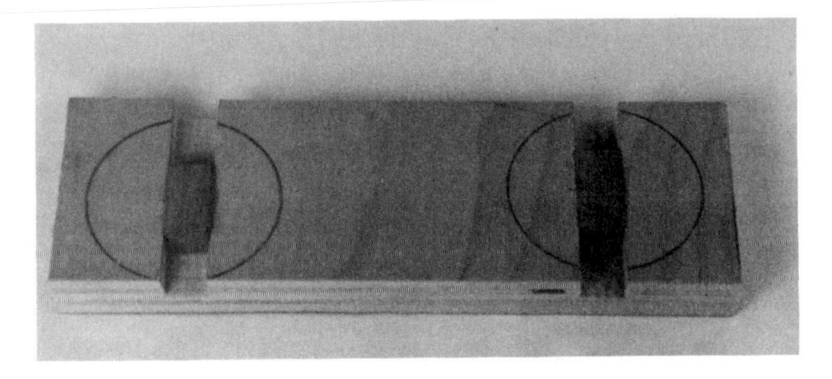

Illus. 8-36. A piece of stock is glued in the dado to hold the T nut.

Glue a piece of stock one inch long in the dado (Illus. 8-36). Cut out the circle and drill a hole through it (Illus. 8-37). The hole should accommodate a T nut. Use the small hole drilled earlier as a pilot hole. Install the T nut (Illus. 8-38) and glue the handle in place (Illus. 8-39).

Illus. 8-37. Drill a hole through the circle to accommodate the T nut. Use the small hole drilled earlier as a pilot hole.

Illus. 8-38. Drive the T nut into position with a hammer. Make sure it is centered and anchored securely.

Illus. 8-39. Glue the handle in position. Allow the glue to cure before using the handle.

Test the universal jig for ease of movement. Remember to make extra work faces for specialty work. You may also wish to make a few extra lock knobs. These can be used on other jigs you make.

Projects

Building a Chisel Case and Sharpening-Stone Box
The chisel case (Illus. 8-41) is a challenging project to build. It allows you to experiment with finger joints, raised panels (Illus. 8-42), and resawing. The project is small, so any errors are inexpensive.

The sharpening-stone box (Illus. 8-43) has no raised panel on top, yet it can be just as challenging. Begin by studying the drawings for the chisel case (Illus. 8-40). Notice that the box is actually made two fingers larger than the desired size. When the box is cut open, two fingers are removed. This keeps the rhythm of the fingers constant on the case corners. Note the rhythm of the corner of this box (Illus. 8-44). If only one finger were removed, the corner would have two dark fingers (end grain) next to each other.

In some cases, it may not be desirable to remove two fingers from a box. Another approach is to use a V-shaped cutter to shape all four faces where the kerf is to be made (Illus. 8-45). A fine-tooth blade can cut through the center of the V cut (Illus. 8-46). The same cutting procedure for opening the box is used (Illus. 8-47). The remaining portion of the V cut accents the separation line and minimizes the clash of two fingers or two cuts.

Review the procedures for resawing (pages 180–185), cutting raised panels, and cutting finger joints (pages 194–207) in Chapter 6. Make sure you understand the procedures before you begin. Develop a bill of materials for your case or box.

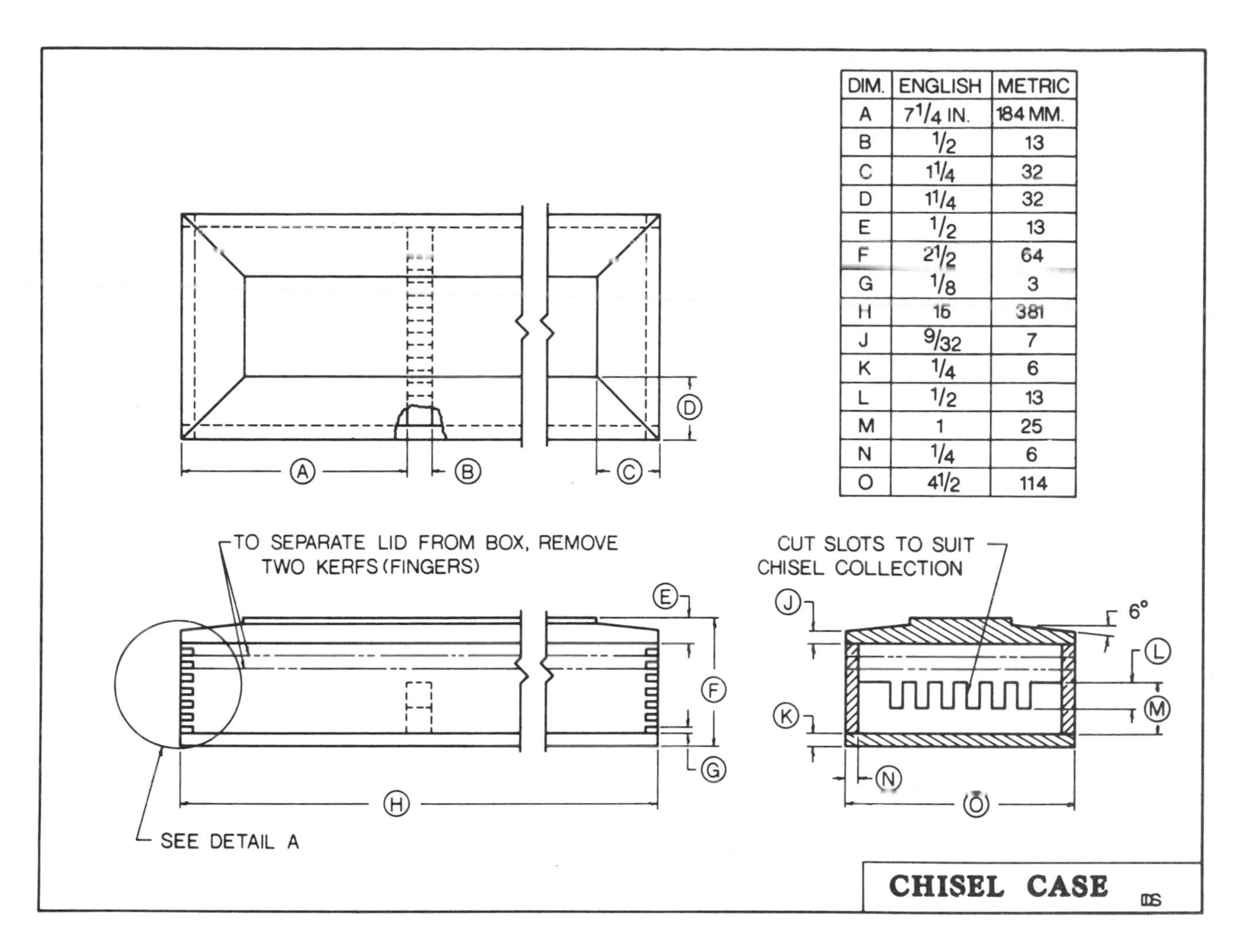

DIM.	ENGLISH	METRIC
A	$7\frac{1}{4}$ IN.	184 MM.
B	$\frac{1}{2}$	13
C	$1\frac{1}{4}$	32
D	$1\frac{1}{4}$	32
E	$\frac{1}{2}$	13
F	$2\frac{1}{2}$	64
G	$\frac{1}{8}$	3
H	15	381
J	$\frac{9}{32}$	7
K	$\frac{1}{4}$	6
L	$\frac{1}{2}$	13
M	1	25
N	$\frac{1}{4}$	6
O	$4\frac{1}{2}$	114

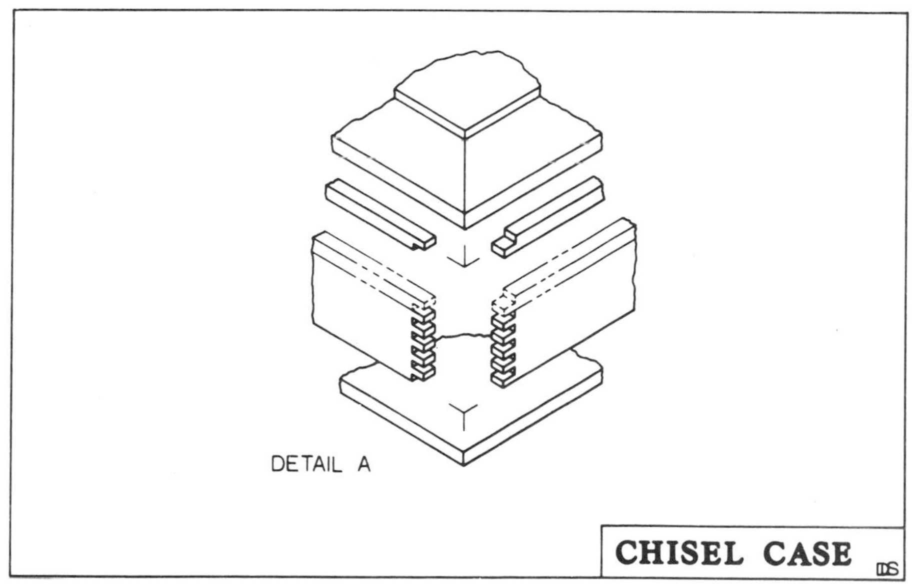

Illus. 8-40. Study these drawings carefully before beginning the chisel case or sharpening-stone box. See Illus. 8-41–8-44 for a look at the chisel case and sharpening-stone box.

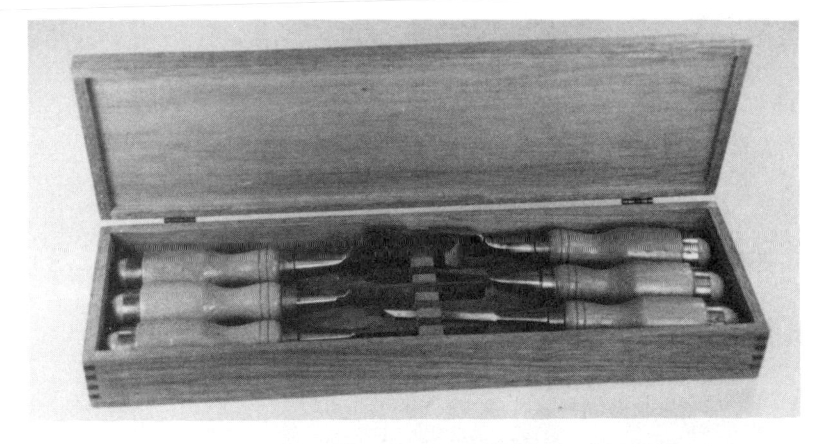

Illus. 8-41. This chisel case has finger joints.

Illus. 8-42. The raised-panel lid on the chisel case adds to its appearance.

Illus. 8-43. This sharpening-stone box also has finger joints.

Illus. 8-44. Two fingers were removed when this box was cut open. Note the uninterrupted rhythm of the fingers because of this.

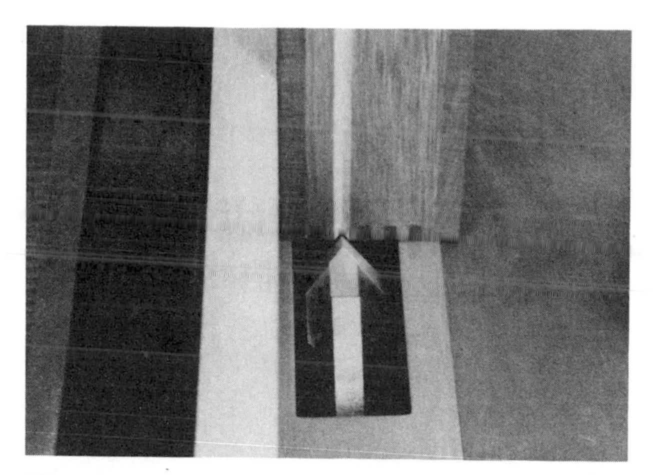

Illus. 8-45. A V-shaped cutter can be used to mark the separation line of a box. Only one cut is made on this box.

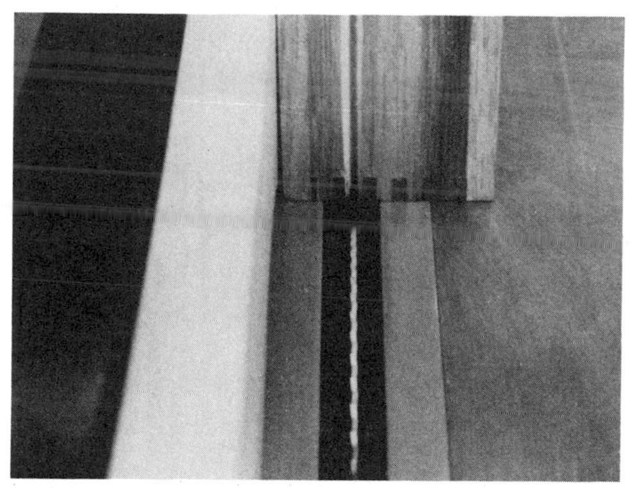

Illus. 8-46. A fine-tooth blade cuts a kerf down the center of the V-shaped cut.

Illus. 8-47. This box is opened with a dovetail saw or backsaw. Note how the kerfs go through the stock on the long faces.

Make some detailed drawings for the sharpening-stone box if you decide to build it.

If you make a sharpening-stone box, the length and width of your parts will equal the length (or width) of your stone plus two times the thickness of your stock. The width of your parts will equal the thickness of the stone plus two fingers. This is the exact size. You may want to make the parts longer or wider for trimming purposes (Illus. 8-48).

Illus. 8-48. These fingers extend beyond the end of the box, so they can be trimmed and sanded. Make an allowance on your bill of materials if you plan to do this.

For the chisel case or other finger-joint boxes using hinges, select the hardware first (Illus. 8-49). Sometimes the hardware available for small boxes is limited. It is best to select it first. Not finding the correct hardware for something you have already built is disappointing.

Illus. 8-49. Select hardware that is correct for your project. It is wise to buy the hardware first.

Make the jig with the correct-sized spacer. If possible, select a saw blade that cuts a kerf with a flat bottom. Attach the jig to the miter gauge (Illus. 8-50) and make a test cut (Illus. 8-51). Make adjustments according to the procedures outlined in Chapter 6.

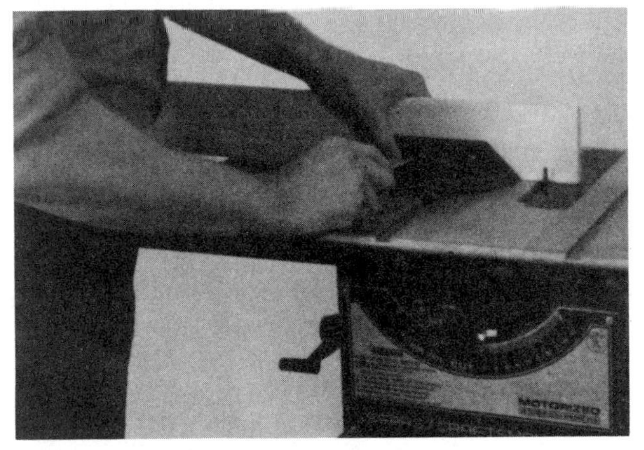

Illus. 8-50. Attach the finger-cutting jig to the miter gauge. See Chapter 6 (page 195) for additional setup details.

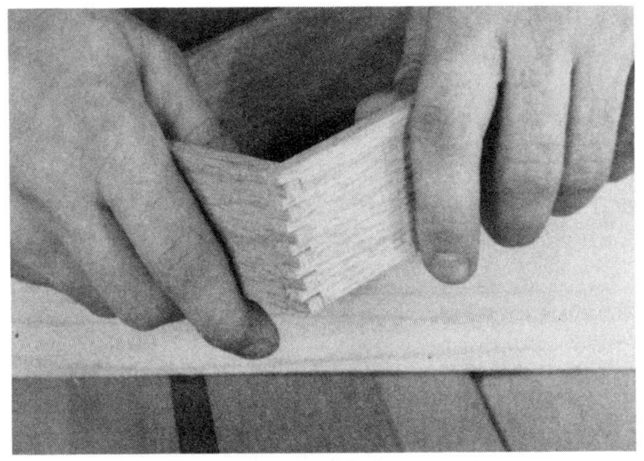

Illus. 8-51. Make a test cut and adjust the jig accordingly. Use the same species of wood for the test cut that you plan to use for the project. The fit varies according to the hardness of the species.

Test the fit of the parts first. Glue them together carefully. Make sure the box or case is square. The stone box is now ready for the top and bottom. Cut them slightly oversize and glue them in position (Illus. 8-52). You may have to sand the top and bottom of the box to produce a smooth surface. Check the surface before gluing the top and bottom in position.

Make the raised panel lit for the chisel case and sand it smooth. Glue and clamp it in position (Illus.

Illus. 8-52. Cut the top and bottom oversize and glue them to the box. Then sand the entire box smooth.

8-53). The lid may be slightly oversized, for sanding purposes. Sand the case or box completely before cutting it open.

Illus. 8-53. Also make the raised-panel lid slightly oversize. Sand it after the glue cures.

Use a fine-tooth blade to cut the case or box open (Illus. 8-54). Set the blade height to slightly less than the stock thickness. Cut a kerf on all four faces. This kerf is on the edge of a finger. Make four more kerfs at the edge of a cut. Raise the blade height to just over more than the thickness of the stock. Saw through the long faces again (Illus. 8-55).

The kerf placement on the sharpening-stone box (Illus. 8-56) and the chisel case (Illus. 8-57) will be different. Both boxes are held together by the stock remaining in the kerfs on the short faces. Use a

Illus. 8-54. A fine-tooth blade is used to cut the box open. The first kerf is set at the edge of a finger.

Illus. 8-55. Make four more kerfs at the edge of a cut or slot. Then raise the blade to cut through the long faces.

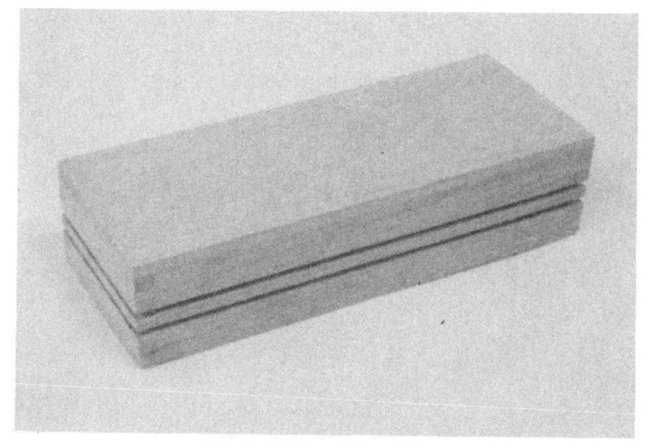

Illus. 8-56. The kerfs are almost centered on the sharpening-stone box. The stock remaining in the kerfs of the short faces holds the box together.

Illus. 8-57. On the chisel case, the kerfs are placed closer to the lid.

dovetail saw or backsaw to separate the top and bottom (Illus. 8-58).

Illus. 8-58. Separate the box with a dovetail saw (as shown here) or with a backsaw. Use the kerfs as a guide for the saw.

Attach hardware and make the slotted rack to hold the chisels. Use your own chisels as models for this part. Apply the finish of your choice to complete the sharpening-stone box and chisel case.

Building a Tool Case Building a tool case (Illus. 8-59) is similar to building the chisel case and sharpening-stone box. The chief difference is that a dado head is used to cut the slots between the fingers. The parts are also larger and thicker. More support is needed behind the parts when the slots are cut. A special finger-cutting jig was made to make the tool case (Illus. 8-60). This jig is controlled by the fence, so minor adjustments can be made by moving the fence.

This jig is easy to make. Study Illus. 8-61 to see how the parts fit together. The slide attaches to the fence. It guides the finger jig. The backing board is attached to the finger jig. The backing board can be changed for fingers of different widths and lengths.

Begin by making the slide (Illus. 8-62). The slide attaches to the fence. Make the mating part of the finger jig (Illus. 8-63) next. Assemble the finger jig and test its operation on the slide. The cabinet glide or thumbtack on the finger jig reduces friction. Make sure it is in place before testing the operation.

Illus. 8-59. This tool case has finger joints that must be cut with a dado head. Larger projects mean greater challenges. Large pieces are apt to warp; this can make cutting fingers or assembling the work more difficult.

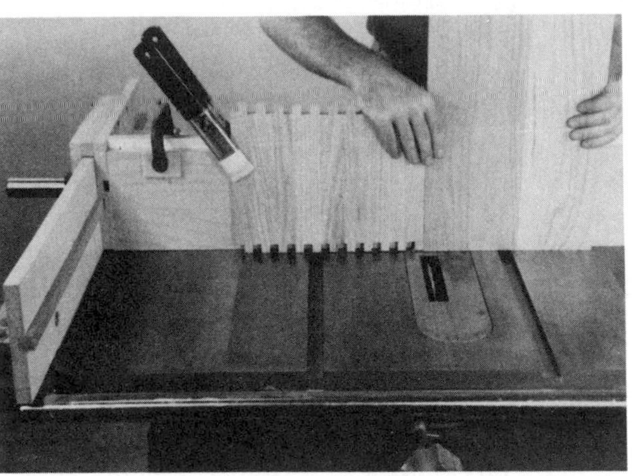

Illus. 8-60. The jig used to cut large fingers is controlled by the fence. Minor adjustments of finger size can be made by moving the fence.

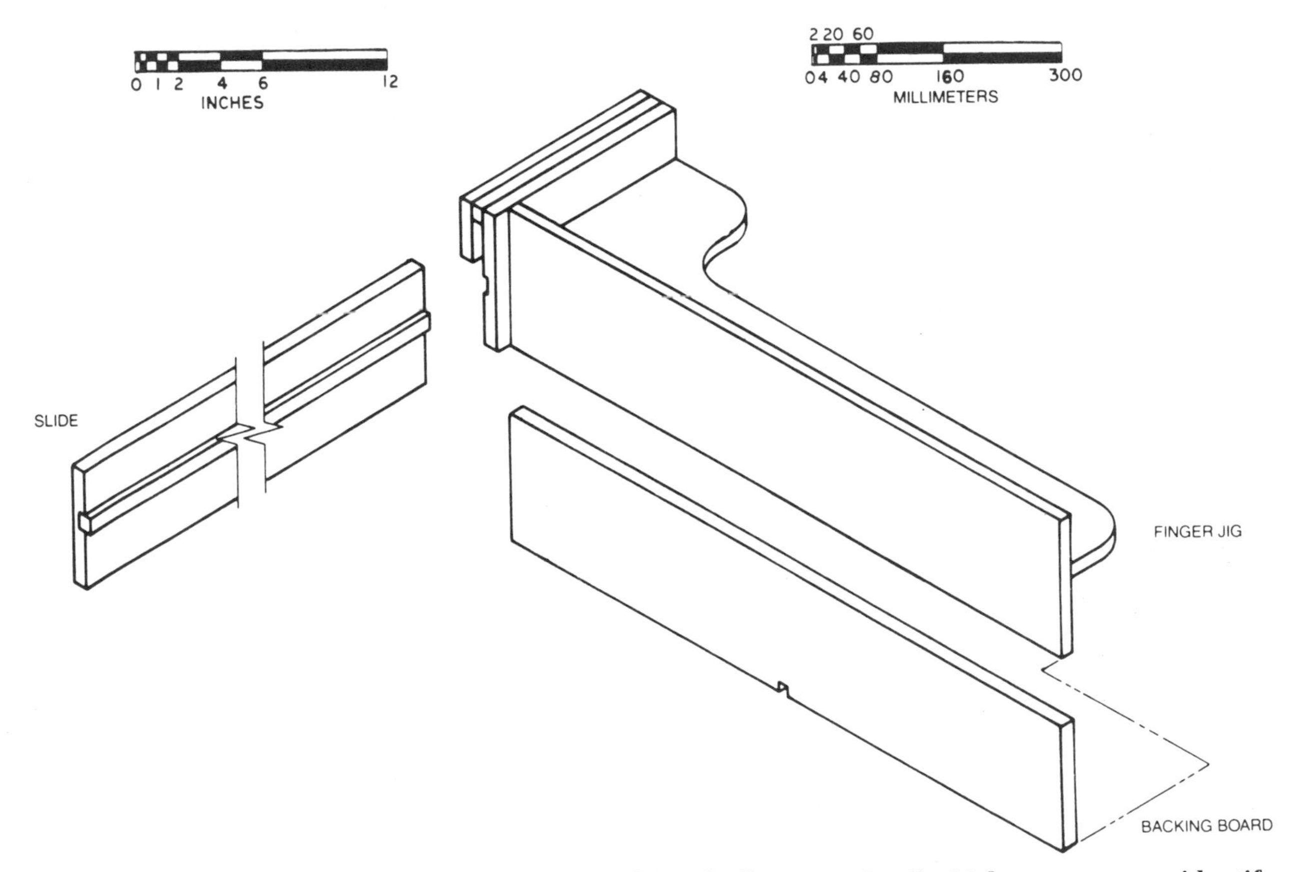

Illus. 8-61. Study this assembly drawing before making the finger-cutting jig. Make sure you can identify each part and how it fits in the assembly.

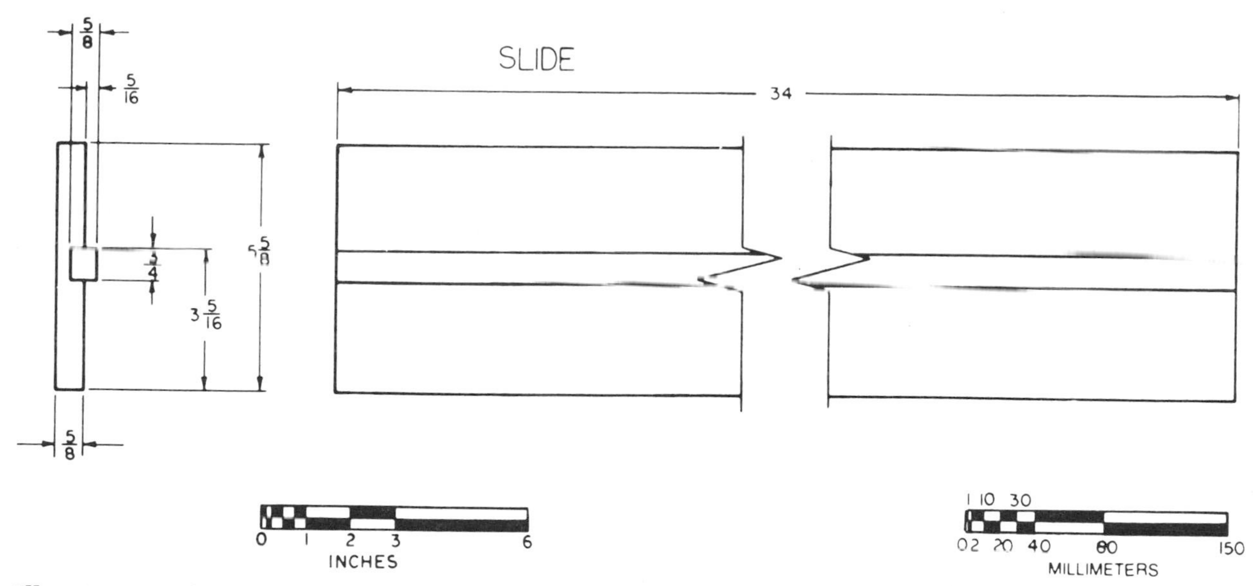

Illus. 8-62. Study this drawing of the slide. Lay out your stock carefully.

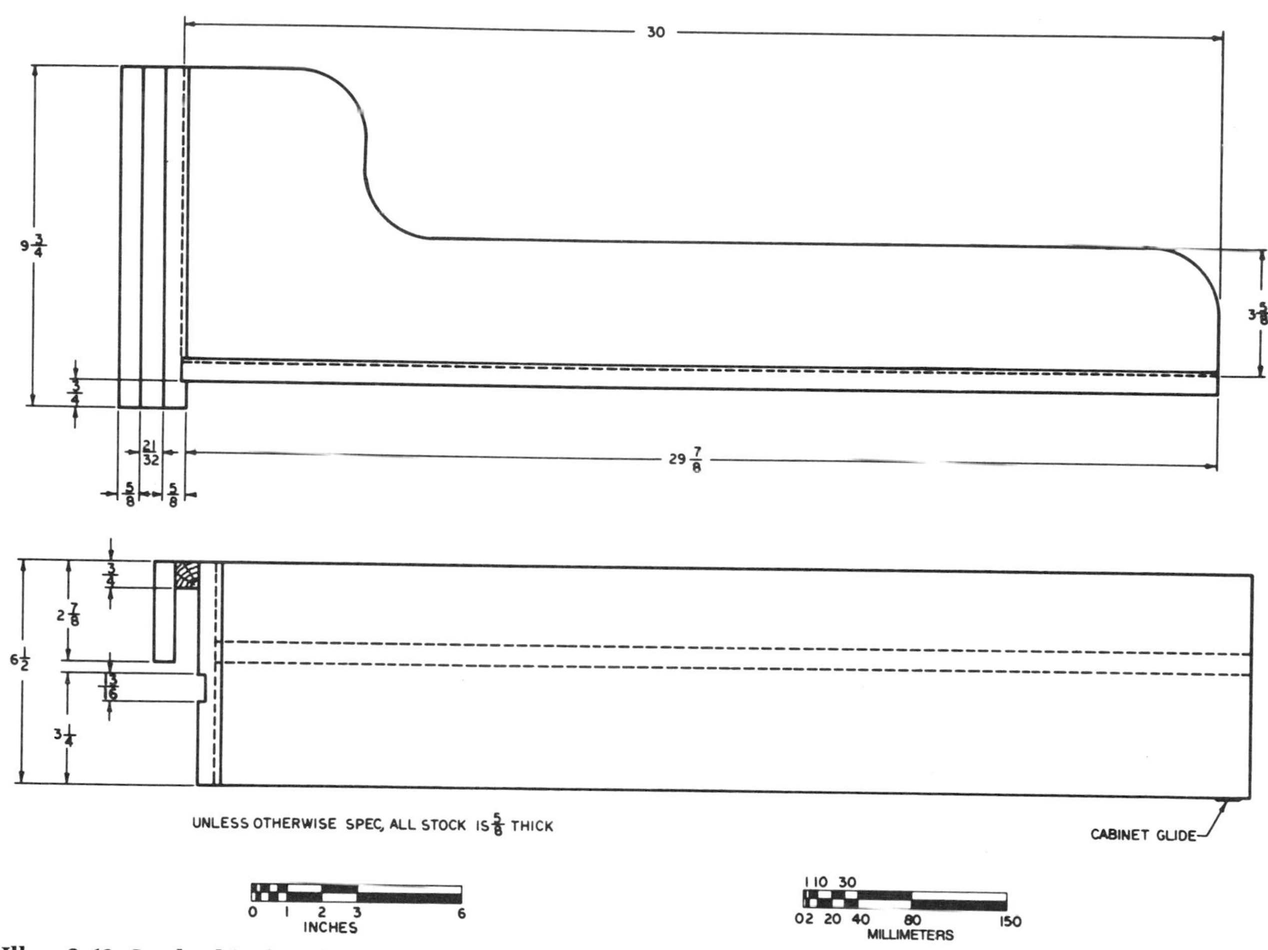

Illus. 8-63. Study this drawing of the finger jig before you begin construction. Make the part that fits the slide first.

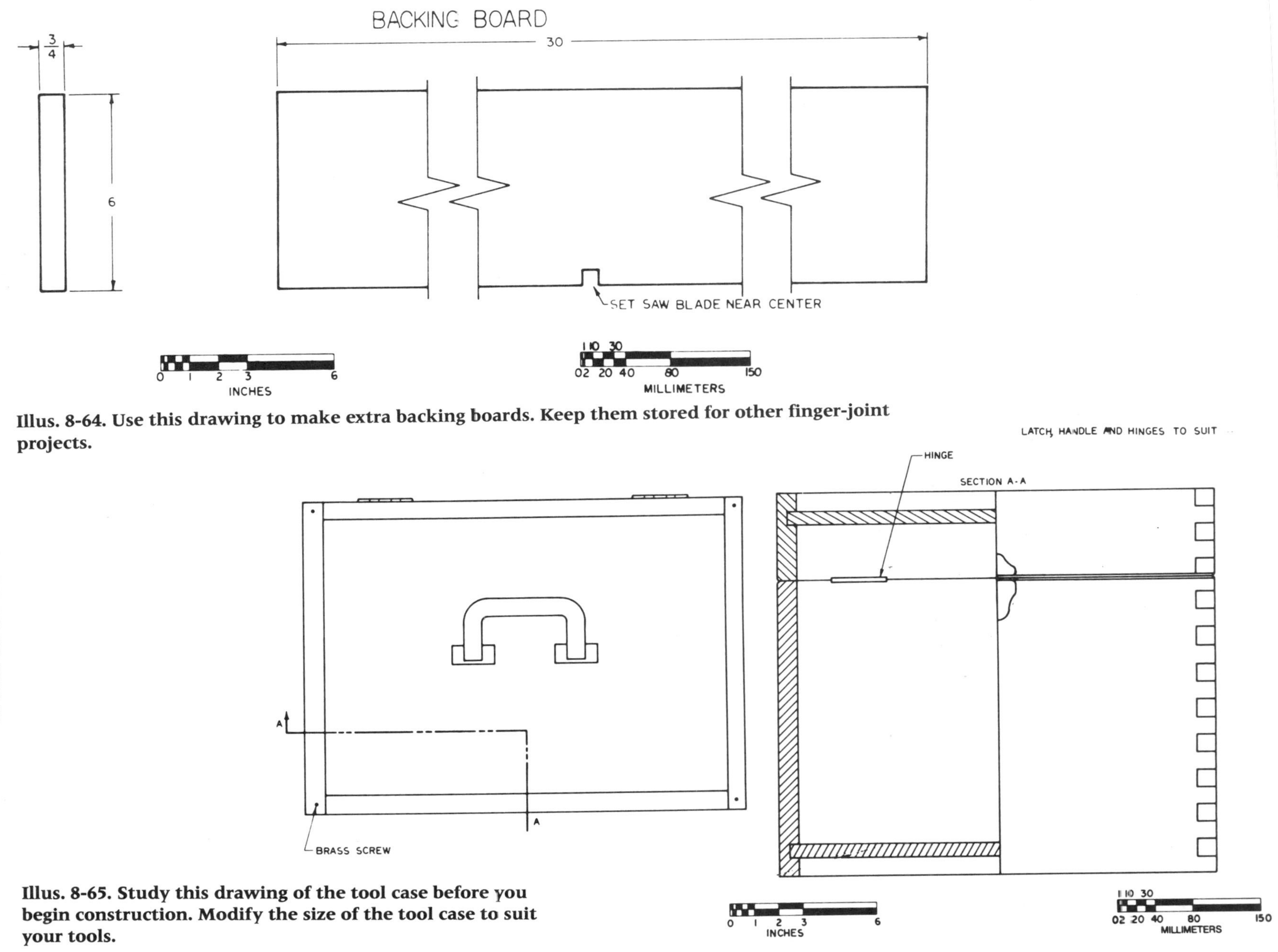

Illus. 8-64. Use this drawing to make extra backing boards. Keep them stored for other finger-joint projects.

Illus. 8-65. Study this drawing of the tool case before you begin construction. Modify the size of the tool case to suit your tools.

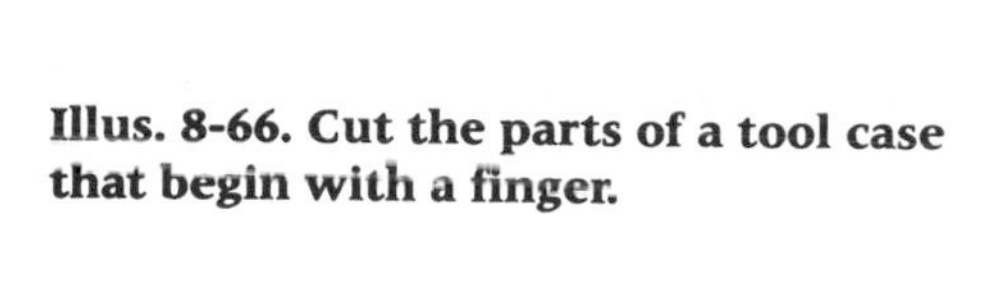

Illus. 8-66. Cut the parts of a tool case that begin with a finger.

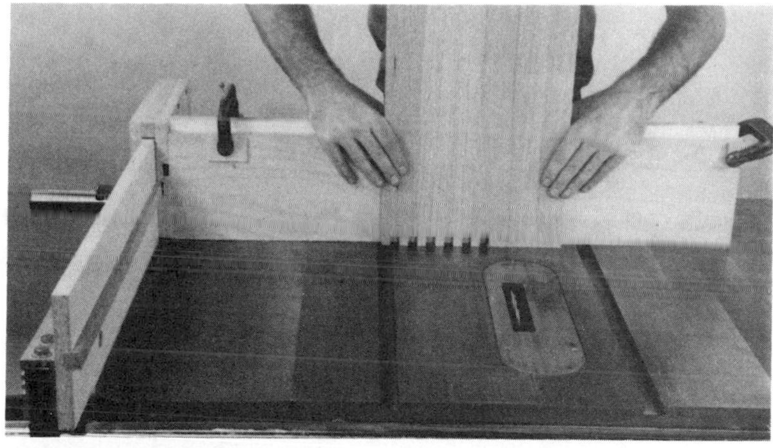

Illus. 8-67. Use a full finger to locate the first slot on the mating sides. Hold stock securely while making this cut.

Illus. 8-68. Test the fit of the fingers without glue. Lay out the dadoes for the top and bottom from this assembly.

Make two or three backing boards (Illus. 8-64). Keep them on hand for other finger cuts. Attach a backing board to the finger jig. Lock the fence at the right edge of the table (Illus. 8-60). This will help you determine where the slot will be cut and where the stop pin should be placed. Cut a kerf and install the stop pin. Make it smaller than the slots you plan to cut.

Install the desired-size dado head and make a trial cut. Adjust the fence until the fit between the fingers is correct. Allow some clearance for glue. A tight fit will become tighter when glue is applied.

Begin your tool case by studying Illus. 8-65. You can scale the drawing to make a case of the same size, or you can measure the tool you wish to house and develop a bill of materials. Make the parts wide enough to inset the top and bottom; if you don't, the case may not hold the intended tool. The tool case size in the drawing will house a 2-horsepower Milwaukee router.

First cut the parts that begin with a finger (Illus. 8-66). Then cut the parts that begin with a slot (Illus. 8-67). Use one of the parts that has a full finger as a guide. Test the fit of the fingers in a dry assembly (Illus. 8-68). Determine where the dadoes for the top and bottom must be cut. Lay them out and cut them with a router. *Note:* Both ends of the dado are blind. This operation should not be attempted on the table saw.

If so desired, you can make the top as a raised panel. This adds to the appearance of the case. Sand the top and bottom (both sides) and the inside of the four sides before assembly. Use a slow-setting glue to assemble the tool case. I used hide glue. This allowed plenty of time to shift the pieces into place. Do not glue the top and bottom into the dado. They should be free to expand and contract in the dado. Use plenty of clamps and strong backs (Illus. 8-69) to hold the parts together. Keep the clamps in place until the glue cures. Hide glue cures in about 12 to 16 hours.

Illus. 8-69. Use plenty of clamps and strong backs to hold the parts together.

Sand the case after the glue cures. It can now be cut open. Since the fingers are so large, a saw cut is all that is needed. Do not remove two fingers, as was the procedure with the chisel case and a sharpening-stone box. Make a V-shaped cut at the desired opening line (Illus. 8-70). Take light cuts, to avoid tear-out. Cut the box open with a fine-tooth blade (Illus. 8-71). Do not cut completely through the box. Separate the top and bottom with a dovetail saw or backsaw.

To lock the box together, I drove brass machine screws into all the corners (Illus. 8-72). Make the hole small enough so that the screw cuts a thread in the wood. Cut the head of the screw off with a hacksaw (Illus. 8-73) and file the screw smooth (Illus. 8-74). These screws add strength and beauty to the box. If desired, you can use a dowel instead of a brass machine screw.

Illus. 8-70. After sanding the case, make a V-shaped cut at the opening line. Take light cuts, to avoid tear-out.

Illus. 8-71. Cut the box open with a fine-tooth blade. Do not cut through the stock. Separate the parts with a dovetail saw.

Illus. 8-72. Drive a brass machine screw through the corners to lock them. Drill a hole small enough so the screw cuts threads in the box.

Illus. 8-73. Cut the head of the screw off with a hacksaw.

Illus. 8-74. File the screw flush with the surface of the wood.

Fit the handle and hinges in position. Apply the desired stain and finish.

Making Picture Frames Pictures frames are fun to make. They incorporate many woodworking operations and challenges. Many picture-frame operations allow you to use the shaper head. Flutes (Illus. 8-75), rabbets (Illus. 8-76), and coves (Illus. 8-77) are all common shaper operations employed on picture frames.

The rabbet for a frame that has compound miters

Illus. 8-75. The flute on this picture-frame part was cut with a shaper head.

Illus. 8-76. The rabbet for the glass on this frame part was cut with a shaper head. Two light cuts were required.

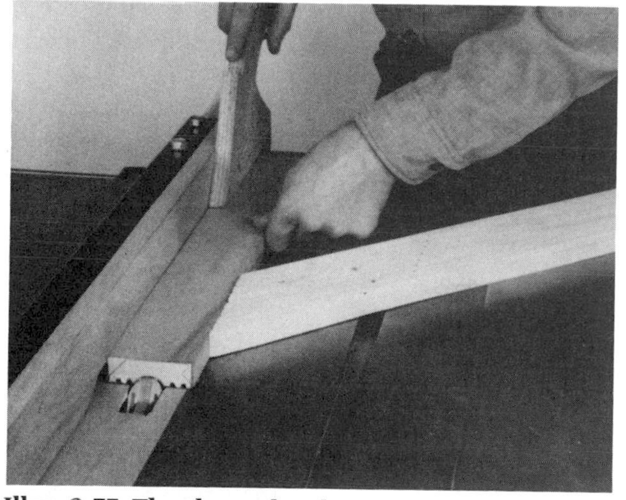

Illus. 8-77. The shaper head cuts an attractive cove on picture-frame parts.

can be made with a V cutter or a planer cutter (Illus. 8-78). The planer cutter is tilted to the 45-degree position for this cut. Remember to take light cuts.

Illus. 8-78. This planer cutter was tilted 45 degrees to cut a rabbet. This part is for a frame with compound miters.

Compound miters can also add a challenge to picture frames. The stock can be tilted to the desired angle and cut like a simple miter (Illus. 8-79). It can also be cut in the flat position, but this requires tilting both the blade and the miter gauge. Picture frames may incorporate special coves that must be cut with an inclined fence (Illus. 8-80). Review the procedures in Chapter 6 (page 194) before attempting this cut. Remember to remove most of the stock with a blade or dado head before making a cove cut.

Illus. 8-79. Compound miters make picture frames more challenging.

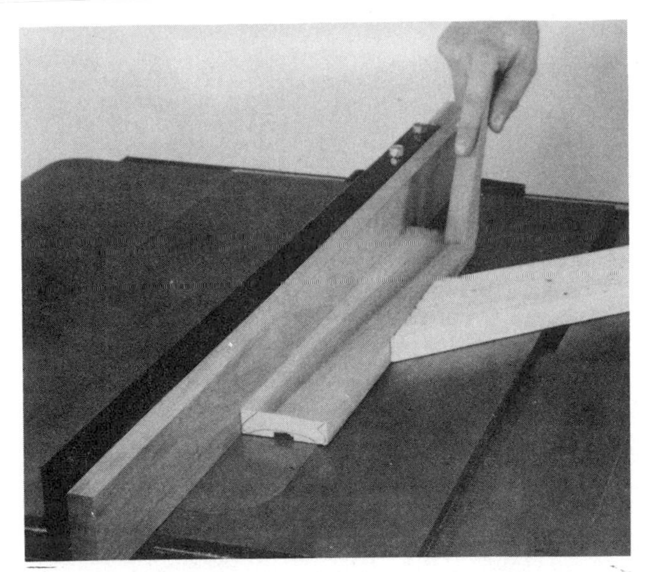

Illus. 8-80. The cove on this picture frame is cut with an inclined fence. Most of the stock is first removed with a dado head.

Begin with picture frames using simple miters. Stock with chamfered profiles (Illus. 8-81) is easy to fit when the corners do not match. Pare away the chamfers until the corners appear to fit perfectly.

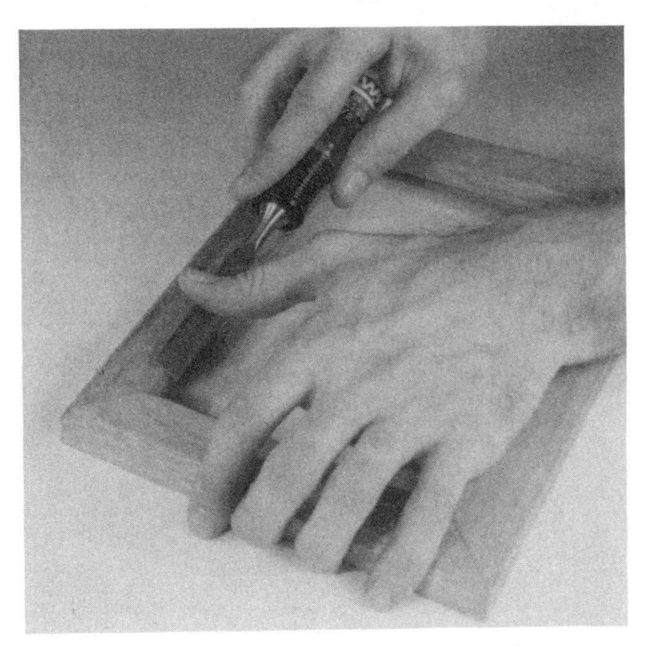

Illus. 8-81. Stock with chamfered profiles is easy to fit when the corners do not match.

The miters can be cut using the miter gauge (Illus. 8-82). Make sure your setup is accurate and the blade is sharp. A miter jig can also be used to cut miters. The stop block clamped to the fence ensures that all parts are of equal length (Illus. 8-83).

Illus. 8-82. Set up the miter gauge carefully to obtain accurate miters.

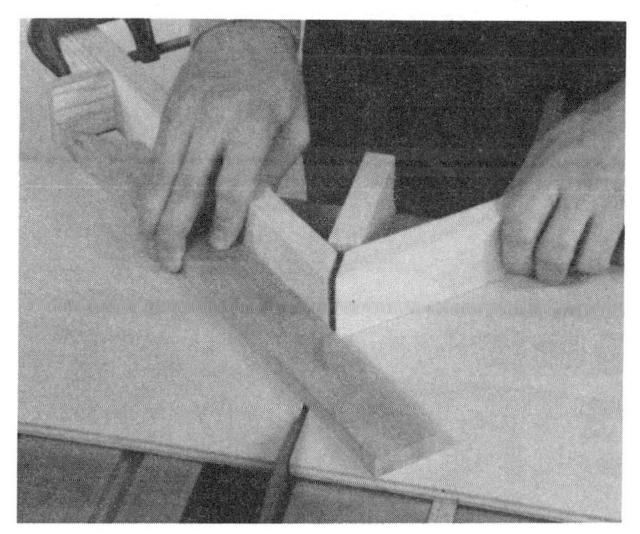

Illus. 8-83. The stop block clamped to the miter jig ensures that all parts are the same length.

Illus. 8-84. Mark the glass size along the rabbet. Make the frame parts ⅛ inch larger than the glass. This allowance is for trimming the miters.

Be sure to consider glass size when making picture frames. Measure along the rabbet (Illus. 8-84). Project these lines to locate the cutting line (Illus. 8-85). It is more difficult to project the lines on frames with compound miters (Illus. 8-86). Mark the rabbet and adjust the mark with the blade's path. Cut one end of all the parts with compound miters first (Illus. 8-87). A stop rod can be used to control the length of all the parts when the second miter is cut.

Illus. 8-85. To locate the cutting line, project the marks on the rabbet onto the face of the frame.

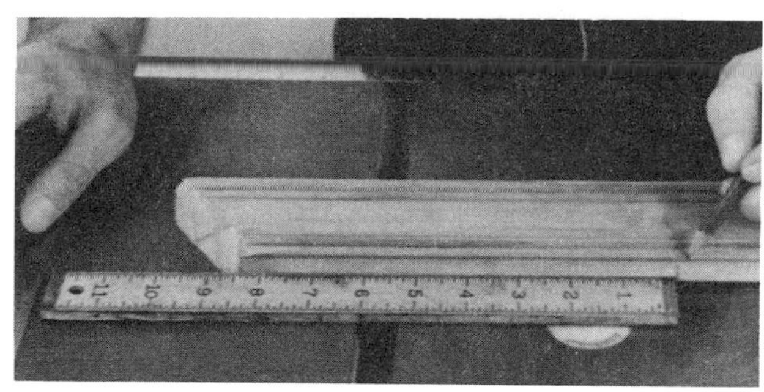

Illus. 8-86. It is difficult to project lines on stock with compound miters. Mark the rabbet and make the setup carefully.

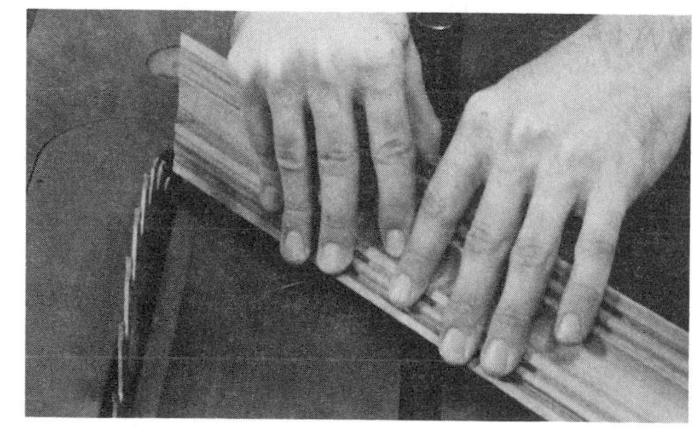

Illus. 8-87. For accuracy, cut one end of all compound miters first. A stop rod can then be used to control length.

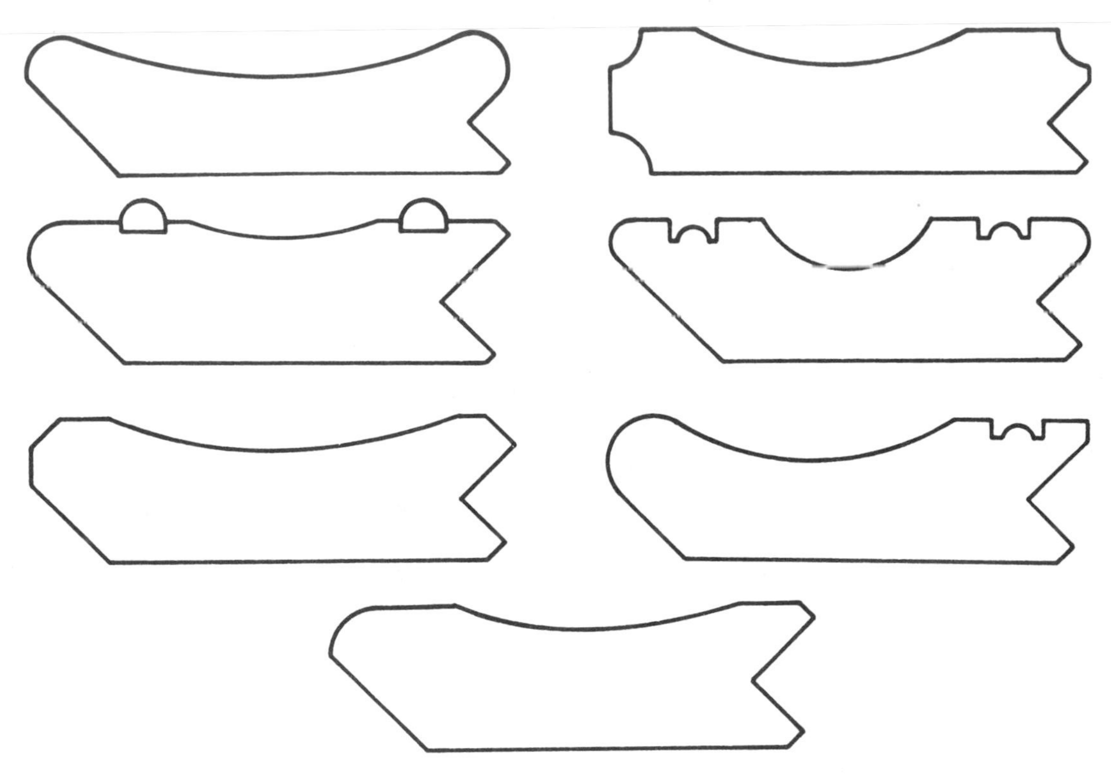

Illus. 8-88. These profiles will challenge your table-saw skills. Photocopy them and glue them to your stock.

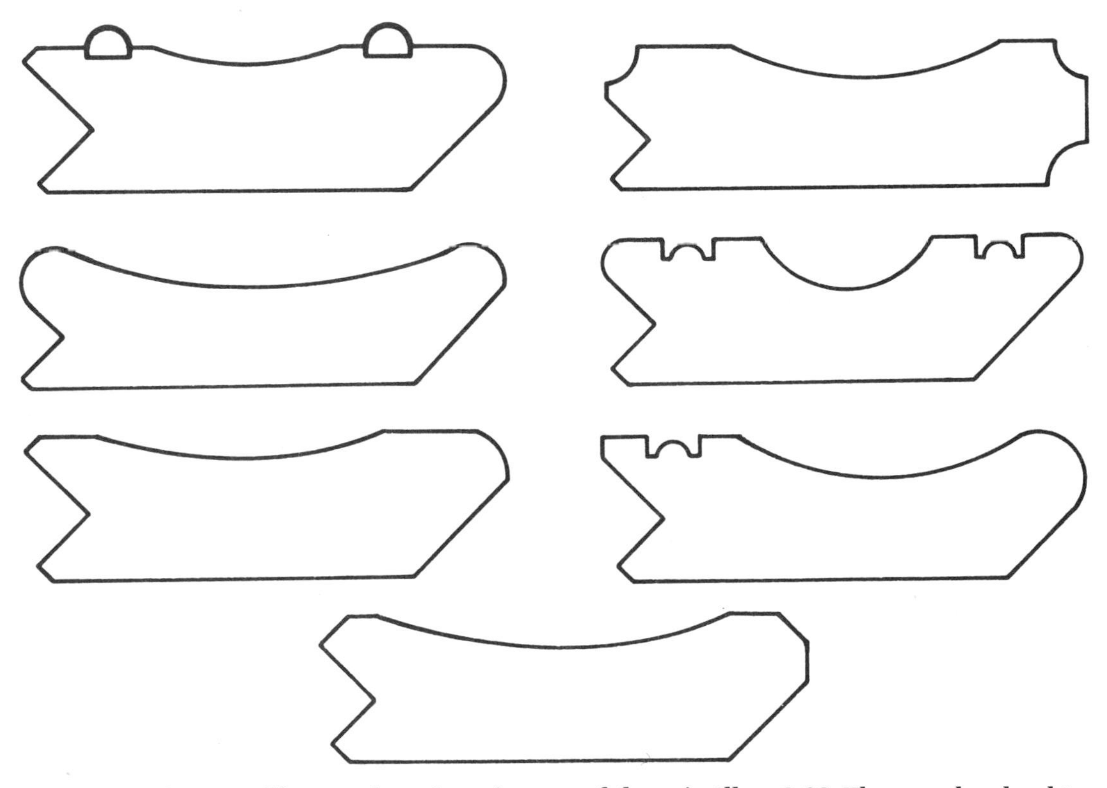

Illus. 8-89. These profiles are the mirror images of those in Illus. 8-88. They can be glued to the other end of your parts.

If you wish to attempt advanced coves and compound-miter frames, try some of the profiles in Illus. 8-88 and 8-89. These profiles are full size; they are mirror images of each other. Photocopy them and glue them to both ends of your stock. They can guide the setup of the saw.

One of the best ways to glue up picture frames is with a band clamp (Illus. 8-90). The clamp pulls uniformly on all four corners. When clamping frames with compound miters, turn the frame upside down. As the band clamp is tightened, the parts lift like a pyramid (Illus. 8-91). This is the easiest way I know to assemble frames with compound miters.

To reinforce miter joints and to keep them from opening up due to moisture changes, cut a key in the corners. The jig shown in Illus. 8-92 or the universal jig presented earlier in the chapter (pages 301–308) can be used for cutting the keyway (groove). A keyway is cut into all four corners. A key or feather is then cut and glued in place (Illus. 8-93). These keys are then trimmed flush with the frame (Illus. 8-94). Keys can be used on simple or compound miters. Remember to keep the keyways shallow or they will come through the front of the frame.

Illus. 8-90. A band clamp pulls all four corners uniformly. It is easy to adjust pieces held with a band clamp.

Illus. 8-91. Turn frames with compound miters upside down for clamping. As the clamp is tightened, they lift like a pyramid.

Illus. 8-92. This jig can be used to cut keyways in all four corners of the frame.

For simple miters, a spline can be cut. A universal jig (Illus. 8-95) is used to cut the groove. A spline is then used to reinforce the miter. The spline locates parts and keeps them from slipping when they are glued together. Remember to keep all faces

Illus. 8-93. Glue the keys in the keyways. Make the keys out of a different wood, for contrast.

Illus. 8-94. The keys are sanded flush with the edges of the frame. The contrasting color gives a decorative effect.

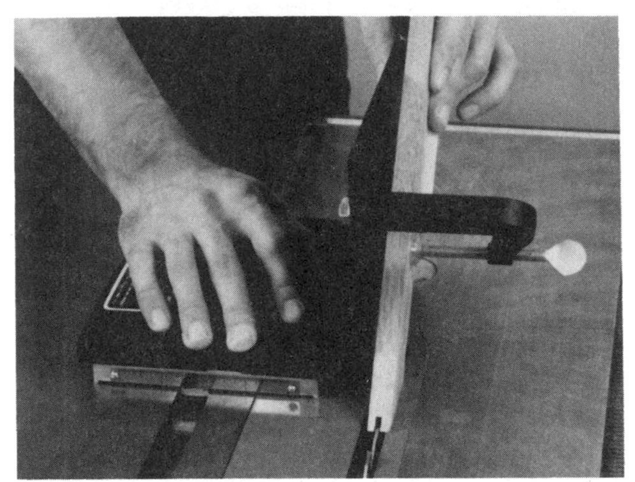

Illus. 8-95. Grooves for splines can be cut with this universal jig.

(or backs) in contact with the jig. Any error will be doubled if you do not. This means that the miters will not line up.

Mats and finish can affect the overall appearance of any frame. Plan ahead. Remember that the objects within the frame (Illus. 8-96 and 8-97) are more important than the frame.

Study the following tips before beginning any picture-frame project:

1. Review the miter section in Chapter 5 (pages 122–128).
2. Plan your shaping and cutting sequence and mark your stock before you begin. Keep one face and edge true for controlling the stock.
3. Allow at least 40 percent more stock than you need, to allow for setup and miter errors.

Illus. 8-96. This pecan frame was stained black and filled with white paste wood filler. The photo draws your eye.

Illus. 8-97. This frame and its message are hung prominently at Cliffe Cabinets.

4. Use a sharp, hollow-ground combination blade to cut the miters. Dull blades waste time and wood.
5. Make sure the blade is perpendicular to the table.
6. Use a jig and stop rod for accurate miters. Lines drawn on the stock are not accurate enough.
7. Cut stock oversize. This way, if the miters have to be trimmed, the glass will still fit.
8. Work from the longest to the shortest parts. Longer parts with errors can always be cut shorter.

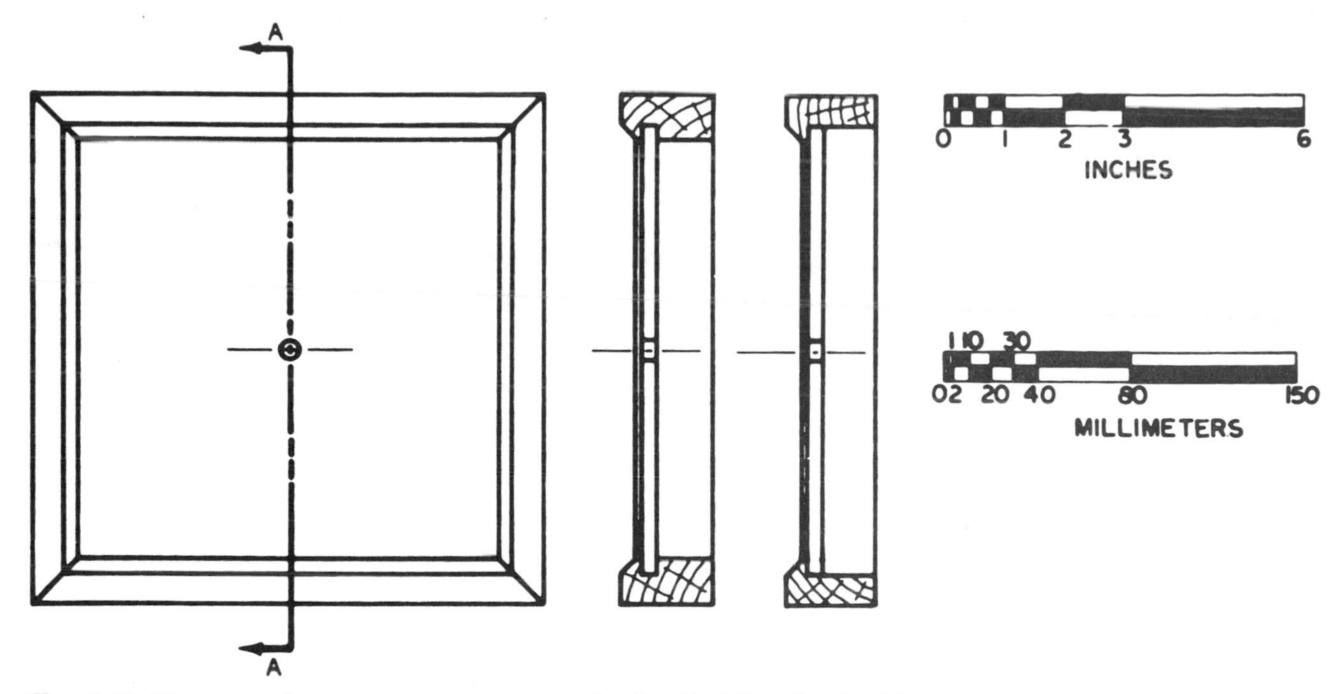

Illus. 8-98. These are the two most common methods of holding the clockface in position.

9. Fit the parts together without glue. Test the fit of the glass. Mark the position of the pieces at the corners. This allows you to put them back together the same way.
10. Sand all the parts well before assembly. It is difficult to sand the molding on an assembled frame.
11. Use glue sparingly. It is difficult to remove glass from the corners of an assembled frame.

Making Wall Clocks Wall clocks are similar to picture frames. The clock frame holds a clockface, and the picture frame holds the picture. Clocks are deeper and have less wood showing on their faces. Usually the edge grain shows on the front of a clock, and the face grain shows on the front of a picture frame. Typical clock profiles are shown in Illus. 8-98. The clockface is either housed in a dado or held in a rabbet. Both methods hold the dial equally well.

There are many types of faces, motors, and hands available. I made a burl-face clock with veneer (Illus. 8-99). Inexpensive paper faces (Illus. 8-100 and 8-101) and porcelain-glazed metal faces (Illus. 8-102) are also available. Select your materials from the many suppliers of clock parts. You can design your own faces or buy them from manufacturers.

The size of the motor determines the position of the face in relation to the frame. Use the motor to determine placement of the dado or rabbet. Deter-

Illus. 8-99. This clock has a burl-veneer face. The veneer face provides an additional woodworking challenge.

mine what type of decorative edge you wish to have surrounding the face, and rip your parts accordingly. Some faces look better if they are set back from the front of the frame. Others look better with less wood around them. Experiment with scraps or cut-offs for best results.

Begin with the faces. Paper faces must be backed with plywood. Make sure the glue you use is com-

Illus. 8-100. The inexpensive paper face on this clock must be glued and clamped carefully to avoid wrinkles.

Illus. 8-101. This paper face has a plastic coating that makes it easier to work with.

Illus. 8-102. This porcelain-glazed metal face is very easy to work with. It is thick enough to require no backing.

patible with the face (Illus. 8-103). Wood glue does not hold thin metal faces to wood very well. Smooth out any bubbles (Illus. 8-104), and clamp the face to the plywood backing. Thin metal pieces may not require clamping, since other types of glue will be used.

Use the face to determine dado size. Cut the dado with a saw blade or dado head. Check the fit

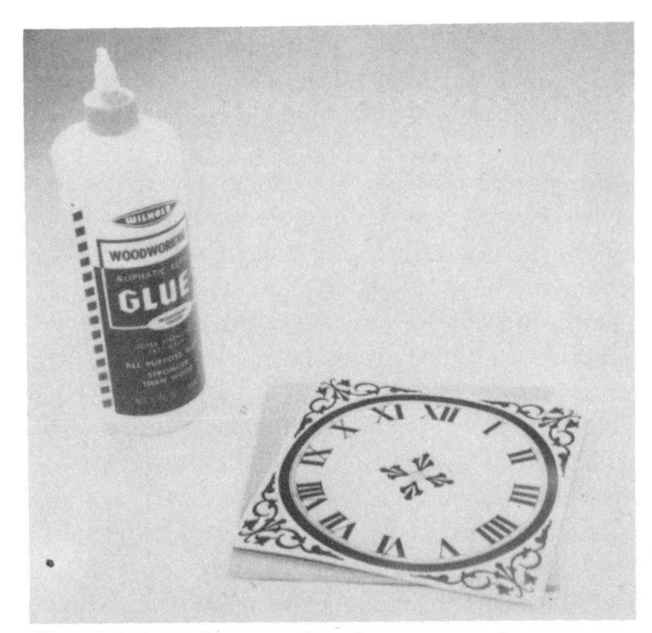

Illus. 8-103. Make sure the glue you use is compatible with the face. White or yellow glue works well with paper faces.

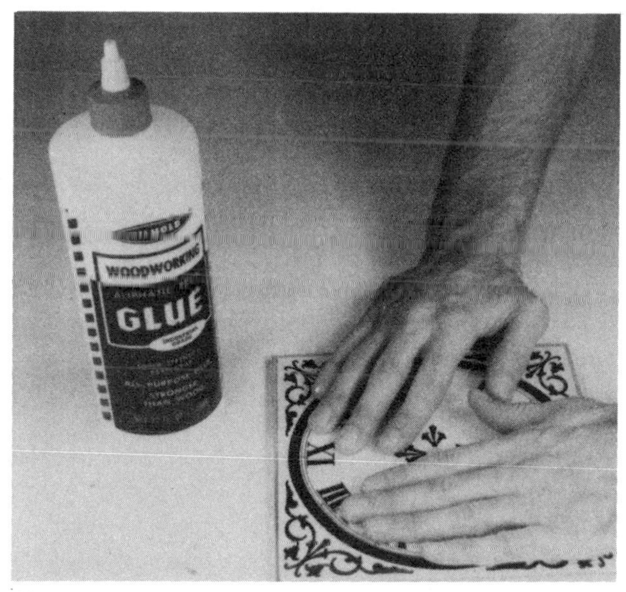

Illus. 8-104. Smooth out any bubbles before clamping the face to a backer.

Illus. 8-106. Miters can be cut with the stock on edge. The blade is set at 90 degrees, and the miter gauge is set at 45 degrees.

of the face in the dado (Illus. 8-105). It is easier to shape and dado pieces 12–18 inches long. Long pieces tend to be warped or twisted. They do not shape as well as shorter pieces. Crosscut longer pieces into parts that are easier to handle. Avoid pieces under 12 inches. They are likely to kick back or cause an accident.

The miters can be cut several different ways. The stock can be placed on edge and fed with the miter gauge (Illus. 8-106). The miter gauge is turned 45 degrees for this operation. This method will not work with very wide parts.

A miter jig will also work for cutting the clock miters. A shop-made jig or commercial jig will work equally well. Set the jig up carefully. The blade can also be tilted to cut the miters. Set the miter gauge at 90 degrees and tilt the blade to 45 degrees (Illus. 8-107). Adjust the blade and miter gauge carefully. Adjustment errors will make the miters difficult to fit. Use a stop block or rod to control part length. All parts of a square frame must be of equal length if the miters are to fit well.

Illus. 8-105. The groove cut in this piece is used to hold the clockface. Miters will be cut later to make this frame.

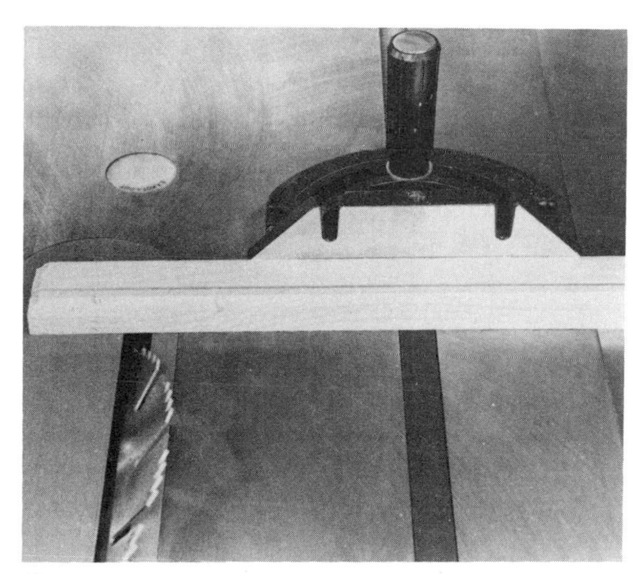
Illus. 8-107. To cut the miter, you can tilt the blade to 45 degrees. Set the miter gauge to 90 degrees before tilting the blade.

Review the section on miters in Chapter 5 (pages 122–128) before beginning. There are many tips on blade selection and saw setup, and a discussion of the causes of poorly fitting miters.

After the parts are cut, dry-fit the clock (Illus. 8-108). You may wish to stain inner parts before gluing the clock together. This will keep stain and finish off the clockface. Do not stain and finish the miters. This will affect the strength of the miter joint. The miters can be reinforced with a spline or feather, if you desire. Clean off any excess glue after assembly, and select hands that look attractive with the face (Illus. 8-109). Bolt the motor in place (Illus. 8-110) and attach the hands. Install a battery and test the movement. Handle the motors carefully. They are precision movements, and can be damaged easily.

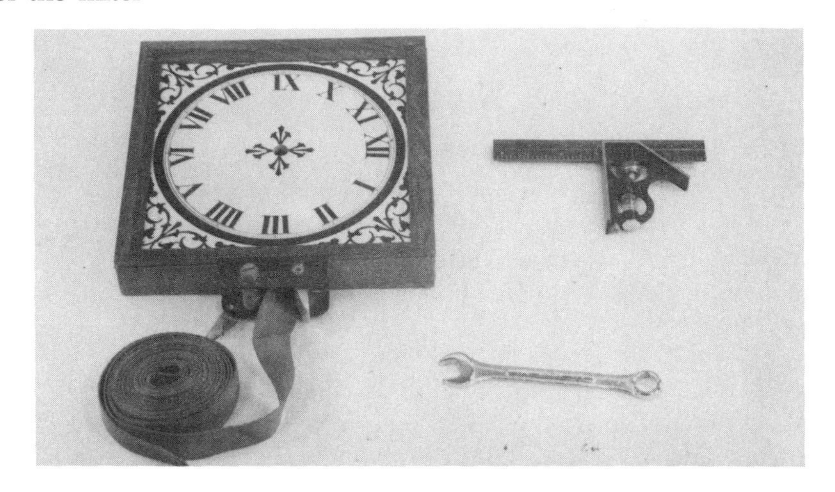

Illus. 8-108. Clamp up the clock dry to make certain the parts fit together well. Be sure to sand (and possibly finish) the inner surfaces before gluing the clock parts.

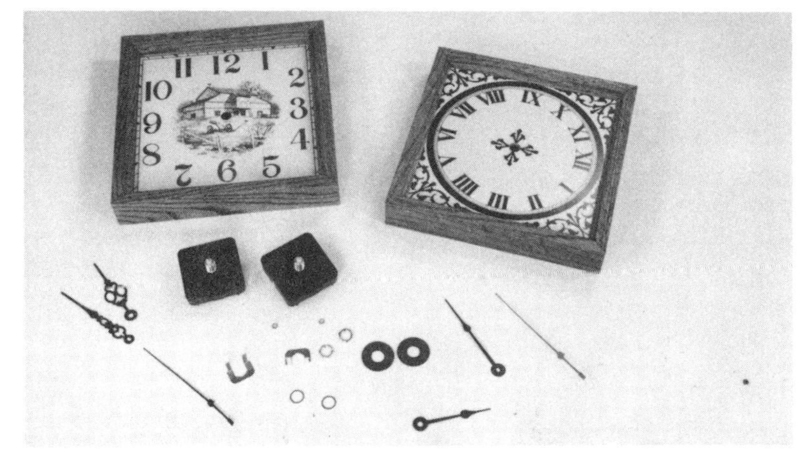

Illus. 8-109. Assemble the motor and select hands that look nice with the face.

Illus. 8-110. Bolt the motor in place before attaching the hands. Handle the motor carefully. It can be easily damaged.

Building a Nightstand The nightstand (Illus. 8-111) is one of the most challenging projects in this section. There are many table-saw operations included in this project. The cabinet can be built with or without a door. In addition to being used as a nightstand next to the bed, it can also be used as an end table next to your favorite easy chair.

Illus. 8-111. This nightstand offers many challenges to the table-saw user. It can be made with or without a door, and also looks nice as an end table next to your favorite chair.

Study Illus. 8-112–8-115 carefully before you begin. Make sure you know how the parts are to be machined and assembled. Develop a bill of materials and a plan of procedure. Break the plan of procedure down into subassemblies such as faceplate, top, cabinet assembly, door, and drawer. This will allow you to work on different areas of the project when certain assemblies are in the clamps.

Rip the faceplate stock to size. Cut the parts to length and make the lap joints. Make a trial cut in some cut-offs so you are certain the lap joint is set up correctly. Glue and clamp the parts together after a trial fit.

Cut the parts of the cabinet, and then assemble them to the faceplate (Illus. 8-116). Sand and trim the faceplate before assembly. Cut notches in the corner blocks so clamps can be used to hold them in place. After the glue cures, install the base molding.

Lay out the parts for the top (Illus. 8-117). Cut the spline joints and the miters. Glue and clamp the parts together after a dry fit (Illus. 8-118). Sand the top and remove any excess glue (Illus. 8-119). Cut some keys into the miters (Illus. 8-120). Keep them below center so they will not be cut away when the edge is shaped (Illus. 8-121). Use the shaper head (Illus. 8-122) or a router to shape the edge of the top. Use the same setup to shape the top edge of the base molding (Illus. 8-123).

Cut and sand the raised panel (Illus. 8-124). Make the other door parts and assemble the door (Illus. 8-125). Cut rabbets on all four edges of the door with a shaper head (Illus. 8-126), dado head, or router. Center the panel, and then pin it in position (Illus. 8-127). Locate the hinges on the door, drill pilot holes, and screw the hinges in place (Illus. 128).

Locate the door on the faceplate and mark the positions of the holes (Illus. 8-129). Drill pilot holes and screw the hinges in position.

Cut the drawer parts, and then fit the drawer together without glue. Stain and finish the drawer front before gluing the drawer together. This gives the nightstand a professional look (Illus. 8-130).

Install the drawer guides, and then fit the drawer to the opening. Screw the top in place. Remove the hardware and sand all the parts. Apply the stain, and then finish and reassemble the nightstand.

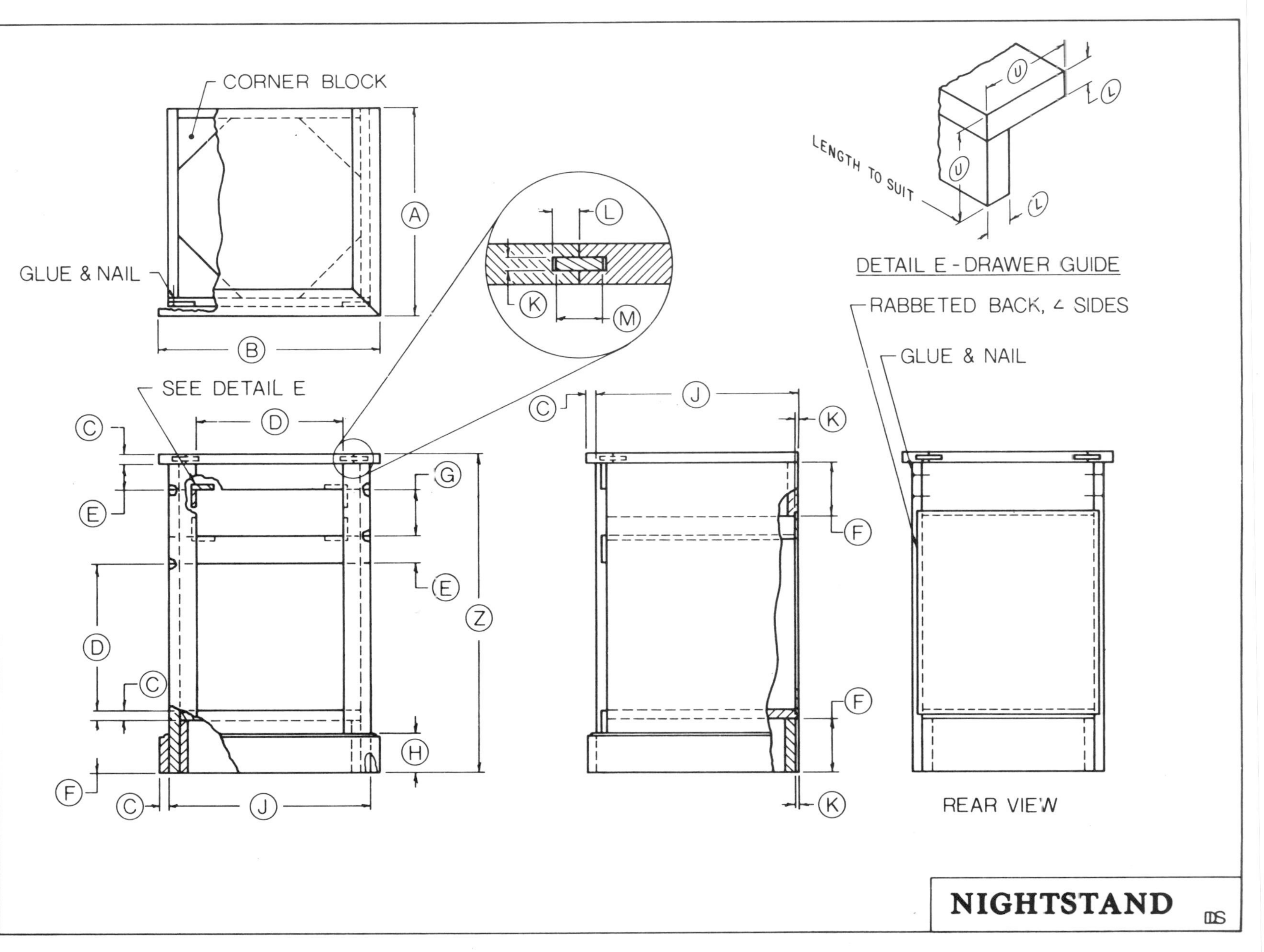

Illus. 8-112–8-115. The drawings for the nightstand are complex. Study them carefully before you begin.

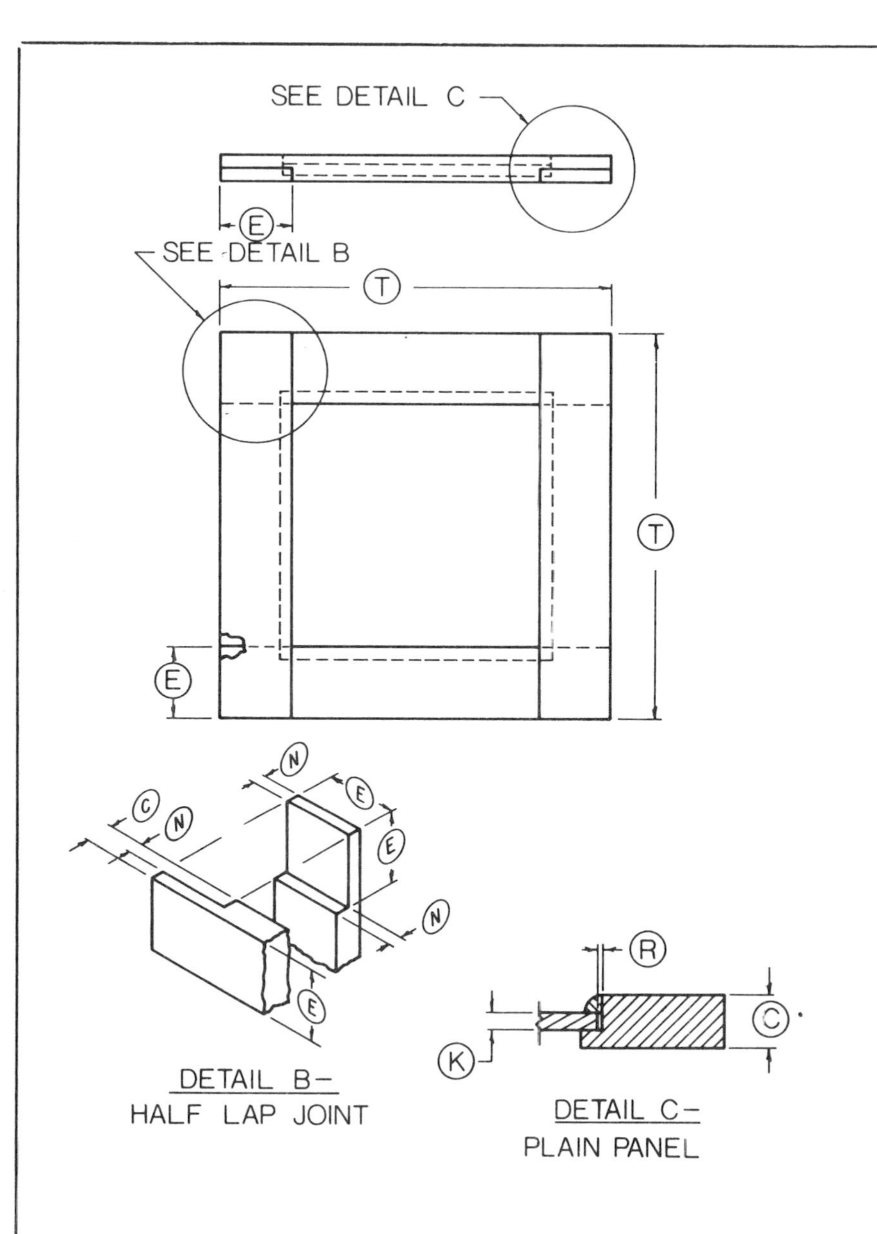

DIM.	ENGLISH	METRIC
A	15 3/4 IN.	400 MM.
B	16 1/2	419
C	3/4	19
D	11	279
E	2	51
F	4	102
G	3 1/2	89
H	3	76
J	15	381
K	1/4	6
L	1/2	13
M	7/8	22
N	3/8	10
O	11 1/2	292
P	1 1/4	32
Q	1 5/8	41
R	1/16	2
S	5/16	8
T	10 7/8	276
U	1 3/4	44
V	3/16	5
W	3 7/16	87
X	13 1/2	343
Y	10 3/8	262
Z	24	610

NIGHTSTAND DS

Illus. 8-113.

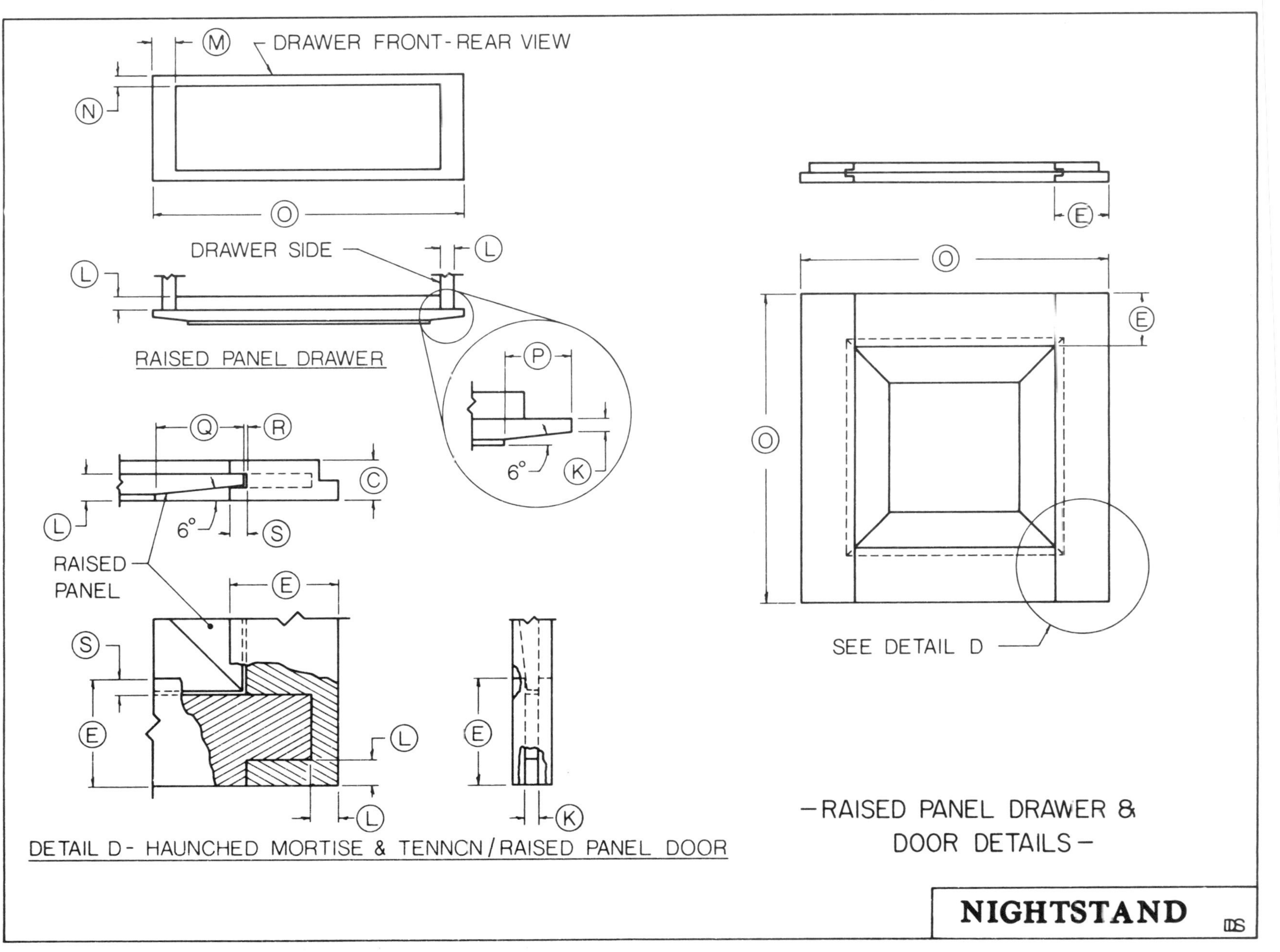
DRAWER FRONT-REAR VIEW
M
N
O
DRAWER SIDE
L
RAISED PANEL DRAWER
P
K
6°
Q
R
C
S
RAISED PANEL
E
DETAIL D- HAUNCHED MORTISE & TENNCN/RAISED PANEL DOOR
SEE DETAIL D
-RAISED PANEL DRAWER & DOOR DETAILS-
NIGHTSTAND
DS

Illus. 8-114.

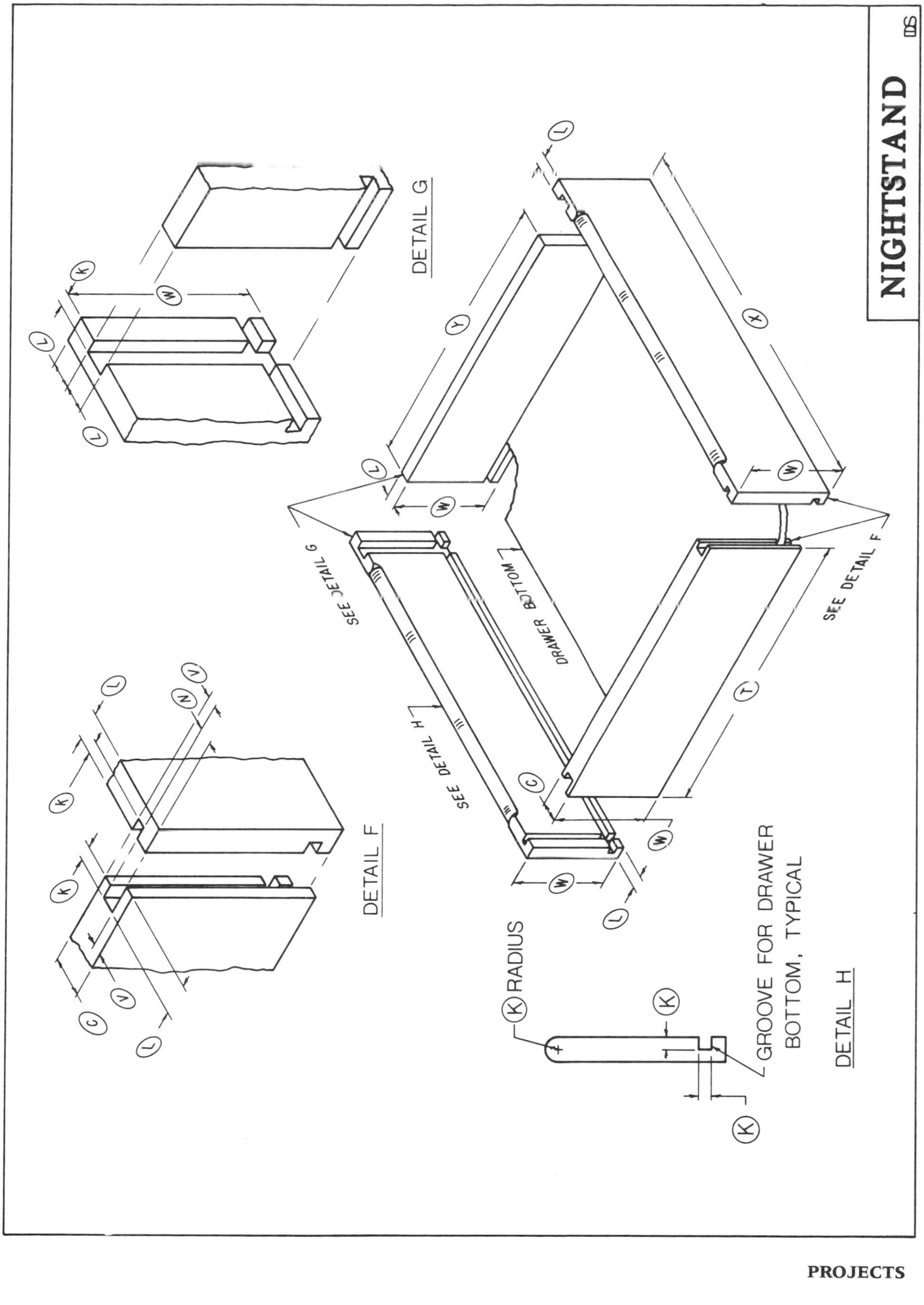

DETAIL F
SEE DETAIL G
DETAIL G
SEE DETAIL H
K RADIUS
DRAWER BOTTOM
GROOVE FOR DRAWER
BOTTOM, TYPICAL
DETAIL H
SEE DETAIL F
NIGHTSTAND

Illus. 8-115.

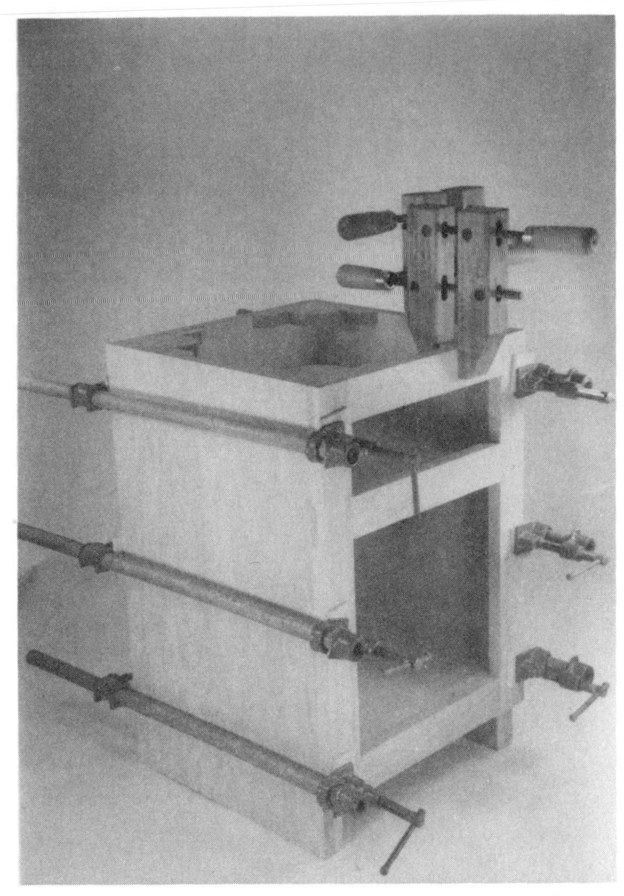

Illus. 8-116. Trim the faceplate and glue it to the cabinet parts. Nails can be used to reinforce the butt joint. Notch the corner blocks so they are easy to clamp.

Illus. 8-117. Lay out the parts for the top and mark them carefully. Chalk works well because it is easy to remove.

Illus. 8-118. Assemble the top after cutting the splines and miters. Clamp the parts securely.

Illus. 8-119. After the glue cures, sand the top carefully.

Illus. 8-120. Cut keys into the miters. A universal jig was used for this operation.

Illus. 8-121. The keys are below the centerline. They will not be cut away when the edge is shaped.

Illus. 8-122. The shaper head can be used to cut a decorative edge on the top. Take light cuts!

Illus. 8-123. The base molding is shaped on the same setup as the top. Work slowly and take light cuts.

Illus. 8-124. Cut the raised panel using the procedure outlined in Chapter 6 (pages 237–243).

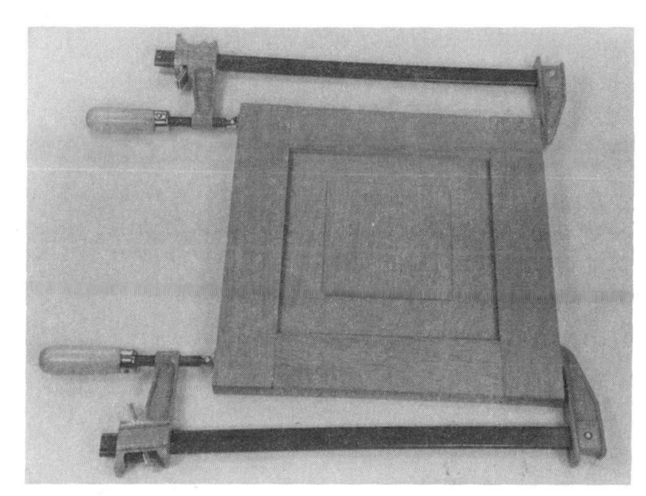

Illus. 8-125. Glue and clamp the door after fitting the parts together. Make sure the door is square and the panel is centered.

Illus. 8-126. The shaper head was used to cut the rabbet on the four door edges.

Illus. 8-127. Pin the panel (top and bottom) at the centerline. Make sure it is centered before pinning it.

Illus. 8-128. Locate the hinges, drill the pilot holes, and screw the hinges in position.

Illus. 8-129. Locate the door carefully. Mark the screw holes with an awl and drill pilot holes. Attach the door and test the fit.

Illus. 8-130. This drawer front was stained and finished before the drawer was glued together. This gives the nightstand a professional look.

Building a Food Preparation Table The food preparation table shown in Illus. 8-131 was designed for a client who wanted a cutting area and food preparation surface for his kitchen. The drawers store knives and other kitchen tools. The drawer fronts (Illus. 8-132) are made of bird's-eye maple. A locking corner joint was used to join the drawer front to the sides.

This table was made of maple. It features knock-down construction. The rails go through the legs, and are held securely with wedges (Illus. 8-133). The top is located on two dowels, and rests on top of the legs.

The top can be glued up and planed to thickness or it can be purchaed as a complete benchtop. The completed benchtop is more expensive, but less labor and machinery are needed. The drawer guides are screwed to the tabletop. The drawer guides are screwed to the tabletop. The drawer sides are dadoed to travel on the guides.

Study Illus. 8-134–8-138 carefully before you begin. Closed-grain woods are best for this table. Start the building sequence with the legs and rails. Then make the top and construct the drawers. Select your wood with care. Avoid checks, knots, and cracks. All parts of the leg and rail unit should be free of defects. Set aside any stock with interesting grain patterns. This stock can be used for drawer fronts.

Lay out the tenons on the rails and cut them with the dado head. Read the section on mortise-and-tenon joints in Chapter 6 before you begin. Make the tenons slightly oversize. This allows you to smooth the exposed surfaces with a chisel.

Lay out and cut the mortises on the edges of the legs. Fit the tenons, and then glue up the leg assembly. After the glue dries, the mortises can be cut for the rails. Keep the unit square while fitting the rails. After the joint is made, the holes for the wedge must be drilled and fitted. Use details A, B, and C as shown in Illus. 8-134 and 8-135 for laying out mortises and wedges. Note that the hole is larger than the wedge. This allows the wedge to pull the unit together snugly.

Cut and carve the wedge carefully. When it is installed (Illus. 8-133), it can enhance the overall appearance of the table. Make an extra wedge or two, in case they are lost when the table is disassembled.

Glue up the tabletop and plane it to thickness. A water-resistant glue would be best for the tabletop. Glue the dowels into the top of two opposing legs (Illus. 8-134). Position the top on the legs. Mark the location of the blind holes into which the dowels will fit. Bore these holes and test the fit of the top on the legs. If the top is warped, some shimming or planing may be needed.

Illus. 8-131. This food-preparation table can make a nice addition to a pantry or country kitchen. It is held together with wedges, and can be dismantled so it can be transported.

Illus. 8-132. The locking corner adds to the quality of this table. Note the bird's-eye maple drawer fronts.

Illus. 8-133. Wedges hold these through mortise-and-tenon joints securely. Contrasting wood color adds accent to the table.

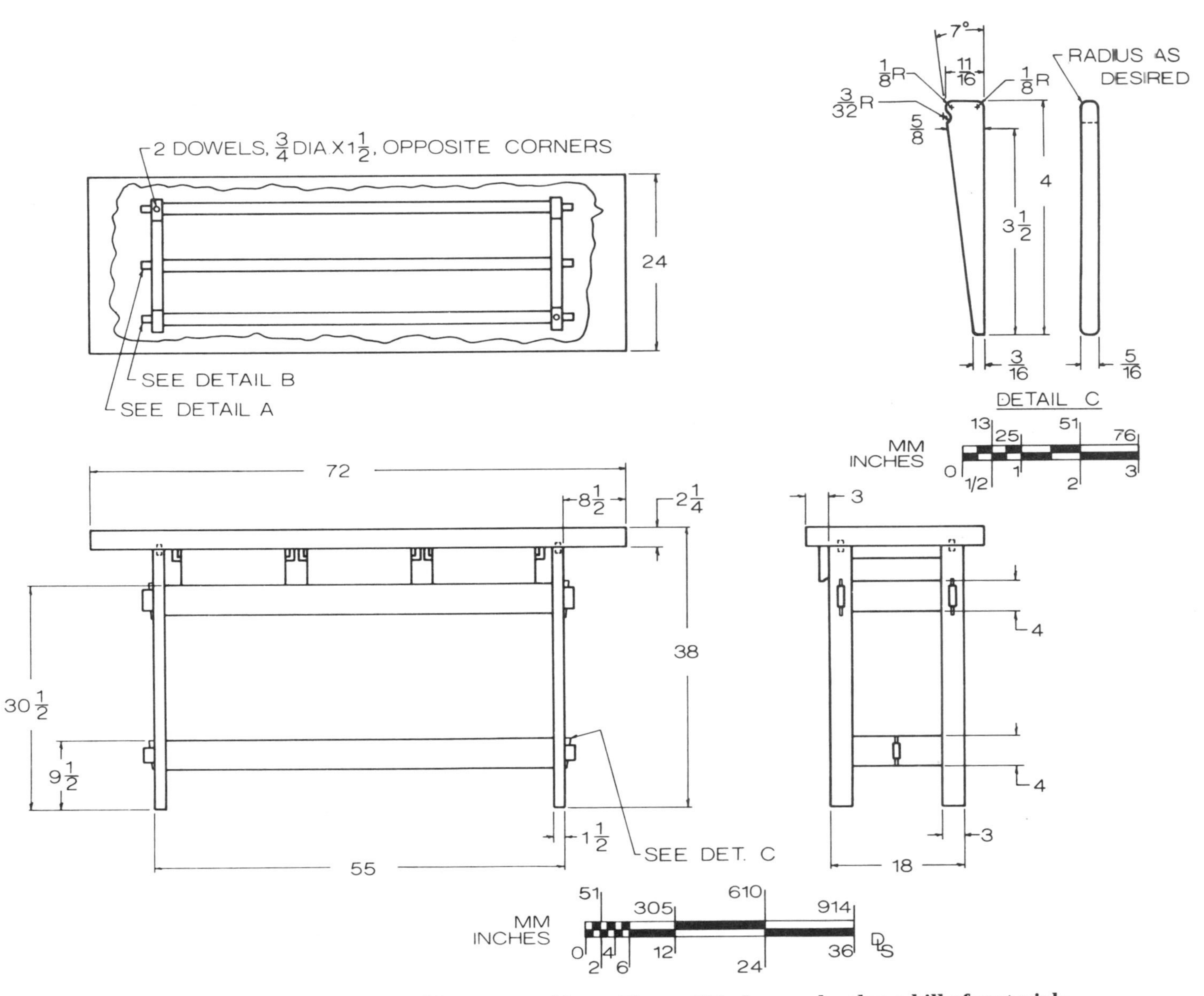

Illus. 8-134. Study the three views of the table presented here. They will help you develop a bill of materials.

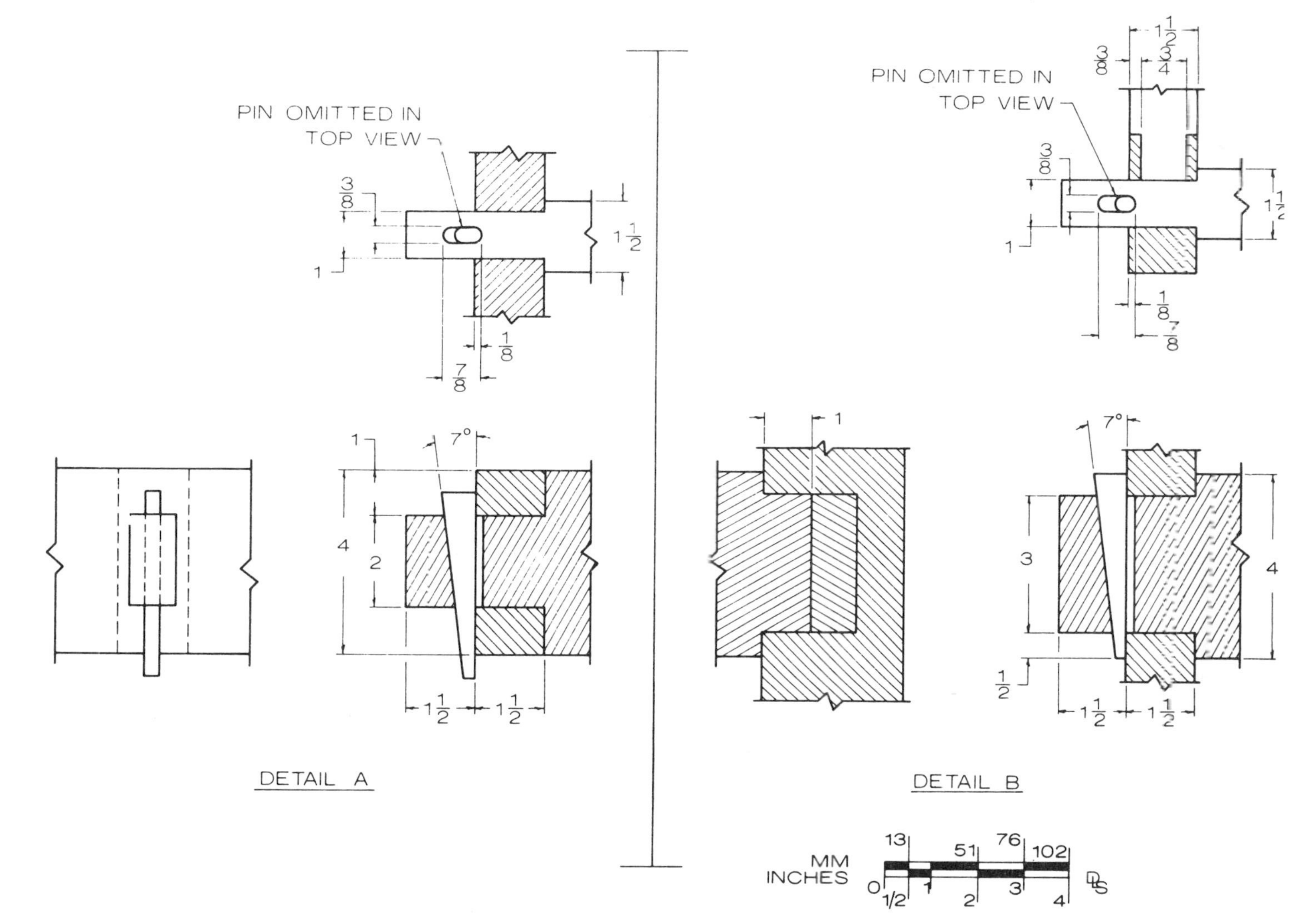

Illus. 8-135. These details will help you see how the mortise-and-tenon joints are designed. See Illus. 8-134 to locate the joints in their correct positions.

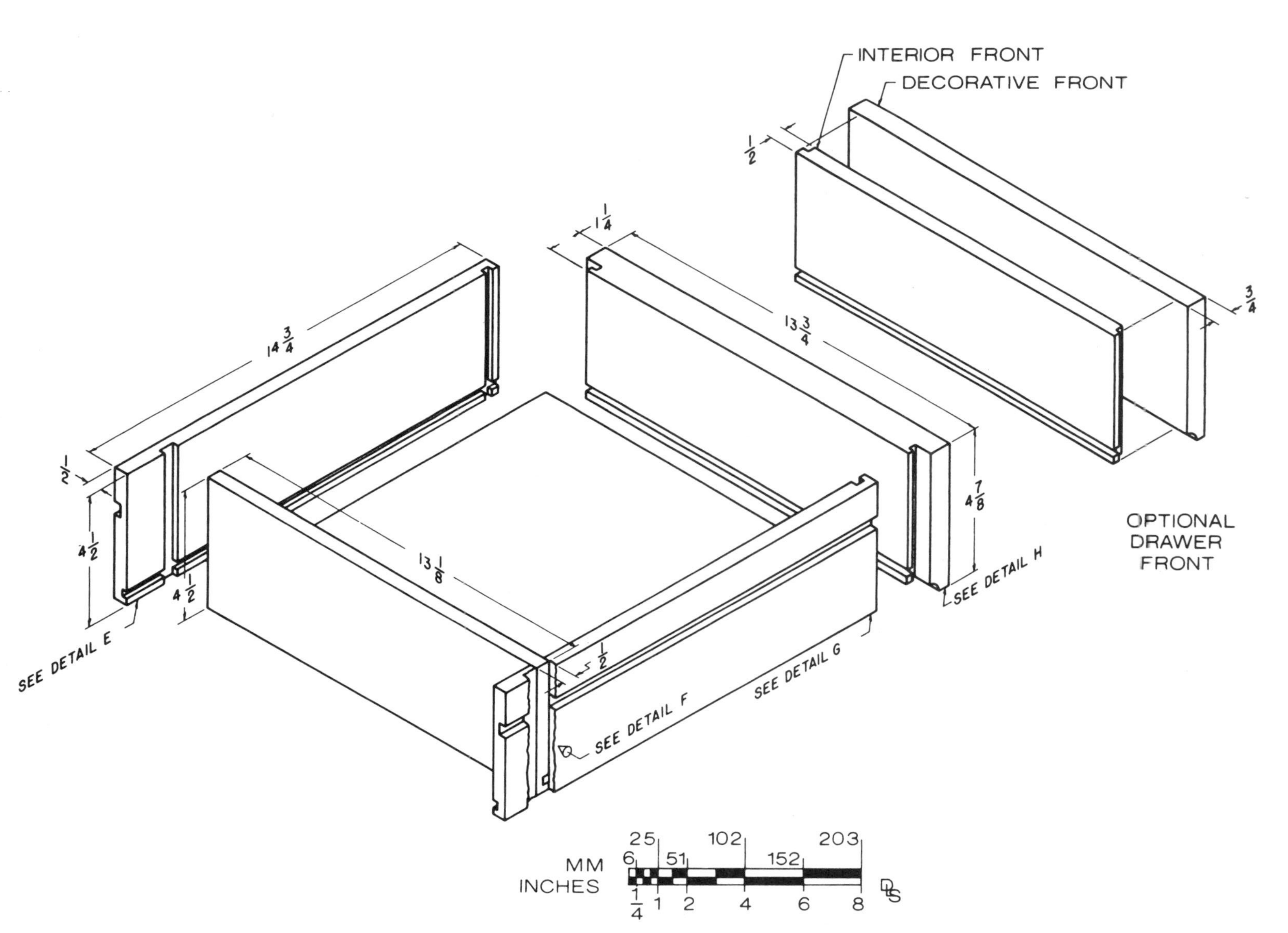

Illus. 8-136. This drawer detail gives you two options for drawer fronts. Others can also be developed. (See Illus. 8-137 for details E–H).

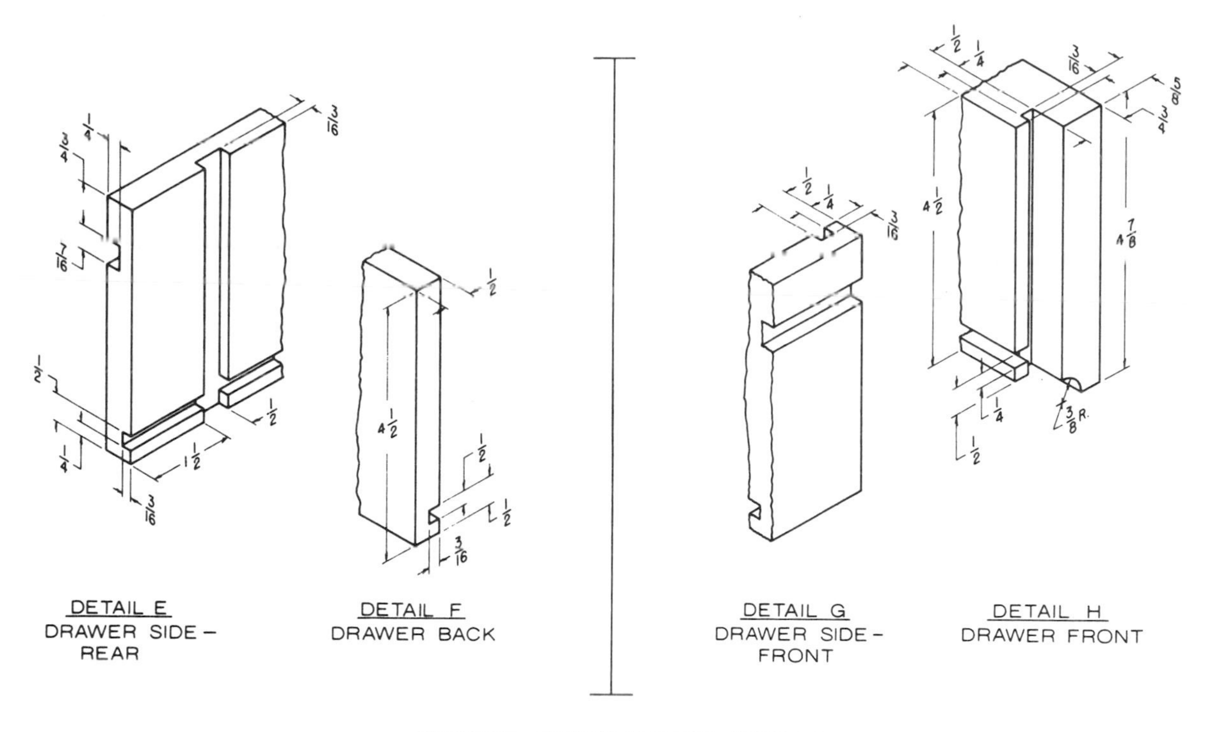

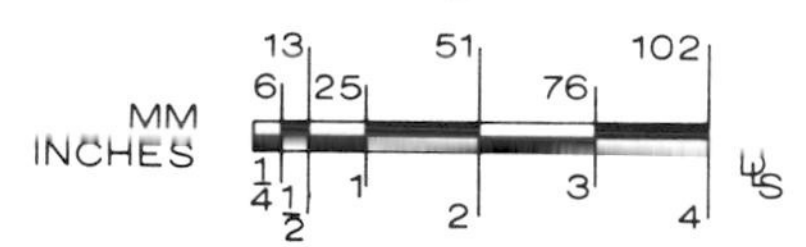

Illus. 8-137). The drawer details presented here will help you visualize what you see in Illus. 8-136.

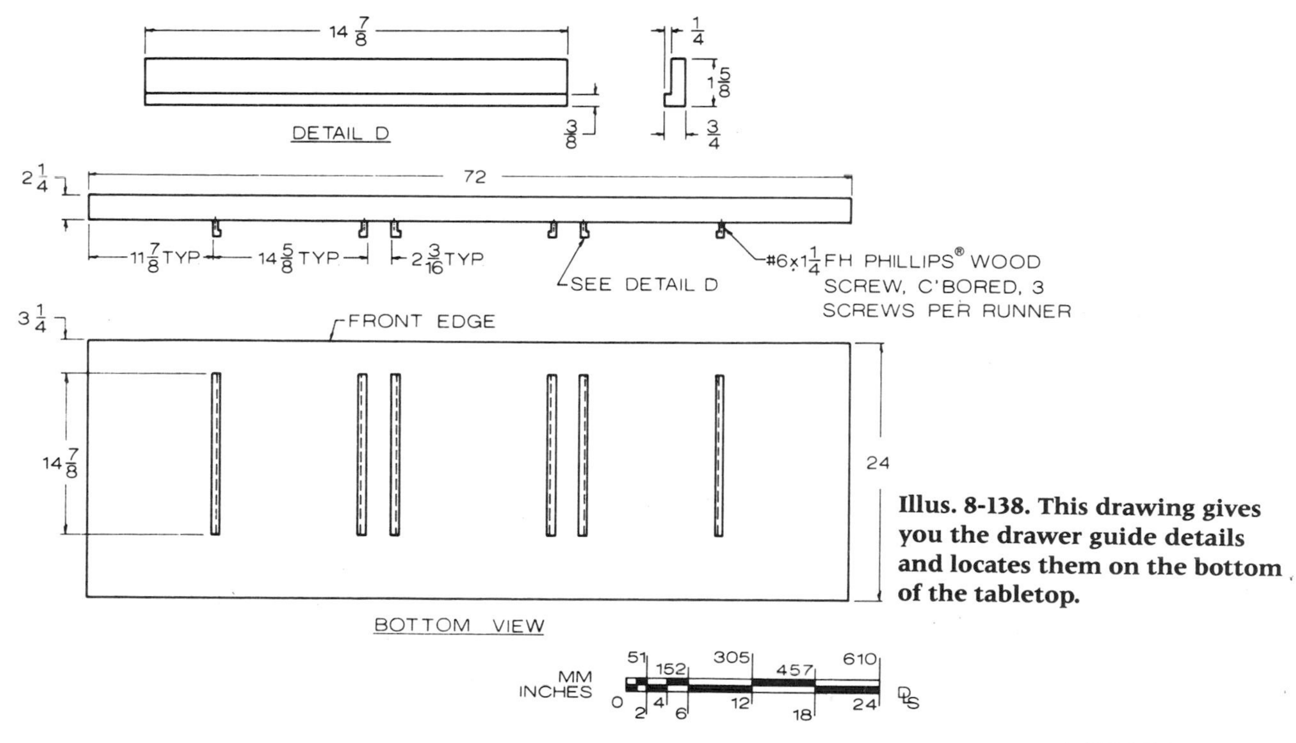

Illus. 8-138. This drawing gives you the drawer guide details and locates them on the bottom of the tabletop.

Study the drawer details and assembly drawing (Illus. 8-136 and 8-137) before cutting the drawings. Note the alternate drawer front, and decide which drawer you wish to make. Cut the joints accurately, Study the drawer section in Chapter 6 (pages 245–254) before you begin. Assemble the drawer without glue to test thc fit of thc parts. Make any needed adjustments, and then glue the drawers together.

Cut the drawer guides (Illus. 8-138) to fit the dadoes on the drawer sides. Locate the guides on the underside of the tabletop. Use Phillips head screws to secure the guides (Illus. 8-139). The Phillips screwdriver will go into the hole without interference. Adjust the drawers for smooth operation and apply the finish. I used a nontoxic oil finish on my table. I also made some knife racks to fit in the drawers. These racks were designed to fit my client's knife assortment.

Illus. 8-139. Use a Phillips screwdriver to mount the guides. It fits easily into the counterbored holes.

Building a Hall Chest The hall chest (Illus. 8-140) offers many of the same challenges as the nightstand and gun cabinet. Study the plans and dimensions (Illus. 8-141) carefully before you begin. Note the door detail and drawer detail (Illus. 8-142 and Illus. 8-143). The doors can be made in many different ways. The decorative drawer front should match the door style. If you use an overlay door, you should also use an overlay dresser.

The doors can also be made out of plywood and banded with decorative molding similar to that in Illus. 6-245 and 6-246. Decide on which type of door you wish to make before you begin.

Illus. 8-140. This hall chest makes a nice storage cabinet for gloves and sweaters. It can be adapted to many other uses.

Begin by making the faceplate. You can use mortise-and-tenon or lap joints. Practice your setup on scrap stock to be sure it is correct. The sides and bottom of the case can now be cut. Note that the carcass assembly uses butt joints (Illus. 8-141). You can substitute a dado joint if you wish.

The top is edge-banded plywood. The solid edge band is splined to the plywood. The miters can be keyed for reinforcement. Keep the keys below center so that they will not cut away when the edge is shaped. Be sure to shape the base molding at the same time. Install the base molding and fasten the top to the cabinet.

Now make the drawers and doors. If your shop is crowded, it may be easier to make the doors and drawers before you assemble the cabinet. Once the cabinet is built, it takes up a lot of bench or floor space. Metal drawer guides with rollers may be substituted for the wooden guides if desired. Remember, this will alter the drawer dimensions. Purchase the slides before you make the drawers. This will ensure a correct fit.

Install all hardware and adjust the doors and drawers. Mount the decorative drawer front to the drawer. Remove the hardware and prepare to finish. Stain and finish as desired.

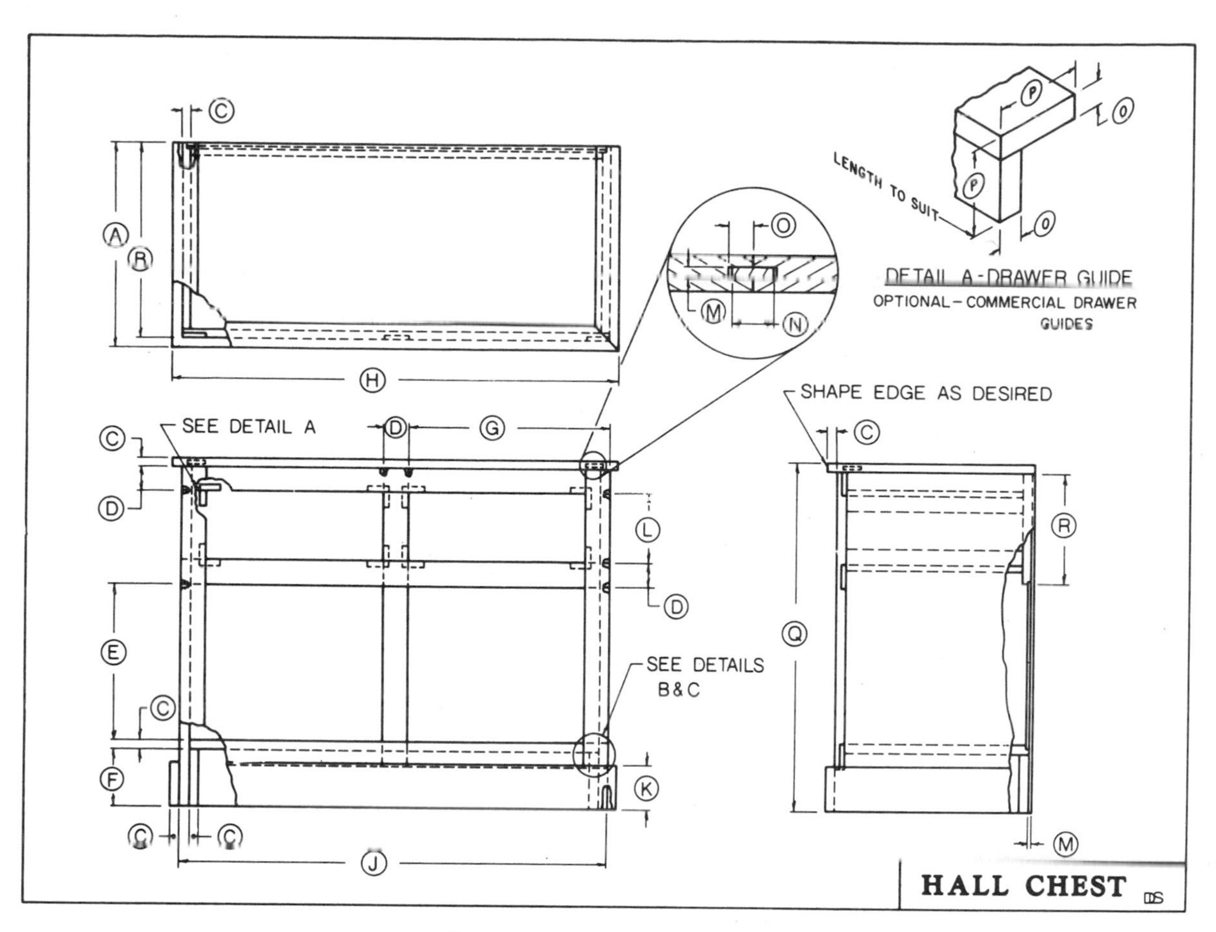

DIM.	ENGLISH	METRIC
A	16 3/4 IN.	425 MM.
B	16	406
C	3/4	19
D	2	51
E	15 3/8	391
F	4 1/2	114
G	16 1/4	413
H	36	914
J	34 1/2	876
K	3 1/2	89
L	4 5/8	117
M	1/4	6
N	7/8	22
O	1/2	13
P	1 3/4	44
Q	30	762
R	9	229
S	3/8	10
T	1 1/4	32
U	1/16	2
V	13 3/4	349
W	13 5/8	346

Illus. 8-141. Study these three views of the hall chest carefully before beginning. You may want to change the butt joints in the base to dado joints. Make additional drawings if you change joinery.

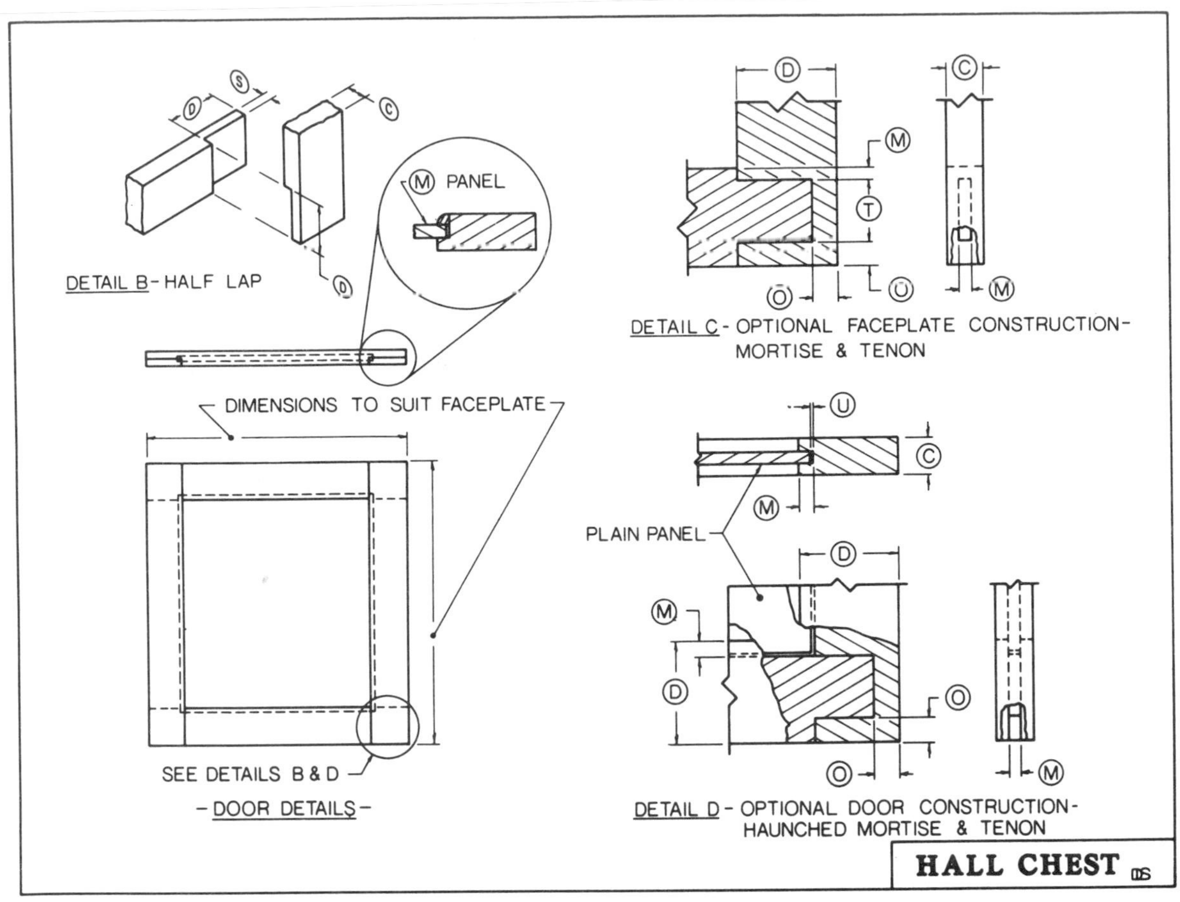

Illus. 8-142. Study your options for door and faceplate construction. Lap joints are easier to make, and mortise-and-tenon joints are more challenging. Overall door dimensions are not given. You must first decide if they will be flush, rabbets, or overlay rabbets.

Building a Raised Panel Chest The raised panel chest is one of my favorite projects. I have built approximately 20 of them and supervised the construction of 100 more. The banak chest (Illus. 8-144) is all solid stock. The walnut chest (Illus. 8-149) has a veneer top. A burl veneer was used, and it added to the overall beauty of the piece. This piece is in a prominent lawyer's private collection.

Hinges and lid supports are the only hardware. You could add a locking mechanism, but the cleaner the chest, the better it looks.

The plan (Illus. 8-147) shows a plywood top with a solid-stock frame. This frame is a challenge because all four corners must be tight. Make sure your plywood top is perfectly square. This will make it easier to cut the frame.

The section view (Illus. 8-146) shows raised panels in the chest. There are 10 panels. This requires a great deal of gluing, cutting, and sanding. You can substitute ¼-inch plywood panels for the raised panels. These also look very nice. If you are making raised panels, make three large ones. The extra panel can be used as a replacement for all three sizes if needed.

The front view (Illus. 8-145) shows stub mortise-and-tenon joints in the corners. These joints should be replaced with a haunched mortise-and-tenon joint, for strength and durability. The extra face-grain gluing makes a joint that is less likely to fail.

The leg detail (Illus. 8-148) shows a leg that is quite a challenge. The top is rounded over with a shaping cutter, and the front is cove-cut. The two parts are mitered and cut on the band saw for extra lines. A plywood triangle is attached to the rabbet

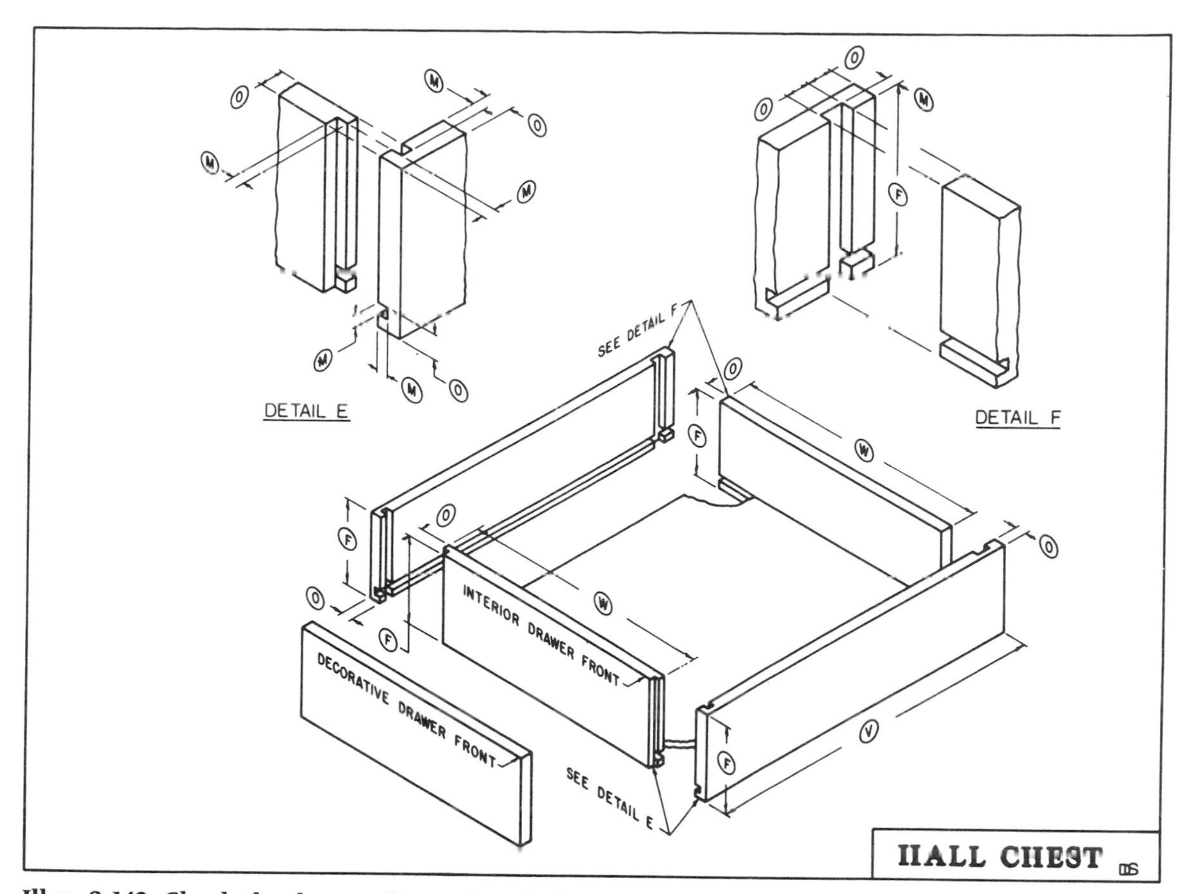

Illus. 8-143. Check the drawer dimensions before you begin. Any error in the faceplate will change these dimensions. Metal drawer guides will also change them.

Illus. 8-144. The banak chest is all solid stock. Banak makes sanding of the panels very easy because it is soft.

for support. This also allows the legs to be attached to the bottom of the chest.

Look over the plans before you begin. Review the related operations in Chapters 6 and 7 before you cut the parts. This review will reduce the chance of error.

Begin by cutting all the rails and stiles. Allow additional length for the joints. Cut the groove on

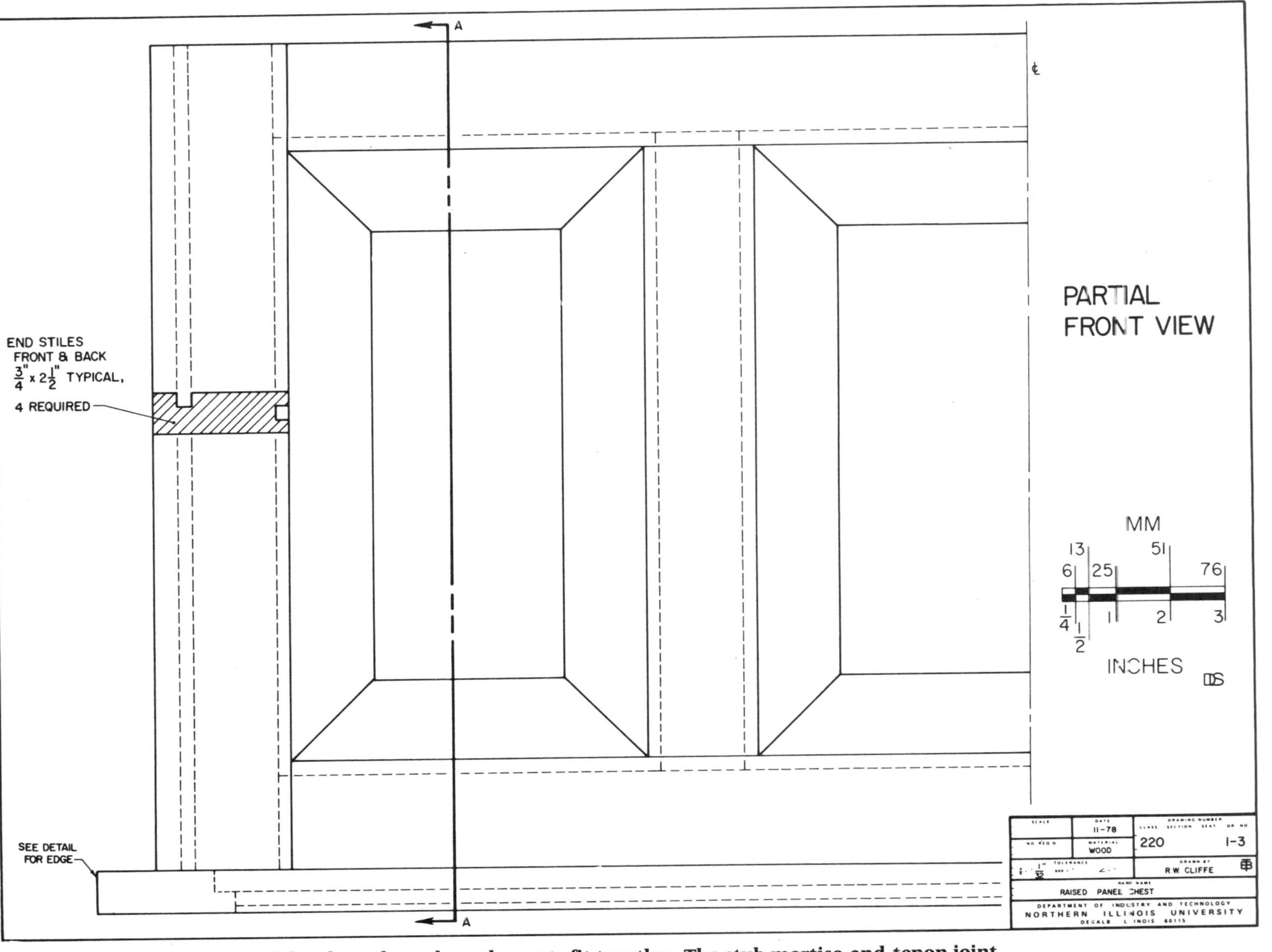

Illus. 8-145. This front view of the chest shows how the parts fit together. The stub mortise-and-tenon joint is not as strong as a haunched mortise-and-tenon joint. You may want to modify this joint.

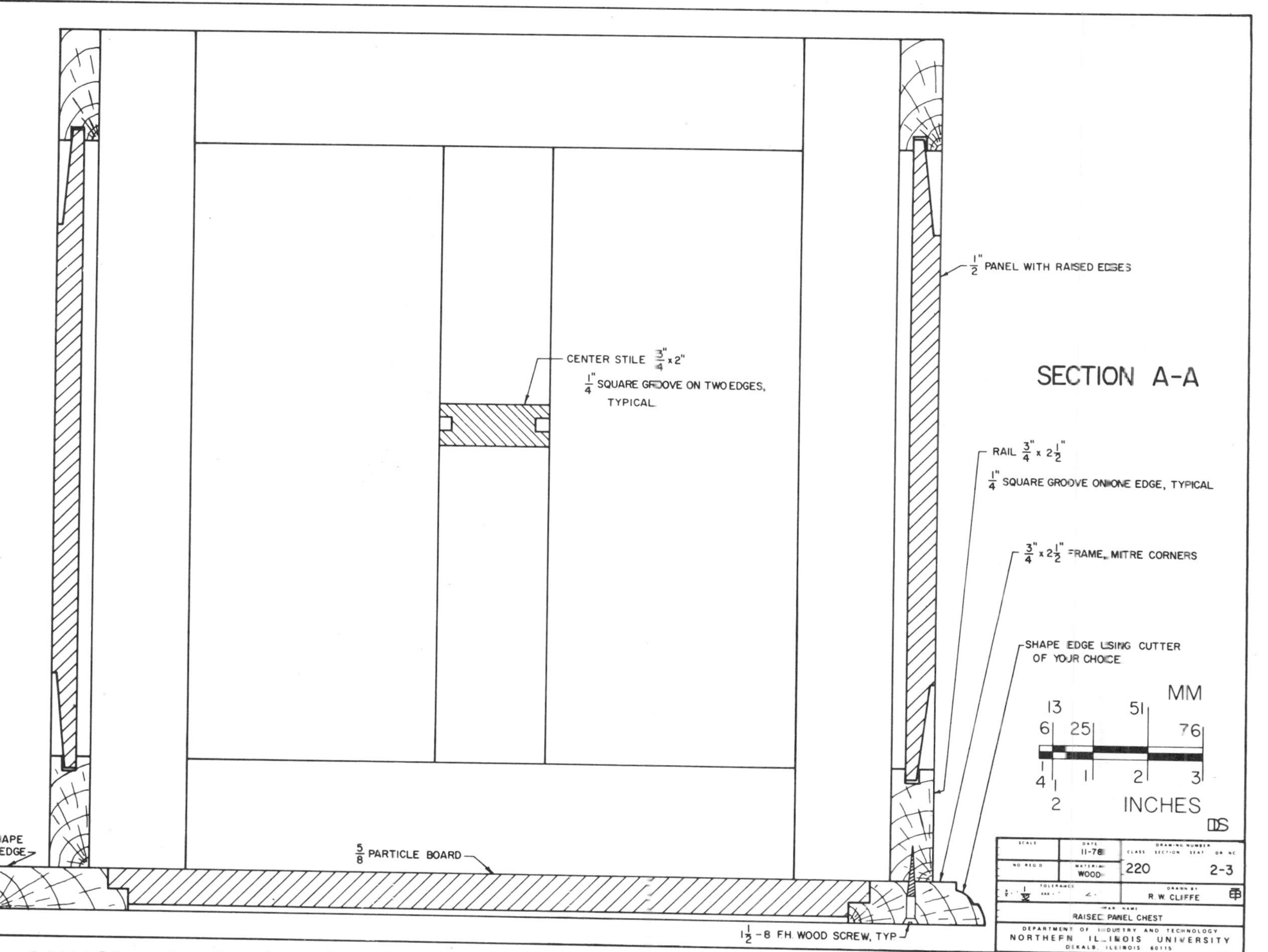

Illus. 8-146. This section view shows the raised panels in the chest. This view will help you lay out the panels. Be sure to review the section in Chapter 6 on raised panels (pages 237–243).

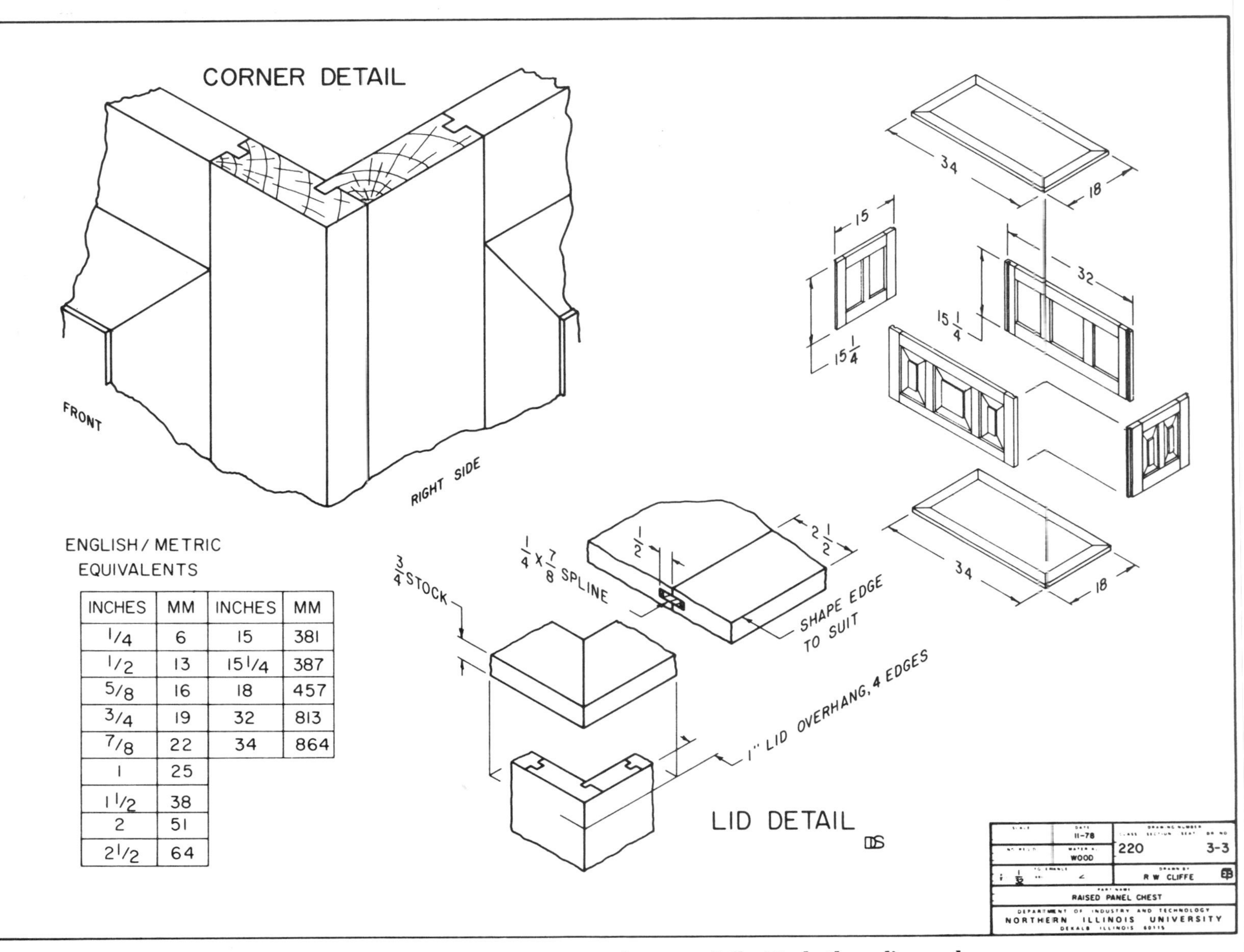

INCHES	MM	INCHES	MM
1/4	6	15	381
1/2	13	15 1/4	387
5/8	16	18	457
3/4	19	32	813
7/8	22	34	864
1	25		
1 1/2	38		
2	51		
2 1/2	64		

Illus. 8-147. The miters for the top and bottom must be tight. Cut them carefully. Study the spline and corner details before you cut any wood.

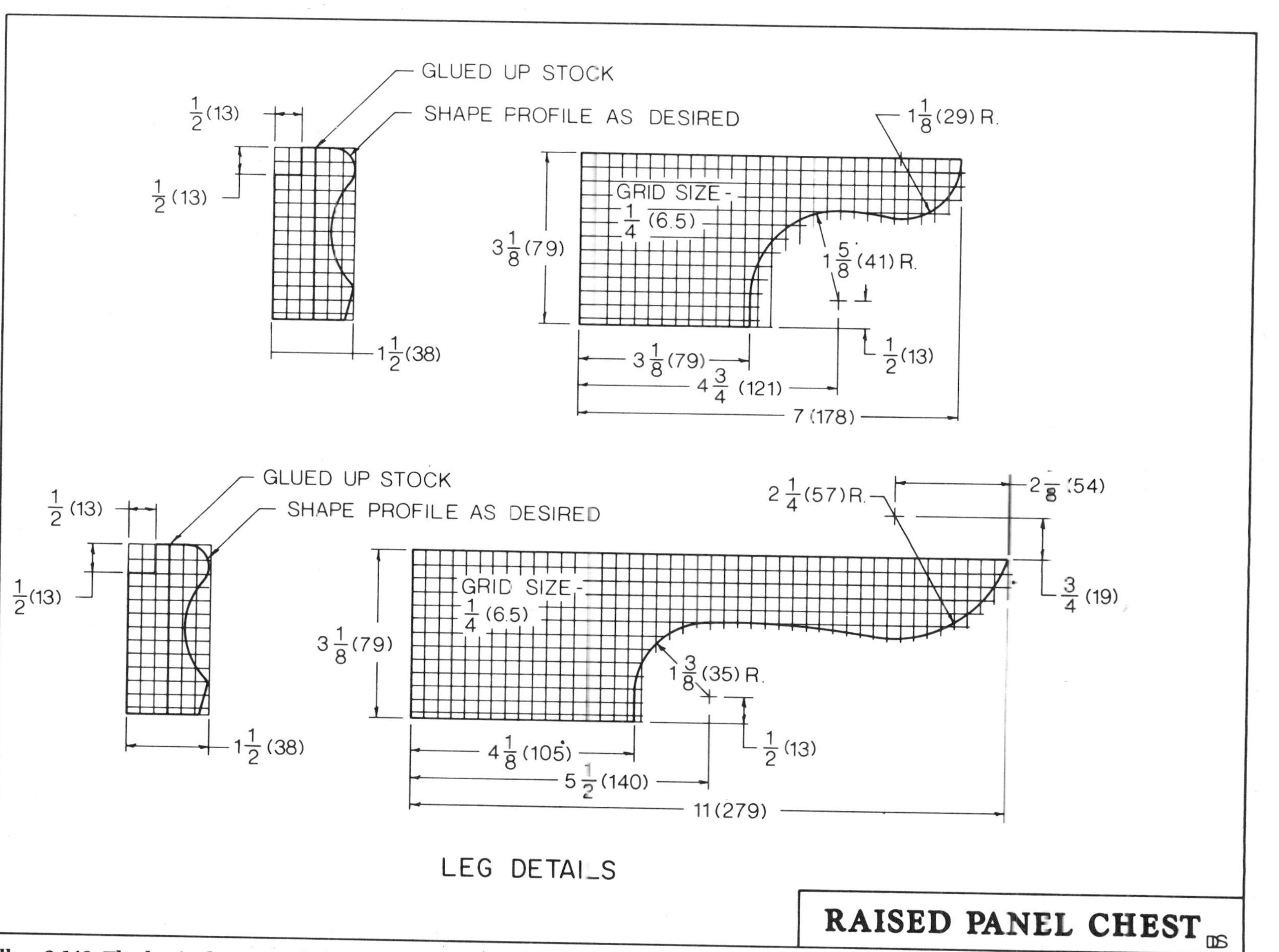

Illus. 8-148. The leg is the most challenging part of the chest. Shown here are the leg details. Plan your cutting sequence carefully.

Illus. 8-149. This walnut chest has a veneer top. Clear solid stock for the top was hard to find.

the inside of all the rails and stiles. Make the tenons to fit the groove. Cut the haunch on the tenons, and drill out the mortises. Clean up the mortises with a sharp chisel. Dry-fit the frames and measure the openings to determine panel size. The panels should be ⅛ inch shorter and narrower than the groove-to-groove measurement.

Cut the panels and sand them. Fit them to the rails and stiles. Send all the parts and assemble them. Do not glue the panels in place. They should be free to move. Pin them in position, so they do not move off center.

Cut the rabbet on the ends of the sides. Cut a matching groove on the ends of the front and back. Glue the chest parts together and clamp them with bar clamps. Protect the surfaces of the box with clamp pads. Make sure the assembly is square before the glue begins to cure.

Cut the parts for the bottom, and rabbet the inside of each part. Cut the edge banding for the top, and cut a groove on the inside edge. This groove will accommodate the spline. Shape the edges of the edge banding and bottom frame parts. Miter the bottom frame parts and glue them together. Use a band clamp to hold them in alignment until the glue cures.

Fit the edge banding to the top and glue up the assembly. A band clamp will pull the miters together. If necessary, a few bar clamps can also be used to pull the edge banding closer to the plywood.

Cut the bottom and rabbet it. Glue it into the frame. After the glue cures, you may wish to put a feather in the miters. Use a universal jig to guide the stock while cutting the kerf. Feathers can also be cut in the lid.

Cut the stock for the legs (Illus. 8-148). You may have to glue up two pieces of stock of different thicknesses for the legs. Lay out the arcs and the coves on the legs. Cut the coves first, and then cut the rabbets. Shape the arc at the top, and blend the curves together with a hand plane or abrasives.

Cut the miters and fit the pieces together. Lay out and cut the curves in the leg parts. This is done with a band saw or saber saw. Sand the curves smooth. Cut the plywood triangle and glue up the legs. Keep the parts aligned and held firmly. Nail the plywood triangle in position if desired. Sand the legs and mount them to the box.

Fit the hinges to the box and install the lid supports. Adjust the lid supports. They should keep the lid from slamming. This protects the hands and fingers of the user.

Remove all hardware, and sand the parts one last time. Apply stain and finish as desired. *Hint:* You may wish to stain the raised panels before they are installed in the frame. This ensures that the whole panel is stained. If the panel ever shrinks, no unstained wood will show.

Index